PELICAN BOOKS

THE MAKING OF MODERN RUSSIA

Lionel Kochan, who is married and has three children, was born in London in 1922 and educated at Haberdashers, Hampstead, at Corpus Christi College, Cambridge, where he was a scholar, and at the School of Slavonic and East European Studies. He took a Ph.D. at the London School of Economics. After lecturing in modern European history at the universities of Edinburgh and East Anglia, he was appointed to the Bearsted Readership in Jewish History at the University of Warwick. His works include *Russia and the Weimar Republic* (1954); *Acton on History* (1955); *The Struggle for Germany 1914–1945* (1963); *Russia in Revolution 1890–1918* (1966); and *The Jew and his History* (1977). He also edited *The Jews in Soviet Russia since 1917* (1972). Lionel Kochan completed his war service in the Intelligence Corps; he is very fond of chess.

Richard Abraham was born in Tetbury, Gloucestershire in 1941 and educated at the Crypt School, Gloucester. He won an exhibition to Downing College, Cambridge, and later spent a year at Kansas State University. He researched and taught Russian History at the University of East Anglia, before returning to school teaching in 1971. Since 1973, he has been Head of Social and Environmental Studies at Battersea County School, a mixed comprehensive school in inner London. He was elected to an Education Fellowship at Keble College, Oxford for the Michaelmas Term of 1982. Richard Abraham lives with his wife and their four children a short distance from the school where he works.

THE MAKING OF
MODERN RUSSIA

LIONEL KOCHAN
AND
RICHARD ABRAHAM

SECOND EDITION

PENGUIN BOOKS

Penguin Books Ltd, Harmondsworth, Middlesex, England
Penguin Books, 40 West 23rd Street, New York, New York 10010, U.S.A.
Penguin Books Australia Ltd, Ringwood, Victoria, Australia
Penguin Books Canada Ltd, 2801 John Street, Markham, Ontario, Canada L3R 1B4
Penguin Books (N.Z.) Ltd, 182-190 Wairau Road, Auckland 10, New Zealand

First published by Jonathan Cape 1962
Published in Pelican Books 1963
Reprinted 1965, 1967, 1968, 1970, 1971, 1973, 1974,
1975, 1977, 1978, 1979, 1981, 1982
Second edition 1983
Reprinted 1983

Made and printed in Great Britain by
Richard Clay (The Chaucer Press) Ltd,
Bungay. Suffolk

TO
NICK, ANNA AND
BENJAMIN

AND TO
SHARON, JULIA, CLAIRE·
AND MARK

Contents

Maps

Foreword to the Second Edition

This book was first published more than twenty years ago. For this new edition the original text has been revised and several entirely new chapters added to bring the book up to date. This has very largely been the work of Richard Abraham, a former pupil of mine whom I am happy to welcome as co-author. The text, as revised, has been edited by us jointly.

New times bring new interests. A number of themes that seemed dormant in the Russia of 1960 have acquired a new urgency. This applies in particular to the national minorities and Russia's relations with Islam. The Chinese cultural revolution and Soviet imports of western technology during the 1970s have led to a reconsideration of precedents in earlier Soviet history. World-wide interest in the history of women has begun to alter our perceptions of Russian social history, though this process is still far from complete. Greater international contact has led to much greater awareness of the details of Russian political culture since the 1930s and has prompted a reconsideration of the sources of that culture in the Russian past and in Marxism. Historians have had to face the demands of sociologists for greater conceptual rigour. The teaching of history in Britain has also followed the American precedent in introducing historiographical controversy at a somewhat earlier stage. These are some of the factors which have affected our revision of this book.

We would like to thank John Biggart of the University of East Anglia for his criticisms of the final chapters of the book; he is not to be blamed for such faults as remain. We are also deeply indebted to Wendy Abraham for making this work possible and for producing most of the final typescript.

LIONEL KOCHAN

CHAPTER 1

The Rise and Fall of Kiev Rus

The formative centuries of Russian history had their setting in a
vast exposed plain, stretching from Eastern Europe to central
Siberia. To the north and north-east, the White Sea and the Arctic
Ocean formed the boundary. To the south lay the Black Sea, the
Caspian, and the Caucasus mountains. The Urals are no kind of
climatic or even physical barrier. Nowhere does their altitude
exceed 6,000 feet. They rise from gradual foothills to a mean
altitude of some 1,500 feet. Numerous valleys and passes make
transit easy, both eastwards and westwards. Where does Europe
end? Where does Asia begin? It is impossible to say. It is this
geographical indeterminacy that helps to account for the perennial
question: does Russia belong to Europe or to Asia, or does it
form some complex world of its own?

The distinctive features of the plain are the uplands that form
the watersheds of the area's river system. The Valdai Hills, for
example, some 200 miles north-west of Moscow, are nowhere
more than a thousand feet above sea-level. Yet they are the source
of such major rivers as the Western Dvina, flowing into the Baltic;
the Dnieper, flowing into the Black Sea; and the Volga, the greatest
of all, which empties into the Caspian. These rivers and their
tributaries linked the territory they watered to the countries
beyond the seas. Portages connected one system with the next. It
was at strategic points on these interlocking routes that the first
Slav towns developed – Kiev, Novgorod, Polotsk, Chernigov,
Smolensk. In the fourth century B.C., Herodotus already knew the
Dnieper as 'the most productive river . . . in the whole world,
excepting only the Nile . . . It has upon its banks the loveliest and
most excellent pasturage for cattle; it contains abundance of the
most delicious fish . . . the richest harvests spring up along its
course and, where the ground is not sown, the heaviest crops of
grass . . .'

This describes, of course, the fertile southern reaches of the

Dnieper. Such vegetation was by no means uniform throughout the vast Eurasian plain through which the river slowly meandered. In the far north lay a belt of cold, barren tundra. Then comes a well-watered forest zone of enormous expanse, ill-suited to agriculture but nourishing well-nigh inexhaustible numbers of wild animals to provide food, clothing, and furs. Throughout the south lie the exceptionally fertile black earth regions, which begin in the Ukraine and stretch eastwards into southern Siberia. These, in their turn, give way to the arid, semi-desert, sandy steppes to the north and east of the Caspian.

When in the sixth and seventh centuries A.D. the Slavs settled on the Russian plain, they were by no means the first people to have established themselves there. There is evidence that for a thousand years there had been continuous settlement and occupation by nomadic and semi-nomadic tribes – Scythians, Sarmatians, Goths, Huns, Avars, Khazars. One after another, warlike hordes from the east and north had made their way across the exposed steppe-lands and along the navigable rivers.

This was the world in which the Slavs made their appearance in about the sixth century. They first began to move eastwards from the Carpathians during the great Migration of Peoples. After the death of Attila in 453, and the collapse of the Hun empire, this process quickened and a threefold division of the Slav migratory stream emerged: to the Elbe, Oder, and lower Vistula went the western Slavs – forerunners of the Czechs, Slovaks, and Poles; to the Balkan peninsula went the southern Slavs – Serbs, Croats, Slovenes, and Bulgars; and to the Dnieper, the upper Volga, and the shores of Lakes Ilmen and Peipus, the eastern Slavs – forerunners of the Great Russians, Ukrainians ('Little Russians') and Belorussians (White Russians).

Those tribes of the eastern Slavs who settled along the waterways of the middle Dnieper and the northern lakes were rapidly drawn into the trading network of the area. Their closest neighbours, and also their conquerors, were the Khazars, a people of Turkic origin who had become converted to Judaism. But it was a mild form of conquest, entailing little more than the payment of tribute.

The Khazar Khaganate had the rough shape of a triangle. Its

1. Waterways of Eastern Europe

base ran from the Caspian Sea to the Sea of Azov; the two sides
rested on the Volga and the lower Don. Originally nomads, the
Khazars had later become agriculturists and traders. They were
advantageously situated to become a centre for transit trade between the rich Arab Caliphate to the east and commercial Europe
to the north-west. From the subjugated Slav tribes came slaves,
honey, wax, and furs. From the Trans-Caspian areas, including
Bokhara, came silks, textiles, and metals *en route* to Byzantium
and Asia Minor. North Africa, Italy, and Spain were also among
the recipients of products from Trans-Caspia, routed via the
Khaganate.

Into this network of trading relationships the Slavs were drawn.
The Dnieper area of Slav settlement was in fact the southern
portion of what was later known as the great 'way from the Varangians to the Greeks', that is, from Scandinavia to Byzantium. This
route, one of the most important trade-routes of early Europe,
began in the far north with the Gulf of Finland; thence to Lake
Ladoga by way of the River Neva; by way of the River Volkhov
to Lake Ilmen; by way of the Lovat to the vicinity of Velikie Luki.
Here the trader took to *terra firma* to reach the upper waters of
the Dvina. Above Smolensk, the Dnieper itself was reached. To
the north of Zaporozhe there was one further trans-shipment to
avoid the cataracts. The west coast of the Black Sea finally led to
the great trading and metropolitan centre of Byzantium.

Under Khazar auspices, there also developed independent Slav
trading-routes to the east; and both the Khazar capital, Ityl (on
the Volga, near the present-day Astrakhan), and Sarkel (on the
Don), another important Khazar metropolis, had large Slav
populations. One of the chief characteristics of the early Slavs was
the large number of towns to which their trading activities gave
rise. The number has been variously estimated at between 300 and
600. To the Varangian traders of Scandinavia and the Baltic, the
Slav territories were known as *gaardariki* – kingdom of the towns.

This extreme decentralization was countered in the ninth century
by a process of consolidation as each town attempted to seize the
territory contiguous to it and dependent on it. The result was
incessant strife. The victims were sold into slavery in Byzantium.
A special square in Constantinople was set aside for the sale of

slaves from the north. It was in these circumstances that the ancient chronicle records the invitation to the Varangians to restore order in the Slav lands: 'Our land is great and rich but there is no order in it. Come, then, to rule as princes over us.' It is in terms similar to these that the *Anglo-Saxon Chronicle* accounts for the arrival of the Angles and Saxons.

In 862, Great Novgorod, on the River Volkhov, one of the most important Slav towns, fell to Rurik, the Varangian chieftain. Rurik died in 879. His successor, Oleg, led a campaign southwards down the river route to Byzantium. He took Smolensk and Lyubech, and Kiev in 882, which he fortified and made his capital.

The Varangians or Norsemen were known to half Europe in the easily interchangeable roles of trader and pirate. They sacked the towns of England and France and founded towns in Ireland; they sailed up the Seine, and through the Straits of Gibraltar into the Mediterranean; about the year 1000 one of their forays even reached the coast of North America.

In Rus, as the Slav lands were known to the people of the north, the Varangians, even before the 'invitation' to Rurik, had become familiar with the route to Byzantium through acting as armed bodyguards to the Slav traders. Their assumption of power over the Slav tribes may well be seen as an extension of their previous role. They did not come to build a state; rather they became the ruling stratum of princes over the mass of Slav society. Even this may be an exaggeration. Rus, with Kiev as its later capital, may also be seen as the conquest of the less organized Slav tribes of the south by the more organized ones of the north, aided by Varangian merchant-adventurers and princes. In any event, it was less than a century before the first signs appeared of the absorption of the Varangians by the numerically far superior Slavs. Oleg's successor, Igor, for example, had a son, born in 942, who was given a Slav name – Svyatoslav.

The relationship between the Varangians and the Slavs was limited in the main to plunder and the imposition of tribute. The Byzantine Emperor, Constantine Porphyrogenitus, describes the Varangian princes and their retinue moving among the Slav villages and homesteads at the onset of winter. They collected tribute in the form of marten, squirrel, and fox furs, honey, wax, and other forest products. The seizure of slaves for sale in Byzantium was another purpose of these winter forays. In summer the proceeds were disposed of, after the journey southwards to Constantinople.

Given this rule at home, the foreign policy of the Varangians aimed to keep their routes open. As early as the year 860, they had descended without warning on a terrified Byzantium in search of plunder. In 907 Oleg led another fleet to Byzantium, this time in search of a trading partner. He was successful in forcing on the Greeks a trade treaty favourable to Kiev. This assured the Slav and Varangian merchants of access to the Byzantine market, accommodation and food at the expense of the Byzantine State, as well as a supply of provisions, sails, and anchors for the return journey northwards. In exchange, the Slavs submitted themselves to close supervision and control at the hands of their suspicious hosts and fellow traders. They had to be registered, they undertook to refrain from looting, not to appear in groups of more than fifty at the market, and not to carry arms.

Igor's successor, Svyatoslav, developed widespread schemes of conquest. He was evidently a true Viking. He left internal matters to his capable mother, Olga, an early Russian Christian, reserving to himself the task of expanding to the maximum the frontiers of Kiev Rus. Whereas his predecessors had made Byzantium their main objective, Svyatoslav turned his efforts towards the Volga basin, the route linking Russia with the East. He overthrew the Khazar Khaganate when he took its principal towns, Sarkel and Ityl. He seized the Kuban area in the northern Caucasus and penetrated in force to the Sea of Azov. He finally came to grief after his overthrow of the Bulgarian kingdom on the Danube. When he turned back to Kiev in 973 he and his troops were attacked at the Dnieper cataracts by Pecheneg tribesmen, the most recent nomadic invaders of the steppes. The Slavs were overwhelmed. Svyatoslav's skull, it is said, was made into a drinking cup for a Pecheneg prince. Never again did the history of Kiev Rus know a realm that stretched from the Volga to the Danube and northwards to the Finnish Gulf and Lake Ladoga.

The next half century or so saw the efflorescence of its culture and the emergence of Kiev Rus as an acknowledged European power. Under the rule of Vladimir, this was considerably facilitated by the adoption of Christianity, in its Byzantine form, in 988. But the preliminaries to the conversion of Rus clearly show the widespread influences to which the State was exposed. To Vladimir came Jews from the Khazar Khanagate, Muslims from a Bulgar state on the Volga, Catholics from Germany, and a Greek philosopher from Byzantium. The latter's victory was no doubt dependent in part on Kiev's commercial relationship to Constantinople.

Once Christianity was established there came an organized Church under a Metropolitan, nominated from Constantinople and usually a Greek. The Greek prelates accepted the use of Slavonic as the language of the Church and educated a literate elite which swiftly created a new, national literature of chronicle and epic poetry. The new religion made its visual impact in the construction of churches in Byzantine style and in the form of frescoes, icons, and mosaics. The use of the icon followed the defeat of Byzantine iconoclasm in the ninth century. Unhappily, the Christianity brought to Russia was heavily impregnated by a monastic misogynism which sanctified the unconditional subjection of women.

Christianity brought moments of joyful piety at Christmas and Easter but Orthodoxy turned a stern face to any form of levity in social intercourse. This was partly a reaction against the indigenous pagan religion which had placed laughter at the centre of its rituals. The Shamans of the old religion did not accept conversion meekly. Eventually they found a precarious niche for themselves as travelling entertainers, bearers of a popular counter-culture which mocked prince and bishop alike. Inevitably, they suffered waves of repression as supposed instigators of popular revolts.

The schism of 1054 between the Eastern and Western forms of Christianity, occasioned by the doctrine of papal supremacy, had as yet no part in separating the Kiev state from Western or Central Europe. Nothing shows more clearly the European acceptance and standing of Kiev than the marriage alliances concluded by Yaroslav, the ruler of Kiev in the second quarter of the eleventh century, and his family. He himself was married to a daughter of the King of Sweden. His sons had German and Polish wives.

Three of his daughters, Anna, Elizabeth, and Anastasia, were married to the Kings of France, Norway, and Hungary. Anna, consort of Henry I of France, was able to sign her name – whereas her French husband was illiterate.

On the other hand, the ethos of Byzantine Russia would later differ profoundly from that of Western Christianity. First, through the use of the Slavonic vernacular as a medium of communication, it was less able to share in the European culture of Greek and Latin. Secondly, it set greater store by piety than knowledge, so that the Eastern Church had a pronounced anti-intellectualist colouring. Thirdly, it stood in much more intimate contact with the State than did the Church in almost any country of Western Europe. When the Mongols came to make their own contribution to the development of the Muscovite state, the consequence would be a reinforcement of the collective at the expense of the individual.

The basis of the Kievan economy was agriculture. This applied with particular force to the area around Kiev and Chernigov. Here the climate and soil were both favourable. To the north the abundance of swamplands and wooded areas made agriculture far less productive and predictable. In the south, however, there was ploughing by horse, and the sowing of wheat, millet, barley, corn, rye, flax, peas, and poppies. The early records also make mention of almost every species of domestic animal – horse, bull, cow, dog, goat, lamb, sheep, oxen, and hog.

The hunting and trapping of fur-bearing animals was the speciality of the north. Here the expanse of forest and water was the home of sable, beaver, marten, polar-fox, and fox. Squirrel skins were dealt in by the tens of thousand and were also used as small change. Trade in honey and wax and the fishing industry were other occupations of the north.

At the top of the social hierarchy stood the prince, whose functions were chiefly military and judicial. He had to defend his principality and to supervise the administration of justice. In both capacities he was advised and aided by a council of boyars, i.e. independent landowners, a nascent landed aristocracy. Urban government was controlled by the *vyeche*, a popular assembly of all free adult males. The towns, and they probably numbered

more than 300, were the home of the emergent class of artisans –
mainly carpenters, masons, bridge-builders, joiners, saddlers, and
the like. These were the men who built the wooden homesteads,
market-places, cattle-sheds, and bath-houses that urban life
required. There were also metal-workers and artisans, who specialized in the processing of leather and the manufacture of linen
and other types of coarse textiles.

Kiev itself was, of course, the paramount town in Rus. Yaroslav
in the eleventh century hoped to make of it a Slav Constantinople,
and it did undoubtedly become one of the showpieces of the
Middle Ages. One account mentions no fewer than 400 churches,
the work of Byzantine architects, stone-masons, mosaic workers,
and painters. The town was surrounded by protective walls. Inside
there were eight great market-places attended by merchants from
all the regions with which Kiev Rus traded – Germany, Bohemia,
Hungary, Poland, Scandinavia, Byzantium, and the countries of
the Orient. Adam of Bremen, the German chronicler, found Kiev
'the fairest jewel' in all the Greek world.

The bulk of the rural population was composed of *smerdi*. These,
during the ascendancy of Kiev Rus, were more or less free farmers
or rural householders with their own homestead, animals, plough-
land, and primitive farming implements. They were their own
masters to the extent of being able to bequeath property, almost
without qualification. The Russkaya Pravda – the eleventh-cen-
tury code of laws which is the chief source of information on the
social relations of this early period – describes other rural classes
in a complex network of obligation. The *zakupi* were landless
peasants whose existence depended on the labour they performed
for others, including the smerdi. They had no agricultural tools of
their own; they used their masters' ploughs and harrows. The
zakupi did, however, possess independent households of a kind,
which they maintained apart from those of their masters. They
were legally free, and their dependence theoretically ceased as
soon as they had discharged their debt by labour. If they failed in
this, or if they took to flight to evade their obligations, they fell
into the lowest status of all – that of *kholopi*, who were barely
distinguishable from slaves.

Yaroslav died in 1054, and with his death the decay of Kiev set in at an increasing rate. Weaknesses in this first Russian state became all too obvious. Thus, its unity and integrity were endangered by the system of rule that Yaroslav enjoined on his deathbed. In principle, all his heirs – and he had five sons and a grandson – undertook to rule Russia collectively. The eldest heir ascended the throne of Kiev, receiving the title of Grand Prince. His brothers assumed rule over the lesser towns and adjacent territories, called apanages, depending on their position in the family hierarchy; the youngest brother, for example, received the smallest town. But this apportionment was in no wise final. When the grand prince of Kiev died, the throne was assumed by his next surviving brother, and this in turn led to a general 'moving up' among all the members of the ruling dynasty. This system inevitably became a source of dissension among the princes and their families. In 1097 a conference of princes at Lyubech attempted to give some order to the system of succession, but no lasting result was achieved. By about 1100 there were some twelve separate principalities on the territory of Kiev Rus, all virtually unconnected by any central power.

These internecine feuds naturally left the country less fitted than ever for self-defence against the latest wave of barbarian nomads from the East – the Cumans. Their raids and depredations, not only on the trading routes but also against villages and homesteads, led to the increasing depopulation of the Dnieper basin. From the Smolensk region, for example, in 1160, Cuman raiders carried off into slavery some 10,000 Russians.

The Crusades were a second external factor tending to undermine Kiev's economic existence. The development of the Mediterranean as a trading highway to the Orient inevitably diminished the importance of Kiev and the Black Sea route to Byzantium and beyond. What Venice and Genoa won, Kiev lost. The capture of Constantinople during the fourth Crusade in 1203–4, expressly at Venetian instigation, was a powerful blow to Kiev's foreign trade.

In the meantime, other enemies were appearing in the northwest – the Teutonic Knights, the Lithuanians, and Swedes. From the south-west came the Hungarians, pressing eastwards. To the smerd threatened with enserfment, to the free population exposed to wholesale kidnapping, to the traders with their livelihood menaced, the response to deteriorating conditions was flight.

One route led south-westwards to Galicia, but in the main the route led north-eastwards, from the Dnieper basin to the region of the upper Volga basin, and the Oka, where new centres of Russian life began to form, based on the natural economy of an environment hitherto peopled by the pagan Slavic and Finnish tribes of the northern forests.

The transfer of power to the north-east was dramatically illuminated in 1169. In that year a coalition of twelve princes under Andrei Bogolyubsky sacked Kiev; and Andrei removed the capital of Rus to the township of Vladimir on the Klyazma River, in his native principality of Rostov-Suzdal. But Vladimir was no more the capital of a united country than Kiev had been. When the Mongols or Tartars invaded Rus in the last thrust westwards of the Eurasian nomads – successors to the Scythians, Sarmatians, Huns, and Cumans – they found a dismembered country before them. Their conquest of 1237–40 decisively broke Slav contact with Europe, or at least Western Europe, and turned the country eastwards. Not until the sixteenth and seventeenth centuries, for example, did such former centres as Kiev and Smolensk rejoin the Russian State. The Dnieper basin was replaced by the more remote region of the Oka and the Volga as the dominant locale of Russian history. It was in this area under the aegis of the Mongols that the small principality of Moscow asserted its position as nucleus of the future Russia.

CHAPTER 2

The Mongol Conquest and the Rise of Muscovy

It was in 1223 that the Mongols first swept into Rus. By 1240 they had conquered in two major invasions all the Slav principalities, and in 1242 they established their headquarters at Sarai, on the lower Volga, not far from where Volgograd stands today. Thereafter, for the best part of two and a half centuries, they dominated political and economic life over a vast area of Eastern Europe. By the end of that period two new Russian states had come into existence – Lithuania, stretching from the Baltic to the Black Sea, and Muscovy, an inland principality, centred on Moscow, and dominant over all the other Slav principalities.

This was a situation very different from that which the Mongols had encountered at the beginning of their sway. Then they had found perhaps a dozen Slav states, from Novgorod in the north to Ryazan in the south, with no tradition of unity that would enable them to combine against the invader. What was the nature of Mongol dominance over this conglomeration of states? The Khans ruled indirectly and made no attempt to interfere with the internal affairs of the Slavs except where and when their supremacy was threatened. They exercised their power, not by colonization or by imposing their own system of government, but by levying tribute on the Slavs and by reserving to themselves the right to confirm in office each new ruler in each of the principalities. Before any ruler could ascend his throne he had to travel to Sarai, and there receive, or more likely intrigue for, his *yarlyk*, or authorization. More than 130 princes made this pilgrimage. Many took their families with them. It was customary for the prince to draw up his will when he left for Sarai, lest he fail to return alive. Economically, Mongol overlordship expressed itself in the levying of taxes and conscription. Mongol officials and census-takers were soon at work throughout the whole of Rus, listing all adult males on their paper scrolls. They imposed a fixed *per capita* tax, known as *yassak*, and also tolls and duties on salt, ploughs, bridges, ferries,

2. Kiev Rus at its Height, and its Chief Enemies

and the movement of cattle across internal boundaries. Mongol troops quartered in the chief towns of each principality bloodily suppressed the frequent Slav uprisings. Modern Russian, in its use of words of Tartar origin to express such ideas as 'goods', 'money', 'toll', 'exchequer', shows the impact made by Tartar financial depredations during these early centuries of the people's history.

In fact, for all the indirectness of the Mongols' rule, they did exert considerable direct influence – and for the most part in a destructive sense. During the period of their dominance there was decline and degeneration in the level of craftsmanship, in artisanry, in the position of the town, which lost its free urban institutions, in the artistic level of the chronicles and religious writings, and politically, in the increasing fragmentation of the political unit. Above and beyond all this, the rule of the Mongols cut Rus off from the rest of Europe. Only Novgorod and Pskov still enjoyed contact with the north German towns. As Mongol rule weakened, some contact did again develop with the Balkans. But when Constantinople fell to the Turks in 1453 and there was a spread of Turkish influence, this access to the West was blocked. There is no doubt that Russian cultural backwardness in the centuries following the collapse of Mongol rule was intimately related to the impact of that rule. From one point of view, the country's subsequent history can in fact be seen as a prolonged attempt to regain contact with the West.

Mongol rule provided future Russian rulers with a model: a state with universalist aspirations, subordinating everything to efficiency in matters of military administration and relying on a class of serving men bound to serve their khan with absolute obedience.

It took some two centuries – from the mid thirteenth to the mid fifteenth – before Muscovy had won for itself undisputed supremacy over the other Slav states of north-eastern Russia as the paramount successor-state to the Mongols. It has been said:

> The history of Moscow is the story of how an insignificant *ostrog* (blockhouse) became the capital of a Eurasian empire. This insignificant *ostrog*, built in the first half of the twelfth century, on an insignificant river by an insignificant princeling, became, in the course of time, the pivot of an empire extending into two, and even three continents.*

*G. Vernadsky, *The Mongols and Russia* (Oxford, 1953), p. 390.

The chronicles first mentioned Moscow in 1147. It was then nothing more than a village domain belonging to the prince of Rostov-Suzdal, and evidently a defence outpost against the south. In 1237 it was sacked by the Mongols and razed to the ground. In 1263 it re-enters history as the permanent capital of a minor principality ruled by Daniel, the youngest son of Alexander Nevsky, conqueror of the Swedes and Livonian Knights. ('Nevsky' is derived from 'Neva', the name of the river on which Leningrad stands, the scene of Alexander's victory over the Swedes.)

What was it that made Moscow the nucleus of a national Russian state? There was the geographical factor, as in the case of Kiev. Moscow, situated on the river of the same name, enjoyed a sheltered position that was of inestimable advantage in the thirteenth and fourteenth centuries. At a time when the west and south-west were harassed by an expanding Lithuania which eventually reached the Black Sea, when the trans-Volgan territories were the prey of free-booters from Novgorod, barely distinguishable from pirates, and when the other outlying territories of Rus to the south and east were the repeated victims of Tartar raids, the site of Moscow offered shelter and protection. No serious attack was made on it in the century and a quarter that separated a Tartar raid of 1238 from a Lithuanian foray of 1368. Moscow became a centre of settlement for the uprooted subjects of the more exposed principalities.

Moscow also drew strength from its position in the Russian Mesopotamia, in the *Mezhduryechie*, the area bounded by the upper Volga and the Oka. The axis of the future Muscovy was to be the Baltic–Volga–Caspian trade-route. But before this stage was reached, Moscow already enjoyed a geo-commercial location on which, fundamentally, its expansion depended. Lying as it did on the Moscow River, flowing from north-west to south-east, and linking the system of the middle Oka with the system of the upper Volga, the principality, and later grand-duchy, was thus connected with all the important river systems of northern and western Russia. Through a complex of portages and tributaries Moscow had access to the Volga on the north, east, and south, and to the Dnieper and Western Dvina on the west. Farther afield, waterways led to the Baltic and the Black Sea. Moscow was thus situated at the centre of the two supremely important trade-routes and water-ways crossing Rus from north to south and from west to east – the Baltic–Caspian and the Western Dvina–Volga.

Many of Moscow's geographical advantages were shared by Tver, and the fourteenth century opened with a bitter contest between the princes of the two towns. Moscow was favoured by political factors of crucial importance: both Tartar Khans and Orthodox primates supported Moscow as the lesser evil. As the increasingly desperate Tverites turned to the growing power of Lithuania for support, this motivation was reinforced. The Metropolitans of the Orthodox Church feared their Tartar over-lords less than they feared the Catholic rulers of Lithuania, and from 1326 they began to reside in Moscow. The support of the eternal institution was unwavering and was often vital at moments of dynastic weakness. With the support of these powerful patrons, the Muscovite rulers were able to reduce the debilitating effects of the apanage system and to adopt, alone in medieval Russia, something approaching primogeniture.

In seeking to extend their rule, a variety of methods was prac-tised, few of them pretty. There was purchase, outright conquest, acquisition by diplomatic means, and the conclusion of treaties with petty princelings that left them masters in their domain but bound to Moscow by ties of service. Finally, there was coloniza-tion. The various processes were all in motion at the very beginning of the fourteenth century. When Daniel, the first ruler of Moscow, died in 1303 he was able to bequeath to his successor a principality that had doubled its area in a single reign. From that point, by and large, the history of Moscow shows a record of steady expan-sion. Among the earliest acquisitions were Mozhaisk and Kolomna. The first lay at the source of the Moscow River, the second at its junction with the Oka. The two towns thus gave control of the whole course of the river. Success here opened the way to further penetration northwards. Ivan Kalita (= 'money bags'), who ruled Moscow from 1325 to 1341, bought control of the important trans-Volgan territories of Uglich, Beloozero, and Galich. These were not incorporated in his domains, but their rulers thereafter retained their positions by virtue of the grace of Muscovy.

Ivan strengthened this dependence by his policy of ransoming Slav prisoners from the Mongols and subsidizing their settlement on his newly dominated territory. In the second half of the fourteenth century and the first half of the fifteenth, Muscovy completed its most impressive phase of expansion. The seizure of Vladimir and Starodub gave command of the Klyazma River, and the gradual erosion of the independence of Nizhny Novgorod and of other eastern principalities set Muscovy athwart the Volga itself. Nizhny Novgorod, the gateway to the lower Volga, brought Moscow within striking distance of the road to Asia, with its particular prize the silk trade of the East.

The slow emergence of Muscovy as the paramount Slav principality was bound to influence the Slav–Mongol relationship. Concerned at the rise of Lithuania, the Mongols fostered the growth of the power destined to eclipse them. No Slav prince was more assiduous in courting the reigning Khan, or more humble in his diplomacy, than the prince of Muscovy. Cash, at Sarai, was all but omnipotent. This weakness the wealthy rulers of Muscovy were well fitted to exploit. They also derived much of their influence at Sarai from the share they took in crushing any movement hostile to the Mongols among the lesser Slav principalities. The troops of Muscovy functioned more than once in this role. It was also not infrequent for Muscovy – no less of course than its rivals – to use Mongol troops in this struggle against the other principalities.

It was through such devious methods that, as early as the reign of Ivan Kalita, Muscovy acquired the undignified but influential right of collecting the taxes imposed by the Mongols on the Slavs. This gave further pressure to Muscovy's financial squeeze. Moreover, in 1353 the principality became acknowledged by the Tartars as the judicial authority over the other princes of Rus. This gradual accretion of strength and influence resulted, in 1380, in the first serious Slav attempt to cast off Mongol rule. At the field of Kulikovo near the Don the whole of northern Rus, led by Dmitry Donskoy, of Muscovy, fought and won a pitched battle against the overlord. But, though the victory was striking, it was in no way conclusive. Barely two years later the Mongols returned in force and utterly devastated Moscow. Vladimir, Mozhaisk, and other towns were similarly laid waste. In 1408 a renewed Mongol invasion led to further widespread ravages in Nizhny Novgorod, Rostov, and Serpukhov. But despite these, and despite losses to Lithuania in the west and an outbreak of internecine feuds in Moscow itself, the dominance of the grand duchy was firmly established by the middle of the fifteenth century.

CHAPTER 3

The Formation of a National State

Ivan III, also known as Ivan the Great, ruled Muscovy from 1462 to 1505. For the first time a clear personality emerges from the ruck of warring princes and grand dukes. Contarini, a Venetian traveller, describes Ivan in a report of 1476 as tall, lean, and handsome. Some forty years later another visitor to Moscow, Baron Herberstein, an envoy of the Holy Roman Emperor, was told that Ivan's mere appearance was enough to send into a swoon any women who encountered him unprepared. If, writes Herberstein, drunkenness caused him to fall asleep during a banquet – and this was not infrequent – his guests would await in fear and trembling his return to consciousness, when he would resume his jocularity.

In political and military matters Ivan avoided frontal combats. His father had blinded one of his rivals for the throne and had been blinded in his turn. Ivan had learnt to achieve his aims through calculated and devious diplomacy. Force and violence he used as a last resort.

As the creator of a centralized state, Ivan has been well compared with his contemporary, Louis XI of France. His reign was without doubt a watershed in the development of the future Russian State. For all the conquests of his forerunners, he found Muscovy flanked to the north by the great commercial republic of Novgorod, which dominated a vast area from the Gulf of Finland to the Urals. To the west stretched the combined Polish–Lithuanian empire, lying along the Western Dvina, the Dnieper, and the Black Sea. South of Tula and Ryazan lay a vast expanse of steppe-land, as far as the Black Sea and the Caspian, dominated by the Tartars of the Crimea and the lower Volga. To the east, the Tartar Khanate stood athwart the Volga.

Apart from the absorption of the lesser Slav principalities such as Yaroslavl, Tver, Rostov, and Ryazan, it was no longer possible for Muscovy to advance farther without meeting head-on opposition from powerful empires. It is a measure of Ivan's success that by the end of his reign the Mongols were no longer a threat. They themselves, on the contrary, were now on the defensive. Novgorod and the other Slav states had lost their independence, and battle had been joined with Lithuania and Poland for expansion to the west.

Internally also, the growth of absolutism with a Pan-Russian ideology, and the emergence of a class of military serving land-owners, mark the second half of the fifteenth century as a turning-point in Muscovy's political and economic development. When Ivan the Great came to power four main national tasks stretched before him: to elevate the power of the grand prince over his fraternal rivals and their apanages; to complete the 'ingathering' of the Slav lands, including Novgorod, under the standard of Muscovy; to win back from Lithuania the south-western lands that had once been part of Kiev Rus; and to complete the over-throw of the Mongols.

Ivan was unremitting in his attacks on the power and privilege of his brothers and the other apanage princes. In 1472, he un-ceremoniously annexed the apanage of a brother who had died intestate. When his remaining brothers predictably objected he put them in their place, though he left them rope enough to hang themselves. In 1486, he annexed the largest of the apanages not owned by a brother. By the end of his reign, the capacity of the apanage system to disrupt the Russian state was radically reduced.

In dealing with the independent Russian principalities, Ivan strode ahead along the same path that had been marked out since the early years of the fourteenth century. In 1463 the princes of Yaroslavl submitted to Muscovy, lost their independence, and accepted service with Ivan. In 1472 it was the turn of Perm, with its lands on both sides of the Kama River. Two years later the Rostov princes sold what remained of their territory to Moscow. Tver, at one time the most hostile to Moscow of all the Slav groupings, was undermined from within by the defection of its boyars to Moscow. An alliance between Tver and Lithuania brought the conflict to a head, and in 1485 the town of Tver fell without a blow to Ivan's encircling army. The ruler fled to Lith-uania and Galicia, never to reappear on Muscovite soil. This same process was continued by Ivan's successor, with the absorption of Pskov and Ryazan.

Of all the areas annexed by Ivan, the most important was Novgorod. Novgorod was a thriving trading centre with access to the Baltic. It was also an ideological adversary: a commonwealth in which the conflicting interests of church, aristocracy and artisans found expression in republican institutions. Its symbol was the bell that summoned its citizens to free discussion in their own assembly. Such a state was increasingly anomalous in a Russia torn between aristocratic Lithuania and the Muscovite grand princes obsessed with the 'Patrimony of Yaroslav'. The struggle for Novgorod reached its culmination in Ivan III's reign. It had long been in the making. Repeated efforts to dominate Novgorod had been made over the past century and a half by the Muscovite princes. As far back as the days of Ivan Kalita, Novgorod had been forced to pay tribute to her south-eastern neighbour and to accept foreign governors (who did not, however, intervene in the republic's internal affairs). But whereas the stakes had originally been river routes and furs, they were raised, when Lithuania emerged to press Novgorod on the west, to nothing less than the continued existence of Muscovy.

The fact is that the Novgorod policy of manoeuvring between her two powerful neighbours could succeed only as long as the latter were in relative equilibrium. This was threatened by the growing power of Muscovy and by a crisis in the Orthodox Church. The decline of Byzantium had reached such proportions by the early fifteenth century that the Emperor John VIII and many of the leading clergy, including the Metropolitan of Moscow, decided that only with the help of the West could the Orthodox world be saved from the Turks. At the Council of Florence in 1437–9, the Orthodox leaders submitted to the Pope. The Orthodox hierarchy in Lithuania accepted this union and aligned itself with the Catholic Church in Poland, but in Moscow the union was violently rejected. Metropolitan Isidore was ejected from his seat and the Russian Orthodox Church ceased to accept instruction from Byzantium. Both sides sought to obtain the adherence of Novgorod to their view of the split.

In the competition with Moscow, Novgorod was hopelessly

handicapped by its vulnerability to economic blockade, its outmoded military system and its open politics. From time to time power passed to an aristocratic faction that seems to have been willing to join the Lithuanian aristocracy in the creation of a West Russian State. Politics of class were also involved, though there is evidence that the lower classes were as reluctant to accept incorporation into Moscow as the oligarchs.

Early in 1471 the pro-Lithuanian party inside the city sought an agreement with Casimir IV, King of Poland and Grand Prince of Lithuania. Casimir was to respect the Orthodox Church and to support Novgorod against Moscow. The treaty would also entitle Casimir to install a Polish governor in Novgorod on condition that no change be made in the constitution. In May 1471 Ivan and his Council of War decided to take up the challenge. Novgorod's new alliance enabled him to proclaim a religious war, a sort of crusade. The campaign took in not only Novgorod proper but also the far north. By August 1471 all resistance was over. An unexpectedly hot summer, which dried up the intervening swamps, helped to accelerate victory – as did the inefficient resistance put up by the Novgorodians. Demoralized by famine and inflation, many could see no point in fighting a hopeless war against the Grand Prince of Muscovy. In the battle along the River Shelon, for example, a Muscovite force of some 4,000 or 5,000 men overcame a Novgorod force many times stronger in number.

The peace that Ivan imposed was comparatively mild. He cancelled the treaty with Lithuania; an indemnity of 15,000 rubles was exacted; he forced Novgorod to yield up to Muscovy certain of its colonies and also to recognize his, Ivan's, sovereignty. This was not quite the end of Novgorod's independence, but there remained little left to lose. The end was a protracted affair and came after almost two decades of anti-Moscow riots and tumults inside the city and half-hearted attempts to reassert a claim to independence. Ivan fomented some of the disorder from outside in order to provide a pretext for intervention. He was also able to interfere with Novgorod's grain supply. By 1489 all was over, with the deportation of many thousands of Novgorod's boyars, merchants, and landowners. Their confiscated estates were bestowed on lesser boyars and other people from Muscovy who undertook, in return for the land, to render military service. As an independent political unit, Novgorod the Great no longer existed. It disappeared as a factor in European trade in 1494, when Ivan arrested all the Hanseatic merchants on Novgorod territory, closed their yard and church, and confiscated all their goods. Not for the last time the rulers of Moscow showed that while trade might be desirable, the elimination of political contamination was even more important to them. Muscovy now enjoyed unchallenged sway over a vast fur-bearing empire that stretched from Karelia, on the Gulf of Finland, to the Urals. The bell which had once called the citizens of Novgorod to their assembly would now praise autocrats in the Moscow Kremlin.

The subjugation of Novgorod left Ivan free to deal with his two other main opponents – Lithuania and the Mongols. This was a complex interdependent problem, with Ivan manoeuvring uneasily between the west and the south, endeavouring to prevent a union of the two fronts. His technique of exploiting his enemies' divisions could be used to better advantage than ever, now that the centralized Mongol empire had begun to disintegrate. At least three separate centres had replaced the former empire. There were Mongol Khanates at Kazan and in the Crimea, and a third group located between the Don and the Dnieper, the heir to the main Golden Horde. The earlier position was thus reversed. The united Mongols had once confronted the disunited Slavs; it was now a dismembered Mongol empire that came to grips with a united Muscovy.

In the 1460s Ivan had begun to withhold his due tribute from the Mongols. Strengthened by an alliance with the Crimean Tatars against the Golden Horde, he acted as though no dependent relationship existed. Ahmed, the Khan of the Golden Horde, twice summoned Ivan to his capital – without response. The climax came in 1480 when, by agreement with Lithuania, Ahmed launched a campaign against Muscovy.

Two and a half centuries of Mongol domination ended in a strange anticlimax. The two forces came to face each other across the banks of the Ugra River, the south-west frontier of Muscovy. There was only one skirmish – and nothing more. The help that Ahmed was expecting from Lithuania never materialized. This made any full-scale campaign against Muscovy impossible. He had no choice but to withdraw his troops. But because Ivan for his part feared the possibility of a Lithuanian attack, he dared not involve himself in a war with the Mongols, not even when they were retreating. Ivan also withdrew from the banks of the Ugra. All along, he had in fact played a very cautious, evasive role; so cautious as to earn the reproach both of the clergy and of the populace. At one time he had even prepared to evacuate his family and treasure from Moscow to the north. The fear inspired by the Mongols still bit deep.

The tragi-comic end to this last attempt of the Mongols to restore their suzerainty was underlined in 1502 when the Golden Horde itself ceased to exist as a cohesive force. It dwindled into the Khanate of Astrakhan. The Mongols still remained a local threat of course – invasion was mounted from the Crimea in 1521, and again half a century later – but never more would they threaten the actual existence of Muscovy, let alone assert a claim to over-lordship.

Ivan had now dealt with both Novgorod and the Mongols. There remained only Lithuania and the recovery of the lands of Kiev Rus. Here Ivan was less successful. A number of campaigns in the 1490s and early 1500s pushed Muscovy's frontier westwards to the upper stretches of the Western Dvina, and the Dnieper, and this brought Smolensk and Kiev within range.

THE CHARACTER OF MUSCOVY

What sort of Muscovite state was it that emerged from the long struggle with the Mongols and the lesser Slav principalities? It can be seen in so many ways – as the victory of the forest over the steppe, as the transition from a society of independent principalities to an absolutist autocracy, or, economically, as an evolution from a system of diffused landholdings and power to a concentration of land and power in the hands of an autocrat backed by a dependent class of service-landholders. But one fact is clear: the ultimate defeat of the Mongols by no means put an end to Mongol influence. On the contrary, the departing Mongols left an indelible impress on Muscovite life and society.

3. The Growth of Muscovy, 1300–1584

This may be seen in such matters as Muscovite military organization, Muscovy's method of collecting taxes, its criminal law, its diplomatic protocol. Not for nothing had Muscovy fought the Mongols or collected their taxes or applied their legal sanctions for the best part of two centuries. The Mongol presence had also justified the extreme seclusion and segregation of aristocratic women. But more important than all this was the impetus that Mongol rule gave to the development of the Muscovite autocracy. This was the kernel of Mongol influence. The Mongol empire was not only erected on the principle of unquestioning, unqualified service to the State; the Khan also demanded the complete obedience of the individual to the State. The Khan alone embodied the State, and all those who shared in it (through, for example, the 'possession' of land or the holding of office) did so on sufferance and not as a matter of right. Not all these consequences, of course, had as yet made themselves felt in the reign of Ivan III. But already they were all evident in a more or less developed state:

... the increasing regimentation of Muscovite society from the time of Ivan III onwards, the imposition of compulsory service to the State, and the assumption by the Muscovite sovereigns of the political inheritance of the Golden Horde owed much to Russia's resistance to, and counter-offensive against, her Mongol overlords.*

It was this specific Mongol colouring that distinguished Muscovite absolutism from that in the contemporary West – in England, say, or France. Ivan III, for example, was the first ruler of Muscovy to claim ownership of all the Russian lands; he vastly extended the internal authority of the grand prince; and he asserted the position of the autocrat as military leader.

The association of Church and State was much more intimate than anything comparable in Western Europe. As a result, the 'apostasy' and defeat of Byzantium had an enormous impact on the religious and political culture of Russia. In the words of James Billington: 'Muscovy at the time of its rise to greatness resembled an expectant revivalist camp.' † Enlightenment was proferred by Nil Sorsky, formerly a monk at Mount Athos, who preached a life

*D. Obolensky, in *Oxford Slavonic Papers*, v (Oxford, 1954), p. 30.
†J. Billington, *The Icon and the Axe* (London, 1966), p. 61.

of 'non-possessing' contemplation and direct contact with God, and by his philosophical opponent Joseph of Volokolamsk. Joseph stressed the importance of external observance, strict regulation and the centralization of authority. He fiercely defended the possessions of the monasteries and his 'possessing' faction increasingly dominated the most important monastic centres. He sought to deflect the greed of the grand princes by appealing to their sense of mission and their need for the Church to sanction their new authority. 'The Tsar,' he wrote, 'is in nature like to all men, but in authority he is like to the highest God.' According to this theory, the autocrat was the divinely ordained fountainhead of an undifferentiated concentration of authority – political, in that the tsar was the only political authority, the ultimate patriarch; economic, in that he claimed ownership of the totality of the land; military, in that he led the country in war; religious, in that he ruled by divine right so long as he defended the rights of Orthodoxy.

This truly momentous conception, even if for the present it was more a matter of theory than of practice, produced equivalent changes throughout the hierarchy of Muscovite society. The first to suffer were the aristocracy, known rather inaccurately to history as the 'boyars'. In the early days of Muscovy, or any of the other principalities for that matter, the boyars had been the prince's advisers, of no very different status from the prince himself. The prince had been only the first among equals. The boyars were not his vassals in the sense of Western feudalism. They were independent freeholders; and this was signalized in the contractual relationship that existed between the prince and boyar which usually contained the condition: 'the boyars who dwell among us shall be at liberty to come and go'. The boyar could have his lands in one principality but serve a prince in another.

It is easy to see how the rise of Muscovy to sole dominance affected not only the boyars but also the princes who were displaced by Muscovite conquest or purchase. They lost all opportunity to move. Where could they go? To Lithuania or Poland, perhaps? But that was tantamount to treason. Such princes and boyars did not indeed lose their rights as landowners, although their rights were somewhat circumscribed by Ivan. What happened was that by losing their right to depart from service they dwindled into the category of 'serving princes'. They could no longer choose whom to serve but had to serve Muscovy.

The status of the aristocracy was further jeopardized by Ivan's policy of creating a new form of landholding. The centralized government of the reign, combined with the growth of an army to defend and expand the new state's frontiers, created the demand for more bureaucrats and soldiers. Their reward took the form of land grants held on conditional tenure for life. These were the so-called *pomestiya*. The *pomeshchiki*, as such landholders were known, owed their position and their land to their dependent position *vis-à-vis* the tsar. They held their land only so long as they served. Pomestiya were often granted to princes and boyars as well as to commoners so it is still far from clear whether this involved the creation of a new class. This policy was first applied in the 1480s in conquered Novgorod, whence many thousands were deported in order to make room for 'service men' from Moscow. This whole practice may also in part be an indirect inheritance from the Mongols, for they had known it centuries before its appearance in Muscovy.

For all Muscovy's indebtedness to the Mongols in matters of class structure and power, however, it was Byzantium that continued to give the new State its cultural superstructure. This was all the more the case on Ivan's marriage in 1472 to Zoë (known in Russia as Sophia) Palaeologus, the daughter of Thomas Palaeologus and niece of the last Byzantine Emperor. In 1453, when the Turks conquered Constantinople, Sophia and her father took refuge in Rome. In papal circles the plan then evolved of a marriage between Sophia and Ivan, in the hope of bringing the latter into communion with Rome in the sense used by the Council of Florence of 1439, which had sought to reunite the Eastern and Western churches. On the Muscovite side, Ivan's master of the mint, an Italian named Giovanni Battista Volpe – known in Moscow as Ivan Fryazin (= Frank, and, by extension, Westerner) – drew Ivan's attention to the Byzantine heiress in Rome.

The Tsar's first wife had been a member of the ruling house of Tver. Her widower quickly grasped the potentiality for enhanced prestige in the proposed alliance. It would raise him to equal status with the ruling houses of Western Europe. Accordingly, a

Muscovite mission led by Ivan Fryazin travelled to Rome in 1472 and returned with Sophia, by way of Lübeck, Reval (Tallinn), Pskov, and Novgorod. Among the company was the Papal Legate; his mission was unsuccessful. In fact, it is said that when he was seen to bear the Latin cross at the head of the Princess's cortège, the Metropolitan Philip, Ivan's spiritual adviser, threatened to quit Moscow in protest.

If the attempt at religious infiltration was without consequence, the same can by no means be said of the implications of a Byzantine princess on the throne of Muscovy. It was during the reign of Ivan and his son, Vasily III, that Moscow came to be referred to as the 'Third Rome', and the Russians as the 'New Israel' of the Church. Philotheos, a monk from a Pskov monastery, wrote to Vasily III that the Church of ancient Rome fell by reason of heresy, the Churches of the second Rome, Constantinople, fell to the grandsons of Hagar; '. . . two Romes have already fallen but the third remains standing and a fourth there will not be'. The hopes of all the Christian empires were now centred on Muscovy, concluded Philotheos. At the same time it was 'discovered' that St Peter's brother Andrew had introduced Christianity to Russia before it had arrived in Italy and that the grand princes of Moscow were descended from ancient Roman emperors. In actual fact, the hopes of Ivan and his successors lay more in the West than in any Byzantine political legacy. But for all that, the ecclesiastical doctrine gave an ideological hallowing to the new State.

This new status enjoyed by Ivan III clearly called for an enhanced physical setting. A number of Italian artists and craftsmen had already been included in Sophia's entourage in 1472. But not until 1475 did Ivan seriously concern himself with the re-modelling of Moscow consistent with its new dignity as the successor to Constantinople. It was then that he summoned from Italy five architects, led by the famous Bolognese, Aristotle da Fioraventi. The latter was entrusted with the rebuilding of the Cathedral of the Dormition, originally built in the Kremlin in the days of Ivan Kalita. Both here and in the city's other churches, there developed a blend of Byzantine plan, Russian onion-shaped domes, and minor Italianate architectural features. The Tsar's residential and official quarters were also complemented by the

construction of two stone buildings – the Palace of Facets, used
for Court ceremonies and the like, and the Terem Palace, for the
royal family's private occupation. The walls of the Kremlin were
strengthened and furnished with towers and gates.

Ivan the Great's outward panoply, his success in foreign policy,
his establishment of abolutism, and his consolidation of a national
Russian State – all these were but the prelude to the upheavals in
the reign of his grandson, Ivan the Terrible. There was a spectacular political explosion; and the policy of creating pomestiya
wholesale rapidly brought on a land crisis – the immediate cause
of so many of the convulsions affecting Russian history, in the
sixteenth century no less than in the twentieth.

CHAPTER 4

Ivan the Terrible
and the Birth of Russian Autocracy

During the course of his long reign of more than fifty years, Ivan IV initiated a radical transformation of Russian society. At his accession in 1533, the north Russian forest was dotted with small peasant families carving out an adequate living. Many were dependent to varying degrees on temporal or spiritual landholders but many more acknowledged no lord but the Grand Prince himself. Clannish aristocrats, descended both from former independent princes and from old Moscow boyars, expected to be consulted on important matters of state in the Boyar Council or *Duma*, and vied with one another for commands and offices. The impoverished offspring of the well-born, the so-called 'boyars' children', competed with the aristocrats for grants of fiefs (pomestiya). The unlucky could expect to become peasants. In flourishing towns, wealthy merchants and manufacturers exploited the work of a growing class of hired labourers. It was a society in which vertical divisions of geography and patronage were still, for all but the urban poor, more important than the horizontal divisions of class.

By Ivan's death in 1584, this had substantially changed. The frontiers of the state had been pushed south to Astrakhan and far into Siberia, but otherwise the picture was bleak. The new military settlements in the south were no answer to the economic and social collapse of town and country in central Russia. The peasants, forced to subsist on barely adequate plots while providing free labour for their masters, bitterly resented the status of bound serfs to which most were now condemned. Unable to meet the exactions levied upon them by their masters on behalf of the State, they fled in thousands to the new lands in the east and to the growing free cossack communes in the 'wild plain' to the south. Nobles and surviving aristocrats had been taught that the tsar-autocrat expected of them the obedience of a monastic order. The autocrat now consulted whom he wanted to when he needed to, for Ivan the Terrible had invested his borrowed Byzantine titles with new and fearsome significance. By the 1580s Russian society had assumed the essential shape it was to retain until 1861; despite war and revolution vestiges of it have survived until today.

During and since Ivan's lifetime Russian and foreign writers have argued bitterly about the Terrible Tsar. The last twenty-five years have seen the emphasis shift from passionate assertion to passionate inquiry but three major questions are still far from resolved. To what extent was the disturbed personality of Ivan IV itself responsible for the events of his reign, and therefore for the transformation of Russian society? What was the nature of the conflicts which caused so much blood-letting among the Russian landholding classes in the sixteenth century? In what sense can the outcome of Ivan's policies be seen as 'progressive' or were they entirely 'reactionary'?

Ivan IV came to the throne at the age of three in 1533. In his early childhood, his mother, a Lithuanian princess, dominated the Regency Council. He was only eight when she died, perhaps a victim of poison. After that, aristocratic factions manoeuvred for the right to use Ivan as their pawn with no regard for his sensibility or any other considerations of propriety. Ivan was only thirteen when he intervened by having one of the leading aristocrats murdered. At the age of seventeen, Metropolitan Makary had him crowned with the title of Tsar (Caesar) so that he was the first Russian monarch to claim an imperial title. In the same year he took the unusual step of marrying Anastasia Zakharina, an attractive young woman of his own choice. That same summer, a terrible series of fires and social upheavals occurred in Moscow and Ivan had to watch impotently as his uncle was dragged off to be killed by the enraged population. Frightened by the rising and by the visions of damnation conjured up by his confessors, Ivan began to rule but relied heavily on advisers. The two principal advisers were a young nobleman, Alexei Adashev, and the priest Silvester; they formed the nucleus of the so-called 'Chosen Council', a body with no clear status but more real influence than the Boyar Duma. The 'Chosen Council' was responsible for pragmatic but far-reaching reforms in almost all aspects of state administration, civil and military, and for taking a critical look at the immunities of the Church. It was largely responsible for a new code of secular law, a reformed statute for the Orthodox Church and the famous *Domostroy*, a manual of household management based on the comfortable and orderly way of life of the merchants of Novgorod. Later the *Domostroy* came to epitomize the subjection of women among Russia's upper classes but in its own time its harsh and unloving language seemed unremarkable, while its suggestions for honourable and useful tasks for women probably enhanced their status. They also extended the obligation to serve to holders of patrimonial estates as well as of pomestiya.

These policies were rewarded by some spectacular successes with the conquest of the Tatars of Kazan in 1553 and of those of Astrakhan in 1556. The trade with England was opened by Chancellor's first voyage to the White Sea in 1553. Despite these successes, the Russian state suffered a severe crisis between 1558 and 1562 that involved the disgrace of the 'Chosen Council', the launching of an adventurous war against the German-ruled bishoprics of Livonia and a mass purge of the 'boyars' by Ivan's personal armed force, the *oprichniki*. After a number of setbacks and the defection of some leading military figures in the Livonian war, Ivan left Moscow in fury in 1562 and retired to a makeshift court at Alexandrova Sloboda. He refused to return until he was given a free hand to do what he wanted. When this was duly proffered, Ivan established a special court or oprichnina which he ruled despotically through his oprichniki, a uniformed force subject to rigid monastic discipline. The oprichnina ruled part of Russia directly. In theory, the rest was handed over to members of the aristocracy whom Ivan temporarily spared. A reign of terror now began in which one 'plot' after another was discovered; it ran its course without regard to the status, age or sex of its victims – even a Metropolitan was murdered for protesting when its excesses touched his own clan. The terror reached its greatest extent in 1567 when the Staritsky clan, Ivan's closest relatives and potential rivals, were eliminated and in 1569–70 when Novgorod and Pskov were sacked. Russia's conflict in Livonia and the disaffection of a large part of the population encouraged the Crimean Khan to invade Russia and sack Moscow in 1571, incidentally destroying many of the documents that might better explain this period in Russian history. In an apparent charade whose purpose has never been fully established, Ivan resigned the throne to a converted Tatar prince in 1575, though he soon resumed it.

By 1582, he had to admit defeat in the Livonian war where the weak German barons had been augmented by Poland and Sweden, then at the height of their power and intent on excluding Russia from the Baltic. The conquest of Siberia in his last years may have provided some comfort, though it tended to confirm the wisdom of his former advisers who had urged expansion to the south and east in preference to the war in Livonia. Also in 1582, Ivan killed his son and heir and his pregnant daughter-in-law, leaving only the mentally and physically handicapped Theodore Ioannovich to succeed him when he died two years later. Were these apocalyptic events the result of a 'class struggle' as so many from Giles Fletcher onwards have suggested? Or could it be that a powerful but deranged individual was able to impose himself on a country in which the social classes had not yet developed to the point at which effective resistance could be organized?

It would have been surprising had the first Russian tsar not been a seriously disturbed person; he may well also have suffered severe mental illness. Neither Ivan nor his mentally handicapped younger brother ever knew their father. As regent their mother was a busy woman in more ways than one; the son of one of her lovers became one of Ivan's early victims. She died when Ivan was only eight and he complained later that from then on they received 'no human care from any quarter . . .', an exaggeration only partly designed to excuse his later crimes. He may have looked for avuncular affection from the leaders of the aristocratic cliques, whose rule followed. If so, he was disappointed, meeting at best indifference and at worst contempt. Encouraged by the clergy to believe that God had intended him to rule absolutely, he resented the way his wishes were ignored. His apologetic writings lack any sense of proportion about this; for Ivan it was as outrageous to be told when to eat as to be refused the company of a friend. Some Western psychologists have speculated that the 'swaddling' of Russian babies develops personalities in which long periods of apparent quietism are interrupted by brief outbursts of exuberance

or violence. Ivan's 'swaddling' continued beyond the nursery:
while still a small child he was forced to endure heavy ceremonial
robes during endless court and religious ritual. His excesses
included an unusual amount of violent horseplay and the torture
of animals.

If Ivan's assumption of the imperial title in 1547 was suggested
by the clergy, his marriage to Anastasia Zakharina was very much
his own idea. The seventeen-year-old monarch organized a sort of
all-Russian talent contest and chose the winner himself. As the
fifteen-year-old daughter of a Moscow boyaral house, the family
of the future Romanov tsars, Anastasia was considered an upstart
by a number of the princely families. She has been credited with
the relative moderation of Ivan's behaviour until her death in
1560. She performed her dynastic duty with fortitude, bearing six
children, only two of whom survived her. Ivan showed his affection, and also helped to ruin her health, by dragging her after him
on his continual pilgrimages and hunting trips, though he still
found time for other women. In 1553 Ivan fell seriously ill and a
crisis erupted over the succession. Many of his advisers feared a
repetition of the internecine struggles that had marked Ivan's
childhood. They preferred to see Ivan's cousin, Prince Vladimir
Staritsky, as tsar or regent, rather than Ivan's infant son. Above
all, they feared the rule of Anastasia's family. On his recovery,
Ivan seemed to overlook this 'treason', but in the years that
followed, as the vengeful patriarch displaced the pragmatic statesman in his mind, it came to assume greater importance. He did
not, however, draw the 'rational' conclusion that the apanage
system should be ended but insisted that a generous apanage
should be earmarked for his younger son.

As time went on Ivan's mind was soured both by the deaths of
his children and by the Josephan clergy resentful of the influence
of the 'Chosen Council'. 'If you wish to be an autocrat do not
keep beside you a single counsellor wiser than yourself' one of
them told him. Impoverished members of the gentry such as Ivan
Peresvetov also forsaw opportunities for themselves in upheavals
which only a radical autocrat could initiate. Anastasia died in
1560, shortly after the removal of Adashev and Silvester, though
before their formal disgrace. Silvester himself had urged Ivan to

take better care of Anastasia's health but Ivan now accused Silvester of using witchcraft to kill her. 'If only you had not taken
from me my young wife, then there would have been no "sacrifices
to Cronos",' he wrote later. So unhinged did his behaviour become
at her death that the Metropolitan begged him to remarry immediately. He followed this advice in his own time – five times in
all, rather more than the rules of the Church permitted. These
marriages brought him neither happiness nor reinforcements for
his dynasty. Nor did he appear to find much solace in his lovers of
both sexes.

The apogee of Ivan's sadism was reached with the sack of Novgorod and Pskov, recorded by one of his German oprichniks:

Mounting a horse and brandishing a spear he charged in and ran people
through while his son watched the entertainment or joined in the sport.
When one horse grew tired, he called for another, until weary but unsated
he shouted for his Oprichniki [assassins] to lay about them and chop
everybody to pieces.*

On other occasions his sadism was laced by a macabre humour.
There was another side to Ivan, pious and superstitious. He was
punctilious in fulfilling his obligation to ease the souls of the dead
aristocrats, even when these were his own victims. He laid no
hands on the 'holy fool' who publicly upbraided his bloodlust in
Pskov. His 'resignation' in 1575 may well have been prompted by
a prophecy that a tsar would die in that year, for, like many of his
contemporaries, he was a sincere believer in witchcraft. Of course
the mentally ill may have moments of cool rationality, but a
measure of scepticism is called for when we are told that all his
policies were the fruits of such moments. It is more likely that
unscrupulous clerics and gentry played on his insecurity to their
own advantage.

Ivan the Terrible's reign left such an indelible imprint on the
minds of those that followed that he has never ceased to evoke
ethical judgement. For his immediate successors he was obviously
a tyrant. Nineteenth-century historians rescued him from obloquy
by ascribing grandiose motives to him. He was credited with far-
sighted and rationalistic statesmanship aimed at transforming the
Russian state and finding new alliances in Western Europe. Thus,

*H. von Staden, in *Canadian American Slavic Studies*, ix (Toronto, 1975), p. 234.

the displacement of the aristocracy by the serving gentry was a statesmanlike plan for overcoming feudal disunity while the Livonian war was undertaken in pursuit of rational mercantilistic economic policies. In the last few years, these assertions have begun to receive the empirical investigation they deserve. It seems unlikely that either will survive intact. Ivan's relative indifference to sound economic policy will be illustrated below, but an examination of the events leading to the Livonian war suggests that agreement with the Livonians on Russian trade with Western Europe and on the undisturbed passage of Western exports through Livonia to Russia had been reached by 1557, *before* the outbreak of the war. By that same year, Russia had also built a port at the mouth of the Narva and had obtained the necessary consent of Sweden for its use, a situation not to recur until the reign of Peter the Great. Ivan's invasion of Livonia has, therefore, to be seen in other terms: as the response of a patriarchal ruler, determined to regain the 'patrimony' of his forefathers, as the Orthodox clergy had continually urged him, and furious at the contumacy of the Livonians. During the invasion he was also able to take the edge off the appetites of some of his supporters by allocating them fiefs in the conquered territory. In this he followed the precedent set by Ivan III at the conquest of Novgorod.

In recent years Ivan's famous 'Correspondence' with the exiled Prince Andrei Kurbsky has been denounced as a forgery, but overwhelmingly vindicated in the subsequent polemic. In it, Ivan described his domestic enemies as 'boyars and grandees'. He accused Kurbsky himself of wishing to become 'master of Yaroslavl' but later directed some irony at '[The old apanage] power of our vassals' and 'their tattered finery'. The brevity and humour of these references are clear enough. Ivan himself did not seriously believe that the 'boyars' were really interested in feudal disunity. The accusation that dominates the letters is quite different. He resented intensely what he considered had been the usurpation of the government between 1547 and 1560 by Adashev and Silvester, the leaders of the 'boyar party'. 'Or do you consider this to be "light", for a priest and overweening, cunning servants to rule and the Tsar to be held in honour only by virtue of his presidency and for the sake of the renown of the kingdom, while in power he is in no way better than a servant?' In fact, the two men were of fairly humble origin, and despite its formal irregularity, their disgrace elicited not a murmur of resistance from the boyars. Kurbsky himself seems to have been surprised at Ivan's belief that they had led a boyar party. So why did Ivan unleash his reign of terror?

A 'boyar' in old Russia was an aristocrat holding the senior court rank obliging and entitling him to participate in state business in exchange for economic and juridical privileges. More loosely, the word was used to describe any aristocrat. By 1550, the boyars were mainly recruited from the untitled Moscow aristocracy which had supplied the grand princes with boyars for generations from the scions of the former apanage principalities. During Ivan's minority, it had been the princes rather than the Moscow boyars who had usurped authority. No evidence has been found to suggest that the princes had separatist ambitions to a greater extent than the Moscow boyars – or than Ivan had when he created an apanage for his younger son. No convincing evidence has ever been discovered demonstrating the existence of coherent policies favouring the interests of their 'class', though there were many conspiracies aimed at promoting the interests of particular clans. It is not at all clear that they constituted a distinct class in any definable sense. Of course, in all pre-industrial societies, human and natural disasters ensured that some old families fell while new ones rose, and Ivan's wrath was an unparalleled disaster for many. It remains to be shown that by the mid sixteenth century, the landholding class was divided into distinct groups; the holders of patrimonial estates (*votchiny*) and fief-holding serving gentry (pomeshchiki). It is not even clear that there was any economic difference between them at all. There were few *votchinniks* who held no pomestiya. In the late fifteenth century at least sixty-one princes had been granted pomestiya in Novgorod, while in the 1560s the oprichnik von Staden received grants of votchiny and pomestiya as though the difference between them was insignificant. Prince Vladimir Staritsky's apanage was probably brought to an end in 1569 because Ivan suspected Staritsky's serving gentry of entertaining a dangerous loyalty to their master. For economic and military reasons, such loyalties must have made sense but they imply that many of the poorer serving gentry were likely to seek advancement through patronage, not class struggle against fellow landholders. On the other hand, one effect of the terror was of course to persuade the poorer serving gentry that the Tsar was the only worthwhile patron.

It is central to later justifications of Ivan's rule that a *strong* aristocracy was, in some reprehensible sense, oppressing the state, perhaps to the extent of trying to introduce an oligarchal 'Lithuanian' constitution. Ivan enjoyed reminding Polish kings that he enjoyed his throne through the grace of God alone. There are reasons for believing that the Russian aristocracy was actually very weak in facing a determined autocrat. The sudden influx of princely families that followed the elimination of Moscow's rivals, the absence of primogeniture amongst the aristocracy, and the alleged demographic upsurge of the early sixteenth century must all have weakened the aristocracy. It is possible that it was precisely this weakness that permitted a deranged tsar, urged on by impoverished 'boyars' children' and his Josephan advisers, to redefine autocracy as despotism. In this case, the 'boyars and grandees' of Ivan's letters become not a sociological category as so many have supposed, but a psychological one: the enemies invented by paranoia. Ivan made enemies of almost all the men who had the courage to stand up to him. In a feudal society, it is hardly surprising that most of them were aristocrats.

Some light is cast on these matters by the institution of *mestnichestvo*. This was the method of establishing the relative merits, as understood by feudal aristocrats, of rival candidates for promotion to places at court and hence to offices and commands. The system was abolished by a later tsar, Theodore II, who felt it generated needless disputes and prevented him promoting able commoners and lesser gentry to high office. Since then, historians have often argued that it damaged the Russian State by preventing the nomination of the best men to military commands. This is surely anachronistic. In 1588, the hereditary senior Grandee of Spain led the Great Armada into battle against the hereditary Lord High Admiral of England. It is not at all obvious that such a system was a relative handicap for Russia. In any case, a despotic ruler like Ivan IV had his own reasons for keeping troops out of the hands of leaders able enough to inspire loyalty. The disastrous consequences of this were painfully apparent when the Tatar Khan Devlet-Girei swept all before him in 1571.

During the years of the 'Chosen Council', the aristocracy had been obliged to submit their records of service and genealogy to the scribes of the grand prince, and service had replaced birth as the major criterion in making appointments. So far from showing an interest in abolishing the system, Ivan showed some interest in manipulating it to increase his overall authority over litigants. Princely families that had recently arrived in Moscow found themselves in competition with other families of the same kind and with old Moscow boyaral families. Even for those with large patrimonial estates near Moscow, the practice of bequeathing equal shares to all the sons meant that the family had to tread a narrow tightrope between extinction and impoverishment. The consequences of decline were highly visible and the large number of princely paupers amazed foreign visitors.

Good husbandry and good luck in the demographic lottery might put a brake on such a decline but only service with the tsar could reverse it, hence the importance of place. So great was the pressure for places and fiefs that Ivan found it easy to recruit informers, even against their own relatives, once the terror had begun. Another sign of aristocratic weakness came in 1550 when service was made compulsory for votchinniki also. There is not the slightest sign that this provoked any aristocratic opposition. In common with aristocrats everywhere, however, the Russian princes and boyars set great store on their pride in their own dignity. Attached as they were to the idea that their ancestors had once rivalled those of the tsar, they felt entitled to consultation on matters of state and they wanted his help in maintaining a show of magnificence. This was probably as far as their 'programme' went.

Many historians have observed the similarities between six-teenth-century Russia and Spain. Both states overcame feudal dis-unity and Islamic opponents at more or less the same time, only to find themselves bearing the heavy burden of defending the one true faith against heresy. In incorporating new territories with ethnically mixed populations they both required a strong ideological justification for their policies of assimilation. The new burdens on the state exacerbated social tensions which were met by institutions which sought to impose the totalitarianism of monastic life on the whole community and which did not shrink from terror. Church and State were prepared, in both cases, to apply a rationalist approach to administrative and military affairs, but they did their best to restrict the influence of the Renaissance (rather easier in Russia than in Spain) and to root out all manifestations of the Protestant Reformation.

Russia was 'God's Land', a religious civilization in which tsar and peasant revered 'holy fools' like the Blessed Vasily and happily saw meat-eaters burnt for desecrating Lent. It was a state in which Orthodoxy far outweighed race or language as the test of nationality. Beyond its confines lay damnation as well as treason: 'Just as Rome is enticement, so are you darkness', thundered Ivan in answer to a request by Polish Protestants to enter Russia. It would be unwise to take these protestations of religious orthodoxy entirely at face value, however: this was still a Russia in which paganism survived and where a belief in witchcraft was almost universal.

Both tsars and clergy were shocked and terrified by the collapse of authority in the German Reformation; symptoms of reformism were apparent in the Russian Church, too. It is not surprising that there was a closing of ranks between the grand princes and the leading clergy. To the ascetic followers of Nil Sorsky at the time, and to materialist critics since, this has appeared an unholy compact. The Grand Prince undertook to defend the temporal possessions of the Church so long as the Church sanctified the despotism of the Grand Prince. By the middle of the sixteenth century the other-worldly 'non-possessing' followers of Sorsky had been virtually eliminated from the Church hierarchy.

In 1550, when Ivan inquired of a Church Council whether it might be right to secularize church lands, the Church responded with a resounding 'no', basing its case on such ancient forgeries as the 'Donation of Constantine'. Like the contemporaneous Council of Trent, it was prepared to put its own house in order by standardizing the liturgy, improving the training of priests, rooting out sexual misconduct everywhere, and especially the 'sin of Sodom' in the monasteries. In view of the other problems facing him at the time, Ivan had to be satisfied with this modest compromise.

The Church was the only disciplined propaganda machine in Russia. It fostered the unity of the State and respect for the authority of the Tsar. It demanded and received the suppression of dissent of all kinds. Maxim the Greek, the chief representative of Renaissance learning in the Russian Church, was hounded into conformity. Freethinkers, evangelical Christians, and primitive Christians bold enough to challenge the moral bases of feudalism were tried for heresy and imprisoned in monasteries. The attitude towards thinking Christians was best expressed by the prelate who advised an ascetic elder: 'Don't read many books and you won't fall into heresy.' The borders were closed and the people were diverted from more dangerous thoughts by the burning of witches and announcements of miracles associated with the showing of relics.

To understand just how indispensable the support of the Church was to Ivan we must consider an aspect of sixteenth-century Russia on which all historians agree: the latter half of the sixteenth century was a period of unmitigated disaster for the Russian peasants. As the violence of exploitation and warfare destroyed more and more of the basic cells of which Russian peasant society was constituted, something approaching a social class in the modern sense began to emerge, though its distinctive ideology had to wait for the collapse of the dynasty at the end of the century. A number of processes were involved. For a start the creeping but extensive colonization of the forest by nuclear families was coming to an end in central Russia anyway as 'axe met axe'. The residual independence of the 'black peasants' was lost as they were granted in fiefs to pomeshchiks or monasteries. The landholders themselves were faced by demands for more money and turned increasingly to new forms of cultivation such as the three-course rotation and three-field systems which gave them more control over peasant labour. Moreover, the great insecurity that even oprichniks felt during the terror was a spur to heedless exploitation rather than good husbandry. Faced with impoverishment, the landholders vigorously asserted their control over the means of production.

The peasants resisted these processes in the only ways they

could. They killed tax collectors, and resisted attempts to subordinate them to landholders. With the reduction in fear following
Ivan's death, more organized forms of resistance took place such
as the rent and labour strike on the estates of the Joseph-Voloko-
lamsk monastery in 1589–91. Overwhelmingly, however, the peasants responded by fleeing to the new lands of the east and south.
As Giles Fletcher observed:

... you shall have many villages and towns of half a mile and a mile long
stand all unhabited, the people being fled all into other places by reason of
the extreme usage and exactions done upon them. So that in the way
toward Moscow, betwixt Vologda and Iaroslavl (which is two nineties,
after their reckoning, little more than an hundred miles English) there are
in sight fifty *derevni*, or villages, at the least, some half a mile, some a mile
long, that stand vacant and desolate without any inhabitant.*

The Law Code of 1550 had attempted to regulate the transfer of
peasants from one estate to another by laying down a strict procedure. Peasants were only to leave after harvest time (St George's
Day in the autumn) and on payment of a dwelling tax. The shortage of hands following the oprichnina was so severe as to cause
serious fighting between landholders for peasant labour. In 1581,
the government intervened once more, this time by announcing
'forbidden years' during which there could be no transfer and by
conducting a census of the land and those working on it. It was
only a matter of time before the peasant finally lost the freedom to
move from one employer to another and became a bound serf.
Whereas economic differences between peasants remained, and
would increase during periods of recovery (the 1590s and 1620s),
differences of status, which had formerly divided the peasantry,
were no longer of any great significance. Something like the Russian peasantry known to modern history was coming into being.

How then could their explosive resentment be contained? The
Church succeeded in persuading the peasants that Ivan himself
was not to blame for their difficulties. He was the God-given tsar
who had been abused by the boyars in his childhood and had
chastised them in his maturity, the victor in the struggle with the
infidel in the East and the defender of Orthodoxy in the West.

*G. Fletcher, *Of the Rus Commonwealth*, ed. A. J. Schmidt (Ithaca N.Y., 1966), p. 66.

Unless they themselves were directly affected, the peasants were willing to take a lenient view of Ivan's purge of the landholding 'boyars'. His excesses were put down to the malice of his advisers.

If the test of 'progress' in a fundamentally medieval society is the emergence of capitalist modes and relations of production, the Russian countryside provides the contrasting case of a society in which there was an intensification of exploitation and a clarification of class relations but, at the same time, a reversion to labour service and social immobility characteristic of a much earlier period in Western European history. The situation of the towns is more confusing still, though some new towns, mainly military settlements, were founded. Soviet historiography has so far failed to pay much attention to the *posads*, the sections of townships devoted to commercial, capitalistic activity, during the late sixteenth and early seventeenth centuries. The existing evidence contrasts too painfully with the assertion that the achievement of national unity facilitates the creation of a national market, and hence of capitalistic relations in general. This does seem to have happened in the early sixteenth century but there is every reason to believe that the commercial activity of the Russian towns actually declined between the crises of 1547 and 1648. In Russia, the creation of new pre-capitalist markets was to be the work of the manorial economies rather than the townships.

The unity of the State may foster market relations but whether or not it is 'progressive' depends on circumstances. The unification of Italy must have seemed 'progressive' to a native of Turin in the 1860s (and more briefly to a native of Palermo) but without the disunity of the fourteenth and fifteenth centuries there would have been no Italian Renaissance. The policies that most favoured the merchants of the posads were those that made the exactions of the State less arbitrary and unpredictable. The most significant were the reforms in local government which eliminated the old system of *kormlyenshchiki*, governors living off the land, and instituted a partly elective system of local government. Again, these were the policies of the 1550s, the period when Ivan and his 'Chosen Council' worked more or less harmoniously together. The period that followed, the period of the oprichnina, was one of massive insecurity in which merchants were subjected to additional taxation to pay for warfare and straightforward protection rackets at the hands of the oprichniki. For this reason, there was a tendency for productive activity to move out of the posads and onto the estates of the monasteries during the latter part of the sixteenth century.

The conquest of Kazan and Astrakhan in mid century gave Russia control of the Volga and the upper part of the Caspian Sea. This was the work of the armed might of the Muscovite patriarchal State. The subsequent conquest of Siberia foreshadows the pattern of westward expansion in the United States. It was organized by the Stroganov merchant dynasty which hired Yermak and his band of lawless Cossack warriors on the basis of a rather vague charter from Ivan. Yermak's campaign also resembles Spanish American precedents; his was a small body of men intruding into a vast alien land where the only advantage lay in its monopoly of firearms. There were differences, of course. Yermak did not burn boats, he simply drowned the doubters and complainers. In 1582 he defeated Kuchum, Khan of the Siberian Tatars, and installed himself in his deserted capital (later Tobolsk). They then had to withstand a long siege until Ivan's greed overcame his caution. The Tatars succeeded in killing Yermak but by that time regular troops were on their way to complete his work. Siberia provided the state with massive additional reserves of forest products and mineral ores and, despite the oprichnina, the Stroganov family were able to make massive profits from their salt-mining operations in Siberia. Expansion into the East created opportunities for Russian merchants to take the initiative in a way that they rarely showed in trade with the West and to build up large reserves of capital that might one day create a more productive economy.

In a world polarized between Russia and the United States, the origins of the uncomfortable relations that have often existed between Russians and Anglo-Saxons is obviously a fascinating subject. In 1553 the *Bona Fortuna*, commanded by Richard Chancellor, the sole surviving vessel of the three which had originally set sail from London in the quest for the North-East Passage, arrived at the mouth of the Northern Dvina. Chancellor travelled on to Kholmogory and thence to Moscow. Here he was warmly welcomed by Ivan, only too willing to relieve his dependence on

German traders. This was the prelude to the formation of the 'Russia Company'. Ivan's charter of 1556 granted the Company extensive trading privileges, which included the right to customs-free trade and tax exemptions for English trading counters established in Kholmogory, Vologda, and Moscow. The reactions of the English traders were on the whole hostile and condescending. They found Muscovy ruled by an all-powerful tsar, they found the Russians drunkards and hypocritical, the Orthodox Church rife with superstition and with morals subverted by homosexuality. George Turberville, a poet and secretary to one of the English embassies, penned in verse a number of such criticisms:

A people passing rude, to vices vile inclined,
Folk fit to be of Bacchus train, so quaffing is their kind.

Devoutly down they duck, with forehead to the ground
Was never more deceit in rags, and greasy garments found.

Turberville even compared them to the Irish, surely the ultimate insult for an Englishman:

Wilde Irish are as civil as the Russians in their kind,
Hard choice which is the best of both, each bloody, rude and blind.

It is, of course, too much to expect that the more flexible sexual mores of the Russian countryside, such as the cohabitation of widowers with their daughters-in-law, might have been seen as a natural response to the precarious economies of nuclear peasant families, or that homosexuality among the upper classes might have been seen as the inevitable result of the seclusion of women. On the other hand, Chancellor found much to praise in the leniency of Russian penal laws, and Fletcher's *Of the Russe Commonwealth*, written in the period after Ivan's death, is an indispensable source for any understanding of sixteenth-century Russia. Relations with England included some very cordial correspondence between Queen Elizabeth and the Russian tsars; Ivan showed an interest in an English wife and in asylum in England. The real significance of these incidents is that they testify to the extreme military and diplomatic isolation felt by both England and Russia at this time. They shared only their enemies.

Economically, politically and militarily, Russia's most important neighbour in the sixteenth century was Poland–Lithuania. Up to half Russia's foreign trade passed through her western rival, and the Lithuanian State with its aristocratic 'West Russian' pretensions had long posed a constant danger of subversion to the Russia based on Moscow. Ivan's own disappointment at his failure to achieve any further consolidation of the Russian lands to the west was probably premature. It is true that Kurbsky was able to taunt Ivan with the loss of Polotsk to the Poles, but its re-capture in 1563 had caused panic among the Lithuanian aristocracy. The result was the Union of Lublin in 1569 which established a new Polish–Lithuanian state, albeit with only Crown and Sejm (Assembly) as sole joint institutions. A period of diplomatic probing followed, facilitated by the Polish interregna of 1574 and 1587. The old vision of a unification of Russian lands under Lithuania had gone; in its place appeared ephemeral notions of a federation of all the Eastern Slavs under the cultural and political leadership of the Polish gentry or the Russian autocrat. Serious negotiations took place in the 1570s; if successful, they might have established Ivan or one of his sons on the combined thrones. The talks foundered in the face of Russian fears of religious heterodoxy and Ivan's hostility towards the tradition of autonomous political activity amongst the Polish gentry. Kurbsky and other opponents of Ivan encouraged the Lithuanian and Polish aristocrats to resist Ivan's demand to rule personally as hereditary autocrat.

The failure of these negotiations was followed by a decade of truce and then by a new period of decisive conflict between Poland and Russia. With the decline of the West Russian state, the Lithuanian gentry converted in increasing numbers to the Polish language and the triumphalist Catholicism of the Council of Trent. They were compensated by admission to some of the freedoms long enjoyed by the Polish gentry. No such compensation was available to the peasants of the borderlands, where the processes of increasing exploitation and flight were analogous to those in the rest of Russia. As the linguistic and religious cohesion of Lithuania declined, the outlines of two new nationalities, the Belorussians and Ukrainians began to emerge; new ethnic groups who saw their future in alliance with the tsars in Moscow, though not necessarily in subjection to them. Far to the south, in mountains only recently subjugated by the Islamic Turks and Persians, the Christian Georgians began to look to Moscow for their ultimate deliverance.

To nineteenth-century West Europeans (including Karl Marx), the evolution of England epitomized 'progress'; the gradual – or dialectical – development of limited representative government had been both cause and effect of economic development based on extensive private ownership and commodity production for the market. Simon De Montfort and Oliver Cromwell might be 'selfish' representatives of the baronage or the mercantile bourgeoisie but they, and not centralizing kings, represented progress. Those who see the centralized state as the only reliable employer may well take a different view. Yet it is a striking paradox, and a challenge to our preconceptions, that it was precisely Ivan (during the years of the 'Chosen Council') who established the Russian equivalent of Parliament, the *Zemsky Sobor*, or Assembly of the Land. Originally conceived in the late 1540s as an integrating alternative to the aristocratic Boyar Duma and to the tradition of the vyeche, the popular assembly that re-emerged in Moscow during the revolt of 1547, the Assemblies of the Land rubber-stamped Ivan's demands during the terror but assumed a leading role in the affairs of state after his death. Their ultimate decline and disappearance suggests that the emergence of aristocratic and bourgeois limited government was inhibited in Russia by more than the personal eccentricities of the Terrible Tsar.

Ivan's death was as dramatic as his life. When his health began to fail he called in the aid of witches and soothsayers from the north. Sir Jerome Horsey, an agent of the Russia Company, has left a vivid description of the Tsar's last days:

The Emperor began grievously to swell in his cods, with which he had most horribly offended above 50 years together, boasting of a thousand virgins he had deflowered and thousands of children of his begetting destroyed.

Every day the Tsar would be carried into his treasure-chamber, where he would fondle and discourse on the curative powers of precious stones – torquoise, coral, diamond, ruby, emerald, sapphire, onyx. But none could help. The verdict of the soothsayers

IVAN THE TERRIBLE   59

was at one with that of some spiders used as a means of divination. The end came while Ivan was preparing to play a game of chess:

He sets his men* ... the Emperor in his loose gown, shirt and linen hose, faints and falls backward. Great outcry and stir, one sent for aqua vita another to the apothecary for 'marigold and rose water' and to call his ghostly father and the physicians. In the mean he was strangled and stark dead.

Special guards were thrown round the Kremlin in case of disorder. But the succession passed easily enough to the Tsarevich, Theodore Ioannovich. This was in fact wholly deceptive. Ivan's social convulsions and his last twenty-five years of war had brought Muscovy to the verge of anarchy. The true, prophetic verdict is that of Giles Fletcher, the English Ambassador to the new Tsar:

This desperate state of things at home maketh the people for the most part to wish for some foreign invasion, which they suppose to be the only means to rid them of the heavy yoke of his tyrannous government.

*'All saving the King, which by no means he could not make stand in his place with all the rest upon the plain board.' (Horsey's note)

CHAPTER 5

The Time of Troubles

The Moscow branch of the dynasty of Rurik came to an end in the person of Ivan the Terrible's younger son, Theodore. A line of strong tsars reached a sudden nadir when a physically and mentally enfeebled autocrat, altogether unfitted for his place in the Muscovite scheme of things, ascended the throne of Muscovy. The new Tsar, crowned in 1584 at the age of twenty-seven, amid the full panoply of the imperial Byzantine ceremony, had a perpetual simper playing about his mouth. He was of devout character; his favourite pursuit was bellringing. But he also enjoyed the antics of dwarfs and court jesters, and combats between men and bears entertained him.

The hazard that brought such an incapable tsar to the throne was all the more fateful in that his reign coincided with the burgeoning of the problems inherent in his father's policies. 'God hath a great plague in store for this people' prophetically wrote Sir Jerome Horsey, an agent of the Russia Company.

The death of Ivan IV came as a relief to everyone in Muscovy save the oprichniks: within weeks the aristocrats and plebs of Moscow had combined to overthrow Bogdan Belsky, the surviving leader of the oprichnina. During the next twenty years the princely Shuiskys and Mstislavskys, the boyaral Romanovs and the oprichnik Godunovs contested the throne. Their inconclusive conflicts gave representative institutions an opportunity to develop; tsars were obliged to rule in consultation with the Boyar Duma and with frequent Assemblies of the Land. Weak central governments were at first unable to resist feudal demands for the intensification of serfdom but the end of the century brought climatic and demographic catastrophes and, with them, a new awareness throughout Russian society of the awesome potential of anti-feudal feelings. Led by the cossacks of the south-west, the peasantry challenged the very basis of Russian feudalism in a series of uprisings. Once the explosive force of peasant resentment was understood, a rash of adventurers sprang from the impoverished gentry and cossacks to see a brief moment of glory as the 'true' tsar or tsarevich. Russia's rivals, the Poles and Swedes, were quick to seize the opportunity to occupy important areas of Muscovite territory. In those years, Muscovy came near to collapse into utter anarchy. At the same time, the Russians demonstrated those qualities of resilience, personal, institutional and economic, that have so often amazed foreign observers.

A loss of manpower was one of the most potent factors in the economic crisis that followed. Flight was not the only expression of peasant discontent. For the first time in Muscovite history, the early years of the seventeenth century were marked by large-scale peasant revolts – elemental and chaotic in organization and aims, but no longer local or regional. Given this disarray inside a weakened country, there was ample leverage for foreign intervention, of which the Poles and Swedes were not slow to take advantage. In fact, the 'Time of Troubles' – the period between the death of Tsar Theodore Ioannovich in 1598 and the coronation of the first of the Romanov dynasty in 1613 – is often known as the period of peasant wars and foreign intervention. Class rose against class. Tsar followed tsar, dubious pretenders gathered support as best they could.

Theodore was so patently unfit to govern that recourse was had to a regent, the first being Nikita Romanov, a maternal uncle of the Tsar. But he died in 1586. There followed the enigmatic figure of Boris Godunov, familiar to lovers of poetry and opera from the works of Pushkin and Mussorgsky. The familiarity is misleading, however, for in this instance great artists made poor historians. Godunov hailed from a family of Mongol origin that had first taken service with the Grand Prince of Moscow in the fourteenth century. Under the oprichnina he rose to rapid eminence, and succeeded in marrying his sister Irene to Theodore, thus making himself the new tsar's brother-in-law. This upstart rise provoked envy and hatred among the old aristocratic families; and in the early years of Godunov's regency there were several plots against his life, as well as attempts to alienate him from his proximity to the throne by trying to bring about a divorce between the Tsar and his childless consort. These attempts failed, and their instigators – the princely families of Mstislavsky and Shuisky – were executed, tortured or exiled. A number of merchants were also publicly beheaded.

Godunov removed Metropolitan Dionisy, a member of the opposition, installing his own nominee, Job, a cleric of modest talents who had served the oprichnina without a qualm. He then exploited the indigence and insecurity of the visiting Patriarch of Constantinople and forced him to create a Patriarchate of Moscow and All Russia in 1588. This astute move improved the prestige of Job and Godunov within the church, averted the danger that Russia's church might come under the influence of the foreign, Islamic power which now controlled Constantinople, and bolstered Moscow's claim to be the Third Rome.

By 1587 Godunov had disposed of or silenced all his rivals. He now ruled supreme, even though he was still nominally regent. Despite his modest education, Boris Godunov was the consummate bureaucratic politician. He had the temerity to tear up Ivan IV's will which had neglected to name him regent. He took care to base his actions on accurate information. He was a masterly tactician who knew when to lie low, when to make alliances and when to denounce his erstwhile allies as 'traitors'. He was vastly superior as a diplomat to Ivan IV and he personally participated in the drafting of diplomatic correspondence with foreign monarchs.

The impoverished men at arms posed an even greater threat to the sickly Theodore and his insecure governments than they had to Ivan IV. In 1584, the Boyar Duma moved swiftly to abolish the special tax exemptions of the major church and lay landholders. This pleased the lesser gentry and replenished the Treasury at the same time. During the last years of the Livonian War, the government had tried to protect the interests of the fighting gentry by denying their peasants the right to depart in specified 'forbidden years'. Under Godunov, administrative decrees attempted to tie down the peasantry, ostensibly to protect the lesser gentry but actually to stabilize the tax-paying population. In 1597, a general law was issued permitting the forcible recovery of all peasants who had left their masters within the previous five years. In effect Boris Godunov had retroactively abolished the peasants' right to depart on St George's Day. Like other politicians of his time, Boris appealed to the poorer gentry when his fortunes were uncertain but attempted to gain allies among the aristocracy once he had reached the top.

Abroad, Godunov pursued a largely defensive policy. He made a serious attempt to unite Poland–Lithuania and Russia under Tsar Theodore during the Polish election of 1587 and concluded an enduring peace with the Poles when this failed. In the steppe-zone, fortress towns such as Kursk, Voronezh, and Byelgorod were established. Godunov even succeeded in recapturing from the Swedes some of the areas on the Gulf of Finland yielded up by Ivan – Ivangorod, Yam, and Karelia.

But these were the years before the storm. Apart from Theodore, Ivan had one other son—Dmitry, the offspring of his marriage with Maria Nagaya. Early in the reign of his half-brother, Dmitry and his mother had been exiled to Uglich, lest they serve as a tool for disaffected magnates anxious to unseat Godunov. If Anastasia Zakharina exemplifies one facet of the lives of aristocratic women in sixteenth-century Russia, Ivan's last wife exemplifies another. Brought up in the stifling confines of the veiled women's quarters, Maria Nagaya was married to an unloving tyrant who expected perfect virtue of her, and was regarded by her male relatives as a step-ladder to fortune. All her affections and hopes were pinned on her pampered, epileptic son. In 1591, she found him bleeding to death from stab wounds. Without a moment's hesitation, she accused the agents of Boris of murder and incited a riot against them. What mother would have done otherwise? And yet she was almost certainly mistaken; Dmitry probably stabbed himself in an epileptic fit. Yet even before Dmitry's death the aristocratic rivals of Boris had whispered accusations that he intended regicide; this seemed to prove them right. Maria Nagaya's shriek of maternal anguish contributed to the birth of a legend that would avenge her wasted life.

Be that as it may, the death of Tsar Theodore in 1598 further thickened the atmosphere. Power passed briefly to Tsarina Irene, but Muscovy was not yet ready for a woman ruler and she immediately took the veil. There was no choice but to tread the Polish path and *choose* a tsar – an unprecedented situation in Muscovite history. Godunov, by virtue of the power that he had in fact exercised, was the favoured candidate. But before he would accept the throne, he insisted upon election by the Zemsky Sobor. When it met in 1598 it consisted of 474 representatives drawn up from the clergy, the boyars, the lesser nobility, officials, and merchants. Godunov's agents were active among the Sobor so that its choice was eventually unanimous. Even so, Godunov insisted on repeated pleas before he would accept the throne. Given the abundant evidence of aristocratic opposition and his reputed murder of the legitimate heir to the throne, the new Tsar had to ensure that his election appear but a reluctant response to the demands of the Sobor.

In this Godunov succeeded, and, until famine nullified his efforts, his reign looked promising. He was, for example, the first tsar to take an interest in education, and he even toyed with the idea of establishing a university, and sent a number of young Russians to study abroad in the West. Four came to England. For about twelve years Muscovy lost track of them. The only one who could then be traced was found to be earning his living as a minister of the Anglican Church. Godunov also tried to eliminate the more flagrant abuses in the workings of the judicial machinery.

Boris was a sick man at his election, oppressed by his fears for the future of his dynasty. He knew that he was resented both by the former oprichniks and by more aristocratic competitors for the throne. At first he tried hard to ingratiate himself with them, but as he felt his health and popularity wane, he took to repression. In 1599, Belsky was publicly humiliated and exiled for treasonable words. In the following year the Romanovs, relatives of Anastasia Zakharina, were accused of plotting to bewitch the Tsar and his family. These excesses were reminiscent of Ivan IV's oprichnina but it is important to note that the victims survived in monastic comfort to found a new ruling dynasty.

A succession of disastrously poor harvests from 1601 to 1603 completed the social isolation of Godunov's regime. The basis of Muscovite subsistence, and especially of Moscow and the surrounding districts, rapidly succumbed to the resulting speculation in grain, and to the depopulation and earlier agrarian collapse of the central provinces. Whole villages died of starvation. Men and women were reduced to eating grass and birch bark; they took to cannibalism. Many landowners, unable to feed their peasants, drove them from their estates; or peasants would voluntarily engage themselves as slaves, for the mere promise of food. One immediate consequence was the formation of marauding bands of homeless peasants, their sole aim being to attack and raid the granaries of the pomeshchiki and the merchants. In 1603, the first major outbreak, led by a peasant called Khlopok, almost reached Moscow before it was bloodily suppressed. It lacked, however, the unifying force of clear leadership and ideology, revealing the limitations of purely peasant activity.

Godunov faced this catastrophe helplessly and hopelessly. Given the inflated price of grain, the government, it has been calculated, disbursed to the starving populace only about a third of the sum needed for subsistence. Moreover, he concentrated in the cities such famine relief as there was. In Moscow, for example, the announcement of free grain supplies attracted an unmanageable throng of the needy, thereby intensifying the crisis still further.

It was at this moment of governmental collapse that Polish intervention began to play its part. Its instrument was the first false Dmitry, and it found allies among the aristocrats. As early as 1598, when the election of a successor to the feeble-minded Theodore was in train, there had been rumours that either Godunov or the Romanovs would put forward a pretender to the throne in order to sabotage the election of the other. The obvious choice was Dmitry, the nine-year-old son of Ivan the Terrible who would now be of age had he survived. The circumstances of his death were so ambiguous that belief in his survival was not altogether impossible. The need of the peasantry for a legitimator and co-ordinator of their anti-feudal struggles coincided with the needs of disgraced aristocrats and impoverished gentry to produce the characteristic ideology of peasant protest, the belief in a 'just tsar'. In Western Europe the same yearning for a hidden Messiah produced the false Manfreds and false Friedrichs of the Hohenstauffen era. In Russia, in the seventeenth and eighteenth centuries, it produced hundreds of false Alexeys, false Peter IIs, and false Peter IIIs. Each would unveil his true identity at a pre-ordained time and rescue the people from their misery.

All the same, the first false Dmitry had sound power-political backing. A mountebank of talent, Grigory Otrepyev was originally a poor gentleman who had served the Romanovs, only to fall in their disgrace. He made a second career in the Church, joining the staff of Patriarch Job, but left during the famine to seek his fortune in Poland. Soon after the turn of the century, rumours of the reappearance of Ivan the Terrible's son began to circulate in Poland and Lithuania. In 1603 the rumours took on tangible form when Otrepyev, claiming to be Tsarevich Dmitry, appeared at the Ukrainian castle of the Polish aristocrat, Adam Wisniewicki. Wisniewicki introduced Dmitry to others of the Polish nobility, in particular to the heavily indebted George Mniszek, governor of Sandomir, who saw in the prospect of backing the putative Tsar of Muscovy a means of saving his family fortunes. He also affianced his daughter Marina to the Pretender, on condition that her suitor made himself tsar within a year. The Papal Nuncio in Poland was interested as well. He saw in the Pretender, who did in fact secretly leave the Orthodox Church for Catholicism, an instrument for the eventual conversion of Muscovy. At Jesuit instigation, Marina secured from her future consort the promise of the right to maintain Catholic priests at her court in Moscow, provision for the Catholic form of worship, and Catholic schools and churches in certain areas.

The Polish King Sigismund III was not taken in by the Pretender's claims when he first met him at Cracow in 1604. But he gave him a pension, recognized him as the legitimate tsar, and announced, although he did not officially declare war on Muscovy, that Poles were free to engage themselves voluntarily in the small private army that the alleged Tsarevich was forming. In the early autumn of 1604 this army of not more than some 4,000 men set out for Moscow.

Godunov, in the meantime, unsuccessfully sought to discredit the Pretender and to whip up Orthodox sentiment against 'Latin and Lutheran heresy' No distinction was made between the two in Muscovy. But the demoralization of Godunov's regime was evident in the Pretender's easy advance along a general north-easterly route from Lvov to Moscow. His army rapidly grew, swollen by warring bands of malcontents, homeless peasants, and, at a later stage, the Cossacks of the Donets.

Along the lower reaches of the Dnieper, the Donets, the Don, and the Volga rivers lived a nomadic mass of humanity, sustained by plunder, brigandage, fishing, hunting, bee-keeping, cattle-raising, and agriculture. The Cossacks were organized in semi-military communities, in so far as they were organized at all, and served as a Slav outpost against Crimean Tatars and their Turkish overlords. But since the Cossacks were largely formed of runaways from the serf regimes of Muscovy and Poland, there was no clearly defined political allegiance.

A few months after it had set out, the Pretender's army had almost quadrupled in size. Godunov's forces, by contrast, disintegrated through mass desertion, treachery, and defeatism. Who knew, perhaps they were indeed up in arms against their legitimate ruler?

Suddenly, in April 1605, Godunov died – whether from a stroke or from self-administered poison is another mystery of the Time of Troubles. Two months later, after the virtual extinction or exile of the whole Godunov family, the Pretender entered Moscow, to the uproarious tumult of the populace. Maria Nagaya was brought from her convent and, delighted at the fall of the Godunovs and anxious to save her own neck, she acknowledged the Pretender as her long-lost son. He was crowned tsar at the end of July 1605.

The new Tsar was assuredly one of the strangest rulers ever to occupy a throne. The French captain, Margaret, who was one of his commanders, found him aged about twenty-five, of small but vigorous stature, with an ugly, beardless face, a wart on his nose, and spiky red hair. His temperament was quite un-Russian in its liveliness. In the Boyar Council his quick-wittedness marked him out. He took his responsibilities as tsar lightly, doubled the pay of his officials and serving officers, was easily accessible to all with a grievance, confirmed and extended the privileges of the Orthodox clergy, and liberated a quarter of the bond slaves and forbade the recovery of the serfs who had fled during the famine. There was an altogether fresh spirit of religious tolerance in the Kremlin and a welcome for foreigners. The Tsar even refused to use terror as a political weapon.

This period lasted less than a year. The Pretender's downfall was precipitated by the arrival of his fiancée, Marina Mniszek, from Poland. The future tsarina's Polish entourage set Muscovite teeth on edge. But this was not the only reason for the Pretender's downfall. Even if such had been his sincere desire, he could not have been of much use to the Catholic cause in Russia. To the Polish Jesuits and the Papacy, who were among his most ardent sponsors, this was necessarily a handicap. Far more important was the opposition of the Russian aristocrats. Their motive in using the Pretender was purely negative – to get rid of Godunov – and not to install another tsar. Positively, their aim was a tsar drawn from their own ranks, and this the false Dmitry obviously could not be. For once their views coincided with those of the city poor, infuriated by the fact that those whom they had brought to power were now flaunting their new wealth and leaving feudal relationships largely unaltered.

The aristocratic revolt, led by Vassily Shuisky, broke out in Moscow one May night in 1606. The Pretender was soon disposed of, his body burnt, and the ashes shot from a cannon to the four winds. Shuisky himself replaced the false Dmitry on the throne. He was not elected by the Zemsky Sobor, only nominated by his supporters, who commanded a majority of the Boyar Duma, and acclaimed by a well-prepared crowd of Muscovites. His election owed much to his promises not to disgrace or punish members of the landholding or merchant classes without fair trial and not to punish innocent relatives. This was not quite a Magna Carta but it was undoubtedly a retreat from the unconditional autocracy of Ivan IV.

The desire of the possessing classes to make life more predictable owed a lot to their memories of Ivan the Terrible but more to the approaching social revolution. The very bases of Russian feudalism were challenged in the years that followed as an ever increasing proportion of the population was mobilized in class struggles. Their belief in the State as such, eroded by the grain-hoarding and speculation of the famine years, undermined by the turbulence of events in Moscow, was yet further shaken by the success of the false Dmitry in mobilizing the Cossacks and the disaffected elements of the south-western regions. Shuisky's seizure of the throne marked the end of one phase of the Time of Troubles – the internal aristocratic struggle for power as against various forms of autocracy – and the opening of the second. Peasant revolt, combined with open foreign intervention by the Poles and Swedes, characterized the new period.

Shuisky's writ did not run much outside Moscow. Perhaps as much as half of Muscovite territory was outside his control. Tula and Ryazan rose against him and defeated government troops from Moscow. Rebels besieged Nizhny Novgorod; Astrakhan produced no fewer than three false pretenders.

At its apogee, the movement found a political and military leader of genius in Ivan Bolotnikov, an impoverished 'boyars' son' whose family had been forced into slavery by the economic catastrophe of the 1570s. He escaped to join the Cossacks but was captured by a Tatar gang and sold to the Turks as a galley slave. A German ship captured him at sea and released him in Venice. He returned to Muscovy via Hungary and Poland at the head of 10,000 Cossacks. As an agitator and revolutionary, he was the first to put into political terms the land-hunger and despair of the peasantry. His 'excellent charters' called on peasants and slaves to rise against their masters, to seize the estates of the pomeshchiki, and to overthrow the existing social order. For a time, especially in the south, this heady call swelled Bolotnikov's following to a vast movement that carried him to the gates of Moscow. There it began to disintegrate when, through the accession of the lesser provincial nobility, the movement lost its homogeneous peasant character. Bolotnikov's new recruits aimed only at unseating Shuisky – not at inaugurating a social revolution. Bolotnikov had to withdraw from Moscow to Tula. Then, although he had hitched his star to 'Tsarevich Peter', the soi-disant son of Tsar Theodore Ioannovich, the rebels eventually succumbed to Shuisky's siege in the autumn of 1607.

Hardly was the threat of a peasant revolution overcome than yet another centre of revolt arose. Under the leadership of a second false Dmitry – like the first, a man of humble origin who gave out that he had not only escaped death at Uglich in 1591 but also at Moscow in 1606 – a mixed array, composed in the main of Polish plunderers and swashbucklers, marched on Moscow from Staro-dub, some 300 miles to the south-west of the capital.

Despite the support of Marina Mniszek, who bore him an heir, and of Philaret Romanov, promoted to Metropolitan by the first false Dmitry and to Patriarch by his re-incarnation, the second false Dmitry had less success than the first. Usually known as the 'Thief' or 'Scoundrel', the label applied by the Shuisky camp to discredit him, his forces never quite reached Moscow. He estab-lished himself at Tushino, a village some six miles to the west, and there he set up a sort of 'anti-Government' with a separate court and appurtenances. Moscow and Tushino confronted each other. Many popular elements abandoned Shuisky for the Thief, for the latter was generous in his promises and bestowal of titles. This confrontation lasted about two years. Shuisky had lost the south, but the Thief was not strong enough to blockade the city and starve it into surrender. At the head of a force of more than 20,000 men, Jan Sapieha, the Polish noble and one of the powers behind the Thief, attempted to cut Moscow off from the north and the trading centre of the White Sea by seizing the strategic monastery of the Trinity of St Sergius. But its fortifications withstood the siege, to the enormous prestige of the Church as a national and centripetal force, and also helped to rally the pro-Shuisky forces in the north.

On the other hand, Shuisky came no nearer to overcoming the Thief, and in this extremity he called in Swedish aid. In return for the renunciation of Muscovy's claim to Livonia, Charles IX of Sweden placed at Shuisky's disposal a force of 6,000 French, German, Scottish, and English auxiliaries under General de la Gardie. This in its turn provoked Sigismund III, King of Poland, to declare open war on Shuisky, lest the whole of the Baltic coast fall into enemy hands. In 1609 Sigismund laid siege to Smolensk, the classic key to Western Russia.

This precipitated the final phase of the Troubles. The Thief's camp disintegrated, Tsar Shuisky was deposed, and a Polish gar-rison was master of Moscow. Meanwhile, negotiations opened between the Boyar Council and Sigismund on the terms that would make a Polish tsar acceptable to Moscow. In the upshot, the council recognized Sigismund himself as tsar. This was perhaps the nadir of Muscovite misfortune. Those Russian nobles opposed to the Poles were at loggerheads with the Cossacks, ostensibly their allies. Smolensk fell to Sigismund; and the Swedes had seized Novgorod. Apparently no force existed able to arrest the utter disintegration of the State. The only comparison possible is with the territory that the Bolsheviks controlled at the end of the First World War, when they too were simultaneously subjected to foreign intervention and civil war.

The solution eventually came from a combination of the influence of the local councils, formed on the same basis of representation by estates as the Assemblies of the Land, and of the Orthodox Church. The first nationalist levy to attack and besiege the Poles in Moscow in 1611 was formed largely of the provincial nobility. But it also included a large force of Cossacks, and the Poles were able to instigate dissension between the two elements to such good effect that the levy dispersed.

The second attempt, made in the following year, was rather better prepared. It took its inspiration from the leaders of the most famous and most ancient of all Russian monasteries – that of the Trinity of St Sergius, already prominent through its sixteen months' resistance to the besieging troops of the Polish princes, Lizowski and Sapieha. The cellarer and bursar of the monastery, Abraham Palitsyn, has left a remarkable account of this period. By the summer of 1611, a full Assembly of the Land was able to elect a provisional government. A stream of appeals was directed to many of the towns of the Russian east – Kazan, Perm, Nizhny Novgorod – exhorting them to rise against the invader and the usurper. In Nizhny Novgorod the response, organized by the mayor of the town, a merchant named Kosma Minin, was particularly strong. A second national levy, made up of townspeople under Minin and of the lesser nobility under Prince Pozharsky, was rapidly formed. Although there was a last-minute dissension with the Cossacks, still attacking the Polish garrison in Moscow, the two forces were able to combine in a final supreme effort that freed the city.

Early in 1613, a freshly elected Assembly of the Land, including the boyaral leaders of the aristocracy, the clergy, representatives of the gentry and merchants of forty-eight towns or districts and even a few free peasants, met in Moscow. Large Cossack forces were on hand to ensure that popular interests were not entirely neglected. The Assembly decided against an elective monarchy but fixed its choice, not on the kings of Poland or Sweden, the Russian princely families, nor on the military hero Prince Pozharsky, but on the sixteen-year-old Michael Romanov. The choice was satisfactory both to the Assembly and to the Cossacks. The new Tsar was related to Ivan IV through Anastasia and had not been involved in aristocratic intrigue. His father, Philaret, though still with the occupying Poles, excited the sympathy of the aristocrats for his sufferings under Boris Godunov and the sympathy of the Cossacks for joining false Dmitry II at Tushino.

In theory, then, the autocracy was restored to the status quo of 1550. The reality was somewhat different. The possessing classes, purged from above by Ivan the Terrible, had now been subjected to a massive challenge from below and had paid a heavy price for survival. A youthful monarch was obviously going to need the co-operation of a cohesive Boyar Duma. Though individual churchmen had helped to rally resistance to the Poles, the hierarchy was discredited by the absence of a recognized Patriarch and a widespread awareness of the compromises made by church leaders during the Time of Troubles. Since 1598, the Assembly of the Land had been recognized as the legitimate source of autocratic authority. Only it now had the prestige to forge some new order out of the chaos of class war, civil war, and foreign intervention.

CHAPTER 6

The Growth of Absolutism: The Early Romanovs

The election of the first of the Romanov dynasty by no means marked the end of the Troubles. The Poles and Swedes still occupied parts of Muscovy. The treasury was empty. Large areas of the country fell prey to wandering bands, and the disruption and flight of the population resulted in a steep decline in agricultural productivity. On the estates of the monastery of the Trinity of St Sergius, for example, arable land, which had formed 37·3 per cent at the end of the sixteenth century, fell to 1·8 per cent by 1614–16. Over the years 1621–40 it rose again, but only to 22·7 per cent. Not until the 1640s was the upturn evident. The poverty of the court and the government can be seen in the Tsar's plea, a bare few months after his election, to the Stroganov family. In humiliating terms he had to ask for a loan in cash and kind – fish, salt, grain – to meet the urgent demands of his officials and military personnel. In these inauspicious circumstances the Romanov dynasty entered on its long career.

It must not be assumed that a decline in general economic activity mirrored the decline in the profitability of feudal estates. The Russian economy of the early seventeenth century was remarkably resilient. However bitter the peasants might feel about their fruitless attempts to throw off the yoke of servility, however much increasing exploitation might force them to work harder, at least some of the peasantry ended up more prosperous as a result. The same was true in the towns. The Time of Troubles caused only slight interruption to trade conducted by the Moscow *gosti* at Archangel with the English and, increasingly, the Dutch. Muscovy was not the exploited and junior partner in this profitable trade: the Dutch and English had to pay for a substantial proportion of their purchases with bullion that stayed in Russia and speeded the growth of a money economy and a national market. This economic resilience was to have important political consequences for the whole of Europe. Of course events in the Russian plain had always affected the rest of Europe but Russia was now an acknowledged part of a European *system* of states. During the Thirty Years' War European townsman scanned their periodical newsheets in hope or fear for news of Russian moves against Catholic Poland. Extracts from these newspapers were transmitted to an increasingly professional Foreign Ministry (*Posolsky Prikaz*) in Moscow where they were translated and used to brief the Tsar and Boyar Duma. Encouraged by Richelieu and the Orthodox Patriarch of Constantinople, it was the Russians who forced Poland to make peace with the Swedes and thereby unleashed Gustavus Adolphus on Germany in 1630 to turn back the high tide of Catholic–Habsburg success. The Swedes repaid this debt by sending some of their best military experts to train a new Russian army. Traders and military experts formed the nucleus of a sizeable foreign quarter in Moscow. This foreign quarter was ultimately to bring to the heart of Muscovy the perplexity of its historical destiny, fated to prove an explosive source of intellectual tension.

The Time of Troubles had revealed the extreme fragility of Muscovite society and the ease with which its social arrangements could be upset when discontented minor gentry set out to articulate mass grievances. This lesson was repeated at regular intervals throughout the century, most notably in the spectacular revolutionary movement led by the Don Cossack Stenka Razin in 1667–71. Despite this, the dynamics of the age, both economic and military, demanded an intensified exploitation of labour by State, Church and gentry alike. In view of the resistance to this process offered by the peasantry, this meant increased serfdom as well. A new kind of compromise was required if the possessing orders were to confine their differences within safe bounds. Given their newly-acquired habits of autonomous political activity this would not be easy. The new dynasty had just been elected so it was in no position to practise despotism. There remained a surplus of poor gentry clamouring for pomestiya or for the return of their fugitive serfs; not all could be satisfied. It was also vital to avert the risk that the remaining aristocrats might subvert the Romanovs as they had subverted the Godunovs and Shuiskys.

Following the truce with Poland, Philaret Romanov returned from captivity in 1619 to become Patriarch and effective head of his son's government. What sort of people were the early Romanovs? Of course, our reactions to them have been conditioned by the cult of their illustrious successor, Peter the Great. The stereotyped view that they were unenlightened and inefficient rulers is totally false. Without exception, they strove to achieve a thorough grasp of European innovations, despite the deference they publicly paid to xenophobia. Philaret was a statesman of European dimensions, his survival during the Time of Troubles was no accident of fate and he used his Polish captivity to acquire a thorough knowledge of contemporary Polish and European politics. As head of the government, he instituted the Assembly of 1619 which attempted to solve Russia's political and administrative problems. Later, he attempted to forge an alliance of Orthodoxy and Calvinism that had important consequences in Russia and Europe. His son Michael relied first on his father and then, after 1633, on aristocratic ministers to lead the government, but his choice of advisers was sound and he, too, was interested in European science.

Alexis, who ruled from 1645 to 1676, was pious but a courageous soldier whose mind was sharpened by the experience of war against Poland and Sweden. He was determined to master the latest developments in European military technology and aristocratic lifestyle. His acquisition of Kiev was almost as important to Russia as his son's foundation of St Petersburg. Theodore II, who ruled from 1676 to 1682, was not a strong ruler but he was highly educated and his government held together well enough to abolish *mestnichestvo*, the system of precedence so long cited as a reason for Russia's military reverses, and to introduce a major reform of the tax system based on Russia's first census.

From 1682 to 1689 – for the first time for six hundred years – Russia was ruled by a woman, the Regent Sophia. Sophia was both educated and forceful. She led her aristocratic sisters out of inane seclusion and herself presided at a vital theological debate between the factions of the Church. She protected unfortunate members of her own sex by moderating the penalties for women who killed tyrannical husbands and by insisting that rape be treated as a serious offence whatever the rank of the offender. It is true that the incapacity of Peter's elder half-brother did create problems that permitted an increase in the influence of the musketeers (*streltsy*). From the vantage point of the mid 1680s, however, an average member of the possessing classes must have felt that the decision of 1613 in favour of an hereditary monarchy under the Romanovs was indeed the 'Will of God'. The Romanovs certainly compare favourably with their European contemporaries.

Philaret Romanov seems to have been a convert to early modern notions of absolutism. As a practical politician, however, he knew he would have to work with the means that were available and that meant the Assembly. His immediate concern lay with the restoration of government finances but he was realistic enough to know that this depended on economic recovery. The main beneficiaries of the reforms of 1619 were the towns, where the tax burden was to be equalized and which were permitted to recover some of their tax-paying citizens who had accepted enserfment to monasteries or secular lords to avoid paying taxes. The Assembly demanded a further meeting at which grievances might be aired but Philaret seems to have avoided such a dangerous confrontation; it is probably no accident that the Assembly did not meet for ten years after 1621. The government resorted to the energetic use of its monopoly of the grain market and the manipulation of the bullion market to raise revenue, but Philaret was no more able to abolish the Assembly than Charles I was able to dispense with Parliament. The Assembly of 1648–9 which approved the new Law Code (*Ulozhenie*) was actually summoned at the instigation of the poorer soldiery and gentry of Moscow. If this was not enough to damn it in the eyes of the government, its reluctance to support war with Poland over the Ukraine was probably the last straw. After the 1650s the membership and powers of the Assembly were strictly limited. This was a European development. With the achievement of national unity, absolute monarchs no longer required the support of traditional forms of representative assembly.

In this unprecedented situation for the Russian autocracy, the first Romanovs had no choice but to turn to the Boyar Duma as an alternative source of support. For this to be effective, the Duma had to represent the aristocracy in fact and not merely in theory. A compact with the aristocracy was implied by the promises made at Michael's election; it was reinforced by such commonsense considerations as the need for experienced leadership and a desire to avoid offending those who might subvert the new dynasty. Philaret packed the Boyar Duma with eldest sons of senior lines of aristo-cratic families which had been prominent in the mid sixteenth century (and which were to do very well in the eighteenth century). Large land grants followed nomination to the Duma, in those cases where they had not preceded them. This reconstituted boy-aral aristocracy, as it has been called, led the government through-out the century. When a general census was conducted in 1678, it was discovered that there were some 833,000 households in Russia of which 65 per cent were owned by the Church or by lay landlords. Around 100,000 were owned by the Church, nearly 9,000 by the Moscow Patriarchate alone. The seventy-three members of the Boyar Duma owned some 42,000, some 11 per cent of the total in secular hands. Of these, twelve owned more than 1,000. Every one of them came from families already prominent in the mid sixteenth century and all but two were princes. Several princes, including the national hero, Prince Pozharsky, became boyars as a result of their military successes during the Time of Troubles. As the cen-tury went on, however, military leadership became less and less important to the aristocracy, which contented itself with the reality rather than the appearance of power. There were several reasons for this. The prevalence of peasant disturbances automatically meant that military service became less obviously patriotic and 'honourable'; the risk of a really humiliating death was much greater. Military failure might be punished in other ways as well. After a brief war of 1632–4, the unsuccessful General Shein was sacrificed by the government to appease the discontented popula-tion. In view of the increasingly technical nature of warfare, it seemed wise to let foreign advisers take the risks of actual combat. All this may help to explain why it was that in 1682 mestnichestvo could be abolished without resistance despite the pre-eminent status of the aristocracy in the government.

According to some historians, the privileges granted to the new 'noble' (*dvoryansky*) caste in the Law Code of 1649 demonstrate that the serving gentry or the pomeshchiki had by now become the ruling class. In the light of recent research this seems unlikely. On the contrary, it may well be that the gentry had good enough reason to be envious of the Church and the aristocracy in view of the demands made on it by the State. Male members of the gentry were regarded as potential officers in their younger years and as tax-collectors and judges as they grew older. Often their estates were very small, comprising as few as ten peasant households. They might be away for years while their estates were managed by peasant bailiffs and their wives and children left at the mercy of peasant risings. Elections to the Assembly cast an interesting light on the gentry. In the larger centres where both rich and poor gentry were well represented, real political differences surfaced in genuine election campaigns. In smaller centres, the available gentry, perhaps no more than a dozen, would beg to be relieved of the burden of sending a representative to Moscow. The government was obliged to reward those who did attend to save them from indigence as well as to incline them to support its projects.

Other aspects of Russian society in the seventeenth century suggest a rather insecure gentry. At the centre, there was a gradual improvement in the organization of the prikazy or ministries along functional and rational lines. Paradoxically, in the localities there was a tendency for older, undifferentiated forms of authority to reassert themselves. The voevodas or governors had arisen as co-ordinators of national resistance during the Time of Troubles. They remained when the troubles subsided, a sign of the insecurity of the possessing classes. They rapidly assumed the vices of the kormlyenshchiki (tax-farming governors) abolished in the previous century. Townsmen and lesser gentry petitioned the Tsar for relief from their insults, corruption and outright violence but rarely got any. With the sole exception of Ordyn-Nashchokin, himself a commoner, who was a reforming governor of Pskov in the 1650s, the early Romanovs and their mostly aristocratic advisers showed no sympathy for the sort of elective local self-government by the gentry which Ivan IV had tried to introduce during his early years. The gentry showed little capacity to fight for it and the petitions they occasionally submitted in favour of elective judges were flatly rejected by the government.

Changes in military organization further reduced the political significance of the gentry. The dvoryane were still mobilized as cavalrymen in military emergencies but since the 1550s there had been a steady expansion of the standing army. At first this consisted of musketeer regiments, made up of men quartered in special parts of Moscow and the other chief towns who would in normal times pursue an occupation in handicrafts or trade, but who could be rapidly mobilized in time of war. The streltsy received a fixed annual salary, and through their closeness to centres of power and their caste-like character were at times politically important – especially if their salary was late or if they were ordered to spend long periods away from their home garrisons. The real novelty lay in creating a standing army, recruited from and officered by foreign mercenaries, a practice copied from Sweden during the Thirty Years' War. It absorbed many of the veterans of that war once relative peace had returned to Western Europe. They included Germans, Swedes, Poles, and Scots. These regiments 'of the new formation' made up two-thirds of the Russian army by the 1680s. Their loyalty was a vital asset to the government in dealing with internal disorder.

One final feature of Muscovite society in the seventeenth century also suggests how limited was the influence of the gentry. As far back as the previous century, they had complained about ecclesiastical landholding. On several occasions in the sixteenth and seventeenth centuries, governments – at moments of weakness – had promised to limit the acquisition of land by the church in the future; they did so again in 1649. These promises were never kept. The estimate of Dr Samuel Collins, an English physician, that the Russian Church owned almost two-thirds of Muscovy was a grotesque exaggeration but it certainly echoed the view of much of the gentry in the latter part of the seventeenth century. Despite this resentment, the government made no attempt to confiscate church lands at this time. The explanation of this is not hard to seek. The churchmen were efficient landlords who kept detailed records. The government had only to permit the gentry to suggest limitations on church ownership of the land for the clergy to accept an increased burden of taxation. The technique of permitting the church to retain its votchiny while alienating its revenues to the government was already practised by Alexis and would be brought to perfection by Peter. In sum, the gentry could be dissuaded from radical measures by the fear of the peasantry while the government continued to entrust the expropriation of peasant surpluses to the churchmen. For their part, the clerics could hardly object to policies justified by the need to militarize society to face the 'threats', real and imagined, posed by Catholic schismatics and Protestant heretics.

The basic contradiction of Muscovite society remained the conflict between the demands of the State and the whole feudal class and the desire of the 'burdened' peasantry and townsmen to pursue their own economic activities limited only by the collective interest as agreed at ad hoc assemblies. In the immediate aftermath of the peasant rebellions, Philaret could not afford to offend the strong, but as the economy recovered, his policies began to assume a coherent shape. The practice had already grown up of designating certain periods during which runaway peasants could be sought out and forcibly returned to the estates they had quitted.* By 1642 the set interval was ten years. But this was far from satisfying the smaller landowners, whose estates, in their absence on service, were frequently robbed by the larger landowners in search of manpower.

A more lasting though still unsatisfactory solution had been in the making since 1619. A census was then ordered, with the aim of bringing back the runaways and also of unmasking those free peasants who, during the Time of Troubles, had 'commended' themselves to some large landowners, lost their freedom, and thereby relieved themselves of the liability to taxation. The work went at a snail's pace and then came to a complete standstill: all the results were burnt during the great fire of Moscow in 1626. But it was resumed and quickly concluded in 1628.

This was the basis of the famous code of 1649 which entirely abolished 'fixed years' in the search for runaways and established the landowner's legal, unlimited right to them. The principle was that the peasants should be sent back to the estates where they had been registered in the census returns. There was also provision for fining those landowners who retained peasants to whom they were not entitled. In the circumstances of the time, much of this decree remained a paper right. In 1658 it had to be reinforced by a further decree that introduced special officials to seek out runaway

*See pp. 62–3 above.

peasants; and in 1661 and later years, flogging and a severe scale of monetary fines were prescribed as punishments for those landowners who took in runaways. Also, as a penalty for such infringement of the law, the guilty landowner had to surrender four of his own peasants for each runaway peasant whom he illegally harboured.

The code of 1649 was the climax to a development extending over the previous century and a half; and during the next two centuries it remained substantially unaltered as the predominant factor in the Russian economy – not only in agriculture, but also in the State industries of the seventeenth, eighteenth, and nineteenth centuries. Its effects and ramifications were so far-reaching, and so intimately identified was the State with serfdom, that reform or abolition of the institution as such was the starting-point for almost every liberal, radical, or critical observer of Russian conditions.

In the middle of the seventeenth century this code served the dual purpose of providing the small and middling landowners with a ready supply of attached labourers, attached not only to a particular estate but also to the estate-owner. The eighteenth century saw probably the apogee of the landowner's powers over his serfs. But in the seventeenth century, despite certain anomalies and contradictions in the law, a landowner could already sell his serfs, exchange them, punish them, force them to marry, split up families, and, in general, treat the serfs as chattels. He could not, however, turn them into slaves in law, for this would deprive them of their taxable status. It is true that the code of 1649 expressly warned the landowner not to kill, wound, or starve his serfs, but there was very little sanction to prevent such maltreatment.

In the main, the landowner used the serf as a performer of *barshchina* – labour – on his estate. This might take up between one-third and one-half of the serf's working time. The system operated predominantly in the central regions of Muscovy. The north-east, Siberia, and the steppe-lands of the south were still largely untouched. Elsewhere the distinction between the slave and the serf grew gradually less and less.

Neither the serf nor the poor townsman ever reconciled himself to the exactions of the State and the landowner fuelled by the

inexorable demands of international competition. The seventeenth
century was marked by a number of elemental movements of
revolt, as well as many sporadic individual outbursts. A tax on
salt led to an upheaval in Moscow in 1648; the government's
exports of grain to its European allies caused a serious inflation in
food prices; and in 1650 revolt came to Pskov and Novgorod. In
1656, the Tsar's debasement of the currency (he replaced silver
coins by copper) provoked further unrest throughout all Muscovy
and led to the deportation and torture *en masse* of many thousands
of the disaffected. As on previous and subsequent occasions, the
government employed a variety of tactics: the sacrifice of 'wicked'
advisers, short-term economic concessions, the rejection of reforms
affecting the power-structure, accusations of treason, the co-
option of moderate critics to break the unity of the mutineers.
Military force was used as a last resort only. The rebels showed a
persistence in creating workable, elective forms of self-government
that was at variance with received notions of happy slaves or
peasant anarchists.

The most significant of these outbreaks was the movement led
by Stenka Razin – a Don Cossack. In the vast area of east and
south-east Muscovy he incited a peasant revolt, aimed not against
Tsar Alexis, but against his 'traitor' boyars and the feudal order.
As the hostility of Alexis became manifest to the rebels, they had
to co-opt a false 'Alexis Alexeievich', an open rejection of the
reigning tsar. Razin even arranged for a false Patriarch to bless
their proceedings. His rising was the successor to Bolotnikov's
movement of the Time of Troubles and the herald of Bulavin's
revolt under Peter the Great, and Pugachov's even more tumultuous upheaval under Catherine. Razin had been embittered by the
execution of his brother by a tsarist commander, and, coming
from the freer Don, he seems to have been genuinely shocked by
the brutalities of serfdom he witnessed on his pilgrimages to north
Russia. Razin's first raids set aflame the lower Volga region and
the shores of the Caspian Sea. Then, in 1670, he turned northwards
and conducted a veritable *jacquerie* against the landowning classes,
winning over tens of thousands of serfs and also many of the
peoples not yet reconciled to Muscovite exploitation – Bashkirs,
Kalmyks, Mordvinians. The mobilization of the oppressed pea-

santry on this occasion was so great that a peasant woman called Alena is supposed to have led a detachment of peasant women against the Tsar's forces in the Arzamas district. The movement spread through the whole Volga region and as far northwards as the Oka. But regular Muscovite troops defeated Razin near Simbirsk on the Volga, and in 1671 he was executed. He survives as the hero of one of Russia's great folk songs, a popular art form with a universal appeal.

It is symptomatic of the relationship of town and country in the seventeenth century that even Razin's followers felt obliged to invest major towns like Astrakhan and Simbirsk. The kremlin at the heart of every major Russian town was the centre of political and religious authority for its region, a fortress sheltering governor, gentry, merchants, and leading clerics, to say nothing of the state tavern. From the government's point of view the town's importance could be given a precise expression. Whereas the tax burden on the peasantry increased many times during the seventeenth century ('musketeer money' increased tenfold from 1619 to 1633), these receipts were far outweighed by the tolls and tavern revenue collected from the towns. Evidently, the government had a very strong motive for a close alliance with the townsmen and yet, to this day, historians are deeply divided as to the fate of the Russian towns. Those who have examined the legal position of the townsmen in conjunction with the government's records of population and taxation have usually painted a rather gloomy picture of stagnation and oppression in urban life. Those who have looked closely at essentially economic evidence have come to quite a different conclusion. While research on this vexed matter continues, all we can do is attempt to explain a paradox we cannot fully resolve.

The first point to be made is that those called 'townspeople' (posadskie) were only a small proportion of those living in towns. Often, especially in the military settlements of the south, they were outnumbered by military serving men. In some cases they were also outnumbered by the servants of large estates or monasteries. Many of these people performed exactly the same economic activities as those officially recognized as 'townspeople'. The picture was further complicated by the fact that the division of labour was so undeveloped that the town and the countryside used exactly the same methods of handicraft production. The peasants were able to satisfy from their own resources their requirements in clothing, housing, and household utensils.

During the Troubles, a large number of townspeople had taken refuge with large monasteries or estates (this form of 'flight' was often a legal convention involving little or no physical movement). In return for evading state taxes, they became the serfs of their new masters, a process which seriously eroded the 'tax base'. In view of the power of these new masters, the first Romanovs trod carefully, but in 1619 it was agreed that such former townspeople should be returned to the urban tax-paying community. According to legal theory, the merchants and townspeople performed commercial and industrial activity. In return for this, the merchants had to act as tax-collectors while the townspeople bore the heaviest tax burdens. The Law Code of 1649 attempted to convert the Russian classes into closed hereditary castes performing mutually exclusive functions, and the urban classes were to be no exception. Commercial and industrial activity was now to be their monopoly; tax-exempt suburbs belonging to lay or clerical lords were annexed to the towns. The townspeople themselves were to be bound to their towns as the serfs were to the soil; they could not leave them even if they were prepared to pay the same taxes elsewhere. They also did not gain any additional self-government; their own forms of self-government, largely restricted to the election of an official to apportion tax burdens, continued to be overshadowed by the governor. Records of population compiled by the government for taxation purposes suggest that whereas the number of towns increased in the seventeenth century the growth in the number of 'townspeople' was very sluggish. Some of this sluggishness was the result of fire, plague, and civil disturbance but the oppressed state of the urban population also probably played its part.

For all that, the towns were centres of handicraftsmen who formed a significant portion of the urban population. In Moscow in 1683 there were 2,367 artisans, in Kolomna 159 (22 per cent of the adult population), in Mozhaisk 224 (40 per cent), in Serpukhov 331, in Kazan 318 (more than 50 per cent), in Novgorod about 2,000, in Nizhni Novgorod about 500. The non-industrial urban groups included such people as coachmen, porters, apothecaries, midwives, bloodletters.

It is possible to distinguish various categories of urban workers. Most numerous were the producers of foodstuffs – bakers, brewers, distillers, fishmongers. A second large group was comprised of clothing workers. These men were hatters, furriers, coatmakers, tanners, tailors. They worked mainly with the wool and flax processed by rural spinners and weavers. Lastly came the metal workers, who produced both articles of military use – swords, armour, axes, arrows – and household utensils. These men were tinsmiths, locksmiths, and needlemakers. It seems that the level of technique was extremely low. According to one observer, not even saws were used by the carpenters. The boards and planks were hewn straight from the log with an axe, though we must not forget that the magical churches of Kizhi were built by men using axes. Generally speaking, the urban artisans and craftsmen were the town poor. Even such a skilled worker as the silversmith sold his products for not much more than the cost of the metal. Labour was very poorly rewarded.

Precisely because there was so little differentiation between town and country, all the town's activity was duplicated on the larger estates and monasteries, where, in fact, there was probably a higher degree of specialization as well as a greater diversification of crafts. In fact, the first large-scale production of commodities such as salt, the precursor of factory production, was conducted on private estates. The work might be performed by serf artisans; but there were also 'free' artisans who received cash for their products, either per unit of product or per half-year. Much of this work was for immediate consumption and use. But some of it was for the market and the requirements of a money economy, on the pattern manifested in the sixteenth century. Local and regional fairs in hamlets and villages were often arranged by monasteries to coincide with Church holidays. An enormous variety of goods was bought and sold – farming implements, animals, vegetables, fruit, poultry, clothing, salt, and meat.

The most important trading centre was undoubtedly Moscow. It stood at the centre of the new trade-routes criss-crossing the country: the road to Western Europe by way of Smolensk, Vitebsk,

Riga; the immensely important route to Archangel; while the Moskva and Oka river system joined Moscow with the Volga as far south as Astrakhan, and also with Siberia. There was also a radial network of shorter routes linking Moscow to such towns as Tula, Ryazan, Kostroma, Vladimir, and Kaluga. Almost one-third of the 20 per cent tax levied in 1634 on the whole commercial and industrial part of the population came from Moscow alone. This further illustrates the capital's commercial predominance. Here were transported the products of fishing, trapping, and hunting, the agricultural wealth of the central and southern districts, iron-ware from the Ural and Tula ironworks. Here were two bazaars every week and ever-open market-places. Foreigners in Moscow were of one voice in their surprise at the number of shops in the city. This was noted by the Jesuit father, Possevino, at the time of the false Dmitry, and by the Dutchman, Kilburger, towards the end of the seventeenth century. Moscow, said the latter, had as many shops as Amsterdam. But shops were not much more than booths, stands, trestles, or barrels with a few articles on top. One shop in Venice had more goods than a whole row of shops in Moscow, wrote Possevino.

Commerce was concentrated around the Kremlin and in the specialized trading quarter – the *Kitai-gorod*. The 'shops' were grouped in rows in accordance with the nature of their stock. Pedlars circulated between the rows, hawking trinkets, miscellaneous wares, and foodstuffs. The retailers were not all Russian; they might also be from Western Europe or the Orient.

Moscow was the centre of foreign as well as of internal trade. Silk from Persia and China, wine from France – Muscovites favoured Anjou and Bordeaux – were some of the more noteworthy items. Altogether, the seventeenth century saw considerable expansion in Russian imports and exports. This is well illustrated in a curious by-product of the period – the development of a postal service with the West. It was first handed over to a Dutch entrepreneur who organized two main postal routes – Moscow–Smolensk–Vilna and Moscow–Novgorod–Pskov–Riga. From Vilna the post went on farther to Königsberg, Berlin, and Hamburg. Letters took four weeks from Moscow to Hamburg; to Danzig a week less. The letters arriving in Moscow were first

opened at the rudimentary foreign ministry so that no private
individual should know what was happening, inside or outside the
country, before the Court. This was one of the most frequent
criticisms of the postal service. It was also accused of irregularity,
and its officials of diverting to their own pockets any valuables or
currency found in the opened packets. But it undeniably fulfilled a
service.

Trade with Poland declined during the seventeenth century.
The merchants of Pskov and Novgorod continued to trade via the
Baltic, though the German merchants of Reval and Riga (not the
Swedish crown) insisted that they use local middle-men. Archangel
remained the sole direct opening to the West. About the middle of
July, the merchants of Muscovy set out on the fourteen-day trip
northwards. So great was the efflux that activity in Moscow
slackened perceptibly. In July also, the foreign ships arrived for
the annual fair. This lasted until September. Despite the long and
hazardous sea journey, it was cheaper than the overland route,
which would have involved excessive tolls and transit taxes.

The Russians exported grain, leather, furs, canvas, hemp, flax,
lard, wax, and caviar. The most important imports were cloth,
copper, and other metals and bullion. Another major import was
pepper. They also imported gun powder and arms from England,
Sweden, and Holland. Special purchasing agents were appointed
to procure the muskets, daggers, shot, and books on military
engineering and fortifications that the armies of Moscow required.
Later, articles of luxury and adornment came to occupy a large
part of the trade. In 1671, imports through Archangel included
diamonds, articles wrought in gold and silver, gold coins, 28,000
reams of paper, 10,000 German hats, 837,000 pins and needles,
wines, spices, muscatel, and herrings.

There was as yet no merchant marine so Muscovy was entirely
dependent on foreigners for its trade with the West. They even
made inroads into Russia's internal trade. But this source of
weakness was partly cancelled out by the competition for what
was a very profitable two-way traffic. The merchants of Muscovy
made repeated attempts to restrict the activities of foreign merchants. Tsar Alexis, frightened already by the 1648 Moscow Rising
and horrified by the news that the English 'Assembly of the Land'

had executed King Charles I, immediately revoked the trading privileges of the English. This changed little, since the Dutch had long overtaken the English as the main foreign traders in Russia. In 1653 the first discriminatory tariffs were applied generally to all foreign traders in Muscovy and in 1667 The New Trade Regulation attempted to restrict them to foreign trade in border cities and increased the discrimination in favour of Russian merchants.

Owing to the multiplicity of retail outlets and of producers, the poor communications and sheer distances involved, home trade could not be regimented to the same extent as foreign. But both were dominated by three corporations of merchant-entrepreneurs, the chief of whom were gosti ('guests'). They worked in intimate co-operation with the Tsar as the foremost representatives of mercantile capital. In Moscow there were about thirty gosti. Comparisons with Dutch merchants suggest that their dynasties were as stable and successful as those of their Western equivalents. Their visible wealth offended the prejudices of soldier, monk, and artisan alike, making them highly vulnerable to attack in times of upheaval. No doubt it eased their path around the more irksome restrictions of the new Law Code. They enjoyed such privileges as tax immunity, the right to unrestricted travel abroad, and the right to distil vodka for their own consumption. They also functioned as the administrators of the customs, the State fisheries, and salt works. They purchased goods for the Tsar and also traded on their own account; they operated leases and also handled the Tsar's foreign and internal trade. One 'guest', a certain Nikitinov, was prominent in textiles, salt, and fish. He also owned a fleet of vessels that plied up and down the Volga as far as Astrakhan. Others were Gruditsyn and Voronin, who owned villages, stores, ships, ironworks, and functioned as army contractors. The most noteworthy 'guest' was the Tsar himself, who could buy imported goods at the prices asked and then, by way of the corporation, dispose of them at inflated prices on the home market. Conversely, through the operation of the royal monopoly he could buy advantageously on the home market and secure the market price at Archangel. In this the tsars of the seventeenth century were following the tradition set by Ivan the Terrible and Boris Godunov.

Trade, as a source of wealth, was paralleled by the exploitation of such natural products as potash. Here, the boyar Morozov was the pioneer in large-scale enterprise. He used the labour of thousands of serfs to work the deposits. Mining and metallurgical industries, directed by foreign masters and specialists, were other significant developments. On a larger scale, this continued the policy initiated by Ivan III and Ivan the Terrible, and anticipated the efforts of Peter the Great – with the same aim of lessening dependence on the foreigner, combined, at first, with a pronounced military emphasis. Towards the end of the century, cameralist and mercantilist ideas began to seep in from the West to suggest that the terms of trade might be further improved if Muscovy produced her own finished goods.

In pursuance of the Romanov policy of developing the army, the first foreign-managed enterprise of importance was an ironworks at Tula. Here, a Dutchman, Andreas Vinnius, established in 1632 on State land a plant that would supply the government with cannon, cannon-balls, and musket barrels at agreed prices. In 1644 Vinnius was joined by a second Dutchman, Peter Marselis, who was granted permission to establish ironworks in certain northern districts. There was also a third ironworks near Moscow that belonged to the Tsar. This, too, was intended for the casting of cannon and other army requirements. The arrangement was in the nature of a concession for a limited number of years, after which the establishment reverted to the State. The foreigner supplied the technical skill and undertook to instruct Muscovite apprentices. In view of the remoteness of the raw materials, these new enterprises could not take advantage of the homeless hired labour that milled around in the river ports so the State had to supply the labour, consisting of the serfs directly employed in the enterprise, or those obliged to deliver fuel or perform other auxiliary services. This was the origin of the 'factory peasants' of the eighteenth century. We must remember that this was the time when the plantation system flourished in the Americas. New 'efficient' forms of exploitation were being pioneered on Europe's periphery, East and West alike.

On this general model other enterprises developed during the seventeenth century – a glass works, leather and silk factories, a paper mill. Not all of these were successful and in any case they were all on a very small scale. But they did at least signify the establishment of a type of industry fundamentally different from manorial handicrafts.

WAR IN THE WEST

For a short time Muscovite territorial losses during the Time of Troubles threatened to make the country more of a Eurasian state than ever before. The position in Siberia and east of the Urals remained unaffected, whereas important towns in the west, such as Novgorod and Smolensk, were still held by the Swedes and Poles respectively. Muscovy's seventeenth-century wars were largely devoted to completing the unification of all the Russian lands and breaking through the barrier of Sweden, Poland, and Turkey which separated Russia from the rest of Europe (although, of course, penetration eastwards never ceased). In the unremitting impulse westwards, the balance of power slowly moved in favour of Muscovy and against Poland. In fact, events on the western borders of Muscovy seem to foreshadow the Polish partitions of the late eighteenth century.

The immediate task after the Time of Troubles was to clear Russian soil of the Swedes and Poles. The former were the easier to deal with. After desultory fighting, which included a vain Swedish assault on Pskov, the Swedish occupation of Novgorod and its surrounding area was ended by the Peace of Stolbovo in 1617. Dutch and British mediation, for commercial motives, and a British loan, helped to ease the settlement. Muscovy paid an indemnity of 20,000 silver roubles, in return for which Sweden evacuated Novgorod and renounced its claim to the Muscovite throne, while retaining the entire coast of the Gulf of Finland. This established Sweden's contact with its Estonian possessions and left Muscovy still cut off from the Baltic. For two decades, Sweden and Russia were allied against Poland. There was a resumption of war against Sweden in 1656 over the control of Poland and Lithuania, but in 1661 the Muscovites were beaten back.

Poland proved a harder nut to crack. With Smolensk still in their possession at the end of the Time of Troubles, the Poles were

able to launch a new offensive that brought them close to Moscow
in 1618. But the capital withstood the assault, and this did in fact
mark the last occasion when Polish troops entered central Muscovy. At the end of the year an armistice for fourteen and a half
years was concluded at Duelino. Poland retained the provinces of
Smolensk and Seversk, but did not renounce a claim to the throne
of Muscovy, a claim that stemmed originally from the Troubles.
In 1630 Philaret denounced the armistice and encouraged Gustavus Adolphus to attack the Habsburg Imperial forces in Germany. After initial successes the Swedes retired to North Germany
to await the promised Muscovite attack on Smolensk. The short
war for Smolensk was a fiasco, doomed by the deaths of Gustavus
and Philaret, by the inconstancy of the Turks who had promised
support, and by Tatar intervention and peasant rebellion in Muscovy. As in 1914 a Russian defeat contributed to the defence of
the liberties of Western Europe. In 1634 an 'eternal peace' was
concluded, as distinct from the earlier armistice. Apart from the
final abandonment of the Polish claim to the Kremlin, it did not
change the *status quo*. Poland remained the principal enemy, to be
absorbed by military force or dynastic union. Muscovite single-
mindedness on this point was illustrated when in 1642 the government forced the Don Cossacks to give up Azov which they had
conquered in a heroic siege five years earlier. Muscovy was not yet
ready to take on the Turks.

The 'eternal peace' lived barely longer than the armistice. It
came to grief in the 1650s in the Ukraine (or Little Russia), where
a most complex conflict was building up between the Poles, the
Russians and the Cossacks. With fine impartiality, the Cossacks
would fight for the Holy Roman Emperor against the Turks, for
Muscovy against Poland, for Poland against Muscovy. Their aim
was to live unhampered by any ties save those of military brotherhood. However, as Muscovy gradually expanded southwards,
and as Poland, after union with Lithuania in 1569, also began to
bring the Lithuanian territories in the Ukraine under some form
of regularized control, Cossack autonomy came under a two-
pronged attack. The conflict was further envenomed by the formation of a Uniate Church, under Jesuit inspiration. The Uniates
accepted the authority of the Pope but retained the Orthodox

form and ritual. The conflict of Orthodoxy and Catholicism thus moved south.

After 1651, after more than a decade of inconclusive Cossack wars and uprisings against the Poles, Bohdan Khmelnitsky, the *hetman*, who had also distinguished himself by his merciless attacks on the Jews of the Ukraine, had to appeal to Tsar Alexis for help. Would he make the Ukraine autonomous under Muscovite suzerainty? Muscovy, mindful of its uniformly unsuccessful wars against Poland, hesitated, but finally agreed. In January 1654 the Cossacks swore their oath of allegiance to the Tsar. At Pereyaslavl an agreement was solemnly and emotionally concluded between Khmelnitsky and Buturlin, the envoy of Alexis; to the Cossacks it was a treaty, to the Tsar it was an act of homage. The Ukraine thereby received confirmation of its autonomy, and the right to entertain independent diplomatic relations, except with Poland and Turkey.

This treaty by no means settled the future of the Ukraine, but this aspect of the Russo-Polish conflict was quickly overshadowed by the outbreak of war between the two countries. For the first time, Muscovite superiority was evident. Smolensk quickly fell, to be followed in 1655 by Vilna, Kovno, Grodno, and large parts of Lithuania. The Muscovites had not only Cossack help, but Swedish also, for Charles X, invading from the north, captured Warsaw and Cracow and proclaimed himself King of Poland. This was too much of a good thing for Alexis, who himself aspired to the Polish crown. He broke off his Polish campaign and turned on his ally, hoping to secure part of the Baltic coast. But his fight against Sweden brought him no success. Muscovy came to grief at Riga. Once again, the desire to re-incorporate all the Russian lands took precedence over maritime interests. Muscovy concluded with Sweden the Peace of Cardis in 1661. All Livonia was returned to Sweden and the latter's possession of Estonia was confirmed.

In the south, Khmelnitsky died in 1667, eventually to be commemorated by a grandiose equestrian statue in Kiev, capital of the Ukraine. Under his successors, there were rapid and bewildering changes in Ukrainian foreign policy as Moscow systematically disregarded its promises of non-intervention and began to move its voevody and their garrisons south-westwards. At close quarters,

Muscovy did not seem such an improvement on the Poles.

The consequence was a renewal of the Muscovite–Polish struggle. Some nine years' fighting ended in 1667 with the armistice of Andrussovo, which split the Ukraine. The left bank, the area east of the Dnieper, fell to Muscovy, together with Smolensk and the province of Seversk. Kiev too returned to Muscovy – after an absence of some four centuries. Kiev stood on the right, western bank of the river and was to have been relinquished by Muscovy after two years. But this provision of the armistice was never carried out. In the following year, John Casimir, the Polish king, renounced his throne and withdrew to the more congenial soil of France and to the lands bestowed on him by Louis XIV.

Muscovy's possession of the left-bank Ukraine and of Kiev could be uncertain only so long as it depended on the armistice of Andrussovo, and even more, on its violation. Their final acquisition was bound up with the formation under papal patronage of the anti-Turkish coalition of the 1680s, consisting of Poland, the Holy Roman Empire, and Venice. Muscovy's two campaigns in the Crimea (in 1687 and 1689) were scarcely successful, but the essential preliminary *rapprochement* between Poland and Muscovy involved the final cession of the conditional gains made under Andrussovo. Just over a century later, in 1793, the second partition of Poland united the right bank of the Dnieper with the left. Not only in a territorial sense did the 1680s significantly foreshadow the future. It was the first time that Muscovy was acknowledged as an ally of some consequence in a European coalition.

Expansion to the east, which even the Time of Troubles did not interrupt, encountered fewer difficulties than expansion to the west. During the seventeenth century, Muscovite bands of military adventurers, sometimes criminals on the run, conquered all eastern Siberia and the whole of the Lena valley. There followed the subjugation of the extreme north-east, beyond the Kamchatka peninsula and the Sea of Okhotsk. By the end of the seventeenth century, Muscovy, landlocked to the west, was already bordering on the Pacific. Penetration beyond the Amur River was limited by the Treaty of Nerchinsk with China in 1689. More regular authorities from Muscovy followed the adventurers. Strongpoints and fortified centres were established, as well as customs-houses to levy and collect tribute from the nomadic tribes of the region.

WESTERN INFLUENCES

In the wake of foreign policy and foreign technicians came a slow seepage into Muscovy of Western ideas. Ecclesiastical control had hitherto stultified such little speculative or scientific thought as existed. The Renaissance, Reformation and Counter-Reformation were carefully excluded. Apart from certain obscure Judaizing heresies, involving the denial of the Trinity and of the divinity of Christ, the observance of Saturday rather than Sunday as the Sabbath, the rejection of the Madonna as an object of worship – heresies that seem to have emanated from Novgorod at the end of the fifteenth century and then infiltrated into Moscow – the Orthodox Church was able to enforce a more or less complete separation from developments in the West. Whereas to the West, Greece signified Hellenic antiquity, to Muscovy it signified Byzantium. Russia rejoined a Europe torn by politico-religious warfare and regained her independence in a spirit of national exaltation which regarded contact with the West as a form of contamination. Church and State had to be seen to repress any incipient intellectual penetration. This was carried to such lengths that Tsar Michael, in the first half of the seventeenth century, would have a golden jug and basin beside his throne in the audience room of the Kremlin. After receiving a Western ambassador, he would then wash away the stain of occidental pollution.

It was noted by Masaryk in the nineteenth century that European ideas necessarily had a revolutionary effect in Russia. The same was true of the seventeenth century. This first became apparent in the field of religion and followed on the conquest of the Ukraine. Politically, it was desirable to bring Muscovite and Ukrainian Orthodoxy into the closest possible harmony, in order to facilitate the absorption of the conquered territóries. Moreover, the Ukrainians, who came directly under the authority of the Constantinople Patriarchate, had remained closer to the original Byzantine usages. On the whole, their clergy were more educated than the Muscovites'.

There was thus considerable inducement to reform Muscovite Orthodox liturgy and ritual and to accept the offer of the Ukrainian clergy to help in this task. Did one cross oneself with two fingers or three? Did one recite a double or a triple Hallelujah? Such trivia as these provoked the most intense conflict. Nikon, the masterful and imperious Muscovite Patriarch, began to introduce the reforms in 1653, and at once met with fierce opposition. This was not only religious, of course. The Orthodox Church, since its earliest days, had identified itself very intimately with the life of the people and the State. The 'white' parish clergy lived the life of their neighbours in the villages. The Church was undoubtedly at a low intellectual level, but – perhaps for that very reason – at one with its congregation, so that Nikon was in fact launching an offensive against the long-cherished popular associations of Moscow – The Third Rome, the heir to Byzantium, the Christian bulwark against the Mongols – and against all the self-sufficiency of Muscovy. Again, to accept ideas from the West, as distinct from techniques, savoured somehow of treachery. The rationalizing approach of Nikon's supporters, partly derived from Catholicism, threatened the simple, uncritical faith of patriarchal tradition. This was the reality that made sense of the fanatical opposition that faced Nikon. Hitherto, religious uniformity had preserved Muscovy from the type of religious conflict practised in the West in the sixteenth and seventeenth centuries. Now this blessing was lost as the reforms were pressed home with fire and sword. Dissenting ecclesiastics were exiled, if not burnt at the stake. The latter was the fate of the Arch-priest Avvakum, the most outspoken opponent of the reforms. The climax came with the attack on Solovetsky monastery, which had to endure a siege of eight years. This was a foretaste of the sort of opposition that Peter the Great's Western-inspired reforms would provoke half a century later.

Muscovite isolation was, then, already beginning to break down in the seventeenth century. It is significant that this period produced Prince Khvorostinin, the first Muscovite free-thinker of Catholicizing tendencies, sometimes considered a remote precursor of Chaadaev in the nineteenth century. It is also no coincidence that the seventeenth century provoked a minor Muscovite diplomatist, Gregory Kotoshchikhin, to pen a highly unflattering description of the institutions and customs of his native country: illiterate and inarticulate boyars resting their long beards on the table of the boyaral council chamber; criminality in Moscow; loveless marriages and dissolute family life; universal arrogance, corruption and oppression. This indictment was actually written in Stockholm, whither Kotoshchikhin had fled. But there were also sources of comparison in Moscow itself. Of these, the most important was the Nemetskaya Sloboda, that is, the German Settlement. (To the Muscovite masses all foreigners were Germans; in actual fact many of the 'Germans' were Scots and Dutch.) The first foreign settlement grew up in the vicinity of Moscow in the reign of Ivan the Terrible. It was destroyed during the Time of Troubles and abandoned. During the next three decades or so it underwent a renaissance inside the capital itself, where foreigners could purchase houses and even establish their own churches. But in 1643, following a fracas at one of the churches, the Patriarch ordered its demolition. The eventual result was the creation of a new Nemetskaya Sloboda outside the capital, in which were assembled all the foreigners evicted from their previous residences. It quickly developed into a handsome suburb with three Lutheran churches and one Calvinist – Catholics might only worship privately – and a population of several thousand. A number of foreigners accepted Orthodoxy and assimilation and went on to spread Western influences less obtrusively throughout the country.

The enclave proved to be a centre of Western influence and Western amenities. The impact did not go very deep and it certainly did not go beyond a small stratum of the Muscovite aristocracy. For all that, the Sloboda is not unimportant historically. To the West as a source of power was added the concept of the West as a source of comfort and amenity.

Through their influential position in Muscovite society, the 'Germans', who were military men, merchants, teachers, artisans, doctors, apothecaries, midwives, paper manufacturers, iron-smelters, glass-workers, formed something of a European community, asserting a system of values that transcended mere practical usefulness. Western-style music would be organized to accompany the banquets of the Kremlin; the residences of leading boyars would house European furniture, clocks, mirrors, pictures. The boyars and the tsar would ride in carriages upholstered in velvet and fitted out with glass windows. One of the most remarkable innovations of the period was the erection of a building in the village of Preobrazhenskoe for use as a theatre. The director was Johann Gregory, the pastor of a German Lutheran church in the Sloboda. The Tsar's religious scruples were overcome by reference to the example of the Byzantine emperors. The first performance of a stage play in Muscovy took place in October 1672. It was a Biblical tragicomedy on the theme of the Esther story, composed by Gregory, and performed by pupils of the German school, with specially trained Muscovite serf-musicians providing the musical accompaniment. It lasted ten hours. The next performance was of the tragedy *Judith and Holofernes*. With the establishment of a 'Palace of Amusements' within its walls, the Kremlin itself soon witnessed theatrical performances. The conduct of the theatre was entrusted to the boyar Matveyev, a true connoisseur of European recreations. There followed the additional novelty of representations in Russian – in the case of the German pieces, Alexis had to rely on an interpreter for a running commentary on the action – and the foundation of a theatre school, under the direction of Pastor Gregory. The students were all male. Not until a century later did women take the female parts. As an index of Russian cultural immaturity, this general situation may be usefully contrasted with the Restoration comedy of contemporary England or the French theatrical world of Racine and Molière.

Alexis's own attitude to these Western European innovations fluctuated. A definite reaction followed his death in 1676. The activities of Pastor Gregory, Matveyev, and the Palace of Amusements were all suspended. Even so, intensified contact with the West was moulding a generation of the Muscovite aristocracy into something very different from Kotoshchikhin's portraits. Thus, although the circulation of Latin and Polish works and the importation of foreign literature were formally forbidden in 1672 – Moscow already had its own printing press, the Government argued – a man such as Matveyev had a library in some four or five European languages, and maintained with his wife, a Scottish lady named Hamilton, something of a European *salon*. Of comparable significance was Vasily Golitsyn, whose house, said a French diplomatic envoy, La Neuville, was one of the most magnificent in all Europe, recalling the court of an Italian Prince. Another such boyar was Ordyn-Nashchokin, the Muscovite equivalent of Foreign Minister.

The same spirit that produced these men also provoked the first faint intimation of systematic education in Muscovy. The virtual illiteracy of the Church had not precluded it from dominating such educational facilities as existed. In the middle of the seventeenth century the first school in Moscow came into being. It met with much opposition from the stauncher minds of Russian Orthodoxy; all the more so as the first teachers were Ukrainian monks from the Latinized Academy of Kiev, and Latinity spelt national and spiritual damnation. The school was organized largely through the efforts of another westernized boyar, Rtishchev, at the Andreyevsky monastery near Moscow. The monastery had been founded and endowed by Rtishchev and he himself studied there, his subjects being Greek, Latin and Slavonic languages, rhetoric, and philosophy. One of the monks on the staff was commissioned to produce a Greek–Slavonic lexicon. In other ways too the school was influential, attracting some of the less hidebound monks and priests of Muscovy.

In 1687, Rtishchev's institute was joined by the Greek–Latin–Slavonic Academy in Moscow, modelled on that of Kiev. It issued from the merger of two hitherto independent schools, where Greek and Latin respectively were taught. This was a compromise between the partisans of westernism and the traditionally minded. In actual fact the new Academy became as much an instrument of censorship and intellectual supervision as of learning. For example, only those who had been its pupils could own foreign books; only the Academy might teach foreign languages; the Academy too had to approve the requests of all applicants for foreign-language tutors. Foreign scholars in Muscovy also came under the supervision of the Academy. Still, supervision by scholars was an improvement on supervision by prelates. In the event it was far from being able to fulfil these various tasks, and by the beginning of the eighteenth century it found itself in a state of utter collapse.

The state of Muscovite intellectual life corresponded generally to the almost complete lack of any provision for education. Arithmetic, which in any case was handicapped by the use of Slavonic characters, since Arabic numerals did not come into general use until the eighteenth century, was limited to addition and subtraction. Euclidean geometry was hardly known, nor were the new astronomical theories of Galileo, Kepler and Copernicus. Letters were in an equally parlous state. However, even if every allowance be made for Muscovite cultural and economic backwardness, the fact remains that certain fermenting influences were at work. And it was these that helped to produce and formulate the pregnant question: what was the place of Muscovy in history?

Muscovite self-criticism was clearly evident in the writings of Kotoshchikhin. More portentous still were the views of Krizhanich. Typically, Yuri Krizhanich was an outsider. He came from Croatia and was thus a Catholic subject of the Sultan. He was born in 1617 and studied theology at Zagreb, Vienna, Bologna and Rome, in the Congregation for the Propagation of the Faith. As a Slav, he was eminently suited for missionary activity in Muscovy, which he had made his adoptive fatherland. His first visit took place in 1647; the second some ten years later. He concealed his priesthood lest he be refused entry to Muscovy. He died in 1683, in the defence of Vienna against the Turks.

Krizhanich distinguished himself in Muscovy by offering his services to Alexis as a translator, scholar and political adviser. But he aroused suspicion and was exiled to Tobolsk in Siberia for fifteen years, during which period he also received a small salary from the State. This enforced leisure gave him an opportunity to compose his unfinished *Political Considerations*, in which he tried to define the historical role of the new Muscovy. Much of this was fantasy in the conditions of the mid seventeenth century, but it was all relevant to the future. Krizhanich did not conceal from himself or his readers any of the evil sides of the life he found in Muscovy – the ubiquitous drunkenness, ignorance, official and judicial corruption and bribery, economic and military inefficiency, personal degradation in matters of hygiene, honour, and punishment. All the same, he was one of the first to contrast the spirituality of Muscovy with the materialism of the West. Krizhanich looked on Muscovy with the eyes of the first Pan-Slav. He called on Muscovy to rescue and unite all the stateless Slav peoples – the Serbs, Croats, Bulgars, Czechs, and Poles – and restore to them their national honour. The Slavs, Krizhanich argued, were the young people of the future. Krizhanich sought to ally Russia with Rome and this meant undoing the tacit alliance of Greek Orthodoxy and German Protestantism that had grown up since the Polish invasions. He argued that if Muscovy was to realize its mission to the full, it must guard against the danger of losing its national identity, and succumb neither to the reactionary spirit of the Greeks nor to the heedless progress of the 'Germans'. The Germans, with their superior civilization, were the more formidable danger, and had already greatly humiliated the Slavs. On the other hand, in the interests of its mission, Muscovy must reform itself through the introduction of Western culture and enlightenment – translate foreign works on agriculture and trade, develop a mercantilist trading policy, organize its artisans into guilds and its merchants into self-governing corporations, and generally create a system in which every subject of the tsar would serve the State.

All this, had he known of it, would have been heady stuff to Peter the Great, for Krizhanich's *Considerations* strongly resembled his own policy. As it is, however, they are even more important as the first attempt to give Muscovy a new *raison d'être* in the changed circumstances produced by the impact of the West.

CHAPTER 7

Expansion and Bureaucracy: The Age of Peter the Great

Hereditary autocracy is a highly unstable form of government. Sooner or later it must be subverted by the all too human realities of weakness, illness, sterility, and untimely death. Whenever this happened in Russia, furious contests erupted for control of the government. Alexis was twice married – first to Maria Miloslavskaya and then to Natalia Naryshkin. For a few years after his death in 1676 there was something of a repetition of the feuds that had disfigured the Kremlin during the minority of Ivan the Terrible – family against family, clan against clan.

Theodore, one of the thirteen children born to Alexis and Maria, succeeded his father on the throne. Under this regime, the Naryshkins, their supporters, and Natalia's eldest son, the four-year-old Peter, were ejected from power and pushed into the background. But in 1682 Theodore died childless. Peter, now ten, was at once plunged into the vortex of a bloody struggle for power. He was proclaimed tsar by a hastily convened Assembly of the Land; the claims of his half-brother Ivan, almost blind and an epileptic, were passed over. Barely a fortnight later, the streltsy invaded the Kremlin, thirsting for the blood of the Naryshkins. There were drunken orgies, there was wild clamour, and in the midst of it all, many of Peter's family were done to death. Peter looked on very calmly, it was said, as the streltsy cut up the bodies of their victims in the courtyards of the palace. In the upshot he was proclaimed joint tsar with Ivan, under the regency of Sophia, Ivan's sister, by a re-convened Assembly. Peter did not become sole ruler in his own name until 1696. By then Sophia had been overthrown, and Peter's mother and Ivan had both died.

The events of Peter's youth may well have fostered an urge to have done with Moscow and all the dead weight of its Byzantine past, its ignorance and inefficiency, its internecine disputes, its complacency, its uncouthness and hostility to change. Be that as it may, Peter was certainly the most venturesome and vigorous of all the tsars in his efforts to create a Russia (as Muscovy was renamed in his reign) able to rank with the West. It is this that made him not only the most unpopular of all the tsars during his lifetime but also the most controversial afterwards. Was he a German imposter or the anti-Christ in person? Did his reforms wrench Russia from its natural path and force the country into an alien mould? Was he a calamity for his country or its saviour? Did he introduce a split in Russian culture, for ever afterwards setting a Westernized upper class against an unregenerate mass of peasants? Then there is the ambiguous verdict of Pushkin's poem *The Bronze Horseman*: does one admire above all the Tsar's vaulting ambition and creative energy, or does one give one's heart to the unnumbered victims of his policy? In all these ways the phenomenon of Peter has dominated the Russian imagination.

The recurrence of despotism in twentieth-century Russia suggests another perspective, for Peter was one of the three great despots whose use of terror continues to horrify many people while arousing the ill-concealed admiration of others. Certainly, there are some striking similarities in their personal biographies. Both Ivan and Peter killed their heirs while Stalin did away with many a possible successor. A closer examination of these similarities leads to the conclusion that Peter, though subject to fits of tyrannical fury, remained much more human than Ivan or Stalin; to the end of his days he retained a capacity for spontaneous affection and physical courage that finds no parallel in the lives of his fellow despots. He lived and died a giant in body and spirit and while this helped to make him a despot it may have saved him from the most corrupt of the vices of tyrants.

Peter was born in the Kremlin in 1672. At the age of five he began to receive the normal education of a tsarevich. This comprised the rudiments of reading and writing, elementary arithmetic, and the Scriptures. This came to an end in 1682, with the eclipse of the Naryshkins. Peter and his mother were forced to leave the Kremlin and to take up residence in the village of Preobrazhenskoe, one of the favourite country seats of Alexis. Here Peter was left very much to his own devices. The games and interests that he now developed prefigure very closely the man he was to become. Foremost was his predilection for military toys and pursuits – bows and arrows, cannon, toy soldiers. More serious games followed when Peter, still in his early teens, began to drill his companions into regiments and organize manoeuvres around a fortress built on the River Yauza near Moscow. All the paraphernalia of a miniature army were present – cannon and firearms supplied by the royal arsenal, barracks, stables, uniforms, money. Soon Peter had at his disposal two regular regiments, the Preobrazhensky and the Semenovsky. The officers were mostly foreigners drawn from the German Sloboda, conveniently close to the village. The soldiers, drawn from the Muscovite nobility were, in effect, cadets at the first Russian military academy.

The other great interest in Peter's early life was nautical. In his youth he stumbled across an old, crumbling English sailing-boat preserved at the village of Izmailova and conceived a life-long passion for this novel form of transport (which can only be compared with the enthusiasm invested in projects like Concorde or the Space Shuttle today). Peter later referred to this boat as the father of the Russian fleet. In the heart of landlocked Russia it spurred him on to nautical experiment on nearby ponds and lakes. Then, aided by Dutch sailors, he progressed from sailing to building and could indulge to the full his passion for the navy and the art of seamanship. Not until some years later did Peter actually see the open sea at Archangel and travel far into the White Sea.

These early years, a world away from the oppressive, intrigue-laden air of Moscow, were filled also with the eager acquisition of practical knowledge and techniques of all kinds. Peter learnt to lay bricks, work metal, use a printing press, wield an axe; he became a skilled carpenter and joiner. A Dutchman, Franz Timmermann, first initiated him into such subjects as mathematics, geometry, the theory of ballistics, the art of fortification, and the use of the astrolabe. All in all, Peter mingled even more freely with the members of the Sloboda than with Russians. His boon companion, for example, was the veteran Scots soldier of fortune, General Patrick Gordon, born near Aberdeen in 1635 and a mercenary under the Emperor, the Swedes, and the Poles. Gordon's friendship was of critical importance to Peter in 1682, when he rallied the foreign mercenaries to Peter, thereby sealing the doom of the Regent Sophia. There was Franz Lefort, a cosmopolitan

Genoese adventurer and Peter's drinking associate in many a bout. The Sloboda also supplied Peter's first mistress, Anna Mons, the daughter of a German wine-merchant. Peter's Russian companions might be scions of the aristocracy or obscure nobodies, chosen for their convivial qualities. But the Sloboda and its inhabitants could never be more than a substitute for the real thing; they could not replace first-hand contact with the West. Hence Peter's desire to see and learn for himself. For a tsar to leave Russia to take instruction from foreigners was a revolutionary affront to traditional Russian ideas. He set out on his own version of the Grand Tour in 1697, travelling under a transparent incognito so that he could dispense with irrelevant protocol when he chose to. The serious purpose of the Great Embassy was underlined by the fact that most of his entourage of 250 were fellow students rather than servants. The aim was to acquire instruction in the latest methods of shipbuilding and to recruit naval and military specialists. The political aim of organizing a grand alliance against the Turks failed through the reluctance of the Western powers.

The Baltic ports of Riga and Libau gave Peter his first view of the Baltic—thence to Mittau, Königsberg, Berlin, Holland, and England. In all, the party was away a year and a quarter. No tsar had ever been outside Muscovy before. Still less had any tsar done what Peter would do. At Zaandam and Amsterdam he and his companions worked every day as prentice shipwrights in the wharves of the Dutch East India Company. In their leisure they visited hospitals, mills, workshops of all kinds, schools, and military and naval centres.

After four months in Holland, Peter went on to England. He sailed in the royal yacht presented to him by William III. This was the real climax of the journey. With his headquarters at John Evelyn's house at Deptford, conveniently near the King's Wharf, Peter was able to study the latest shipbuilding techniques. But he also visited Oxford, London, the Tower, the Mint, and, of course, Woolwich Arsenal. There were other visits to Chatham and Portsmouth for fleet reviews and mock naval battles. All of this, Peter meticulously noted in his diary. From Bishop Burnett he learned of the advantages of a state-controlled church. The lighter side of the English stay produced damages to Evelyn's house estimated by Sir Christopher Wren at £350. Wren's report noted a ruined lawn, destroyed furniture, pictures used for target practice, walls scratched and smeared.

After some four months in England, Peter set out on his return journey, by way of Holland to Vienna. He had not been long in the Imperial capital when a letter from Prince Romodanovsky, Peter's governor in Moscow and Minister in Charge of Flogging and the Torture Chamber, urgently summoned him back – the streltsy were in revolt. The secret police had already uncovered one plot against Peter led by a colonel of the streltsy. This was shortly before he left for the West. The ringleaders were tortured and executed. This new mutiny had wider ramifications. It drew its strength from the streltsy's awareness that their power was waning. To their perennial grievances over arrears of salary had been added the humiliation of virtual exile to Azov and the south-western frontier under heretical foreign commanders. Many of them were Old Believers. Hoping to attract the sympathy of Sophia, and fortified by rumours that Peter had died abroad, a number of regiments marched on Moscow in the early summer of 1698. Gordon's troops helped to defeat them and punished the ringleaders, but with Peter's sudden and unexpected return a massive bloody purge was conducted. It was of a scale and type that Moscow had not seen for many a long day. Day after day, in September and October of that year, and again in January 1699, men were flogged with the knout, broken on the wheel, roasted over a slow fire. Report had it that Peter himself wielded the executioner's axe, displaying the strength needed to decapitate a man with one blow. His favourites, Menshikov and Romodanovsky, certainly did so. Some 1,200 men died this way. Their corpses, often mutilated, were left for months on show to the public. The revolt of the streltsy was the first test for the Preobrazhensky Prikaz (literally 'Transfiguration Office') which had grown out of Peter's new regiment and which now became the first regular secret police department in Russian history.

It is no coincidence, perhaps, that this first merciless onslaught on a characteristic feature of old Muscovy was accompanied by another, though lesser, attack – this time on Muscovite beards. Aided by his court jester Turgenev, Peter in person, the very day following his return from the West, shaved off the beards of his principal boyars and also enforced the wearing of Hungarian or German dress as distinct from the long-sleeved topcoats worn hitherto. Every Russian, except for the clergy and the peasants, had to comply with the new laws on pain of a fine. This effort to westernize the outward appearance of Peter's subjects had little success outside the court and military milieu. Most Russians preferred to pay the fine rather than lose their beards.

In those early years after the return from the West, Peter also set about reforming local government and finance, replacing the voevoda system by elected elders and reorganizing the collection of certain direct and indirect taxes. Most of his ideas came from Holland. He also devoted these years to the expansion of the fleet and the creation of a new army. An Admiralty was set up, and shipbuilding feverishly carried on at Voronezh, in which many foreigners recruited from the West were engaged. One vessel, a sixty-gun warship, was designed by Peter himself and built entirely by Russian shipwrights. 'Companies', compulsorily financed by the Church, the merchants, and the larger landowners, unwillingly supplied the cash. An army of sorts was raised by levies on the landowners and monasteries. Domestic serfs, slaves, and semi-attached retainers were taken for preference, so that agricultural production would be affected as little as possible. At first, the officers were foreigners and the conscripted gentry.

Both apologists for Russian despotism and exponents of Anglo-Saxon military and naval expansionism have found it convenient to assert that Russia has always wanted to become a major maritime power. Closer examination suggests that the Russian people have always been more interested in colonizing contiguous land masses, and this includes the great majority of the Muscovite ruling class. The merchant class was still segmented; the merchants of Novgorod and Pskov who wanted Russia to develop the Baltic trade were remote from government while those of Moscow who could influence the government favoured the Archangel trade they had come to dominate. The truth is that while Peter's foreign policy had some precedents, they were exceptions that proved the rule. Peter's foreign policy was truly revolutionary – the 'Patrimony of Yaroslav' might provide pretexts but his motives were mercantilist. He seems to have learnt from his foreign friends that western riches had come from trade between the fabulous East and key western ports like Amsterdam. The grandiose task he set before himself was the creation of a trade route of comparable significance through Russia. As a soldier, Peter felt this could best be achieved if existing trading-routes were annexed to Russia. First of all he moved south, annexing Azov from the Crimean vassals of the Turks in 1696. This move was dictated as much by the hunger of his gentry supporters for southern pomestiya, and by a misreading of Turkey's temporary weakness, as by Peter's genius. It brought him great prestige in the short term but in the end it led to a disaster from which he was only saved by events that still seem miraculous or inexplicable to historians.

THE GREAT NORTHERN WAR

In July 1700, a number of minor campaigns against Turkey came to an end. Russia secured Azov and Taganrog, the right of pilgrimage to Palestine, the abrogation of the duty to make any further 'gifts' (tribute) to the Crimea, and the right to maintain a resident minister at Constantinople.

Peter had discovered during his Grand Tour that the Europeans had no intention of fighting a crusade against the Turks. This led him to consider that other obstacle to Russian trade, Sweden. Ever since the Thirty Years' War, Sweden had been the master-power in northern Europe. Its hold on Finland, Karelia, Ingria, Estonia, Livonia, Pomerania, and Schleswig-Holstein made Sweden the Baltic power *par excellence*. Peter's allies in his challenge were Denmark and Poland. The Poles attacked first, followed by the Danes. The very day he heard of the signing of peace at Constantinople, some five weeks after the event, Peter joined in. On that same day, too, the Danes were knocked out of the war. This was an inauspicious beginning. But worse was to come.

Peter's forces, all 40,000 of them, under the command of Eugène, Duc de Croy, Prince of the Holy Roman Empire, were before the Swedish port and strongpoint of Narva. Suddenly the Swedish troops appeared, led by the eighteen-year-old Charles XII, and overwhelmed the Russians in a thick snow-storm. The Russian troops fled in disarray or gave themselves up. Peter was in despair. Peace at any price was his first agonized cry. But this defeat evoked new strength and resilience, for Peter made the reform and reconstruction of the army his first concern. Levy after levy was imposed on the peasants and townspeople, usually in the proportion of one man per twenty households. This produced about 30,000 men a year. Training, drill, and tactics were all revolutionized. Peter stepped up the production of flint-locks and bayonets, of siege guns and field-artillery. New ironworks and powder factories in the Urals were the chief centres of arms manufacture. He made every effort to attract more and more military specialists from abroad; and in 1702 issued a decree inviting all foreigners to Russia, promising them religious freedom and their own law courts, as well as free passage and employment. Russians who attempted to take advantage of this promise of religious freedom were brutally chastised. At home, further measures of conscription were imposed on the landowners. To finance all this effort, Peter sequestered the Church's revenues; all in all, about 80 per cent of the State's income went to feed the needs of war.

For all his urging and impatience, Peter also needed time. Here Charles came to his aid. He failed to follow up his victory at Narva by a march on Moscow; instead he moved south and involved his forces in innumerable minor campaigns against the Poles. Peter himself kept Charles bogged down in Poland as long as possible by sending Augustus II, the Polish King, reinforcements and money. But at the end of 1706 the Polish front finally collapsed. By the Treaty of Altranstädt a Swedish–Polish peace was concluded. Augustus had to give up his throne and acknowledge Charles's nominee, Stanislas Leszczynski, as the new Polish king.

In the meantime, however, Peter had also to some extent been able to strengthen his position, especially to the north. He had retaken Ingria, the port of Dorpat, and stormed Narva (1704). In 1703 he had founded St Petersburg (now Leningrad) near the mouth of the Neva River and constructed the fortress of Kronstadt to protect it from the open sea. But none of this could be of great avail against Charles, who was now freed from the incubus of the Polish campaign. Peter had already made several attempts to secure a mediated peace, on the sole condition that he retain St Petersburg. Their failure left him all the more exposed to Charles's imminent attack. In addition, it was at this time that his repeated levies, programmes of forced labour, and oppressive taxation provoked uprisings in the Russian interior. There was one revolt at Astrakhan in 1705. Two years later the Don Cossacks rebelled, led by their hetman Bulavin. Survivors of Razin's rebellion and Old Believers were also among the leaders of the revolt. The movement rapidly spread to a mass of peasant refugees from serfdom in the Don country. From there it engulfed the Voronezh area and the workers conscripted to build the Volga–Don canal. Eventually, Bulavin's uprising dominated a vast area between the Volga and the lower Don. At the same time there were rebellions among certain of the oppressed non-Russian nationalities – the Bashkirs, Tartars, Cheremis.

The suppression of these revolts urgently demanded the transfer of troops needed in the West; even so, the task was mercilessly carried out. Foreign observers were saying, with evident truth, that had Peter's campaign against the Swedes failed, he would have had to face a revolution.

In 1706, Charles began to march eastwards into Poland. The Russians systematically retreated, avoiding pitched battles as far as possible, and carrying out a scorched-earth policy. In July the enemy crossed the Dnieper and took Mogilev. Would Charles then strike northwards at Novgorod and Pskov and make his ultimate goal St Petersburg? Or would he aim directly eastwards at Smolensk, the classical key to Moscow, only some sixty miles away?

At first, Charles dismissed the Livonian area which had been fought over too much already to withstand further campaigning in an age when armies lived off the land. He resolved to aim at the Russian centre – Moscow. The capital hastily prepared for the imminent siege. But the central area had also been thoroughly scorched. Charles changed his plan. He decided on a detour by way of the Ukraine. Here there would be no lack of food supplies for his troops, for Mazepa, the hetman of the Ukraine, had promised him supplies if he would patronize Ukrainian independence.

This move southwards proved fatal. The Ukrainian Cossacks were divided, many were undoubtedly intimidated by Menshikov's bloodcurdling threats while others remembered Mazepa's hostility to peasant rebellion and regarded his monarchical ambitions with suspicion. In the event, he carried only 2,000 with him. Meanwhile Charles had moved farther from his supply and baggage train, which was slowly advancing southwards from Riga under the command of General Löwenhaupt.

The two Swedish forces were isolated. At the small town of Lesnaya, to the south-east of Mogilev, the Russians attacked Löwenhaupt's army and inflicted a heavy defeat. The vast bulk of the supplies of arms and munitions eagerly awaited by Charles had to be destroyed. This was in October 1708. An unusually severe winter followed. The Swedish forces, not much more than 20,000 by now, suffered from the climate and shortages of food and arms. The climactic battle came on 27 June 1709 (8 July new style). Charles besieged the small fortress-town of Poltava – and suffered a crushing defeat. The Swedish survivors retreated to the Dnieper. But their boats were burnt and they fell before the onset of Russian cavalry. Charles and Mazepa fled to Turkish territory. In a phrase, Peter crystallized the meaning of the victory: 'Now the final stone has been laid on the foundations of St Petersburg'.

The 'most glorious victory' of Poltava was far from ending the war, however. The Great Northern War, as it came to be called, dragged on with intermissions for another twelve years. But at least Russia was freed from the threat of invasion. This was perhaps its most important immediate consequence. By the same token, it gave Peter the opportunity to exploit the Swedish collapse so that he could consolidate his position to the west and north. There was a radical transformation in the Russian diplomatic position. Peter could overrun Livonia and Estonia and control the whole Baltic coast from the Western Dvina to Vyborg; he could reinstate Augustus on the Polish throne; he could create a powerful Russian fleet on the Baltic and station Russian forces on the territory of his petty German clients, an unprecedented phenomenon; he could marry his nieces to the rulers of Mecklenburg and Courland and dabble, more or less successfully, in North German politics; he could even aspire to a marriage between his daughter

Elizabeth and the young Louis XV of France; he could conquer Finland and raid the Swedish coast.

The beginning of the end of the Great Northern War came in 1718; direct Russo-Swedish negotiations opened on one of the Åland islands. They dragged on inconclusively for nearly eighteen months. A further year and a half later, the final peace was concluded at Nystad. Russia received the territories of Livonia, Estonia, Ingria, part of Karelia, with the city and district of Vyborg, and the islands of Ösel and Dagö (Hiumaa and Saaremaa). In return, Russia bound herself to restore Finland to Sweden, to pay a compensation of two million Dutch thalers, and to refrain from interference in Swedish internal affairs. These terms signalled nothing less than the emergence of Russia as one of the great powers of Europe.

The expansion of Russia created terrible dilemmas for the smaller nationalities that lay across its path. These were exemplified by the careers of the two famous 'traitors', Mazepa and Patkul. Mazepa tried and failed to make Russia's emergency the Ukraine's opportunity, though he managed to save his neck in exile. Patkul helped to forge the coalition that eventually defeated Sweden. Charles XII had him hanged but the Baltic German gentry and merchant class he came from found greater security and a vital role in Peter's new Russian Empire.

Before Peter could consolidate his control over the Baltic territories, his victory at Poltava was very nearly cancelled out by his defeat and virtual capture in a disastrous war with Turkey. The indomitable Charles XII, an insecure and unwelcome refugee in Turkey, joined forces with the Crimean Khan and the Turkish governor of the Dnieper ports to bring down a neutralist Turkish government and replace it with one bent on war with Russia. The war which opened in 1710 brought out all Peter's revolutionary opportunism; he saw a chance to secure outlets for Russia's Mediterranean trade by relying as much on the Orthodox sympathies of the Balkan peoples as on Russian military activity. The rulers of Montenegro and Moldavia rallied to him and his army was welcomed as a liberating force in Jassy. The military side of the war was another matter. Russian supplies ran out and Peter and his wife were surrounded with the main Russian army on the banks of the Pruth; they were forced to sue for peace. At this point Peter was prepared to sacrifice all his conquests and even the ancient Russian city of Pskov to save his new capital. Miraculously, the Turks insisted only on the return of Azov and the destruction of Russian forts on the Dnieper; they merely requested the Russians to permit Charles XII a safe passage home. Shortly afterwards two of the Turkish negotiators were executed for corruption.

Peter was more successful in the Far East and central Asia. He was able to develop the trade in silk and furs with China, while leaving unchanged the political relationship established by the treaty of 1689. In the far north-east he advanced the Russian frontiers to Kamchatka and annexed the northern Kurile islands in the Pacific but in central Asia his efforts to subdue the two Moslem Khanates of Khiva and Bokhara failed.

Peter's most striking, if ephemeral, successes were in Persia and along the shores of the Caspian. He sent his first envoy, Volynsky, to Isfahan in 1715, hoping to expand trade with Persia, explore the possibility of a route to India, and enforce a rerouting of the Armenian silk trade through St Petersburg, cutting out the route through Turkey. Volynsky did indeed conclude a trade treaty that opened up Persia to Russian merchants. More important, he reported that the country was in a state of collapse; nothing more than a small detachment would be needed to carve it up. For the moment, preoccupation with the Great Northern War inhibited Russian aggression. But in 1722, on the pretext of aiding the Shah to restore order in his territory, Peter set sail down the Volga to Astrakhan. Derbent soon fell to the Russians, then the port of Resht, and in 1723 Baku. In the eventual peace, Russia retained these ports, and also certain Persian provinces along the southern and south-western littoral of the Caspian. As ever, Peter had grandiose ideas for developing these areas. He would build fortifications, deport the Moslems to make way for Christian settlers, carry out mineral surveys ... But it came to nothing in the end. Soon after his death, the nearly-acquired provinces had to be abandoned. The anticipated revenues failed to meet the costs of defending them. For the Orthodox Georgians, on the other hand, centuries of encirclement by Islam seem to be coming to an end.

THE REFORMS

For most of Peter's reign, Russia was at war. This very largely determined the nature, scope, and success of the Tsar's activities as a reformer. Many of his reforms were desperate expedients born of immediate military necessity but as he matured he came to see the need for greater consistency in his legislation. Throughout his career, he was inspired by the same vision of a people devoted to the State which had inspired the rulers of Muscovy since the fifteenth century. Peter was pragmatic in his approach and his reforms were addressed to two objectives: to educate the Russian ruling class in his own rationalist ethos and to harness all the resources of the country for total war. He shrank from no measure that seemed calculated to advance his purposes, however great the opposition he met with. 'The Tsar pulls uphill along with the strength of ten, but millions pull downhill,' wrote Pososhkov, an early apologist for the Petrine regime. To drag these millions with him, Peter had to deploy a widespread system of spying and informing, in addition to the punishments traditional in Muscovy. He made his subjects, particularly the peasants, pay a heavy price for their country's rise to the status of a great power.

Money engaged Peter's attention from the start. How could he cover an ever-mounting military expenditure – 2·3 million roubles in 1701, 3·2 millions in 1710, over 4 millions in 1724? There were a number of expedients to hand, all of which Peter made use of. He confiscated the income of the estates of the Church; he debased the currency; he introduced any number of indirect taxes, which were often suggested by a special corps of 'profit-makers'. There were taxes on beards, coffins, bee-keeping, bath-houses, knife-grinding, articles of clothing, the sale of salt, the weddings of non-Russian tribesmen. But by 1710 these measures showed diminishing returns. This led to a transformation in the incidence of direct taxation. This had hitherto been based on a tax on households as determined by the census of 1678. In 1710 a new census was ordered in the confident hope that the result would show an increase. But it actually revealed a decline of about 20 per cent over the whole country, though it is still not clear how much of this was due to evasion of the census. For the time being the old system was retained. In 1719, however, after a further census had revealed an increase in the number of male peasants, the transition was made to a poll-tax on the individual male 'soul'. The penalty for evading the census was death. The new tax succeeded both in increasing revenue, bringing in more than 50 per cent of the budgetary income in 1724, and in extending the cultivated area. The peasants had to cultivate more land in order to pay tax. The new system lasted until 1886.

Peter the Great believed that the engine of a modern state should be an enterprising commercial and industrial class and he made many attempts to associate Russia's merchants with the kinds of economic development he favoured. Despite some notable exceptions, these efforts failed. Peter had little interest in their small-scale enterprises producing for Russia's cellular network of local markets and directed at small-scale consumers. Few of the merchants were happy at the prospect of producing solely for the militarized state, a consumer notoriously demanding and unreliable in settling accounts. For Peter, the need of the military machine came first and this involved the large-scale production of munitions, arms, and textiles for military uniforms. The production of paper – indispensable in a bureaucratic regime – also went forward, so that by 1723 Peter could decree that only Russian-made paper be used in the departments of State. At the end of the reign, Russia had some 200 factories, some of which employed more than 1,000 workers. Among the largest were those that produced wool, linen, silk, leather, cotton, and ornaments.

Mining and metallurgy also progressed. The Ural iron deposits were the scene of the most notable advance in extractive technique and processing. Between 1695 and 1725 fifty-two new ironworks were opened, of which one-quarter were in the Urals. Altogether, the latter accounted for about 40 per cent of all Russian production, equally divided between State-owned and privately owned works. In not much more than a quarter of a century, Russia had come to lead the world in the production of iron. It was Russia which supplied the major part of England's iron imports.

The general development of Russian manufactures and mining depended on State aid, forced labour, and protective tariffs. There was indeed a preponderance of merchants and mercantile capital among the companies formed, at Peter's urging, to develop the country's resources; but State subsidies were also essential in view of the shortage of capital. The State similarly helped to overcome the shortage of labour. It conscripted all sorts of vagabonds, unemployed, and marginal individuals, such as prostitutes and orphans, for service in the factories. In less populated areas the problem would be overcome by forcing peasants from State lands into factory service. Runaway peasants working in a factory could not even be reclaimed by their owners. We should remember that the plantation system was just then at its height in the Americas. Such was the emphasis Peter gave to industrialization. Finally, the State not only helped to subsidize and to man new enterprises, it also gave them the benefits of a high tariff, the right to import machinery and raw materials freely, and exemption from taxation.

Financial and industrial policy had only an indirect effect on the status of the various classes. Peter's social policy, on the other hand, intentionally produced profound changes in their duties and interrelationship. As ever, the aim that overrode all others was to organize the population so that it could best fulfil its duties to the State. This principle of universal and compulsory national service had nothing new about it. But Peter systematized, refined, and intensified its application.

The position of the landowning gentry underwent the greatest change, for Peter was determined that they should be competent to lead the modern Russia he hoped to build. They were forced to undergo instruction in some branch of practical knowledge, either abroad or in certain 'mathematical' schools that Peter established in St Petersburg. The penalty for failing to complete the course was enforced celibacy. This might not affect the man's personal life but it would mean that his children had no claim on his property. At fifteen, the young noble had then to choose between State service in the army, the navy, or the bureaucracy. Russia had no nautical tradition and the noble did not take kindly to the sea; an interesting comment on the theory that Russia had always aspired to the mastery of the seas. The bureaucracy was the most popular. It was safer, less arduous, and more remunerative. To preserve a balance, therefore, personnel were rationed, only one in every three young men being allocated to the bureaucracy. Those who 'chose' the army as their career served in one of the three regiments of Guards. They had to work their way up from the lowest rank before being rewarded with commissions in other regiments, where they received faster promotion than the regimental officers promoted from the ranks, or, if their connections and status warranted it, with a commission in the Guards themselves. It was this special status that later in the eighteenth century gave the Guards their importance as kingmakers. A special official, the Heraldmaster, controlled the noble's career. He maintained a register of each family, ensuring, on pain of the severest penalty, that no leadswinger, slacker, scrimshanker, or defaulter evaded his duty.

Peter reinforced the threat of punishment by a flanking attack that struck at the very roots of the ancient Muscovite law of inheritance. Estates had hitherto been divided equally among the sons of the deceased. This had led to much subdivision into unprofitable units, with consequent loss of tax-paying capacity and also waste of manpower. To overcome these twin disadvantages, Peter issued an unprecedented Entail Law in 1714. He drew largely on English practice in primogeniture. An estate could henceforth be bequeathed to one son only, chosen by the owner. The remaining children, Peter hoped, would be forced off the land and into State service. This calculation was borne out in a paradoxical way; after Peter's death, the dispossessed younger sons in the Guards regiments proved themselves determined opponents of the political pretensions of the magnates and secured the abolition of Entail in 1730.

He had much more success with the institution of the 'Table of Ranks' of 1722; this lasted right up to the Revolution of 1917. Its adoption was followed by the gradual disappearance of the term *shlyakhetstvo* for the gentry or nobility (a word derived ultimately from the German word for family) and its replacement by the word *dvoryantsvo* (derived from the word for court). If the dvoryantsvo had to serve, then it was only logical that those who served should be, or should become, members of the dvoryantsvo. What Peter did was to classify into fourteen parallel grades all the ranks in the army, navy and bureaucracy; Church ranks were completely ignored. Those who reached the eighth rank from the top in the bureaucracy were granted ennoblement. In the army and navy, ennoblement was earned on reaching the lowest commissioned rank. Service in both military and civilian posts began in the lowest grade; promotion depended on merit and seniority. The whole scheme was much more in keeping with Russian tradition than many of Peter's other reforms. The nobility had never formed a closed corporation or caste. Now hosts of newcomers could enjoy the privilege of owning serfs, and also exemption from the poll-tax. Peter was not a social leveller; on several occasions he ordered that 'nobles must not be soldiers anywhere but in the guards'. Nor could he prevent the aristocratic elite from dominating the senior positions in the army and civil bureaucracy. What he wanted was a competent dvoryanstvo. The promotion of competent commoners via the Table of Ranks reminded all the nobility that service mattered more than blood; it brought in new men and kept them on their toes.

The first emergence of the service nobility in the fifteenth and sixteenth centuries had been marked by their intensified control over the peasant. This process continued in the eighteenth century. The serfs in Peter's time made up about 90 per cent of the whole population of some twelve million. This total was enlarged by including the class of slaves, who were thus made liable to military service and to the poll-tax. The State peasants, monasterial retainers, and dependents were also subjected to conditions closely resembling serfdom. The State laid further burdens on these unfortunates. There was the poll-tax; there was forced labour in the new mines, factories, and ironworks; the construction of St Petersburg on marshy, Ingrian swampland demanded the lives of thousands of labourers; the digging of canals and conscription claimed others.

Those who stayed at home by no means escaped. On the contrary, the State subjected them even more tightly to the landowner In 1721, Peter issued a decree denouncing the sale of serfs 'separately, like cattle, a practice which is not supported anywhere else in the world'. But he introduced no penalty for its infringement and could only suggest that whole families be sold; as ever, the landowner remained sole ruler of every aspect of the serfs' way of life. Moreover, the introduction of an internal passport system obliged every serf to secure his owner's written permission before being able to leave his village. This system lasted until the Revolution, and even survived it in a somewhat changed form. (It was only in the 1970s that Soviet collective farmers acquired an automatic right to an *internal* passport.) As we have seen, these measures aroused energetic resistance among the peasantry.

The merchants and the urban population, on the other hand, derived some benefit from the reforms. The municipal autonomy enjoyed by Riga and Revel was Peter's inspiration. He divided the town population into three main groups – the 'first guild' consisting of the upper bourgeoisie of wealthy merchants, professional men; the 'second guild' of small merchants, handicraftsmen, artisans; and the 'common people' of hired labourers and the poor generally. The two guilds jointly elected a magistracy responsible for all the town's affairs, on which, however, only the members of the first guild could serve. Peter also attempted to establish true guilds of craftsmen of the type familiar in the Western European town, but this failed.

On the whole, one may say that Peter had more success in remodelling the organs of central and provincial government than in anything else. But before he found an adequate answer to the problems confronting him he took many a false step. Moreover, owing to the prevalence of bribery, peculation, overlapping functions, ill-defined powers, and the sheer physical difficulty of controlling vast areas suffering from poor communications, Peter had constantly to grapple with the problem: *quis custodiet custodes?* At first he took the path of decentralization. He created eight provincial governments (to which he later added two more), with very extensive powers. In view of the complete disappearance of the old Boyar Duma, this left a gap at the centre, so in 1711, when he left for the second Turkish war, Peter established a Senate of nine members to supervise the work of the provincial governments, to function as the supreme court of justice, and, above all, to ensure that all taxes were efficiently collected. A Guards officer was deputed to attend its meetings and to supervise the senators' conduct – no easy matter if the punishments to which they were subjected is any criterion. In 1715, for example, two senators were

flogged, and had their tongues branded and their property confiscated. In 1722 a general-procurator replaced the Guards officer
as Peter's 'eye'.

The Senate lasted until 1917. Less enduring, but still of fundamental governmental importance for a century, was Peter's introduction of nine colleges, based on Swedish and Danish models.
They completely replaced the old system of Prikazy. Each college
had a functional jurisdiction – army, foreign affairs, revenue,
mining, and manufacturing, for example – and was governed by a
Russian president, assisted initially by a foreign-born vice-president, and a board of eleven members.

It was in his treatment of the Church that Peter broke most
radically with Muscovite tradition. A contemporary historian goes
so far as to say that 'what Tsar Peter did to and with the Church
appears the decisive step in the secularization of Russian society'.*
His father had broken the caesaropapist aspirations of the Patriarchate and had begun to usurp the administration of its estates.
Peter carried these processes to their logical conclusion; henceforth
the Church would serve the largely secular objectives of the State.
Unlike his father, Peter regarded the religious sensibilities of his
subjects with indifference or even hostility. Early in his reign, he
organized his drinking partners into a 'Most Drunken Synod' at
which the rites of the Church were openly mocked. Deprived of
popular esteem by the schism provoked by Nikon's reforms, the
Church lacked the moral authority to oppose him. In 1700, when
the Patriarch died, Peter failed to appoint a successor and in 1721
he replaced the Patriarchate by a Holy Synod, essentially a secular
ministry of religion. The Church thereby lost any form of
independent self-government at the national level. Peter restricted
entry into monasteries and convents and insisted that those remaining in them helped to care for the sick or engage in useful
trades. Surplus parish clergy were conscripted into the army. In
the longer term, the clergy were also profoundly affected by
changes in the system of direct taxation that turned them into a
closed caste. Out of all these changes emerged a clergy that very
gradually became better educated and more efficiently adminis-
tered. The costs were high, however. The churchmen felt slighted

* J. Cracraft, *The Church Reform of Peter the Great* (London, 1971), p. viii.

in status by the secular state while their efforts to emulate the gentry cut them off still further from the masses, who were already suspicious of them for accepting Nikon's reforms and for carrying out the new tasks imposed on them by Peter. Increasingly, peasants and Cossacks looked to the Old Belief and to new fundamentalist sects for religious enlightenment.

Where provincial administration was concerned, Peter's over-faithful adoption of Swedish models led to an artificial system of fifty provinces covering the entire Empire. Its main intent was not only to achieve organizational tidiness but also to separate admin-istration *qua* administration from the administration of justice. Thus the fifty provinces expressly did not coincide with the eleven judicial districts. Peter further complicated the position by remov-ing from the purview of the provincial authorities the collection of the poll-tax and the selection of conscripts. This was tantamount to military rule in the countryside, in view of the importance of these two requirements of State. But the whole system produced so much tension between the rulers and the ruled and was so ineffective and unwieldy that it did not long survive Peter's death. The attempt to separate justice from administration ran clean counter to Russian tradition and to the spirit of indivisible auto-cracy as it had developed ever since the days of Ivan III.

The acquisition of the new Baltic territories and the gradual Russian expansion into the Ukraine posed administrative prob-lems of their own. The German ruling class of landowners in Estonia and Livonia was left undisturbed in the enjoyment of its special privileges, and the position of the Lutheran Church con-firmed. Peter understood that mild treatment of the Baltic Ger-mans would raise his standing in Germany; he also needed the help of the Baltic Germans in his attempts to make Russia a significant mercantile and naval power. In the Ukraine, on the other hand, consistent politico-economic Russification was the order of the day. At Kiev a Russian governor and two Russian regiments wielded power; and Russian nobles would receive grants of land in the Ukraine for particularly distinguished service. In the case of his non-European subjects – the Bashkirs and Tatars of the Urals and the Volga, for example – the policy of Russification could be applied more harshly. No non-Orthodox Russian could own serfs. Such peoples were also exposed to forced conversion by the Orthodox missions. Consequently, Tobolsk became the seat of a Metropolitan as early as 1700. Peter even hoped for the conversion of the Chinese to Orthodoxy; this was inspired as much by his fear of the Jesuits as by his love of the Chinese.

The same spirit of enlightenment, secularization, and practical utility informed Peter's educational and general pedagogic policy. He forced Russia to study – or rather, certain Russians to study certain subjects. The publication of about thirty decrees devoted to education in a broad sense testified in itself to Peter's perennial concern. But it was an uphill struggle and not always successful. When Peter ascended the throne he found only one school in existence, the Moscow Academy, apart from two theological academies in Moscow and Kiev respectively. This was plainly insufficient provision for the hosts of new experts and specialists that the new State demanded. Foreigners supplied many of the trained personnel, but this could be no more than a stopgap. In any case, they fulfilled in the main an executive rule and had little influence on policy. Russians trained abroad in navigation, seamanship, gunnery, economics, languages, and engineering could also help But the bulk of a trained ruling class must obviously be produced inside Russia itself. Peter, concentrating on the needs of the army and navy, first established a number of schools in Moscow and St Petersburg for future officers in the two services. Their curriculum was limited to mathematics, navigation, gunnery, and military engineering. The schools acquired their pupils by conscripting the sons of the nobility. But even this method hardly produced sufficient pupils.

Peter's plan for the introduction of an empire-wide system of elementary education had even less success. In 1714 each province was ordered to establish two 'cipher' (mathematical) schools. The Admiralty bore the cost and the provincial authorities supplied the pupils, again on the basis of conscription, this time primarily from non-noble families. Here also, however, the pupils dwindled away, and the schools with them. In 1722 the number of schools totalled forty-two, with some 4,000 pupils. Three years later the totals were twenty-eight and 500 respectively. By 1744 the whole system had collapsed and was merged with a network of army schools run by and for the local military garrisons. Part of the reason for this failure was the success of the Church from 1721 onwards in organizing a parochial school system for the sons of the clergy. This drew off many of the pupils who would otherwise have attended the 'cipher' schools. Only one school of a non-vocational type existed. Pastor Glück, a Lutheran from Marienburg, founded this establishment in Moscow and also drew up its curriculum – Oriental and European languages, literature, ethics, philosophy, equitation, etiquette and decorum. The teachers were all foreigners, but in ten years its pupils had dwindled to five and the whole institution was disbanded.

Yet more grandiose in appearance, but in actual fact a permanent feature of Russian intellectual life despite Stalin's cultural revolution, was Peter's foundation of the Academy of Sciences. This owed something to the inspiration of Leibniz, whom Peter met twice, and to the examples of the Royal Prussian Academy in Berlin and the Royal Society in London. At first, its professorial fellows and their students had all to be imported from Germany. But this did not later inhibit the growth of a truly Russian institution.

To Peter's educational activity, in the widest sense of the term, there was no limit. He remodelled the calendar, adopting the Julian system in 1700 so that Russia no longer reckoned from the creation of the world but from the birth of Christ; he simplified the old Cyrillic alphabet, reducing the number of characters and approximating the remainder to Latin models; he founded the first Russian newspaper, and urgently promoted the translation of foreign works – those which were overwhelmingly secular and technological in tone; he inaugurated the first public Russian theatre, with performances on Red Square in Moscow; he forcibly ended the seclusion of women; and he instituted *assemblées*, where the nobility of both sexes were forced to acquire the rudiments of *bon ton* by entertaining one another with gossip, dancing, and refreshment. Foreigners commented disparagingly on the 'in-born Bashfulness and Awkwardness' of the first Russian women to 'come out' but not even the most conservative of aristocratic dowagers could resist this chance to see more of the world. Their daughters would soon outgrow their shyness.

In the nineteenth century, nostalgic intellectuals such as Dos-

toyevsky and Khomyakov contrasted the 'inorganic' life of Petrine
Russia unfavourably with the 'organic' life of old Muscovy. In
fact they were bemoaning the creation of the impersonal modern
State. Peter's capital, St Petersburg, epitomized what they disliked,
it was 'a city where all is stone; not only the houses but the trees
and the inhabitants'. To some extent they exaggerated Peter's
radicalism. In his policies for reforming the army, and even to
some extent the Church, Peter followed past precedents. Even
when he undertook a really new departure, he took care to establish such precedents. The 'organic' life of old Muscovy was dis-
rupted by the Time of Troubles not by Peter.

But if Peter did not break with the past, it is also clear that he
did inaugurate some kind of new order, some kind of new departure. Furthermore, it is obvious that this cannot be equated with
the dichotomy of Russia and Europe. A law of Entail *à l'anglaise*,
a collegiate system on the Swedish model, an Academy of Sciences
taken from Berlin, military and naval tactics from Great Britain
and Holland – all these, and much more, do not in combination
amount to the westernization of Russia. All such imported ideas
and institutions had a connotation very different in Russia from
what they had in Europe.

Ever since the Time of Troubles there had been an intermittent
Russian attempt to catch up and surpass the more technically
advanced countries of Western Europe. And it was to this attempt
that Peter's reign came as a partial climax and a logical sequel. It is
implicit in Peter's remarks to the Swedish generals taken prisoner
after Poltava: 'Gentlemen,' he said, 'it is to you we owe it.' Russia
used the West in order to overcome the West. From the Time of
Troubles to Peter the Great – and beyond – the West appeared
first and foremost as a system of power, the adoption of which
would serve as the sole means to ensure Russian survival. It is in
this sense that Peter was a westernizer and in this spirit that he
strove to modernize Russia and make it a part of the West.

Peter the Great found only a blank page when he came to power, and
with a strong hand he wrote on it the words *Europe* and *Occident*; from
that time on we were part of Europe and of the Occident ... The most
marked trait of our historical physiognomy is the absence of spontaneity
in our social development. Look carefully, and you will see that each

important fact in our history is a fact that was forced on us; almost every new idea is an imported idea.*

But who is this 'we'? Who belonged to Europe and the West and who did not? In the early stages of Peter's reforms there was undoubtedly a certain incongruity in turning Muscovites into westerners. Western clothes sat comically on Muscovite shoulders, sometimes literally so. For example, in 1701 the British Ambassador to Turkey drew attention to the contrast between old and new:

The Muscovite Ambassador and his retinue have appeared here so different from what they always formerly wore that ye Turks cannot tell what to make of them. They are all coutred in French habit, with an abundance of gold and silver lace, long perruques and, which the Turks most wonder at, without beards. Last Sunday, being at mass in Adrianople, ye Ambassador and all his company did not only keep all their hats off during ye whole ceremony, but at ye elevation, himself and all of them pulled off their wigs. It was much taken notice of and thought an unusual act of devotion.

This cheek-by-jowl juxtaposition of the old and the new gradually gave way, however, to a more profound influence, even if in absolute terms it never did go very deep. With all its faults, the culture and the intellectual world of Muscovy had been homogeneous, at least until Nikon's reforms forced a breach. From the tsar to the last *muzhik*, however much their differing socio-political roles might set them at loggerheads, there was a basic unity in values, outlook, and prejudices.

It was this unity that Peter's reforms destroyed. In its simplest and most obvious form, a bewigged and clean-shaven dvoryantsvo and bureaucracy, dressed in western style, pursuing a career in some form of State service, and living apart from its hereditary estates, confronted the mass of bearded peasantry. The beard was far more than a symbol. It stood for two worlds of the mind. A tiny minority, educated in Western ideas but as yet by no means permeated with them, lived a very different life from the 'dark mass'. Two cultures lived side by side with the minimum of inter-

* T. Riha, ed., *Readings in Russian Civilization*, Vol. III (Chicago and London, 1964), pp. 311–12.

relationship or interconnection. The mass, steeped in poverty and illiteracy, clung with ingrained conservatism, broken only by spasmodic elemental upheavals, to its traditional religion, way of life, dress, and morals. The alienated upper stratum spoke an entirely different language, thought in different terms, and pursued different ideals. To quote a recent student: 'the Tsar discarded a medieval political theology, borrowed unabashedly from Western political writings, and assumed a role and style befitting a modern secular ruler'.*

The effort to emulate the way of life of the European aristocracy imposed enormous financial burdens on the poor Russian gentry, burdens they sought to transfer to the State and to their own peasants. These burdens pitted peasantry against nobility in a struggle for their very survival and lent a bitter hostility to the basic division in Russian society. This division was a fateful element in Peter's legacy to the Russian future. It needed another, and even more fundamental revolution – Stalin's, to overcome the split.

* G. L. Freeze, *The Russian Levites* (Cambridge, Mass., 1977), p. 1.

CHAPTER 8

The Age of the Nobility

Peter the Great died in 1725 from the stone and strangury. He was unable, without great pain, to retain or discharge his urine. This may have been caused ultimately by syphilis, probably contracted in Holland and aggravated by alcohol. The final attack was certainly hastened by his personal participation in saving the lives of twenty common sailors and soldiers from a shipwreck. Peter left no successor. From a combination of personal and political motives, he had already caused the death of his son Alexis, and had excluded Alexis's son from the succession. By a decree of 1722, Peter claimed the right to nominate his successor in much the same spirit that had animated Ivan III: 'to whom I will, to him I shall give my throne'. But when the time came, Peter was unable to speak. One of his daughters waited at his deathbed for the word that never came.

Given the tensions and the conflicts that Peter's reform programme had let loose inside Russian society, a period of reaction and disorder would have been normal. But what actually happened exceeded all precedents. Between Peter's death and Catherine's accession in 1762, the throne had no less than six occupants: Catherine I, Peter II, Anna, Ivan VI, Elizabeth, and Peter III. Never before or since has Russia been ruled for such a long period by women, two of them foreigners with no real claim on the throne.

So transformed was the whole notion of the *pays légal* that no one gave a thought to the summoning of representative Assemblies. Those thirty-odd years were the palmiest of palmy days for the favourite, the intriguer, the lover, the instigator of the midnight *coup d'état* and palace revolution, the politician of the bedchamber, the king-making Guards, and the assassin. Writing in 1741, Daniel Finch, the British minister in St Petersburg, most accurately summed up the confusion of the Petrine system:

After all the pains which had been taken to bring this country into its present shape . . . I must confess that I can yet see it in no other light than as a rough model of something meant to be perfected hereafter, in which the several parts do neither fit nor join, nor are well glued together . .

But amid the welter of changing rulers two great facts stood out. First, there was no weakening of Russia's position as a great European power. On the contrary, in all the wars and diplomatic transactions of the eighteenth century, such as the carve-up of Turkey, the Seven Years' War, the elimination of Poland, Russia increasingly brought its weight into play. Second, inside the country, the cultural westernization of the nobility was brought to completion.

The background to this development indicates the transition through which Russia was passing in the eighteenth century. It was probably a question of war. Roughly speaking, up to and including Peter's reign, Russia's wars had been wars of existence. At least, they had involved the concentrated exertion of the population's energies and also determined the country's social evolution. But Peter's victories finally did away with the threat of national extinction. There were wars in the eighteenth century, of course, but they were waged from a position of strength, usually not on Russian soil, and altogether lacked the desperate do-or-die quality.

This new security called immediately for a new regulation of relations between government and nobility. Why should the government retain the costly services of incompetent noblemen when a smaller and more efficient civil and military establishment would suffice? Why should the nobles endure a lifetime of hardship and social dislocation when the fate of the country no longer hung in the balance?

The nobility had two main interests: to ease the burden of service imposed on it by Peter and to fend off challenges to its control over the serfs which emanated from the bureaucracy. It largely succeeded in both. As the century went on Petrine absolutism was moderated while the bureaucracy of the State grew apace. There were recurring divisions within the nobility as would-be aristocrats and 'new men' argued over the qualifications for membership in the nobility and the relationship of the class or estate as a whole to the supreme power. The nobles were able to increase their liberties substantially but whether this meant that they were exploiting the State or whether, on the contrary, the State was achieving independence from them is still disputed. What is quite clear is that all attempts to create an aristocratic polity modelled on Sweden or England were doomed to failure.

The first open indication of the way the wind was blowing came as early as 1730. The Supreme Privy Council, a body of would-be oligarchs that had replaced the Senate as the highest judicial and administrative organ, decided to offer the vacant throne to Anna, the widowed Duchess of Courland and a niece of Peter the Great. But there were conditions attached to the invitation, similar to those imposed on the Swedish crown by the Swedish nobility after the death of Charles XII. Without the consent of the Council, Anna must not marry or appoint an heir, make war or agree to peace, levy taxes, grant senior army or civil rank, bestow estates out of Crown land or dispose of State revenue, deprive a noble of his life or estate without due trial. Anna agreed to these restrictions of power. But on arrival in Moscow for her coronation, she dramatically tore up the list of conditions. Supported by the Guards regiments and many of the lesser nobility, she was able to rout the would-be oligarchs of the Supreme Privy Council. The way ahead lay clear for a widespread expansion of the nobility's liberties.

Since compulsory service had replaced enfeoffment, Peter moved to eliminate the distinction between pomestiya and votchina in his last years. Both now became patrimony. His hated Law on Entail – hated, that is, by dispossessed younger sons, many of them guardsmen – was soon abolished. At the end of 1730 the *status quo ante* Peter was restored, leaving the nobility henceforth free to sub-divide its estates among all the heirs. The next sign that the nobility were determined to consolidate their position as a class came the following year, with the establishment of a military academy through which the sons of the nobility were channelled directly to commissioned rank in the army or the bureaucracy, thus avoiding the necessity of starting in the ranks. In 1736, the period of compulsory State service was reduced from life to twenty-five years. Furthermore, if a father had two sons, one was altogether freed from service so that he might devote himself to the care of the family estates. (Owing to the Turkish war, this decree did not come into active operation until 1739.) Another sign of the times was the growing reluctance of the Heraldmaster to grant nobility to petitioners of uncertain status.

The short reign of Peter III (January–July 1762) produced a whole series of liberal decrees, culminating in the emancipation of the nobility from compulsory State service entirely. The Tsar's manifesto put the nobles' obligations on a purely voluntary basis, empowered them to resign from the army or the bureaucracy except in time of war, to travel freely abroad, and to take service with non-Russian powers. (But those who retired from service were prohibited for life from appearing at Court.) 'Altogether, it is difficult to exaggerate the importance of the edict of 1762 for Russia's social and cultural history. With this single act, the monarchy created a large, privileged, Westernized leisure class, such as Russia had never known before.'* Peter abolished the secret police (the public abolition and subsequent discreet re-creation of the secret police was almost a ritual gesture for incoming monarchs in the eighteenth century), prohibited the purchase of serfs by manufacturers for service in the factories, and secularized the estates of the Church. Thereafter, the institutions of the Church and its various dignitaries would receive specific sums for their maintenance and upkeep from a State-administered college. This followed logically on Peter the Great's abolition of the Patriarchate.

In 1767, Catherine summoned a Legislative Commission to advise her on a new code of laws. Its debates brought her up sharply against the determination of the mass of provincial nobles to retain absolute control over their serfs. In the 1770s the Pugachev revolt revealed the fragility of the bureaucracy outside the capitals. Catherine's realization that she could not, after all, dispense with the nobility in her dealings with the peasantry, led in 1785 to the proclamation of the 'Charter' of the nobility. This document reaffirmed and widened all the special status won in the previous half century – the right to travel abroad, enter the service of friendly foreign states, resign from government service, dispose

---

* R. Pipes, *Karamzin's Memoir on Ancient and Modern Russia* (Cambridge, Mass., 1959), p. 15.

of property at will. The dvoryanin could not be dispossessed of his title, estates, life or personal status without trial by his peers. If convicted on a serious charge, his hereditary estates would pass to his heirs and not be confiscated in favour of the State, as had formerly been the custom. The noble enjoyed exemption from the poll-tax, corporal punishment, and the duty to billet troops. He could engage in commerce and industry, and exploit on his own account any mineral or timber resources on his estates.

There was also a provision for the formation in each province of a corporation of nobles who would co-operate with the organs of local government by electing certain of the dvoryane to administrative posts. But where these functions were not decorative, they were much overshadowed in importance by the centrally organized system of provincial and local government. In effect, the decrees of 1762 and 1785 were an eighteenth-century restatement of the alliance of autocracy and nobility that had first been concluded in the sixteenth century. This was all the more significant as Catherine had hoped to render the State less dependent on the nobility. The tsar(-ina) would rule at the centre, the nobles in the countryside. Furthermore, class division among the nobles forced many into government service for economic reasons. In 1777, for example, it seems that as many as 32 per cent had less than ten serfs; 27 per cent had from ten to twenty; 25 per cent from twenty to one hundred; and only 16 per cent more than one hundred. Since the nobles, in general, took little part in economic development and regarded their estates and perquisites purely and simply as a means of support, there was some economic incentive to enter State service. But the effect of this too should not be exaggerated. In 1762 there was quite an exodus from St Petersburg, and the following decades saw the growth of a sizeable class of provincial nobles.

Catherine regarded serfdom with distaste and succeeded in improving the status of peasants in the Baltic provinces and Church and factory peasants in Great Russia. While it is untrue to suggest, as many of her disappointed critics have done, that she made things worse for the nobles' serfs, it is true that the emancipation of the nobles was accompanied by the reaffirmation of their rights over their serfs. All crimes except murder and robbery came within the landowner's jurisdiction. A number of decrees of the 1760s further extended this power to include the right to send criminal or delinquent serfs into Siberian exile as settlers, or to periods of penal servitude in Siberia. To serve in the army was another form of punishment. It is worth adding that Catherine was responsible for real improvements in penal policy: torture was no longer routinely applied in criminal investigations; criticism of herself was no longer deemed treason; and punishments were lightened for all categories of offender.

Upheavals and revolts were regular among the serfs, both on private estates and in the possessional factories. The landowners often needed to call in regular troops to crush the rebels. The climax came in 1773 with the uprising led by Pugachov. This exceeded in scope and terror any peasant uprising of the seventeenth, eighteenth, or nineteenth centuries. The movement drew its vigour not only from the perennial burdens of the peasantry, but also from the widespread hope that since the nobility had been freed from State service, the serfs would also be similarly emancipated.

Pugachov was a Don Cossack who gave out that he was in fact Peter III. After a nomadic life, in and out of prison, in and out of the Russian army, he raised his revolt in the territory east of the Volga in the autumn of 1773. The provinces of Orenburg and Kazan were its centres. In these vast regions grievances of all kinds lay ready to hand – the dispossessed native tribes, misruled and subjected to forced conversion; the repressed national feelings of the Bashkirs; the Old Believers; the forced labourers in the Ural mines and factories; the Cossacks perpetually at odds with the central government; over and above all, the refugees from serfdom. There were some interesting exceptions, including some factory peasants who felt sufficiently attached to their jobs to defend their enterprises.

Pugachov's programme did not differ in essence from that of his predecessors, from Bolotnikov to Stenka Razin and Bulavin. He called for freedom from the landowners, the division of their estates, the restoration of the 'true monarch' and the 'old faith', the end to recruiting levies.

Pugachov's forces, amounting to between 20,000 and 30,000 men, waged guerilla campaigns on an unprecedentedly vast scale from Perm in the Urals to Tsaritsyn (now Volgograd) on the lower Volga. They took the important towns of Saratov and Kazan, but Ufa and Orenburg successfully defied the rebels' siege. Almost invariably, the rebels set about electing free 'Cossack' forms of self-government. Everywhere there was marauding and plundering, the burning of manors and hanging of landowners. Not until regular troops were released at the conclusion of the Russo-Turkish war did Catherine win back control of the insurgent areas. In 1775 the self-styled Peter III was brought in a cage to Moscow and his body dismembered. Catherine confessed herself defeated by serfdom: 'Wherever you touch it, it does not yield'. Despite her intermittent benevolence towards the peasantry, she never began to understand peasants. With the declining influence of the parish clergy over the peasants – to which Catherine was almost completely indifferent – serfdom came to rely more and more obviously on inertia, fear and force.

THE GROWTH OF INDUSTRY

Economic development after Peter mirrored social development and was characterized by a gradual reversion to private economic initiative. But the tempo was quickened through the increase by about one-quarter in the size of the Empire, owing to annexations in the Crimea, Northern Caucasus, Ukraine, Poland and Courland. The population increased by more than 50 per cent – from almost 18 million in 1724 to some 30 million at the end of the century. This represented an increase in absolute numbers, not only the mere addition of the annexed populations. Of this total, serfs accounted for 9,900,000 males. Here was an absolute increase that largely resulted from the incorporation of new territories and from natural increase, though generous land grants to the favourites of Catherine and Paul also contributed. The installation of a private owner had the effect of reducing State peasants to serfs. Very broadly speaking, a growing geographical differentiation took place in the functions of the serf. In the central provinces and to the north-west and south-west he was a performer of *obrok*, making payment in cash or kind to his owner. In the south, east, and north he was more likely working on a barshchina basis, toiling on his owner's land for so many days per week. This division of labour roughly corresponded to those areas where industry and agriculture were most developed. Serfdom was still virtually unknown in the far north and in Siberia.

The character of industry continued to be determined by co-operation with the State. The State was the market for the goods produced, it supplied capital and, to some extent, labour; and it guaranteed certain monopolies by establishing high tariffs and sometimes by banning outright foreign products that would have competed with Russian products.

From the middle of the eighteenth century, the State introduced a number of positive measures to encourage industry. Under Peter, for example, the ports had been able to purchase grain for export only from certain specific areas, and internal trade had suffered from a number of customs barriers. But in 1753 these latter were abolished, and a general sentiment in favour of free trade charac-terized much of Catherine's economic policy: 'No affairs pertain-ing to commerce and factories,' asserted a decree of 1767, 'can be conducted through compulsion, and a low cost of living is achieved as a result of a large number of sellers and an unhampered increase of goods.' A few years later another decree permitted 'everybody and anybody to start any type of mill and to produce in these mills any type of handiwork.'

Encouraged by the State and facilitated by the reduced demands of service, many of the wealthier nobles set out to revive manorial manufacture. And why not? There was cheap and abundant man-power available. In so far as the estate was a self-supporting unit, a certain degree of technical skill in handicrafts had been attained; raw materials, such as hemp, flax, wool, and hides, could be readily used. Equally important, no wages need be paid, since the serfs, in working on a manorial factory, were in fact merely performing their regular barshchina. In 1773, nobles owned sixty-five enter-prises as compared with 328 merchant manufactures, that is, about 20 per cent of the total.

The freeing of the internal market also favoured two other types of low-level industry – the *kustar* or cottage industry, and the serf-owned enterprises. Textiles, including taffeta, silk, cotton, ribbons, as well as coarse, military-type cloth, were the specialities of the first. But specialist goldsmiths, silversmiths, embossers, also produced luxury articles and leather goods to order. The forest areas would specialize in wooden objects, such as wheels and sleighs. In most cases, a merchant would make the rounds of the peasant homesteads and buy up goods for sale at town and village fairs.

The second category of small-scale manufacturers – the serf enterprises – sometimes grew out of the kustar type of production. A landowner, particularly if his estates were on obrok, had a powerful interest in securing the maximum output and productivity of his serfs so that they in their turn would be able to pay him increased obrok. As a result, the more enterprising serfs would be permitted and encouraged to set up small enterprises, employing the labour of other serfs or perhaps even hired labour. Sometimes it also became possible for a serf entrepreneur to buy his freedom from his owner. But to do this he would have to be exceedingly successful.

The paucity and unreliability of the statistics makes it impossible to show in detail the extent of the growth of industry in the eighteenth century. But there is no doubt that it took place. Also important is the fact that new districts were opened up, primarily in the Urals. Most of these had been established in the second and third quarters of the century. The Urals were the predominant area for copper-smelting and iron and steel production. On the other hand, the level of technique still remained very low. Water and horses were the main sources of power; charcoal was used exclusively in the smelting of pig-iron; and manual labour in the forging of iron. Whatever was achieved came about through the employment of a mass labour force, unskilled and miserably underpaid. This applied not only to the actual production, but also to such auxiliary operations as preparing and delivering the wood, water, and coal. Neither in industry nor in agriculture could a serf-economy be productive. Even in the eighteenth century, the arrested nature of Russian technology by comparison with that of Western Europe was abundantly clear.

We must not paint too gloomy a picture of the Russian economy. The productivity of Russia's extensive industries was low and the serfs were exploited. However, famines were rare and localized. Russian peasants had not yet begun to suffer from the over-population that cursed their descendants. Almost half the peasants were not serfs at all but state peasants (a higher proportion than in Prussia). The 100,000 state peasant households in Kursk included 20 per cent owning 10 horses, 10 cows, 10 sheep, and 50 pigs in the late eighteenth century. Absolute misery was still the plight of only a minority.

POLAND AND TURKEY

The Great Northern War had made Russia into a great power, with interests extending from the Baltic and Germany in the north to the Caspian Sea in the south. In the course of its rise to this commanding position, Russia had eliminated Sweden and annexed Livonia, made inroads into Poland, gained some influence in the North German states, and waged the first of many campaigns against Turkey. Each process was now to be taken a stage further. The expansion of Russia brought with it the gradual reduction of its neighbours to the west, north and south.

After Peter's death, Ostermann, a shrewd and experienced Westphalian polyglot, controlled foreign affairs. In the 1730s German influence at St Petersburg enjoyed its heyday, and the Foreign Minister was one of its most distinguished representatives. He based his policy on an alliance with the Austrian Habsburgs in opposition to the French system of alliances, which embraced Sweden, Poland, and Turkey and functioned as a sort of *cordon sanitaire* against further Russian expansion.

Early on, Franco-Russian hostility became centred on the Polish question. Who would succeed Augustus II as King of Poland? A Russian or a French nominee? In the upshot, after a two-year struggle from 1733 to 1735, Russia succeeded in imposing Augustus III. It was during this clash that Russia troops first appeared on the Rhine. They joined up with an Austrian army near Heidelberg. This war also saw the first clash of Russian and French arms, on the Polish battlefields.

The War of the Polish Succession brought with it a renewal of the Russo-Turkish struggle for Azov, the key to the delta of the Don, and to the whole river system of south Russia – the Dniester, Bug, Dnieper, Kuban. The four-year struggle from 1735 to 1739 partially reversed the unhappy verdict of Peter the Great's campaign of 1711. The Treaty of Belgrade of 1739 returned Azov and the adjacent territory to Russia, but the great fortress itself was destroyed. Taganrog was not to be fortified; and Russia, while acquiring the right to trade on the Sea of Azov, was obliged not to make use of its own ships but to allow its goods to be carried in Turkish bottoms. These results were less impressive than might have been expected from Russia's military successes during the war. But the defection of Austria from the campaign and its conclusion of a separate peace gave the Russians no choice. These were ominous portents for the future even though the war had revealed that the Russian forces were far superior to the Austrian. This marked a significant stage in Russian military history.

In the Seven Years' War (1756–63) Russia was one of the mainstays of the Austro-French coalition against Prussia and Great Britain. The fundamental Russian aim was to crush the Prussia of Frederick the Great. In the campaigns of 1759, 1760, and 1761, this was all but achieved, the Russians sweeping into East Prussia and securing some spectacular victories. They brought Frederick the Great to the verge of suicide, notably after the battle of Kunersdorf in 1759. The following year saw Russian and Austrian troops in occupation of Berlin.

But just when Frederick's position was at its weakest, the fortuitous death of the Empress Elizabeth at the end of 1761 saved him from utter collapse. This brought to the throne Peter III, an idolater of Frederick the Great, in whose army Peter's father-in-law had served as a Field-Marshal. Within a few months, Russia had changed sides and had turned to face its previous allies. No wonder Frederick the Great warned his successors in his Political Testament: '*après moi les souverains de la Prusse auront bien raison de cultiver l'amitié de ces barbares*'. This advice was well taken. From 1762 to 1914 there was no serious Russo-Prussian or Russo-German conflict. Russian withdrawal from the Seven Years' War inaugurated a century and a half of peace between the two countries. It would be the Russians who would clear Napoleon out of Prussia and provide Bismarck with the support he needed to make Prussia the leading power in Germany and all Central Europe. But what mattered more in the 1760s was that the conclusion of peace in the West gave Russia the necessary freedom of manoeuvre to move forward in Poland and Turkey.

This was primarily Catherine's inspiration. After having condoned the assassination of her husband, Peter III, she took into her own hands the direction of foreign policy. 'I came to Russia a poor girl,' she declared. 'Russia had endowed me richly, but I have paid her back with Azov, the Crimea, and the Ukraine.' She showed her mettle as a true Russian autocrat by subjecting her conquests and the Baltic provinces to the same uniform centralized form of administration that prevailed in Great Russia itself.

The death in 1763 of Russia's earlier nominee, Augustus III, as King of Poland, very soon precipitated the Polish conflict once again. Once more, Russian bayonets united with an aristocratic Polish party to ensure the 'election' of the Russian candidate – Stanislas Poniatowski. Using as a pretext the protection of the rights of the Orthodox population, Catherine gained further influence in Poland, in 1768, by a Russo-Polish treaty which placed the Polish constitution under Russian protection. This was the prelude to the first partition of Poland in 1772, made in concert with Prussia and Austria. The Russian share took in the White Russian areas of Polotsk, Vitebsk, and Mogilev – altogether about 36,000 square miles and a population of about one and three-quarter millions. Russia and Prussia jointly organized a second partition in 1793; the Western powers were unable to intervene as they were now absorbed by the French revolution. In the following year, the Poles rose in revolt but were put down with the utmost ferocity by Suvorov. Finally, in 1795, the three autocrats carved up the remainder and independent Poland disappeared from the map until 1918. In one sense, this was the logical conclusion of the alliance between Orthodoxy and Protestantism that had emerged at the Time of Troubles. Yet the Poles would not forget their nationhood and their repeated attempts to recover their independence persisted in complicating relations between the three empires until the First World War.

In the meantime, Russia's growing influence in Poland was producing friction with Turkey. The whole territory north of the Black Sea, extending from the Danube to the Don and Caucasus, still lay under Turkish domination; and the Russians were beginning to menace this northern flank. Catherine also tried to undermine European Turkey from within by exploiting the Christian sympathies of the populations of Greece, Crete, Serbia, Montenegro, and Bosnia. Catherine followed Peter's precedent in showing an enthusiasm for Orthodox interests abroad that contrasted oddly with her indifference to the Church at home.

War broke out between Russia and Turkey in 1768. In 1769 the Russians occupied Jassy and Bucharest and moved into the two principalities of Moldavia and Walachia. The next year, the Russian fleet, units of which were commanded by Admiral Elphinstone, formerly of the British Navy, sailed round Europe from the Baltic to the Aegean Sea. It totally destroyed the Turkish fleet off Chios. Thus began a short period in Russian military history when the navy, on which Peter had expended so much effort and treasure, operated successfully and independently of Russian land forces. But these victories were not sufficient to bring the war to an end. Catherine constantly spurred on her armies to throw the Turks out of Europe altogether. It was then that the dream of recovering Constantinople for Orthodoxy – perhaps under Catherine's grandson, portentously christened Constantine – was revived. But the war dragged on for another four years, its end eventually hastened by the Russian necessity to deal with Pugachov's uprising.

Catherine's ally, Frederick II, did his best to rob Russia of the fruits of victory, as Bismarck would a century later. Nevertheless, the Turks had to accept significant Russian gains in the Treaty of Küchük-Kainardji of 1774. The Crimea was wrested from Turkey, to become an independent state. Russia annexed Azov, Kerch, and Yenikale; acquired the right to establish consuls at will, to sail freely on the Black Sea and through the Bosphorus and the Dardanelles, and twisted certain provisions of the treaty into a basis for intervention on behalf of the Sultan's Orthodox subjects. The general effect of Küchük-Kainardji was to give Russia a firm hold on the northern shore and also on the northern Caucasus. In 1783 the logic of this was carried a stage further when the Russians annexed the Crimea; and in 1792 the Russian border advanced south-westwards to the coastal territory between the Dniester and

4. Russian Westward and South-Westward Expansion in the Reign of
Catherine the Great

the Bug. Here the great port of Odessa soon developed. Since the 1750s there had been some attempt to develop the new southern territories by settling foreigners in them. Serbs and Montenegrins were the first to come. A decree of 1762 invited all foreigners – again excluding Jews, as in Peter the Great's decree of 1702 – to install themselves on the empty lands of the Empire and acquire property on favourable terms. These immigrants came from Germany in the main, and by 1768 they had formed more than a hundred colonies, with a population of over 20,000 in the lower Volga areas near Saratov and Tsaritsyn.

These immense accretions of territory, coupled with the more settled conditions that prevailed, had immense significance for the future. They yielded the southern ports through which Russian grain could reach Western Europe, and England in particular. The war against Turkey gave Russia a whole series of harbours. When the Industrial Revolution brought with it a vast increase in population, there were hopes in Russia that Eastern Europe would become the granary of Europe. The black-earth country – a wide belt of land stretching from a line Zhitomir–Kiev–Tula–Kazan in the north to the northern shores of the Black Sea and the Sea of Azov in the south – provided the raw material. Transport costs to the Baltic ports would have been prohibitive. The only practicable alternative was the Black Sea – and this was what Russia now gained. The export of Russian grain jumped from 32,000 chetvert * in 1717–18 to 4,000,000 chetvert in 1793–5. Most of it went through Riga and St Petersburg, but Taganrog was also growing. By 1793, one-fifth of Russia's cereal exports went through the Dardanelles. To complete the list of Russian foreign successes during the eighteenth century, we must mention the Russo-Georgian Treaty of 1783 that led to Georgia's annexation by Russia in 1801.

Catherine's conquests had a highly important demographic significance that did not become fully apparent until the nineteenth century. They provided the agricultural foundation for the three-fold expansion of the Russian population in the nineteenth century. Up to the early eighteenth century the Russian State had developed in the main on a poor type of soil, the full exploitation of which

* 1 chetvert = 5·8 bushels.

was hampered by the inclement climate. Both these factors were particularly operative in the central Moscow area. The 300 per cent population increase in the nineteenth century was largely dependent on the agricultural exploitation of the southern Russian areas annexed by Catherine. By the end of the eighteenth century, central and northern Russia had already become grain-importing areas, which lacked, furthermore, any of the mineral and industrial resources lying beyond the Urals. Had the newly annexed territories to the south not been available as grain-producing areas, agrarian over-population would have soon resulted. As it was, these areas provided the basis for the expansion of the population in the nineteenth century.

THE ENLIGHTENMENT IN RUSSIA

Voltaire wrote a history of Peter the Great and when he spoke of it to Madame de la Fontaine he said: '. . . *rien de plus ennuyeux pour une Parisienne que des détails de Russie*'. He would hardly have said this had he been speaking of the post-Petrine era. This was the period *par excellence* when three Empresses – Anna, Elizabeth, and, most of all, Catherine – set the tone of the social and intellectual life of Russia. Their setting was St Petersburg. This had been the nominal capital since 1712, but only some two decades later did it become the real centre of Russian court life. The architectural magnificence of the Winter Palace, the Hermitage, Tsarskoe Selo, the Tauride Palace, Gatchina, Peterhof, and the lesser but still opulent palaces of the wealthier, newly emancipated nobles gave a flamboyant and sumptuous air to the life of the capital. Not for nothing was St Petersburg known as the Palmyra of the north. The artists and architects who created this milieu were mainly foreign – Rastrelli, Quarenghi, Charles Cameron, Lamothe, Trombara – to mention but the best known. There was, of course, a seamy side to the magnificence arising from the inclement climate and the damp atmosphere. An uncharitable French visitor recalled the phrase: 'It has been wittily enough said that ruins make themselves in other places, but that they were built at St Petersburg.'

The three women who occupied the Russian throne for so much of the eighteenth century have never ceased to inspire malicious gossip. It was not easy for Russian men of that time to accept women rulers and, unlike Maria Theresa of Austria, these were no paragons of domestic virtue but true autocrats, determined to enjoy the rewards of power just like their male counterparts. The German Anna continued Peter's tradition of looking to Germany for cultural importations. She left little mark on the city. She divided her passions between those of the flesh, the shoot, and the hunt. In other respects her court followed the Petrine model which was itself a clear reflection of the High Renaissance, in its abundance of human monstrosities. Midgets, giants, hunchbacks, cripples, the deformed in body and mind were a grotesque and pathetic feature of Anna's entourage.

The francophile Elizabeth was a more sympathetic character. Sir George Macartney, who came to Russia as British Envoy Extraordinary shortly after her death in 1761, rather unkindly described her as 'abandoning herself to every excess of intemperance and lubricity'. In actual fact, pleasure and piety dominated her life. To Elizabeth the cares of State were non-existent. Her days she devoted to relaxing *en déshabille*; her nights to love-making and dancing and masquerades. 'She had not an ounce of nun's flesh about her', said Finch. A particular *penchant* was to have the soles of her feet tickled. The minuet was the most popular measure, as everywhere in Europe. At St Petersburg it shared pride of place with the quadrille (often masked). At some of the Court balls, Elizabeth combined the fetish of the foot with transvestite tastes; the men must dress as women and the women as men. In this way Elizabeth could display her tiny feet and shapely legs which would otherwise have been concealed beneath the enormous hooped skirts of the period. Her favourite male costume was that of a Dutch sailor. This was a tribute to the memory of her father, Peter the Great. The young Catherine, the future Empress, has described in her memoirs something of the strange sights produced by these entertainments:

The women looked like scrubby little boys, while the more aged had thick short legs which were anything but attractive. The only woman who looked well and completely a man was the Empress herself. As she was tall and powerful, male attire suited her. She had the handsomest leg I have ever seen on any man and her feet were admirably proportioned.

Catherine, in her turn, took no less enjoyment in the pleasures of the flesh than did Elizabeth. The older she got, the younger her lovers. All together, the total ran into fifty-odd. But what really made Catherine different from Elizabeth was her compelling interest in State affairs. Never did she allow private concerns to clash with public. Like Frederick the Great, or Peter, or Joseph II, or Maria Theresa, Catherine saw herself as an enlightened despot of the eighteenth century, identifying her own well-being with her people's. By intellect and taste she would have been perfectly at home with Voltaire at Ferney, with Gibbon at Lausanne, with Walpole at Strawberry Hill. Her regular correspondents included such representative men of the age as Voltaire, Diderot, D'Alembert. Her favoured reading was Montesquieu's *L'Esprit des Lois* and Beccaria's *Crime and Punishment*. She drew freely on these works when compiling the famous liberal *Instruction* to her Legislative Commission of 1767.

Chance had it, however, that Catherine was no mere member of the cosmopolitan European intelligentsia of the eighteenth century, but also the Empress of one of the most unenlightened and barbarous frontier areas of Europe. This dual role meant that her performance, like Plato's in Syracuse, would be subjected to a scrutiny not directed at intellectuals whose only power was the power to write. In instructing Russia's educated classes to think for themselves – only to shut some of them up later when they took this too literally – Catherine helped to create what later became known as the Russian intelligentsia. Alexander Radishchev, who suffered as much as anyone from her later intolerance, drew up a remarkably fair balance sheet:

It will be to her great credit before distant posterity that in her *Instruction* she has stressed the basic principles on which societies are founded, and their purpose. Her wish was to reign over a contented people, to use a better expression, to let them govern themselves, leaving to herself only the task of supervising everything.

Radishchev himself excused her suppression of dissent in her later years in view of the 'external and internal disorders' and asked rhetorically: 'who among the mortals has ever succeeded in remaining unchanged throughout his whole life?'* In retrospect, her initial liberalism is more surprising than her retreat to conservatism later in life. It certainly surprised – even perplexed – the vast majority of her subjects when it first became manifest.

With all its obvious opportunities for satirizing the gap between promise and performance, Catherine's long reign marked a definite stage in the education of the top stratum of the Russian nobility. French became the language of the Court. With the language went the thought of the Enlightenment. 'The first lessons in French that Russians learned were lessons in blasphemy,' said Joseph de Maistre of the all-pervasive Voltairian influence in Russia. French tutors were very much *à la mode* in the families of the wealthier nobles. La Harpe taught Catherine's own grandson. In the Saltykov family the tutor was Charles-François Masson, who actually attributed Gallomania to the prevalence of French tutors: 'Les Russes, presque tous élevés par des Français, contractent, dès leur enfance, une prédiliction marquée pour cette nation.' At the same time, the freeing of the nobility from State service coupled with the abolition of restrictions on foreign travel led to the growth of a sizeable aristocratic Russian colony in Paris. Count Paul Stroganov, for example, was the archivist of the Jacobin Club. The Golitsyn, Shuvalov, and Vorontsov families were as well known in Paris as in St Petersburg. Gambling and libertinage distinguished them in both capitals.

During Catherine's reign tentative steps were taken towards a major expansion of primary education. The eighteenth century was also a period of assimilation and experimentation for Russian culture. The first Russian theatre, *maître-de-ballet*, actress, were little to set against the tedious and perfunctory official literature of the period, or the plethora of French and Italian opera and ballet companies. What did emerge in the eighteenth century, however – and this had supreme importance as the precondition and essential instrument of the literary glory of the nineteenth – was a Russian literary language. The remarkable genius of Michael Lomonosov played a decisive part in this process, though many

* K. A. Papmehl, *Freedom of Expression in Eighteenth Century Russia* (The Hague, 1971), p. 135.

others, including Catherine's friend Catherine Dashkova, also played their parts. The son of a White Sea fisherman, Lomonosov developed polymathic gifts as professor of chemistry, scientist, philologist, and historian.

In Peter's time a certain linguistic confusion had developed through the decay of Church Slavonic and its alienation from popular understanding, and also through the introduction of secular literature from the Ukraine and the West. The suicide of one of the translators appointed by Peter the Great to render into Russian a French work on horticulture illuminated the linguistic crisis. He was simply unable to find in Russian the equivalents of the French terms. Lomonosov broke down this isolation by amalgamating the literary language of Church Slavonic with the non-literary spoken Russian. A virtually new language was created. It soon achieved a vituperative vitality in the satirical journals patronized, and sometimes sharply criticized, by Catherine around the Court. Writers like Zhukovsky and Batyushkov went on to achieve a melodious elegance in verse and prose that foreshadows Pushkin.

If the eighteenth century saw only hesitant and uncertain signs of the high Russian culture of the following century, it was very different where the flow of ideas was concerned. If Voltaire's works could circulate, and the *Encyclopaedia*, and Blackstone's *Commentaries*, and *L'Esprit des Lois*, if Russians could study abroad – then it could only be a question of time before some attempt would be made to apply to the Russian reality some of the ideas garnered in Leipzig, Paris, Geneva, Dresden. In view of the unpromising nature of contemporary social reality, it is not surprising that for Court critics such as Novikov – as for Mozart – the first move was away from the enlightened rationalism of Voltaire and into the mystic liberalism of Freemasonry. It was here that the intelligentsia-to-be first acquired the habits of solidarity, independent thought and organization that characterized them throughout the nineteenth century.

The French revolution was enthusiastically welcomed by many people in St Petersburg. Ségur, the French minister, saw passersby in the streets of the capital excitedly embracing each other when news came of the fall of the Bastille. He himself was greeted and congratulated, while walking along the Nevsky Prospect, by Catherine's grandsons, Alexander (the future Emperor) and Constantine, his brother. Catherine's initially cautious reaction towards the French revolution mirrored that of the European aristocracy, as did her horror as all forms of established authority began to crumble and royal heads to roll. She broke off diplomatic relations with France; she put all French-speaking foreigners under police supervision; stopped the sale of the *Encyclopaedia* and confiscated a new Russian translation of Voltaire's works. Frenchmen were anathema. To Grimm she wrote: '*Il faudra faire jeter au feu tous leurs meilleurs auteurs, et tout ce qui a répandu leur langue en Europe, car tout cela dépose contre l'abominable grabuge qu'ils font.*' But by now the damage was done – not so much by actual revolution, but by the slowly gathering impact of French liberal ideas. In 1790 about fifty copies of a work entitled *Journey from St Petersburg to Moscow* were put on sale. The author was Alexander Radishchev, assistant-director of the St Petersburg Customs House, and a member of a family of provincial serf-owners. After serving in the Corps of Pages, he had been sent by Catherine to study at Leipzig University. Here he read for preference the works of Rousseau, Mably and Helvétius.

The *Journey*, printed on a private press – permission for these had only recently been given – is a strange, discursive hotchpotch of prose and verse, autobiography, and descriptive narrative. The technique is ostensibly taken from Sterne's *Sentimental Journey*. But what a difference between the journey through France and Italy and the journey from St Petersburg to Moscow! Radishchev was no revolutionary, rather a sentimental Utopian, who looked 'across a century', as he himself put it. But this did not prevent him from penning the most outspoken criticism of Russian life that had yet appeared.

What did the traveller find on his grisly journey from the new to the old capital? He found serfs forced to toil six days a week on their master's land. He found officials and judges who would sell a verdict or a decision. He found corrupt businessmen. He witnessed a serf auction, where human beings were knocked down like cattle to the highest bidder. He saw a round-up of serfs, press-ganged into army service, as in eighteenth-century England. And everywhere he was overcome by the tragic results of autocratic rule. Radishchev was sentenced to death at Catherine's instigation, but she later commuted his punishment to ten years' exile in central Siberia. He was, in fact, released after seven years, on the accession of the Emperor Paul. This exile heralded the breach between the autocracy and educated men and women of independent mind that became final around 1840; while Radishchev might forgive Catherine, they would never forgive autocracy. By the same token, Radishchev's fate marked, as Berdyayev has truly said, the birth of the Russian intelligentsia: 'I looked around me – my soul was afflicted by the sufferings of humanity . . . I felt that all may take part in helping their fellow-men.' These words, from Radishchev's dedication, became the leitmotif of generation after generation of the intelligentsia. Gradually, they came to see themselves not as poor nobles or priests' sons and daughters but as members of a new class or caste that would liberate the Russian people.

CHAPTER 9

Liberators and Gendarmes

One fine autumn day – it was either Sunday or some festival – we had been at Mass in our parish church dedicated to the Assumption of the Virgin, and we were returning home. We had just mounted the high step outside our house, when suddenly we noticed some commotion and loud talking among the people returning from church. Next, along the street at full gallop came a Cossack orderly; to all whom he passed he cried out, 'Go back to the church to take the oath of allegiance to the new Emperor!' ... The cathedral bells began to ring, the bells of ten other churches chimed in, and the sound spread all over the town.*

In this undramatic fashion, Sergei Aksakov heard the news of Catherine's death in one small Russian town – Ufa. It lay in the heart of the Bashkir country on the southern Urals; it is now the centre of oil refineries and motor manufacture. The new Emperor to whom the population had to swear allegiance was Paul, the son of Catherine the Great. By the time she died in 1796, she had kept him off the throne for thirty-three years and she was planning to by-pass him altogether. Paul I fully reciprocated his mother's sentiments, forcing her mortal remains to undergo the symbolic humiliation of a joint funeral with the bones of his supposed father, Peter III, and issuing a law of succession which forever barred women from the throne of Russia. Paul did not enjoy the last laugh for very long. He made a number of friendly gestures to the peasants, restoring the right of individuals to petition the emperor, for example, which irritated the nobility. More seriously, he curtailed or withdrew a number of the rights Catherine had granted the nobility, including their participation in local government, their freedom from service and their exemption from corporal punishment. Even more dangerous for Russia was his bizarre foreign policy, including a mystical identification with Malta, whose nominal ruler he became in 1798, which earned him the enmity of England and diplomatic isolation in Europe just as

*S. Aksakov, *Years of Childhood* (Oxford, 1923), p. 158.

Napoleon was reaching the apogee of his fortune. His obsession with military trivia earned him the hostility of the officers of the guards and in 1801 a group of conspirators secured the sanction of Paul's son and heir, Alexander, for his deposition. After a brief struggle, Paul was murdered in his own bedchamber.

The nocturnal coup was the end of a phase in the evolution of Russian politics. Thereafter assassinations were to take place in the open streets and would cease to be the prerogatives of palace cliques and guards officers. To put it another way, this was to be the last time that an aristocratic elite would permit itself the luxury of a palace coup. This widened concern with politics, so powerfully promoted by the Napoleonic Wars, was one important symptom of the new age. In foreign policy it saw the growth of Russia from a European power into a world power; culturally it saw an un-precedented flowering of thought and literature; in economic life, there was a significant increase in urbanization and industrializa-tion; politically, it saw the growth of a revolutionary movement that at first embraced a few scattered individuals, but later coalesced into highly organized parties. All these developments had one factor in common: they all called into question the continued existence of the autocracy in the form in which it had hitherto existed.

One of the first problems to confront the new Emperor, Alex-ander I, was Russia's relationship to Napoleon. From the first, of course, the Russian government had been hostile to the French Republic and its military campaigns. But Catherine had taken no direct part in opposing France. She had preferred to combat Jacob-inism on her doorstep in Poland. Paul was more ambitious, sending his armies to expel the French from northern Italy. Aban-doned by their Austrian allies, the Russian armies in Italy marched into Switzerland. There General Korsakov's army was defeated, while Suvorov managed to effect an ordered retreat by crossing the Alps and marching home through Austria. Marshal Suvorov was one of the most remarkable military leaders in Russian history, one of those Russian phenomena that defy Western categories. He introduced greater tactical flexibility while stressing the superiority of 'cold steel' over firearms; he shared the hardships of his men but he terrorized civilian populations in order to sap the morale of his opponents.

Russian reverses in Switzerland, coupled with Russo-British friction over Holland and the Mediterranean, led to Russian withdrawal from the campaign. Moreover, Napoleon's overthrow of the Directory and his installation as First Consul helped to convince Paul that the dangerous, explosive force of the Revolution had been tamed. At home, the war was highly unpopular among the nobles, who lost, in England, their chief foreign market for Russia's exports of timber, flax, and hemp.

Soon after his accession, Alexander made peace with Napoleon and also with England. But this came to an end when Russia entered Pitt's Third Coalition in 1805. Two years later, first Prussia and then Russia were defeated by Napoleon. Yet the defeat was not so overwhelming that Alexander could not negotiate peace terms with Napoleon – and this was done at Tilsit (now Sovietsk) in 1807, on a raft moored in the River Niemen. Russia indeed lost no territories. Russo-French peace, and also an alliance, were sealed largely at the expense of Prussia, which lost all its Polish acquisitions. These were formed into the Duchy of Warsaw. Russia annexed the Bielostok district. On the other hand, it also had to enter Napoleon's Continental System and to suffer all the inevitable consequences to its export trade. Russia had taken advantage of the French wars to seize Dalmatia and the Ionian Islands. These were now forfeit, as was her Mediterranean fleet, despite Admiral Senyavin's unbroken series of victories. Not until 1904 would a major Russian fleet attempt once more to operate independently of her main land forces. Russia had learnt the hard lesson that without the Straits she could not maintain her influence in the Mediterranean. Equally, unilateral action in the Straits would not succeed; only an alliance with Turkey or international agreement could secure the Russian fleet safe passage to and from the Mediterranean. The Russian presence in the Balkans, though short-lived, may well have hastened the Serbian Revolt of 1804 and the growth of Greek resistance to the Turks. As in 1940, partial compensation came in Russia's enjoyment of a free hand on her immediate borders.

To the north-west, Finland was seized from Sweden in 1809, though her autonomous institutions were guaranteed; in the south-west, Bessarabia was taken from Turkey. Farther to the east, the annexation of Georgia in 1801 was followed by a war with Persia in the Caucasus. Here too there were Christians to protect; here also lay a land route to India and the East. After a long, swaying, wayward struggle in this wild mountainous country, Persia at length acknowledged Russian sovereignty over a large area stretching from the Black Sea to the Caspian. In later years this was shown to be the oil-land of the Caucasus.

In the West, meanwhile, the alliance with France was breaking down – mainly as a result of Napoleon's aggrandizement of the Duchy of Warsaw. In June 1812, the Grand Army crossed the Niemen into Russian territory, And then the truth was proved of a remark attributed to Rostopchin, the Governor of Moscow: 'The Emperor of Russia will always be formidable in Moscow, terrible in Kazan, and invincible in Tobolsk.' But it was not only Russian geography and climate that defeated Napoleon and the Grand Army. The invasion of 1812 created one of those occasions, rare in any country's history, when a genuine movement of national resistance emerged to throw back the invader. It was something akin to the rally that had thrown back the Poles in 1612; or to the similar national upheaval that Napoleon had roused in Spain. Nobles and merchants hastened to raise and finance regiments; guerrilla bands spontaneously emerged to harry and harass Napoleon's flanks. The supreme Russian sacrifice came with the burning of Moscow. (Both Russians and French assumed that the barbaric enemy was responsible; it did much to embitter the Russian peasantry against the godless French. We shall probably never know who started it; Governor Rostopchin claimed the credit for it when to do so brought him popularity and then denied it when it seemed it might bring him odium.) The Emperor had no need to withdraw to Kazan or Tobolsk; he had already retired to St Petersburg where he obstinately refused to treat with Napoleon. The flames of burning Moscow consumed Napoleon's hopes of a swift conquest. He had no choice but to retreat.

'The Russian advance did not stop at throwing Napoleon back over the Niemen. It carried on into Western Europe, and at the Congress of Vienna in 1815 secured for Alexander a powerful voice in the settlement of Europe. Convinced that God had extended him His protection in 1812, a certain *folie de grandeur* took possession of his soul. Through the Holy Alliance with Prussia and Austria, later joined by most of the European States, he dedicated himself to the duty of introducing into diplomacy 'holy faith, love, justice and peace', as a criterion of interstate relations. This notion had little importance, and certainly did not affect Alexander's attempts to secure for Russia the whole of Poland as an autonomous kingdom under Alexander's protect-orate. This aroused the opposition of England and Austria. In the end Alexander had to moderate his claims, and to share Poland with Austria and Prussia. But he retained the major portion. The frontiers with which Russia emerged from the Napoleonic Wars remained unchanged until 1914, apart from some readjustments in Bessarabia.

THE LIBERATION OF EUROPE AND THE DECEMBRISTS

Alexander I seems to have been blessed with all the physical and mental gifts required by an autocrat and yet he is best remembered in Herzen's phrase 'Hamlet crowned' for he lacked the crucial qualities of realism and will. It is not surprising that in Alexander's most significant contribution to world history – his refusal to treat with Napoleon in 1812 – he was acting both as a European liberal and a Russian autocrat. More commonly these aspects of his personality were at war with one another. He had been brought up to please both his liberal free-thinking grandmother and his narrow-minded drill-master father. As an adolescent he had ex-pressed the intention of reigning just long enough to endow his people with a liberal constitution. His inability to accept his vocation was intensified by the tragic circumstances of his accession. The first Russian ruler to regard his reign as a form of martyrdom, Alexander's spiritual odyssey from agnosticism, by way of Pietism and semi-Catholicism, to a mystical Orthodoxy, can be regarded as a recovery of nationality, or a fruitless attempt to rationalize the intolerable.

Alexander came to the throne a reputed liberal, and in his early years he went some way to justify this reputation. He abolished the security police; he removed the ban on foreign travel for the nobility and permitted the importation of foreign publications. He even dallied with constitutional reform, and charged Michael Speransky, the son of a village priest who developed into a brilliant administrator, to draw up a scheme for the improved government of the Empire. This was ready in 1809 and, in essence, aimed at reconciling the autocracy with a system of law by introducing the separation of legislative, executive and judicial powers. All these would flow from the prerogatives of the autocracy, but the latter would to some small extent be limited by a State Duma elected on a property franchise, totally excluding the serfs of course. In the end, all this was watered down into a State Council appointed by the Crown and equipped only with advisory powers. It was never any curb on the autocracy. Of Speransky's other proposals, the most important to be adopted was a reorganization of the ministries; this amounted to a relative modernization of the Imperial bureaucracy. Speransky did introduce a more modern ethos into the bureaucracy. According to his biographer, 'he set it a high standard of honesty, devotion to the good of State and country, and concern for the national welfare ... He helped to inculcate a belief in orderly and just administration on the basis of clearly defined rules'.* All the same, by Western standards it remained corrupt, irresponsible and inefficient. It enjoyed none of the prestige attaching to the Prussian or British Civil Service. Hostility to the bureaucracy was further stimulated by the presence in its ranks of a high proportion of Germans.

Alexander's treatment of the serf problem was on a par with his treatment of Speransky's project. It was, of course, an infinitely more explosive topic than any constitutional matter. 'The Emperor cannot rule without slavery,' prophetically wrote de Maistre (meaning by 'slavery' serfdom). To touch serfdom was to touch the very foundation of the State. Yet a number of factors, including the virtual abolition of serfdom in east-central Europe during the French Wars, were making it less and less possible to avoid dealing with it by some means or other. Was serfdom an economic proposition? The Free Economic Society of St Petersburg, which held a competition for essays on this subject in 1812, found that the

* M. Raeff, *Michael Speransky* (The Hague, 1969), pp. 364–5.

authors of the fourteen manuscripts submitted were divided
equally on this point. The conclusions of the winners of the first
and second prizes, both of whom supported free labour, were
reinforced by the fact that the total agricultural yield remained
virtually stationary between 1810 and 1870. Indeed, there was
some attempt, particularly in the south-west, to introduce capitalist farming techniques with livestock rearing, the use of modern
machinery, and the employment of hired labour. But all this
remained a drop in the ocean as compared with the vast extent of
grain farming. The basic requirements of capital, and a free,
skilled, and productive supply of labour were both lacking.

The precarious economic position of the landowners also milit-
ated against agricultural productivity and progress. By 1843, for
example, more than 54 per cent of noble-owned lands were mortgaged to different State institutions. Many estates were also encumbered by private debts. The low productivity of agriculture
and the constant subdivision of estates because of Russian inheritance law resulted in nearly half the Russian nobility having
neither land nor serfs on the eve of emancipation in the middle of
the century.

Serfdom not only posed economic problems, but also had immense political and moral repercussions. However deep-rooted
and old-established, it was none the less increasingly acknowledged
to be an evil that demanded some attention. What was the secret
of emancipation without tears? This inescapable and tortuous
conundrum dominated all thinking on the question in the first
half of the century and formed the leitmotif of the official and
unofficial committees that Alexander established. In general, these
committees were quite unproductive. But they did at least serve to
illuminate the complexity of the problem and to reveal the bitter
opposition that any proposed solution would inevitably provoke.
It was only in the fringe areas of the Empire – Courland, Livonia,
Estonia, and Poland – that serfdom could be abolished, or its
effects mitigated by a system of 'inventories' that codified more
precisely the respective obligations of landlord and peasant.

All that was done in Russia itself was to enact a number of
minor measures that did to some extent ameliorate the position of
the serfs. But these measures only tinkered with the problem. In

1801 a decree made it illegal to advertise serfs for sale. Two years later an interesting attempt was made to create a class of free agriculturists whereby a landowner wishing to emancipate his serfs was obliged to provide appropriate areas of land, on agreed terms, for the use of the freed serfs. Only 37,000 serfs were freed in this way during Alexander's reign. After 1809, landowners could no longer sentence their serfs to penal servitude.

As Alexander grew more and more engrossed in the campaign against Napoleon, as he fell more and more deeply under pietistic and mystical influences, as his self-appointed mission of European saviour absorbed him more and more passionately, his liberalism dwindled into a mere concern for the *status quo*. At home he delegated his authority to honest but brutal martinets like Arakcheev, and reactionary cynics like Magnitsky were permitted to terrorize the universities. To all appearances, there was little to distinguish the state of Russia at the beginning and at the end of Alexander's reign. But this was wholly and utterly deceptive. The fact is that Alexander's campaign against Napoleon had unintentionally given decisive impetus to a new generation of thinking Russians. These were the sons of those of the eighteenth century who had read the *philosophes* and drunk of the waters of the Enlightenment. They were Guards officers, landowning nobles, senior officials and the offspring of the wealthier class of merchants and professional men. But where the fathers had become critics through their reading, the sons had seen the West at first hand. Radishchev was the first of the 'repentant noblemen'; after the Napoleonic Wars he had a host of progeny. Not for nothing did Herzen say that only in 1812 did the veritable history of Russia begin. To put it another way, 1812 was the last occasion when all educated Russians shared a common view of their society and its needs, the last opportunity perhaps for reform to be bestowed from above and welcomed from below. But if Napoleon's invasion had exposed the backwardness of Russian society, the Russian victories that followed were used to legitimize the *status quo*.

The Napoleonic Wars and the Russian entry into Paris brought large numbers of the educated nobility for the first time into immediate contact with unfamiliar conditions of a nature infallibly destined to arouse Russian self-doubt and self-criticism. 'The campaigns of 1812–14,' wrote Prince Volkonsky in his memoirs – and this assertion is typical of many – 'brought Europe nearer to us, made us familiar with its forms of state, its public institutions, the rights of its people. By contrast with our state life, the laughably limited rights which our people possessed, the despotism of our regime first became truly present in our heart and understanding.' If even Poland and Finland had constitutions under Alexander I, why should not Russia also? Two other factors deepened the feeling of dissatisfaction: first, the further contrast between Russia's deplorable governmental system and her role at the Congress of Vienna as one of the great powers of Europe; and secondly, the sentiment of popular unity, generated by the national upsurge of 1812, which led in turn to the notion of a duty owed by the higher orders to the lower, and to the serfs in particular. Rostopchin, the Governor of Moscow in the 1820s, commented dryly on this phenomenon from the point of view of the regime: *'Ordinairement ce sont les cordonniers qui font des révolutions pour devenir grands seigneurs; mais chez nous ce sont les grands seigneurs qui ont voulu devenir cordonniers.'*

The first fruits of the revolutionary spirit of a number of *grands seigneurs* was the Decembrist revolt, so called because it took place in December 1825. It was a curious amalgam, a palace *coup d'état* of the eighteenth century combined with the revolutionary theory of the nineteenth. It looked both to the past and to the future. It fell between two worlds, a dichotomy that may well be the ultimate reason for the failure of the attempted revolt. It was a noble movement, both in the sociological sense that its members were nobles – even aristocrats – and in the sense that they were inspired by liberal ideals rather than individual grudges. Their inflated sense of noble honour played its own part in inhibiting their actions and loosening their tongues when their moment of destiny arrived.

The antecedents of the Decembrist movement reach back about a decade, to the immediate post-Napoleonic period. In 1816–17 a number of highly-placed officers, the scions of aristocratic families – the brothers Muravyov, Colonel Paul Pestel, and Prince Sergei Trubetskoy – formed a Union of Salvation in St Petersburg. Its objects were to abolish serfdom and to install a constitutional regime. Before long the Union of Salvation died. In doing so, it gave birth to the Union of the Public Weal. Here again, military men predominated in a membership that fluctuated between fifty and two hundred. The programme, although it was never homogeneous and fully accepted, showed a certain move leftwards. Certain members, led by Pestel, saw no solution for their problems save in the forcible establishment of a republic.

Again the Union broke up after a few years, to be reformed in St Petersburg at the end of 1822 under the name of the Northern Society. In the meantime, a Southern Society had also come into existence under Pestel, who was stationed with his regiment in the Ukraine. In 1825 the Southern Society merged with the equally conspiratorial Society of United Slavs, composed of representatives of the Slav peoples of the west and south – Czechs, Slovaks, Croats, Slovenes, Serbs, and Ukrainians. The Poles were affiliated through the Polish Society of Patriots.

Pestel, the son of the German-born Governor of Siberia, a former student of Dresden University, knowledgeable in French revolutionary theory and practice, and a veteran of the Borodino battle and other Napoleonic campaigns, was by far the most radical Decembrist. He held that the Imperial family must be assassinated and the autocracy replaced by a republican system based on universal suffrage. Pestel, known to his critics among the Decembrists as 'a Bonaparte, not a Washington', was clearly a Jacobin type. His *Russkaya Pravda* – Russian Truth, or Justice, or Law – which propounded the ideal programme for the morrow of the successful revolt, envisaged a regime that combined compulsory republican virtue with centralized government. He demanded the abolition of serfdom and the division of the land into publicly and privately owned sectors, with every family having enough land to be self-sufficient. Pestel also urged the need for free enterprise, equality before the law, a jury system, equal military service for all classes, and the abolition of a standing army. By means of a police force and secret spying organizations, Pestel's government would forbid all private associations of citizens. The authoritarian form of State was further expressed in a policy of Russification extending to all the peoples of the Russian Empire except the Poles. The Jews too, Pestel argued, must assimilate or undergo forced emigration to Asia Minor. There was a converted Jew among the Decembrists of the Northern Society, a certain Gregory Peretz, and he may have suggested this to Pestel.

By comparison with this authoritarian scheme, Nikita Muravyov, the theorist of the Northern Society, son of a senator and heir to great estates, propounded the idea of a federated constitutional monarchy on the pattern of the thirteen original States of North America, each a self-governing entity. Only four ministries would, he argued, represent the proposed Russian federation as a whole – the Ministries of Foreign Affairs, Finance, War, and the Navy. Civil liberties, trial by jury, and the freeing of the serfs, though not necessarily with grants of land, were other features of Muravyov's programme. Though notably less radical than Pestel, Muravyov was no less a revolutionary in the Russian context.

Secret propaganda, preparation, and recruitment filled the years 1823–5. Officers only were enlisted; the soldiers would obediently follow their superiors. But in which direction would their superiors lead them? After much debate a plan was finally devised, timed to come into operation in May 1826 when the Tsar was expected to attend a troop review in the south. This would provide the occasion for his assassination. The arrest of the Grand Dukes, the occupation of Kiev, a march on Moscow, and the assumption of control over the Guards regiments in St Petersburg – all this would follow fast. But no troop review in the south took place. Alexander inconveniently died at Taganrog on 19 November 1825 (Old Style). A week later the news reached Moscow. A minor dynastic crisis followed. It lasted about three weeks. Constantine was the heir apparent, and it was to him that Grand Duke Nicholas and the Guards first swore allegiance. However, Constantine had been disqualified by Alexander from the succession following a morganatic marriage. He was also clear-headed enough to sense his own unfitness to rule. He adamantly refused to ascend the throne. The Decembrists hoped to exploit the confused interregnum to pull off their own *coup* before Nicholas, the dead tsar's younger brother, ascended the throne.

The hurriedly revised plan called for a revolt on the day when the soldiers were to take their oath of allegiance to Nicholas. But there was treachery. Field-Marshal Ivan Dibich knew of the plot from a non-commissioned officer named John (Ivan) Sherwood, who was of English origin. Information came from Jacob Rostovtsev also, an officer whom Prince Eugene Obolensky had unsuccessfully tried to enlist in the Northern Society. 'In the early hours of the day after tomorrow' (that is the day appointed for the taking of the oath), Nicholas wrote to Dibich, 'I shall either be a sovereign or a corpse.' In actual fact, he became a sovereign while his enemies founded both a legend and the intelligentsia of Siberia. Treachery was not of itself fatal to the plot. What did kill it at the roots was the collapse of the plotters' morale. Some defected at the last minute; others, after leading their troops on to the Senate Square in St Petersburg, where the ceremony of allegiance was due to take place, failed to give the order to rise. For about six hours, until the early winter dusk drew in, loyal and insurgent troops faced each other. Hardly a salvo came from either side. At one point, Nicholas ordered carriages to be ready to take the Imperial family to safety. But he never lost his head; and after dusk had fallen and after the mutineers had rejected the offer of capitulation, he had cannon trained on them, and in two hours had cleared the Square. In the south the march on Kiev came similarly to grief.

The authorities interrogated and investigated about 600 people, many of whom confessed – apparently in the hope that they could bring Nicholas to understand the need for reform; others gave way to mutual recriminations and implicated their fellow conspirators. Nicholas himself displayed great intelligence in eliciting from the prisoners the maximum information. Pestel was one of the few to maintain his sang-froid. 'We wanted the harvest before we had sown', he told his judges. In the end five people were sentenced to death by hanging and more than a hundred exiled to Siberia or to army service in the ranks.

This marked the official end of what Nicholas called a 'horrible and extraordinary plot'. No mention of it was allowed to appear in the Press, and everything was done to destroy the very memory of the abortive revolt, which was euphemistically referred to as '14 December'. But it survived as a myth to inspire all future rebels against the regime – the intelligentsia of the forties, the Nihilists of the sixties, the Populists and Anarchists of the seventies, and the Marxists of the eighties. The resident British Minister in St Petersburg sent Canning a remarkable diagnosis of failure and an equally remarkable prophecy:

> The late conspiracy failed for want of management, and want of a head to direct it, and was too premature to answer any good purpose, but I think the seeds are sown which one day will produce important consequences.

The Decembrists were the only significant Russian representatives of that phenomenon, the military revolutionary, which first emerged in Iberia and Latin America during the Napoleonic Wars. Yet in Russia they failed. Once more, Russia had shown the world that she was not like other countries, not like China where peasant revolt might signal the passing of the 'Mandate of Heaven', not like England, where power passed gradually from king to aristocracy and thence to middle class and people, nor like Spain and the independent Third World. In Russia, such change as there was would only come when sanctioned by established authority until new forms of social and political revolution would be devised.

THE REIGN OF NICHOLAS

To the new Tsar, twenty-nine-year-old Nicholas, the Decembrist revolt came as a traumatic shock. From the first, he was resolved to preserve the status quo intact. Not that Nicholas was not *au courant* with all the abuses, injustices, and corruption stigmatized by the Decembrists. On the contrary, he took the greatest pains to familiarize himself with their criticisms, keeping a bound volume of their testimony on his desk for the rest of his life. But he did very little about them. It was this Russian government that de Custine compared to 'the discipline of the camp – it is a state of siege become the normal state of society'.

All criticism at any level but the topmost was stifled through the operation of the censorship and the closest possible supervision of the activities of the populace. The revolts of 1830–31 in Belgium, France, and Poland, and the revolutions of 1848–9 throughout the continent, gave Nicholas renewed and reinforced incentive to preserve Russia inviolate. The slogan 'Orthodoxy, Autocracy, Nationality', coined by Count Uvarov, the Minister of Education, was intended to serve as an ideological dam that would hold back all critics of the existing order. Uvarov was quite frank about this: 'If I can succeed in delaying for fifty years the kind of future that theories are brewing for Russia, I shall have performed my duty and shall die in peace.' In one way or another a whole generation of Russian thinkers and writers suffered from this oppressive regime: Pushkin, Lermontov, Herzen, Belinsky, Turgenev, Bakunin, Dostoyevsky – these were but a few of the most prominent. By the end of the reign the autocracy had virtually no supporters of any distinction among the intelligentsia.

Nicholas I was personally brave, honourable, and totally dedicated to his job. He was a monstrous anachronism, seeing himself as another Peter the Great, supervising the smallest details of administration, – down to the sacking of schoolmasters whose pupils slouched during lessons. In many respects, he can be regarded as the last real autocrat of Imperial Russia. The characteristic institution of Nicholas's reign was the Personal Chancellery of His Imperial Majesty. It consisted of a varying number of Sections entrusted with the most urgent tasks. The First controlled promotions to all important offices and positions, the Second assisted Speransky's ultimately successful attempt to collate Russian Laws, the Fifth undertook cautious investigations into ways of improving the condition of the serfs. But it was the notorious Third Section which far exceeded all the others in importance. The very formation of this section, concerned with internal security, testified to Nicholas's distrust of the regular governmental machinery, and also to the embarrassment felt by that lonely man, in his austere room in the vast Winter Palace, at not knowing what was going on among his subjects. Where no free expression of public opinion was permitted, the autocrat lived in a vacuum, beset by feelings of uncertainty and insecurity. The Third Section, it was hoped, would overcome the gap that divided the autocrat from the knowledge of what was being felt and thought by his subjects. Most important of all, it would keep track of any subversive ideas and institutions. This was the true and innermost *raison d'être* of the Third Section. Foreigners, dissenters, criminals, sectarians, writers – any exponent of ideas would come under its supervision. The Section was headed by General Benkendorf, who had quickly convinced Nicholas that the Decembrist conspiracy proved the inadequacy of the existing police force. This was an obvious challenge to create improved forces.

These new forces were of two kinds: first, a uniformed Gendarmerie covering the whole Empire, organized and officered on military lines in five (and then, eight) regions; second, the Section operated through a body of secret informers. Very often the Section functioned not only as a police force proper, but also as a judicial body with the power to punish or to exile. But for all the censorship, the Third Section, the supervision of universities and schools, the prohibition of foreign travel, the propagation of official patriotism, there were three main disruptive forces at work against which all the Government's measures were helpless. These were the serf problem, the development of urban life and industry, and the growth of the intelligentsia. If the following pages seem to spend a disproportionate amount of space on the intelligentsia, this is because of the contribution they have made to the culture of the whole world and the importance they still have for Russians today. The other two factors were probably far more important for most Russians of the time and they did just as much to bring change to Russian life.

Nicholas I's police chief Benkendorf called serfdom 'the powder-magazine under the state' and Nicholas himself was quite clear about the desirability of its abolition. However, he was inhibited by the complementary fears that emancipation on terms favourable to the serfs would secure his assassination, while emancipation on terms unfavourable to them might provoke a peasant war. His father's murder and the unrest that plagued the Baltic provinces following the regulation of serfdom there showed that neither fear was groundless. Economically, serfdom was stagnant during the first half of the nineteenth century and an increasing proportion of the nobility had no serfs at all. For those who did, however, their financial interest in the serfs was immense. The gentry of the industrializing north could have little interest in losing the obrok they levied on the industrial earnings of their serfs, while in the south there seemed little likelihood that gentry farmers would be able to pay the market wage that free farm-workers would demand if they were both to expand their grain production and live the lives they were used to. Nicholas introduced certain palliatives in the treatment of the serfs. He prohibited the sale of serfs without land as a means of settling private debts, and also auction-sales of serfs that would have dispersed families. Serfs whose owners went bankrupt received the right to buy their liberty. The number of serfs declined absolutely in Russia in the first half of the century despite a considerable increase in the total population. Historians are still divided between those who put this down to the intolerable extent of serf exploitation and those who suggest that many serfs were in fact escaping serf status. Ironically, it was Nicholas's own determination to maintain a million-strong army that did most to 'liberate' serfs, if twenty-five years at the colours can be called 'liberation'. On the state lands, Kiselyov, the Minister of State Domains, carried through certain reforms which equalized the peasants' land allotments and created some sort of welfare system – schools, a medical and fire service, and agricultural advisory centres.

The statistical analysis of peasant disturbances in nineteenth-century Russia is still far from complete; there are obvious difficulties in deciding what constitutes a disturbance – can the murder of a steward be equated with an obrok 'strike' of 2,000 peasants? Certainly, nothing remotely like the Pugachov revolt recurred though some of the statistical series suggest that peasant violence was on the increase. The climax came in 1848–9 when the inspiration of European revolutions, and the fear of famine and cholera, provoked widespread disturbances. Almost anything was capable of setting off unrest among the peasantry; the accession of a new tsar, the arrival of a new master or mistress, rumours that peasants building railways would be emancipated or rumours of new lands in the south. There was a stream of loyal and very literate petitions to the Emperor, complaining of exploitation and brutal treatment by landowners or their stewards. The events of 1825 produced a crop of false Constantines, and even female pretenders claiming to be Constantine's wife and sister. Constantine was to be the last member of the Imperial family to inspire this vision of a true tsar rewarding his loyal peasantry by lopping the heads off the 'boyars' and granting the serfs their freedom. The only conclusion that can safely be drawn is that the peasants would seize on any pretext and any opportunity to escape the servile status they hated.

If we regard the term 'industrial revolution' as signifying a process in which the whole economy is stimulated, then Russia's industrial revolution did not really begin until after the reforms of the 1860s. In the first half of the century, industry, and particularly light industry, developed at a much faster rate than agriculture. Foreign technological advances were imported into Russia. In 1824–8, for example, some 42,000 silver roubles' worth of steam engines were imported; by 1851–3 this figure had gone up to 2,736,000. Even so, production of pig-iron barely doubled (as compared with a thirtyfold increase in Great Britain over the same period). There was almost no coal, fuel, or petroleum industry and very little in the way of non-ferrous metallurgy. This signified a tremendous reversal of the trend of the previous century, when, for example, Russian production of cast iron had been at least equal to that of England. There were many reasons for this relative stagnation. During the eighteenth century, Russian industry had relied excessively on an export market that was destroyed by the Continental System and by the competition of cheaper and better British goods. Russia's internal market was, as yet, no match for the lost export opportunities. Communications, investment institutions and the productivity of labour were all at a primitive stage as compared with Western Europe. The growth of industry was labour intensive rather than capital intensive. The number of factories rose from 2,402 in 1804 to about 14,000 in the second half of the 1850s. The number of workmen increased correspondingly. In 1804 there were 225,000; in 1825, 340,000; in 1860, 860,000. The proportion of hired labour in these totals rose respectively from $27\frac{1}{2}$ per cent to 33 per cent, and then to 60 per cent. The accelerating tempo of industrialization is shown in the rate of growth in hired labour. It increased in absolute figures 1·9 times from 1804 to 1825, but 4·6 times from 1825 to 1860. Over the whole period 1804–60, there was almost a ninefold increase in the number of hired labourers.

Two industries stood out for their rapid growth (admittedly from almost non-existent beginnings) – cotton textiles and beet sugar. The former was distinguished for its use, from 1840 onwards, of hired labour exclusively. It also benefited greatly from the impact of the most modern English machinery (after 1842, that is, when the English ban on the export of textile machinery was lifted). Knopp, an English entrepreneur, built and maintained the majority of Russian cotton factories. The most developed industrial centres were Moscow, Vladimir, and St Petersburg, but entirely new urban centres developed, too, like Ivanovo, the Russian 'Manchester'.

THE INTELLIGENTSIA

Radishchev and the Decembrists had possessed vision and courage but it was not until the 1840s that they became heroes for a significant section of society. For the first fifteen years of his reign, Nicholas I was regarded with deferential admiration by the vast majority of his educated subjects. Somewhere around 1840 this attituded was replaced by one of increasingly bitter criticism by a growing proportion of thinking Russians. He had not changed but they had. The intelligentsia, as it was to be called, had become a tangible social reality, though it was not yet a class. In the absence of a 'bourgeois market . . . providing a sufficient demand for trained intellectual labour and its products', the intelligentsia could only arise from the nobility and those members of other social groups who aspired to join them by assimilating their culture. The benign myth forged by their greatest representatives, the great writers of the nineteenth century, has become an integral part of our culture. Their deficiencies were, of course, recorded by Goncharov, Dostoyevsky, and Chekhov, but still we tend to idealize them. Many young Russian nobles turned to social criticism because they were incapable of anything else.

Little kings at home, admired by their family and relatives, mostly women, and confident that they were superior in kind to their serf servitors and playmates, gentry children frequently lacked the presence of even the one obvious authority, their father, whose service obligations had taken him elsewhere. They ruled the roost. The awakening, whether in a military school or government office, was bound to be rude.*

Commerce was even less attractive: they were brought up to squander wealth, not invest it, and only the greatest of them were

* N. V. Riasanovsky, *A Parting of Ways* (Oxford, 1976), p. 268.

able to find a market valuation for their labours which they found anything but insulting. Great artists like Pushkin and Gogol were as flawed by idiotic pride and childish greed as their less illustrious contemporaries.

Of course the intellectuals had worthier reasons for chafing at the bit. They could not avoid thinking about the contrast between the heightened Russian patriotism of 1812 and the liberation of Europe by Russia with the growing chorus of liberal European hostility towards Russian autocracy. They were aware of the moral, as well as the economic deficiencies of agrarian serfdom. Increasingly rapid urbanization was failing to produce a more urbane society. On the contrary, Russia's cities were fast becoming prototypes of today's agglomerations in the Third World: awesomely elegant centres surrounded by festering industrial suburbs patrolled by police spies. The discipline of service, while not entirely unjustified considering the upbringing of many Russians, was petty to the point of absurdity. It also reeked of corruption and oppression. The democratization of the intelligentsia was a slow process which did not immediately lead to the emergence of greater radicalism but it did widen the gulf between the rulers and their critics. The very successes of early nineteenth-century Russian culture, the emergence of a Russian academic and literary elite, and educated public and organs to serve them, brought closer the day when government and intelligentsia would speak in mutually incomprehensible tongues. As Nicholas's reign drew on, he showed less and less interest in the popularity of himself and his ministers, while the intellectuals withdrew into their isolated *circles*. The government's ideological bankruptcy became more and more evident, while the intellectuals turned to Utopias. If we turn to consider the dominant ideas of this period, we must first look to history, or rather, to the meaning of Russian history with its manifold political implications.

This was the great age dominated by the historical theories of Hegel and Schelling. As Lord Acton pointed out, the social function of a historical philosophy such as that of Hegel in Germany, of Burke in England, of de Maistre in France, was to form the 'resistance to the revolutionary rationalism' of the eighteenth century, to decry the power of the unaided human mind in its capacity to influence the development of society, and to exalt in its stead the essentially irrational and unthinking weight of the past and of tradition, against which it was futile for the individual to pit himself. But what was a reactionary philosophy in the West had, characteristically, revolutionary connotations in Russia; at the level of ideas, that is to say, and not in terms of practical politics. For what was the Russian past, the Russian tradition, in which men were to seek a guide to the present and the future? Here lay the core of the tense debates in the thirties and forties between Slavophiles and Westerners. The conflict was no new one in Russian intellectual history. What Herzen called 'wounded national feeling, dark recollection, healthy instinct' had characterized a certain movement of opinion and cast of thought from at least the seventeenth century. The Old Believers had been Slavophile, as against Nikon, the Westerner; so had the opposition to Peter the Great; so had Prince M. M. Shcherbatov in his opposition to the Gallomania of the later eighteenth century. All such critics had manifested what is known to sociologists as 'Utopianism of the past' – a tendency to hark back to the good old days. Precisely the same conflict would run through the left-wing and socialist movement of the latter part of the nineteenth century.

What made the conflict particularly acute at the beginning of the century was the nearness of the West and the impact of Western constitutional ideas and ideals. The first fruits of this were the Decembrists, Westerners to a man. To them it was axiomatic that the light came from the West, whether France, England, or the United States. But now the conflict entered a new phase. Hegel himself had slighted the Slav world as 'an intermediate essence between European and Asiatic spirit'. This limbo left Hegel's students all the more freedom to construct their own version of Russian history. The issue was clearly posed: did Russia belong to Western society, albeit in a retarded state; or did Russia embody a civilization *sui generis* that must be saved from the contamination of Western influence?

Peter Chaadayev, an ex-officer in the Hussars and friend of the Decembrists, a dandy, an *habitué* of the aristocratic salons of St Petersburg and Moscow, brought the conflict to the fore with *A Philosophic Letter*. It was written in 1829, but not published in the

Moscow journal *Telescope* until 1836. The 'letter' provoked an immense furore – 'what alarm in the salons!', exclaimed one contemporary. Chaadayev was officially declared insane and subjected to a sort of house arrest. What had he done? He had simply condemned Russian history *en bloc* as sterile and worthless because of its separation from Western influence. Russia had remained apart from the world's developments, stagnant in its isolation.

Confined in our schism, nothing of what was happening in Europe reached us. We stood apart from the world's great venture ... while the whole world was building anew, we created nothing: we remained crouched in our hovels of log and thatch. In a word, we had no part in the new destinies of mankind. We were Christians, but the fruits of Christianity were not for us.

Chaadayev's remedy was a rapprochement with Catholicism, the medium whereby Russia should rejoin the West. Here was a clarion call to the Westerners. Their members included Herzen, the brilliant publicist and father of Russian socialism, Belinsky, the founder of Russian literary criticism, Turgenev, the novelist, Granovsky, the historian, and Bakunin, the future anarchist. Whatever their other differences, there was a fundamental belief in the urgent necessity for closer contact with the West, where the virtues of free thought, rationalism, individual liberty, the values of science existed, and could serve as the means and the model for the regeneration of Russia.

Slavophile doctrine – the doctrine of Khomyakov, the two Aksakov brothers, and of the two Kireyevsky brothers – was a heady romantic mixture. This, too, stood in opposition to Nicholas's regime, which it stigmatized as the product of an alien dynasty, stemming ultimately from the European-inspired reforms of Peter the Great. Slavophilism saw in unperverted Russian history a youthful force with its own innate strength and virtue, rooted in the people and the Orthodox Church, destined to supersede the West and to become the universal civilization of the future. In this context, Slavophile doctrine gave special emphasis to the co-operative peasant commune. This embodied, it was argued, a specifically Russian form of socialism of a type that would enable Russia to avoid both the individualism and the unbridled capitalism that were tearing the Western world apart.

The opposition between Westerners and Slavophiles must not be overestimated. Both shared, albeit for different reasons, a detestation of the regime, and both fervently believed in the Russian future, whether as part of the West or as an independent force. It was Herzen who, in a famous image, compared his allies and his Slavophile opponents to Janus, or the two heads of the Imperial eagle in whose breast the same heart was beating, even though the heads might face opposite ways. Also, as the thirties turned into the forties, events in the West itself helped to bring the two groups together. After 1848 particularly, with the failure of the revolutions in such countries as France and Germany, and the consequent discredit of republicanism and liberalism, the notion of a Russian messianic mission also took root among the erstwhile Westerners. Herzen, who went into voluntary exile in 1847, emerged deeply disenchanted from his first encounter with Western ways, turned a complete *volte face* and was converted to the Slavophile cult of the peasant commune:

... what a blessing it is for Russia that the rural commune has never been broken up, that private ownership has never replaced the property of the commune: how fortunate it is for the Russian people that they have remained outside all political movements, and, for that matter, outside European civilization ...

Bakunin too began to talk of the Russian peasant as the future progenitor of the revolution. Europeanism lost ground and pro-Russian sentiment grew. Ivan Kireyevsky, in his writings of the early fifties, could look back over the past twenty years and point with satisfaction to the decay of Russian faith in the West.

Some of the first fruits of Westernism in a political guise, as distinct from a theoretical attitude, can be seen in the circle organized by Petrashevsky in the 1840s in St Petersburg. M. V. Butashevich-Petrashevsky himself, to give him his full name, was a graduate of the exclusive *lycée* of Tsarskoe Selo. From there he passed as a junior clerk into the Ministry of Foreign Affairs. He was in his twenties in 1845 when he began to bring together the intellectual elite at Friday-evening gatherings in his apartment at

St Petersburg. By now the intelligentsia had lost some of its social homogeneity and the Petrashevsky circle was composed of 'men of different ranks' – middle-rank officials and army officers, students, artists, and young *littérateurs* such as Dostoyevsky, Danilevsky (the precursor of Spengler), and Pleshcheyev, the poet. Here the ideas of pre-Marxist socialists such as Louis Blanc, Fourier, Cabet, and Considérant were read and passionately discussed.

The group had neither formal membership nor common doctrine. But its members were unanimous in their opposition to the autocracy, serfdom, and harsh army discipline. They demanded equality before the law, freedom of the Press, abolition of censorship, and a democratic republic. These demands were conceived, of course, on the Western models. But how were they to be attained? The Petrashevskyites condemned the Decembrist solution of a military conspiracy or palace revolution. On the contrary, the revolution could only be successful if it won the support of the masses. 'The main aim,' said Petrashevsky, 'is that ideas and wishes should take root in the masses of the people, for when the whole people wants something then the army will be unable to do anything.' In the Russia of the 1840s this meant a peasant revolution. It was for this reason that Petrashevsky assiduously studied the Peasant Wars in sixteenth-century Germany, the career of Thomas Müntzer, and the Levellers' movement in England – not to speak, of course, of the Pugachov rebellion as the Russian version of the Western upheavals.

Under the impact of the revolutions of 1848, these interests and studies took on a more radical character. A plan for an uprising was evolved, or, more truthfully perhaps, the ideas of an armed uprising took root in the minds of a few hotheads. One such was Nicholas Speshnev, a wealthy young landowner, a theist, who may have been the original of Stavrogin in *The Devils*. Speshnev said on one occasion

... that the Urals were almost ready to rise, that it was possible to get 400,000 armed men, that this was a terrible force and that the person who controlled it could be almost certain of victory, that ... if anyone with such a force hurled himself into the lower Volga area, where the people remembered Pugachov, then he would be raised on high.

All this soon proved to be empty talk. From early in 1848 the police knew of the Friday-evening meetings, and by the beginning of 1849 they had planted an informer in the group. In April and May, more than a hundred participants were arrested and interrogated, often after periods of solitary confinement in the Peter and Paul fortress in St Petersburg. In the end, some of the group were sentenced to hard labour and fifteen to death. Among the latter was Dostoyevsky. Nicholas used psychological terror against the fifteen young men. He did not make known his clemency and the commutation of the death sentence to hard labour until all the preparations for the execution by firing squad had been completed – until the prisoners had been clothed in shrouds and the first three intended victims brought forward.

LITERATURE AS A SOCIAL WEAPON

In a society in which opposition is forbidden, social criticism will gravitate towards any available mode of expression. Thus, Granovsky's lectures on English parliamentarianism were widely interpreted as an attack on Russian autocracy. But it was literature that inspired most fear in the government. Literature is an impossibly difficult field to police and Russian writers and their readers soon mastered 'Aesopian language'. It was Vissarion Grigorievich Belinsky who welded the various criticisms into a coherent set of attitudes and transmitted them to the whole of the intelligentsia. It was under Belinsky's influence that Russian literature developed its characteristic identification with the life of society. No writer or social critic of the Russian nineteenth century withstood his influence.

Belinsky was born in 1810 (or 1811) in Finland, the son of a retired naval doctor who later settled down to practise at Chembar (now renamed Belinsky) in the province of Penza. The father was something of a drunkard, and the mother a harassed, irritable and embittered woman. Neither parent took at all seriously their precocious son's fanatical devotion to literature and to the search for truth. He won a government scholarship to the University of Moscow, where he almost starved, but studied unremittingly. In 1831 he was expelled from the University for having written a play denouncing Russian conditions, and also perhaps because he lacked the necessary solid intellectual background considered essential by the authorities.

Be that as it may, from 1831 until his death from tuberculosis in 1848, Belinsky had to earn his living by his pen. Much of what he wrote was inevitably nothing more than pot-boiling journalism. Nadezhdin, the professor of literature at the University and also editor of *Telescope*, the periodical which had published Chaadayev's 'Letter', took Belinsky up and commissioned him to write reviews. Philosophically speaking, Belinsky moved from adherence to Hegel, Schelling and Fichte to sympathy with French and German Utopian anarchists and socialists – Feuerbach, Proudhon, Fourier, Louis Blanc, and Saint-Simon. Crudely and roughly, this was equivalent to the transition from an uncritical acceptance of the status quo to a paramount concern for the individual.

It is no exaggeration to say that Belinsky created a new and vastly influential method of literary criticism. A great deal of his achievement is implicit in the famous letter of denunciation with which he overwhelmed the deranged Gogol:

And here the public is right, for it looks upon Russian writers as its only leaders, defenders and saviours against Russian autocracy, orthodoxy and nationality, and therefore, while always prepared to forgive a writer a bad book, will never forgive him a pernicious book.*

Here, in essence, is Belinsky's ideal of the committed writer as the man capable of giving voice to the deepest and most cherished humanist ideals and values. There was a time, as Herzen said, when Germany gave Russia nothing but midwives and empresses. But in the early nineteenth century these yielded pride of place to German philosophy, and Belinsky's ideal is probably derived from German romantic philosophy, with its view of the artist as the mouthpiece and expression of his particular epoch. Under Belinsky's inspiration, however, this developed quite different connotations in Russia.

It involved taking a middle course between the theory of art for art's sake, and moral, social, or political didacticism. Literature would be both narrower and broader in scope – narrower in the

* Belinsky, *Selected Philosophical Works*, ed. Riha (Moscow, 1948), p. 510.

sense that its concern would be first and foremost with ideas, and broader in that it would be responsible to the whole of society. 'To deny art the right of serving public interests,' Belinsky wrote, 'means debasing it, not raising it, for that would mean depriving it of its most vital force, that is, the idea, and would make it an object of sybaritic pleasure, a plaything of lazy idlers.'

Thus the critic's task was to elucidate and assess the idea embodied in a work. Belinsky would have agreed that 'all art is propaganda'. The question was: what sort of propaganda? Did it defend the people from 'autocracy, orthodoxy, and nationality', or did it defend the official patriotism of the regime? Where did the writer, the poet or the novelist stand? This was Belinsky's criterion. In other words, he saw and judged literature in moral and not in literary or utilitarian terms. The work of art had no right to lead an autonomous moral existence in a world divorced from the values of human life. It was part and parcel of the world.

If literature was identified with life, then it followed that there was an even closer identification of the artist with his art. The artist must above all else remain faithful to his vision – and not only when he functioned as an artist but also when he functioned as a man, if indeed the two could be separated. It is this that accounts for the virulence with which writers such as Gogol and Tolstoy, for example, renounced their own earlier writings when they found them incompatible with their later beliefs. They could not look on their works as something apart from their life.

Belinsky's aesthetic, if the word be allowed, had a further consequence. It was a matter of supreme importance to be an artist; for it meant a decision to take an active part in the most momentous struggles of the day. Hence the peculiar strength and the tang of the conflicts that often set one writer or critic against another – Belinsky against Gogol, Chernyshevsky against Herzen, Pisarev against Pushkin, Tolstoy against Turgenev. What gave these conflicts their special force was not simply personality differences or literary theories, but the underlying conviction that the stake was the very future of society itself.

Belinsky's demands that art be coterminous with life, that the artist be committed to portray reality (though not of course without the exercise of his imagination), the inescapability of a theme or a problem located in a certain milieu known to the writer and recognizable as such by his readers – all this did, of course, gain added strength from the censorship. By prohibiting the free public expression and discussion of public issues, it helped to ensure that fiction would become the favoured medium for debates of this type.

In Belinsky's lifetime the impetus that his theories gave to literature was already showing itself. He died in 1848. But by then Pushkin and Lermontov had created, in Eugene Onegin and Pechorin, respectively, the first significant representatives of the 'superfluous man' as a criticism of the regime and of social conditions. The type enjoyed a long life and was variously embodied in the works of Turgenev and Chekhov, and of course in Goncharov's Oblomov, the apotheosis of superfluity in the form of apathy. Although differing in detail, they were men whose energy and talent could find no outlet in public service. They were cut off from the Court and the regime by their contempt for its values. But they were also cut off from the mass of the people by their superior Europeanized education. Hence they lived and moved in a sort of limbo, animated purely by private concerns.

Much of the enduring charm of *Eugene Onegin* stems from the elegance and maturity of Pushkin's diction and the gentle irony of the narration. It tells the story of a bored, blasé, and *déraciné* St Petersburg dandy who rebuffs the love of Tatiana, a serious but romantic provincial girl. Onegin flees the country estate where he had met Tatiana, after a duel in which he kills his friend Lensky. He seeks oblivion in the Caucasus. Years later, in St Petersburg, he meets Tatiana again, this time as a mature beauty – but married to an elderly dignitary. Onegin is now in Tatiana's place – it is he who is rebuffed by Tatiana, in her determination to remain faithful to her vows.

Lermontov's *A Hero of Our Time* gives full vent to similar frustration. The introduction boldly calls it 'a portrait composed of the vices of all our generation, in their full development'. The author's mouthpiece is Pechorin, a young officer whose character is gradually revealed – there is virtually no story to the book – through a series of laconic episodes. Pechorin, *the* man of the thirties, is shown to be something of a Machiavellian character, become sinister in his incapacity to use his undoubted talents and condemned to waste his life in pointless soldiering. Unfathomable and unutterable despair is his end. Although Lermontov's portrait is no objective analysis and not without a certain cool irony, it yet remains a powerful study of a man of vigour gone to seed in a society that denies him the necessary scope. Here the 'superflous man' is blended with the rebel against society, whom Dostoyevsky was later to portray in such characters as Raskolnikov.

Pushkin and Lermontov studied society on a small scale, their viewpoint derived from the position of the isolated Westernized aristocracy. With Gogol, the canvas is immeasurably broadened to include the lives of the small landowner and nobility, as Gogol conceived them, in all their triviality and vulgarity. He himself came from a family of poor Ukrainian gentry. After some years spent as junior clerk, private tutor, and professor of history at the University of St Petersburg, he made literature his career. Pushkin and Zhukovsky, a veteran court poet, were his first mentors.

Gogol's early stories of Ukrainian life, told in a nostalgic, humorous vein, and then his stories of metropolitan St Petersburg – fantasy strangely mingled with big-city realism – soon established him as one of the leading writers of the day. One of these stories, *The Overcoat*, tenderly satirizing and pitying a humble clerk, has become famous as the progenitor of a staple theme of much nineteenth-century literature. It is characterized by a simple story, a meek principal character, an accumulation of small detail, and a tone of fellow-feeling. Dostoyevsky's *Poor Folk* is a prime example of the genre. It was also Dostoyevsky who said: 'We have all come out from underneath Gogol's "Overcoat" '. With *Dead Souls*, Gogol's peculiar vision of a reality given over to spiritual emptiness reaches its climax. (The 'souls' of the title are serfs, this being the term by which they were known in Russia.) Gogol based the novel on an idea given him by Pushkin. The form is picaresque, the loose thread of the story is held together by the negotiations of the hero, Chichikov, in his quest for the 'dead souls'. His idea is simple. After a number of ups and downs in life, Chichikov, the epitome of smooth imperturbability, decides to enrich himself again by trafficking in the dead – the physically, and not the officially dead. He will buy from the landowner those of his serfs who have died since the last census. This deal will benefit both parties. On the one side it will release the landowner from paying tax on a worthless possession; on the other, it will give Chichikov title to a certain number of serfs whom he can then mortgage to a bank, and thus set himself up as a man of substance once again.

This macabre story is the pretext for a widespread panorama of backwoods noblemen and provincial life. As Chichikov goes about his business of purchasing the dead souls – or rather, 'non-existent souls', as he delicately prefers to describe them – he gives Gogol occasion to evoke a satirically distorted but recognizably truthful picture of country life. This is not the wild Caucasus of Pechorin, not the lyrical estate of Onegin, but a cadaverous world, peopled by barely one sympathetic personage. Whom does Chichikov meet on his travels? Grasping, corrupt officials, miserly widows, slothful, brutal landowners, stupid noblemen, gamblers, and a whole array of living monstrosities. At the end it is clear that the 'dead souls' of the title are by no means the serfs but the whole world above them.

When the novel was published in 1842 it created something of a furore. Pushkin had exclaimed some years earlier on hearing Gogol read the first draft: 'God, how sad our Russia is!' Belinsky greeted it as a truthful picture of the country inspired by a profound inner love. The Slavophiles could see in the novel a faith in the Russian future, however much its present might be betrayed. Gogol's comedy, *The Inspector General*, which is a not dissimilar satire on provincial life, could also be understood in this sense. No doubt this was the reason why Nicholas personally intervened so that it might be well received.

In his later years, Gogol became mentally ill and suffered from a form of religious mania, made a pilgrimage to Palestine, and utterly disappointed the hopes of the liberals and even of the Slavophiles. His last work, *Extracts from Correspondence with Friends*, in which he repented of his earlier writings and praised the virtues of the autocracy and of serfdom, brought upon him the wrath of Belinsky. 'Preacher of the knout,' Belinsky reviled the hapless Gogol, 'apostle of darkness, champion of obscurantism and dark ignorance . . .' This magnificent torrent of denunciation made no allowance for human weakness or illness. It set the tone for almost the whole of the literature of the nineteenth century. A bad book – yes; a harmful book – no, a thousand times no!

FOREIGN AFFAIRS

A military despotism can only be justified as long as it is victorious. It was more than a coincidence that Nicholas I's life gave out at the moment when Russia's armies finally faced defeat on Russian soil. A domestic policy which sought to galvanize support by identifying Autocracy and Orthodoxy with nationality was bound to cause trouble abroad where these principles were in conflict. Nicholas the Autocrat might sympathize with the Turkish Sultan but as the defender of the Sultan's rebellious Orthodox subjects he was bound to oppose him. Such contradictions exist in the foreign policies of many states right up to our time. What made them fatal to Russia under Nicholas was the way he extended military rigidity to the diplomatic service and his own indifference to the niceties of diplomacy, or rather, to the feelings of others. He humiliated the Shah and the Sultan with his ultimata, he extended a form of protectorate over the German monarchies in their moment of weakness that proved irksome in the long run and he made the mistake of discussing remote eventualities for the partition of the Ottoman Empire with the pragmatic British. For a long time his diplomatic and military efforts brought him nothing but success, but by the 1850s he had succeeded in isolating Russia from all the major powers. Even then, he saw no need to change his tone.

The reign of Nicholas I brought out all the reactionary potential of the Holy Alliance. Nicholas did eventually give guarded support to the rebellious Greeks, but only when he thought it might bring Russia advantage in the Straits. More characteristically, he was far from displeased when the Polish revolt of 1830 gave him a pretext for tearing up the liberal Polish constitution of 1815. In 1849 his armies restored the young Franz Joseph to the throne of Hungary. The gratitude of Franz Joseph was brief indeed, whereas the hostility of European liberals, for whom Mickiewicz and Kossuth became heroes, was enduring. It was during Nicholas's reign too that Russia engaged in the most truly genocidal of all her wars of conquest. By the 1840s, 200,000 men were tied down in a campaign against the Islamic guerrillas of Shaikh Shamil in Trans-caucasia, another inspiration for romantic Western liberals. This was the period when, after over 200 years of amity, rivalry between Russia and the Anglo-Saxons finally became the normal state of affairs. True, there had been moments of Anglo-Russian tension in the 1780s and 1790s but such hostility had not struck deep roots in the popular consciousness. Ever since the reign of Nicholas, British (and latterly American) conservatives have seen Russia as a threat to imperial interests in the Mediterranean and Asia, while Anglo-Saxon liberals have seen Russia as the arch-enemy of liberty in Europe.

It was Napoleon III, with his own appeals to nationality and religious orthodoxy in France, who finally forced Nicholas into a corner. In 1852, he sought to win the support of French Catholics by challenging Russia's sole right to control the Christian Holy Places in Palestine. The Sultan was delighted at this opportunity to evade the protection of Russia and when Nicholas reasserted Russian claims by means of the familiar ultimatum, the Turks sought to negotiate. Russia then occupied Moldavia and Wal-lachia; a few months later Turkey declared war. The following year, after the Turkish fleet had been destroyed by the Russians and after vain attempts had been made to compose the differences of the two powers, Britain and France allied themselves with Turkey. Austria too joined the coalition of enemies when it called on Russia to evacuate the two Danubian principalities.

The Allies took the Crimean fortress of Sevastopol in 1855, and after that the Russians had no choice but to surrender. The peace terms put a decisive stop to further Russian advance in the south; certain Bessarabian territories were restored to Moldavia, and this threw the Russians back from the Danube; Russia lost the right to maintain a fleet in the Black Sea; the Straits were closed to the warships of all nations; and the great powers themselves undertook to safeguard the integrity of Turkey and not to countenance any intervention in its internal affairs.

This was more than a military defeat. It discredited the whole regime. Ill-led and ill-equipped as the British troops were, the serf armies of the Russians had to do and die in incomparably worse conditions even though they were fighting on their home soil.

They had no modern weapons. The serf labour manning the wool, linen, and leather industries proved incapable of supplying adequate uniforms. A special munitions industry did not exist. The commissariat suffered from the almost entire absence of roads and railways in the immediate hinterland of the fighting area. In these circumstances, what began as a military trial of strength rapidly developed into a trial of the regime's strength. Many of the intelligentsia looked forward to Russian defeat as an essential precondition to reform. In this they were not disappointed.

CHAPTER 10

Reform and Assassination

'Impernickel is dead! Impernickel is dead!' This cry resounded at Twickenham in March 1855. Small boys were echoing in their own jargon the rejoicing of Herzen, now in exile in London, at the death of the Emperor Nicholas. When Herzen first saw the news in *The Times* he had rushed out in great jubilation to distribute largesse to all and sundry. For most educated Russians, hopes for the future were mixed with regrets for the past. As the liberal censor Nikitenko put it: 'The Emperor is dead; long live the Emperor! A long and, I must say, joyless page in the history of the Russian empire has come to an end.'

The death of 'Impernickel' in itself well justified Herzen's excitement. But there was more. If ever a country existed to which Trotsky's dictum applied – that war is the locomotive of history (especially if the war is unsuccessful) – that country was Russia. Defeat in the Crimea opened the way to impressive political and economic changes. Defeat in 1905 by the Japanese helped to produce the St Petersburg Soviet and the Duma movement. Defeat in 1917 helped to create the greatest upheaval of all, the Bolshevik revolution.

Defeat in 1855 exposed the inadequacy of Russia as rarely before. A social system created to endow Russia with a European army came to grief as well as a nation. The challenge was taken up. Out of the debacle came a transformation of the countryside, a significant industrial upsurge and an army that could reassert Russian prestige. Writers, composers, painters and scientists secured for Russia full and undeniable membership in the culture of Europe. Russian women contributed to life as reformers and revolutionaries, scientists and nurses; by 1865 some 200,000 women had joined the industrial working class of St Petersburg. Professional revolutionaries, unlike such well-intentioned amateurs as the Decembrists and the Petrashevskyites, rose up to challenge the State. In the 1860s and 1870s a new realistic, iconoclastic, and utilitarian spirit took hold of the intelligentsia. Much of this flowed from the primary act of the new reign, the emancipation of the serfs. Yet the reign which began with high hopes ended in – assassination. When Alexander II followed his father Nicholas on the throne, he had the wellnigh unanimous support of all groups of Russian society and even of political exiles such as Herzen. A few years before his death, 'the Tsar was isolated from the Russian people, unpopular with the educated public, and cut off from the bulk of society and even the Court. His fate had become a matter of indifference to the majority of his subjects.' * His death, when it finally came, was something of an anticlimax.

Alexander II was the best prepared heir the Russian throne had ever had. Like his uncle and namesake he had been exposed to both liberal and military influences, he was handsome and charming and he also seemed to lack consistency and will. His father's last words to him were 'hold on to everything!' and, unlike his uncle, Alexander II never doubted that Russia required an autocratic government. On the other hand, he differed from his father in recognizing the need for delegation. No sooner had he ascended the throne than it became evident that a break with the past was in preparation. In publishing the terms of the treaty of Paris, he also proclaimed that a programme of social reform was imminent. Furthermore he made it clear that the methods of his father were in abeyance. He released the surviving Decembrists and Petrashevskyites from exile. Many thousands of people were removed from police supervision. He lifted the restrictions imposed by his father on university students, and he put in hand a revision of the censorship regulations. To suspend recruiting, to remit tax arrears, to show more tolerance *vis-à-vis* Poland and the Catholic Church also augured well for the new reign.

More than anything else, Alexander wanted to restore Russia's shattered military prestige. His most articulate soldier, the fortyyear-old polymath General Dmitry Miliutin, explained that what was required was a smaller, better trained and equipped, and more mobile army backed up by a system of reserves. He was bold enough to add that such a reform was impeded by serfdom:

* W. E. Mosse, *Alexander II and the Modernization of Russia* (London, 1958), pp. 162–3.

Serfdom does not permit us to shorten the term of service nor to increase the number of those on indefinite leave so as to reduce the number of troops on hand.

To shorten the term of service from the current twenty-five years would have meant sending hundreds of thousands of freed serfs, trained in the arts of war, back to their serf relations in their prime, a prospect too horrendous for the Russian government to contemplate. The alternative was emancipation, which might ease social tensions in the long term but was certain to increase them for the foreseeable future. As a former member of one of his father's secret committees on serfdom, Alexander could see this clearly. He was determined to re-assert Russian prestige in Europe and this could not be secured by permitting the peasantry to revert to a subsistence agriculture unable to provide for the army – let alone for railways or universities. It was also not feasible to expropriate without compensation the landowning class, the class from which both bureaucrats and officers were largely drawn. Yet emancipation on any other terms was bound to strike the peasants as unfair and unacceptable and to increase unrest in the short term. Despite these risks, Alexander's determination to reform the army and abolish serfdom were unalterable and in this he was warmly supported by his aunt, Elena Pavlovna, and his brother Constantine. The most startling sign of the new order came in an announcement made in April 1856, a month after the end of the Crimean War. Alexander was addressing a gathering of the Moscow nobles. He denied rumours that he was intending to put into effect the immediate emancipation of the serfs.

But [he went on] you yourselves are certainly aware that the existing order of serfdom cannot remain unchanged. It is better to abolish serfdom from above than to wait for the time when it will begin to abolish itself from below. I request you, gentlemen, to reflect on how this may be achieved. Convey my words to the nobility for their consideration.

The element of blackmail in the Tsar's words was increased by their prompt publication. While some of the nobles who lacked serfs were favourably disposed towards the Tsar's ideas, they were deeply resented by the landowning gentry among them, even in the administration. Alexander found it extremely difficult to find loyal collaborators to carry the emancipation through. So great was his isolation that he had to resort to a series of subterfuges to secure the apparent agreement of the gentry to a discussion of abolition by local gentry committees. He needed the gentry to seem to consent to emancipation for the sake of social peace; he needed detailed information on local conditions which only they could provide, and he needed their services in policing the country during what was widely expected to be a troubled period of transition. Leaders of a liberal gentry party were found in the province of Tver (now Kalinin), in the persons of two opinionated young noble graduates, Unkovsky and Golovechev, and they co-ordinated what became a virtual gentry movement between 1858 and 1862. During the summer of 1858 the Tsar canvassed support for emancipation among the gentry of Vladimir, Tver, Moscow, and Kostroma, rebuking the obdurate Muscovites for their initial refusal to discuss the matter. By the following year most of the gentry had begun to accept that emancipation was inevitable and to prepare proposals. In their various projects, they addressed themselves to two sets of problems which emancipation would raise. In the first place, there were the economic problems. How much land would the pomeshchik keep and how much would go to the peasants? Would the pomeshchiks be compensated for the loss of peasant labour as well as land? How could the peasants acquire land without ruining the pomeshchiks? Who would finance the redemption of the land acquired by the peasants? The gentry responded to these questions very much in the way we might expect. There were differences between them that seemed to be due to the influence of particular personalities, age and education. They were also affected by their own individual economic circumstances and by their perception of the interests of their class as a whole. For the liberal minority, especially in areas where land was unproductive and labour valuable, the projects advanced sought to force the peasants to acquire substantial holdings of land. They demanded that the State give them interest-bearing bonds and recover the redemption payments from the peasantry itself. In areas where land was valuable and labour plentiful, the gentry wanted to keep as much of the land as they could and as many of their seigneurial privileges as the state would permit.

The abolition of serfdom raised important political questions as well, and it was here that government and liberal gentry finally came to grief. It was obvious to all that the abolition of the patriarchal authority of the pomeshchik would leave a substantial power vacuum in the Russian countryside. What was going to fill it? In 1859, gentry deputies from the provincial committees were summoned to St Petersburg to discuss emancipation with the Main Committee on Peasant Affairs, or so they fondly imagined. By now, however, the Tsar had found loyal collaborators in the bureaucracy. These were General Rostovtsev and Nicholas Miliutin, respectively chairman of the Editing Commissions and leader of their economic section; these bodies had been specially set up by Alexander to circumvent the reactionaries on the Main Committee. The provincial deputies found that their sole permitted role in the capital was now to provide information on local conditions to the Editing Commissions. The suspicion began to dawn on them that what they were witnessing was a bureaucratic coup, an exploitation of the emancipation by the bureaucracy so that it could 'expand its authority to the very villages of rural Russia'.* In the months that followed, they emerged with their own competing programmes of opposition, one 'aristocratic', the other 'liberal'. The would-be aristocrats, many of them hostile to emancipation in any shape or form, argued that it should only take place by voluntary agreement. In addition, the gentry should elect new organs of local self-government and deputies to participate in national legislation. The liberals, on the other hand, wanted emancipation and redemption to be obligatory for all gentry and all peasants. They wanted to see organs of local self-government elected by all citizens, the introduction of independent courts and freedom for the press to criticize administrative abuses. They did not at first see any need for a national legislature. As they became progressively more disenchanted with the bureaucratic conduct of the emancipation, they began to demand the convocation of an Assembly of the Land to restore the organic unity between tsar and people which they blamed the bureaucracy for breaking. What united all the landowners outside the charmed circle of the upper bureaucracy was the conviction that they should gain political privileges in return for their loss of seigneurial privileges; they

* T. Emmons, *The Russian Landed Gentry* (Cambridge, 1968), p. 260.

were determined not to be levelled down to the status of State peasants. The gentry movement was an unprecedented phenomenon in Russian politics. Although it apparently came to an end by 1863, it succeeded in altering the economic conditions of emancipation in the interests of the gentry and in securing a more liberal reform of local government and the courts than the government desired.

At the beginning of March 1861, nearly five years after Alexander's speech to the Moscow gentry, the Emancipation Resolutions were read out from the pulpits of Russia's churches. Before we consider the deficiencies of the emancipation settlement, it is worth remembering that it was not until eighteen months later, in the midst of a terrible civil war, that Abraham Lincoln was able to use his powers as Commander-in-Chief to begin the process of the *landless* emancipation of the slaves in the U.S.A. Such a reflection would have given little comfort to the Russian peasantry, however. For them, the emancipation was a terrible disappointment, perhaps even a fraud. This was so deeply felt that Alexander soon had to deny forcefully rumours of a new and genuine emancipation to replace the bitter appearance of 1861. At Bezdna in the province of Kazan the peasant Anton Petrov led a rebellion in expectation of a true emancipation and it even came to a massacre by troops of seventy rioting villagers. None the less, despite – and also because of – its limitations, the statute of emancipation marked an epoch in the history of modern Russia. It resounded decisively and perhaps fatally throughout the remaining decades of tsarism. The theme of the reform was the desire to reconcile every conflicting interest. 'The peasant should immediately feel that his life has been improved; the landowner should at once be satisfied that his interests are protected; and stable political order should not be disturbed for one moment in any locality.' Such was the government's laudable ideal. But it was, in fact, distorted into a concern for the preservation of the landowners' incomes, despite which the peasantry remained calmer than almost anyone had anticipated.

The serf, it is true, was at once released from his status and became a free citizen. He was free to marry, own property in his own name, take action at law, and engage in a trade or business on his own account. He could no longer be bought or sold. The principal benefit to female serfs was that they gained the right to determine whom they would marry and when. For all this, the serfs paid a heavy price in economic and financial dependence. This resulted from the principle that the land belonged to the landowner regardless of whether it had been used by him or by his serfs. If, therefore, the serf was to be released with land – and the government was determined to prevent the emergence of a rootless and untaxable rural proletariat – the serf must pay a price for it. Furthermore, the amount of land and also the type of land that the former serf received would depend to a large extent on what the landowner would grant.

To take the latter first – the peasant's pre-reform allotments were to be regarded as adequate, and voluntary agreement was to be sought on this basis. But since there were great disparities among the various regions, as well as within them, maximum and minimum norms were determined for the whole of the country, to which the new allotments had to conform. In most agricultural provinces, however, the owner could retain as much as one-third of the non-waste land, no matter what effect this had on the size of the allotments. There were also 'beggars' ' allotments, one-quarter of the maximum norm, which were acceptable only at the peasant's option and for which he had to pay nothing. About three-quarters of a million families accepted these holdings in the hope of bettering their status in the future; these hopes were to be disappointed.

Except for the beggars' allotments, the land allotted to the peasant did not become his personal, inalienable property until it was redeemed. Thus the redemption operation constituted the second main feature of the reform. The land could be redeemed by service at the rate of thirty or forty days' labour a year on the landowner's estate; alternatively – and this was the more general procedure – the obrok due to the landowner was capitalized at 6 per cent. This sum was then known as the redemption value of the allotment. At this point the State intervened between landowner and peasant, paying the former 80 per cent of the redemption value in interest-bearing certificates negotiable on the Stock Exchange, and yielding a 6 per cent income. The remaining 20 per cent was paid, by voluntary agreement, by the peasants themselves. If the settlement was made at the landowner's request, he or she merely received the certificates to the value of 80 per cent. Whichever was the case the sum advanced by the government to the landowners had to be repaid by the peasants over a period of forty-nine years from the date of issue and at the rate of 6·5 per cent to cover interest and amortization.

The village commune was encouraged and strengthened by the reform in that it became collectively responsible not only, as before, for the payment of taxes, but also for the payment of redemption dues. Similarly, in order to preserve the stability of relations in the countryside now that the peasant's personal dependence was ended, a form of peasant self-government was instituted, composed of peasant householders and elected 'Elders'. Special courts to judge minor cases that involved peasants only also came into existence to serve 'cantons', which were formed by the grouping together of communes.

So much for the landowners' serfs, numbering some twenty-one million. The somewhat larger number of State serfs received more generous treatment, a fact which reinforced the common conviction that the Tsar meant well by the peasants. The average holding of the privately owned male serf was nine acres, that of the State serf twenty-three. (This comparison is not, of course, as straightforward as it appears, given the enormous difference in the agricultural value of the land in the different areas – ranging from Siberia to Poland, and from the north to the Caucasus.) Moreover, the State serf's annual dues were materially less. In other respects, including the attachment of the peasant to the household, commune, and 'canton', there was no essential difference between the two processes of emancipation.

What was the effect of all these measures on the peasantry? The massacre of Bezdna was not an isolated event. The Ministry of the Interior reported no fewer than 647 incidents of peasant rioting in the first four months following the promulgation of the emancipation statute; and during the year of 1861 there were 499 outbreaks of serious rioting in which troops had to be used. This was not yet another *Pugachovshchina*, but looking further ahead, the terms of the emancipation were directly related to the peasant *jacqueries* of 1902 and 1905–6 – and the seizure of the land in 1917.

The fact is that in 1861 the peasants actually received less land than they had utilized in the pre-emancipation era; and for that lesser amount they were to pay more than the land would fetch by sale or rent; more than the land would bear, as it turned out. In general and summary terms, the peasants lost one-fifth of the land previously held. In many cases this was the most valuable part of the land, such as the meadows and pastures in the north and central areas. Very often, this completely destroyed the balance of their farming units, resulting in inadequate supplies of natural fertilizer and the progressive exhaustion of the land. In the black-earth zone particularly, where many peasants took the 'beggars' ' holdings, they lost more than a quarter. On the other hand, in the non-black-soil industrial provinces they were forced to increase their holdings; in effect, this permitted the landowner to tax them on their earnings from trade and industry. The former serfs were paying not merely for their allotments, they were also buying from the landowner their personal freedom.

In both cases the serfs received less than they were paying for. It has been calculated that by 1878 only some 50 per cent of the former serfs had received adequate endowments of land. The rest were below subsistence level. The situation was substantially worsened by the rapid growth of the population. In the forty years after 1861, the rate of increase was double that of the forty years before. There was a 72 per cent increase in the peasant population in European Russia. In the northern areas that underwent rapid industrialization, the surplus was absorbed by the new industries; in the south and east, land was still to be had while emigration to America began in the south and west. It was in the central black-soil provinces close to Moscow that overpopulation was at its worst. The increase was due not to any significant improvement in standards of public hygiene but to an increase in the birth-rate. Following the collapse of seigneurial authority peasant women tended to marry earlier. In the communes where the land was periodically re-partitioned there was an institutional incentive to have more mouths to feed.

In financial terms the landowners did not do very well either. By 1860, about 62 per cent of their serfs were mortgaged to the banks, and about 53 per cent of the value of their estates. Thus, a large part of the vast sums which would otherwise have accrued to them through the redemption operation actually went to pay off their debts. By 1871, for example, 248 million roubles, out of a total of 543 million paid in redemption dues by the peasants, had had to be repaid to various credit institutions. A few owners of very large estates in the black-soil regions succeeded in becoming producers of large surpluses of grain and other products. The remainder of the gentry were now embarked on an irreversible decline.

In the seventeenth century, tsarism had been supported by clergy and landholders. In the eighteenth century the State had condemned the clergy to penury and loss of social influence; now something similar was happening to the gentry. If the State was not to founder entirely, it was essential that new social forces be brought in to support it. Further reforms were therefore inevitable.

The first reform to follow the emancipation was the institution of a system of local self-government, through an agency known as a *zemstvo* (plural *zemstva*). The members of the zemstva were elected on a county and provincial basis through a system of electoral colleges that gave preponderance to the nobility. Those elected then chose an executive board of three members to carry on the routine business of each zemstvo from one annual meeting to the next. This went some way towards meeting the demands of the gentry liberals in 1862. The functions of the zemstva were limited to the maintenance of roads, prisons, hospitals, the encouragement of industry, agriculture, education, poor relief and famine relief, and public health. The zemstva were not fully autonomous because they had no executive power, and a good part of their revenue, derived from rates, was used for the purposes of the central government. On the other hand, particularly after 1878, as the zemstva spread to more and more provinces, they developed into a genuinely liberal force, constantly at odds with the tsarist bureaucracy. What is more, through their employment of experts, that is to say, doctors, nurses, teachers, sanitary inspectors, engineers, economists, and agronomists, they gave employment to a new sub-class drawn from the intelligentsia, reformers, and radicals, intimately aware of peasant conditions and bitterly critical of what they saw.

As a reforming tsar, Alexander II also had to his credit a development of municipal self-government that led to the creation of a primary educational system in the larger towns, as well as an equalization and a lightening of the burden of military service by the institution of conscription and the abolition of the more barbarous forms of punishment. Ultimately the period of service was reduced from twenty-five years to six with the colours and nine with the reserve. Aristocratic privilege in obtaining promotion was reduced to a minimum, better training methods and arms were introduced, and the military bureaucracy was radically reformed. It is a measure of Alexander II's priorities that the liberal bureaucrats associated with the emancipation were thrown to the wolves as soon as it was completed, but he kept his liberal War Minister Dmitry Miliutin with him to the end. In the intellectual and educational field there was a relaxation of the censorship of books and periodicals, and an attempt to re-establish university autonomy and widen the basis of entry to the secondary schools. These had previously been largely the preserve of the nobility.

Finally, the early reforming years of Alexander's reign also produced the new court system that provided for open trial, the use of a jury, the appointment of trained judges who were irremoveable, and the right to defence counsel. Minor offences were reserved for trial by Justices of the Peace elected by the zemstva and municipal representative institutions. Again, *toute réserve faite*, especially since the peasants had access only to their own courts, and therefore equality before the law could not be said to exist, it still remains true that the legal reforms of the 1860s marked a break with the past as indeed did all the other reforms of the period.

Yet how far did they really go? Obviously, they did not amount to the 'revolution from above' that many had hoped for. But it is equally clear that the old regime had gone for ever. Rather, to the existing tensions in the Russian social system was added yet another: that between the autocracy and some intimation of Western European legal, constitutional, and educational practice. Two worlds came to exist cheek by jowl. The emancipation and the associated reforms powerfully accelerated a tendency that had been gaining strength since the end of the eighteenth century. On the one hand, there was the world of the autocracy, its bureaucratic system, its ecclesiastical appendage, its serf economy, and its quasi-monopoly of intellectual life that controlled or spied on virtually every aspect of the national life. There was very little that took place outside the purview of this comprehensive system. The urge to supervise was irrepressible; it extended not merely to the dissident religious sects and the growing national intelligentsias of the borderlands but to all public or private activity that sought autonomy. To some extent this was both cause and effect of the continuing domination of the bureaucracy by the nobility. Of course they had even less choice than before if they wished to safeguard themselves against the economic consequences of the emancipation. The reforms notably failed to integrate any significant new class into the kind of society desired by the bureaucracy. The capitalists and rich peasants might not want revolution but they would not defend autocracy; the peasants revered the Tsar but loathed his government; the intelligentsia, fortified by the opportunities for worthwhile employment with the zemstva, remained almost unanimous in their hostility to the very principle of autocracy.

On the other hand, and increasingly so as the nineteenth century progressed, all sorts of new stirrings and new forces were alive. Autonomy from the State – this was their common characteristic. The administration of justice was separated from the administration of the State. The Church no longer monopolized education, even at the primary level. The Press took on a character of its own, however much hampered by the censorship. And the zemstvo movement, despite the supervision exercised by the Government and its inherent weakness in financial and executive power, constituted a source of authority directly representative of the population. This was the period that saw Russians enrich world civilization with the great realist novels of Leo Tolstoy, Dostoyevsky, and Turgenev while musicians such as Mussorgsky and painters such as Repin made the common people the subject of great art. In this period Timiryazev began his work on photosynthesis, and Mendeleyev devised the periodic table of the known elements and predicted the discovery of three new ones. It was the period that saw Sofia Kovalevskaya leave Russia to become Professor of Mathematics in Stockholm and Mykhaylo Drahomaniv settle in Austrian Galicia to campaign for Ukrainian autonomy. Most of these people got into hot water with the tsarist authorities at some stage in their careers.

All this signified not only the clipping of autocratic wings, but also the rise of new centres of power and influence, opposed in varying degrees to what remained of the old regime. The friction resulting from the juxtaposition of these two worlds was intensified by the economic consequences of the reforms and the increased industrialization of the 1860s and 1870s.

ECONOMIC DEVELOPMENT

Both the landowners and the peasants lost by the reform. Many of the former saw their mortgages and indebtedness reach a figure exceeding the pre-reform total. Many a Chekhovian cherry orchard had to be abandoned to the merchant, emergent industrialist or wealthier peasant. The nobles' landholdings dwindled inexorably; they shrank by something like 18 per cent in forty-one provinces of European Russia in the two decades following emancipation, and at an increasing rate afterwards. Only their predominance within the bureaucracy enabled them to retain something like their traditional social pre-eminence until 1917.

On the whole the peasantry fared very badly in that their standard of living declined to a level that threatened starvation. To begin with there were the four million peasants of both sexes who received no land at all. These were predominantly the former domestic serfs, the serfs employed in manorial factories and mines and the State industrial installations. For the majority of these there was no choice but to join the emerging proletariat.

Many of their counterparts who remained on the land fared even worse. The terms of the emancipation in themselves ensured that the average peasant holding was less than it was before 1861. Even this inadequate amount diminished with the growth of the rural population. Land could be rented for additional cultivation, it is true, but this required cash resources beyond the peasant's purse. In the 1880s, something like one-quarter of the peasants did not even own a horse. Furthermore, emancipation dues and other taxes produced a steadily increasing peasant indebtedness. It was this, in fact, that enabled Russia to maintain a consistently favourable balance of trade, to service all its foreign debt in the second half of the nineteenth century, and to maintain a strong ruble backed by gold. In order to pay their debts, the peasants had to sell their grain for export to Western Europe. But the 'granary of Europe' achieved its position only at the price of impoverishing its own population. The economic pressure was such that the peasants had to sell the grain that they actually needed for their own consumption. Chronic undernourishment in the Russian village was emphasized by the disproportionate effects of crop failure and, even more, by the increased mortality rate – from twenty-four to twenty-seven per thousand at the beginning of the nineteenth century to thirty-five per thousand in 1880.

By and large, the Russian masses completely failed to participate in the rise of the popular standard of living that elsewhere characterized the latter part of the nineteenth century. On the contrary, the acquisition of some degree of personal freedom was accompanied by a decline in living standards, by land hunger, and by rural over-population.

This extremely low standard of living severely inhibited the growth of the Russian internal market; even where the peasants considered themselves well off – as in Siberia – they showed only limited interest in the products of modern industry. None the less, emancipation did give a certain impetus to capitalist development and to the urbanization of Russia. After the reform, for example, the urban population increased almost twice as fast as the rural. Again, during the 1880s the first sizeable influx of foreign capital took place.

The development of the railway network was one of the most impressive tokens of the post-reform decades. The aim was, first, to link the grain-producing areas with the population centres and the internal markets, and, second, to link the former with the ports and thus facilitate the export of grain. Between 1861 and 1880 the track grew from 1,000 to more than 14,000 miles. Here was something akin to the English railway boom of the 1840s. Both foreign and native interests put up the capital. Russian industry was never able to supply all the rails, locomotives, and other capital items that this development needed. Even screws and bolts had to be imported from abroad. Yet the railway boom did encourage Russian heavy industry, for it constituted the latter's chief market. This can be seen in a sixteen-fold rise in coal production, a ten-fold rise in steel, and a 50 per cent rise in iron and pig-iron in the period from 1860 to 1876. To this period, for example, belong Hughes's factory for the production of coal, iron, and rails to the Krivoi Rog basin, the first large-scale exploitation of the coal deposits in the Donets basin, and the oil companies financed by the Nobel brothers in Baku. In the traditional industries, cotton-spinning, and woollen manufactures, similar expansion took place.

The fairs served as the great medium of circulation for the products of light industry and consumer goods. At these colourful assemblies, of which there were more than 6,500 in the middle 1860s, agricultural raw materials were collected and industrial products distributed. The fairs made up for the virtual absence of any modern retail network. The development of the railways, the spread of money relations in the countryside, and the undermining of household crafts, turning the peasant into a purchaser of manufactured goods – all these factors promoted the prosperity of the fairs. Their turnover grew from 360 million rubles in 1870 to 460 million in 1863.

Concomitant with all this development went the inauguration of a budgeting system (before 1862 there had been no proper budget at all); the promotion of private banks; and various attempts to stabilize the currency. None of these really succeeded, and their failure is evident in the fact that to service the public debt in 1860–80 took up between one-quarter and one-third of all budget expenditure.

As Russian capitalism developed, it began to display certain individual features that set it apart from the Western form. Of course, there were also many resemblances. The exploitation of the labour of women and children, low wages, an extensive system of fines, payments in kind, workers' barracks – this was the same harsh regime as in the early stages of the Industrial Revolution in England. But what first set Russian industrial development apart was the high degree of large-scale production. In respect of organization, Russian industry was as advanced as that of any Western state, if not more so. Thus, 40 per cent of the workers, according to calculations made by Lenin, were employed in factories employing more than 1,000 workers. This was in 1879; in 1866 the comparable figure had been 27 per cent. Over the same period the proportionate number of workers in factories employing between a hundred and 999 actually dropped.

This concentration of production was further expressed in Russian industry's characteristically close connection with the state. This had been a feature ever since the days of Alexis Mikhailovich, and, even more, of Peter the Great. It was the State that had made serf-workers available, had supplied a not inconsiderable proportion of the finance, had leased out the concessions, and had also provided the markets. This is connected historically with the failure to develop an industrial and capitalist bourgeoisie, as distinct from a professional and intellectual one. The typical Russian bourgeois was not an independent entrepreneur or manufacturer, but some kind of professional, a bureaucrat or an administrator.

Given this situation, the State stepped in as the promoter of industrial enterprise. Its instrument was the State Bank, founded in 1860. The issuing of notes was a very secondary function; far more important was its role as the keystone of the Russian credit system. The banks, with the State Bank at their head, were 'not only the creditors of many industrial enterprises but also their founders, cashiers, directors of their current accounts, the managers and owners of their shares and their basic capital, in short, the complete masters of their destinies'.*

Naturally enough, therefore, it was the needs of the State rather than the profits of private capital that were the determining factor, though not of course the *exclusive* factor, in laying down the general lines of industrial development. This is best exemplified in the history of Russian railway construction. From the start, the State's participation was extensive and its impetus decisive. The first railway company resulted from an Imperial decree of 1857 establishing a Grand Company of Russian Railways, formed of

* P. I. Lyashchenko, *History of the National Economy of Russia* (New York, 1949), p. 708.

an alliance between the State and a consortium of French, Dutch, and British bankers. The State granted the concession and also determined the direction of the network. This would be operated by the company, which would also receive a State-guaranteed 5 per cent interest on the sums invested. Later, owing to the company's difficulties, the State took on a more direct role in its fortunes. The headquarters were transferred from Paris to St Petersburg and four Russians were appointed to the board of management.

This set the general pattern of participation between the State and private, mainly foreign, capital. In some cases the State would even advance the capital sums required for the construction of the lines. The logical consequence of this policy was reached in the years after 1876 when the government began to buy back the railways shares issued to the public and to encourage the consolidation of the smaller companies into large groupings. This was the first step towards the formal nationalization of the railways. By 1901 the government owned two-thirds of the existing track. This type of governmental economic policy has an obvious affinity with the planning from above practised later by the Bolsheviks.

RUSSIA AND EUROPE IN THE AGE OF NATIONALISM

Only the dynastic confederation of the Austrian Habsburgs suffered as much from the rise of modern nationalism as the Russian Empire. Not more than half the Tsar's subjects were Russians, and while the use of Russian nationalism might, for a time, bind the Russian peasantry to the government, the side-effects were destabilizing in the borderlands. There, the rise of national feeling among ethnic groups with newly literate cultures, the Finns, Estonians, Latvians, and Ukrainians, led some demagogic Russian nationalists such as Yuri Samarin to seek to deflect these new nationalisms from challenging Russia by identifying as 'exploiters' such traditionally loyal groups as the Finnish Swedes, the Baltic Germans and the Jews. The apparent victory over Islamic nationalism in Transcaucasia merely encouraged the intelligentsias of Georgia and Armenia to feel secure enough to turn to revolutionary agitation. In Asia, the government's increasing support for a determined proselytizing movement was bound to offend the Islamic traditionalists among the local populations.

Alexander II and his Foreign Minister Gorchakov had a compelling need to pursue a policy of peace and quiescence. The Crimean War had shown that the country was, in any case, unfitted to wage an extended campaign; Miliutin's army reforms – which would take many years to bear fruit – were only completed in 1874. Moreover the reforms of the early years of the reign entailed retrenchment abroad. Lastly, the Polish revolt of 1863, which took more than a year to suppress, further undermined the prestige of the Russian army and offered foreign powers a justification for intervention in Russian affairs. What with the Italian liberation movement, the struggle for hegemony in Germany between Austria and Prussia, and the ever-present Polish nationalism, it is clear that Russia's best policy was to avoid war. There was no immediate recognition in high places that the unification of Germany posed any kind of threat to Russian interests and no attempt to use Austria's moment of weakness in 1866 to extract from Vienna a more sympathetic attitude towards the liberation of the Christian subjects of the Turkish Empire.

In central Asia and the Far East it was a very different story. These were the happy hunting-grounds of Russian imperialist adventurers, dubious carpet-baggers, and pseudo-viceroys, all the usual amalgam of heroism and brutality, altruism and greed that characterized imperialism everywhere. In many ways the occupation of central Asia was merely a continuation of the age-old conflict with the Islamic nations of Asia that had begun with the overthrow of Tatar authority. Trade followed the flag. If European Russia was becoming in some sense a colony of Western capital, then central Asia was also in some sense a colony of European Russia. By Alexander II's time great inroads had already been made into the Caucasus; and by 1864, after further campaigns against the mountaineers, the two-headed eagle was dominant in the territory between the Black Sea and the Caspian.

It was not long before the Caspian was crossed and a base secured for further penetration south-eastwards. This was one axis of advance. In 1869 it led to the foundation of Krasnovodsk on the eastern shore of the Caspian, and from there to the capture of Ashkhabad and the Merv oasis in the region of the Afghan frontier. This process was barely completed when military engineers were at work building the Trans-Caspian Railway along the Persian border. This line was later extended southwards to Kushk, on the Afghan frontier. All this area was developed as a cotton-growing centre for the Moscow textile industry.

Meanwhile, farther to the north and east, other Russian forces were coming to grips with the ancient Islamic khanates and emirates of Khiva, Bokhara and Kokand. Orenburg, on the Ural River, was the centre of Russian expansionism here. Perovsky, the Governor-General of Orenburg, made his first assault on Khiva in 1839. But inclement weather foiled his Cossack cavalrymen. For the next two decades or so, Perovsky conducted a campaign of subjection by building lines of forts deeper and deeper into the territory of the nomadic Kazakhs. By the 1860s they extended from the mouth of the Syr-Darya River (Jaxartes) to Verny, not far from the Russian border with Chinese Turkestan. Frequent clashes between the Russian invaders and the local populations along these ill-defined borders gave the occasion for further and more successful Russian aggression. Tashkent fell in 1865; Samarkand in 1868. By 1881, Kokand had been annexed to Russia and Bokhara and Khiva transformed into protectorates of the newly-formed Government-General of Turkestan. The Russian frontiers were now contiguous with those of Persia, China, and Afghanistan. A railway, running south-east from Orenburg to Turkestan, where it linked up with the Trans-Caspian line, consolidated the conquest, and made it possible to deploy troops at speed in these far-flung corners of the Empire. With one notable exception, the indigenous peoples of Central Asia gave little resistance to their conquest. Only at Geok Tepe in 1881 did the Turkmen give battle, suffering 8,000 killed for 700 Russian dead and 2,500 wounded.

This Russian expansionism often conflicted with the pacific policies urged by the Foreign Ministry in St Petersburg. And this urge on the part of a Perovsky in Turkestan, of a von Kaufman in Transcaspia, of a Chernyayev in Tashkent, helped to feed the profound Anglo-Russian tension which was crucial in the conversion of the English working class to support for imperialism. Only Afghanistan, where British and Russian envoys jostled for position, separated the two Empires. Would the future see a revival of the Emperor Paul's plan of 1801 to invade India? Such were the thoughts and fears aroused in British circles by the Russian advance. For their part, the Russians feared that the British would descend on central Asia and, to this day, they justify the Russian conquest with the claim that British imperialism would have been a disaster for the native peoples. It is difficult to separate genuine fears from the cynical manipulation of opinion in both countries.

In the Far East the coast was clearer. At first the status of the island of Sakhalin gave rise to friction with Japan. But in 1875 it was agreed that Japan would renounce its claim to the island in return for the Russian cession of those Kurile islands in its possession. This exchange put Russia in a strategic position at the mouth of the River Amur. At first, policy *vis-à-vis* China lay in the forceful hands of Muravyov-Amursky, appointed Governor-General of Eastern Siberia in 1847, and then of Admiral Putyatin and General Ignatiev. None of these three paid much attention to the directions emanating from remote St Petersburg – perhaps because they knew that only failure would be punished – and not much more to the treaties signed at various times between China and Russia. Muravyov himself extended the Russian area of occupation and penetration at the mouth of the River Amur and along its northern bank. This area was later reorganized as a Russian province and the Chinese were forced to accept it as a *fait accompli*. China was weakened by an attack from France and Britain over Canton (Gwangzhou) and Tonkin, and this helped the Russians forward. Putyatin and Ignatiev were able to force the Chinese to grant Russia the same trading rights won by the Western powers and the right also to maintain a legation at Peking (Beijing). Territorially, Russia acquired land along both banks of the Amur and a strip of coast on the Sea of Japan. Here, in 1861, was founded the naval base fittingly named Vladivostok – Commander of the East.

‘ The other important event in the Pacific at this time was the Russian sale of Alaska to the United States for $7,200,000. The territory, first settled in the 1780s, had over-extended Russian communications without proving particularly rewarding. Its sale was a financial necessity that had the added advantage of averting a collision with both Anglo-Saxon powers at a point where Russia was very vulnerable.

To return to Europe – and the perennial 'Eastern Question'. A somewhat similar situation confronted the Tsar as in central Asia and the Far East. Again the nominal autocrat showed himself unable to withstand emotional nationalistic forces. In Asia, it was the Russian version of the white man's burden, albeit without the racial exclusivity that marked Anglo-Saxon imperialism. In Europe, it was Pan-Slavism, a programme of quasi-imperialism masquerading as an ethnographical and historical theory that relied on Russian folk-memories of oppression at the hands of the Tatars. Moreover, Russia, like the other European powers, found that along with their gradual extra-European expansion, matters of foreign policy could no longer be divided into separate geographical areas. What happened at one point on the Russian periphery affected and was affected by what happened elsewhere. There was no longer one single identifiable Eastern Question to harass Anglo-Russian relations, for example, but a whole string of interrelated problems, ranging all the way from Tashkent to the Black Sea. It was part of the process whereby the impact of the conquering West made the world one. Russia, therefore, in its efforts to expand, would inevitably have to meet the same hostility at any point on its borders. On the other hand, it would also be aided by the conflicts among its neighbours. The success of Russian encroachment on China owed not a little to this factor.

In Europe, the same factor gave Russia the opportunity to overthrow the most humiliating condition imposed by the Treaty of Paris. The Russian government had never forgotten that Britain's insistence on the abolition of the Russian Black Sea navy had followed a similar insistence on the reduction of the Chinese navy after the Opium War. In other words, Palmerston had treated Russia like an Asiatic power. The Tsar and Gorchakov were agreed that the favourable conjuncture of circumstances present in 1870 was too good to miss. France had collapsed under the Prussian attack, and Prussia itself was to some degree indebted to Russia for the latter's part in preventing Austrian intervention. In the autumn of 1870 Gorchakov could, with impunity, send to the powers which had signed the Treaty of Paris a note repudiating its Black Sea provisions. At first there resulted a Russo-British diplomatic crisis but the Liberal government of Gladstone had no real intention of going to war for a provision in which it did not believe. Face was saved when a conference in London in 1871 rubber-stamped this solution. Henceforth both Turkey and Russia enjoyed the rights to maintain warships in the Black Sea and to erect fortifications and arsenals on its shores.

The principal flag-waver for Pan-Slavism was M. N. Katkov, the proprietor of *Moscow News*, one of the most influential conservative newspapers of nineteenth-century Russia. The theoretical foundations of Pan-Slavism were laid by others. Two books had special influence – General Fadayev's *Opinion on the Eastern Question* and, to a lesser extent, Danilevsky's *Russia and Europe*. Both argued, in summary terms, that the Russian historic mission was to form a federation of the Slav peoples through their liberation from the dominion of Turkey and Austria–Hungary. Given the repression exercised by Russia in Poland and the Ukraine, this programme had unwelcome and even revolutionary implications. For this reason, Pan-Slavism never won the tsar's favour. But it had such great appeal to influential circles of Russian society – primarily militarist and the official intelligentsia – that it acquired a momentum of its own, overriding the autocrat's hostility.

The test of Russian diplomatic *sangfroid* and military preparedness was not long delayed. The Treaty of Paris had replaced the Russian protectorate over the Christian population of the Balkans by a European guarantee. This proved worthless given that the British Conservatives insisted that the integrity of the Turkish bulwark against Russia mattered more than the fate of the Balkan Christians. In 1875 revolts broke out against Turkish rule in Bosnia and Herzegovina. The area of unrest gradually spread as rumour, atrocity, Pan-Slav agitation and aroused public opinion made their own specific influence felt. In April 1876, the Bulgarians also rose and around 12,000 men, women, and children were killed in the Turkish reprisals that followed. In the summer, Serbian and Montenegrin forces took the field against the Turks, with General Chernyayev, the victor of Tashkent, leading the Serbian army. This was clearly an attempt to force the hand of the Russian government.

The pressure of public opinion was fast converting the government to Pan-Slavism of a kind. The war that seemed increasingly inevitable was Russia's most altruistic war – far more than the great national emergencies of 1610, 1812 or 1941 when the Russians were forced to fight for survival and when they had every prospect of help from powerful allies. Of course there were ulterior motives. Pan-Slav gentry and bureaucrats hoped to divert popular discontent and the intelligentsia hoped that autocracy would reveal its incompetence to the people. For both groups, the coming war offered opportunities for organization and propaganda that the government found difficulty in suppressing. There was no doubt that the cause of the Balkan Christians was immensely popular with the worker and peasant masses also, for they contributed their money and themselves on a massive scale. British Conservatives who suspected the Russian government of wanting war were wide of the mark. Both Finance and War Ministries were aghast at the prospect. The Austrians had gone out of their way to indicate that Russia could make no significant gains for itself from a war. But such was the popular mood that the government had no choice but to fight if it was to retain the respect of its subjects.

At the beginning of 1877 the Serbs were thrown back on Belgrade and the Montenegrin valleys penetrated by Turkish forces. Both were overwhelmed by floods of refugees from other Turkish provinces. After a brief diplomatic pause, the Russians themselves openly declared war on Turkey. Russian prestige was fully committed when the Tsar and his sons joined the Danubian Army. They launched a two-front attack – in the Balkans, in alliance with Romania, and in Transcaucasia, where the Russo-Turkish frontiers met. The war revealed the uneven quality of the half-reformed Russian army and its commanders. It took Miliutin's cool head to correct several disastrous errors and to see that financial and diplomatic considerations did not get forgotten in the heat of warfare. For the Russian people, the images that remained – reinforced by Vershchagin's graphic paintings and Tchaikovsky's *Marche Slave* – were those of weeping Bulgarians greeting their liberators with bread, salt and flowers; Russian soldiers and Bulgarian militiamen manhandling cannon over the Shipka Pass in forty degrees of frost and Baroness Julia Vrevskaya paying the supreme penalty in her efforts to nurse the victims of wounds and cholera.

The Russians gained a military victory over the Turks and imposed the interim Treaty of San Stefano. The Russian government was perfectly well aware that the settlement would have to be ratified by the powers, given the impossibility of fighting both Britain and Austria with an army that had already suffered heavy casualties and with an empty treasury. The result was the Treaty of Berlin of 1878. This confirmed the independence of Serbia, Montenegro, and Romania with improved borders. Russia gained the small section of southern Bessarabia that separated her from the mouths of the Danube and also Kars and Ardahan in Transcaucasia. But the biggest difference between the two treaties lay in the reduction of Bulgaria, much of which was restored to the Turks, while the remainder was divided into two zones enjoying varying degrees of autonomy. The second major difference was the reward paid by Turkey to the two powers which had saved it from total surrender: Austria gained a protectorate over Bosnia and Herzegovina while Britain gained Cyprus. These arrangements, time would show, brought no stability to the Balkans. While the Russian government found these terms a regrettable necessity, the bulk of Russian society found them intolerable and blamed them on Gorchakov's senility. The autocracy was not helped by the knowledge that the Grand Dukes had not, in the main, justified their appointments to senior commands. Russian diplomats were disconcerted by the diplomacy of Bismarck who now sought to recruit Austria as an ally in creating a German hegemony in central and Eastern Europe; the seeds of the Franco-Russian alliance were sown at the Congress of Berlin.

LITERATURE AND REVOLUTION

The missionary idea at the heart of Pan-Slavism had its revolutionary counterpart. If Danilevsky could say that Russia would set an example to the world by creating a united Slav civilization, then, for their part, the radical intelligentsia saw another instrument of salvation in the peasant commune. This co-operative form of landholding would preserve Russia from the bane of a landless proletariat, inhibit the growth of individualism and herald the birth of a Russian socialism *sui generis*. It is symptomatic of the relationship between Western ideas and Russian ideologies that the central feature of a revolutionary thought, the commune itself, was discovered for them by a senior civil servant from Prussia and then idealized by a generation of the intelligentsia. The virtues of the commune were a staple theme of the thought of the 1860s and 1870s. The new age was utilitarian, or, as the music-critic Stasov had it, 'Populism, idealism, realism' was to be the radical reply to Uvarov's trinity. A typical phenomenon of the time was the Society of Wandering Exhibitions – best remembered for Kramskoy's idealized portraits of peasants – which broke with academic art in 1863 to take art to the people. The function of art and literature underwent a certain vulgarization, as compared with Belinsky's theories, and was redefined as the service of society. Values and morals became a creation of the needs of society. The noblest calling was that of the practitioner of some branch of the natural sciences. The urge that service to society constituted the true and ultimate aim of life dominated all minds.

A passage from Dostoyevsky's *The Devils* gives some idea of the intellectual ferment of the 1860s:

They talked of the abolition of the censorship, and of phonetic spelling, of the substitution of the Latin characters for the Russian alphabet . . . of splitting Russia into nationalities, united in a free federation: of the abolition of the Army and Navy, of the restoration of Poland as far as the Dnieper, of the peasant reforms and of the Manifestoes, of the abolition of the hereditary principle and of the family, of children, of priests, of women's rights.

In the end, what crystallized out of all this was a broad sentiment in favour of Populism. It had as its *point de départ* the conviction that a revolution must come, that the revolution would be socialist and that its institutional kernel would be the peasant commune. The driving-force behind all this would be the people, conceived of as the peasantry. This was an echo of Slavophile teaching.

Populism emerged at a time when modern 'scientific' methods of investigating social phenomena were only just beginning to be applied to Russian conditions. It offered no exact prescriptions; it also suffered from a basic dichotomy, between self-assertion and self-abnegation. Could the world be remade best through the individual's capacity to lead and inspire; or should not the individual seek to sink and steep himself or herself in the mass, transforming it from within? These were the two poles of agitational activity to which corresponded two types of political activity: terrorism, or pilgrimages *en masse* to the people. To this there further corresponded two views of the State: was it a Jacobin instrument of coercion or a retrograde survival that must be done away with, in a spirit of anarchism?

Who were the mentors of the revolutionaries in the new decades? At the end of the fifties and the beginning of the sixties, Herzen's *The Bell*, the Russian journal that he published in London, won an extraordinary circulation in Russia, dominating the thought of the younger generation. But Herzen lost much of his influence when his support for the Tsar was undermined by the terms of the Act of Emancipation and also through his support for the Polish Revolt of 1863. But to the Populist movement he left his faith in the commune as a Russian form of socialism that would preserve humanity from both the all-powerful State and the perils of individualism, and two slogans of immense historical resonance: 'To the People' and 'Land and Liberty'. Whether Herzen would have approved of the use to which they were put is a very different matter. In Russia, the future belonged to revolutionaries of a more practical and narrower stamp and outlook. They were less Olympian and European than Herzen, but more in touch with the realities of political life in Russia and more prepared to subordinate their personalities to the exigencies of organizations – especially the women.

In the sixties the iconoclast *par excellence* was the young Dmitri Pisaryov, scion of a gentry family. He scorned all dogma and authority, all aesthetic and metaphysical theory, all religion and morals. The voice of reason and the principles of natural sciences were humanity's sole guide to conduct. To be a 'thinking realist' represented the highest ideal. This led to the most obvious kind of utilitarianism. Down with the romantic view of the artist as an inspired creator, exulted Pisaryov! A poet was nothing more than a craftsman. Better be a shoemaker than a Raphael, for at least the shoemaker created something useful. Nature was not a temple to be revered but a workshop to be dominated. Music, painting, and the arts were illusions, only to be savoured by aesthetes blind and deaf to the human suffering around them.

This doctrine was too individualistic to be fully acceptable over a period, but its inculcation of the ideal of service to the community fitted in with Populist thinking. It was an admirable antidote to the self-indulgent ethos which much of the intelligentsia had picked up from the gentry. Further impetus, in the same sense, came from Nicholas Chernyshevsky, the son of a priest. He was born in 1828 in Saratov and educated in an ecclesiastical seminary. He rapidly threw off Orthodox dogma and emerged as one of the foremost intellectual leaders of the day, radiating an influence that survived twenty years' Siberian exile. Although primarily an economist, what gave Chernyshevsky his influence was his vastly popular didactic novel *What is to be Done?* (1863). This was actually written during the author's imprisonment in the Peter-Paul Fortress in St Petersburg. The directing ideas were taken from Robert Owen, Fourier, John Stuart Mill – whose *Principles of Political Economy* Chernyshevsky had translated into Russian – and William Godwin, the English anarchist. The theme and message are purely Russian, however. The heroine, Vera Pavlovna, the new emancipated woman, studies medicine and runs a co-operative of seamstresses. Kirsanov, the hero, is a free-thinking physician. Rakhmetov, an aristocrat, who has gone over to the people and devotes himself unreservedly to their welfare, is the real key to the novel. He sleeps on a bed of nails to develop his powers of endurance; he will eat no food but what would be consumed by the poorest peasant; he will renounce all pleasure for the sake of the cause. However lifeless in art (though based on a real personality), in real life Rakhmetov becomes the prototype of many a self-sacrificing young person in the revolutionary movement.

The philosophic sanction for self-sacrifice by the more gifted in the cause of the humble came from Professor Peter Lavrov, a teacher of mathematics at the Artillery School in Moscow. His *Historical Letters* appeared in 1868–9 and won even more popularity than *What is to be Done?* He counselled his readers to abstain from the direct political struggle but to stake their all on the social revolution; he did not exhort them to violence. The objective conditions for revolt already existed in the misery of the masses. What was needed was to awaken the masses to the subjective awareness of their misery, and this was the duty of the educated minority. They had acquired their education and culture at the expense of the downtrodden, and now they must repay their debt. They must show the masses the way to a new social order that would transform their status. And by so doing, the minority would at the same time be fulfilling its true function. This was the rationale of repentance.

As always in Russia, intellectual ferment both erupted into and was fed by the novel. The themes of the intellectuals *vis-à-vis* the peasantry are met with, for example, in Leskov's topical novels, such as *Nowhere to Go* and *At Daggers Drawn* and also in Gleb Uspensky's *Power of the Soil*. But it is in the work of the great novelists of the period – Turgenev, Dostoyevsky, and Tolstoy – that the full force of Populist themes and types is dominant.

Turgenev's work, in particular, can be seen as a spectrum, reflecting the whole gamut of intellectual evolution. In his first long novel *Rudin* (1855), he had portrayed the superfluous man of the forties – a *beau parleur*, an idealist, a romantic with no firm footing in reality. In *On the Eve* he showed Insarov, the strong man, who is significantly not a Russian but a Bulgarian, preparing to fight for his country's liberty against the Turks. It is typical of Turgenev's pessimism and detachment that Insarov, who is tubercular, never gets to Bulgaria but dies in Venice. It is Elena, Insarov's Russian fiancée, who takes up the dead man's work.

Vera Pavlovna and Elena, together with the heroine of Nekrasov's poem *Sasha*, were typical of a new phenomenon in Russian literature – the strong woman who succeeds where a man fails. This mirrored a real phenomenon: all too often, the men of the radical intelligentsia were enervated by too much education and a sense of guilt while the women, less spoiled and less guilty, were more effective personalities.

In *Fathers and Sons* (1862), his famous novel on conflict between the generations, Turgenev went one step further and depicted Bazarov, a Russian man of action, representative of his generation, the man of the sixties. Bazarov is a doctor, a realist, and a practical man who shuns all transcendentalism and whose aim is the mastery of nature. This was the novel that launched the term 'nihilist' with its celebrated definition: 'A Nihilist is a man who does not bow before any authorities, who does not accept any single principle on trust, however much respect surrounds this principle.' But in the end the self-styled nihilist and would-be master of nature himself falls victim to nature. Bazarov dies of typhus contracted while attending the stricken peasantry.

This ironical conclusion and the author's love–hate relationship to Bazarov brought down on Turgenev's head the wrath of both camps. To the men of the left, Bazarov was a caricature of their ideals; to those of the right, a monster, an upstart *révolté*. The furore testified to the acuteness with which Turgenev had discerned a type. In later works his ambivalence to political trends lost some of its detachment, and in *Smoke* and *Virgin Soil* he went over to the direct satire of all Populist types. In the end this coalesced with a sense of the futility of action and of the unreal, impalpable, evanescent, smoke-like nature of life, especially Russian life: '. . . Everything is hurrying away, everything is speeding off somewhere – and everything vanishes without a trace, without ever achieving anything . . .'

Neither Tolstoy nor Dostoyevsky ever identified his work with any special political theme, to the same extent as Turgenev did. But since their major novels appeared in the sixties and seventies, and since neither was at all aloof from contemporary topics, it was inevitable that their works would reflect some aspects at least of Populist sentiment. In Tolstoy this took the form of an idealization of the virtues of rural life and of its chief exponent, the peasant. In the Rousseauesque spirit, a consistent theme of Tolstoy's writings was the opposition of nature and civilization, the former alone inspiring life and fertility. Who is it, for example, who saves Levin in *Anna Karenina* from spiritual torment and suicide but an illiterate unreflecting peasant? Who is it but the peasant Platon Karataev in *War and Peace* who incarnates a deeper wisdom and greater power than any general or thinker? This is precisely because the peasants have not been subjected to the debilitating effects of civilization and can thus, *en masse*, act as a regenerating historical force.

Dostoyevsky was the most distinguished of the recanting intellectuals of Russian culture. His perception of the inhumane possibilities of socialism led him to take his stand at the other wing of Russian messianism – the Pan-Slav movement with the Russian Army as its instrument, its deification of the autocracy, and its invocation of God and the Orthodox Church. Here was 'a true preacher of the knout', to borrow a phrase from Belinsky.

Dostoyevsky, like the revolutionaries, could talk of the Russian people's mission to rescue the world from the fate that had overtaken the West. But when Dostoyevsky wrote, 'God will save Russia. Salvation will come from the people, from their faith and their humility', this was no Populist panegyric. This was a call to throw off the sins of nihilism and to emerge as the only God-fearing and God-bearing nation of Europe, in fact as the Pan-European nation *par excellence*. When two such missions clashed, only one could survive. And the Orthodox Church, the autocracy, and the cause of Holy Russia were Dostoyevsky's response to the mission proclaimed by the enemy. If, as Dostoyevsky averred, 'God will save Russia', then there was no room for a competing saviour such as Chernyshevsky, a philosophical materialist who denied God.

'TO THE PEOPLE'

'The road of history is not the pavement of the Nevsky Prospect . . . He who fears dirty boots must not take part in public activity.' This dictum of Chernyshevsky proved itself again and again in the course of Russian history. A state of latent civil war became characteristic of Russian public life – waged now against dissident nationalities such as the Poles and Ukrainians; now against dissident religious groups such as the Old Believers; now against selected political groups such as the Populists; and now against selected social groups such as the peasants, students and emancipated women. Much of this had its counterpart, to a greater or lesser degree of severity, in any European country. But it was in Russia that the tension seemed to switch with unique rapidity from one affected area to another. The immense size of the country, the notional omnipotence of its government, the censorship and total absence of reliable information about the attitudes of key sections of the population all contributed to this atmosphere of paranoia.

In Russia, as in the Anglo-Saxon countries, the decline of the patriarchal family and the emancipation of low-status males had important consequences for upper- and middle-class women. Despite the harshness of the *Domostroy*, Russian noblewomen had performed tasks of real value for society when their husbands were away on state service. They had been managers of home and estate, with all its craft and trading activities, and teachers to their children. Many aspects of medicine, especially midwifery, had been in the hands of women also. The return of the gentry to their estates after 1762 had involved a reduction of scope for their wives. The first revolutionaries, the Decembrists, refused to permit the involvement of women in their activities. Their wives' insistence on sharing their Siberian exile became part of the legend of the whole revolutionary movement and helped to ensure that women were admitted as full participants into later phases of the movement. The emancipation of 1861 threatened women of the gentry with the loss of financial support and social standing that would once have found them eligible husbands. It did not guarantee them access to the newer worlds of professionalized education and medicine monopolized by men. In view of the demands of the gentry for greater political rights to compensate them for their loss of relative status, it would have been surprising had poorer noblewomen not reacted by demanding for themselves the same civil freedoms as male ex-serfs. They were joined by educated young women from the urban lower classes and from the upper echelons of the bureaucracy. Fathers who hoped that their relative wealth would enable them to keep their daughters in the condition of docile ignorance that had characterized an earlier generation were often cruelly disappointed. Despite the element of rebellion implicit in the emancipation of Russian women, the forms of emancipation they chose owed a great deal to the ethic of service they had acquired in their early years and which they internalized more successfully than most of their male counterparts.

Despite the smutty innuendoes of the ultra-right, only a tiny minority of emancipated Russian women showed any interest in sexual experimentation, though they might live with a man to whom they were not married by law. As compared with the aristocratic men who sneered at them, they were models of monogamous propriety. For a few individuals, smoking or wearing male clothing was an essential part of emancipation, but the great majority regarded these as undignified luxuries. What they all aspired to was civil independence – the right to visit their friends unchaperoned, the right to administer their own personal possessions, the right to live where they liked and with whom they liked. By a variety of means, including the occasional fictitious marriage, these rights were successfully asserted. Independence without sustenance was an impossibility, of course, but securing suitable employment was no easy matter. The appearance of a female librarian in the St Petersburg Public Library in the early 1860s was treated as a seven day wonder and demands were made for the dismissal of her husband from State service. In the main, the women gravitated towards education and medicine. The government had to permit them to qualify as midwives. Otherwise, it did all it could to hamper their progress, shutting the doors of the universities to them and recalling female medical students from the University of Zurich.

On the eve of the emancipation of the serfs, Maria Vernadskaya had drawn attention to the need for upper- and middle-class women to prepare themselves for work. Hers was an isolated voice, however, for in the main Russian women were content to leave the theorizing to men. As we have seen, a great deal of this was done in the fiction of the time by Turgenev (unwittingly) and intentionally by other writers. *What is to be Done?* and *Sasha* were formative influences for a whole generation of Russian women. The major theorist of Russian feminism in the sixties was Mikhail Mikhailov, whose article *Women, their Education and Importance in Family and Society*, published in 1860, outlined the nature of the past subjection of women and its corrupting effects on both sexes and portrayed a systematic programme for their emancipation. Those who went on to demand the abolition of marriage and the family were not widely supported. Russian feminism failed to develop an independent ideology at this time largely because of the warmth with which female emancipation was supported by the male intelligentsia, irrespective of politics. Liberal bureaucrats and professors conspired against the autocracy to set up courses for women excluded from universities while the underground revolutionaries welcomed them as equals into their para-military organizations. No doubt this was partly due to the frustration experienced by progressive men in attempting to change Russia, and to their need for allies from any quarter. On the whole, Russian women accepted that their own emancipation was bound up with the emancipation of the whole of Russian society from the grip of autocracy. At a practical level, women were more innovative, seeking in experimental communes and workshops to provide one another with employment as well as education and emotional support.

With the advent of rapid industrialization, lower-class women began to enter the factories in large numbers. In 1859 it was discovered that in the St Petersburg district 44 per cent of the workers in cotton-spinning factories and 34 per cent of those in the tobacco industry were women. They suffered the hardships of the men at work. In addition, they had no right to maternity leave and had to hand over their earnings to their husbands. These women were mostly 'invisible' to educated 'society', behind the barriers of the industrial settlements. Others were more difficult to miss, like the growing number of shop assistants and street-sweepers. Some educated women did try to make contact with the factory workers, though their male comrades tried hard to dissuade them. After a week's factory work, Betya Kaminskaya was described as 'pale, thin, and worn out, but remarkably pleased with herself and very talkative'. Such pioneers had to put up with the suspicions of the supervisors, the indignities of body searches and the obscenities of the male workers. They rarely stayed long. When they did make contact with the workers intellectually, it was with the men. With few exceptions, Russian women of the lower classes were still too inhibited and too concerned with the daily struggle for survival to assert themselves in broader questions, let alone run the gauntlet of the men in the bars where working men discussed them. There were portents of a new attitude even among them, however. Factory women constituted a quarter of the pupils at the unofficial 'Sunday schools' in the early 1860s at which members of the radical intelligentsia taught literacy and socialism. It was typical of the autocracy, even in its most liberal phase, that it closed down these 'Sunday schools' in 1862 but took a further twenty years to begin to protect factory women from the worst abuses of industrial capitalism.

In the sixties violence between government and opposition was only sporadic and organized on a relatively minor scale. It was marked by a great deal of student unrest that led at times to the closure of the universities, to the temporary exile of the ringleaders, and the opening of a 'free university' in St Petersburg by some nonconformist socialist-minded professors.

At the same time illegal pamphlets, appeals, and proclamations appeared (*The Great Russian* and *Young Russia* were two of the best-known series – and a new legal publication, *People's Chronicle*), to give voice to the revolutionary aspirations of the day. It was symptomatic of the contemporary mood that the latter made no mention of the death of the Grand Duke Nicholas in 1865, whereas that of Abraham Lincoln, two days later, received prominent front-page treatment, surrounded by a mourning border. This somewhat inchoate movement produced the first political trial in Alexander I I's reign – a landmark in the period when the reforms were intended to inaugurate a new mood between the autocrat and his subjects. It was the trial of Mikhailov, theorist of feminism and part-author of a famous *Proclamation to the Younger Generation*. He was sentenced to penal servitude in Siberia, where he died. Pisarev was also arrested at this time; and Chernyshevsky was stilled for ever. A sentence of fourteen years' hard labour in Siberia and six years' exile left him a broken man when he eventually returned to European Russia.

The radicalism of the sixties found its sharpest expression in a secret ascetic group of terrorists known as 'Hell'; and in another group organized by Nechayev. Both derived a great deal of their inspiration from the anarchist, Bakunin. The first produced the sickly and ill-balanced student Karakozov, who made an unsuccessful and unauthorized attempt on the Tsar's life in April 1866 which provoked a wave of repression by the authorities. Nechayev's importance comes from the cell type of organization which he pioneered, and also from his collaboration with Bakunin in the compilation of the famous *Catechism of the Revolutionary*. This demanded of every member of the cause the uttermost subjection of the personality. The notorious Ivanov case showed how literally this must be taken. Ivanov, a student at the Agricultural Academy in Moscow and a member of one of Nechayev's cells, had a somewhat independent mind and even doubted at times the existence of a mysterious Central Committee in whose name Nechayev allegedly acted. This 'treason' to the cause – which, since the Committee had no existence, was in fact perfectly justifiable – provoked Nechayev into organizing Ivanov's murder. In this he involved the other members of his cell. Nechayev died after ten years' imprisonment but the incident was never forgotten by educated Russians.

Dilettantism of this type proved its own undoing, at least for a time. Not only did the revelations of the Nechayev trial discredit the radicals, but their impotence was all too clear. There was a reversion to propagandist activity of a more peaceful type, at the beginning of the seventies. In the meantime, the government had made a number of tactical errors which had the effect of further alienating its opponents. First, after renewed outbreaks of student unrest, it expelled large numbers of young men from the universities, depriving them of their professional aspirations, leaving them without career or subsistence, and virtually giving them no hope save for a transformation of society. Second, women students abroad were ordered to return home in 1873 – but not before they had absorbed the teachings of the exiled Russian revolutionaries, especially in Switzerland. Here were more recruits to the cause.

The reaction, not to say revulsion, from the conspiratorial underground, and explicitly political methods of Nechayev, led to the formation of a number of non-conspiratorial student circles. Informality and loose organization were their characteristics. Nicholas Chaikovsky and Mark Natanson founded two of the first circles in St Petersburg in 1869. Others spread to Kiev, Moscow, Kazan, and Odessa. Their members came from the intelligentsia of the upper and middle classes, with a sprinkling of army officers. One girl, Sophia Perovskaya, for example, was the daughter of a former Governor-General of St Petersburg. Prince Peter Kropotkin, the future revolutionary anarchist of ancient Russian lineage, was another member.

The primary purpose of these circles was self-education and self-betterment through study. The next step was to extend this process to the less privileged – the urban workers and peasants. The idea was to draw in the popular masses.

Gradually they came to the idea [writes Kropotkin] that the only way was to settle among the people and to live the people's life. Young men went into the villages as doctors, doctors' assistants, teachers, village scribes, even as agricultural labourers, blacksmiths, woodcutters, and so on, and tried to live there in close contact with the peasants. Girls passed teachers' examinations, learned midwifery or nursing, and went by the hundred into the villages, devoting themselves entirely to the poorest part of the population.

In Moscow, writes Stepniak, another participant in this movement, girls 'became common mill hands, wrought fifteen hours a day in Moscow cotton factories, endured cold, hunger and dirt ... in order that they might preach the new gospel as sisters and friends, not as superiors'.

Illegal libraries were set up, books and pamphlets distributed illegally and published illegally – the works of Marx, Proudhon, Lassalle, Lavrov, Louis Blanc. This all took place in the name of Lavrov, rather than that of Bakunin. Patient preparation and patient sowing of the socialist seed, conceived in a social not a political sense, must take precedence over direct revolutionary action. Besides, the crushing of the Paris Commune in 1871 served to reinforce the view that armed insurrection was foredoomed to failure and that a specifically Russian way must be found.

The opportunity came in the spring of 1874. The previous winter there had been a famine in the Volga region. This brought the ever-present sense of guilt to a new pitch of acuity. The result was an extraordinary phenomenon. Between two and three thousand of the intelligentsia, perhaps a quarter of them women, literally 'went to the people'. In a spontaneous elemental upsurge they put on peasant dress and tried to become one with the peasantry. To the crusaders it was not so much a political agitation, Stepniak wrote, but 'far more a mystical and religious movement'. The elite of Russian youth threw aside their careers, positions, and privileged past in order to spread the gospel of socialism.

One of the most durable myths propagated by Russian conservatives was the claim that the peasants responded to this crusade 'not merely with a lack of trust and a suspiciousness, but with open hostility, refusing the pamphlets handed out to them, arresting the propagandists and handing them over to the authorities'. The truth was more complex. Those of the intelligentsia who directly attacked God or the Tsar were usually shouted down by most peasants. Those who focused on taxations or the depredations of landowners had a much better hearing. A real process of mutual education took place when sensitive members of the intelligentsia and intelligent peasants discussed the practical difficulties of communal action and the joint ownership of property. Where they were denounced to the authorities, this was usually done by village priests or peasant elders who might be called to account for failing to inform.

The government's reaction to this remarkable movement showed that its confidence in the peasantry was strictly limited. It treated the movement as an attempted revolution. By the end of the autumn the police had their hands on more than 1,500 young people. Further arrests were made when a second 'going to the people' took place in 1875.

Two mass trials were staged – the 'Trial of the Fifty' in Moscow in the early part of 1877 and that of the 'Hundred and Ninety-Three' in St Petersburg in the autumn of the same year. The sentences were comparatively light, and most of the accused were acquitted. But there was no sign of any concession by the government to the Populists' demands. In these circumstances, there was a reversion to the type of theory and activity more popular in the sixties – that of a disciplined group with a quasi-terrorist outlook.

Through Natanson's inspiration in the main, the famous organization 'Land and Liberty' was founded in 1876. It demanded that the land be handed over to the peasants and that the State be destroyed in the name of collectivism. What this programme lacked in clarity it made up in organization. Here was a close-knit, disciplined, underground body, organized in regional groups with a membership of not much more than 200, with its own printing press, and network of secret sympathizers and fellow-travellers. A special 'disorganization group' existed to protect members from the police and to plan escapes if necessary. 'Disorganization' also included the assassination of informers and prominent members of the government. 'Land and Liberty' acted in the name of the people, in the true Populist tradition. But it had given up hopes of actually calling in the aid of the people, although, of course, it might and did exploit and encourage all symptoms of popular discontent. Thus one of its first acts was to stage a mass demonstration in front of the Kazan Cathedral in St Petersburg in 1876. More than 2,000 people saw and heard a young student of the St Petersburg Mining Academy, George Plekhanov, deliver a rousing speech and unfurl a red flag bearing the words: 'Land and Liberty'. A decade or so later, it was Plekhanov who would begin the assimilation of Marxism by the Russian intelligentsia.

The same demonstration was also important in giving, indirectly, powerful encouragement to terrorism. Among those arrested in the fracas before the Cathedral was a seasoned young revolutionary, Alexis Bogolyubov. Apparently, Bogolyubov was flogged for an act of personal discourtesy towards General Trepov, Governor of St Petersburg. This provoked a prison riot which was brutally suppressed. Public indignation was intense. A young woman, Vera Zasulich, took the law into her own hands and shot Trepov, wounding him seriously. She made no attempt to avoid arrest and trial. Hers had been an act of pure retribution. She knew neither the prisoner nor the General.

All of Petersburg society followed the Zasulich trial with bated breath. It was held under the new legal reforms of the 1860s, complete with jury and Russia's most distinguished liberal judge. The jury acquitted Zasulich, to the rejoicing, not only of the revolutionaries, but even of some officials and army officers – a most significant criterion of the isolation of the regime. After successfully pillorying the government in court, Zasulich completed its discomfiture by escaping to Switzerland in the mêlée that broke out at the end of the trial. It was of course a disaster for the unfortunate judge, Anatole Koni, and the other remaining liberals within the government. They were now totally discredited in the eyes of the Tsar.

Thereafter, all the trials of those resisting the authorities were to be conducted by military courts. This, together with the increasing use of administrative exile, was symptomatic of the increasing repression exercised by the police in their desperate struggle against the revolutionaries. Terrorist attempts grew bolder and bolder. In broad daylight, in the streets of St Petersburg, the famous Stepniak struck down General Mezentsov, a hero of the Crimea and Chief of the Third Section. In Kharkov, Goldenberg killed Prince Kropotkin, cousin to the anarchist and Governor-General of the city.

Logically, the policy of assassination must end in regicide; and in April 1879 a certain Alexander Solovyov did in fact fire at the Tsar. But he escaped unhurt. 'Land and Liberty' had given Solovyov the gun he used but not the authority to use it. This act, in conjunction with the growing terrorist wave, brought to a head the conflict inside the party on the whole policy of terrorism. In 1879, Plekhanov and Zasulich, with a small group of sympathizers, seceded from the party to form their own group – 'Black Partition' (i.e. all land to the peasants) – which would concentrate on agitation. 'Land and Liberty' was dissolved and a new organization took its place called 'People's Freedom'. Its programme described the aim of terrorism as 'lifting . . . the revolutionary spirit of the people and its faith in the success of the task . . . the Party must take upon itself the start of the overthrow and not wait for the moment when the people will be able to act without its aid'. 'History is terribly slow, it must be pushed forward', said Zhelyabov, one of the terrorists.

The Executive Committee of the new party concentrated its energy on the assassination of the Tsar. He was formally condemned to death in the late summer of 1879. But not until two years later did the terrorists actually carry out the 'execution'. 'People's Freedom' organized at least seven attempts on the Tsar's life before succeeding. The plotters favoured dynamite and high explosives, made popular in Russia through the war with Turkey. The fatal blow came on 1 March 1881. The Tsar was returning from watching two Guards battalions at their manoeuvres. As his carriage and its mounted escort passed along the Catherine Embankment, the first bomb was thrown. But it killed only one of the Cossack escorts and a butcher's boy. The Tsar stepped out of his carriage to have a closer look at the attacker, pinned against a wall, and also the two victims. This took perhaps five minutes. The Tsar then turned to re-enter his carriage and the second bomb was thrown. This was the fatal explosion. He died an hour or so later.

'The nightmare that had weighed down on Young Russia for ten years had vanished', was the sentiment of Vera Figner, a participant in the plot, when she heard of the Tsar's death. But despite all the éclat of success, it was not to terrorism that the future belonged but to the followers of the secessionist, Plekhanov and his pupil, Lenin.

CHAPTER 11

Dress Rehearsal for Revolution

One assassination – even that of a tsar – does not make a revolution. The *coup* unleashed none of the upheaval feared by the government and longed for by the revolutionaries. The masses in town and country failed to budge. The terrorists' appeal to the new Tsar, Alexander III, to call a national assembly and institute a free social order, in return for which they, the terrorists, would suspend their activity, also fell on deaf ears. At both levels – as threat or as trigger – terrorism had failed and was, inevitably, discredited. It did not cease entirely. Alexander Ulyanov, the elder brother of the future Lenin, was executed in 1887 for a plot against the Tsar; nearly twenty years later, the young Socialist revolutionary, Maria Spiridonova, successfully assassinated a brutal provincial governor. Both these incidents had important indirect effects on events to come. At intervals during the three decades after 1881 ministers and lesser dignitaries were picked off by devotees of various populist organizations. But terrorism, as the force that would produce the revolution, died at the moment of its greatest apparent success.

The cause of revolution made a quicker recovery from the general radical discredit. By the end of the century scattered Marxist groups were at work in the Empire of all the Russias, to say nothing of the intensive study of Marxist thought in progress at Geneva and elsewhere. The populists had re-emerged in the guise of a Socialist Revolutionary (S.R.) Party which sought to unite old conspiratorial traditions with modern appeals to a mass audience. Liberal professors and elected members of the zemstvo boards began to plan for peaceful revolution. Similar developments among the non-Russian half of the population posed an increasingly serious challenge to the authorities. A race for the future developed. To whom did the twentieth century belong? To the Tsar or to the revolutionaries? In this contest it soon became clear that the multifarious opposition reacted to changing circumstances far more flexibly than did the government.

All through the nineteenth century one of the most remarkable features of the autocracy was its loss of zeal, its virtual inability to react, its blind adherence to the *status quo*. As compared with earlier periods, it was blessed with a wealth of talent and intelligence shown, for example, in the rapid and successful arrangements made in 1906 for the election of Russia's first modern parliament, the Duma. The Russian Imperial archives are littered with percipient analyses of social, economic and political problems and dire warnings of the consequences of a failure to tackle them. Yet at precisely this moment in its history the autocracy became most clearly identified with one social class, the declining landed aristocracy and gentry, convinced that they stood for Russia and that only policies that slowed down their own decline could save the country.

Increasing scepticism about autocracy called forth a new *rationale* of absolutism in Russia. Its spokesman was Konstantin Pobedonostsev, lay head of the Orthodox Church and one of the models for Dostoyevsky's Grand Inquisitor. He proclaimed a pure theory of repression, decrying freedom of the Press, constitutionalism, rationalism, the goodness of human nature, and exalting the virtues of Orthodoxy, the family, obedience, and governmental coercion. Come hell and high water, the autocracy must be preserved as the safeguard of the Russian future – this was Pobedonostsev's constant refrain to Alexander III and Nicholas II, whom he served as tutor, confidant, and adviser. For him, the reforms of Alexander II were a 'criminal error' and it was he who set out to dominate, or rather to smother, the social and cultural life of the 1880s.

In their own way, Pobedonostsev's Imperial pupils were also populists. For them the ideal Russian was not the cultured aristocrat who graced the court of Catherine but an idealized version of the Russian peasant steeped in superstition and prejudiced against women and foreigners. They preferred to spend their time in peaceful, bourgeois pursuits with their own immediate families but they enjoyed the company of peasant serving men as well. Alexander III was almost the only heir to the Russian throne to express himself vociferously in his own father's councils and come to no harm. His bearish mannerisms and inflexible will were not really redeemed by his interest in and support for the less politically committed writing and music of his time. It cannot be an entire accident that the strong-willed Alexander III was followed by his weak but obstinate son Nicholas II, just as Alexander II had followed Nicholas I. Nicholas II had firm opinions which he kept close to his chest and avoided unpleasant scenes by sacking unwanted ministers by letter. Both Alexander and Nicholas believed devoutly in the virtues of autocracy and both looked to scapegoats, particularly the Jews whom they loathed, to explain the difficulties that beset them.

The first victim of the new reactionary course was a semi-constitutional project drawn up by Loris-Melikov, the Minister of the Interior. It had actually been approved by Alexander II on the eve of his assassination. At the very beginning of the new reign both the project and the Minister were consigned to oblivion. In many ways Alexander III harked back to the dark days of Nicholas I, with their slogan of 'autocracy, orthodoxy and nationalism'. But it was now incomparably more difficult. A more mature opposition had developed in the meantime; and the taste for freedom and local self-government and a relaxed censorship, however circumscribed, was not lightly lost. On the contrary, the emergence of intelligentsias among the national minorities and, in the 1890s, among the workers and peasants, ensured the ultimate failure of the policies of reaction.

To achieve the same result, Alexander's regime had therefore to be far more repressive than that of Nicholas. The first move was an attempt to re-assert the power of the landed nobility and the bureaucracy in the countryside. A new official post was created – that of land captain. He was picked as far as possible from the ranks of the local nobility and exercised judicial and administrative functions. The regime did away with the Justices of the Peace, except in the larger towns, their functions being assimilated to those of the land captains. The latter in fact wielded wellnigh despotic power in the villages.

This was in 1889. The next year saw the revision of the constitution of the zemstva so as to guarantee paramount power to the noble element and correspondingly diminish the peasant element.

Two years later, in a similar spirit, the government raised the property qualification for voters to the organs of municipal self-government. In order to bolster the waning economic power of the nobility, a Nobles' Bank had been founded in 1885. This made loans to landowners at far more favourable terms than did the Peasant Bank. (The latter made loans to peasants to enable them to purchase land over and above their allotment.) The kind of thinking prevalent in high government circles was graphically illustrated by a circular issued by Delyanov, the Minister of Education in 1887, banning lower-class children from secondary schools:

... children of coachmen, servants, cooks, washerwomen, small shop-keepers, and persons of a similar type, whose children, perhaps with the exception of those gifted with unusual abilities, should certainly not be brought out of the social environment to which they belong.

The same motives inspired an attack on the independence of the judiciary and the inviolability of the courts. Emergency powers, military tribunals, a tighter hold over the judges, granting powers to administrative officials – these were typical of the methods used. Refusing Jews the right to practise at the bar was another device.

The government gave equal attention to the spread of ideas at every level – from the village elementary school to the university, from the newspaper to the workers' free library and reading-room. Each sign of intellectual life that threatened to diverge from or contradict the official patriotic line fell under closer and closer supervision. University autonomy was undermined, the Press censorship tightened, village schools subjected to the Holy Synod, and the provision of reading-rooms subordinated to the whim of provincial governors.

With the emergence of national intelligentsias among nearly all the minority peoples, the government had either to concede the need for some local autonomy in the vulnerable borderlands or else seek to convert these new forces to its own beliefs. The upshot was a vigorous policy of Russification. In the Ukraine, White Russia, Lithuania, and Poland, the teaching of the vernacular was restricted or forbidden in schools and the use of Russian enforced. In the Baltic provinces, Livonia, Estonia and Courland, the government exercised similar discrimination against the German element. Forced conversions from Lutheranism to Greek Orthodoxy were common. The Russian nonconformist sects, such as the Doukhobors, the Molokany, and the Stundists, had to suffer religious oppression, deportation, and imprisonment.

It was probably the Russian Jews who now had to undergo the worst torments. Concentrated in the western and southern provinces of the Empire, in the so-called Pale of Settlement, and living at a miserably low level of existence as factory proletariat or in the interstices of the economy – they were petty traders, innkeepers, tailors, cobblers, cabinet-makers – the Jews were exposed, more than any other of the minority peoples, to all the tensions that accumulated in the final decades of tsarist rule. (This did not inhibit members of the Imperial family from investing in profitable companies run by Russia's few wealthy Jews.)

Antisemitism had been endemic in the Russian south-west for generations. But it had only constituted 'a problem' since the partitions of Poland at the end of the eighteenth century, when perhaps a million Jews were incorporated in the Russian Empire. The tsars and tsarinas had unsuccessfully sought to assimilate these newly acquired Jewish subjects. In fact, the Jewish population, despite the various forms of often inhumane treatment to which it was subjected, increased in number, reaching some six millions by the end of the nineteenth century. Moreover, a recognizable Russo-Jewish intelligentsia emerged, particularly when the reforms of the 1860s facilitated entry to Russian schools and universities. In music (the Rubinstein brothers), art (Leonid Pasternak, Mark Antokolsky, Isaac Levitan), journalism and literary criticism (Michael Gershenzon), politics and law (in all parties from the Kadets leftwards) and in literature, writing in Russian, Hebrew, or Yiddish, Jewish participation was evident. But this was for the favoured few. The Jewish masses within the Pale of Settlement lived amidst increasing poverty that for large numbers came close to destitution. It was they who bore the torments of persecution. Even so, what happened after the assassination of Alexander II was unprecedented. A Jewish girl, Hessia Helfmann, had been one of Alexander's assassins. This was some sort of pretext for the ensuing pogroms. In circumstances that are far from clear (it would certainly be simplistic to cast the Jews as a designated scapegoat for the failings of the regime) the Jews in the southern and eastern Ukraine particularly were subjected to physical violence that brought death, injury, and destruction to a multitude of localities. The army and police stood idly by, in the spring and summer of 1881. The outrages were at their worst in Kiev. One-third of the Jews must die, one-third emigrate, and one-third assimilate, said Pobedonostsev. At the end of the year and early in 1882 the movement spread to Warsaw and Podolia.

Government committees of inquiry predictably discovered that the Jews themselves were to blame and the so-called 'May Laws' followed. These forbade Jews to settle in rural districts, even within the Jewish Pale of Settlement. Within the next decade, repressive and discriminatory laws fell thick and fast on the hapless Jews – for example, the quota system in schools and universities, exclusion from the bar, and, for Jewish doctors, exclusion from employment with public authorities, the loss of franchise rights in zemstvo and municipality. The process reached its climax in 1891 and 1892 when, without warning and in bitter winter, the government evicted many thousands of Jewish artisans from Moscow and cleared the Jews from a wide belt of territory on the western frontiers. The Jews were forcibly 'resettled' in the ghettoes of the interior.

Among the measures suggested by the luckless Loris-Melikov had been proposals to ease the burden of redemption payments on the peasantry. These proposals were denounced by Pobedonostsev on the grounds that they might weaken the moral fibre of the peasants by reducing their respect for their obligations. Alexander III therefore insisted on re-checking the studies of his father's experts before reducing the redemption payments and eliminating the poll-tax. The government also made it easier, partly through the Peasant Bank and through the removal of legal restrictions, for village communes to rent or buy additional land.

On the other hand, the commune was preserved, with all its power over the individual member. Until 1903, for example, a peasant still had to obtain a passport to leave his or her village and work outside it. In other respects, the commune was artificially preserved from the free play of economic forces by prohibiting the sale or mortgage of its land except with special administrative permission, and then such sales could be made only to peasant purchasers. But the attempt to 'freeze' the commune could not overcome the division into rich and poor that was steadily making itself more and more obvious among the peasants. Its economic strength sapped by the government's own policies, the rural population was tied to intermittent unproductive work on plots that were increasingly over-exploited in view of the low level of agrarian technology. With the constant increase in rural population, the peasant's allotments proved more and more inadequate. It was the great famine of 1891 that prodded 'society' out of ten years of torpor while the agrarian upheavals of 1902 signalled the eve of the first Russian Revolution. This was the peasantry that made such an important contribution to the upheaval of 1905 and the final cataclysm of 1917.

The contrast between agriculture and industry was startling, though causally connected. The first stagnated, the second flourished. Under the inspiration of Sergei Witte, an outstanding negotiator and organizer, all branches of Russian industry and production showed a remarkable upsurge in the nineties. It was Witte who insisted that the rural population must pay for the rapid industrialization of Russia.

Witte, born in 1849, began his career as a student of mathematics at the University of Tiflis (now Tblisi). Thence he became a clerk in the ticket-office of the Odessa Railways Company. From this curious rung he climbed higher and higher in railway administration and logistics, earning special praise for his handling of troop movements in the Russo-Turkish war of 1878. He passed into the Civil Service in 1891 as Director of the Railway Department in the Ministry of Finance. The next year he became in rapid succession Minister of Transport and Minister of Finance. During the Revolution of 1905, he become Russia's first Prime Minister and attempted to introduce cabinet government to Russia.

Witte's superiority in the government was so manifest that he was for all practical purposes the Tsar's chief minister. While Pobedonostsev was retained as ideological policeman, the tone was increasingly set by Witte. In Russian conditions his economic policies were truly revolutionary, though the harsh taxation policies of his predecessors had already begun to stabilize the Russian currency. Witte convinced Alexander III that Russia's only hope of remaining a great power lay in the development of heavy industry and modern communications. Between 1892 and 1900 two-thirds of the government's expenses went on economic development, mostly of the railways; the railways were of course the main consumers of the products of heavy industry. In the absence of a developed capital market in Russia, Witte turned to Western Europe for investment. In this, he was spectacularly successful: foreign investment in Russia leapt from 97·7 million rubles in 1880 to 214·7 million in 1890, and to 911 million at the turn of the century. Foreign investment could only be secured if the ruble was convertible into gold and this was achieved in 1896. Convertibility could only be maintained if Russia preserved a positive balance of payments. To achieve this, Witte maintained a system of taxation that was indirect and regressive and that depended to a large extent on the alcohol monopoly which he reintroduced in 1894. It was this, together with the redemption payments, which forced the peasants to market their produce; had they consumed at the standard enjoyed by the peasants of central Europe, Russia would have had to *import* food.

To overcome the uncompetitiveness of Russian industry, Witte also continued to impose higher tariffs on imported manufactured goods than existed elsewhere in Europe. Naturally, this did nothing to create the kind of dynamic market in the countryside that Russian industry would require once the helping hand of foreign finance was removed. Altogether, the Russian economy, even at the moment when it was making the greatest efforts to evade colonial status, remained dependent on the capitalist West. As late as 1913 three-quarters of Russian exports were still derived from agriculture and forestry. The whole of Witte's strategy depended on the export of grain at a time when world grain prices were fluctuating and often low. All the same, he had some spectacular successes. The epic construction of the Trans-Siberian Railway will never be forgotten by the Russians.

A few figures are enough to show the astonishing upsurge in production as Russia prepared to enter the twentieth century. In the last decade of the old century the smelting of pig-iron increased in Russia by 190 per cent (the equivalent rate for Germany was 72, for the United States 50, for England 18). By 1900 Russia had moved up from seventh to fourth place in world production. The same applies to the production of iron, coal, oil, and cotton. In every case the rate of growth in Russia far outstripped that of any other nation. Part of this fantastic rate derives, of course, from a low starting-point. Even so, the picture remains striking. In its general lines of development the same characteristics prevailed as in the earlier period, but to an intensified degree – the emphasis being on heavy industry, particularly railroad and rolling-stock construction, the concentration of industry in large units of production, the great extent of governmental financial participation, and the influx of foreign capital. It is remarkable, for example, that by 1902, 49·8 per cent of the factory workers were engaged in factories employing a thousand or more workers. The number of such factories had increased between 1879 and 1902 by 123 per cent. The growth in productivity was concentrated in the larger units.

The government, as ever, took a particularly important part in railroad construction. Not only did it issue special loans for this purpose, but it also guaranteed the interest on private railroad loans. In addition, the Treasury was authorized to buy from private railroad companies both their more important and their less profitable lines. The bulk of the investment capital came from direct and indirect taxes and from the deposits in the State savings banks. There developed a special form of State capitalism with particular interests in railroads, and, through the railroads, in all the ramifications of heavy industry. The State's participation in industry went even further. It founded credit institutions. At the State-owned mines in the Urals, Siberia, and the Altai it processed ores for industrial purposes.

During the years 1891 to 1894, the Franco-Russian Alliance took shape. This decisive alteration in the European balance of power was dictated largely by strategic considerations, by French fears of a second Sedan and Russian resentment at German support for Austria in the Balkans. As usual, however, economics walked hand-in-hand with politics. It was German industry that was hardest hit by Russia's high tariff wall while the French rentier class proved more willing to invest in their Russian ally than in their own industry. This was the background to the astonishing influx of foreign capital in the 1890s. France and Belgium together accounted for the bulk of foreign investments at this period, followed by Germany and Great Britain. The absolute figures are obscure, but it is estimated that foreign investors supplied something more than one-third of all company capital during 1890, a proportion which, by 1900, had risen to nearly one-half. In some industries, such as mining, it actually exceeded the participation of Russian capital. And of course it was not only capital that came from abroad: Russian industry could also profit from the most advanced technical innovations of the West, could use its technicians, its managers, its manifold specialists. Russia jumped several stages in industrial development in a few decades.

Eight main industrial areas developed: the Moscow region – predominantly textile in character; St Petersburg – metallurgical and machine-building; the Polish region – textiles, coal, chemicals; Krivoi Rog and Donets – coal, iron-ore, basic chemicals; the Ural mining region; the Baku petroleum region; the sugar-beet area of the south-west; and the manganese region of Transcaucasia.

The human accompaniment to all this was a sudden, gigantic growth in the size of the urban working class. It more than doubled between 1865 and 1890, increasing not only faster than the population as a whole, but also at a faster rate than the urban population. In the next decade the rate accelerated even more. By the beginning of the twentieth century, the total was touching on two and a quarter million. By now, also, a hereditary working class, or true proletariat was coming into being. Of course the rapidity of industrialization meant that many workers were still only seasonally employed in industry, while many more continued to think in peasant categories. The immigration of workers from Great Russia into industrial centres in the Ukraine and Baku was accompanied by the emergence of some national tensions. With few exceptions, the workers continued to look to the Tsar to alleviate harsh conditions they blamed on their employers.

The workers' dwelling quarters in the new industrial centres were fantastically overcrowded, unhygienic and squalid. The workers were herded into factory barracks, fed in factory canteens, and forced to take their wages in the form of goods and foodstuffs. The conditions were much worse for women than for men. A Moscow study carried out in the early 1880s found male cotton-spinners spending only one-third of their incomes on food while female spinners spent two-thirds, yet the female spinners ate only 71 per cent of the protein and 65 per cent of the fat eaten by male spinners. In view of the greater docility and lower cost of female workers, employers often preferred them to men, yet neither the male workers nor their intellectual mentors raised the issue of equal pay. More surprising was the failure to provide any form of support for pregnant women and nursing mothers. The first factory act of 1882 seemed more concerned to limit the hours worked by children than to protect women. The newly created factory inspectorate published just one report; its findings were so disquieting that they were regarded as subversive by the government and future reports forbidden.

In the pages that follow, we will examine the responses of the intellectual leaders to the changes taking place in Russian society and their attempts to influence the workers and peasants through publications and political parties. It would be an error to see the Russian workers as an inert mass meekly awaiting enlightenment by socialist intellectuals, however. Their inclination to follow Bolshevik, Menshevik, Socialist-Revolutionary injunctions, police-sponsored trade unions, or even the proto-fascist Black Hundreds, was a function of their own experience, not a result of some arcane power exercised by philosophical magicians. What is more, the workers were very often ahead of the intellectuals when it came to putting general ideas into practical effect. The worker intelligentsia, educated by socialist intellectuals in the late 1880s and early 1890s, were a disappointment to their mentors, often more concerned with self-betterment than class struggle. From the early 1890s, however, in a wave that moved east from Poland, through the Jewish Pale to St Petersburg, the workers discovered the power of the (illegal) strike weapon. This movement was legitimized and encouraged by the pamphlet *On Agitation* (1894) composed by Kremer and Martov, two leaders of the Jewish Social-Democratic movement. While Lenin was excoriating those who sought to detach the workers from dependence on the intellectuals as 'Economists' at the turn of the century, the workers themselves were already taking to the streets to object to political as well as economic abuses. The emergence of Soviets in the 1905 revolution came as a surprise to the theoreticians of Russian social democracy and nearly all the leading Russian Marxists were honest enough to admit their surprise at the February revolution of 1917. Furthermore, there is plenty of evidence that many of the worker-socialists, and even worker-Marxists, actively resented the tutelage to which the intellectuals often subjected them. Some of them became sufficiently alienated from socialism to lend their support to the trade unions sponsored by the unconventional Sergei Zubatov, police chief of Moscow at the beginning of the century, or Father Gapon's equivalent non-political union in St Petersburg.

Whatever the frictions between workers and peasants and members of the intelligentsia, it is quite impossible to conceive of the mobilization of the Russian working people in the early twentieth century without the intelligentsia. Their role was not restricted to theorizing, educating and agitating. Their mastery of the techniques involved in conspiratorial publishing did an enormous amount to ensure that the workers went into battle in an informed and co-ordinated manner, using tactics that created the maximum difficulty for the authorities. It is symptomatic that the journal *Workers' Thought*, denounced by Lenin for its 'Economism' and dedicated in theory to securing the autonomy of the workers from the intellectuals, was itself run by members of the intelligentsia. These points could be made with even greater force about the relationship between the Socialist Revolutionaries and the peasantry. The S.R. Party began to emerge in the late 1890s and was using terrorism once more to advertise its existence by the early 1900s. The first major peasant disturbances occurred in 1902 in areas where S.R.s had been active, but most peasants did not begin to recognize the party as their own until the revolution of 1905–6. The creation of a programme capable of rallying neo-populist intellectuals, the peasant intelligentsia, and the mass of the peasantry was, however, the creation of a single intellectual, Victor Chernov.

THE OPPOSITIONS

The existence of a large number of minority nationalities on Russia's vulnerable borders was one of the main justifications for the autocracy in its final decades. It was also a source of unending weakness. It would be impossible in the confines of this small book to tell the complex story of the rise of conservative, liberal, revolutionary-socialist and Marxist groups among these nationalities and the contribution made by each one to the weakening of the tsarist state. In view of later events in the Soviet Union, it is worth mentioning the work of the Crimean Tatar, Izmail Gaspraly, who sought to avert the disruption of the Russian Islamic community into separate nationalities by creating a Turkic lingua franca and a common educational system. It was in these years, too, that the Armenians, long loyal to Russia because of their harsh experiences at the hands of the Turks, were finally alienated by the Russian bureaucracy. In revenge, the authorities incited their Moslem neighbours to subject them to pogroms. Such examples could be multiplied indefinitely. One of their consequences was the over-representation of the oppressed minorities in the socialist movements in Russia itself. Another was the creation of new methods of mass struggle in the borderlands which were then imitated by the workers and peasants of Russia. It was in Russia itself, however, that the campaign had to be waged if the autocracy was to be defeated, or even seriously modified. For such a campaign to be successful, there had to be organizations to co-ordinate 'elemental' outbursts against the government in the widely scattered localities. By the beginning of the twentieth century, three main currents could be discerned. Very soon these assumed the form of political parties with mass support; they were the Social-Democrats (Bolshevik and Menshevik), the Socialist Revolutionaries and the liberals (the Constitutional Democrats).

With the accession of the last tsar in 1894, the Russian autocracy missed perhaps its final opportunity to reform itself. Pressed by the perennially liberal zemstvo gentry of Tver to introduce some kind of constitutional order, the new Tsar denounced such thoughts as 'senseless dreams'. In the same year, the censorship was relaxed against the works of Marxist theoreticians, provided they were sufficiently abstruse and provided their authors were not known to be political criminals. The first fruits of this new policy were two works which rocked the radical intelligentsia, shattering its faith in traditional populist ideas. They were Peter Struve's *Critical Notes on the Question of Russia's Economic Development* and Plekhanov's *In Defence of Materialism: On the Question of the Development of the Monistic View of History*. These two works began the process of assimilating Marxist ideas to Russian reality on a systematic basis. Their influence over the radical intelligentsia was overwhelming.

George Valentinovich Plekhanov was born in 1856, the scion of a middling estate-owner; he always retained his father's physical courage and martial bearing, his sympathy for the oppressed he took from his mother. Early experiences convinced him that the peasantry was too unscientific a social force to realize the advance in civilization expected with socialism and so he looked to the industrial workers. Plekhanov founded the Russian, and ultimately Soviet, school of Marxist philosophy which is renowned for its uncompromising materialism. In applying the analysis of the development of capitalism in the West in the first volume of Marx's *Capital*, Plekhanov came to the conclusion that Russia's revolution would be in two distinct stages, bourgeois and proletarian. In other words, he was the author of the political scheme later associated with the Mensheviks. In the final years of his life, he moved towards neo-Kantian idealism and support for the Russian war effort in the Great War. Struve's evolution was even more rapid and more extreme. Reasoning that the most urgent task was the bourgeois democratic revolution, Struve joined the liberals and ultimately became a conservative Russian patriot.

Plekhanov was by no means the first Russian to interest himself in Marxism. As early as 1860 Professor Babst of the University of Moscow had delivered a lecture on the first part of the *Critique of Political Economy*. Professor Ziber of Kiev was another academic expounder of Marx. In the early 1860s Bakunin had translated into Russian the *Communist Manifesto*; and in 1872 appeared a Russian translation of the first volume of *Capital*, the first translation from the original into any foreign language. Moreover, both Marx and Engels were in regular contact with Russian exiles such as Lavrov. There were assuredly any number of channels through which Marxist influence could flow into Russia. As early as the 1870s there were small and short-lived Marxist groups calling for the overthrow of the autocracy. Important as these pragmatic, piecemeal efforts were, they did not yet constitute the assimilation of Marxism into the Russian intellectual framework.

Plekhanov had begun his political career as a member of 'Land and Liberty', but had broken with the party when it decided that its main energies should be devoted to terror rather than mass agitation. At the end of 1879, to save him from arrest, he was sent abroad to live in Switzerland. Here, together with other ex-Populists – Vera Zasulich, Paul Axelrod, and Leo Deutsch – he founded a group known as the 'Emancipation of Labour'. This was in 1883. It was a tiny group numerically, so tiny that when the members were out boating on the Lake of Geneva, Plekhanov once quipped: 'Be careful: if this boat sinks, it's the end of Russian Marxism.' Throughout its history, Russian Marxism has managed to be witty without real humour; it has rarely suffered from too much modesty.

As it happened, for better or for worse, the boat did not sink. But why should it have carried a cargo of Marxists? Why not one of the other revolutionary doctrines of the West? This is no easy question to answer. There are, of course, obvious affinities between Marxism and Populism, such as the belief in violent revolution and the belief in the masses as its agent. There is a strong messianic element common to both. Moreover, even though the industrial proletariat formed a minute proportion of the population of Russia, it was at least growing fast, whereas the peasantry seemed incapable of responding to any truly revolutionary appeal. There was also the immense attraction of joining a movement which, with its powerful Marxist parties in Germany and France, seemed invincible to the Russians.

To understand the magnitude, and even the scandalous nature of Plekhanov's undertaking, we must remember that he set out to crush Populism and defend the progressive mission of capitalism at a time when capitalism was bringing famine to the villages and brutal oppression to the industrial barracks of the Russian towns. The struggle was fought out in terms of Russian economic development. More particularly, it was concerned with the role of capitalism in Russia. Was it an alien, unnatural growth, condemned to a premature death? Or was it to be the inevitable next stage in Russia's economic development? Populist economists such as Vorontsov and Danielson argued that capitalism in Russia could make only slow progress because Russia had neither capital nor a bourgeoisie, that the internal consumption level was too low to absorb its products, that it was too weak to conquer markets abroad in the normal imperialist fashion, and that it was kept alive only through massive State subsidies and bounties of all sorts. In the end, therefore, neither having markets at home nor being able to acquire them abroad, it would infallibly collapse. They felt that the contemporary misery of the villages proved their case.

The Populists concluded from this analysis that Russia could well represent a special case and escape the capitalist phase of economic development. By fortifying the commune and its collective virtues, Russia could evolve its own form of socialism without undergoing the preliminary capitalist phase of exploitation and wage slavery. While the hopes pinned on the commune may strike us as rather sanguine, it is now clear that many parts of the Populist economic analysis were correct. Just as Russia may be said to lie somewhere along a 'cultural slope' between Europe and Asia, so one might describe nineteenth-century Russia as lying somewhere in the middle of an 'economic slope' between eighteenth-century England and present-day India. Marx had begun to sense that Volume 1 of *Capital* could not be applied mechanically to Russian conditions and he sided with the Populists, though his own notes on these matters were censored by the Russian Marxists. Later on, Lenin and Trotsky would have to re-open the question. In an important sense, twentieth-century leaders as diverse as Mao and Nyerere are heirs to the nineteenth-century Russian Populists.

To all this, in the polemic-filled eighties and nineties, Plekhanov opposed two basic arguments. First, in such works as *Socialism and the Political Struggle*, *Our Differences*, and *In Defence of Materialism*, he reiterated time and time again that 'the present as much as the future belongs to capitalism', and he added, 'we suffer not only from the development of capitalism, but also from the scarcity of that development'. Second, Plekhanov argued, Russian capitalism was a progressive movement in that its further expansion would require the overthrow of the autocracy and at the same time lead to the ripening of the industrial proletariat; and the latter in their turn would inaugurate the socialist revolution. At the Foundation Congress of the Second Socialist International in Paris in 1889, Plekhanov summed up his creed in its application to Russia: 'The revolutionary movement in Russia can triumph only as the revolutionary movement of the workers. There is no other way out for us, and cannot be . . .' Already, Plekhanov was able to predict the plight of a revolutionary group that seized power prematurely and sought to run national production on socialist lines without either adequate objective conditions or popular approval: 'it would have to seek salvation in the ideals of "patriarchal and authoritarian communism", introducing into those ideals only the change that a socialist caste would manage the national production instead of the Peruvian "Children of the Sun" and their officials.'

In practical political terms, Plekhanov's analysis required that the emphasis be shifted from the peasantry to the workers as the principal revolutionary force. In the initial bourgeois revolution, the workers would supply the discipline, energy, and sheer force required to topple autocracy, but they would not sacrifice their ideological or organizational autonomy. This autonomy would be a vital factor in shortening the subsequent interval between the bourgeois and the proletarian revolution.

The second great Russian Marxist thinker is known to us as Lenin, a conspiratorial name derived from the great Siberian river. Plekhanov had pre-empted the use of the name 'Volgin' by using it himself. It was, however, in Simbirsk (now Ulyanovsk) on the Middle Volga that Vladimir Ilyich Ulyanov was born in 1870. His father was a progressive-minded schoolteacher who rose to become director of elementary schools for the province of Simbirsk. The mother had been a schoolmistress. All their surviving children became revolutionaries after the execution of their eldest son, Alexander, in 1887 for his participation in a plot to kill the Tsar.

At the local high school Lenin had a brilliant record. His headmaster – even in Russia it was a small world for the educated classes in those days – was the father of Alexander Kerensky, the leader of the Provisional Government overthrown by Lenin in October 1917. 'Highly gifted, industrious, and punctual,' ran the verdict of Kerensky *père*. Lenin then entered the local university of Kazan. A few months later, the authorities sent him down because of his part in a student demonstration. Not until 1891 was he permitted as an external student of the university of St Petersburg to qualify as a lawyer. He emerged with a first-class diploma and top results in every subject. A little while later he returned to Samara, on the Middle Volga, where he practised as a lawyer.

It was not a successful bourgeois career that Lenin sought. He had already familiarized himself with Marx's *Capital*, using his dead brother's copy; and in St Petersburg and Samara he was already in contact with Marxist circles and known for his sharp criticism of Populist ideas. In his first work, *The Position of the Peasants in Russia*, he emphasized the disintegrating influence of capitalism in the countryside. In *What the Friends of the People are and How They Fight against the Social-Democrats* Lenin carried on the underground struggle against the Populists, displaying a remarkable mastery of Marxist method, the art of polemical writing, and the arguments of his enemies. From some of his populist opponents, he learned how to caricature his enemies the better to attack them; his own biting sarcasm has rarely been surpassed. Lenin was no mere thinker, however. He used his time in Samara to interrogate exiled populists of the older generation on the methods required by a conspiratorial organization at war with the government.

Lenin combined his theoretical work with practical instruction to Marxist study circles, composed mainly of intellectuals but not without a sprinkling of working men. Many of Lenin's audiences came through introductions from Nadezhda Krupskaya, a schoolteacher, and his future wife who was destined to become the archetypal party secretary.

Vladimir Ilyich [she writes] read with the workers from Marx's *Capital*, and explained it to them. The second half of the studies was devoted to the workers' questions about their work and labour conditions. He showed them how their life was linked up with the entire structure of society, and told them in what manner the existing order could be transformed. The combination of theory with practice was the particular feature of Vladimir Ilyich's work in the circles.*

In 1895 Lenin had belonged to the St Petersburg Union of Struggle for the Liberation of the Working Class, which supported the great strikes in the middle and later 1890s. In the same year Lenin applied for a passport, ostensibly on health grounds, to which colour was given by a recent attack of pneumonia. But it was in actual fact to meet Plekhanov and the other exiles in Geneva. Lenin spent four months in Western Europe – France and Germany, as well as Switzerland. Axelrod noted afterwards: 'I felt that I had before me a man who would be the leader of the Russian Revolution. He was not only a cultured Marxist – of them there were many – but he also knew what he wanted to do and how to do it. He had something of the smell of the Russian soil about him . . .' This was precisely what the exiles had been missing during their long years in Switzerland. Now their labours, it seemed, were beginning to bear tangible fruit in the person of the brilliant young man from Simbirsk.

Lenin returned to St Petersburg in the autumn of 1895. He had with him a double-bottomed trunk full of illegal literature printed in Geneva. A month or so later the police picked up his trail, aided probably by spies abroad and an *agent provocateur* planted in the study circles. In four years of imprisonment and Siberian exile, Lenin was able to turn his prison cell and then his peasant hut into a well-stocked library. He drew on these resources for his major dissertation *The Development of Capitalism in Russia*. He was also able to translate Webb's *History of British Trade Unionism*, to attack the Populists, the 'economist' Marxists who would water down the revolutionary theory in the fight for economic aims and leave political issues to one side, and also the 'legal' Marxists who limited themselves in the main to economic analysis. Thus, when Lenin was released at the beginning of 1900, the world to which he returned had lost none of its familiarity. He took up the struggle where he had left it four years earlier.

His first thought was to found a paper and, through it, a party. An attempt had been made at Minsk in 1898 to establish a Russian

*N. K. Krupskaya, *Memories of Lenin* (1942), p. 7.

Social-Democratic Party, rallying the scattered Russian Marxist groups around the *Bund*, the organization of the Jewish Social-Democrats based on Vilna. But barely was the party founded than the police seized the founders. The coast was clear for Lenin to overcome the political and doctrinal fragmentation inherent in the conditions in which Russian Marxism had grown up.

Now the two streams came together – that of the active Marxists in Russia and that of the theoreticians in European exile. It was not an easy marriage. Lenin, Martov (a product of a comfortable and well-connected Jewish family from Odessa who had won his spurs with the movement in Vilna and the Pale), and Potresov, who had access to funds through wealthy relations, made their way to Geneva, one by one. The union was eventually consummated, and in December 1900 the first number of *Iskra* (*The Spark*) appeared. The editorial board consisted of Plekhanov, Axelrod, and Zasulich on the one hand, and Lenin, Martov, and Potresov, on the other.

Iskra was printed in Munich, Leipzig, Stuttgart, and London, in tiny characters on thin cigarette paper, and smuggled into Russia by way of Romania, Prussia, and Austria. (It was as illegal in Germany as it would have been in Russia itself. The capitalist international was no less alert than the socialist.) A network of agents saw to its further distribution in the great industrial centres. The distribution system under Lenin's control was in fact an instrument for securing the loyalty of the scattered Marxist groups in Russia, the organizational network of a party that did not yet exist. These men (for so they were with very few exceptions) had no local loyalties or attachments but moved around Russia, constantly changing their identities and living off the membership, obedient to the will of the impersonal organization and its authoritative head. The tool with which Lenin sought to transform Russia bore more than an accidental resemblance to the bureaucracy of Peter the Great.

Iskra set out to create a clear ideological identity for the nascent Russian Social-Democratic Party, and simultaneously to help the Socialist International purify itself of the siren call of revisionism. Lenin therefore chose as his targets the 'economists' (those who felt the workers would be better off without the tutelage of the intellectuals) and the 'legal' Marxists, whose academic approach was too remote from the workers to command much support. As the demonstrations of 1901 were to show, the workers were perfectly capable of working out for themselves that their economic demands could not be satisfied without radical political changes. In 1900 a new enemy had appeared – the Socialist Revolutionary Party, heirs to the Populists and soon to become the largest party of the left, far superior in numbers to the Social-Democrats. In a society undergoing rapid industrialization, it was inevitable that many workers would be attracted towards the peasant party. But mere numbers would not in the end be decisive. Organization and policy would be, and it was to these that *Iskra* made a crucial contribution. The very first issue contained an article by Lenin closely anticipating the sort of party he hoped to form:

> Not a single class in history has reached power without thrusting forward its political leaders, without advancing leading representatives capable of directing and organizing the movement. We must train people who will dedicate to the revolution, not a spare evening but the whole of their lives . . .

This was the immediate prelude to the formation of such a party of revolutionaries. A second congress – so named in deference to the first, abortive congress held at Minsk in 1898 – opened in Brussels in 1903. Half-way through, the delegates moved to London to escape the attentions of the Belgian police.

This was the crucial congress. It saw the birth of Bolshevism as a political organization and a special form of political warfare that had no precedent in the West, and it also saw the split with Menshevism. Present were forty-three delegates with fifty-one votes, representing mainly Russian underground organizations. This in itself was something of a triumph. Lenin had seen to it that most of them were *Iskra* supporters. The disued flour warehouse in Brussels, swarming with rats and fleas, witnessed some of the stormiest and most emotional debates that even the Russian revolutionary movement had produced. The decisions of the congress were to impress an indelible stamp not only on policy in 1917, but also on the type of ruling party that would emerge after the revolution.

After the singing of the 'Internationale' the congress turned to business. Some of the early disputes concerned the representation of groups opposed to *Iskra* at the congress. Lenin was anxious to exclude Ryazanov's *Struggle* group which had subjected his own programme to expert criticism. In the row over this, he was able to discredit not only the *Struggle* group but also most of Martov's leading supporters. Lenin wanted the Jewish *Bund* to remain within the new party, but only on condition that it gave up its organizational autonomy. He put up Martov, Trotsky, and other leading Jewish Social-Democrats to deny the right of the *Bund* to represent all Jewish workers in western Russia. With the departure of the *Bund*, Lenin's supporters gained in relative significance.

The party programme was divided into a minimum and a maximum. The first demanded the overthrow of the autocracy, the erection of a democratic republic on the basis of a constituent assembly elected by free, equal, direct, and universal suffrage, freedom of speech, Press and assembly, equality before the law, and the introduction of the eight-hour day. The second called for the socialist revolution and the establishment of the dictatorship of the proletariat. It was in connection with a hypothetical conflict between the unexceptionably democratic demands of the first part and the dictatorship explicitly called for in the second part that Plekhanov made his celebrated declaration: he denied that universal suffrage was 'a fetish', and emphasized that '*salus revolutiae* [*sic*] *suprema lex* . . . If the salvation of the revolution should demand the temporary limitation of one or other democratic principle, then it would be a crime to hold back . . .' With an implicit reference to Cromwell, Plekhanov continued:

If the people, seized by revolutionary enthusiasm, were to elect a good Parliament, then we must try to make of this a Long Parliament. If the elections, on the other hand, go badly, then we must try not to wait two years to dissolve Parliament, but to do so after two weeks if possible.

Acclamations and also some hisses greeted this exposé. But, saving one abstainer, the congress adopted the programme. It is worth noting that the delegates did not crystallize into proto-Mensheviks who attached great importance to a joint struggle with the bourgeoisie in the pursuit of the minimum programme as against Bolsheviks who looked to the peasantry to help the workers move directly to the achievement of the maximum programme. Nor was the future Menshevik Plekhanov any less 'Jacobin' than Lenin at this point.

The basic conflict emerged in the debate on Paragraph 1 of the party statutes. How define a party member? What was his duty? To Lenin a party member was 'any person who accepts its programme, supports the party with material means, and personally participates in one of its organizations'. To Martov the criterion was less rigid. He would replace 'personally participate' by 'co-operate personally and regularly under the direction of one of the organizations'. This trifling verbal distinction did in fact conceal and involve far-ranging divergencies on an interrelated hierarchy of values. Was revolution an inevitable and spontaneous process or did it require the intervention of a conscious force? More specifically, must the Russian socialist revolution wait on the achievement of a bourgeois revolution, or could it be the by-product, as it were, of the bourgeois revolution? Finally, and as a consequence, must a socialist party in Russia be organized so as to be a minority, bringing to the workers 'from outside' their revolutionary consciousness, or must it seek to envelop as many of the workers as possible? In other words, was the party to be a disciplined body of professional revolutionaries, or was it to be a mass party somewhat similar to those that had developed in the West?

Lenin's determined insistence on the need for professional revolutionaries, as distinct from party members who might be nothing more than well-wishers and sympathizers, did not spring forth fully armed, like Minerva from Jupiter's head. It was drawn from the experience of the Russian revolutionary movement extending over the best part of a century. Tsarism, to a very large extent, imprinted its own image on its enemies. A centralized authoritarian autocracy called into being a precisely similar revolutionary movement. Already Pestel, the Decembrist, had understood the need for conspiratorial groups. But Tkachev, a follower of the French revolutionary Blanqui, and one of the leaders of the People's Freedom Party, was probably Lenin's closest precursor in his view that revolutionary success depended on the work of an underground corps of professional workers for the cause. Lenin himself once paid tribute to his predecessors:

> The magnificent organization that the revolutionaries had in the seventies should serve us all as a model ... no revolutionary tendency, if it seriously thinks of fighting, can dispense with such an organization ... the spontaneous struggle of the proletariat will not become a genuine class struggle until it is led by a strong organization of revolutionaries.

This in itself could not, of course, guarantee success. But in Russia at least experience, or so Lenin insisted, showed that anything else invariably succumbed to the police. These were the Russian roots of Bolshevism. From the same environment stemmed the need for secrecy, the impossibility of public discussion of policy, and the election in open forum of party leaders. While some of the future Mensheviks were uneasy at this line of argument, their methods – and even those of their Socialist-Revolutionary rivals – were often very similar. It might have been argued that experience showed that the workers were capable of moving from spontaneous struggle to class struggle once the Marxist seed had been sown and that centralized organizations were also highly vulnerable to infiltration and suppression; but it was not.

Lenin made the same point in his criticism of the 'economists'' proposals for the organization of workers' factory circles. Their rules demanded, for example, keeping a record of events in the factory, collecting funds regularly, presenting monthly reports on the state of the funds. 'Why,' exclaimed Lenin, 'this is a very paradise for the police; for nothing would be easier for them than to penetrate into the ponderous secrecy of a "central fund", confiscate the money and arrest the best members ... only an incorrigible Utopian would want a *wide* organization of workers, with elections, reports, universal suffrage, etc., under the autocracy.' (Italics in the original.) Once again, Lenin used sound pragmatic arguments to justify a position in which he believed on principle. When the fall of the autocracy led, unavoidably, to the growth of a mass party, Lenin and Sverdlov would re-create a new elite of party functionaries within the party.

The counterpart to Lenin's demand for a disciplined corps of professional revolutionaries was the insistence that the masses of themselves could only develop what he called a 'trade-union consciousness', i.e. could not rise above the level of immediate economic demands. But this, he suggested, would make a political revolution impossible. Thus

Lenin's theory of Bolshevism amounted to acknowledging that the revolutionary forces had to be re-created and organized outside and even against the 'immediate interests' of the proletariat, whose class-consciousness had been arrested by the system in which they functioned. The Bolshevik doctrine of the predominant role of the Party leadership as the revolutionary vanguard grew out of the new conditions of Western society (the conditions of 'imperialism' and 'monopoly capitalism') rather than out of the personality or psychology of the Russian Marxists.[*]

Right up to the present day, Russian conservatives have seen in Lenin an 'un-Russian' phenomenon imposing Western doctrines on Russia. They cite Lenin's mixed ancestry in support of this claim. Nothing could be more absurd. The creation of a Russian from Slavic, Tatar, and German ancestry is typically Russian, far more so than the 'Germanization' of the Imperial family. What is more, recent sociological analysis of the sources of support for Bolshevism and Menshevism in the Russian Empire make it quite clear that it was precisely in the most Russian industrial centres, close to the capitals, that Bolshevism was most popular during both revolutions. Menshevism, on the other hand, had a greater appeal to the more Europeanized Social-Democrats of the west and south. What Lenin did was to assimilate to Russian conditions the notion of the unity of theory and practice in Marxism. As he himself said: 'Different in England from France, different in France from Germany, different from Germany in Russia.'

Not all this was by any means evident in 1903. After the congress Lenin himself sought for reconciliation with some of his defeated opponents. But it was not to be. Lenin lost the debate on the party status by twenty-eight votes to twenty-two. On the other hand, the Leninist group was victorious in the elections to the editorial board of *Iskra* and to the Central Committee. It is characteristic of Lenin's brilliance as a propagandist that he was able to claim for

[*] H. Marcuse in *Continuity and Change in Russian and Soviet Thought*, ed. E. J Simmons (Cambridge, Mass., 1955), pp. 348–9.

his majority the description *Bolshevik*, from the Russian word for majority, and for his opponents the description *Menshevik*, from the word for minority. But there was still no hard and fast division and the Mensheviks never became a cohesive group like the Bolsheviks. In 1904 the Central Committee fell to Lenin's rivals, Lenin resigned from *Iskra* and published his own journal, *Vperyod* (*Forward*). In 1905, however, the split went considerably further when the Bolsheviks and Mensheviks held separate congresses in London and Geneva respectively.

Lenin's victory was not only short-lived; it was also achieved at great cost. Both Martov, his closest collaborator for the previous few years, and his younger admirer, Trotsky, were thoroughly alienated by the events of the congress. Martov had already had reason to worry about Lenin's willingness to recruit henchmen of disreputable personal morality and this was confirmed when one of them opportunely slandered him at the congress. He was to end as one of the main theoreticians of Menshevism. Leon Trotsky belonged consistently to neither faction. But it was he, on the very morrow of the split, who brilliantly foresaw one consequence of Lenin's theory of organization. 'The Party is replaced by the organization of the party, the organization by the central committee, and finally the central committee by the dictator.' The split also perplexed many of the most active Social-Democrats among the workers. For two years effective leadership over the working class of the capitals passed to the patriarchal, monarchist, and xenophobic organizations established by Zubatov and Gapon.

In April 1902 a young Socialist-Revolutionary, Balmashev, assassinated Sipyagin, Minister of the Interior. In the same month, peasants in Poltava and Kharkov provinces took over the assets of their landowners and in some cases burned down their manors. Subsequent investigations suggested that the peasants had been propagandized by S.R. agitators. The S.R. Party had arrived as a force to be reckoned with in Russian politics.

The first steps towards the re-constitution of a populist party had been undertaken by the veteran ex-convicts Catherine Breshko-Breshkovskaya and Mark Natanson, upon the expiry of their terms of exile in the 1890s. Their pioneering efforts revealed the existence of two partly overlapping groups in society with an interest in a revolutionary alliance. There were the radical members of the intelligentsia who could not yet bring themselves to accept Marxist materialism and who felt that the time was once more ripe for the use of terror to establish political democracy. There were also spokesmen and women for the growing peasant intelligentsia who wanted a resolution of the land problem in the sense desired by the peasants and who felt this might best be realized through the achievement of political democracy. Only in a democracy could the numerical strength of the peasantry be deployed to maximum effect. From its inception, the leadership of the Socialist-Revolutionary Party was divided between terrorist activists, such as Grigory Gershuni, Yevno Azef and Boris Savinkov, and political intellectuals with a penchant for peasant interests, such as Victor Chernov and Breshkovskaya. The party programme urged the socialization of land, treading a middle path between the peasant egoism that demanded its immediate repartition, albeit within the commune, and the Marxist insistence that it be nationalized. It carefully avoided committing itself on such details as whether peasants in areas of land shortage would be permitted to claim plots in areas of land surplus. The party's fighting organization, referred to in awed tones as 'The Central Terror', seemed at first to suffer from no such equivocation, and successfully assassinated several leading bureaucrats, including Plehve, who displaced Witte as the Tsar's leading minister in 1903, and even an uncle of the Tsar. The S.R.s were no more successful in avoiding ethical complications than the Bolsheviks, however, and the fighting organization – floating in a miasma of intrigue and betrayal – soon evolved its own cult of violence. Given its commitment to the physical annihilation of leading figures of the tsarist regime, it is not surprising that the S.R. Party suffered even greater repression than the Social-Democrats and was even less able to organize a mass membership than they were.

Under Witte's inspiration, the State, staffed largely by aristocratic landowners in its higher strata, undertook to transform the Russian economy in a direction desired by its small but burgeoning capitalist class. The capitalist bourgeoisie in Russia, as a result, was nationalist and monarchist. Despite this, the turn of the century saw the emergence of a specifically bourgeois liberal third force within the opposition. Its father-figure was the venerable Ivan Petrunkevich, standard bearer of the liberal tradition of the Tver zemstvo. Its ideologist and tactician was the history professor Paul Milyukov. With Peter Struve, Milyukov brought out the first number of its journal *Liberation* in Stuttgart in 1902. The liberals suffered not merely from the relative weakness of their social base but also from the tension between their non-revolutionary natures and their bourgeois revolutionary demands: '. . . we propose to unite those groups of Russian society which do not find it possible to express their indignation by means of either the class or the revolutionary struggle'. Yet their programme demanded personal inviolability, equality before the law, freedom of the Press, assembly and association, the right of petition, the calling of a 'classless representative body', the annulment of extra-legal administrative circulars and a general amnesty. The liberals soon began to make headway in the zemstvo movement, which now demanded for itself wider administrative powers and the right to nation-wide organization. These demands gave some colour to the Menshevik thesis that the break between the bourgeoisie and the autocracy could not be long delayed. At the end of 1904 a meeting of zemstvo leaders demanded by a considerable majority the abolition of the autocracy and the installation of a parliament with power to issue laws and to control the budget. The zemstvo programme reiterated the demand for the introduction of civil liberties.

It is remarkable that the liberals made no serious attempt to capture the leadership of the masses from the parties of the left; it was as though they tacitly accepted the validity of the Marxist view that only Marxists could represent the workers and only revolutionary socialists the peasants. All the same, on this basis, the Union of Liberation, embracing zemstva, municipalities, professional men, corporations of the nobility, and even the Socialist Revolutionaries, instituted a bold campaign of reform through political banquets, public assemblies, and nation-wide agitation in the autumn of 1904.

PORT ARTHUR AND BLOODY SUNDAY

After 1878, with its hopes for the Balkans dashed, there was a natural tendency for the Russian government to give priority to the Far East. In 1875 there had already been a Russo-Japanese deal whereby Russia abandoned to Japan the Kurile Islands in her possession in return for the Japanese renunciation of all claims to the island of Sakhalin. Quite apart from the general trend eastwards, the Sino-Japanese war of 1894–5, with its dual revelation of Chinese weakness and the emerging power of Japan, and the construction of the Trans-Siberian Railroad, pulled Russia into the competitive imperialisms of the Far East. The special area of penetration was Manchuria. A treaty with China in 1896 gave Russia the right to construct a railroad across the north-western part of the territory. A later treaty entitled Russia to construct northwards from the military and naval base of Port Arthur (Lü-shun) and the commercial port of Dalny (Ta-lien) the South Manchurian Railroad, to link up with the Chinese Eastern Railroad. Despite the conclusion of the Franco-Russian alliance in 1892, Russia was anxious to avoid complications with major powers at this time, so much so that she took the initiative in summoning the first major disarmament conference in The Hague in 1899. The tangible and enduring result of this was the International Court of Justice.

The Boxer Rebellion of 1900 gave a further boost to a forward Russian policy in the Far East by justifying the stationing of troops in Manchuria. But in 1903, the planned evacuation of these troops, forced on Russia by Anglo-Japanese diplomatic pressure, the opposition of the United States, and the reluctance of France any longer to support her ally's Far Eastern advances, failed to take place. Moreover, Nicholas II, who had by now largely taken the control of foreign policy into his own hands, sanctioned the infiltration of Russian troops into Northern Korea, and the exploitation of a timber concession and shipping depot on the Yalu River.

The tension between Russia and Japan in 1903 might have been resolved had the former accepted a Japanese proposal for the mutual acknowledgement of each other's respective preponderance in Manchuria and Korea. But Russian aims were confused and her under-estimation of Japanese strength fatal. On 8 February 1904, the Japanese attacked Port Arthur. The war was widely blamed on Witte's rival in the government, the cynical Vyacheslav von Plehve whose comment about a 'short, victorious war that would stem the tide of revolution' received wide currency. In fact, Plehve realized the futility of the war as well as Witte did and advised against it. Nevertheless, the remark reminded society of the pogroms instigated by the authorities under Plehve – at Kishinyov on Easter Sunday 1903, and again at Gomel in August–September 1903 – in the hope, it was said, of 'drowning the revolution in Jewish blood'. Jewish blood had indeed been shed. But it had not produced the desired effect. On the contrary, the revolutionary wave swelled to unprecedented size and scope, and all the more so when the war in the Far East turned out to be far from short and far from victorious. If the government was initially weaker with the departure of its best troops to the Far East, the army was probably more loyal as a result of the war. Even the more liberal of the army officers were scandalized by the defeatism of many radicals and liberals, and more willing to suppress disorders as a result.

The sparks came on 22 January 1905 (9 January Old Style). Port Arthur had fallen a few weeks earlier, the latest and the most crushing of a series of Russian defeats in the Far East. At much the same time a strike broke out in St Petersburg at the Putilov engineering works. It rapidly spread to other factories. Here, overnight almost, was a mass workers' movement of unprecedented dimensions. The tension rose to such a pitch that it forced a certain Father George Gapon, who led a police-sponsored labour union, either to take some positive action or to abdicate entirely and leave his members to follow an even more radical path. Gapon, in collaboration with some of the zemstvo leaders, intelligentsia, and Socialist-Revolutionaries, drafted a petition for presentation to the Tsar. It was couched for the most part in plaintive terms – 'we are not considered human beings . . . we are treated like slaves'. But it also contained outspoken political demands: freedom of the Press, religion, assembly; the calling of a constituent assembly: equality before the law; labour legislation and the eight-hour day; a reduction in indirect taxes and the introduction of a graduated income tax; an amnesty for political prisoners; and an end to the war. One hundred and thirty-five thousand people signed the petition.

And so, on Sunday 22 January, about 150,000 people marched

under Father Gapon's leadership, in a series of columns from the various suburbs to the Winter Palace. They were peaceful processions. The marchers intoned hymns, and bore icons and portraits of the Tsar. What followed was not only a crime but a political error of colossal dimensions. The military authorities were under instructions to accept no petitions (the Tsar was not in residence in the capital) but to disperse the crowds by whatever means proved necessary. In a series of incidents, the marching columns peacefully singing their hymns were met by stentorian commands to disperse which could not possibly be carried out quickly. Salvo after salvo poured into the terror-stricken marchers. At the end of 'Bloody Sunday' there were perhaps a thousand dead and many more thousands wounded. The Tsar's pitiful gesture in inviting a group of workers to share tea and cakes with him some weeks later failed to efface the reputation he now acquired as 'Bloody Nicholas'.

This was the spark that set alight the flame of revolution. In all social groups, in all parts of the country, revolt flared up. By the end of January nearly half a million workmen were on strike. The professional intelligentsia joined in. Doctors, lawyers, teachers, professors, engineers, formed unions to press political claims on the government. The terrorist movement flared up with the killing of the Tsar's uncle, the Grand Duke Sergei, who had made himself infamous for his cruelty during his Governor-Generalship of Moscow. Industrialists also joined in the clamour for a constitutional regime. A new feature of the popular movement was the formation of an All-Russian Peasants' Union – the first time that a political organization open to peasants had arisen on Russian soil. It soon joined the Union of Unions, led by the liberal leader Milyukov. In many parts of the country a state of anarchy prevailed that all the Tsar's courts martial and repression could not repress.

The Tsar, meanwhile, was hoping for military victories that would re-establish his shattered prestige and allow him to recall the armies from Manchuria. There came, instead, defeat at Mukden in Manchuria, and the destruction of the Russian Baltic Fleet at Tsushima in May 1905. The epic voyage of Rozhdestvensky's fleet halfway round the world to tip the balance of forces in the Far East had ended in total disaster. In a sense this was the end of one of the dreams of Peter the Great. No Russian fleet has fought a battle on the high seas since. In August, the Tsar bowed to the mounting pressure by issuing a law promising a consultative assembly, to be known as the Duma, to be formed from an electoral body weighted in favour of high property qualifications and also the peasantry. But this succeeded in splitting off only the wealthier and more right-wing liberals. To the rest of the population it was a matter for derision and boycott. To the workers, the proposed Duma meant nothing. They would have no vote in it at all.

In the spring the first wave of strikes petered out, and the initiative passed to the middle classes. But in the summer and autumn the workers' movement suddenly revived. Not that the summer had seen any real break in the movement: troops had been called out in Lodz, and in the Black Sea fleet the crew of the battleship *Potyomkin* had mutinied – the subject of one of Eisenstein's most famous films. Also, of course, there were few provinces, especially in the border regions, where the peasants were not plundering the manors, despoiling the landowners' estates, raiding store-houses, burning land registers.

The events of the autumn eclipsed even these. In the second half of September, a printers' strike in St Petersburg touched off, with unexampled rapidity, what was in all but name a general strike. It came so swiftly and so spontaneously that even the revolutionaries were taken by surprise – as indeed they had been by most of the events of the year. Barricades sprang up on the streets of Odessa, Kharkov, Ekaterinoslav. The whole life of the country was paralysed. There were further mutinies among the troops. The countryside was ablaze with peasant violence. The climax came, both from the government's standpoint and that of the revolutionaries, in the middle of October. In view of the mounting chaos and the inability of the military hard-liners to guarantee a speedy return to order, Nicholas II was persuaded to issue a manifesto promising civil liberties and some sort of constitutional order and to appoint Witte as Russia's first Prime Minister. Simultaneously, he called on loyal Russians to rally round the throne; sure enough, riots broke out in which Jews and socialists were killed. At the

5. The Russian

OCEAN

Bering I. St.

Anadyr Mts.

Koryak Mts.

Chersky Mts.

Verkhoyansk Mts.

Vilyuisk Mts.

Kolyma Mts.

Kamchatka

CIRCLE

R. Lena

Dzhugdzhur Mts.

SEA of OKHOTSK

Yakutsk

Sakhalin

Stanovoi Mts.

Bureinsk Mts.

Yablonovy Mts.

Khabarovsk

Krasnoyarsk

Lake Baikal

Blagoveshchensk

Nerchinsk

TRANS-SIBERIAN RLY.

MANCHURIA

Irkutsk

Vladivostok

MONGOLIA

SEA of JAPAN

KIANG

Port Arthur

KOREA

Tsushima Str.

JAPAN

0   200   400   600   800   1000
Miles

EST.   • ESTHONIA
LAT.   • LATVIA
LITH• LITHUANIA

Empire in 1914

same time, a new instrument of revolutionary democracy, the St Petersburg Soviet, emerged. These phenomena towered above the chaos and tumult of the year.

The October manifesto proclaimed fundamental civil liberties, promised to extend the franchise beyond the limits announced in July, and promised also that no law would be promulgated without the approval of the State Duma. Witte's premiership lasted just six months. During that time, he presided over Russia's first nation-wide elections, prepared a major peasant reform and negotiated a massive loan with foreign bankers that enabled the Tsar to dispense with both him and the Duma. Yet Witte's experiment was a failure. No part of the opposition would openly side with a government which continued to employ the military reactionaries to suppress the revolution. For his part, Nicholas II loathed and hated Witte for divesting him of some of his inherited prerogatives – particularly when he failed to restore order.

The St Petersburg Soviet, formed of some 500 delegates elected by about 200,000 workers, represented the peak of working-class achievement. It has been called a spontaneous creation; this just means that its creators were neither famous themselves, nor operating under the instructions of the organizations of the revolutionary intelligentsia. But it was a lesson in revolution, not the revolution itself – the manifestation of the class autonomy urged by Plekhanov, not the revolutionary instrument of class power for which Lenin was hoping. The Soviet, of which Trotsky became co-chairman, followed on the whole a moderate policy. It supported the general strike, but sought rather to educate the workers in the limitations of the Duma than to organize an immediate armed insurrection. 'A constitution is given, but the autocracy remains', said Trotsky. The most revolutionary act of the Soviet was to issue an appeal for the non-payment of taxes and the withdrawal of bank deposits.

Whatever they might think of the government, the liberal members of the middle classes were appalled by the emergence of the Soviet and even more by the revolts occurring throughout the country. The government, despite its own inner tensions and low morale, could proceed with the repression of the revolution. The leaders of the St Petersburg Soviet were arrested and an armed uprising in Moscow put down with relative ease. But even at the end of the year, with mutinies in the Sevastopol fleet, and revolts in Siberia, Batum, and Kharkov, it might seem that a renewed upsurge was in the making. In actual fact, the autumn had seen the climax. Not for more than a decade would it be overtopped by a second and even more tumultuous upheaval. One thing was clear: there would be no western-style bourgeois revolution in Russia. At the first sign of independent activity by the lower orders, the Russian bourgeoisie had dissociated itself from the revolution. The peasantry, on the other hand, would go on fighting for months and months after the workers had been put down. The Menshevik view of Russia's future development had been struck a blow from which it never fully recovered.

CHAPTER 12

Forebodings, 1881–1917

By the 1880s the great age of Russian realism was over. A Russian La Bruyère might well have said: '*Tout est dit*'. The poet Nekrasov died in 1878, Dostoyevsky in 1881, Turgenev in 1883, the dramatist Ostrovsky in 1886, and Goncharov, the creator of Oblomov, in 1891. What could remain to be said? What could still be written that would be more than repetition? The dripping pathos of Tchaikovsky provided the defeated intelligentsia of the 1880s with some consolation. Yet this mood of defeatism was misplaced. Tolstoy was still to produce his powerful didactic novel *Resurrection* and a final artistic gem, *Hadji Murad*. New talents and new forms would emerge. The democratization of the intelligentsia would pose a terrible dilemma for their artistic leaders: what, after all, was the point of being an intellectual if the people themselves could not only produce but think as well? Faced with the prospect of redundancy, would the intelligentsia maintain its commitment to democracy, or would it retreat into mysticism and exoticism?

To Gorky, speaking in 1934 at the first Congress of Soviet Writers, 'the main and basic theme of pre-revolutionary literature was the tragedy of a person to whom life seemed cramped, who felt superfluous in society, sought therein a comfortable place, failed to find it and suffered, died, or reconciled himself to a society that was hostile to him, or sank to drunkenness or suicide'. His own life, and that of his friend and mentor Chekhov, illustrated another theme: the struggle of gifted people to avoid the many snares that lay on the road to their full development as human beings. Despite their debt to Tolstoy, Chekhov and Gorky were both westernizing humanists.

The onslaught on society through the description of the fate inflicted on its more talented members was indeed a basic theme, both before and after the 1880s. But it ceased to be treated on the same scale, and it ceased to resound with the same note of protest. The isolation of the individual from society came to be matter for acceptance rather than matter for attack. But this was no joyful acceptance. The Russian masses who were beginning to find themselves in a world of individuals experienced little of the sense of elation that an eighteenth-century aristocrat may have felt on being awakened to European civilization. For the displaced ex-peasants of Russia, the process was experienced as a series of losses: the loss of warmth and comfort of primitive economy and commune, and the loss of moral dependence once provided by the beating patriarchs who traditionally assumed the sins of their 'children'. These psychological traumas were intensified by real economic hardships and the cruel indifference of the authorities. There was also no guarantee that the emergence of a more democratic and humane society could be accomplished in a tolerably humane fashion. The acceptance of individualism was therefore combined with a fierce rejection of the values of society and a very strong undercurrent of foreboding. It was the note that Tolstoy struck in a diary entry in 1881: 'An economic revolution not only may come but must come. It is extraordinary that it has not come already.' The famous words that Chekhov put into the mouth of Baron Tuzenbach in *Three Sisters* are even more prophetic:

> The time has come, an avalanche is moving down on us, a mighty, wholesome storm is brewing, which is approaching, is already near, and soon will sweep away from our society its idleness, indifference, prejudice against work, and foul *ennui*. I shall work, and in some twenty-five or thirty years everyone will work too.

Round about the turn of the century such thinkers as Freud, Sorel, and Nietzsche had already given voice to a sentiment of collapse, that a world was dying, that the old order had had its day, that forces of unreason and violence were struggling to the surface. This foreboding and anticipation of the future was sensed in Russia perhaps more deeply than anywhere else – if only, perhaps, because violence and the regime's unvarying policy of repression were so patent a feature of the national life.

Thus to those unable to share in the hope of revolution the future was bleak indeed. And never more so than in the period of intensified reaction, of pogroms and oppression, that followed the assassination of Alexander II. It was then that Tolstoy, having renounced literature, became the moral conscience of the nation, and grew to such stature that although the government might prohibit the publication of his works, it dared not silence the man himself.

'Who is mad – they or I?' Tolstoy asked this question after a family discussion in which he had heard conventional pro-governmental views put forward on the topics of the day. The question would not obsess him much longer. His positive doctrine was ascetic and strikingly similar to the doctrines of Gandhi in India – the gospel of universal love, undogmatic Christianity, sexual abstinence, the renunciation of tobacco and alcohol, non-resistance to evil. But his disintegrating criticism of society and its values, his corrosive and derisive scepticism, made him into an anarchist more anarchic and a nihilist more nihilistic than any whom Russia had yet produced or would produce in the future.

'What is science?' he asked. Had it done anything important or unique when it determined the weight of Saturn's satellites? What was universal suffrage? A means for the prisoners to elect their own gaolers. Had industrialism raised the standard of living? Then look at the slums and doss-houses of Moscow. In his powerful work *The Restoration of Hell* (1903), he derided division of labour as a device for turning men into machines, book printing as a medium for communicating 'all the nasty and stupid things that are done and written in the world', philanthropy as plundering by the hundredweight and returning by the ounce, socialism as fostering class enmity in the name of the supreme organization of man's life – and as for reform, 'it taught people that though themselves bad they can reform bad people'. No iconoclast ever made such a *tabula rasa* of the hopes and beliefs cherished by the men and women of his time. Despite this, the hand of friendship he proffered Gorky was to ensure an essential continuity in Russian literary culture well into the twentieth century.

After Tolstoy's denunciations, the voice of Chekhov must inevitably sound muted and anticlimactic. But Chekhov too had his own specific contribution to make to the revolt against society that marked the Russian *fin de siècle*. It was couched primarily in personal terms. To politics Chekhov was more or less indifferent. He was explicitly apolitical.

Great writers and artists [he wrote in defence of Zola's intervention in the Dreyfus case] must take part in politics only in so far as it is necessary to put a defence against politics. There are enough prosecutors and gendarmes already, without adding to the number.

Chekhov, however, in his own way, and despite himself, was also a prosecutor; and the indictment that he drew up against Russian society is redolent of Gogol's *Dead Souls*. But it is expressed with a mitigating touch of sympathetic humour where Gogol had been satiric. To Chekhov Russia was a country where men, kindly men and men of goodwill, were isolated both from one another and from society, and where their women were condemned to hysteria. It was a chaotic, frustrating world of alienated individuals, victims of their own sentiment of inferiority *vis-à-vis* an impossibly imposing environment. It was a world where the individual was powerless, and reduced to finding his or her *raison d'être* in the expression of his or her own feelings. It was a world where nobody was happy save dogs and children.

Chekhov did indeed have faith in a better future. His vision was not irretrievably and inconsolably bleak, as was Tolstoy's. It was easier for the *intelligent* doctor to see the possible benefits of the new industrial world than for the aristocratic landowner. But the situation was so desperate that half-measures were a mere palliative; and he could not conceive of revolution. In the end, all that was left to comfort Chekhov was a belief, as he himself put it, 'in individual personalities, scattered here and there throughout Russia, whether they be intellectuals or peasants'. How substantial could this hope be, in the face of the overwhelming preponderance of the trivial, the humdrum, the shoddy, and the pretentious?

The third major figure in Russian literary culture in these years was Gorky. The pseudonym 'Gorky' means bitter; the man was both portent and patron of that bitter awakening to individualism endured by the Russian peasants and workers in this century. Lionized by the intelligentsia as the long-awaited proletarian writer of the turn of the century, he quarrelled with most of them over their passivity in 1905. Ironically, his reputation with the intelligentsia declined as his artistry improved. His popularity among socialists all over the world and the newly-literate Russian peasants and workers was never in doubt. After the revolution he decisively rejected the notion that the workers needed intellectuals to provide them with a synthetic proletarian culture. He supervised the translation and cheap publication of the classics of world literature so that the people could decide for themselves.

Gorky was not the first writer to record the degradation to which Russian society subjected so many men and women of the lower classes. What was new about his anti-heroes and anti-heroines was that 'they were wrathful, forceful human beings, ready to challenge the very order of things that turned them into thieves, drunkards and derelicts'. His sentimental and didactic novel *Mother* suffers from a degree of linguistic poverty and a faith that simple characters can be artistically satisfying. Its importance lies in its portrayal of the moment when workers and peasants began to take hold of the message of socialism and wield it as a weapon in their own struggles. His support for the Bolsheviks and for the 1905 Moscow Rising showed him to be more than a mere writer. His willingness to publish the polemical writing of the revolutionary feminist Alexandra Kollontai showed that he was more than a mere Bolshevik. Against all the odds and in defiance of the pessimism which afflicted a large proportion of the intelligentsia after 1905, Gorky insisted that the future belonged to the people in a society that was both socialist and humane.

The Russian *fin de siècle* began in earnest after the failure of the 1905 revolution. The specifically Russian form of the decadent movement emphasized the impossibility of communication between one human being and another, which is, for example, the leitmotif of Andreyev's writings. There was also the turning away from public themes to private pursuits – the glorification of sex, the resurrection of myth and legend, the invocation of death, the exploration of the emotions. These last were the favoured matter of the symbolist poets, the closest Russian equivalent to the Western exponents of art for art's sake. At a more light-hearted level, the cult of Sherlock Holmes enjoyed a brief vogue among the literate members of Russian society in these years.

Despite an element of hyperbole, there was some truth in Dmitri Merezhkovsky's assertion that previous generations of Russian artists had merely reacted to the West while his own aspired to lead it. These are the years that saw the first flowering of the

Moscow Arts Theatre of Stanislavsky and Nemirovich-Dan-chenko, the work of Meyerhold at St Petersburg, the 'Diaghilev period' of the Russian ballet, the first works of Stravinsky and Rakhmaninov, and the shift from post-impressionism to con-structivism in painting associated with Larionov and Goncharova, Chagall and Alexandra Exter. For the first time in their history St Petersburg and Moscow became intellectual and artistic centres comparable to any in the West. In 1904 Pavlov earned the renown of all the world when his work in psychology brought him Russia's first Nobel prize.

All the intelligentsia sensed the ground shaking under their feet: some in their fear of what was to come blamed the radical and rational tradition of the intelligentsia itself and sought to return to Christianity via neo-Kantianism. While they might overcome the pitfalls of instrumental ethics, their philosophy failed to rehabili-tate the normal economic motives of ordinary people. While they might dislike Bolshevism, they could not bring themselves to like capitalism. This group, best known by the titles of the essays they published – *Signposts*, was unable to stem the outburst of chiliastic, apocalyptic, and eschatological thought and sentiment that emerged in the decades preceding the First World War. This had always been a feature of Russian social criticism, of course. Baku-nin's anarchism, for example, has been seen as the direct con-tinuation of chiliastic attitudes in the modern world; and the messianic conception of Moscow as the Third Rome had been preserved in many of the dissident sects, less subject to the westernizing influence of St Petersburg. It even emerged in the Petrashevsky circle, where French Utopian socialism took on at times an unusual note.

A life of wealth and bliss, to cover this beggar's earth with palaces and fruits and to adorn it with fruits – this is our aim [wrote one of the members]. Here in our country will we begin this revolution, and the whole world will bring it to fulfilment. Soon the whole of mankind will be freed from unbearable suffering.

The nearer the revolution came, and particularly after 1905, the more acute and pervasive this feeling grew. It can be found in Merezhkovsky, the theoretician of symbolism, in the poems of his wife Zinaida Gippius, one of the movement's best poets, and in the influential novel *Petersburg* by Bely, in which the anxiety and alienation of the characters bring the city itself to life. It informed the religious philosophy of Rozanov and Solovyov. It even survived the Bolshevik revolution of 1917 and inspired the 'Scythian' movement of Ivanov-Razumnik and the peasant-poet Esenin. The 'Scythians' saw the revolution as the outburst of a newborn, unlimited, maximalist spirit that would sweep away the corrupt old world, as Christianity had once burst asunder the decadent Roman Empire. In the 'Internationale' Ivanov-Razumnik could hear the words 'Peace on earth, goodwill to men'. This cast of thought reached its climax in Blok's poem, 'The Twelve' of 1918. Blok, probably the greatest of the symbolist poets and a sympathizer with the left Socialist Revolutionaries, who were themselves allied for a time to the Bolsheviks, depicts twelve riotous, rowdy Red Guards marching through the snowy streets of Petersburg, shouting, shooting, cursing, blaspheming. They are led by a man bearing the red flag – Jesus Christ. Blok in turn helped to inspire the loudspeaker poet of the victorious revolution, Mayakovsky.

In his essay of 1918, 'The Intelligentsia and Revolution', Blok compared the revolution to a mighty phenomenon of nature. 'We Russians,' he exclaimed, 'are living through an epoch which has had few things equal to it in grandeur.' The aim is –

To remake everything. To build everything anew, so that our lying, dirty, boring, monstrous life becomes a just and clean, a joyous and beautiful life ... The range of the Russian Revolution aimed at embracing the world. A true revolution cannot wish for less ... 'The peace and the brotherhood of the people' – that is the symbol under which the Russian Revolution is taking place. It is of this that its torrent is roaring. This is the music which those with ears must hear.

This dithyrambic outburst was not typical of all the intelligentsia; all too many contributed to the culture of the world in exile after 1921 and Blok himself died disillusioned in that year. But it forms an apt prelude to the last decade of the autocracy. Blok's cry, 'We are Scythians, we are Asiatics, with slit and hungry eyes', was tantamount to a rejection of the whole St Petersburg tradition. A Russian wind was blowing from the endless plain that would sweep the official nihilism of St Petersburg from the map forever. Artistically speaking, all that would be left were the heirs of the Acmeists, a small group of poets dedicated to the integrity of language. It was they who foresaw the corruption of the revolution, when it came, and bequeathed to the Soviet intelligentsia a vital critical tool with which to appraise the avalanche of Russia's 'Second Revolution'.

CHAPTER 13

From Revolution to War

The revolution of 1905 did not end with the arrest of the St Petersburg Soviet or the crushing of the Moscow armed uprising. In the early part of 1906 the peasant movement raged as intensively as ever. To take one instance: in one district of the province of Voronezh the peasants razed to the ground all the landowners' houses and farms. Mutinies in the army and navy were almost as frequent in 1906 as in the preceding year. But it is clear in retrospect that the high-point had come, and gone. The officer corps was intact, the peasant soldiers had honoured their oaths and tsarism had won a reprieve.

'La Revolution est morte, vive la Revolution', exclaimed Trotsky. The words had a challenging ring, but also a somewhat hollow sound. One of the government's achievements in 1905–6 was to inflict a serious defeat on the workers' movement, sufficient to demoralize it for five years and to prevent it re-organizing on a national scale until 1917. The declining number of strikers tells its own story: in round figures, 1905 – three million; 1906 – one million; 1907 – 400,000; 1908 – 174,000; 1909 – 64,000. No wonder Lenin's wife, Krupskaya, could lament in 1909: 'We have no people at all.' The active membership of the underground revolutionary groups declined from some 100,000 in 1905 to some 10,000 in 1910. Despite their moderation, the Russian liberals, organized in Milyukov's Kadet (i.e. Constitutional Democratic) Party, suffered a similar fate – the party's membership declined from 100,000 in 1906 to only 25,000 in 1908. From 1912 a new upsurge began, triggered by the massacre of the striking gold-miners in distant Siberia. Once again strikes, both economic and political, took on a momentum that began to rival 1905. One-and-a-half million struck in the first half of 1914. The left wing of the Kadet Party began to demand a rapprochement with the socialists. Some Russian industrialists showed their dissatisfaction with the government and the desire to form a united opposition expressed itself in the creation of a political freemasonry immune to the secret police.

Internationally, as Lenin pointed out, the abortive revolution had given 'rise to a movement throughout the whole of Asia. The revolutions in Turkey (1908), Persia (1909), and China (1911) prove that the mighty uprising of 1905 left deep traces, and that its influence expressed in the forward movement of *hundreds and hundreds* of millions of people is ineradicable.'

And yet, and yet . . . by 1906 the revolutionary elite lay in tsarist gaols, in Siberian deportation, or in European exile. Lenin was back in Finland. A year earlier he had been zealously translating into Russian a manual on street-fighting tactics. Trotsky, clad in drab prison garb, was on trial for his life. He would shortly be on his way with fourteen others to serve a sentence of life deportation in Siberia.

The year of revolution had shown the astonishing resilience of the regime. It could yield ground on every front, face the bitter opposition of almost all the articulate strata of society, endure a crippling general strike, see outbreaks of mutiny in the army and navy, lose a disastrous war in the Far East, be discredited internationally – and still survive. And not only survive; it could also go over to the offensive. As early as October 1905, the Tsar's appeal for support brought hundreds of pogroms to the towns and hamlets of the Jewish Pale and initiated a campaign of assassination of socialists and liberals. A government wedded to industrial capitalism and reliant on its bureaucracy could not make consistent use of proto-fascism, any more than police trade-unionism. The fascist Union of the Russian People took only 5 per cent of the Moscow vote in 1906 and was allowed to decay once the moment of danger seemed past. Antisemitism periodically revived, however. In 1911, for example, the government even went so far as to accuse a Kiev Jew, Mendel Beilis, of murdering a Gentile child for ritual reasons. The case, a *cause célèbre* in its day throughout the world, ended two years later with the acquittal of Beilis.

For a moment, however, a more immediate task was to confront the Duma and the new political parties that sprang into being. Before the Duma could meet, the government prepared its position. First of all, and in defiance of the terms of the October Manifesto, it issued a kind of constitution, the Fundamental Laws. These drastically limited the powers of the Duma and permitted the tsar to reassert autocratic power in emergency circumstances. It also created a buffer between itself and the Duma in the shape of the State Council, an upper chamber with equal rights to the Duma, consisting of imperial nominees and representatives of the wealthier commercial and professional classes in equal numbers. The State Duma was elected on the broader franchise introduced by Witte. The electors were divided into six *curiae*, depending on whether they were landowners, town-dwellers, peasants, or workers. Each *curia* elected electors in the proportion of 1 to 2,000 (landowners), 1 to 7,000 (town dwellers), 1 to 30,000 (peasants), and 1 to 90,000 (workers). This rigged assembly was further hampered by the narrowness of its competence. The Duma could exercise only a very limited control over the State finances. There was no responsibility to the Duma on the part of the ministers; they were responsible only to the tsar. Lastly, no law could become effective without receiving the approval of both houses and the sanction of the tsar, anything but a foregone conclusion.

Given these handicaps, it is a tribute to the optimism of the voters that this first experiment in Russian constitutionalism yet gave birth to a number of parties and groupings, and that by 10 May 1906 around 450 deputies were present at the opening of the Duma.

There were about twenty-six political groupings and some twelve national groups. The Constitutional Democrats or 'Kadets' – who represented the zemstvo liberals and the majority of the intelligentsia – had 170–80 seats. The more conservative liberals, the Octobrists – i.e. those who regarded the October Manifesto as a satisfactory basis for Russian development – had 30–40. The national groups – Polish, Ukrainian, Latvian, etc. – with some 60 seats were radical and nationalist. A Labour group formed from radical but non-party peasants had a combined membership of about 100. There were another 100 peasant members of no definite affiliation, and 18 Social Democrats, mainly Georgian Mensheviks. (The Mensheviks had become *the* national party of

Georgia.) Officially, both wings of the R.S.D.L.P. and the S.R.s boycotted the elections.

It was a tense opening session in the throne-room of the Winter Palace! To one side of the Tsar stood senators and the Imperial entourage; to the other the newly elected deputies, many in peasant blouses, workers' overalls, and rough boots. So charged with hostility was the mood that Stolypin, Minister of the Interior, whispered to his ministerial colleague, Kokovtsov, that he feared a bombing attempt. The Dowager-Empress noted 'a strange, incomprehensible hatred' on the faces of the deputies – as well she might.

The storm burst at the Duma's first session. Speaker after speaker brought forth flaming demands – an amnesty for political prisoners, the abolition of the death penalty, the resignation of the government, the elimination of the upper house, ministerial responsibility, the confiscation of the large estates, the right to strike, equality before the law, the reformation of the whole tax system, and a democratic electoral system. Gradually, Milyukov – not a member but the most influential person in the first Duma – forged a programme of radical reform from these potentially revolutionary demands.

From the point of view of the government each demand in itself was tantamount to a declaration of war. Taken together, they destroyed any possibility of co-operation between the government and the Duma. In ten weeks it was all over. On 22 July (9 July Old Style), a Sunday, large bodies of troops surrounded the Tauride Palace, where the Duma met, and simultaneously the Tsar decreed its dissolution on the grounds that it had exceeded its competence, shown itself incapable of efficient work, and addressed illegal appeals to the people. The Tsar gave no date for new elections, as he was legally obliged to do, but merely proclaimed that the second Duma would convene in February 1907. Two hundred left-wing and Kadet members thereupon made their way to Vyborg in nearby Finland. Here they appealed to the public to refuse to pay taxes and to refuse to register for military service. The appeal went unheeded; the Kadets themselves were so embarrassed by it that they conducted no agitation in its favour.

The second Duma followed a similar path to the first and was dispersed after a three-month session on trumped-up charges against the Social-Democratic deputies. They were accused of plotting the assassination of the Tsar and of inciting the troops to mutiny. The 'Coup of 3 June 1907' illegally narrowed the franchise to secure the elimination of the voice of the poorer peasants and most of the border nationalities from subsequent Dumas. The third Duma ran its full course, not without further conflict with the government. The fourth found itself obliged to yield to the February revolution of 1917. Altogether it was not a happy history. The Duma suffered from what has been called

... the dilemma of attaining complex, specifically Western objectives in an illiberal, under-developed society. Were the only alternatives those of conciliating the illiberal government or changing it by illiberal means ...? On each occasion the range of plausible Liberal answers was narrowly circumscribed by the same environment, the same Russia.*

To return to the first Duma – the dissolution was precipitated by the land issue, or, more precisely, by the need to alleviate the peasants' land-hunger. This was not fortuitous. As Russian politics became more democratic, the largest social class in Russian society was bound to receive more attention. Both the government and the parties of the centre and left – in addition to the Socialist-Revolutionaries who regarded themselves as *the* peasant party – were beginning to concentrate their efforts on fortifying the peasants as a bulwark of the State, or, alternatively, on mobilizing the discontent of the peasantry as a positively anti-governmental force rather than allowing such discontent to dissipate itself in futile, sporadic, and short-lived *jacqueries*.

Ever since the late 1890s some sort of agrarian reform had been in the air. Arrears of redemption payments were mounting, and the size of the individual allotments was becoming tinier and tinier as a result of population growth. The issue soon began to centre on individual as against communal tenure. Would Russia become a country of peasant proprietors? Under the pressure of events, the government gradually came to look in this direction. The power of the commune was weakened in 1903 when, in many provinces, it was relieved of joint responsibility for the State obli-

* G. Fischer, *Russian Liberalism* (Cambridge, Mass., 1958), p. 203.

gations of its members. Then, in 1905, a decree cancelled all further redemption payments after the peasants should have paid half the sums due for 1906. This was a radical concession to necessity.

In the first Duma, Professor Herzenstein, a Kadet member and Moscow agricultural specialist, proposed that the State expropriate the large landowners on payment of fair compensation. The land would then be distributed to the peasants in return for a form of payment. This foundered on the absolute refusal of Nicholas II to contemplate any form of compulsory alienation of private property. Respect for the notion of private property, especially in land, had been very slow to grow in Russia. The gentry felt confident that one of its few tangible gains from the settlement of 1861 was the respect of the State for its property rights. In fact the conversion of the autocracy to respect for property was almost absolute; men like Herzen and Lenin might suffer the loss of their rights as citizens, but as property owners the State never ceased to respect them. Many of the intelligentsia came to share this feeling; the veteran Populist Peshekhonov wanted to protest against the Soviet seizure of private presses during the February revolution. In 1906 the question was: could this sentiment be transmitted to the Russian peasantry?

It was from the government itself that some of the most radical measures relating to Russian land tenure finally emanated. Many of them were conceived under Witte but they have always been associated with the name of Stolypin, for it was he who attempted to carry them out. Peter Stolypin was born the son of a landowner, graduated from St Petersburg University, and, like his father before him, took up a career in the bureaucracy. By 1905, when Stolypin was forty-four, he had risen to become Governor of the province of Saratov. In that year of revolution he made himself notorious for his cruelty to peasants and revolutionaries. His later actions, especially his ruthless treatment of Jews and Poles, further justified his reputation and the gallows was popularly known as 'Stolypin's necktie'. The field courts martial and extraordinary powers given to governor-generals were responsible, between September 1906 and May 1907, for the execution of more than 1,100 people. Stolypin became Minister of the Interior and chairman of the Council of Ministers in 1906 and held these offices until 1911.

Witte's experience showed him that true cabinet government was still impossible in Russia but Stolypin attempted to be a genuine Prime Minister. Even this was too much for Nicholas II, a man of average endowments truly happy only with nonentities. Stolypin, the last considerable politician of Imperial Russia, died of a police agent's bullet in the autumn of 1911 – to the great relief of his master.

Repression was only one half of Stolypin's policy. Under his premiership, government and Duma achieved a measure of co-operation, introducing universal, free, elementary education and moving towards the first social insurance schemes. Stolypin's name is associated most of all with the end of the commune. The ultimate idea was to introduce almost completely free trade into the buying and selling of land. The more able peasants would then emerge as small landed proprietors with a strong stake in the existing order; and they would hold in check the less able, who were destined to dwindle into a landless rural proletariat. In Stolypin's words, 'the government relied not on the feeble and the drunk, but on the solid and strong'.

This policy came into effect in 1906, when peasants were allowed to obtain passports on the same terms as anyone else and when the land captains lost their power over the peasants. It continued until 1911, when the final land-settlement act was passed. The intervening legislation was almost as complex as the Emancipation Act of 1861. But essentially what it did was to entitle every house-holder in a commune where the land was periodically redistrib-uted to turn his share of arable land into his inalienable, individual property. The commune could not oppose this. Where the communes were based on hereditary tenure, the government simply decreed that individual ownership was now in force.

Many other rural institutions went into limbo together with communal tenure. Communally owned pasture and grazing land was divided up; the traditional scattered strips of land were con-solidated into one farmstead; finally, joint family ownership was, as a rule, abolished by acknowledging the family elder as the owner of the household's allotment.

Altogether some twelve million peasant households were involved and 320 million acres. The reforms got off to an excellent start in 1907 with some 50,000 householders leaving the commune; the number soared the next year to half a million, and in 1909 to nearly 580,000. The machinery came to an end at the beginning of 1916 because those peasants in uniform were naturally unable to take part in the negotiations over their property rights. By then about two million householders had received legal title to their new lands and started out on their own. Many, of course, later sold their land to the more able peasants, and in this process the enlarged Peasant Bank played a growing and important role. The net result was growing social stratification in the village. This was accompanied by the spread of modernized methods of farming, increased production by the purchase and rent of extra land, and expanding output in the more profitable branches of agriculture like dairy-farming. Peasant co-operatives flourished during these years. Internal colonization was another means of attack on the peasant problem. Between 1905 and 1915 about three-and-a-half million people emigrated to Siberia, most of them with government assistance.

It turned out to be too little, too late. This would probably have been so even had Russia enjoyed another decade of peace after 1914. The problem was only partly one of redistributing the land. The average peasant holding in Russia by 1905 was actually larger than its French or German counterpart. But agricultural technique was so low that its yield in crops was no more than between one-half and one-third. Also, Stolypin's reforms were insufficient to offset the growth in rural population that amounted to some one and a half million per year; much of this was in the politically sensitive Black Earth zone south of Moscow. Thus, even if he had thrown into the balance the 140 million-odd acres that were still in the hands of the nobility – which neither he nor his sovereign would countenance – he could still not solve the problem. In fact, he may actually have exacerbated it by increasing the number of landless peasants and grinding them down both absolutely and relatively. What was needed was the raising of agricultural pro-ductivity and accelerated industrial development and to this the reforms made only an insignificant contribution in relation to the scale of the problem.

Lenin, and the revolutionaries generally, no less than Stolypin, could draw their own conclusions from the peasant upheavals of 1905 and the radicalism demonstrated by the peasants in the Duma elections just as they had from the caution displayed by the Russian liberals. The land issue came up at the fourth Congress of the R.S.D.L.P., attended by both Bolsheviks and Mensheviks, at Stockholm in 1906. In all respects this congress showed a determination to square the facts of recent Russian experience with the dogmas of the Marxist factions. In view of the Kadet success at the polls, Plekhanov's view that the working class had demonstrated its 'hegemony' over the bourgeoisie was somewhat shaken. While the explosive potential of peasant discontent was now clear to all, it was far from clear what the Marxists should do about it. The Mensheviks argued in favour of expropriating the land and municipalizing it for the benefit of local peasant bodies. Lenin advocated the nationalization of the land with a view to blunting the accusation that he was less than orthodox in his attitude towards the peasantry. Obviously, this only made sense if he envisioned a speedy transition to a socialist state. It was left to Stalin, the sole Bolshevik representative from the Caucasus, to come out with a piece of obvious revolutionary common sense: the revolutionaries must promise to give the peasants the land or encourage them to seize it for themselves.

In the long run, of course, Marxists were opposed to the creation of a propertied petty-bourgeois stratum, backward and essentially reactionary. But Lenin was forced to admit that in 1905 he had underestimated 'the breadth and depth of the democratic or rather bourgeois-democratic movement among the peasantry'. He asserted that what the Russian peasantry were carrying out was not the struggle against large-scale farming, but the struggle of the dispossessed against feudalism. Thus they were carrying the class struggle into the countryside and clearing the way for the emergence of capitalist farming, which would produce its own proletariat: '... in this instance,' Lenin declared, 'we want to support small property, not against capitalism but against feudalism.'

If the Mensheviks were gambling on the possibility of the emergence of open mass politics, and even, perhaps, on some further advances towards a genuinely constitutional order in Russia, Lenin was gambling on the failure of Stolypin's policies. Of course a landless rural proletariat would be created with a burden of discontent that could easily be exploited in town and country alike. As against this, however, a bourgeois peasant class might come into existence, clinging to its new status and property, and – like the peasantry of the Third French Republic – constituting a far stronger barrier to revolution than a declining rural gentry, riddled with debts, incompetent, and often only too happy to dispose of its property at a reasonable price. By 1911, Lenin could discern the failure of Stolypin's attempt 'to pour new wine into the old bottles, to reshape the autocracy into a bourgeois monarchy'. He drew comfort from the fact that this failure 'is the failure of Tsarism on this last road – *the last conceivable road* for Tsarism'. (Italics in the original.)

In 1931, Stalin declared that it was 'axiomatic' that Leninism and Bolshevism had always been identical. Remarkably, historians outside the Soviet Union have accepted this view almost as readily as those in Russia. And yet, in 1907, Lenin lost the leadership of the Bolsheviks to Bogdanov and was driven into a new alliance with Plekhanov and the Social Democrat 'centrists'. Only in 1912 was he able to re-launch his own party. The crisis in the Bolshevik faction was brought about by the events of 1905–7. The revolution brought a substantial recruitment of revolutionary socialists to the Bolshevik ranks who were reluctant to accept the need to work with the Duma after 1906. There is some evidence that suggests that Lenin was even considering the possibility that his party would have to work along the same lines as those of the 'centre' Social Democrats in Germany at this time. Lenin used a variety of weapons in re-establishing a Bolshevik party under his authority during these years. One was organizational: Lenin's party centre simply expelled Bogdanov from the party in 1909. However, this was merely the culmination of a process in which control of party funds and philosophical polemic were essential preliminaries. The financial struggle was waged in 1907. At first, Lenin seemed to have lost out when Krasin sided with Bogdanov and refused to allow Lenin to monopolize the profits of the notorious bank-raid carried out by the Georgian Bolshevik Kamo in Tiflis. (The bank-raid was exposed and provided the Mensheviks with a useful weapon against all the Bolsheviks in the Socialist International.)

The methods used by Lenin's ally Taratuta, to even the score, were only slightly less scandalous, involving a matrimonial intrigue to get hold of a millionaire's inheritance. Thus armed, Lenin could ensure the continuation of his own journal and the subsidy of like-minded groups in Russia on condition that they voted for him in intra-party conflicts. The philosophical battle was only joined in 1909. Lenin had known since 1903 that Bogdanov's views were in conflict with the Party orthodoxy established by Plekhanov but had refrained from criticizing them in public so long as they had agreed on revolutionary tactics. He now saw Bogdanov's philosophy as his Achilles' heel; an attack on it would discredit Bogdanov with the rank-and-file and might bring about a rapprochement with Plekhanov. In 1909, Lenin published his contribution to Marxist philosophy under the title *Materialism and Empiriocriticism*. In view of Lenin's reputation for voluntarism, it is ironic that his sole excursion into epistemology should be a 'plea for a rational, experimental approach to nature and society'.* It provides striking confirmation that with Lenin, the unity of theory and practice invariably subordinates theory to practice.

After further skirmishes with both Mensheviks and 'left-Bolsheviks' Lenin finally took the plunge in 1912 and, at a conference of his supporters in Prague, announced the formation of a separate Bolshevik Social-Democratic Party. Its organ, *Pravda* (*Truth*) soon commanded a circulation inside Russia five times greater than that of its Menshevik rival. At no time, in fact, did the Mensheviks make any serious attempt to adopt the tight discipline and sectarianism of Lenin's organization. Many of Lenin's colleagues lacked the erudition and high-mindedness of the Menshevik leaders but their capacity for action was at least equal. Only the Georgian Mensheviks had the cohesion and élan of the Bolsheviks.

Lenin's other rivals on the left, the Socialist-Revolutionaries, were in even greater trouble. Several voices demanded tactics applicable to an age of mass politics, e.g. the intimidation of capitalists or bureaucrats by the masses. When the critics of centralized terror were expelled from the party and denounced as 'maximalists', S.R. chances of capitalizing on its support in the towns were seriously damaged. In general, there was a tendency for

* B. Wolfe, *Three who Made a Revolution* (London, 1966), p. 570.

ex-peasants to turn to the Bolsheviks as they came to accept that their futures lay in the towns rather than in a return to the peasant communes. In 1908 it emerged that the key figure in the S.R.'s terrorist organization, Yevno Azef, had been a police spy all along. Inevitably, this unleashed a furious debate among the S.R.s about the tactics of the party. December 1908 saw a scandalous row split the women's movement in Russia when Alexandra Kollontai's revolutionary feminists barracked a meeting called by middle-class feminists who hoped to win women the vote on the same restricted terms as men. From Lenin's point of view, this cannot have been unwelcome. Nor did the failure of the Kadets displease him during these years. For all their willingness to endure the Stolypin reaction they failed to extract any significant concessions from the regime. Even when they went out of their way to support the government over foreign policy, for example, their gestures were spurned. As war approached, the influence of 'dark forces' over the throne grew and Nicholas showed increasing interest in schemes to transform the Duma into a merely consultative assembly.

The years of bitter polemic, intrigue and faction fighting were as important in the education of the future leaders of the Soviet state as the preceding period of revolutionary enthusiasm. Lenin gathered around himself the economist Kamenev and the fiery orator Zinoviev, while the young Bukharin was graduating from student politics to membership of the Bolshevik committee in Moscow. Krupskaya continued to supply vital organizational skills, while Inessa Armand, future head of the Women's Departments, represented the Bolsheviks on the Women's Bureau of the Socialist International. An important recruit to Lenin's new Central Committee was the crude Georgian conspirator Stalin; after 1913, he found himself exiled to Siberia with the revolutionary bureaucrat Sverdlov. Many future Bolshevik leaders stayed outside Lenin's party at this time. They included Trotsky and Lunacharsky, interested in broad cultural matters as well as narrowly political ones, and Kollontai, who laid down the basis for a socialist solution of 'the women question' in Russia. The cosmopolitan Krasin gradually withdrew from active politics but his skills as engineer, financier and conspirator were there when needed. Many future Soviet leaders were still Mensheviks at this time, such as the aristocratic Russian Chicherin and the Jewish intellectual Litvinov, who would one day become the foreign affairs experts of the Soviet state. The Bolsheviks and future Bolsheviks compared favourably to the Kadet leadership as they did to the leadership of the other opposition parties. As the influence of Rasputin and other favourites combined to weed out the last remaining independence of spirit from the higher reaches of the government, the contrast between the Marxists and the Tsarists was as Hyperion to a satyr.

FROM THE ENTENTE TO THE WARTIME ALLIANCE

After the defeat of 1905, the story of Russian foreign relations can largely be told in terms of the conversion of the Russian government from its traditional policy of friendship with the Germans to one of accommodation with, and ultimately reliance on, France and even Britain.

An essential preliminary was a drawing together of victor and vanquished in the Far East. The threat of American, British, and German economic intervention in northern China, an area where both Russia and Japan had staked out their own claims, hastened this rapprochement. In 1907 a Russo-Japanese convention confirmed the division of Manchuria into a northern, Russian sphere of influence and a southern, Japanese sphere. Russia thereby accepted the abandonment of its more ambitious plans in the Far East and affirmed the *status quo*. Later revisions of this agreement gave it more bite. Japan annexed Korea while Russia fostered the autonomy of Mongolia and increased its influence in the Singkiang border areas.

Peace with Japan was followed by a settlement of differences with Japan's ally, Britain. The Anglo-Russian convention of 1907 defined the relations of the two countries in three disputed areas. As such, it was a classical specimen of the diplomacy of the period. In Tibet, both powers acknowledged Chinese sovereignty and undertook to refrain from intervention; in Afghanistan, Russia recognized an English sphere of influence; Persia was carved up, the north with its oilfields falling to the Russians, the south, of more use to a naval power anxious about India, falling to the British. A central, buffer zone was left free. The agreement did not prevent the British from trying to control all the Persian oil industry, nor the Russians from trying to control the Persian government whose capital lay in their zone. Finally, the British, now securely established in Egypt, offered vague promises of support for Russian policy in the Dardanelles. There was nothing at all in this agreement to suggest that either power would support the other in a major European war.

In July 1908, the Ottoman Sultan Abdul Hamid was overthrown by the 'Young Turk' revolution led by Mustafa Shevket and Enver Pasha. As we have seen, this development was greeted with enthusiasm by Lenin; the Russian liberals, ideologically closer to the 'Young Turks', were equally pleased. Predictably, perhaps, the Russian government was anything but pleased. Turkey, the ancestral enemy, had become an important, though unacknowledged, ally of Russia in south-east Europe. In calling into being the independent nations of Greece and Bulgaria, Russia had helped to create two more rivals to the heritage of Byzantium; the Russians were willing to forego the conquest of Constantinople ('Tsargrad') but only on the understanding that the other Orthodox states did the same. Good relations between Russia, Bulgaria, and Greece therefore depended on a strong Turkey. Turkish strength was also vital if the Straits were to be properly controlled. The Russians had announced their intention of re-militarizing the Black Sea during the Franco-Prussian War, but in fact they had done little about this, allowing the Turks naval supremacy on the Black Sea on the assumption that they would continue to deny access through the Straits to the navies of other nations. Since then, the Ukraine had become increasingly vital to Russia's economic success, providing the bulk of her grain exports and harbouring major industrial centres. The Straits had therefore become vital to Russia for economic as well as military reasons.

Unfortunately for the Russians, Austria-Hungary was better placed, both economically and strategically, to exert its influence in the Balkans. Germany, so tantalizingly close to hegemony over the whole of Europe, gave increasingly uncritical support to its sole reliable ally in the years that followed. In the end, this ensured that Germany and Russia would fight on opposite sides. For some time, Russian Slavophiles had encouraged Czechs and Serbs in their hostility towards Austria while the Austrians had permitted Polish and Ukrainian nationalists – to say nothing of Russian revolutionaries like Lenin – to operate on their soil. Despite this, Russia's first approach towards Austria after the Young Turk revolution was pacific. Foreign Minister Izvolsky suggested that Austria annex the Serbian-speaking Bosnia and Herzegovina, already subject to Austrian military rule, in return for Austrian support for Russia's right to send warships through the Straits. This suggestion ruined Izvolsky when the Austrians annexed the Bosnians before Russia had gained the sanction of the other powers for an alteration in the *status quo* at the Straits. Russia's attempt to work in concert with Austria had been brutally rebuffed.

Stolypin was furious with Izvolsky and had him sacked. His view was clear: 'only after some years of complete quiet can Russia speak again as in the past'. Until his death in 1911, he played the decisive role in Russian foreign policy, though his Foreign Minister Sazonov gradually gained in authority. Stolypin's plan aimed to create an all-Balkan alliance which would serve as a buffer against Austria-Hungary in the peninsula. By 1912 a Balkan League had emerged, uniting Serbia, Bulgaria, Greece, and Montenegro. But instead of recruiting Romania and Turkey to an alliance against Austria, the League attacked Turkey, with almost total success. The Greeks were in Salonika, the Serbs in Albania, and the Bulgarians before the gates of Constantinople. By the spring of 1913, the Sultan was forced to concede almost all Turkey's European possessions.

This display of Balkan independence dismayed the Russians and appalled the Austrians. The Austrians were determined to show that their power could not be thus ignored and simultaneously to bind Serbia closer to them. They therefore insisted that Serbia could not receive a port on the Adriatic. Denied their hopes of expansion to the west, the Serbs decided to hang on to Macedonia, which everyone took to be inhabited by Bulgarians. The Bulgarians attacked the Serbs but the Greeks, Romanians, and Turks combined with the Serbs to force further concessions from Bulgaria. Bulgaria, with a German dynasty since 1882, now had a strong motive in supporting Austrian moves to undermine the newly demonstrated power of Serbia.

The overall effect of these wars was, most importantly, to create further hostility between Russia and Austria-Hungary and to align the Balkan states with one or the other. Bulgarian support for Austria was matched by Serbian and Montenegrin support for Russia. The Romanian people were wooed by Sazonov, who enticed them with the prospect of annexing their fellow-Romanians in Transylvania. But it was Russia's failure in Turkey that confirmed that the real enemies of Russia were not merely in Vienna and Budapest, but in Berlin.

The first sign of German interest in Turkey was the project for a railroad from Constantinople to Baghdad, the concession for which was to be financed by a German group. The Russians knew only too well to what use a concession in an economically weaker country might be put. Russian opposition in this case was bought off by German acknowledgement of Russian supremacy in northern Persia. In November 1913, a major row blew up between Russia and Germany when a German general, Liman von Sanders, was made head of the Turkish army and commander of the garrison at Constantinople. The Germans intended to modernize the Turkish army, but to Sazonov this looked like 'a Prussian garrison under our noses!'. Russia's failure to regain the friendship of the Turks ensured that she would fight the First World War with the crippling disadvantage that the Straits would be closed to her.

From 1912 to 1914, Nicholas II was gradually converted into a reluctant believer in a full alliance with Britain as well as France. This defied the presentiments of Rasputin and intelligent reactionaries such as Durnovo who foresaw the consequences of war with Germany with uncanny precision. In 1912 the first naval conversations between Britain and Russia were agreed, and on the eve of the war a vast loan was floated in Paris for the construction of railways that would facilitate Russian mobilization. The role of Russian public opinion, or rather the opinion of liberals and capitalists, in this process was considerable. When the time came, Nicholas II felt he had no choice but to support Serbia, since

'Russia would never forgive' a new capitulation. Russia mobilized to protect Serbian independence, unsure of the support of France and without regard to the support of Britain. The fate of Russia now depended on men in Berlin, Paris, and London. It would take the Bolshevik revolution and the brutal peace of Brest-Litovsk to bring it back to Moscow.

CHAPTER 14

The Collapse of the Tsarist Order

Despite its economic and organizational inferiority, relative to its enemies, the tsarist Russian State entered the war in fairly good order. The inefficiency and incompetence of large parts of the bureaucracy did not show through immediately. The call-up of men and animals was successfully conducted; the old men and women left in the villages responded to the challenge and maintained agricultural production at its previous level. Had the war been the short one universally predicted the demise of the old order might have been postponed. In the event, the Great War was to demonstrate both the brittleness and senility of the tsarist order and the remarkable resilience of Russian society.

This resilience had shown itself more than once in Russian history. In the seventeenth century, during the Time of Troubles, the combined efforts of civil war, foreign intervention, and economic collapse had been followed by a speedy restoration of the State. Napoleon's invasion in 1812 saw the tsarist State in retreat; the subsequent movement of national resistance catapulted Alexander I into the position of arbiter of the fate of Europe – a lesson Hitler notoriously failed to learn from. But the Russian people have shown a good deal more discrimination than many other peoples in distinguishing between brutal invasions threatening Russian independence and conflicts on Russia's borders which did not seriously threaten Russia. Neither the Crimean War nor the war with Japan aroused any real echo among the masses. For most of the First World War, the Russian armies fought on non-Russian territory, in Poland, Lithuania, western Ukraine, and Romania. Few Russians ever forgot that Teuton and Turk were hereditary enemies but the time came when they began to wonder whether the internal enemies of Russian freedom should not be dealt with first.

Even so, as in all the other belligerent countries there was something of a *union sacrée* at the beginning of the war. The war was all things to all men. The ruling classes, as in Germany, could see in war the opportunity of diverting the labour movement onto less dangerous paths. The Russian liberals could console themselves with the hope that alliance with the Western democracies might lead to some relaxation of the autocracy, perhaps to a government responsible to the Duma. As in 1878, they intended to demonstrate that the zemstvo organizations, under the benign presidency of Prince Georgi Lvov, could compensate for the inefficiency of the tsarist bureaucracy. Although the Russian workers were keen to defend Russia from German aggression, the Russian socialists were less affected by war hysteria than socialists anywhere else. The obverse of patriotism is of course treason; the labelling of enemies as 'traitors' is one of the most unpleasant symptoms of war psychosis. The first victims were the Bolshevik deputies of the Duma and Lenin's emissary, Kamenev. Defended in court by the leading populist in the Duma, the young Alexander Kerensky, all but one had denied agreeing with Lenin's position on the war. Shortly before the war Lenin had written that 'a war between Austria and Russia would be a very helpful thing for the revolution', but, he added regretfully, 'it is not likely that Franz Joseph and Nikolasha will give us that pleasure'. His own response to the war was typically uncompromising: the imperialist war must be converted into civil war everywhere.

The first Russian offensive culminated in the defeat at Tannenberg in August 1914. The campaign was undertaken in response to urgent French pleas for a manoeuvre that would take some of the pressure off Paris. And save Paris it did. The East Prussian campaign forced the Germans to divert eastwards two corps needed for the crucial first battle of the Marne, a debt the French were quick to forget. But the Russian losses were 170,000; a few weeks later the Russians suffered another disaster in East Prussia. The next year, on the southern front in Galicia, there came further disasters, with casualties reaching unprecedented totals. By the end of the first ten months of war they have been estimated at 3,800,000. In 1915 also, Poland, Lithuania, and Courland all fell to the Central Powers. The zigzag path towards the restoration of Polish independence had begun. In 1916 an offensive against Austria-Hungary dealt the Dual Monarchy an irreparable and overwhelming blow; Russia's prestige among the Slavs was shown by the enthusiasm with which the Czechs let themselves be captured. It also saved the Italian army, materially helped the Allies during the battles of Verdun and the Somme, and brought Romania into the war on the Allied side. But again Russian casualties and prisoners ran into millions. By now, the end of 1916, in a welter of corruption, incompetence, abysmal military leadership, and unimaginable human suffering, the Russian Army had all but lost its capacity to fight. Ironically, the Russian Army was better equipped in 1916 than it had ever been at precisely the moment when its human resources were on the brink of giving out. In January 1917, forty-year-old men and youths of the class of 1919 were called up. Politically, the Army had been transformed as career officers from the landowning class were replaced by ensigns of the intelligentsia. The garrisons of St Petersburg were reduced to training battalions, officered by an unstable mixture of unfit believers in autocracy and youthful members of the intelligentsia.

Collapse at the rear matched disarray at the front. The mood of August 1914 proved ephemeral. Very soon an unbridgeable chasm opened up between the government and the people. In fact, who or what *was* the government? The cool response to the tercentenary of the Romanovs in 1913 had shown the weakness of the dynasty. The growing influence of Rasputin, the licentious, hypnotically gifted monk, rendered the Court more and more odious; his bizarre assassination in the winter of 1916 provoked a last feeble echo of the unanimity of 1914. Nicholas II sealed his own fate as an autocrat by assuming the Supreme Command of the armed forces; despite his modest gifts he had none of the humility of Alexander I. The task of nominating his ministers he passed to his hysterical wife Alexandra. The ministers changed so quickly, no one really knew or trusted them: in the first two years of war, four prime ministers, three foreign ministers, three defence ministers, and six ministers of the interior came and went. The right-wing Kadet Maklakov wrote openly of the 'Mad Chauffeur' and Milyukov asked in the Duma whether the government's incompetence was stupidity or treason.

Despite a massive wartime programme of railroad construction, the railway system in the western provinces was totally disorganized by the German occupation of Poland and a huge jam of railway waggons grew up around Moscow. The German navy's failure at Jutland did not prevent them from closing Russia's Baltic ports and the Turks defied all attempts to prise them from the Straits. Russia was virtually cut off from her allies. Only the port of Archangel remained open, and this was icebound for about half the year. Furthermore, only a winding single track railroad connected it with the interior. Entry through Vladivostok entailed a journey halfway round the world. The low level of technical and economic development produced an army suffering a paralysing shortage of equipment and trained personnel. Sometimes soldiers had to arm themselves from the discarded rifles of the killed and wounded. One-sided artillery barrages wrought havoc on Russian morale. Hospitals and medical services, in the hands of volunteers from the union of zemstva and town councils, were too thinly spread to provide adequate assistance. Chaos was piled on chaos through the influx of millions of refugees, mainly Jews and Poles. They fled from Poland when the western provinces were placed under martial law and their population moved out of the fighting zone. Nicholas II's military protégés had been unable to resist the temptation of evicting the Jews on the grounds that they were traitors. Inflation (the convertibility of the rouble was abandoned in July 1914), food shortages, and a fall in real wages, at least as severe for the white-collar workers as for the factory workers, produced an increasing ordeal for the urban population. The villages had food and to spare – Czech and Slovak prisoners were willing enough substitutes for the absent village lads – but less and less incentive to deliver food to the towns which had nothing to offer them after war production had taken over the factories. In 1916, large-scale strikes, often political and economic, erupted once more. On 9 January 1917, 145,000 workers went on strike in St Petersburg in commemoration of Bloody Sunday. 'Down with the Tsar' was the ominous cry beginning to be heard.

This went hand in hand with an atmosphere that Trotsky has described with characteristic verve:

Enormous fortunes arose out of the bloody foam. The lack of bread and fuel in the capital did not prevent the court jeweller, Fabergé, from boasting that he had never before done such flourishing business. Lady-in-Waiting Vyrubova says that in no other seasons were such gowns to be seen as in the winter of 1915–16, and never were so many diamonds purchased ... everybody splashed about in the bloody mud – bankers, heads of the commissariat, industrialists, ballerinas of the Tsar and the Grand-Dukes, Orthodox prelates, ladies-in-waiting, liberal deputies, generals in the front and rear, radical lawyers, illustrious mandarins of both sexes, innumerable nephews, and more particularly nieces.*

At the end of 1916 and the beginning of 1917, almost every voice spoke in tones of an imminent upheaval. General Krymov told a Duma delegation: 'The spirit of the army is such that the news of a *coup d'état* would be welcomed with joy. A revolution is imminent and we at the front feel it be so.' Despite this, Krymov and his fellow conspirators failed to act. Their failure was fatal to the reputation of the officer corps in the eyes of the revolutionary masses after the revolution. The peasants were saying: 'When ten or fifteen generals are on the gallows we shall begin to win.' A Police Department report noted 'a marked increase in hostile feelings among the peasants not only against the government but also against all other social groups . . .' The same report stated:

The proletariat of the capital is on the verge of despair . . . the mass of industrial workers are quite ready to let themselves go to the wildest excesses of a hunger riot . . . The prohibition of all labour meetings . . . the closing of trade unions, the prosecution of men taking an active part in the sick benefit funds, the suspension of labour newspapers, and so on, make the labour masses, led by the more advanced and already revolutionary-minded elements, assume an openly hostile attitude towards the government and protest with all the means at their disposal against the continuation of the war.†

In a word, the war had utterly destroyed any confidence that still remained between the government and the people. Despite this, the 'Progressive Block' of liberals and moderate conservatives led by Milyukov refused to do anything to destabilize the regime.

* Leon Trotsky, *History of the Russian Revolution* (Eng. trans., London, 1934), pp. 46–7.

† See M. T. Florinsky, *The End of the Russian Empire* (Yale, 1931), pp. 232, 205, 175–7.

Kerensky felt that the only way to avoid an anarchic revolution was to engineer a popular demonstration to nudge the Duma into taking power. He tried to organize this for 14 February 1917, the day the Duma re-convened. The planned demonstration was denounced by Milyukov and the underground Bolsheviks alike, a portent of things to come. Undaunted, Kerensky called for regicide from the Duma tribune, provoking the tsarina's comment that he 'should be hanged'.

The political activists had refused or failed to conduct the revolution. The housewives of Petrograd (formerly St Petersburg) now took a hand. Infuriated by endless queuing for bread that quickly sold out, they began to demonstrate, and then to attack the bakeries. The revolutionary intellectual Sukhanov overheard one typist say to another: 'Do you know what, I think it's the beginning of the revolution! . . .' His reaction was typical of his caste: 'these young ladies had no idea of revolutions. I didn't believe them for a minute.' On 22 February, the militarized management of the giant Putilov factory in Petrograd poured fuel on the flames by locking out their increasingly militant work force. On 23 February, International Women's Day, working men and women poured from the working-class suburbs into the centre of Petrograd where they confronted the forces of order. At once it became obvious that neither soldiers nor cossacks wanted to open fire. Forced to fire on the demonstrators on 26 February, the soldiers of the Volhynia Guards Regiment returned to barracks in a state of mental anguish and mutinied the following morning. By the end of that day, the majority of the Petrograd garrison had joined the uprising.

Despite the massive demonstrations after 23 February, the majority of the Duma politicians had refused to do anything illegal and when the Tsar, erroneously blaming them for the disturbances, ordered the prorogation of the Duma on 27 February, they complied. There was no heroic oath taken on the royal tennis court, only a decision to let the steering committee meet in a side hall. This committee turned down Kerensky's demand that it assume the leadership of the revolution and merely set up a committee 'for the re-establishment of order in the capital'. Kerensky was nominated to this committee, and simultaneously elected vice-chairman of the Petrograd Soviet quickly re-established by the Mensheviks and Trotsky's followers. The Bolsheviks complained that they were left out only because they were rallying the masses on the streets. The same day Nicholas I I entrusted the suppression of the revolt to a military dictator, General Ivanov. The peaceful sabotage of Ivanov's expedition was one of the most comical interludes of the whole revolution. On 2 March (15 March by our calendar) the Tsar, mindful of the ill-health of his infant son, abdicated in favour of his brother, the Grand-Duke Michael. Urged to stand up to the revolution by Milyukov and to abdicate by Kerensky, the Grand-Duke sought the same assurances for his physical safety that Michael I had demanded in 1613. He did not get them; for the first time in three centuries, Russia was without a tsar. This was not all. Russia was now totally without a legitimate government of any kind at all.

Amazingly enough, the provisional government which emerged from the Duma committee on 2 March was soon acclaimed by almost the entire population of the Russian Empire, apart from a few cantankerous monarchists on the right and Bolsheviks and left-wing S.R.s on the left. The key to this unprecedented legitimation by acclamation lay in two factors. One was that the revolution was, as yet, largely confined to Petrograd. It was assumed by both high command and revolutionaries that the remainder of the army, if not the country, would obey the call to suppress the revolution. When the generals were assured that the revolution would continue the war, they put pressure on the Tsar to abdicate in favour of the Duma politicians. The other was the ideology of the Mensheviks and most S.R.s which insisted that this was a 'bourgeois' revolution and that the bourgeoisie would have to govern on their own, receiving the support of the Soviet only 'in so far as' it carried through the democratic reforms everyone claimed they wanted. Kerensky's oratorical gifts enabled him to evade Menshevik dogma and to remain in both government and Soviet, the fulcrum of the political life of Russia so long as the politics of class conciliation held sway at the centre. These policies, the immediate promulgation of liberal democratic reforms, and the postponement of radical social, economic and constitutional changes until victory over the Germans or the convocation of the

Constituent Assembly, suited the intelligentsia as a whole more than most of them liked to admit. Few of them were yet prepared for the 'maximum' programme they had preached to the workers and peasants. The authors of the recanting anthology *Signposts* had been wrong. If anything, the intelligentsia were encumbered by *too great* a respect for private property, legality, Christian ethics, and conventional patriotism.

Elected, as they were, by workers in factories and soldiers in the barracks, the Soviets – and soon they spread across the length and breadth of the former Empire – enjoyed much more prestige in the minds of the masses than the provisional government. 'The provisional government,' said one minister, 'possesses no real power and its orders are executed only in so far as this is permitted by the Soviet of Workers' and Soldiers' Deputies, which holds in its hands the most important element of actual power, such as troops, railroads, postal and telegraph service.' The Soviet had also issued the famous 'Order No. 1' which enjoined all soldiers to obey only the Soviet, form their own committees, and safeguard their arms lest they fall into counter-revolutionary hands. The existence of parallel government and soviet committees throughout Russia gave body to the concept of 'dual power'. Certainly, that is the way it looked to rural landowners seeking redress at the hands of the government for the activities of rural soviets. At least until the autumn, when the Bolsheviks and their allies came to control the Soviets of Petrograd and Moscow, this was an illusion. In reality this was the period of dual revolution. There was a democratic political revolution at the centre, presided over by a more and more brittle coalition of the Kadet Party, now the party of order and property, and by the moderate socialists who led the Soviets. At the same time, there was a massive social revolution egged on, but not caused, by the Bolsheviks. In the words of the historian of this second revolution:

From the very depths of Russia came a great cry of hope, in which were mingled the voices of the poor and down-trodden, expressing their sufferings, hopes and dreams. Dream-like, they experienced unique events: in Moscow, workmen would compel their employer to learn the bases of the workers' rights in future; in Odessa, students would dictate a new way of teaching universal history to their professor; in Petrograd, actors would take over from the theatre manager and select the next play; in the army, soldiers would summon the chaplain to attend their meetings so that he could 'get some real meaning in his life'. Even 'children under the age of fourteen' demanded the right to learn boxing, 'to make the older children have some respect'.*

Such a revolution was the culmination of generations of experience by the Russian people. It was inherently, even ruthlessly, egalitarian. It followed that all those whose position or authority derived from the accident of birth, possession of great wealth, title, age, divine right, or even revolutionary experience alone, felt threatened. Burnt-out revolutionaries such as Khrustalev-Nosar, president of the 1905 Soviet, or Plekhanov, founder of Russian Marxism, were cast aside with only slightly more ceremony than tsarist generals or Islamic mullahs. Ordinary Russians wanted an egalitarian society and common-sense answers to their basic problems.

The majority of the provisional government was quite sincere in its support for the democratic promises made during the first month or so of revolution. There was an amnesty for political prisoners; discriminatory legislation against national minorities was abolished; moves were made towards the introduction of the eight-hour day; the autonomy of Finland was restored; Poland, still under German occupation, was promised its independence; there were also to be democratic elections for local government and ultimately for the Constituent Assembly. Despite the fact that the government lacked any other legitimation than its acclamation in March, there was no hurry actually to convene the Constituent Assembly. The Kadets hoped to postpone the general election until revolutionary sentiment had died down, while the moderate socialists sensed that the coalition might not survive the discussion of radical reforms of the land question and nationalities. Unfortunately, it was all too obvious that the government had conceded only what the rebellious soldiers, workers, and peasants had already taken for themselves.

In its brief existence, the Russian provisional government suffered three major crises, in mid April, early July and late August. The first crisis erupted over foreign policy, though there

* M. Ferro, *October 1917* (London, 1980), pp. 1–2.

is every reason to believe that Kerensky and the other former political freemasons, Nekrasov, Tereshchenko and Konovalov, used this as a pretext for the elimination from the government of Milyukov and Guchkov, neither of whom believed in the revolution. The substance of it was that Kerensky insisted that the soldiers would only renew the fight against the Germans if the government promised to drop its former 'imperialist' war aims, especially the annexation of the Straits. Milyukov, sensible of the immense damage done to Russia's war effort by the closure of the Straits and still mourning a son who fell the year before, could see no reason why Russia should continue to fight if she could not share in the spoils. He blamed British diplomacy, keen to get Russian support for nothing, for encouraging Kerensky. The issue was settled when soldiers of the Petrograd garrison demonstrated their hostility to Imperialist war aims on the streets. The fiery garrison commander, General Kornilov, was transferred back to the front after being denied the authority to put down the demonstrators by force. It was the orators of the Soviet that finally brought them to heel.

As a result of the April Crisis the leaders of the Petrograd (and now the All-Russian) Soviets had to abandon their objections to participation in the government. Irakli Tsereteli, the Georgian heart of Russian Menshevism, and Victor Chernov, the 'village minister', now represented 'democracy' in the government. Kerensky became Minister of War; he was soon known as the 'Persuader-in-Chief' as he embarked on a surprisingly successful tour of the front lines. There he harangued the soldiers into accepting the need for a further offensive against the Germans. This took place in late June. By early July, it had obviously turned into rout. In the meantime, anti-war demonstrations had broken out in Petrograd and the Ukrainian nationalists had extorted Kerensky's agreement to the creation of a Ukrainian executive in Kiev.

The armed demonstrations in Petrograd were put down by a mixture of force and black propaganda alleging that Lenin was a German agent. The Kadet ministers who had resigned in protest at Kerensky's deal with the Ukrainians came back or were replaced. In theory, Kerensky was now a dictator; in an attempt to bluff the right and left, he assumed mannerisms made famous by real dictators later in other lands.

Kerensky's coalition soldiered on until its final crisis late in August. After the fiasco at the front in July, he had authorized the appointment of General Kornilov as Supreme Commander. Encouraged by right-wing politicians and industrialists, Kornilov began to demand the re-introduction of the death penalty in the rear, the re-militarization of communications and war production and the end of the conciliation of the Soviets. An army corps of supposedly reliable troops was moved towards Petrograd. At the end of August, Kerensky suddenly denounced Kornilov for planning a coup. Weapons were handed out to workers disarmed in July and Kornilov's men were soon swamped by agitators from the Soviets. Once again, Kerensky had prevented a rallying of conservative forces and had postponed the civil war. By now, however, the radicalization of right and left was such that Kerensky, once the fulcrum of Russian politics, was reduced to an impotent refugee marooned on a tiny island of moderation eroded by the flood tide of civil war.

THE SOCIAL REVOLUTION AND THE BOLSHEVIKS

How did it come about that 'the Russian revolution of 1917, an elemental popular movement inspired by the most egalitarian and libertarian ideals, gave birth to the twentieth century's most durable dictatorship'?* The historian who posed this question has supplied part of the answer by describing two of the revolutions of 1917, those of the peasants and the workers. There was in fact a multitude of revolutions in Russia in 1917. Before we consider those that were politically decisive, a brief glance at two others that have been largely ignored by historians illustrates the weaknesses of many of these movements.

On May Day 1917, 900 Russian Moslems met in Moscow to consider their needs. Under the presidency of Selima Yakubova, and over the noisy protests of the 200 mullahs present, the congress voted in favour of the absolute equality of women. On the future of Russia's Islamic peoples they were much less united. While the

* J. L. H. Keep, *The Russian Revolution* (London, 1976), p. vii.

Tatars, now well integrated in Russian commercial and educational life, wanted to provide the leadership for a united Moslem minority within Russia, the majority voted for a federal order in which nationality would prevail. The implication was that they would seek to develop their own separate nations and abstain from intervention in Russian political life.

Another organization that achieved a sudden, but transitory, prominence in the spring of 1917 was the Russian League of Women's Equality. The spirit of coalition now brought together the Kadets Tyrkova and Shishkina with the socialists Breshkovskaya, Figner, and Kuskova. To all of them it was axiomatic that the revolution meant equality for women, and when Prince Lvov failed to assure them that women would get the vote they organized a massive demonstration to the Soviet. Once again, the Bolshevik Kollontai found herself heckling the moderate feminists; like Lenin, she wanted soviet power and immediate peace. The last tragic episode in the history of middle-class feminism in Russia was the Women's Battalion formed by M. L. Bochkaryova. Unlike their British counterparts, these brave women did not merely hand out white feathers. They went off to the front to fight the Germans and remained with the provisional government until the last bitter moment of defeat.

Other examples of social movements doomed to ineffectuality could be given. This does not mean that Moslems and women gained nothing from the events of 1917. Only that religious background and gender were forced to give way to the imperatives of class. The largest social class in Russia was still the peasantry. Their reaction to the coming social conflict would be crucial – not least because peasant lads in grey coats were armed.

As we have seen earlier, the conversion of industry to war production had ended by destroying the incentive for the peasants to produce a surplus of food for the market. The relatively high level of agricultural production depended to a considerable extent on the labour of prisoners of war and one of the grievances of the peasants was that these were assigned to the large estates producing for the market instead of substituting for their own absent or killed husbands and sons. The February revolution was greeted with enormous enthusiasm in the countryside. Led, to begin with, by the S.R.-inclined rural intelligentsia, it fully supported the demands for democracy, a just peace and social reforms sanctioned by a properly elected Constituent Assembly. Peasant views of democracy and legality (to say nothing of property) were by no means the same as those of the landlords and the Europeanized intelligentsia and they saw no reason why the immediate needs of the countryside should not be met in a democratic manner. Everywhere there was a revival of the historic commune, and the isolated peasant farmers (*otrubniki*) were faced with the bleak choice of rejoining the commune on equal terms with the rest of the peasantry, or being relegated to the ranks of the historic enemy, the pomeshchiki. How the latter were dealt with appears from their own accounts.

Everything has been quite orderly ... we own about 3,000 *desyatins*, and employ nearly 100 people ... A few weeks ago the situation began to change. Letters from our steward show that the peasants have seized part of the land and left us forty-five desyatins only; they are themselves cultivating the rest. They use our meadows and pasture for their cattle. After a short time the 'village committee' prohibited us from selling cattle, and there is no point in feeding the cattle, because we have to sell it to keep our property going. Finally, following a decision of the '*volost* committee', our prisoners of war were removed as well as the day-labourers we had employed. The estate is in a hopeless position. Our stewards' speeches and objections have been fruitless, and the peasants are still aggressive.

It was this situation on the land that destroyed the reputations of both Prince Lvov, the leading landowner in the provisional government, whose inability to preserve the rights of his class pending the Constituent caused his resignation in July, and of Chernov, the most left-wing member of the government of coalition, who was accused of fomenting peasant disorder without being honest enough to say so. Of one thing we may be sure; while the peasants were overwhelmingly loyal to the S.R. Party, they remembered the suppression of peasant disorders in 1906 only too well. They would react violently against any party that looked like returning with 'Stolypin's necktie' to the villages.

The industrial workers also meant to use the collapse of authority in February to inaugurate a new era in industrial relations. No longer would they submit to the mixture of modern business efficiency and autocratic Russian brutality that passed for labour relations in most Russian factories. The workers whose strikes had sparked off the revolution did not return to work with the fall of the Tsar, nor even with the constitution of the Soviets. The first widespread demand was for the eight-hour day. This was finally conceded by the Petrograd employers on 10 March and by those in Moscow eleven days later. The provisional government would not legislate on this matter itself. Between February and July, a series of strikes and negotiations took place in the capitals and elsewhere over wages. There was a tendency for the workers to demand a basic minimum for every worker, and to equalize the basic rates between men and women, and then to calculate the differentials for the more skilled workers. This was also the period of 'wheelbarrow rides', scenes of bucolic revenge in which disliked foremen were carted through the gauntlet of their former charges and dumped in ponds. The workers still respected the Soviets, despite their Menshevik and S.R. leaders, but the focus of their own energies was their own factory committees. The committees quickly asserted their rights to see the accounts and to sack unpopular colleagues. The Petrograd conference of factory committees at the end of May was the first major assembly to give overwhelming support to the Bolsheviks. The Bolsheviks, for their part, were careful to hide their belief in the necessity of nationalization of industry at this stage. Their anarcho-communist competitors were still too strong for the time being.

It was the continuing collapse of the economy and the spread of factory closures and redundancies that forced the workers to consider their factories not merely as an urban equivalent of the self-sufficient village commune, but as part of a system of relationships that must be mastered. Naturally, the employers claimed that the closures and dismissals were the result of supply difficulties and escalating wage rates. The Bolshevized workers were equally sure that they were caused by malicious bosses, prepared to sacrifice war production to force the proletariat back into line. P. P. Ryabushinsky, one of Russia's leading industrialists, referred ominously to 'the bony hand of hunger' which would 'clutch by the throat . . . the members of various committees and Soviets, forcing them to come to their senses'. The apogee of the workers' self-manage-ment movement, and of the fortunes of the Bolsheviks' rivals, the anarcho-communists, occurred in the early summer of 1917. There-after the workers began to look to the trade-union organizations to provide the kind of discipline and co-ordination that the factory committees lacked. As the economic situation became more and more terrifying in the early autumn, they listened with increasing receptivity to Bolshevik calls for nationalization and workers' power.

The third element in Russian society that no one could afford to ignore was the army. Overwhelmingly, the soldiery were peasants but their residence in urban centres and their concern with the progress of the war had given them far wider horizons than their fathers and younger brothers in the villages. To understand the reactions of the soldiers in 1917, we must remember that the Feb-ruary revolution succeeded because of a mutiny by the soldiers *against their officers*. Few officers actually resisted their men, but still fewer came out with them. On the evening of 27 February Peshekhonov found only one subaltern, himself a well-known socialist schoolmaster, among the rebellious soldiers at the Duma. 'Order No. 1' became the touchstone of the free army for the men and its message swept like a forest fire through the ranks of the Russian Army. There were enlightened commanders like Alexeyev and Brusilov, and conservatives with the common touch like Kor-nilov and Krasnov, but they were the minority. All too many of the officers were obsessed by the humiliation they suffered when they could no longer address the men with the intimate 'Thou' – as used to children and animals – and when the men no longer saluted them. Kerensky understood this situation well enough; he even asked Merezhkovsky to write a pamphlet explaining to the men that many officers of the past had been revolutionary democrats. He hoped that the offensive would bring officers and men together once more in the comradeship of battle. Most of the Petrograd garrison had no desire to face the Germans and were easily per-suaded by anarchists and communists alike that the offensive was simply a means to the restoration of traditional discipline. This impression was confirmed when the desertions at the front were followed by the restoration of the death penalty. Kerensky, who had abolished the death penalty for the Tsar, was now restoring it for the ordinary soldiers, or so it seemed.

The reaction to the 'July Days' evoked the spectre of a 'white terror'. In retrospect this may seem rather unfair. After all, only a few hundred leading Bolsheviks were arrested, only one agitator killed out of hand, a few Bolshevik printing presses smashed up. To recapture the anti-socialist hysteria of July 1917, we must dismiss from our minds any thoughts of the 'Red Terror' of 1918 – let alone the GULAG. The Russians of 1917 had no foreknowledge of those terrible events. They remembered the reaction of 1906–7 and they watched with horror, or enthusiasm, as the once left–liberal Kadet Party became the refuge not merely for the former Octobrists, but for members of all the tsarist right-wing parties that had disappeared in February. The word that men and women used to indicate their intentions towards one another during the Great War was 'treason'. The tsarist government had accused the Bolsheviks, the Jews, and expatriate German capitalists of 'treason' during 1914 and 1915. The liberals had retaliated by suggesting that Rasputin and Empress Alexandra were guilty of potential 'treason' during 1916. Kerensky's government accused the Bolsheviks of 'treason' in July 1917, and the Bolsheviks retaliated by accusing the government of 'treason', of planning to surrender Red Petrograd to the Germans in the autumn of 1917. During the First World War the meaning of the word was clear: to accuse someone of treason was to threaten him with death. The successful appropriation of the word 'treason' by the government in July and then by the Bolsheviks in the autumn of 1917 suggests the enormous hold it had over the minds of the Russian soldiers. We will never know how unreal the fears of rebellious soldiers and workers were. In neighbouring Finland, where the Reds took power in 1918, only to lose it to the Whites, over 50,000 Reds were killed. In the light of Russia's enormous population, this is equivalent to a casualty figure for Russia of 3 to 4 million. Lenin was quite well aware that once the civil war had begun, men and women would fight against those who threatened them with death.

Apart from the rebellious soldiers, those who stood most to lose from any form of conservative reaction were the staffs of the

Soviets and the other working-class institutions. The Soviets rapidly spread from one end of the country to another; in some cases uniting soldiers with workers, in others uniting peasants with workers. At the national level, the peasants' Soviets retained their separate identity until after October. The plenary meetings of the local Soviets were important at moments of crisis, but at other times, the crucial instances of the Soviets were the hierarchies of committees and their plethora of specialized commissions. Overwhelmingly, the responsible members of these organizations were drawn from the intelligentsia and those members of the working class who had worked with revolutionary organizations for so long that they had as much in common with the intelligentsia as with the members of their own class. In Moscow, for example, 37 per cent of the executive committee of the Soviet were intellectuals, though intellectuals made up only 4 per cent of the deputies. It is worth noting that the Bolsheviks were probably slightly more successful at co-opting workers into Soviet institutions than the other parties. All parties were guilty of bureaucratization from the very beginning of the February revolution: the creation of elite inner bureaux; party nominations to executive posts that were merely ratified by plenary meetings; longer and longer intervals between meetings of the plenary bodies, and so on. The members of these institutions were not yet a class but their sources of income and their activities were quite distinct from those of rank-and-file workers. The Bolshevik dictatorship owed as much to the emergence of this social group as to Lenin's ideas about a core of professional revolutionaries. They shared with the more democratically recruited Red Guard an institutional interest in Bolshevik success. 'All power to the Soviets' meant power for them. The Menshevik and S.R. idea that they would only exist until the Constituent Assembly had far less attraction.

The second stage in the Russian revolution began with Lenin's arrival at the Finland Station in Petrograd on 2 April 1917. From the first Lenin had been in no doubt that the imperialist war must be turned into a civil war. But he had no idea that the transformation was so imminent. As late as January 1917 he was telling his audience at a Zurich meeting (Lenin spent the bulk of the war, from September 1914 to March 1917, in Switzerland), that 'we of the older generation may not live to see the decisive battles of this coming revolution'. And when the first news of the formation of the provisional government reached Zurich, Lenin, like the other revolutionaries, did not anticipate all the possibilities that were opening up. Kollontai in Norway arranged to act as Lenin's emissary to the Bolsheviks in Russia. His message was radical: 'Our tactics – absolute distrust, no support for the provisional government. Distrust Kerensky above all. No alliance with other parties.' But how could he return to Russia with such a message? Neutral Switzerland was surrounded by Allied powers which might be expected to impede his passage and by Germany and Austria where he would be an enemy alien. His return came under the aegis of the German government. This contrasted ironically with Lenin's view that 'the German proletariat is the most trustworthy, the most reliable ally of the Russian and the world proletarian revolution'. In reality, the contrary was true.

From 1915 onwards, the Germans, like the Japanese in 1904–5, had been fishing in the waters of the Russian left-wing parties. They promoted revolutionary propaganda in Russia as an act of political warfare, just as they did in Ireland and as the British did in Arabia. Through Stockholm, in the main, such funds flowed into Russia and were used, it may be conjectured, for the publication of pamphlets and the financial support of left-wing groups. At the end of September 1917, on the eve of the October revolution, Kühlmann, the German Secretary of State, summed up these activities with pardonable self-congratulation (and some exaggeration?):

The military operations on the Eastern front ... were seconded by intensive undermining activities inside Russia on the part of the Foreign Ministry. Our first interest in these activities was to further nationalist and separatist endeavours as far as possible, and to give strong support to the revolutionary elements. We have now been engaged in these activities for some time, and in complete agreement with the Political Section of the General Staff in Berlin ... Our work together has shown tangible results. The Bolshevik movement could never have attained the scale or the influence which it has today without our continual support. There is every indication that the movement will continue to grow, and the same is true also of the Finnish and Ukrainian independence movements.*

*Z. A. B. Zeman, ed., *Germany and the Revolution in Russia* (Oxford, 1958), Doc. No. 71.

But this is to anticipate. In March 1917, as one item in this policy, the return of Lenin and a group of other Bolsheviks and other revolutionaries was decided on, for the purpose of facilitating further disintegration in Russia. Thirty-two people in all left Switzerland – nineteen Bolsheviks, six Bundists, three Mensheviks, and four miscellaneous. The most important were Lenin, Krupskaya, Armand, and Zinoviev.

The journey to Petrograd took Lenin and his party through Germany, Sweden, and Finland. Tumultuous crowds greeted Lenin in Petrograd, the *Marseillaise*, anthem of revolutionary Russia, thundered forth from a thousand voices, a searchlight played over the faces of the throng, Bolshevik posters and slogans decorated the platform walls and station buildings. A curious and significant encounter then took place in the waiting-room, previously reserved for the tsar's personal use. Chkheidze, the Menshevik president of the Petrograd Soviet, welcomed Lenin with the assertion that the principal task of the workers was now to defend the revolution, and for this unity was the requisite of the day. But Lenin ignored Chkheidze and spoke of the Russian revolution as the harbinger of world revolution. It was not something that had come to a full stop. Its greatest hour was still to come.

This preliminary brush was but a foretaste of the thunderbolt that Lenin was preparing to hurl into the Bolsheviks' ranks. After a triumphal procession with speeches at every street corner, Lenin, in an armoured car, eventually arrived at Bolshevik headquarters, formerly the sumptuous house of Kshesinskaya, prima ballerina and one-time mistress of the Tsar. Here there was a reception, snacks, more speeches. It was late at night before Lenin proclaimed the policy that he had been slowly hatching both before and during the return from Zurich. The following day, at the Tauride Palace, he presented this policy to a congress of Bolsheviks in the famous 'April Theses'. He demanded the overthrow of capitalism as the only way to end the war; no further support must be given to the provisional government; the power of the Soviets must be built up, and the influence of the Bolsheviks inside the Soviets; there must be no parliamentary republic; the land and the banks must be nationalized; the Soviets must take production and distribution into their own hands; a new International must be founded to replace the defunct Second International.

To understand the furore this caused, at first within the Bolshevik party and subsequently between the Bolsheviks and the other socialist parties, we must remember that the Bolshevik party of 1917 was quite unlike Lenin's professional revolutionaries of 1903 and equally unlike the bureaucracy, against which Lenin himself so often complained, that came to run the party in the years following the conquest of power. Lenin had largely lost control of his own party in the wrangle over participation in the Duma elections after 1906. The Bolshevik party of 1917 had become the kind of mass party Lenin disapproved of. Its members were linked in bonds of comradeship with members of the other socialist parties. Together they had helped to overthrow the Tsar and set up the Soviet. They had acquiesced when the moderate socialist leaders of the Soviet had prevailed on the soldiers and workers to abandon slogans hostile to the war and to the government. At first, only Alexandra Kollontai supported Lenin. Of the others, Molotov stood closest to him. But to the majority he was a 'Bakunin', 'a madman', a dealer in 'abstractions'. It was not until the morrow of the October revolution that the centre and right in Russian politics were rudely disabused of the notion that Lenin had abandoned Marxism for anarchism. Yet the key to the Theses is clear enough – that the bourgeois-democratic phase of the revolution was concluded and that what must now be prepared was the transition to the socialist phase, which would be incorporated in government by the Soviets. All that Lenin left open was the timing of the socialist revolution. For the moment the slogan was – 'All power to the Soviets'.

After the first upheaval, the new line was carried at the Petrograd Party conference, and then by the 150 delegates to the All-Russian Party Conference. (Kamenev, who had returned with Stalin from Siberian exile at the time of the February revolution, maintained a consistent opposition to Lenin's policies throughout the year; Stalin soon abandoned him to support Lenin on most issues.) Lenin's views carried because they were supported by elements among the workers and soldiers and because of the sheer power of his intellect and the inexorable logic of his oratory.

Thus, by the end of April 1917, the Bolsheviks had committed themselves to opposing any collaboration with the provisional government and to transferring power to the Soviets. As the mood of the masses was still favourable to the government all the party could do to begin with was criticize the government and build up its own support. As spring turned into summer, this gained them recruits like Trotsky and Lunacharsky – who would never have joined a purely Leninist revolutionary elite – and allies like the left–S.R. Maria Spiridonova, increasingly disgruntled at the concessions made by Chernov towards his colleagues in the government.

As we have seen, Kerensky's offensive was enormously unpopular with the Petrograd garrison. Heavy-handed actions threatened by the government brought unprecedented sympathy for the anarchists in June 1917 and the Bolshevik military organization was obliged to join the movement initiated by them in July in order to retain its own following. The suppression of the Bolsheviks following the July Days was a half-hearted affair. The Kadets wanted blood but the government feared that they really intended to abolish the Soviets and precipitate civil war on their own terms. The government refused to close down the Sixth Bolshevik Party Congress in August and took some measures against anti-semitic newspapers at this time. Nevertheless, the dislocation in the higher reaches of the party was considerable. *Pravda* was banned. Lenin and Zinoviev sought assurances of a fair trial and fled to Finland when these were not forthcoming. Kamenev, Trotsky (who had returned from New York at the beginning of May), Kollontai, and Lunacharsky were arrested shortly afterwards. On the face of it, the Bolsheviks were now back to where they had started in February. This impression was fundamentally misleading, however. The government had still not found answers to the problems facing the country; the war continued, industrial production continued to decline and the agrarian revolution went from strength to strength. The government now came under massive pressure from the army high command and from the Kadets to take vigorous action to restore traditional discipline in the army and to stop the social revolution in its tracks. The only results of this pressure were that the government became totally identified in the minds of millions of soldiers, workers, and peasants with their traditional oppressors. Elections to the city dumas in August showed that the Bolsheviks were again gaining ground. Just as important were the splits that were finally emerging in the S.R. party.

The Bolshevization of the Soviets was immensely accelerated by the abortive revolt under General Kornilov. The episode – it was not more – brought the government into disrepute and made the soldiers and workers feel that safety now lay in supporting the Bolsheviks. Within a week they had majorities in the Soviets of Petrograd and Moscow. Trotsky, on his release from prison, was elected chairman of the former. The number of party members increased some ten-fold to 200,000 between January and August 1917. This pattern was followed in many local and provincial soviets. In the countryside also, as peasant disorders spread, Bolshevik influence grew.

Revolution was now on the agenda. The moment anticipated in Lenin's 'April Theses' was approaching rapidly. Lenin himself wrote on three successive days in mid September to the party's central committee, urging that the moment had come. At the end of the month, he moved from Helsinki to Vyborg, nearer the Russian frontier. 'History will not forgive us if we do not seize power now.' Again, he met with resistance from Kamenev and the right, who wanted all the socialist parties to take power together through the Soviets, and from the Bolshevik military experts whose fingers had been burnt in July and who had no wish to repeat the experience.

On 23 October (10 October old style) the supreme decision was taken, though still only in principle. Lenin emerged from hiding to take part in the debate. By a majority of ten to two – Lenin, Trotsky, Stalin, and seven others against Zinoviev and Kamenev – it was resolved to initiate an armed insurrection. Zinoviev and Kamenev took the struggle to the membership, whence it leaked to Gorky's newspaper and so to the general public. On 29 October (16 October old style) the Petrograd Soviet established a Military-Revolutionary Committee, under the presidency of Trotsky by virtue of his chairmanship of the Soviet. It included forty-eight Bolsheviks, fourteen left Social-Revolutionaries, and four anarchists. It was the provisional government itself that converted this committee from an organization to defend the Soviets into an organization destined to overthrow it. It tried to arrange for Bolshevik units of the Petrograd garrison to be transferred to the front and for troops loyal to itself to replace them.

After a week's existence, the Military-Revolutionary Committee had its plan ready. Insurgent troops, numbering some 20–25,000, would be used to occupy the key points in the capital. The date for the uprising was fixed for 6–7 November (24–25 October old style), the day before the second All-Russian Congress of Soviets was scheduled to meet. It was Lenin's determination that the congress, 'irrespective of its composition, would be confronted with a situation in which the seizure of power by the workers is an actual fact'.

Early in the morning of the crucial day the Central Committee, except for Lenin, Zinoviev, and Stalin, met for the last time before the night of decision. Their headquarters were at the Soviet in the Smolny Institute. It had been in former days a convent and school for young ladies; now it resounded to the final orders for the uprising. Trotsky assigned to each of his colleagues responsibility for supervising key services – food supplies, posts and telegraphs, railways, and liaison with Moscow. Trotsky himself directed the overall strategy of the *coup*. Lenin, back in hiding, once again urged immediate action. 'We must at all costs, this very evening, this very night, arrest the Government . . .' Later that night, disguised by a bandage wound round his face, Lenin arrived at Smolny.

Early the next morning revolutionary troops and Red Guards went into action. They met no resistance. They methodically occupied one key-point after another – the railway stations, the power station, the telephone exchange, the State Bank, the bridges over the Neva. It was almost bloodless.

Kerensky departed for the front to find troops to put down the revolution. This was about ten in the morning. At about the same time, Trotsky's posters appeared on the streets: 'To the citizens of Russia – the provisional government has been overthrown.' This was not quite true. The Winter Palace was still occupied by those ministers who remained, guarded by about a thousand officer cadets and the Women's Battalion. Not until early the next morning had enough Red Guards and sailors infiltrated the enormous building and its grounds. Kerensky's ministers were finally arrested by Vladimir Antonov-Ovseyenko, a man wearing pince-nez and a broad-brimmed hat. To the last the *coup* was virtually bloodless. But it still remained a *coup*. Before the Bolsheviks held firm power, much blood would be shed.

CHAPTER 15

The Bolsheviks Conquer Power

PART ONE: THE DEFEAT OF THE WHITES

The Bolshevik *coup* in Petrograd had been inefficient but almost bloodless. The Kadet newspapers alleged (untruthfully) that the Women's Battalion had been raped but the opera and ballet went on, theatres, schools and some government offices were still functioning, though many civil servants refused to accept orders from the Bolsheviks. What met the eyes of the British Ambassador, Sir George Buchanan, as he walked towards the Winter Palace on the afternoon of 7 November (new style)? 'The aspect of the quay was more or less normal,' he remarked, 'except for the groups of armed soldiers stationed near the bridges.' Since the beginning of the year so many upheavals had swept over the capital that each one made less and less impression. The next morning, 8 November, it still seemed as if nothing had happened. Anti-Bolshevik newspapers continued to appear on the streets, reporting the arrest of the government and Kerensky's flight. They anticipated that the Bolshevik *coup* would prove no more than a temporary reversal. The same views were held in Kadet and official circles. What can account for this extraordinary complacency? The answer is that, ever since April, Lenin had appeared to be the prophet of anarchism. To some extent, this accounted both for his popularity with soldiers, workers and peasants, and for his unpopularity with the possessing classes. Had they been able to read the theoretical work, *State and Revolution*, he had been preparing in the underground, they might have felt less complacent. Lenin never wasted his time on 'pure' theory, of course. His works of theory were always tailored to specific tactical objectives. Thus, his attack on 'empirio-criticism' after 1906 was merely part of an assault on Bolshevik groups that threatened his control over the party. Similarly, *State and Revolution* constituted an attack on both right-wing Bolsheviks like Kamenev, who might feel tempted to support a 'people's state', and left-wing Bolsheviks inclined to support the view ascribed to the anarchists that the State must wither away immediately. To these heresies, he opposed the notion of a transitory state on the road to the classless society to which Engels had given the name 'the dictatorship of the proletariat'. Lenin had arrived in Russia with the thaw; his revolution began as the first snowflakes of winter filled the Petrograd air.

For the moment, *State and Revolution* was strictly for the cadres. It was Lenin at his most 'anarchistic' who emerged at Smolny, while naval guns were still using blanks to bombard the Winter Palace. Late that night the second All-Russian Congress of Soviets met to the sound of continuing shell-fire; and this sound mingled with Menshevik denunciations of the *coup d'état*. The Bolsheviks and their supporters, the left Socialist-Revolutionaries, had a considerable majority in the Congress – and this was sufficient to confirm in office an exclusively Bolshevik government according to the new theory of legitimacy. There were, it is true, certain Bolshevik leaders, of whom the most prominent was Kamenev, President of the Central Executive Committee of the Soviets and titular head of state, who urged that Menshevik-Internationalists and S.R.s be invited to share office with the Bolsheviks. They argued that a one-party government would be able to maintain itself in power only 'by means of political terror'. But this was anathema to Lenin and Trotsky. Had they seized power in order to share it with their opponents, those opponents whom Trotsky now verbally consigned to the 'dustbin of history'? Despite these bold words, Lenin was forced to temporize for some days in the face of the hostility or neutrality of the vital communications workers. Only when he knew that the revolution had triumphed in most of Russia's great cities could he insist on a government of his own choice.

When Lenin, in his capacity as President of the newly-formed Council of People's Commissars (as the Bolshevik cabinet was named), rose to address the Congress, he was greeted with an indescribable ovation. There he stood, in John Reed's description –

a short, stocky figure, with a big head, set down in his shoulders, bald and bulging. Little eyes, a snubbish nose, wide, generous mouth and heavy chin ... Dressed in shabby clothes, his trousers much too long for him.

Unimpressive, to be the idol of a mob, loved and revered as perhaps few leaders in history have been . . .*

These were the halcyon days of the October revolution. But, as the Russian proverb has it: 'Don't praise the day till evening comes'.

Lenin, in his first public appearance since his flight to Finland in July, would now read out the first two historic decrees of the Council of People's Commissars – the decree on peace and the decree on land. The first invited 'all the belligerent peoples and their governments to open immediate negotiations for an honest democratic peace', that is, a peace without annexations or indemnities. The Soviets also abolished all secret diplomacy and undertook to publish all the wartime secret agreements from which they would, Lenin declared, refuse to derive any territorial gains. For the general purpose of the decree, Lenin proposed an immediate armistice to last not less than three months. He ended with an appeal to the working classes of Britain, France, and Germany to support the Soviets' peace policy. This was a disguised appeal for a European revolution, belief in which had been one of Lenin's foremost arguments for urging on a Russian revolution in September and October.

After peace came land. Lenin's second decree abolished without compensation and nationalized all private property in the form of landowners' estates, and apanages belonging to the Crown, monasteries and the Church. Local land committees and peasant Soviets would take into custody all such land, together with all livestock and implements, for distribution among their members. The decree prohibited the use of hired labour and also the sale, mortgaging, leasing, or alienation of the land. This was seemingly the most far-reaching agricultural reform in Russian history. In actual fact it merely recognized a *fait accompli*. The peasant seizure of the land had been in full spate for months before Lenin spoke and would continue throughout the early part of 1918. It was a movement, unchallengeable by any force that the Bolsheviks could conceivably have mustered. It expressed, as nothing else could have done, the dual nature of the October revolution. On one side, the Bolsheviks – on the other, the peasants.

*John Reed, *Ten Days That Shook the World* (New York, 1960), p. 170.

In order to realize the Soviet State [wrote Trotsky] there was required a drawing together and mutual penetration of two factors belonging to completely different historic species: a peasant war – that is, a movement characteristic of the dawn of the bourgeois development – and a proletarian insurrection, the movement signifying its decline. That is the essence of 1917.

It is not necessary to accept Trotsky's historical framework to perceive the justice of this analysis. The Bolsheviks' attitude to the land question was probably the crucial factor in the civil war. Could the White generals offer anything more than the return to a landlord economy? And who would fight for that? On the other hand, so many peasants returned from the towns to secure their share in the distribution that the average holding increased only very slightly. Land-hunger was by no means appeased, and Bolshevism found itself saddled with about seventeen million smallholders working tiny plots collectively, but by the most inefficient methods. Given the condition of industry, Lenin could not give both land to the peasants and bread to the towns. Already, there was a suggestion of future conflict with the peasants. They were not given the land as property, only permitted its usage.

On the morrow of the revolution, Lenin's land policy was primarily of political importance in consummating the separation of the left Socialist-Revolutionaries from their mother-party. Chernov complained that the Bolsheviks had stolen his clothes; they retorted with equal justice that he had never had the courage to wear them.

In the days and weeks that followed the rising in Petrograd, all the major industrial centres in Russia were taken over by their Soviets, anxious to support the new order. The rising in Moscow was less well organized and had to contend with stiffer opposition. It took a week of bloody fighting before Soviet authority prevailed. If the Bolsheviks and their allies controlled most of the towns, the same could not be said of the countryside. In south Russia, the Cossacks of the Don and Kuban moved towards autonomy and provided a haven for right-wing generals. The Ukraine was torn between the Bolshevized Soviets and the local agencies of the Ukrainian national Rada. Throughout Moslem Russia, the native peoples looked on with sullen indifference as Russians fought one another. It was in this curious interval of undeclared civil war that Russia's only democratic general election took place.

Lenin had foreseen the difficulties that the Constituent Assembly might cause him. Like all the socialist parties, the Bolsheviks had vigorously campaigned for the summoning of the Assembly. It had been one of their chief weapons in belabouring Kerensky that he was purposely delaying its convocation. It says much for the prestige of the Assembly, and the unpreparedness of both right and left for civil war, that the elections went ahead with almost no interference. Lenin knew, of course, that the city-based Bolsheviks stood no chance of victory in an election based on the principle of 'one man, one vote'. His Council of People's Commissars wanted no rivals for power.

The election results confirmed Lenin's fears. The Bolsheviks received about a quarter of the forty million votes cast and 175 seats. The left S.R.s got forty, the S.R.s 370. There were a mere fifteen Mensheviks and seventeen Kadets. There were also about eighty representatives of national groupings, in addition to the eighty Ukrainian autonomists who had gone to the polls as Social-Democrats or S.R.s. Of the proto-fascist 'Black Hundreds', the fear of which had so often rationalized the moderation of so many socialists (and even a few Bolsheviks) during 1917, almost nothing remained. They secured less than 2 per cent of the votes and only two seats; one for a general and one for an archbishop. The pro-Bolshevik votes came from the industrial centres and the army, particularly those units stationed in Petrograd and Moscow.

The S.R.s had won the election, or so it seemed. Yet already, those who had not followed the left S.R. faction were splitting into undisciplined splinters. Chernov wanted the Assembly to attempt peaceful legislation and bring popular opinion to bear on the Bolsheviks to restore 'democracy'. From his hideaway, Kerensky urged a massive armed demonstration of support for the Assembly which, he hoped, would become an anti-Bolshevik revolution. A small group of young S.R. militants went even further. They now believed that Lenin was a tyrant and should be dealt with by means of the traditional S.R. weapon of terror. On 14 January 1918, they tried to assassinate him as he drove along the Fontanka quay. When the Constituent Assembly finally met (in the absence of most Kadet and many nationalist deputies), its members were mocked and insulted. When they elected Chernov President over the left S.R. Spiridonova, their fate was sealed. They barely had time to approve Chernov's land law before they were dispersed by trigger-happy Red Guards and sailors. The small groups of demonstrators who gathered to support it were dispersed by gunfire, an event that Gorky likened to 'Bloody Sunday' of 1905. Lenin argued that the Soviet form of democracy represented a higher type than mechanical and formal majorities. Be that as it may, the forcible dissolution of the Constituent Assembly was not only a break with the great bulk of the revolutionary aspirations of the nineteenth century, it also widened the gap between the Bolsheviks and all the other left-wing parties and groupings, apart, of course, from the left S.R.s and anarchists. While it was members of the intelligentsia who led the Bolshevik uprising, the mass of the intelligentsia was bitterly hostile to it. The workers could not understand this coming from people who had preached socialism to them to win their support for the assault on the autocracy. Indeed, it is striking how little interest the moderate socialists in 1917 showed in any theoretical or practical aspect of socialism. Their socialism seemed to have disappeared in the February revolution; what took its place was often, even in life-long socialists like Gorky and Sukhanov, an ill-concealed intellectual and social snobbery. Some workers sensed this and resented it, not least because they were conscious enough of their own limitations to sense that a revolution without the intelligentsia would involve needless mistakes and sacrifices for everyone. They pursued the intellectuals in the streets with cries of 'borzhooi'. The last straw for most intellectuals was the murder by Red sailors of the left-wing Kadet deputies Shingarev and Kokoshkin. They felt that this signalled the beginning of the civil war.

The Bolsheviks had now disposed of what constituted *as yet* their most serious internal danger. They then turned to the greatest external menace – the German and Austrian armies on the soil of what had once been the Russian Empire. At this time the German lines ran southwards from east of Riga to east of Lvov. They then sloped south-eastwards to the Black Sea, to include most of Romania.

Lenin's original peace decree had brought no response from either the Allied or the central powers. This did not prevent him from taking the policy a stage further. About a fortnight afterwards, the Bolshevik government ordered fraternization on all fronts and instructed General Dukhonin, the Russian Supreme Commander, to propose to the Germans an immediate cease-fire. On the same day, Trotsky, the Soviet Foreign Commissar, informed the Allied Ambassadors in Petrograd of the Russian peace move. But Dukhonin rejected the order and the Allied governments refused to entertain Trotsky's plan.

The Allied military missions accredited to Dukhonin's headquarters at Mogilev (except for the U.S. mission) threatened that 'the gravest consequences' would follow any unilateral Russian violation of the treaty of 5 September 1914. Trotsky denounced this as intervention in Russian domestic affairs. 'The soldiers, workers, and peasants of Russia,' he said, 'did not overthrow the governments of the Tsar and Kerensky merely to become cannon fodder for the Allied imperialists.' Dukhonin was displaced by the Bolshevik, Krylenko. Krylenko left for Mogilev on 23 November. He took his time on the journey in order to depose *en route* as many hostile generals as possible. He did not arrive until 3 December. A few hours later Dukhonin was killed by his troops. The Allied military missions had left for Kiev, where resistance to the Bolsheviks was already building up. Relations between the Allies and the Soviets were further inflamed through the Soviet repudiation of all tsarist debts to foreign powers. (This threat had first been made by all the anti-tsarist parties in 1906 when the French made their largest ever loan to date to stabilize tsarist Russia.) They were equally inflamed by Trotsky's calculated publication of all the secret Allied agreements that could be found in the archives of the Foreign Ministry. Matters such as the Anglo-Russian agreement of 1907 and the Sykes–Picot agreement of 1915 for the carve-up of Turkey's Arabian Empire seriously compromised and discredited the Allied cause, especially in the United States. Wilson's Fourteen Points did not entirely overcome the effects of these disclosures.

In the meantime, the Germans had agreed to negotiate with the Bolsheviks and a Russo-German armistice was signed on 15 December. The ensuing Treaty of Brest-Litovsk was finally ratified by the Fourth Congress of Soviets on 16 March 1918. This long interval was due in part to Trotsky's stalling tactics. He hoped to use the negotiations to stimulate revolution in Germany and Austria so as to take the weight off Russia. But nothing came of his efforts, apart from a wave of fairly widespread strikes. At one time there was also a possibility of some kind of agreement with the Allies, perhaps for further military assistance. This was even more of a chimera. His Marxist background suggested to Trotsky that the Allies and the Germans might already be collaborating against the Russians, though this did not mature until a year or so later. In the end, the Soviets had no choice but to accept a truly brutal peace, foreshadowing Versailles. They had to yield up Estonia, Latvia, Lithuania, most of Byelorussia, and all of Russian Poland to Germany and Austria, to recognize the independence of the Ukraine, Georgia, and Finland, and to evacuate the areas of Kars, Ardahan, and Batum in favour of Turkey. In addition, reparation payments of 6,000 million marks had to be made. In concrete terms, this meant that Russia lost one-third of its agricultural land and its population; more than four-fifths of its coal-mines; over half its industrial undertakings. Geographically speaking, Russia was pushed back from the Black Sea, and virtually cut off from the Baltic. It was almost the Grand Duchy of Muscovy over again.

No wonder the acceptance of these terms gave rise to the most violent polemics inside Russian society, the Bolshevik Party and the government! In the crucial Central Committee meeting of 23 February, the voting went seven for acceptance, four against, and four abstainers. A left Communist group led by Bukharin and Radek split off from the main Bolshevik Party so as to be free to urge forward a campaign for a revolutionary war against the Germans. Similarly, the left S.R. members of the Council of People's Commissars resigned their posts and denounced the treaty as a 'betrayal of the international proletariat and of the socialist revolution begun in Russia'.

To all such arguments Lenin reiterated his complete and utter disbelief in any further Russian capacity to fight. Moreover, to attempt to fight would, he believed, jeopardize the revolution.

'Germany,' he said, 'was only pregnant with revolution.' But to the Bolsheviks quite a healthy child had been born – 'which we may kill if we begin war'. Who would risk a live child for one as yet unborn, all the more so as Russia could act as the German *accoucheur*? This was Lenin's conclusive argument. Russia sacrificed space in order to gain time. Russia won a breathing space that would enable her to consolidate the revolution in preparation for the imminent struggle for the world. Russia accepted Brest-Litovsk in the same spirit in which the Germans had once accepted the Peace of Tilsit – 'and just as the Germans freed themselves from Napoleon,' wrote Lenin in *Pravda*, 'so will we get our freedom'. In fact, of course, it had been the Russians who had freed the Germans then and it would be the Allies who freed Russia from Germany – not without plotting adventures of their own on the periphery of Russia.

A curious situation now arose. In order to help stimulate revolution in Germany, Adolf Joffe, the first Bolshevik Ambassador in Berlin, was actively in touch with the German left. He aided them with pamphlets and funds. In Moscow (whither the Soviet capital had been transferred in March) these activities were held to be so important that the reparation instalments due to Germany continued to be paid even *after* the German request to the Allies for an armistice. The aim was to minimize any danger of a Russo-German rupture that might unseat Joffe.

Similarly, the German Ambassador to Moscow, Count Mirbach, was exhorted to continue to give financial support to the Bolsheviks.

Please use larger sums [he was adjured by his Foreign Minister in May 1918] as it is greatly to our interests that Bolsheviks should survive . . . As a party, Kadets are anti-German; Monarchists would also work for a revision of the Brest peace treaty. We have no interest in supporting Monarchists' ideas, which would reunite Russia. On the contrary, we must try and prevent Russian consolidation as far as possible and, from this point of view, we must therefore support the parties furthest to the left.*

As we have seen, this analysis is as fallacious as it is understandable. The confrontation with the central powers, closely followed

* Zeman, *Germany and the Revolution in Russia* (Oxford, 1958), Doc. No. 129.

by counter-revolution and foreign intervention by the Allies, was to consolidate a 'dictatorship of the proletariat' that would reunite and consolidate the former Russian Empire.

During 1918 all these movements became inextricably intertwined. At first Allied intervention aimed at helping those forces opposed to the Germans, though the White generals supporting the Allies were receiving military supplies from the German protégé, the Ataman Krasnov of the Don Cossacks. But as the White generals were at the same time opponents of the Bolsheviks, the two movements inevitably coalesced into one. Even after the armistice of 1918, when there could no longer be any question of reviving an Eastern front against the Germans, intervention was not simply anti-Bolshevik *tout court*. Each of the interventionist powers – Great Britain, France, the United States, and Japan – had its own axe to grind, and this disunity helped the Bolsheviks to survive. During the whole campaigning period of some two years, the Bolsheviks held fast to the historic heartland of Russia, the territory around Moscow and Petrograd. Their transfer of the seat of government to Moscow had deeply patriotic overtones. At the same time, it indicated their intention to overcome the social and cultural gulf that had riven Russian society since Peter's time. The Bolsheviks were thus able to concentrate their forces at any threatened point on the periphery. Trotsky's famous armoured train, with its dazzling array of equipment and its elite guard romantically attired in black leather, rushed from front to front exhorting and organizing whenever and wherever it was needed. On the other hand, the Whites had the advantage of surprise and also of access to the sea. Unfortunately for them, the areas in which they gathered were themselves riven by social and national divisions and they wasted much of their strength rescuing local chieftains from their own subjects. The sea, the source of supplies, was also a tempting invitation to the faint-hearted to give up the battlefields of Russia for the cafés of Paris.

The first White Army formed in the territory of the Don Cossacks. It was led by Generals Kornilov, Denikin, and Alexeyev, the former tsarist Chief of Staff. But it was not from here that the first major blow came – it was from the Czechoslovak Legion of about 40,000 men.

This was formed originally of prisoners taken from the Austro-Hungarian Army. The Czech leader Masaryk hoped that a Czech contingent, fighting alongside the Allies, would ensure Czechoslovak independence, rather as Cavour had used the Sardinian contingent in the Crimean War to bring about the unity of northern Italy. For the French, who financed them and enrolled them in their own army, they represented a source of relief from the endless bloodletting along the Western front. This assumed that the British would spare the shipping to evacuate them. It was a period of bewildering uncertainty in British foreign policy. The desire to defeat the Germans and a kind of contemptuous hostility towards the Russians were axiomatic. Otherwise confusion reigned. For their part, when it came to dealing with the Czechs in 1918, the Bolshevik leaders showed a lamentable lack of the grasp of psychology that had enabled them to assume the leadership of Russian soldiers in 1917. The upshot was that the Czechs came to believe that the Bolsheviks intended to disarm them and turn them over to the Austrians to be shot. The last straw was the feeling of the Czechs that the Bolsheviks were treating the repatriated German and Austro-Hungarian prisoners better than themselves. Within a matter of weeks a row of towns, from Samara on the Volga to Vladivostok on the Pacific coast, was in Czech hands. Soviet power in the Volga region and in Siberia was overthrown. The Soviet government abandoned the idea of a trial for Nicholas II and liquidated the entire Imperial family rather than risk their escape. In the West, the S.R. Party formed a government in Samara called the Committee of the Constituent Assembly. The forces of the Committee were finally halted at Kazan, where Trotsky, as Commissar for War, personally intervened in the battle, rallying the demoralized and retreating Red forces.

This was a strictly limited defensive victory. It did not prevent Japanese, American, and small British, French, and Italian detachments landing at Vladivostok. The pretext was 'aid to the Czechs'. Thence the interventionists moved westwards into Siberia, where, with British and French support, a series of coups were mounted against the 'democratic' S.R. government in Samara and an authoritarian government, under Admiral Kolchak, former commander of the Black Sea Fleet, was established. The government of the S.R.s never stood much of a chance. Its leadership was impeccably democratic, but deprived of mass support, the only people it could count on to fight the Reds were officers and cadets of monarchist or proto-fascist views. These views were fully supported, if not entirely shared, by the Allied military missions that dispensed aid.

In the meantime, Allied troops were landing at the White Sea ports of Murmansk and Archangel. Simultaneously, an anti-Bolshevik government consisting mostly of S.R.s was set up in Archangel under the leadership of Chaikovsky, the former populist. A White Russian government, almost entirely working class in composition, was set up under British aegis at Ashkhabad in Turkestan. The British troops had advanced through Baluchistan and Persia, and occupied the Transcaspian area. By August 1918 about thirty different governments were functioning on Russian soil.

Superimposed on the turmoil that same summer was the apparent risk of a rapprochement between the left and right S.R.s, both equally enraged by Brest-Litovsk. There were a number of assassinations: that of Count Mirbach, the German Ambassador; of Uritsky, the head of the Petrograd Cheka (the new secret police of the regime); and an attempt on Lenin's life by a Jewish girl, Dora Kaplan. Meanwhile, Savinkov led the right S.R.s in a rebellion in Yaroslavl, helped by the French Ambassador. By far the most serious outbreak was the revolt of the left S.R.s in Moscow. The attempt failed: its sole result was to legitimize the 'Red Terror' now wielded against the enemies of the regime. To start with, the Cheka shot five hundred 'bourgeois' hostages in Petrograd; this was just the beginning.

It was in these circumstances that Chicherin, the former Menshevik who followed Trotsky as Commissar for Foreign Affairs, approached the Germans with a proposal for their collaboration in parrying the Allied forces in the north. The Germans, Chicherin proposed, should advance to prevent a possible southward advance of the British in Murmansk, while the Soviets withdrew their troops around Vologda in order to protect Moscow. But nothing came of this. The Germans by now had enough troubles of their own.

The end of the war in the West forced the Entente to clarify its intentions with regard to Russia. In December 1917, an inter-Allied agreement at Paris, signed by Milner and Lord Robert Cecil for Britain, and by Clemenceau for France, had tried to lay down which power would be responsible for Allied efforts in the different borderlands of Russia. The French were allotted Bessarabia, the Ukraine, and the Crimea. To the British fell the Cossack lands, the Caucasus, Armenia, Georgia, and Kurdistan. Pursuant to this agreement, both Powers sent ships to Novorossiisk with arms for Denikin. Later, a French naval division landed at Odessa and British troops moved into Batum and Baku, attracted, it has been said, 'by the smell of oil'. The summary execution of the twenty-six Bolshevik commissars of Baku by Russian Mensheviks under British protection is still commemorated in the U.S.S.R. as the greatest single atrocity of British imperialism against the Russian revolution. Other White generals to be helped by the Allies were Miller in north Russia and Yudenich in the west. Everywhere the Allies went there was a tendency for the anti-revolutionary governments to move from an initially democratic set of policies to those of outright reaction, restoring the land to the landowners and suppressing all independent labour organizations.

As the war in the West ended, with the Soviets hemmed in on all fronts and under increasing Allied pressure, Lenin expected a concerted attack by world capital. The answer to world capital was world revolution. In fact, we now know that capital was hopelessly divided, not least by national differences over how to deal with Russia, and world revolution still remote. Still, Lenin's hopes were not unreasonable on empirical grounds alone, to say nothing of their theoretical justification in Marxist eyes. Habsburg and Hohenzollern fell. Soldiers' and Workers' Councils spontaneously formed themselves in Germany on the Russian model. *Pravda* proclaimed on 1 November 1918: 'The world revolution has begun ... Nothing can hold up the iron tread of revolution.' A month later, Radek, the foremost Soviet journalist and recent inmate of a German prison cell, predicted that the spring of 1919 would find all Europe communist. Zinoviev, the President of the Communist International, the embryonic world communist government, looked forward to transferring the headquarters of his organization from Moscow to Paris.

The Soviets combined revolutionary propaganda with offers of surrender. In a note of 4 February 1919, Chicherin offered to meet Russia's foreign debts, to lease concessions, and to give up territories to be occupied by armies drawing their support from the Allies. Russia, should these terms be accepted, would then undertake not to intervene in the internal affairs of the powers. But they were not accepted, as Lenin had foreseen. The Bolsheviks were also unable to take advantage of President Wilson's attempt to mediate between themselves and the White forces at a meeting to be arranged on the Island of Prinkipo in the Straits. The onus for this failure was allowed to fall on the French and the Whites.

In these circumstances, revolutionary propaganda continued unabated. Germany was the focal point of Russian hopes. It was here that Lenin made his greatest effort. Ill-nourished as Russia was, he still set aside a store of grain for transport to a Germany suffering under the Allied blockade. He also assembled a small delegation of diplomats to represent Russia at the Berlin Congress of Soldiers' and Workers' Councils. But the new German government, predominantly social-democratic, refused to admit both the grain and the diplomats. The Russians remained as isolated as ever. Nor were they helped very much by the fiery proclamations and optimistic prognoses of the third Communist International. The ephemeral successes of the Soviet Republics in Hungary and Bavaria were the exception that proved the rule. However, the 'Hands off Russia' movement in Britain limited the supply of military equipment sent to the Whites while the mutiny of the French fleet in the Black Sea forced the evacuation of French forces from Odessa.

In 1919, as in 1918, the Soviets had to win through on their own. In one way they were in a weaker position because they were now blockaded by the Allies; also, the Allies, by Point 12 of the Armistice agreements with Germany, tried to ensure that the German troops on the Eastern front would return only to 'within the frontiers of Germany as soon as the Allies shall think the moment suitable, having regard to the internal situation of these territories'. (This condition was repeated *vis-à-vis* the Baltic countries in Article 433 of the Versailles Treaty.)

Early in 1919 Kolchak, to whom the Allies looked to form the future non-Bolshevik government of Russia, moved westwards across the Urals in the direction of Moscow. This was the opening move in a year of incessant campaigns that would reach its climax in the autumn. At first Kolchak's three armies rapidly advanced. Ufa fell and then, in April, Samara and Kazan were menaced. The bulk of the Red Army was in the south, holding the line against Denikin. But by the end of April Kolchak had reached his farthest point westwards. His southern wing, with its over-extended external lines, was outflanked in a wide sweep ordered by General S. Kamenev, the Soviet commander on the eastern front and one of the 30,000 former tsarist officers mobilized by Trotsky for service with the Red Army. Kolchak was forced back from Ufa and eastwards across the Urals. He lost pitched battles at Chelyabinsk and Omsk. By the end of the year, Kolchak's troops had simply disintegrated and he himself, abandoned by the Czechs, had fallen into Red hands. He was executed early in 1920.

Hardly had the main threat from Kolchak been repelled than the southern front under Denikin came alive. Here a virtual state of chaos prevailed. The unfortunate Ukrainians were only intermittently masters of their own land, and their independence movement lost the support of the peasantry as the authoritarian and antisemitic Petlyura, backed by the largely Galician officers in the Ukrainian army, ousted the socialist Vynnychenko from the leadership. The Poles, anxious to re-establish control over the territories they had ruled long ago, intrigued and threatened them all. The peasants themselves produced an authentic prophet of peasant socialism and xenophobia in Nestor Makhno. They attacked the supply lines of all the other combatants. Red and White Russians continued to fight over the Ukraine with sublime disregard for its claims to independence. At first Denikin made good headway in this quagmire. By the end of June he had taken Kharkov and Tsaritsyn (subsequently Stalingrad and now Volgograd), and Kiev by the end of August. At the same time, a diversionary attack was launched by General Yudenich against Petrograd. His base was in Estonia and he enjoyed British advice and naval backing. This was the second such attack. The first had been thrown back in May under Stalin's leadership. Soon Yudenich was in the suburbs of the city and, but for the railway link with Moscow, had cut it off from the outside world. So critical was the situation that Lenin contemplated abandoning Petrograd altogether. This time Trotsky rallied the defenders. Yudenich was not strong enough to besiege the city and he dared not risk street fighting that would break up his forces. He had no choice but to retreat. A month later he was back in Estonia where his army broke up.

This reverse severely weakened Denikin in the south. He was no more popular with the local population than any other Russian force. Like most of the White armies, his administration was marked by corruption, brigandage, and political reaction. He soon found himself out-fought with the weapon which had brought him so much success, when the 1st Red Cavalry Division, formed under Stalin's patronage, pursued his own cavalry to the Black Sea. The end of the year saw him inexorably on the retreat. He withdrew, with British aid, to the Crimea, and turned over his command to General Wrangel.

Wrangel tried hard to avoid some of the worst political errors of his predecessors but it was too late. All the more so as both the British and French had pulled out of the Black Sea and Transcaspian area and were preparing to lift the blockade. This was in fact withdrawn in January 1920. The Soviet government was finally able to eliminate the threat to Petrograd when peace with the conservative Finnish government was concluded in February of that year.

The last obstacle to peace was Poland. In April 1920 Pilsudski advanced eastwards into the Ukraine, and on 7 May took Kiev. But a Ukrainian revolt, on which he had counted, did not materialize. A swift turn came in the tide of battle. The Poles had to evacuate Kiev, and soon the Russians, carried forward on a swell-tide of revolutionary patriotism, were on the River Bug, the rough ethnic border between Russian Ukraine and Poland proper. It was at this time that Brusilov, the former Supreme Commander of the provisional government, offered his services to the Red Army. Lenin, desperate at the continued isolation of the Russian revolution, succumbed to the temptation offered by the Polish flight. He would take the revolution westward by force of arms, 'probe Western Europe with Russian bayonets', as he put it. The target was, as ever, Germany.

At this time the Second Congress of the Comintern was in session and the delegates could see pin-pointed on a map the advance of the Russian armies.

With a clutch at their hearts [said Zinoviev], the best representatives of the international proletariat followed the advance of our armies . . . We all understood that on every step forward of our Red Army there literally depended the fate of the international proletarian revolution.

In the event, Lenin's gamble did not come off. The Russians were thrown back before Warsaw and were soon themselves on the retreat. Early in 1921 the Treaty of Riga between Russia, Poland, and the three small Baltic States, brought an end to the war in the West. The Bolsheviks had maintained themselves in power; and the non-communist world had perforce to acknowledge failure. The process took longer in Transcaucasia, Central Asia and the Far East. But by February 1921 three anti-Communist republics in Georgia, Armenia, and Azerbaijan had been conquered. The overthrow of the popular Menshevik government in Georgia did much to confirm Western socialists in their hostility towards Russian Communism; the duplicity of the Soviet government in assuring the Georgians of their peaceful intentions while preparing to invade them followed a similar deception in the Ukraine. It showed that old habits died hard. In 1921, also, youthful revolutionaries in the Islamic protected states of Khiva and Bokhara in central Asia failed to sustain themselves in power and had to summon the Russian Communists to their rescue. The exiled Enver Pasha, hero of the Young Turk revolution in 1908 and one of the best Turkish commanders in the Great War, arrived to stoke a nationalist revolt. His heroic campaign and death continued to inspire imitators until 1930. Many of the refugees from Central Asia took refuge in Afghanistan; there they awaited another opportunity to raise the banner of Islam in Soviet Central Asia. At the end of 1922 Red troops at last entered Vladivostok, reluctantly evacuated by the Japanese under Allied pressure. The White cause was over.

Many of the Whites had paid for their hopeless courage with

their lives, cut off by lead or typhus. One such was the Cossack teacher and socialist Fyodor Kryukov, whose great novel about the civil war on the Don is still partly visible as a palimpsest, so it is argued, beneath the famous work claimed by Sholokhov.* Nearly a million Russians were evacuated in the melancholy steamers across the Black Sea to Gallipoli or under the grim eyes of Cheka frontier guards on to the trains to Finland, Poland and the Baltic States. In 1921, 120,000, mostly poorer Cossacks, returned to find the remnants of their families. Half the remainder went to France. Nina Berberova describes how most of them lived:

> A factory whistle sounds. Twenty-five thousand workers flow through wide iron gates onto the square. Every fourth man is a high-ranking officer of the White Army, military in bearing, his hands roughened by work. These are family people, obedient taxpayers and readers of the Russian daily newspapers, members of every conceivable Russian military organization who keep their regimental distinctions, St George's Crosses and medals, epaulettes, and dirks at the bottom of what are still Russian trunks, together with faded photographs – chiefly group ones ... I saw them at work: pouring steel into open-hearth furnaces, next to Arabs, half naked, deafened by the noise of air hammers, ...

A small minority were driven into crime or into hiring themselves out as the assassins of reaction in the Balkans and the Far East. A number of the exiles were more fortunate: the cadres of the Kadet, Menshevik, and S.R. Parties gathered in Paris, Berlin, and Prague to hurl abuse at the Soviets and at one another. A few managed to retain their wealth and gain acceptance in Paris society; Stravinsky continued to compose and Chagall to paint. None would forget what they had been, for in the words of Khodasevich:

> ... I have packed my Russia in my bag,
> And take her with me anywhere I go.

For the Russia that continued, they represented a frightful loss of human capital, and a mortal threat.

The end of the civil war forced the Soviet government to confront the relationship of the nationalities to the centre. Lenin's

---

*R. A. Medvedev, *Some Problems in the Literary Biography of Mikhail Sholokhov* (Cambridge, 1977), *passim*.

espousal of the right to self-determination had been of enormous value in winning sympathy for Bolshevism among the minorities of the borderlands. It had even created an unspoken common interest between the Bolsheviks and such unpromising allies as the peasant parties of Finland and the Baltic States. At the same time, Lenin's own insistence on the hegemony of the industrial proletariat and the subordination of the national to the class struggle lent support, on the other hand, to those who sought to re-annex as much as possible of the old Empire. At the level of practice, the unity, centralization and omnicompetence of the party, which transcended national boundaries within the former Empire, also ensured that the Soviet republics would be independent in name only. This seemed obvious to Stalin, the commissar for nationalities, who signed himself 'Muscovite' at this time. The fierce struggle which broke out between Lenin's and Stalin's friends in 1922 concerned the domineering style of the latter in handling the Georgians, not the substance of Georgian independence. Yet Lenin was certainly sincere in believing that the nationalities should have more real independence in cultural matters and in the implementation of locally sensitive policies concerning agriculture and religion. In 1922, the Soviets once more rejoined the international community, though still excluded from the League. As such it was vital that they spoke with one voice. The Soviet republics first transferred their rights over foreign policy to the Russian Republic and then, in December 1922, submerged their sovereignties in the notionally supranational Union of Soviet Socialist Republics.

The fundamental reason for the success of the Bolsheviks against their White and nationalist opponents was that they promised to satisfy the demands of the peasantry – the great majority of the Russian people – and to respect the independence of the minorities. Yet the defeat of the Whites was far from total. They had done as much as Bolshevik dogma to destroy Lenin's experiment with 'state capitalism' in the spring of 1918 and proceed to the militarization of Soviet society, or 'war communism'. The war that they fought forced the Bolsheviks to rely, to a considerable extent, on their brothers and cousins, the so called 'bourgeois specialists' in the army and in industry. The civil war had also turned politicians like Trotsky and Stalin into 'field-marshals'. Though the conflict between these two should not be exaggerated at this time, there was something portentous about the terms of their differences. Trotsky embodied the passionate rationality of those members of the intelligentsia who had opted for Bolshevism. He admired the training of his tsarist officers and had no hesitation in using them to command his disciplined infantry, deployed from front to front on the militarized railways. For Stalin, imbued with plebeian resentment against the bourgeois specialists, they were to be replaced by proletarian officers as soon as possible; his favoured weapon was the Red Cavalry which chased Denikin off the south Russian steppe.

PART TWO: THE DEFEAT OF THE WORKING CLASS

During the whole of the Georgian affair that haunted Lenin's last months of real political activity in 1922, one incident caused him the greatest distress. Ordzhonikidze, a friend of Stalin, had gone to Georgia to investigate complaints made by leading Georgian Communists against Stalin's friends in Georgia. When one of the complainants spoke out, Ordzhonikidze struck him in the face. Neither Dzerzhinsky, the 'incorruptible' head of the Cheka, who was present, nor Stalin could see anything wrong with this. To Lenin, this recalled the *khamstvo* or boorish brutality of eighteenth-century Russian provincial governors. The political culture of tsarist Russia was reproducing itself before his very eyes. There had been many such worrying symptoms. In 1918, he had discovered that someone had raised his salary without consulting him and had taken no action when he had protested. What kind of salary structure had such people in mind and for whose benefit? In 1920, he and Dzerzhinsky had decided to mark the end of the civil war by abolishing the death penalty. The operatives of the Cheka had defied the decree by shooting several hundred prisoners on their own responsibility. Lenin's ceaseless campaigns against bureaucratic 'red tape' are well known. As the realization began to dawn on him that he might have presided, unwittingly, at the birth of a new form of ruling class, he clung with increasing desperation to a form of Hegelian dialectics increasingly remote from Russian reality. His hostility to any form of sociology became more and more emotional. He would not admit that the warnings of Bakunin, Plekhanov, and Machajski could have any validity. At the same time, he was sensitive to the lessons of history. Unlike Robespierre, he and his government would change course, when forced to, rather than go down into oblivion.

During the first half of 1918, the Russian workers and peasants were, first economically and then politically, deprived of the most crucial gains of the October revolution. The Bolsheviks had claimed the mantle of Winstanley and Babeuf, not Cromwell and Bonaparte, and they had ridden to power by encouraging the masses to believe in the imminence of utopia; now they would perform the remarkable task of disappointing these hopes while retaining power. For many of the workers, these disappointments were lessened by the realization that they were economically necessary; for others there was the prospect of co-option to the ruling bureaucracy. Few such positive incentives existed for the peasantry. The Bolshevik honeymoon with the peasantry and the left S.R.s who sought to represent them lasted only half a year.

Lenin began to tackle the question of labour discipline immediately after the conclusion of the Treaty of Brest-Litovsk. As we have already seen, it was usually the workers themselves who had insisted on the nationalization of their enterprises when the capitalists had proven unable or unwilling to pay their wages. They had demanded state financial support for their industries and, at first, this was met by the simple expedient of printing money. In April 1918, Lenin announced that in future the workers must be subjected to capitalist techniques for maximizing exploitation ('Taylorism') and one-man management:

And our task ... is to appreciate this change, to understand that it is necessary, to take the lead of the exhausted masses who are wearily seeking a way out and lead them along the true path, along the path of labour discipline, along the path of co-ordinating the task of discussing at mass meetings the conditions of labour with the task of unquestioningly obeying the will of the Soviet leader, of the dictator, *during work time*.

The combination of nationalization, one-man management and labour discipline would enable the central bureaucracy to appropriate the surplus product, one of the crucial attributes of any ruling class. These theses provoked almost as much bedlam within the Bolsheviks as had Lenin's April Theses of a year before. Once more, Lenin relied heavily on his party manager, Yakov Sverdlov, to ensure that they carried. During the spring of 1918, Lenin was anxious for a truce between the government and what remained of Russian capitalism; he was even willing to defend a period of 'state capitalism' to the party. It was the intensification of the civil war in the summer of 1918, rather than the opposition of his comrades, that forced him to drop this idea.

Relations between the Soviet government and the peasantry were at first cordial enough. In many ways, they echoed those of the factory committees. Thus, in the spring of 1918 the left S.R.s urged the peasants to establish communes and demand that the Soviets in the towns give them economic assistance. The commissars replied by insisting on rights of inspection and control. As a British journalist who visited the Volga put it, 'a controlling commissar was to them an element of bureaucratic tyranny'. It was the sheer hunger of the townspeople and soldiers which finally forced a more vigorous assertion of Soviet authority, however. As we have seen, the peasants had suffered from low fixed prices for their produce and an absence of consumer goods as a result of the war. Their natural reaction had been to grow only as much food as they needed for themselves. The Bolsheviks had made matters worse by encouraging the disruption of such industry as continued to function and by relieving the peasants of all their financial obligations to the former landlords. The predictable result was a further decline in deliveries of food to the towns. In May 1918, the government introduced a 'food dictatorship' which effectively allowed armed townsmen to confiscate peasant 'surpluses' at their discretion. In June, this became a full-scale attempt to disrupt the villages when 'committees of the poor' were set up. These were recruited from the former household servants of the landlords and from the least efficient of the peasants. Lenin's grasp of the economics of peasant life was probably sound but he underestimated the extent to which the vertical ties of family and economic patronage overlay the differences of class within the village. Many of the former 'kulaks', i.e. village money-lenders, had themselves had to re-enter the commune and reduce their holdings. From the point of view of the peasants, there was no justification for an attack on them which masqueraded as an attack on 'kulaks'. From the point of view of the town-dwellers, on the other hand, virtually the entire peasantry now came to be seen as a bunch of tight-fisted (*kulak* means just this), selfish exploiters of their misery.

Inevitably, the economic expropriation of the working classes was accompanied by their political expropriation. The technician of this process was Yakov Sverdlov. It was he who had inherited the party organization from Krupskaya and Elena Stasova. Sverdlov was another of the party's ascetic intellectuals, a man with an extraordinary memory for people and a commanding bass voice that came, surprisingly, from an emaciated physique. His command of organization and procedure had given Lenin his victory over the doubting in April 1917. It was this that commended him to Lenin as Kamenev's successor at the head of the All-Russian Central Executive Soviet early in 1918. As Trotsky put it: '. . . unwittingly and potentially the political administration Sverdlov headed was the precursor to the one-party State'. Sverdlov soon set to work on the body that had become Russia's parliament, inventing 'technical' rules to limit debate, changing the formulae for representation, removing effective control from the plenary sessions to those of the Presidium and denying Martov's request for a roll-call vote on this issue. This process continued at the 4th Congress of Soviets in summer 1918 when a whole series of procedures was established to clamp down on the rights of minorities and Sukhanov was denied an opportunity to put a motion on Brest-Litovsk. He then introduced new rules prohibiting discussion by the Central Executive Committee of any item not previously discussed by its Presidium. With the left S.R. rising of July 1918, the opposition was expelled from the Central Executive Committee. Before this had happened, however, Sverdlov had summarized his work in the Soviets in this unforgettable line: 'Who is for not opening debate? Accepted; debate is not opened!' With the taming of the Soviets, Sverdlov could return to the party apparatus which moved towards the formation of local secretariats and files on all party members. They could proceed to the taming of the local Soviets in turn. It was precisely the Soviets which, in

Lenin's view, enabled the proletariat to demonstrate the 'historical, creative spirit'. What would happen if they became mere 'transmission belts' of the party apparatus?

A second aspect of the political expropriation of the working class was the elimination of choice. The Bolsheviks had won the support of the majority of the industrial workers and much of the peasantry by open agitation and in free elections in 1917. But what if the workers and peasants should change their minds? Lenin had no intention of letting this happen but that does not mean that either he or Sverdlov set out with a master plan for the one-party state. To a large extent what they did was in response to particular emergencies; they benefited considerably from the errors of their opponents. The Kadet Party, and its press, were suppressed in December 1917. The elimination of the party that had come to represent property was not mourned by the working class; it seemed even more just when it emerged that it was the Kadets who were behind the first White Army in the south. The suppression of the socialist parties, and their publications, was more difficult. The totally illegal closure of *Forwards*, the paper of the Menshevik-Internationalists, at the end of April for an alleged 'slander' by Martov on Stalin, was exceptional. The right S.R.s, Kerensky included, were still able to publish their views in Moscow in June 1918. It was the revolt of the left S.R.s that totally changed the atmosphere, not least because the Russian regiments refused to support the Bolsheviks who were driven to rely on the Latvians and Cheka. This last example of the muddle-headedness of the S.R. tradition failed as much because the left S.R.s did not know what they wanted as for any other reason. Apparently, they really believed they could revolt against the Bolshevik government and force it to change course without being treated as traitors to the revolution. With the failure of their venture, Soviet Russia became a one-party state, the remaining left Mensheviks and anarchists sharing in the defeat of the left S.R.s. In the spring of 1918, working-class confidence in the Bolsheviks was still high. Many leading Bolsheviks had encouraged working-class demands in 1917, seeing in them more than a mere tactic to overthrow the bourgeois state. The reaction against Lenin's plan for 'state capitalism' was therefore shared by members of the Communist Party as well as the ordinary workers. They predicted that Lenin's new policies would lead to 'bureaucratic centralization, the supremacy of various commissars, the loss by local Soviets of their independence, and . . . the abandonment of . . . government from below – of the "commune state" '. The defeat of the left Communists does not seem to have led to any real swing to the anarchists. The degeneration of anarchism into 'small expropriations', i.e. outright thefts from individual members of the bourgeoisie, helped to discredit them, and in their August congress in 1918 they had to admit that the policies of the Bolsheviks had moved the working class 'to the right, towards the Constituent Assembly'. As we have seen, the Committee of the Constituent Assembly was unable to wield effective power and the counter-revolution soon revealed a much more reactionary face. Until it was defeated, the industrial workers supported the Bolsheviks in opposing it. The anarchists were unsuccessful in their attempt to supplant the Bolshevik leadership of the working class. They were better at prophecy; the anarchist Sergven wrote:

The song [Lenin's policies] goes thus: management implies responsibility, and can responsibility be compared with ordinary labour? Responsibility demands special rights and advantages. Such is the source of privilege and of the new anti-socialist morality.

The first major popular revolt against Bolshevism occurred in the Ukraine. There were several reasons for this. In the first place, the Bolsheviks had abandoned the Ukrainians to the Germans and Austrians and their puppet, the Hetman Skoropadsky, with the Treaty of Brest-Litovsk. Resentment of this was widespread within the Red Army itself. The action of Kollontai's lover, the Ukrainian sailor Paul Dybenko, in deserting the Red Army to set up a partisan movement in the Ukraine was not an isolated phenomenon. A second factor affecting the Ukraine was probably the fact that Red Army units operating from the industrial centres were led entirely by Russians. As a Ukrainian Communist put it later: 'The army still remains a weapon of Russification of the Ukrainian population . . .' A final influence was perhaps the extremism of the Ukrainian Communists with their intolerance of any form of autonomy and their enthusiasm for enforcing col-

lective, and even state, farms. The centre of the Ukrainian movement was the village of Gulyai-Pole, home of the youthful and
handsome leader, Nestor Makhno, a convinced anarchist. Initially,
the movement embraced four communes, whose members shared
meals, brought their children up according to advanced educational ideals and insisted on regular physical work from all their
members. It was supported by a penumbra of sympathetic, but
more conventional, peasant settlements. At first the battle was
with the Germans, then with the Ukrainian nationalists, and
finally with the Bolsheviks. The movement was widely discredited
by its alleged antisemitism. Thus, in 1919, Makhnovites were using
the slogan: 'Down with the Communists, Jews and Russians; long
live the rule of true Soviets!' In this context, Jews and Russians
probably means intellectuals and industrial workers. They committed atrocities, like all participants in the events of the period,
against Jews as against gentiles. On the other hand, many Jews
served with Makhno and a Jew was his chief of staff.

If the ruling Soviet bureaucracy was to avoid degenerating into
a new ruling class, its relations with the working class were obviously of the greatest importance. The working class itself was
terribly weakened by the civil war and war Communism. Between
1917 and 1920 over half the working class disappeared. Many of
them fell on the many fronts or fell victim to the typhus epidemics
of those awful years. For many more, the only alternative to
starving in the city was to return to the villages from which they,
or their parents, had come. As an industrial country, Russia had
been thrown back decades, industrial production standing at less
than a third of the 1913 total. Some industries, like iron and steel
and sugar production, had virtually ceased to function. Only
agriculture had retained some of its resilience. It is hardly surprising that the attrition of the workers was the opportunity of the
intelligentsia. The proportion of workers in the Communist Party
went down from 59 per cent in 1918 to only 41 per cent in 1920. Nor
does this give an adequate idea of the qualitative change in party
membership. Many of the members who had freely chosen their
party in 1918 had fallen at the fronts. Their places had often been
taken by pure opportunists aware of the fact that while Communist
rations were still very modest (the maximum permitted wage dif-

ferential was 4:1), they were at least regular. Very soon, a caste spirit developed among senior party members and administrators that continued to glorify manual work while seeking to have as little as possible to do with it. All these factors seemed to justify the increasing tendency of the party bureaucracy to appoint to positions of responsibility rather than permitting election by the workers. In 1920, the *Uchraspred* was formed under the aegis of the Central Committee; this was the first step towards the creation of an agency which would come to control *all* appointments to positions of responsibility within the U.S.S.R. Within a year, Kollontai was complaining: 'The procedure of appointments produces a very unhealthy atmosphere in the party, and disrupts the relationship of equality among the members by rewarding friends and punishing enemies.'

As the civil war came to an end, the workers themselves became more restive. The excuse of civil war could no longer be used to rationalize the discrepancy between the conditions they experienced and the promises of 1917. At first this mood found expression within the party and its subordinate institutions, the trade unions. When rebuffed, it broke out in strikes and finally into open rebellion. The most articulate spokeswoman for the Workers' Opposition was Alexandra Kollontai, its most influential leader within the working class, Alexander Shlyapnikov. It was supported by the entire metal-workers union, perhaps a quarter of the members of the Moscow Party, by workers in south-east Russia and by the Ukrainian Communists. In the first place, the Workers' Opposition demanded that the trade unions play a central role in the management of industry and that workers elect the economic planning authorities. There were also calls for compulsory periods of manual labour for non-working-class recruits to the party, extreme egalitarianism of rewards, etc. Trotsky allowed Lenin to appear to tread the moderate centre by coming out with an extreme alternative which would have subjected the unions totally to state control. Two things were obvious to the workers themselves. One was that the party was deeply divided. The other was the total hostility of the Central Committee, not just to the proposals of the Workers' Opposition, but even to the articulation of the actual grievances of the workers themselves.

At the end of February 1921, the Kronstadt naval garrison took matters into their own hands. When their demands were answered by the Soviet President Kalinin with threats of merciless reprisals, they went into open rebellion. The Soviet press asserted that they were acting under the command of a White general, a cynical fabrication. Despite this, news of their real programme seeped through the working-class districts of Petrograd and there was an immediate general strike. On all sides, there were reports of refusals by troops to fire on the demonstrators in the streets. The Kronstadt commune, led in fact by the naval rating S. M. Petrichenko, came as a tremendous shock to the Bolsheviks. 'Red Kronstadt' had been the most militant centre of the 1917 revolution. Now it was leading what claimed to be the 'third revolution', demanding political freedom for the workers, an investigation of repression, an equalization of rations and an end to unnecessary interference with peasant agriculture and food supply. Despite the impassioned pleas of many internationally respected Communists and socialists, there were no negotiations. On 17 March Tukhachevsky led the assault over the ice. Several hundred men were killed on either side; the Cheka later shot a similar number of captives. Petrichenko escaped to Finland. The chief effect of the revolt was to make it easier for Lenin to overcome the resistance of the party fundamentalists towards his proposed new economic policies and the imminent clamp-down on democracy within the party. His own mind on these matters had already been made up by pressure from a different quarter.

Makhno's movement had continued to flourish after the collapse of the Germans in 1918. For a time, it appeared that Communists and peasant anarchists might work in harmony; they collaborated in the final campaign against General Wrangel. The honeymoon was shortlived. The moment Wrangel was safely despatched, Trotsky's forces turned on Makhno. In November 1920, his headquarters was attacked and many of his closest collaborators killed. He himself escaped to Romania and thence to France, where he survived in alcoholic exile until the 1930s. His reputation had spread across Russia, however, and his example was followed all over the country. As one historian has aptly put it:

In the late winter and spring of 1921, small fires nearly everywhere in Russia threatened to merge with half a dozen major conflagrations into one vast funeral pyre for the Communist hierarchy.*

The best documented of these rural uprisings is the peasant rising in Tambov province, which broke out in August 1920 and was not put down until the summer of 1922. The Tambov rebels were blessed by a strong S.R. tradition, a sense of solidarity deriving from their membership of an independent Union of Toiling Peasantry, and a leader of real administrative and military talent in the person of Alexander S. Antonov. Like Makhno and Petrichenko, Antonov escaped; he left a legend in peasant doggerel – perhaps the last legend of a peasant hero to come out of Russia:

> Antonov doesn't drown in water, he doesn't burn in fire,
> the bayonet doesn't touch him, the bullet doesn't hit him.

To judge from Lenin's own words, however, it was the revolt of the Siberian peasantry that finally made up his mind that the government would have to change course. On 24 February 1921, before the outbreak of the Kronstadt Rising, he told a meeting of Moscow party members:

There are no deliveries from Siberia now, because the kulak rebels have cut off the railway . . . The Siberian peasantry are not yet used to privations, although they are bearing less than the peasantry of European Russia . . .

His explanation of these 'kulak' risings was extraordinarily confused:

In the banditism one feels the influence of the Socialist-Revolutionaries. Their main forces are abroad; every spring they dream of overthrowing Soviet power. Chernov wrote about this recently in a Russian newspaper abroad. The S.R.s are connected with the local instigators. This connection is to be seen in the fact that the uprisings take place in the very districts from which we take grain. The surplus-appropriation system here met with tremendous difficulties.†

Within days, Lenin had moved from the most fanatical de-

*O. H. Radkey, *The Unknown Civil War in Soviet Russia* (Stanford, Cal., 1976), p. 3.

†V. I. Lenin, *Collected Works*, vol. 42 (Moscow, 1969), pp. 272–3.

termination to eliminate private trading by punitive means, to a decision in favour of a tax in kind on the peasants which would allow them to keep part of their surpluses, and thence to the restoration of the market. He seems to have understood that he would himself preside over the Thermidorean reaction to his own revolution; it was better than seeing the collapse of the State he had helped to create.

To Lenin it was quite clear that though the 'special detachments' and Cheka might exterminate the leaders of the peasant rebellions, the peasantry had, collectively, inflicted a serious defeat on the Communist Party. A *modus vivendi* with the peasantry would have to be found. But if the party was not to be corrupted by the sea of petty bourgeois individualism that surrounded it, then it would have to give up some of its bad habits and return to the discipline of Lenin's ideal party in *What is to Be Done?* At the Tenth Party Congress, he waited until the last day to introduce resolutions condemning the Workers' Opposition and banning all factions on pain of expulsion from the party.

Marxism teaches . . . [he asserted] . . . that only the political party of the working class, i.e., the Communist Party, is capable of uniting, training and organizing a vanguard of the proletariat and of the mass of the working people that alone will be capable of withstanding the inevitable petty-bourgeois vacillations of this mass and the inevitable traditions and relapses of narrow craft-unionism or craft prejudices among the proletariat.*

With such a radical reduction of possibilities for democratic organization and debate within the party, the real power to decide party policy passed rapidly into the hands of the central bureaucracy of the party itself. At the end of 1922, the new post of General Secretary was created. The first occupant was Joseph Stalin.

After some years of relative social peace, the party would return to the offensive and inflict a conclusive and crushing defeat on the peasantry. Some years later, the intelligentsia would be subjected to a series of frightful purges. When all these events were examined in retrospect, the legend would grow up that the wicked tyrant

* R. V. Daniels, *A Documentary History of Communism*, Vol. I (New York, 1960), p. 210.

had subjected the peasants to forcible collectivization despite the socialist humanism of the intelligentsia. Like the German middle classes, educated Russians were victims of runaway inflation and the assertiveness of the 'lower orders'. Nothing illustrates this better than the penetrating and scandalous essay brought out by Gorky following his departure from Russia in January 1922. It was a vicious attack on the whole Russian national character and, paradoxically, an apologia for the entire Russian intelligentsia:

Accusations of egotistic self-interest, ambition and dishonesty I consider altogether inapplicable to any one of the groups of the Russian intelligentsia; all who bandy such accusations about are well aware that they are unfounded.*

No doubt Gorky was trying to build bridges between Kadets and Bolsheviks in the wider interests of Russian culture. The redundancy is striking: the Russian white-collar workers who were altruistic were members of the intelligentsia; the intelligentsia were altruistic. We are reminded of the claim of the intelligentsia to be a caste, not a class. White-collar workers who were not altruistic were always dismissed as mere *meshchanye*, vulgar commercial townspeople. This extraordinary apologia was provoked by the class-consciousness of the peasantry, that very class-consciousness that the intelligentsia had sought so hard to awaken. But Gorky finds it less attractive now that it has been turned against the intelligentsia. He had no sympathy for the peasant who tells an intellectual, 'we used to wait still longer for your favours', when selling him food. What frightened him about the food shortages of War Communism was that 'the countryside clearly understood that the town depended on it, while until this moment it had only felt its dependence on the town'. Nor does Gorky suggest that concessions to the peasantry can be regarded as anything other than a retreat before a class enemy. He regales his readers with tales of peasant brutality but regards similar accusations against the Bolsheviks as 'lies and slander'. This hostility towards the peasants did not die in 1922. Throughout the whole period of the New Economic Policy (or N.E.P. as it came to be known), the intelligentsia as a whole manifested unremitting hostility towards

*R. E. F. Smith, ed., *The Russian Peasant 1920 and 1984* (London, 1977), p. 26.

that policy and its visible representatives, the men who took food to the towns and consumer goods to the villages. Famine had taught the intelligentsia that they depended for their lives on the expropriation of peasant surpluses; the peasants would not fund any Shakespeares of their own free will.

To progressives of all kinds, it is axiomatic that the maturity of a society can be seen from the way it treats its women. The story of Russian women during the revolution is one of massive advances towards equality combined with the total suppression (sometimes by co-option) of any independent leadership. The Bolsheviks were enormously helped by the rigid patriarchalism of the tsarist State. It provided neither the vote for the well-off, nor a welfare net for the poor. The rich women suffered from marriage laws known to the whole world from *Anna Karenina*. Poor women suffered from exactly opposite difficulties. The total inability of the Orthodox Church to adapt to urbanization meant that they simply could not get married; the Church that enjoined chastity on them would not help them to get maintenance for their illegitimate children but it turned a blind eye to the thousands of licensed prostitutes who catered for male needs in the capitals and elsewhere. The war made the whole of Russian society crucially dependent on women in field and factory. By 1921, 65 per cent of the factory workers of Petrograd were women. Over 70,000 women served in the Red Army, usually behind the lines, but a small number fought in the same detachments as men in the front line, producing such authentic heroines as Nina Rostovtseva who saved her detachment by knocking out a White machine-gun nest.

For the very beginning, the Soviet government set out to secure the support of working-class women. In December 1917 its first marriage law was issued, converting marriage into a simple civil transaction conferring no advantage on either party, providing for simple divorce proceedings and maintenance for children. The revolutionary feminists were not entirely happy with a measure that appeared to rehabilitate marriage rather than abolish it; Kollontai had to be content with the concession that the woman would not have to take her husband's name. To demonstrate her support for the law, and the new classless spirit, she registered her marriage with Dybenko. During the civil war, the government also proclaimed the (unenforceable) principle of equal pay for equal work. As a concession to the needs of hygiene they finally conceded the right to abortion on demand; it was happening anyway. Real strides were taken towards the provision of eight weeks' maternity leave both before and after the birth of a child, and on full pay. Already, tensions were appearing in the government's thinking on the issue, not in any case a high priority during the civil war. If women were to play a full part in politics and production, how could they simultaneously provide all the citizens the new society would need in the period of reconstruction that would follow the seven years of the Apocalypse? This is a dilemma that has never been fully resolved; women continue to bear the 'double burden' in Russia. The utopian ideals of Kollontai and other feminists from the intelligentsia for the sexual liberation of women were roundly condemned when she tried to 'meddle' in high politics as a member of the Workers' Opposition. Even had the mass of Russian women been ready for them, which they were not, efficient methods of birth control were not available on the scale required. Kollontai's experiments with crêches and communal eating did lighten the burdens of some women during the civil war, but when the Red Army veterans returned they wanted their jobs back and their women back at home. Despite this mood, Russian women retained most of the benefits for which they, like women in other countries, had worked so hard. Legally speaking, Russian women were better off than women anywhere in the world. The path to their further emancipation would lie through their involvement in the world of work.

CHAPTER 16

New Economic Policy, Nomenklatura and the Rise of Stalin

By late February 1921, Lenin was to conclude that the alliance with the peasantry – the temporary coincidence of interests that had been the very foundation of the 1917 revolution – must be re-established. He had already submitted to the Party Central Committee a project for a new economic policy. A few weeks later this emerged, after due discussion by the delegates, as the starting point of an economic programme that entirely scrapped the policies of war communism. It began primarily as an agricultural measure that would give an incentive for the peasant to produce more food for the towns; it then broadened out into a medium for the development of commodity exchange between town and country; and, lastly, into an encouragement to industrial productivity.

At the back of it all was the necessity of saving the revolution. This was the point that had been reached, a 'peasant Brest', as Bukharin put it. It had always been held by Lenin that in Russian conditions – that is, in a country where bourgeois capitalism had remained underdeveloped – there could be no direct transition to socialism. The accomplishment of a socialist revolution would depend, Lenin argued, either on a socialist revolution in the more advanced countries of the West, or on 'a compromise between the proletariat which puts its dictatorship into practice or holds the State power in its hands, and the majority of the peasant population'.

In the absence of the first of these conditions (and hope in the European revolution survived until 1923), the second automatically moved into first place. To this necessary compromise Lenin's New Economic Policy made its own specific contribution.

What it did initially was to replace the requisitioning of the peasants' food surpluses and labour services by a graduated, agricultural tax in kind (from 1923 onwards in money only). This latter was calculated as a proportion of the surplus left over after providing for the minimum subsistence needs of the peasants' families and dependants. The new policy did indeed contain a residue of the previous requisitioning element. But it had a vital difference in that, since it took only a fixed proportion of the surplus, it gave every incentive to the peasant to produce to the maximum and thus to increase his or her share of the surplus; or, as the official decree put it, 'every peasant must now realize and remember that the more land he plants, the greater will be the surplus of grain which will remain in his complete possession'. In 1925 the wealthier peasant was further favoured in being allowed to use hired agricultural labour. A progressive scale of taxation was devised to mollify the conscience of the party and defend it from the accusation that it was abandoning the 'poor peasant'.

But what would happen to the peasants' surplus? It was here that N.E.P. developed its second arm. It implied that there was a right of free trade in agricultural produce. In other words, the market was re-created. It was at first limited to local fairs and marts. This limitation later fell away and a class of so-called *Nepmen* came into existence. They dominated retail distribution and also played an important role as wholesalers. In 1922–3, for example, private traders controlled about 75 per cent of the retail trade of the Soviet Union. The share of state and co-operative trading respectively was about 14 per cent and 10 per cent. The *Nepmen* functioned as the medium through which trade between town and country was re-established.

The New Economic Policy was thus a 'retreat', a partial surrender to the peasant majority. On the other hand, the State retained what Lenin called the 'commanding heights' of the economy. These were primarily the largest industrial installations. According to a census of 1923, although quantitatively the share controlled by the State was comparatively small – of 165,781 enterprises 88 per cent belonged to private individuals, 8·5 per cent to the State and 3 per cent to co-operatives – *qualitatively* the share of the State enormously outweighed that of its partners. Thus, the 88 per cent privately owned enterprises employed only 12·5 per cent of the total number of workers employed in industry, whereas the State owned enterprises employed just over 84 per cent of all industrial workers. Put in another way, the average number of workers in a State-owned enterprise was 155; in co-operative and private enterprises it was fifteen and two respectively. We would simply call the latter self-employed in small family businesses. Altogether, private enterprises accounted for only 5 per cent of gross production.

Moreover, the State controlled all such vital services as credit and banking, transport, and, of course, foreign trade and merchant shipping. All these remained State monopolies. The overall consequence was an economy in which the State virtually monopolized industrial life, acted as the arbiter of commercial life, and left agricultural production under the control of an ever growing number of small producers. This was an inherently unstable mixture, as was shown by wild fluctuations in prices. It seemed that the peasant producer held the whip hand over the industrial proletariat. The peasant had only the obligation of a taxpayer to the State. The town worker, on the other hand, was exposed to all the hazards of food rationing and unemployment. At this time the quip was current that the initials N.E.P. denoted 'New Exploitation of the Proletariat'. By early 1924 there were nearly one and a quarter million unemployed, the result of a ruthless drive to re-establish sound money and the profitability of individual enterprises. At its height the total was to reach two million, over a quarter of the Russian proletariat. Other casualties of the new market rationality were Lunacharsky's efforts at providing universal free education on progressive lines, Semashko's attempts to provide a universal free health service, and Kollontai's efforts at replacing women's domestic labour by providing communal facilities for housework. All this came as a terrible shock to many Communists; the disillusionment suffered by the rank and file workers must have been as great. Driven by unemployment to set themselves up in small businesses, they were naturally drawn to ask whether the capitalist mode of production was such a bad thing after all.

Until 1928 there was no basic change in this mixed economy, though after 1926, when pre-war production levels were regained in most branches of industry, attempts at planning investment became more systematic. Though the volume of private trade rose, the proportion of trade in the hands of the co-operatives rose sharply as political suspicion of these former S.R. and Menshevik institutions declined. Still, given their obsession with the criterion of ownership of the means of production, it was not implausible for Communists to look for possible Thermidorians among the petty merchants and wealthier peasant farmers. To head off this danger, the remaining S.R. cadres in Russia were rounded up and accused of conspiring with White generals to overthrow the revolution. To Lenin's fury, Kamenev promised foreign socialists that there would be no executions. Still, the point was made.

N.E.P. Russia and Weimar Germany shared all the symptoms of defeat and disillusionment. They inspired revulsion at the time and tremendous nostalgia from then on. For despite all the penury and hardship, all the cleft between the dream of abundance and the reality of hardship, it still seems true that in many respects the twenties were the halcyon days of the Soviet regime. Once economic stabilization was achieved, there was increasing expenditure on social insurance, sanatoria, workers' housing, hospitals, convalescent centres, and general welfare. These were, of course, goals the Communists also shared with Social-Democrats and even Fascists. Educationally, progressive methods in schools and the treatment of orphans and delinquents made Soviet Russia a centre of experiment and research. The 'Road to Life' pioneered by Makarenko for the reclamation of the millions of unsupervised orphans left by seven years of war and famine was conducted under the aegis of the Cheka. The Cheka itself was brought under stricter Party control, renamed the G.P.U., deprived of its power to execute and purged of its more psychopathic members.

The Soviet government made enormous efforts to overcome the suspicions of the intelligentsia. Private publishing houses were encouraged, non-Marxist historians still enjoyed positions of prominence and freedom of publication, provided, of course, that their work did not contest the legitimacy of the new regime. There was as yet no government-inspired historical schema. The Academy of Sciences was allowed to continue its work with a secretary who was a former Kadet Minister in the provisional government. Some of the pioneers of the new science of development economics that emerged in Russia in these years were former S.R., Menshevik, and even Kadet economists. In the arts, Lenin, Trotsky, and Lunacharsky all poured scorn on the idea of a purely proletarian culture, and it was possible for the 'Serapion Brotherhood', poets such as Mayakovsky and Yesenin, novelists and short-story writers such as Isaac Babel, Pilnyak, Vsevolod Ivanov, and Leonid Leonov, to choose and develop their themes with a broad degree of freedom. Often, they described the civil war, and truthfully discussed the ambivalence with which the intelligentsia and religious dissenters had met the revolution. Yesenin was even permitted to mourn the impending doom of the peasant way of life with unrivalled poignancy:

> The little thatched hut I was born in lies bare to the sky,
> And in these crooked alleys of Moscow I am fated to die.

During these years the Soviet government tried hard to make up for tsarist attempts to suppress the cultures of the national minorities. By far the most remarkable of these compensatory policies was the policy of 'Ukrainization' launched in 1923. Ukrainian national sentiment has always posed a greater challenge to Great Russian chauvinism, as Lenin called it, than anything else. Yet by the mid twenties, Stalin was happily looking forward to the day when the industrial cities of the Ukraine, those bastions of Great Russia, would become 'Ukrainized'. The greatest coup for the party was the return in 1926 of Mykhaylo Hrushevsky, former President of the Ukrainian Central Rada and one of the principal exponents of Ukrainian history and culture. During these years, the Ukrainian national intelligentsia developed a distinctive literature but their penetration of the party apparatus was much weaker. By 1929, Ukrainians had still only one-third of senior party members in the Ukraine.

Formally, the Soviet Union was a democracy, though the principle of 'one man, one vote' was subordinated to that of proletarian democracy. The former bourgeoisie, clergy, and adherents of the White regimes were disenfranchised. The remainder of the population was represented in the All-Russian Congress of Soviets. This was the pinnacle of many thousands of Soviets throughout the Union, elected indirectly on the basis of one deputy for each 25,000 urban voters and one deputy for each 125,000 rural inhabitants. But the All-Russian Congress met for only about one week in the year and consisted of almost 2,000 members. Its Central Executive Committee of about 300 members was scarcely less cumbersome. Thus power devolved on to the ten-member Council of People's Commissars elected from the Central Executive Committee and the formal equivalent to a Western European cabinet of ministers. But after 1921, all the commissars and almost all the members of the Central Executive Committee were members of the Communist Party, itself subordinated to its Politburo. Below the Politburo was the party secretariat headed by Stalin. It was he who supervised the work of the Orgburo for the Politburo. His devotion to the painstaking work of cadre selection conducted by the Uchraspred, a section of the Orgburo, earned him the nickname 'Comrade card-index' from those who foolishly under-estimated this kind of activity. In 1924, the Politburo belatedly recognized the importance of Uchraspred and re-organized it as *Orgraspred*, directly subordinate to the Politburo. Its head was Stalin's protégé, Lazar Kaganovich. Lenin's death provided a perfect opportunity to maximize the influence of these organs of selection. The civil war had seen a massive increase in the size of the party and, by 1921, it was obvious that many of its 6–700,000 members were not the kind of people the party leadership required. By early 1924, their numbers had been reduced to 350,000. In a move designed to promote the infusion of proletarian talent into the party, the two years that followed saw the admission of the 240,000 members of the so-called 'Lenin enrollment'. At the Twelfth Party Congress in 1923, Stalin had given his own view of how to select cadres:

It is a matter of selecting functionaries of such a kind that positions will be occupied by men who know how to draw up directives, to understand directives, to consider these directives as their own directives and to transform these directives into realities. Otherwise politics loses its point and gets lost in hollow speeches.

Molotov observed shrewdly that 'the development of the party in the future will undoubtedly be based on this Lenin enrolment'. At the Fourteenth Party Congress in 1925, the Leningrad party machine, controlled by Zinoviev, would fall before the onslaught of the central party machine controlled by Stalin. Thereafter, organized resistance to Stalin would become increasingly difficult.

From the beginning, the central bodies concerned with cadre selection drew up lists of two kinds; rather confusingly both were endowed with the Russified Latin term *Nomenklatura*. One was a list of the most responsible positions in Soviet society, the other was a list of those considered qualified to hold them. Political reliability was always more important than mere professional competence and there was a scattering of real proletarian bombasts to remind the able that they owed their promotion to the party, not just to their own talents. The All-Union and republican Nomenklaturas can be considered the ruling group in Soviet society to the present day. The question naturally arises: who were these people and which of their characteristics was most important? To what extent were they drawn disproportionately from the industrial working class in line with the ideology? Or did they bring with them elements of the traditions of the intelligentsia, the peasantry or even the despised and ignored meshchanye? Was it a conflict of generations or a conflict of class background that separated them from the Old Bolsheviks? Was their brusqueness in command a result of their modest education or their experience of warfare as N.C.O.s in the Great War and the civil war? Not all the answers to these questions are yet clear. In general, those like Trotsky, who champion the revolutionary intelligentsia, blame the degeneration of the party on 'the green and callow mass which was [rapidly being moulded and shaped] to play the role of [snappy yes-men] at a prod from the professionals of the machine'. The champions of the workers blamed degeneration on the 'petty-bourgeois elements, peasants, or . . . the faithful servants of Capital – the specialists'. Vera Dunham's study of the evidence provided by official Soviet literature suggests that the influence of the mesh-chanye must be taken into consideration. This group, descended from the unprivileged townspeople of Old Russia, had been schooled by generations of servility to accommodate itself to every demand of autocracy. By the late nineteenth century the occupational distinction between such people and the intelligentsia was no longer so clear; the difference between them was one of caste, of culture, not class. The role of women as bearers of this conformist culture cannot be ignored. It is hard to believe that they were not well represented among the typists of the Moscow Commissariats. This would not have mattered had the family lost its importance, but it had not. The re-marriage of Dybenko in 1922 to a young, conformist woman was another sign of the times. It was precisely these women, and the children they would bear, who would have an incentive to perpetuate their status, and hence reproduce a ruling class. Whatever the contributions made by the former social classes to the culture of the Nomenklatura, it is clear that it was a hybrid and not simply the product of any one social class.

In his analysis of the Soviet 'Thermidor', Trotsky made the following comment on the nascent Nomenklatura: 'The question of appointments came to have more and more to do with the question of personal life, living conditions of the [appointee's] family, his career'. Nomenklatura wives have left few published memoirs, though Stalin's daughter has given us a few hints. Another 'Soviet aristocrat' whose foreign nationality enabled her to survive to tell the tale was Aino Kuusinen, first wife of the senior Comintern official and loyal Stalinist, O. W. Kuusinen. When she arrived in Moscow in the early twenties, she moved immediately into the most privileged ranks of the new establishment. Typically, she saw little of her husband, who preferred never to leave his office. How did he compensate her for this unavoidable neglect? For a start, there was a flat on the tenth floor of Government House with new large rooms, two balconies, and lifts that actually worked. For company, she could seek out the wives of Rykov, Bukharin, and Radek who also lived in the block. Everything was free: the apartment, a *dacha*, a new car each year, a chauffeur and a housekeeper (who had worked for wealthy people before the revolution also). At a time when ordinary mortals received only 100 grammes of butter after queueing for hours, the Kuusinen housekeeper would take their three ration books (for dairy, butcher and fishmonger), show them to the alert militiaman who would put her at the front of the queue, and buy as much as she wanted. The Kuusinens did not find it necessary to tell her that while lower-ranking officials also had unlimited rations, at least they paid for theirs. Unfortunately, other women in the queue had the temerity to shout abuse at queue-jumpers of this kind. No doubt it was to eliminate this source of embarrassment (and at a time of growing shortages of consumer goods), that the system of special shops for the privileged was established in 1928. As if these material privileges were not enough, they were matched by an almost feudal sense of power over persons. The Kuusinens got rid of their over-loquacious chauffeur by getting him accepted as a new proletarian playwright. It would perhaps be unfair to make comparisons between the life of women like this and the re-appearance in the streets of Moscow of thousands of prostitutes in the N.E.P. period. Nevertheless, both phenomena demonstrated that the failure to achieve more progress towards sexual equality had corrosive social implications. On the other hand, these rewards were probably necessary if the bureaucrats were to resist corruption by *Nepmen*; they were hardly lavish by comparison with the ostentatious luxury of the tsarist aristocracy.

Between 1921 and 1929 Joseph Stalin became the undisputed 'Boss' of the emerging Nomenklatura and 'Leader' of the Soviet State. What were the formative influences on the man Trotsky described, with only slight exaggeration, as 'neither a thinker, a writer, nor an orator'? Born in 1879 to parents described as Georgian 'peasants', he nursed a lifelong resentment against the noble '-idzes' and '-adzes' who led the Georgians into Menshevism. After an unsuccessful attempt to become an artisan, his father died around 1890, a proletarian and an alcoholic brawler. Stalin's mother was determined that he should succeed and that meant getting an education. The only way a poor Georgian could achieve such an ambition at that time was by entering an Orthodox theological seminary. Some of the hair-splitting, witch-hunting mentality of the Orthodox Church may have rubbed off on Stalin, but on the whole the atmosphere of the seminary repelled him, as it did many of the other students. He quickly gravitated to participation in the revolutionary movement, becoming an enthusiastic Bolshevik. His proletarian background condemned him to 'practical' rather than literary work for the party. This included underground activity supervising the Baku Party press and participating in some of the 'expropriations' of the 1905–6 period. Stalin's first wife, Catherine Svanidze, died in 1910, having born him a son for whom he never had much time. Did he, perhaps, resent the destruction of his personal life, the result of decisions by exiled intellectuals that he should continue his underground work inside Russia while they carried on their polemics in the safety of exile? We have already noted the independence of judgement he displayed over the peasant question. He was initially highly unsympathetic towards Lenin's attack on the dissident Bolsheviks after 1905, but by 1910 he had made it up with Lenin and his reward came in 1912, when he was made a member of the Central Committee of the Bolshevik Party, reconstituted at its Prague Congress. It was at this juncture that Lenin sent Stalin to Vienna for a short period of study so that he could write the party statement on the national question, his admission ticket to the Council of People's Commissars in 1917. This was the Vienna Hitler both admired and loathed; Stalin never recorded his impressions of his sole foray to a Western capital. Lenin wanted a non-Russian to write a document for which he himself provided many of the ideas. In the event, Stalin's own views and experience are clearly visible in *Marxism and the National Question*. Stalin's new prominence guaranteed his arrest by the Okhrana in 1913. The atmosphere of suspicion and betrayal which had surrounded him from the moment he entered the movement had born bitter fruit. He was treated with the utmost severity then available, being deported to the desolate Yenisei-Turukhan region. Many revolutionaries were afflicted by depression in exile, but Stalin's rudeness and egotism ensured his ostracism from the society of local exiles. It was from there that he returned to the February revolution.

By the end of the civil war, Stalin had founded a new family. In 1918, he had married Nadezhda Alliluyeva, a secretary in his Commissariat and a daughter of Old Bolsheviks; in 1920, she bore him a son. By 1922, he was General Secretary of the party's Central Committee, in charge of liaison between the Politburo, of which he was a member, and the Orgburo. He was Commissar of Nationalities and Commissar of the Workers' and Peasants' Inspectorate, the body that was supposed to co-opt teams of rank and file workers and peasants to weed out bureaucratic abuses. He was the obvious candidate of the Politburo to supervise the ailing Lenin, once they resolved to insulate him from politics. The role of 'nanny' to the sick leader inevitably led to conflict between Stalin's and Lenin's female aides and supporters, and this was taken into account by the other oligarchs when they decided to discount the criticisms made of Stalin in Lenin's 'political testament'. After all, none of them escaped criticism either. Thus Zinoviev and Kamenev supported the suppression of the testament, while Trotsky denied publicly that such a document existed.

The struggle for the succession to Lenin had already broken out in 1923, with the first steps towards the reduction of Trotsky's influence. After Lenin's death in 1924, it became much more open. Stalin at first allied himself with Zinoviev and Kamenev in order to complete the destruction of Trotsky. This first phase of the conflict began in 1923 and came to an end in January 1925. Trotsky was then forced to resign his post as Commissar for War and his presidency of the Revolutionary-Military Council. A few months later he was appointed to a post on the Council of National Economy with largely nominal and potentially compromising duties in the field of foreign concessions, electro-technical development, and in an industrial-technical commission.

In the middle of 1925, Stalin moved against Zinoviev and Kamenev; they responded by forming a rather implausible alliance with Trotsky. As a result, all three lost their membership of the Politburo and Zinoviev his seat on the Executive Committee of the Communist International. The climax came in November and December 1927, when the three fallen leaders and seventy-five of their followers were expelled from the party. Early in 1929 Trotsky was sent into exile and later deported from Odessa.

Hardly had this so-called 'left opposition' been dealt with, than Stalin discovered a 'right opposition' in the Politburo, headed by his erstwhile ally, Bukharin, the editor of *Pravda* and secretary of the Comintern, Tomsky, head of the trade unions, and Rykov, chairman of the Council of People's Commissars. By 1930, all three had been removed to lesser posts. Stalin now dominated the Politburo, seconded by Molotov, Voroshilov and Kalinin.

Evidently, Stalin employed the time-honoured methods of 'divide and rule' against his rivals. The question is: why did these methods succeed? After all, his rivals knew the story of Napoleon as well as he did. Again, it is Trotsky who suggests the answer:

'Stalin's first qualification was a contemptuous attitude towards ideas'. The full meaning of this remark can only be understood when rescued from the looking-glass of the prejudices Trotsky shared with the other oligarchs. For a start, they all expected Lenin's successor to be a theoretician – the Revolution demanded it – and in this respect Stalin was clearly not a threat. Their Marxist training misled them into making social relations more transparent, not a recommendation in the eyes of the burgeoning Nomenklatura. The negative side to Marxist thinking is the insistence that since all thought is a manifestation of the class struggle opposing opinions must represent hostile class influences. This completely blinded the oligarchs to the fact that their differences were minimal in comparison with their common interests. Schooled in class theory as they were, it seemed obvious that 'Thermidor' must make its appearance. To the 'right', Trotsky, with his supercilious arrogance and intellectual snobbery, his fondness for bourgeois experts and militarization, his support among the young officer cadets, must represent the reaction of the bourgeois intelligentsia. To the 'left' on the other hand, Bukharin's overtures to the kulaks represented the reaction of the peasant bourgeoisie. It was not, therefore, that Stalin had too little respect for ideas; his opponents just had too much.

Stalin had his own use for ideas – as weapons. He was adept at picking up other people's ideas and using them as labels. Zinoviev also made a fetish of Leninism, but it was Stalin who profited from it; his own differences with Lenin were minor as compared with the fact that Trotsky had not joined the party until 1917, while Zinoviev and Kamenev had denounced the October revolution. His own sole contribution to theory, the idea of 'socialism in one country', was hardly a theory, more a sop to the *amour propre* of the Nomenklatura. After the death of Sverdlov in 1919, Stalin had no rivals as an administrator. On more than one occasion, his opponents suggested diluting his control over the Secretariat, but backed off when he offered to resign. He was a master of flattery and arcane manoeuvre, setting up even trusty supporters such as Molotov to be attacked the more to confuse his opponents. By abusing his authority as *Gensek*, and by sheer force of personality, he early acquired the assistance of the security apparatus. The fear he inspired, but also the open nature of Party politics, are illustrated by the 'medical murder' incident. In May 1926, the writer Pilnyak published a 'story' suggesting that Stalin had medically murdered Defence Minister Frunze so that his henchman, Voroshilov, could take his job; this probably attracted precisely the right mixture of fear and sympathy. It was only in defeat that Stalin's rivals began to understand the significance of 'the personality factor' in Soviet politics. On his defeat in 1928, Bukharin confided to Kamenev his fears about 'this Gengis Khan who is going to kill all of us . . .'

Stalin's victory was Trotsky's defeat. Pursued by diplomatic pressure, and eventually by Stalin's assassins, to Turkey, Norway, and Mexico, Trotsky worked ceaselessly to demonstrate that he had not joined the Mensheviks on the 'garbage heap of history'. He did all he could to keep alive the spirit of critical Marxism, which Stalin's emissaries were everywhere trying to extinguish. The Fourth International he founded has had only limited success (the only avowedly Trotskyist Party to hold office has been in Sri Lanka under conditions Trotsky would probably not have approved), but the parties of this International and refugees from them have forced socialists everywhere to confront Marxist ideas. It was also during these years that Trotsky consolidated his reputation as the great historian of the Russian revolution. As long as men and women are capable of being moved by the grandeur and pathos of the Russian revolution, they will return to Trotsky. He has left one of the most priceless political and literary legacies of Russian culture.

CHAPTER 17

The Second Revolution: 1928–33

One of the casualties of the struggle between the factions was rational economic policy. After 1925 there was increasing agreement that the kulak would have to be taxed more heavily to pay for industrialization. In 1926, the government moved in this direction by cutting procurement prices for agricultural goods. Had they done this across the board, the peasants might have continued to produce at equal or higher levels. In fact, the highest cuts (20–25 per cent) were made in procurement prices for grain, leaving the peasant with barely enough to cover costs of production. Yet this was precisely the crop upon which the government most depended for feeding the soldiers and workers and for exporting to pay for the importation of badly needed machine tools. Predictably, the peasants switched to producing the crops which promised a better return. Meat sales reached new heights but many peasants simply fed their grain to livestock or used it to brew *samogon* (home-made vodka). By January 1928, the State had collected some 300 million poods of grain as compared with 428 million the year before. Some kind of price adjustment seemed imminent. But that same month, Stalin decided on a response of a very different kind. We must remember that Trotsky had just been exiled to Central Asia while the three future leaders of the 'right opposition' were apparently still Stalin's allies. Without any authorization from anyone, Stalin went on a tour of Siberia by train and, in summary language, he lectured officials of party and government on how to get in the missing grain. 'You people are not really concerned to help the country get out of the grain crisis', he told them. The kulaks were hiding 50–60,000 poods of grain each, he told his incredulous listeners. He urged the use of criminal sanctions against speculation and threatened those who would not resort to them. 'We cannot,' he insisted, 'allow our industry to be dependent on the caprice of the kulaks.'

Thus began the upheavals which have been described as a

'second revolution', a 'second civil war' and a 'war against the nation'. Industrialization has always been the work of a minority and peasants have always tended to resist rapid change, but Stalin's 'second revolution' was perhaps the most abrupt and violent transition to industrialization ever experienced anywhere. By the time he brought some order into the proceedings in June 1931, the political economy of the Soviet Union had been profoundly modified. Gone for ever were the substantial private traders and self-employed artisans of the N.E.P. period; gone, too, were the prosperous individual farmers, the khutoryane and otrubniki on whom Stolypin had once based his hopes. The old intelligentsia would be matched by a new 'technical intelligentsia' recruited from the working class. Its cultural elite would be purged by a 'cultural revolution' and allowed to retain its material privileges on condition that it gave up its ideological and institutional autonomy. The industrial workers would gain the right to work; in the short term this meant that both they and their wives would *have* to work out of sheer necessity. Again, in the short term, they would suffer a reduction in living standards only partly offset by greater provision of educational opportunity and health services. After a devastating rearguard action by the peasantry, the regime would be forced to give up its dream of expropriating them totally. Instead, they would be left with tiny plots of land, very small numbers of animals and access to a limited urban market. For all other purposes, they would be dragooned into massive collective farms and subjected to contractual exploitation and political surveillance by the new Machine Tractor Stations. At least three million people would die in these upheavals; the effects on some pastoral peoples like the Kazakhs would be entirely comparable to those of the buffalo hunts upon the Plains Indians. Millions more would be uprooted from their homes to remote settlement or would quietly merge with the burgeoning urban working class. These losses are still remembered with pain in Russia today. Yet Stalin survived with his reputation enhanced and his powers vastly magnified. For his victories were also the victories of those he promoted. In the words of a historian of our time:

... the First Five-Year Plan must be regarded as a period of enormous upward social mobility, as peasants moved into the industrial labour force, unskilled workers became skilled, and skilled workers were promoted into white-collar and managerial positions and higher education.*

Two men promoted in this way were Nikita Khrushchev and Leonid Brezhnev. Several years later they were to benefit from another upheaval. Their 'class' still forms the core of the Soviet ruling group in our own day.

During the 1920s, a famous and intellectually distinguished debate took place in Russia on the 'sources' of the capital required for the coming development of industry. Stalin carefully distanced himself from both extremes of this debate. For him, as for the Soviet Nomenklatura as a whole, economic objectives, however desirable, always took second place to considerations of power. The gamble he took in January 1928 was dictated by the perception he shared with the party that Soviet power was still not secure in Russia, that the October revolution had not yet been won. He understood and shared the sense of shame inspired in party members by the continued existence of superstition, illiteracy, unemployment, and prostitution in year eleven of the revolution. Like them, he alternated between the conviction that the 'contradictions of capitalism' were so fundamental that they could be manipulated at will and the fear that the capitalists would sink their differences for a final assault on the fortress of socialism. He shared their impatience at Bukharin's idea that N.E.P. might last for decades and he understood the nostalgia for war communism that fuelled criticisms of 'bureaucratic degeneration' made by the Young Communist League (Komsomol). He was keenly aware of the conviction of the party that *Nepmen* and kulaks were dangerous rivals for power, bloodsucking vampires that deserved all that was coming to them. He had every reason for confidence that the party would forgive every conceivable deviation from socialist legality in order to uproot these evils. And even though many, even most, of the party were initially horrified by the barbarism of his behaviour, in the end he was proved right.

Stalin's enemies suggest that he exaggerated the dangers of 'capitalist encirclement' in the late twenties to make the opposition of his rivals seem like treason. To some observers, the 1927 war

*Sheila Fitzpatrick, in *Cultural Revolution in Russia* (London, 1978), p. 3.

scare did seem artificial. Those who knew British politics were confident that the British Tories were more interested in blaming the Russians for labour unrest in Britain than in fighting wars against them. It was at this moment, too, that Trotsky made some of his most stupid and tactless criticisms of Stalin when he implied that he (like Clemenceau!) might try to seize power should an enemy arrive at the gates of Moscow. Still, if the scare of 1927 was overdone, in the long term there were solid reasons for concern at Russia's isolation. In 1926, the ex-socialist Pilsudski had taken power in Poland and allied himself with reactionaries dreaming of ancestral estates to the east. A conflict with Poland, or with Finland, Romania, or Iran, all with violently anti-Communist governments, could not be ruled out indefinitely. The massacre of the Chinese Communists in 1927 was all the more worrying in that the new Chinese dictator, Chiang Kai-shek, looked likely to unite the whole of China. Meanwhile, his Japanese friends were tightening their grip on Manchuria; in 1928 they assassinated the local war lord Chang Tso-lin. The British decision to break off diplomatic relations with the Soviet Union in 1927, and simultaneous complications with France, suggested that the time was not far off when Soviet Russia might have to fight for her life once more.

In 1927, party leaders in Soviet Central Asia embarked on an experiment that illustrated the frustrations of the militants, the limits to Soviet power and the dangers of external intervention in the most lurid light. From the beginning of the Soviet regime, the activists of the Women's Departments had known that their greatest challenge would lie in the east, especially in Uzbekistan, where women's inferior status was visibly expressed in the *parandja*, the shapeless robe that concealed them from the eyes of any man bar their husbands. They had been able to persuade a minority of Uzbek women to give up the parandja but they had always been rewarded with divorce and loss of their children, sometimes with physical violence, rape, or murder. To the alarm of party activists, news began to arrive of moves to regulate the *kalym*, or bride price, in Afghanistan and to outlaw the veil itself in Turkey. As it turned out, Kemal Atatürk did not propose to outlaw the veil. Still, the idea that feudal or bourgeois Islamic regimes might outdo the Soviet regime was distinctly discomforting. There was also the hope that if women rallied to the Soviet regime its basis of support in Central Asia might be broadened. After preliminary meetings of militants and the widespread showing of the propaganda film 'The Moslem Woman', ceremonies were held on Women's Day, the tenth anniversary of the February Revolution, at which some 10,000 Uzbek women tore off their veils. By April, the number had risen to 70,000. The operation was given the title *khüjüm*, or assault, and that is how most local males perceived it. The mullahs warned of the horrors to come, including the ritual deflowering of the emancipated women by the Communists, an invasion by England, and even the End of the World. Unspeakable reprisals followed; public humiliation of unveiled women, mass rapes involving even local Communists, bizarre murders, often by relatives of the women concerned. The net effect was to drive even poor Moslem men into opposition to the regime; they then quarantined their wives and children from Soviet influence. In 1929, the policy was abandoned.

The situation in the Russian countryside was nowhere near so difficult for the party, and yet Sir John Maynard recorded that children in rural Russia, when asked during the N.E.P. period if they were for the Soviets, replied: 'We are not Soviet people. We are peasants.' This attitude was deep-seated. It expressed an important social reality. Of Russia's 100 million peasants, only 123,000 were Communists by 1929. Inevitably, they became richer themselves and joined the ranks of the kulaks. Such was the indifference to Soviet institutions that less than half the peasants voted in the village Soviet elections in 1925–6. Only 10 per cent of village Soviet chairmen were Communists. Only one-third of the peasantry were involved in the co-operatives, supposedly the starting point for socialist development. Again, these were usually the wealthier peasants. The party itself showed virtually no interest in the pitiful number of Soviet and collective farms that survived from the war communism period. The mutual indifference of the central party authorities and the peasantry did not always assume such innocuous forms. The only Soviet archive to have fallen into Western hands reveals far more serious signs of friction. In the spring of 1926, the town of Bely, Smolensk province, witnessed some stirring events. When the local party leadership tried to gain control of the Credit Union, it was rebuffed by the better-off peasants who controlled it. Even more alarming, on 3 April some fifty posters appeared on the walls of the town on market day carrying slogans such as 'Leninism leads to poverty'.

As the people of Poland have proved, there are other ways of showing opposition to a ruling Communist Party than committing illegal political acts. In the Russia of the 1920s, it was quite clear that no one could be both Christian and Communist; though this did not prevent religious-minded peasants serving in the Red Army. Of course, not all peasants were religious. Gorky commented on the crude materialism of many of those he met and on their lack of surprise when relics were shown to be faked. Still, in a country with millions of grieving women a religion of consolation is bound to find some support. Fortunately for the regime, Russia's religious communities were sharply divided. For the former established Orthodox Church, the October revolution had been followed by expropriation and vigorous persecution, since the hierarchy had mostly backed the Whites. Lenin had humiliated the Patriarch Tikhon in 1922 when he refused to hand over sacred vessels to pay for famine relief. The party had fostered the growth of a dissenting 'living Church' of young, socialist priests with only limited success. The peasantry had reacted to all these developments with some detachment, but they took exception to the arrival, after the mid twenties, of members of the League of Militant Atheists in their villages when they took to desecrating 'their' church. The government had to intervene to damp down the ardour of the atheists. Catholics and Jews were also lost after the revolution. The secession of the Poles and the Lithuanians explained Soviet hostility towards the Catholic hierarchy; French involvement in an attempt to revive a hierarchy for Russia was one element in the cooling of relations with France in the mid twenties. Jewish religious and cultural activity associated with the synagogues was subjected to intense persecution; a thousand Jewish schools were closed in 1922–3. This was mostly the work of enthusiastic Jewish Communists who were anxious to demonstrate that their loyalties were with the revolution.

This was not the whole story, of course. For the revolutions brought an unprecedented period of growth and prosperity to the dissenters. Relieved of the persecution they had suffered under tsarism, they grew by leaps and bounds after 1921, so that by the late 1920s, it was said jokingly, there were more members in the Bapsomol than in the Komsomol. During this time the Old Believers built up a hierarchy of twenty-one bishops, the Molokans formed a Union, the Seventh Day Adventists doubled their numbers, while the Baptists were able to found theological schools in Leningrad and Moscow. In 1928, Nikolai Odintsov was able to represent them at the World Baptist Congress in Toronto. So far from giving up 'superstition', the Soviet peasants were turning to religion in unprecedented numbers in the 1920s. Furthermore, these new forms of religion implied a much higher degree of personal commitment than Orthodoxy had ever done.

As if all this was not enough for the party, at the beginning of 1927 S. F. Oldenburg, the ex-Kadet Education Minister of the provisional government and academician, attacked Lunacharsky for not increasing the educational budget and professorial salaries. By current Soviet standards, professors had high salaries, good housing, and privileged access to higher education for their children. Sympathetic though he was, Lunacharsky had to warn Oldenburg and others not to fall into the danger of preaching a 'Populist *Intelligentokratia*'.

THE CULTURAL REVOLUTION

In 1927, thousands of Young Communists began to stage what they called 'light cavalry raids' on the bureaucracy. Large groups of them would march into government offices and denounce red tape, incompetence, and corrupt officials, particularly those who had served under the tsarist regime. Undisciplined activity was not unknown in the Young Communist League, yet this time the party leadership looked on with benevolence. The 'cultural revolution' had begun. In view of the date at which it started and the influence of the 'left opposition' within the Komsomol, it is tempting to believe that the movement was started by circles sympathetic to Trotsky. If so, they miscalculated. As Stalin began to move in an increasingly radical direction, he saw the advantages of a movement that promised to isolate and intimidate established experts and institutions. As he told the Komsomol Congress in May 1928, the immediate task of the party was 'to wage a ruthless struggle against bureaucracy, to organize mass criticism from below, and to take this criticism into account when adopting practical decisions for eliminating our shortcomings'. Stalin personally made a number of contributions to the cultural revolution. The show trials on spurious charges of the Donbas Mining engineers in 1928, the 'Industrial Party' in 1930 and the surviving Mensheviks in 1931 were mainly intended to provide scapegoats for industrial difficulties, but they also alerted all Communists to the need to sniff out enemies of the revolution. Young Communists who had missed out on class struggle were now able to participate in the 'storming of fortresses' like the Bolshoi Theatre and the Academy of Sciences. They set out on 'Cultcampaigns' in the country to spread literacy; their local 'Cultstaffs' touted for funds among the population, trade unions, and local enterprises. Between 1929 and 1930, the Workers' and Peasants' Inspectorate and *ad hoc* groups of Moscow workers purged the central governmental institutions of 164,000 workers (out of more than a million and a half). Between 1929 and 1930 over a hundred workers in the Academy of Sciences were arrested while 17 per cent of the engineers were purged in 1929. Leopold Averbakh and the other members of the Russian Association of Proletarian Writers (R.A.P.P.) were delighted at this opportunity to overthrow the influence of Bukharin, who had blocked their demand for a 'proletarian hegemony' over literature in 1925. No one wanted to be left out. A group of painters informed Voroshilov:

We artists with our works want to shoot at our class enemies as Red Army soldiers have shot and will shoot. You have taught us fighting art, class art.

The cultural revolution fostered plenty of 'hare-brained' scheming as cranks of all kinds saw a chance to gain official backing for their ideas. It saw would-be dictators of various areas of national culture seek to establish control over their intellectual superiors. It saw foolish attempts to define proletarian mathematics and surgery. On the other hand, the debates on Russian history that so nearly cost M. N. Pokrovsky his leading place in the academic establishment were genuinely interesting. Under the impact of the new ideas, Soviet historians began to look at ancient and Oriental societies and emerge with new critical tools to supplement those provided by the Marxist classics. By 1931, Stalin had had enough while the cultural elite were only too glad to have the State rescue them from their tormentors. The result of class struggle in culture was State control. In June 1931, as he was announcing his 'Great Retreat' in industry, including the abolition of the equal wage movement, a new organization was set up to subject all publication to rigorous preliminary censorship. The formation of *Glavlit* was followed in 1932 by the dissolution of the R.A.P.P. Finally, in 1934, a single Union of Soviet Writers was set up with the task of licensing *all* writers and preventing the emergence of faction fights in future.

Conflicts with the peasantry soon created conflicts between the regime and all those alternative forms of leadership available to the peasants. The situation was particularly acute in the Ukraine where the campaign against the kulaks was being waged largely by Russian workers (both Khrushchev and Brezhnev were Russian workers from the Ukraine). For Stalin it was obvious that 'the deviation towards local nationalism reflects the dissatisfaction of the moribund classes of the formerly oppressed nations with the regime of the proletarian dictatorship'. In 1929 the Ukrainian universities were closed and in 1930 Hrushevsky was deported to Kislovodsk in the Caucasus. The policy of 'Ukrainization' came to a halt. Soon it would be replaced by one of cautious Russification. The suicide of Mykhaylo Skrypnyk, the Ukrainian Minister of Education, in 1933 marked the end of Lenin's policy of opposing 'Great Russian chauvinism'.

The other alternative sources of leadership were mainly religious. In 1929, a new Law on Religious Associations came into operation, which confined the Churches to the performance of services. They saw their publications closed down, their buildings confiscated, and their leaders exiled and imprisoned. The League of Militant Atheists, now swollen to some three million volunteers, went around the countryside showing films in which nuns cohabited with kulaks, insulting clergy and desecrating former churches. The Moscow Cathedral of the Redeemer was dynamited to make room for a gigantic Palace of Soviets. Of the 54,000 Orthodox churches open in 1914, only a few hundred survived until the war. The dissenters were treated no better. The Baptists lost their theological schools and their journal. It was a time of martyrdom for all Russia's Christians and for members of other religions, too. Some years later, a Baptist, Anna Ivanova-Klyshnikova, wrote to her husband, already five years dead: 'You left me young, in the flower of youth and strength, and now I am different . . .' Such introspection was unusual, however. A large number of the banished clergy continued their witness as alms-seeking, wandering priests in true Apostolic tradition.

To solve Russia's economic and cultural backwardness, as well as to capture the allegiance of Russian youth, Stalin knew they must create 'a new technical intelligentsia capable of satisfying the needs of our industries'. For some time now, there had been concern in the party about the formation of the future leadership of the party and State. During the 1920s, this task had been entrusted to the Sverdlov and Zinoviev Communist Universities, the Plekhanov Economics Institute and the social science faculties of the universities in the capitals. They did indeed produce many of the radicals of the cultural revolution but while they might be capable of journalism and polemic – Mikhail Suslov was the last prominent member of this group – they did not seem to have the right qualities to build Russian industry. In the spring of 1928, Stalin and Molotov moved towards the idea of mobilizing 'thousands' of working-class members of the party for short engineering courses at the re-constituted Technical Universities. They became known as the *vydvizhentsy* ('promoted ones'). By these means, further education was opened up to the working classes on a scale that dwarfed all previous efforts. In 1928, there were 40,000 students of working-class origin (a quarter of the total); by the end of 1932, there were 290,000 (over half the total). At a conversation witnessed by the American writer W. H. Chamberlin, an older member of the intelligentsia taxed the younger generation with being 'dry, crude rationalists'. A young woman answered him indignantly:

Here is Pavel Ivanov, who is absorbed in organic chemistry and can quote fifty complicated formulas from memory. He pronounces them with the inspiration of a great poet. He dreams of making artificial proteins.

Another of our students wants to be a city planner and to lay out the socialist cities of our future. And one of our hydrotechnicians has thought of a scheme by which he will steal all the warm currents from the capitalist countries and envelop Siberia with them. Our epoch is so full and varied; there is so much to dream about.

THE LIQUIDATION OF THE KULAKS AS A CLASS

In his reminiscences, Leonid Brezhnev writes:

> Together with other Y.C.L.ers I clashed with kulaks in the fields and argued with them at village meetings. We were threatened with cudgels, pitchforks, and vicious letters, and stones were thrown through our windows.

For Brezhnev, as for all Young Communists of his generation, hostile peasants were obviously kulaks. 'Squeezing the kulak' was both an ethical and an economic imperative for them. Still, we are entitled to ask: who were these kulaks and what contribution did their expropriation make to the industrialization of Russia?

During the 'Great Debate' of the N.E.P. period, the Communist economist Preobrazhensky had described N.E.P. itself as a period of 'primitive socialist accumulation', i.e. a period in which the State should accumulate capital for the industrialization of the country. In the absence of foreign investment or colonies, such accumulation could only arise from the interception of surplus value produced by the peasants and from voluntary 'self-exploitation' by the ruling class, the workers. With the abolition of land rent and the reduction of the tax burden, the only way to intercept peasant surplus value lay through the manipulation of prices so that the peasant sold cheap and bought dear. As we have seen, incompetent pricing policies caused the failure of this policy, for – despite the disclaimers of Stalin and Bukharin – this was the policy in operation after 1926. It is important to remember that, for Marxists, 'exploitation' is not a description of misery but a technical term. Thus, a medieval serf may be oppressed, but for a Marxist, he is less 'exploited' than a modern industrial worker, since the latter produces incomparably more surplus product for the benefit of his employer. It follows that any private individual who employs another is, in Marxist terms, an 'exploiter' no matter how favourable the conditions of his workers. Equally, it is open to the socialist State to expropriate surplus value from peasants without implying their impoverishment. Thus, the arguments of the civilized Marxists of the twenties about the 'sources' of Soviet industrialization are largely irrelevant to collectivization. They did, however, help to create an atmosphere in which ill-trained 'Marxist' workers could acquiesce in Stalin's policies.

Recent Soviet studies suggest that Soviet agriculture made a *negative* contribution to Soviet industrialization during the period of the First Five-Year Plan (1928–32). At a time when foreign exchange was desperately needed for the importation of industrial equipment, the regime was briefly forced to *import* grain. The only claimed success of collectivization, the eventual increase in deliveries of grain to the State, owed more to the slaughter of livestock than to anything positive done by the State. This same slaughter drastically reduced the number of draught animals in the countryside and forced the State to spend enormous extra sums on agricultural machinery. The reluctant decision to permit the peasants to market the produce of their private plots permitted them to regain much of what they had lost economically by charging very high prices to urban consumers. Of course, collectivization might have produced much better initial results, including more capital for industry, had the wealthier peasants, the kulaks, co-operated with the process rather than sabotaging it by slaughtering their animals. But what reason was there to expect that the kulaks would co-operate loyally with a process that had begun with threats, the liberal use of prosecutions for 'speculation', forced loans, and extra personal taxes, and had ended with the promise to liquidate the kulaks as a class? Can there be any economic rationality in a policy that ignores the motivation of those who must work with it if it is to succeed?

Who were these kulaks anyway? The old money-lending *miroyedy* (village eaters) had been eliminated during the agrarian revolution of 1917. No doubt time and the operations of the market would once more create a rural capitalist class. In 1928, most agrarian experts and many leading Communists doubted whether that had yet happened. Indeed, 'blindness' towards the class struggle in the villages was one of Stalin's most serious accusations against the 'right opposition'. Yet no one seemed to have a clear idea as to the real identity of the kulak. The official definitions lacked 'class content'. In other words, the relationship of the kulak to the means of production was no different from that of any other peasant. He was just better off, as the party had encouraged him to be since 1921. Stalin insisted that 5 per cent of the peasants were kulaks yet the R.S.F.S.R. Minister of Agriculture could find only 2·1 per cent of peasant farms employing anyone outside the family for more than fifty days a year. Only 0·8 per cent of peasant farms had mills or powered churns; these were obviously kulaks. Almost half the kulaks hired out machines or rented additional land from poor peasants. Already, we can see just why the poor peasants might resent richer peasants, but also why they might respect them and feel obliged to turn to them for economic, and sometimes even political, leadership. In 1928, a typical kulak was the proud owner of 3–4 cows and 2–3 horses. He was an 'exploiter' by virtue of the fact that he hired a *single* agricultural labourer for fifty days a year at a time of widespread unemployment.

The first moves towards collectivization were comparatively mild and fully within the limits established as prudent by Lenin in his last years of activity. At the end of 1927 the party congress proclaimed collectivization by example, and also imposed limits on the leasing of land by 'kulaks' and their hiring of labour. Everything suggested that Stalin was approaching the peasant question very gingerly.

The first clashes came at the beginning of 1928 when Stalin decided to break peasant resistance rather than alter the price structure. In the short term the 'Urals–Siberia' method seemed to do the trick. Stalin got in the grain. By a combination of prosecutions, searches, fiscal impositions and denunciations by hastily convened Committees of Poor Peasants, the grain was secured. However, the introduction of 'class war' in the villages was powerless to avert a further reduction of the sown areas.

Even so, at the end of 1928, the first Five-Year Plan did not propose any radical change. In fact, its original version spoke, with disarming frankness, of 'the unusual difficulties [that] are involved in the problem of reorganizing farming on a collective basis . . . The fact must be frankly faced that in this field we are still feeling our way . . .' The object was to encourage the poorer peasants to enter collective farms, which would be favoured with financial and technical aid in the form of tractors and modern agricultural machinery; similarly, the middle peasant would be encouraged to improve his agriculture; and the kulaks would be crushed by additional taxes and other measures of financial discrimination. But was this consistent with the objective of financing industry from the profits of agriculture?

At first the policy had some success. The number of collective farms rose from 33,000 to 57,000 between 1 June 1928 and 1 June 1929, embracing respectively 417,000 and more than a million peasant households. But this success applied overwhelmingly to the poor peasants, those without land, horse, or cow. Those peasants who had something to lose, the kulaks and the so-called 'middle peasants', were unresponsive or hostile to the government's plans; war communism had not been forgotten in the countryside. The autumn sowing of 1928 and the spring sowing of 1929 gave further evidence that the peasants had lost interest in maximizing their incomes, given the intention of the State to expropriate them at will or to persecute them should they be too successful. This development was all the more unwelcome to a government which had set its heart on raising the pace of industrialization and absorbing a vastly greater labour force into non-agrarian occupations.

Would industrialization be held up by an unregenerate, hostile peasantry? This was the prospect that opened up before Stalin. His answer came in the winter of 1929:

. . . We must break down the resistance of this class [the kulaks] in open battle and deprive it of the productive sources of its existence . . . This is the turn towards the policy of eliminating the kulaks as a class . . . the present policy of our party in the rural districts is not a continuation of the old policy, but a turn . . . to the new policy of eliminating the kulaks as a class.

And since Stalin simultaneously declared that they could not be allowed to join the new collective farms, the implication was that the kulaks would have to be removed from their homes, too. It was but a short step from the elimination of a class to the elimination of three million individuals. Spurred on by Stalin, terror and repression came to the countryside. It was indeed, 'open battle', akin to civil war. On the one side stood the power of the State, embodied in the dispatch of picked party 'members to the countryside, and with the occasional use of Red Army and G.P.U. units and police detachments. Also, the government encouraged poor peasants and village Soviets to seize from the kulaks machinery, cattle, and farm appliances for the benefit of the new collective farms. The kulaks retaliated by killing their cattle, burning their crops, and destroying their homesteads; they had a last good meal before they went into slavery. The frantic pace, but not the human tragedy, can be seen in the triumphant statistics of the change; between 20 January and 1 March 1930, the number of collective farms almost doubled and the percentage of collectivized peasant households rose from 21·6 per cent to 55 per cent. This went far beyond the modest totals envisaged in the Plan.

Then, in one of those *ex cathedra* pronouncements, in which Stalin implied that any excesses committed had been the fault of unregenerate 'Leftists', Stalin called a temporary halt. His article *Dizzy with Success*, published in March 1930, greeted the tremendous increase in the number of collective farms and their successes in storing seed as an enormous achievement. 'They inspire our party with a spirit of confidence and faith in its own power.' But he warned against the use of compulsion: 'Who benefits by these distortions, this bureaucratic decreeing of the collective farm movement, this wretched threatening of the peasants? Nobody but our enemies!'

Living premises, small livestock, and poultry were to be left alone. The next few years did in fact see significant relaxations. When the collective farms had delivered their fixed quotas, they were allowed to sell surplus wheat, meat, vegetables, and fruit on the open market, and those peasants who so desired were allowed to withdraw from the collectives with their land stock. In two months, March and April 1930, about nine million households took advantage of this freedom. This was not what Stalin had intended. A combination of renewed coercion and concessions was launched and, by the end of 1932, there were again some fourteen million collectivized peasant households, more than half the total number.

Hand in hand with the collectivization of agriculture went the establishment of Machine-Tractor Stations. These had more or less a monopoly of heavy agricultural machinery, with which they ploughed the collective's land and harvested its grain in return for an exorbitant share of the crop. They also sheltered Political Departments, the eyes and ears of the G.P.U. and the Party in the countryside.

It was many years before Russian agriculture made a recovery from the turmoil and destruction of 1929–32; the cost is still being paid to this day. Not until 1934 could Stalin bring himself to reveal something of the cost of the 'advance' to large-scale farming. There were thirty-three million horses in 1928 – and fifteen million in 1933. The respective figures for horned cattle were seventy million and thirty-four million; for pigs, twenty-six million and nine million; for sheep and goats, 146 million and forty-two million. This is to say nothing of the millions of kulaks and their families deported to forced-labour settlements in the Arctic and the new industrial areas beyond the Urals. In some areas the actual loss of life reached unimaginable proportions. This applied to the Ukraine, for example, where famine conditions prevailed in 1932 as a direct result of the disorganization of peasant agriculture. In Kazakhstan, where the depletion of livestock was probably greater than anywhere else (seventy-three per cent of the cattle, eighty-seven per cent of the sheep and goats, eighty-eight per cent of the horses) 'the number of Kazakhs ... was less by one million or more than the number that would normally have been expected in 1939'. In 1937, a census was conducted; the results were so shattering that they were suppressed. The kulaks were joined by 'wrecking' statisticians.

THE BATTLE FOR INDUSTRY

The idea of a rationally planned economy is central to any notion of a perfect society. For Marxists, the common ownership of the means of production provided society with the opportunity to make conscious decisions about economic development where previous forms of society had been obliged to respond blindly to market forces. The first intimation of comprehensive socialist planning in Russia goes back to 1920, when the State Commission for Electrification was established in order to draft a programme for the electrification of the Russian Soviet Federated Socialist Republic. It was then that Lenin coined his famous aphorism: 'Communism is Soviet power, plus electrification of the whole country'. Then, in 1921, the State Planning Commission – Gosplan for short – was set up to draft a unified economic plan for the whole country. It started with a staff of forty economists and certain technical personnel. Their number increased rapidly and so did the scope of the work, with the establishment of many regional planning offices throughout the Union. But this was far from constituting a plan in the modern sense. Gosplan conceived its task somewhat on the model of capitalist economic planning and limited itself in the main to the forecasting of trends and the analysis of the socialist trade cycle. Also, of course, Gosplan could not but point to the inherent contradiction of attempting to plan an economy in which the agricultural sector was totally unamenable to planning. All the same, the control figures that Gosplan produced from 1925 onwards as an extrapolation of current trends did in fact serve as a preparation for planning. By 1927–8 they already filled a thick volume of 500 pages. The leitmotif of Gosplan thinking was that once the pre-war rate of production had been achieved, only limited progress could be expected thereafter.

But in December 1927 the whole leisurely tenor of Gosplan's activity was revolutionized. It was instructed by the Fifteenth Party Congress to produce a Five-Year Plan for the overall development of the Soviet economy. This followed the epoch-making decision of the party in December 1926 that demanded 'the transformation of our country from an agrarian into an industrial one, capable by its own means of producing the necessary equipment'.

Still, the decisions of 1926 were a long way from the ambitious targets finally ratified in 1929. Within Gosplan, the Bolshevik Strumilin fought the ex-Menshevik Groman. Kuibyshev, the head of the Council for the National Economy, was an enthusiastic industrializer but the Commissariats of Finance and Agriculture did their best to hold back the pace of industrial investment to levels that the peasants could stand and to levels that did not involve unacceptable rates of inflation. Once Stalin had dealt with the 'left opposition', he unequivocally supported the rapid indus- trializers. At the same time, he provided himself and the Russian people with a scapegoat for the inevitable difficulties ahead. In the spring of 1928, he announced the discovery of a 'major wrecking organization' involving engineers in the coal-mines of the Donetsk basin, and paid by 'former owners, currently abroad, and counter- revolutionary capitalists in the West'. They were even violating the labour laws and safety regulations. Later in 1928, he explained the need for a plan which would put the 'production of the means of production' above all else. 'The independence of our country cannot be upheld unless we have an adequate industrial basis for defence.'

After two years haggling, purging, and study, the plan went into operation on 1 October 1928. The whole of Russia was hurled into a gigantic struggle to build socialism, to transform Russia from a backward agricultural into an advanced socialist country. Class A industries – coal, iron, steel, oil, and machine-building – were scheduled to triple their output; Class B industries, producing consumer goods, were to double their output. Overall, the gross output in 1932–3 was scheduled to rise to 236 per cent of the output of 1927–8. To support this effort, the production of elec- trical power was to rise by 600 per cent. Much of this was to come from the Dnieper Dam, already under construction since 1927 and destined to be the largest power plant in the world. It would provide power for the exploitation of the Krivoi Rog iron-mines, the steel plants of the new towns of Zaporozhie and Dneprope- trovsk and the coal mines of the Donetsk Basin. Massive motor and tractor works would be built at Gorky (formerly Nizhny Novgorod), Kharkov, and Stalingrad. An entirely new industrial complex would be created beyond the Urals, virtually invulnerable to attack from the West or Japan, centred on the mountain of pure iron at Magnitogorsk. There, the second largest steel works in the world would arise; its coal would have to come 1,500 miles by rail from the Kuznetsk Basin further east. There would be a massive new asbestos mine, a massive expansion in Georgian manganese production and oil production in the Baku oilfield.

Rostov would receive a massive new factory for agricultural machinery; machinery works would appear in Smolensk and the central Moscow industrial region. The Chelyabinsk tractor plant alone would cover an area larger than all the old city of Chelyabinsk. Side by side with all this development would go the vast enlargement of towns, not only of such old-established urban centres as Moscow, Leningrad, and Kharkov, but also of lesser centres such as Tashkent, Minsk, Vladivostok, Voronezh, Sverdlovsk, Novosibirsk.

It is well known that the contrast between the Soviet plan and the 'Great Crash' in the capitalist world created a wave of enthusiasm for Russia among Western radical intellectuals. It is less well known that the Soviet drive for industry created enormous opportunities for Western capitalists. While they might have scruples about investing their own money in a country that defaulted on its debts, they willingly sold their technology for good Soviet gold, especially when demand for their products was depressed in the capitalist world. No single pattern was followed, though Stalin showed a distinct preference for American engineers and firms over European ones. The most famous American in Russia was Colonel Hugh L. Cooper, builder of the largest dam in the Tennessee Valley, who insisted on a contract guaranteeing himself and his team every amenity of American upper-class comfort in the starving Ukraine. He was one of the few foreigners who could gain access to Stalin. The turbines of the dam were imported from America but the construction, at rates never before achieved anywhere, was by Soviet workers. The Magnitogorsk plant was constructed by a team headed by Max MacMurray of the Arthur C. McKee Co. of Cleveland, and then handed over to the Soviet engineers for production. H. F. Mitre headed the construction team for the Gorky Works, built by the Austin Co. under licence from Henry Ford. John K. Calder headed the construction team for the Stalingrad Tractor Plant, which acknowledged the patent of International Harvester Co. and for the Chelyabinsk Tractor Plant, which pirated the designs of the Caterpillar Co.

The purpose of all this investment in American technology was to enable Russia to overcome her technological backwardness in one great leap forward. Here is how H. R. Knickerbocker described the Stalingrad Tractor Plant:

> The assembly building, bristling with an endless forest of lathes, drills, gear-cutters, and a hundred machines that only a specialist could name, all of them bearing American trade-marks, stretched 446 yards long and 105 wide, enclosed by glass walls that let in light like a studio ... The motor conveyor, with a normal speed of two feet per minute, was working at six inches a minute, and at that frequently had to stop ...

This was, of course, the problem. Importing technology is one thing; using it efficiently is quite another. It depends on the level of technical education of the work force, its organization and motivation.

Some of the sites of the major plants, especially in Siberia, may have been cleared by forced labour. Solzhenitsyn has described the way in which kulaks and other prisoners were made to work with the most primitive technology in the construction of the White Sea Canal. Such labour could not be relied on for anything but removing the primeval forest. It was the opposite extreme of the labour force, the highly motivated Communist workers, especially the younger ones, who formed the core of the force which actually built and worked the new plants. John Scott, an American engineer who worked for five years at Magnitogorsk in the thirties, writes:

> I was going to be one of the many who cared not to own a second pair of shoes, but who built the blast furnaces which were their aim. I would wager that Russia's battle of ferrous metallurgy alone involved more casualties than the battle of the Marne. All during the thirties the Russian people were at war ... In Magnitogorsk I was precipitated into a battle. I was deployed on the iron and steel front. Tens of thousands of people were enduring the most intense hardships in order to build blast furnaces, and many of them did it willingly, with boundless enthusiasm, which infected me from the day of my arrival.*

The Spanish Communist Lister remembers similar scenes in the Moscow Metro. Even in these prestige projects, idealism alone was not enough. Many of the young engineers working in Kuznetsk or Magnitogorsk were sent there by the organizations which

---

*John Scott, *Beyond the Urals* (London, 1943), p. 9.

had sponsored their training. Additional workers had to be hired from collective farms by recruiting agents sent out from the factories. Furthermore, while the construction of housing was often well behind the construction of the factories, the workers in the prestige projects benefited from better diets and more of the meagre supply of the scarce consumer goods than those workers who remained in the traditional industrial centres. Many of them padded about in slippers during these years.

The abolition of industrial unemployment posed Soviet managers with acute problems of labour discipline. How could the new industrial workers, used as they were to the natural rhythms of rural life, be turned into a reliable and efficient modern labour force? In view of the impossibility of achieving the improved levels of consumption indicated by the plan simultaneously with the high rates of investment foreseen by it, what incentive could the workers have to increase productivity? Part of the answer lay in propaganda. Not since the days of the First World War had such attention been paid by government propaganda to the common man and woman in their roles as producers. In any Russian newspaper of the time, it has been said,

The workers speak with their own voices and write with their own pens; on four pages of very poor paper, with very poor print, the vocal soldiers of industry shout themselves hoarse, with boasting, with exhortation, with criticism of failures, with challenges to socialist competition, with offers of 'tow-ropes' to less forward enterprises, with promises, with indignation ... Next we come upon a grave article upon the problems of technical construction in the coal industry ... Our correspondent complains of short production of coal in the Donets Basin, there is absenteeism of labour on a large scale ... The repair of locomotives on the Murmansk line is unsatisfactory ... A locomotive came back from the Vologda repair shop, after overhaul, with seventy defects ... Next we have a page devoted to agriculture, with a great headline across it: 'Quick collection of seeds shows Bolshevik leadership' ...*

And so it went on, in newspapers, books, films and plays – an increasing flow of criticism and exhortation, always and everywhere associating and identifying the worker with the national effort.

*Sir J. Maynard, *The Russian Peasant* (London, 1942), pp. 240–41.

Even before June 1931, when Stalin denounced wage equality as a leftist deviation, sticks and carrots were much in evidence. The very existence of a vastly expanded system of forced labour camps, the *G U L A G Archipelago* as we know it today, acted as a powerful incentive to the workers to avoid obvious breaches of labour discipline. Then there were non-monetary incentives to the shock-workers (*udarniki*), such as opera tickets, holidays in trade-union hostels, and access to the impossibly scarce consumer goods. The period of the First Five-Year Plan saw the paradoxical development whereby the peasant was forced to abandon his traditional autarky and enter commodity production while the suppression of the *Nepmen* and artisans obliged the workers to seek non-monetary compensation for their efforts. Despite all these pressures, Russian workers showed a remarkable instability. During 1929–30, for example, the coalmines of the Don Basin had a turnover of about 150 per cent in the labour force. It was this phenomenon of 'fluidity' in the labour force that led Stalin to reintroduce wide differentials in rewards.

After 1931, there was an increasingly urgent search for sanctions which could enforce labour discipline. It was as though the ex-peasant workers were now to be subjected to the disciplines which Peter the Great and Nicholas I had once imposed on the upper classes.

In the absence of foreign investment, Russia had to finance her own industrialization. In the face of peasant resistance to collectivization, the State was determined to recoup from the peasantry the additional inputs of tractors and equipment required by agriculture. The 'squeezing' of the kulak provided significant capital in 1927–9, though obviously this could not be repeated. Peasants and workers alike were obliged to subscribe to massive industrialization loans. After 1930 a general turnover tax was introduced, especially on goods like vodka. The State bought grain cheap from the peasants and sold it dear to the consumers. Forced to import grain briefly in 1929, the State exported around 5 million tons of grain in 1930 and 1931 and continued to export grain in 1932 and 1933 despite the famine in the latter year. In 1966, a Soviet writer published figures illustrating the effect of these burdens on the diets of urban and rural workers. In 1928, the average urban worker ate 174·4 kg of grain, 87·6 kg of potatoes, 51·7 kg of meat and lard, and 2·97 kg of butter while the rural worker ate 250·4 kg of grain, 141·1 kg of potatoes, 24·8 kg of meat and lard, and 1·55 kg of butter. By 1932, this picture had changed radically. The urban worker was now eating 211·3 kg of grain, 110·0 kg of potatoes, a mere 16·9 kg of meat and lard, and 1·75 kg of butter. The rural worker was now eating less of everything. He ate 214·6 kg of grain, 125 kg of potatoes, 11·2 kg of meat and lard, and 0·7 kg of butter. Evidently, the Russian peasantry made a quite disproportionate contribution to the financing of industrialization. The industrial worker was not exempt from these pressures. The monthly average wage of the Russian worker went up from 75 rubles in 1929 to 125 rubles in 1933 but there was a massive inflation of the currency. There were 1·7 milliard rubles in circulation in 1928 and 5·7 milliard in 1932. Chamberlin reckoned that a chocolate cake which had sold for about 30 kopecks in 1926 sold for 12 rubles by 1933. The trouble was that such luxuries were often not to be had for any amount of money. Furthermore, industrial workers were under the same pressure to subscribe to industrialization loans as everyone else.

Soviet industrialization was not an entirely rational process. Perhaps no rational economist could have insisted on such a massive rate of capital accumulation. The concentration of such a high proportion of it in massive projects such as Magnitogorsk, which were bound to take time to show any real return, may have resulted in a slower rate of industrial development than might have been achieved by more modest but discriminating investment. The ability of the Russian economy to employ the ultra-modern American technology was limited by a variety of factors. In the absence of a labour force trained to a satisfactory minimum standard, continuous-flow production could not be maintained; in 1931 Stalin sanctioned its abandonment in the Stalingrad Tractor Factory. Other problems arose from the large variety of parts Russian factories were forced to make and their tendency to go in for vertical integration, inevitable in a country where there was almost no progress towards the standardization of components. Given the poor quality of production, factories receiving components from elsewhere often had to re-machine them before they could use them. There was little attempt to mechanize such auxiliary processes as loading, one reason for the fact that the plan was vastly over-fulfilled in respect of the expansion of the labour force.

The first Five-Year Plan was not achieved; it never could have been. Despite this, a mighty engineering industry had been created. Russia, the country where two-thirds of all ploughs had been wooden until 1910, now boasted industries producing machine-tools, turbines, tractors, and metallurgical equipment and produced more electricity than it could use. At a time when industrial production in the principal capitalist powers had actually declined below the level of 1913, that of Soviet Russia showed an almost four-fold increase over the level of 1913. It did indeed seem that there were no fortresses that Bolsheviks might not storm.

CHAPTER 18

The Great Retreat and the Great Terror

In 1920 Yevgenii Zamyatin, fascinated by the science fiction of H. G. Wells, wrote the first of the great anti-Utopian novels of the twentieth century. In *We*, the numbered citizens of the future socialist Single State are protected from subversive thoughts by an operation with the sinister title of fantasiectomy. As the cultural revolution gained momentum in 1928, the militants of the R.A.P.P. picked out the publication abroad of *We* as one of the most heinous crimes of the 'bourgeois' writers in Leningrad. Evidently, they found Zamyatin's novel uncomfortably effective as an antidote to their own propaganda. To this day, neither *We*, *Brave New World* nor *1984* has ever been published in the Soviet Union. For Stalin's Russia was about to embark on a course which would culminate in the deification of the Leader and the subjection of everyone else, from the highest Nomenklaturist to the lowliest peasant, to an equality of fear. The militarization of Russian culture, used as a metaphor by the Komsomols of 1928, would become a literal reality so that a child would find it quite normal that his mother would disappear on an 'assignment' without so much as a word of farewell. The more public manifestations of this culture, the massive parades, the constant use of stereotyped clichés, the fostering and channelling of hysteria and hatred, were only the most visible signs of much deeper processes. Everywhere, allegiances to caste, locality or nationality were destroyed. While allegiance to the family came to depend on its political loyalty, the primary reproductive and child-rearing functions of women were stressed once more. Recent social historians have noted the contradiction of despotic politics and massive social mobility. Historians can still not be sure whether the revival of a political culture reminiscent of sixteenth-century Russia was the product of the mental disturbance of the despot or the rise of a ruling group drawn from sections of the population that had never emerged from patriarchal xenophobia.

An understanding of Stalinism was made even more difficult by the fact that most of these same processes occurred simultaneously in Germany, a society with a radically different culture, economic system, and ideology. Despite their differences, Soviet Russia and Nazi Germany seemed to go far beyond previous authoritarian regimes in the demands they made on their subjects. With some exaggeration, these demands were described as 'total'. To some it seemed that labels like 'left' and 'right' had been superseded by the emergence of the totalitarian State. This idea now seems exaggerated. The police terror that afflicted Berlin, Tokyo, and Moscow in the late thirties was a feature of societies undergoing rapid modernization from above at a time of real international insecurity. Similarities of style seem to derive from such factors as the rapid assimilation of semi-literate peasants into urban life and the rise to power of a generation brutalized by war.

Yet the Great Terror, which has justifiably attracted so much attention, was preceded by a 'Great Retreat', a period of several years in which the Soviet regime abandoned some of its more Utopian objectives in favour of the more mundane but realizable aims of industrial and social modernization. Unlike the 'retreat' of 1921, the 'Great Retreat' involved the conversion of the Soviet ruling group to more modest goals. Stalin's abandonment of 'leftism' in 1931 caused none of the heart-searching associated with the introduction of N.E.P. For a few short years, the strategic interest of the Nomenklatura in maximizing the expropriation of the surplus product gave way to a tactical interest in securing their own physical survival against the risks that threatened from the Scylla of popular wrath and the Charybdis of Stalin's paranoia. The abandonment of 'leftism' in 1931 was followed by the reduction of those norms of industrial construction that Stalin had said could not be reduced. The famine of 1933 brought a mood of greater realism into the second Five-Year Plan, introduced in that year. In 1932 a second-rank Communist called Ryutin had suggested removing Stalin as *Gensek*. The Politburo would not even have him shot. This was a time when the head of the Lenin library still found it possible to refuse Stalin's request to purge the library holdings. Stalin himself seemed to confirm the mood at the

Seventeenth Party Congress in 1934 when he uttered the famous words, 'Life has become better, Comrades. Life has become gayer.' Though there were few lucky enough to benefit from the importation of American Victrola gramophones, life did become somewhat easier with the abolition of food rationing in 1935. The subordination of the G.P.U. to the People's Commissariat of Internal Affairs (N.K.V.D.) seemed at first to promise that the security organs would be brought back under party control once more.

One of the most striking symptoms of this Indian summer of Communist toleration was the re-emergence of Bukharin into public life. After recanting his former 'right deviation', he was permitted to participate in the Seventeenth Party Congress, the 'Congress of Victors', and pay his tribute to Stalin in person. He was rewarded with the editorship of *Izvestiya*, the government newspaper. At the First Congress of the Union of Soviet Writers in August 1934, he spoke for the government in offering an olive branch to the cultural intelligentsia. The 'paraphrasing of newspaper articles' and 'rhymed slogan', he said, 'is, of course, not art at all'. He went so far as to praise the apolitical Pasternak and the majority of his listeners cheered him enthusiastically. In February 1935, a commission was set up under the nominal chairmanship of Stalin to prepare a new Soviet constitution. Bukharin was made a member of the commission and later boasted that he had written the document 'from first word to last'. The constitution was impeccably democratic, restoring equality of suffrage for all free citizens and guaranteeing an impressive list of human rights. Even the exiled Mensheviks and S.R.s were impressed. The public discussions that took place before the promulgation of the 'Stalin Constitution' in December 1936 revealed a widespread desire for a return to civil peace as against the institutionalized civil war of the preceding years.

Temporarily thwarted in his desire to execute disloyal members of the party hierarchy, Stalin turned to a peaceful purge of the party's rank and file. Between 1932 and 1936, there was one long series of expulsions affecting hundreds of thousands of members. *Pravda* published some of the comments for which people were expelled from the party at this time:

We have no meat because we began to liquidate the kulak before we created a base for meat supply.

The material position of the workers is deteriorating.

Our pace of development was excessive and the liquidation of the kulaks was untimely.

You can only talk about the favourable side of things; if you talk about difficulties you become a Right deviationist and are out of harmony with the decisions of the party.

A Leningrad party member called Grushetsky went so far as to say: 'the party invented sabotage and the people who were shot allegedly for creating hunger were innocent victims'. A large number of the party members sent to extract grain from the peasants were so appalled by what they found that they courageously and foolishly asked for procurements to be lowered. Clearly, it would take time to rid the party of such free-thinkers as these.

In the early 1930s, Russians did not yet suffer from 'atomization', that disease of totalitarianism. In the words of Osip Mandelshtam,

> ... whenever there's a snatch of talk,
> it turns to the Kremlin mountaineer.

Mandelshtam was one of many observers who knew where to lay the blame for the country's current difficulties:

> He forges decrees in a line like horseshoes,
> One for the groin, one the forehead, temple, eye.

Nor was such percipience limited to men of brilliance like the poet. In 1933, W. H. Chamberlin collected a series of current jokes which suggest a wide popular understanding of the realities of Stalin's Russia: a worker saw big-wigs passing in a limousine and wryly commented: 'I am the boss. Those people are just my clerks'. The 'voluntary' expropriation of the surplus purchasing power of the working class was mocked in the tale of the man found drowned in the Moscow River 'with no signs of violence, except a few bonds of the five-year plan loan'. The persecution of ordinary peasants as kulaks gave rise to the story of terrified rabbits fleeing to the Polish border because the G.P.U. had ordered the arrest of all the camels in Russia. When the naive Polish frontier guards tell them they have nothing to worry about since they are not camels, they reply: 'Just try to prove that to the G.P.U.' In an ironic comment on the 'guilt' of the purged specialists, a woman told her friend: 'I have three sons. One is an engineer; one is an agronome; the third is also in prison'.

During the early 1930s, the regime fought against the critics and doubters with propaganda, appeals to the competitive spirit, and administrative measures. With the formation of *Glavlit* and the Union of Soviet Writers the period of class struggle in literature was replaced by a period in which 'socialist realism' became the only permissible approach to the arts. Where the tsarist censorship had once hindered the writer by chopping out subversive references without regard to sense, the 'engineers of human souls' of Stalin's time found the servants of *Glavlit* full of helpful suggestions for improvements in their work. This was the period that saw the publication of some of the most characteristic monuments of Soviet literature. Valentin Katayev's *Time, Forward!* provided a breathless account of the construction of Magnitogorsk; Sholokhov's *Virgin Soil Upturned* allowed the regime to convey a franker picture of collectivization than hitherto while continuing to blame the disasters on the malice of kulaks and the idiocy of 'leftists'.

With the growing unreality of official propaganda, literature of the official variety became increasingly important as a medium of communication between the government and its subjects. The pride of Soviet literature at this time was, and is, Nikolai Ostrovsky's *How the Steel was Tempered*. This semi-autobiographical work has now nurtured three generations of Young Communists. It tells the story of a working-class youth who grows up during the revolution and civil war. During and after the war he suffers injuries that ruin his health. Determined not to miss the task of socialist construction, the crippled and blind man turns himself into a writer through sheer hard work. The book contains enough anti-kulak material to justify the author's belief that he had indeed returned to the ranks. However, the direct style and the sincerity of the author raise it far above the level of most official literature. It is the most convincing attempt produced by Russian literature to identify the cause of humanism with that of Bolshevism.

At the opposite end of the spectrum lies the attempt by Gorky and several other socialist humanist writers to justify the growing system of forced convict labour in *The White Sea Canal*. Contemporary socialists can only echo Solzhenitsyn's comments on this shameful work. There is one point that Solzhenitsyn misses, however. The book, published in 1934, identifies nearly all the leading slave-drivers on the White Sea canal project as Jews. Gorky, one of the great campaigners against antisemitism in tsarist Russia, was helping to encourage antisemitism in Stalin's Russia. In Ostrovsky's book, however, there was a strong suggestion that Russians had a duty to protect Jews from pogroms. Despite the increasing tension of the later thirties, it was then that Mikhail Bulgakov wrote *The Master and Margarita*, a great satirical novel which cast ironic sidelong glances at the new Soviet man and raised a vital ethical problem for the new society. Could there be good without evil? The work was not published but nor was Bulgakov purged.

All the arts were expected to pull together at this time. Eisenstein was nudged away from revolutionary agitprop, past an abortive attempt to portray collectivization in the direction of historical epics. It is to this that we owe the knowledge that in the late 1930s Stalin came to identify himself with Ivan the Terrible. For once, Stalin was being unfair to himself; still, it suggests he recognized his own growing paranoia. The Bauhaus style which had held sway in Soviet architecture during the twenties was now replaced by that massive yet fussy brand of neo-classicism, dubbed 'Stalinist wedding cake' by westerners. Fortunately, the Palace of Soviets planned for Moscow was never built. In painting, the competent landscape artist and water-colorist Gerasimov was prevailed upon to portray the Leader and sundry collective farm chairmen in leaden oils. Only the most undisciplined of the arts, music, retained a degree of freedom. Thus it was that Shostakovich's *Lady Macbeth of Mtsensk* was able to convey the dark passions of those who plot for power; there was more social realism in this than in nearly all the official literature.

For the young and vigorous, there were real adventures to lift the imagination and stimulate a desire to achieve great things. This was the period of the competition in airship construction with Germany. It was the period of the *Chelyushkin* rescue, the drama of a Soviet icebreaker caught in the Arctic, whose crew were heroically rescued by a fleet of Soviet airmen. The technique of offering intangible rewards such as publicity and medals to victors in productivity contests was taken to new extremes. In 1935, the miner Alexei Stakhanov supposedly exceeded the norm for coal production in a single day fourteen times over. He quickly became a celebrity and eventually a deputy to the Supreme Soviet. The message was clear: social mobility is open to those who assist in intensifying the exploitation of labour. In case the point should be missed by the overworked and underpaid working class, ample material incentives were also made available to the small minority who took the initiative in raising work norms.

Unfortunately, the mass of the working class, both peasants and workers, showed far too little interest in productivity. As a result, the regime turned increasingly towards administrative methods of controlling the population. In 1932 internal passports were introduced for all Soviet citizens except collective farmers; they now reverted to a civil status reminiscent of their ex-serf forebears, having to beg for special permits to visit large towns. In the same year, employers were given the right to dismiss workers for a single day's absence; the shortage of labour meant that this provision could only be used with discretion. Such were the thefts of socialist property that in 1934 the death penalty was provided for this and other crimes, for twelve-year-olds upwards. The worst case of desertion from the 'labour' front was the refusal of working-class women to endure all the demands made of them. Rapid industrialization and falling living standards had forced them into work and eroded the humane labour legislation of the twenties. The lack of investment in transport and the shortages of foodstuffs condemned them to fight their way on to overcrowded trams and to stand for hours in queues. They responded by refusing the 'double burden'; the number of abortions rose alarmingly, so that in 1936 abortion was made illegal once more.

From 1936 until the outbreak of the Second World War, the personality of Joseph Stalin became the determining factor in Soviet politics.

It was then that he became sole dictator, no longer responsible in any real sense to the Politburo and the Central Committee. Increasingly, he was a person coarsened and corrupted by the civil war he had himself unleashed on the peasantry, his old sense of inadequacy demanding the humiliation and, finally, the physical destruction of his enemies. His wife responded to the deterioration in his personality by committing suicide in 1932. Thereafter he seemed to take particular interest in the destruction of all those who had been personally close to him. His announcement of the Marxist 'law' whereby the class struggle intensified as socialism approached rationalized his own need to engage in unceasing repression to eliminate those who must seek to pay him back for the excesses of collectivization. Such people did exist. When Kirov was shot in December 1934, Young Communists in the Smolensk countryside began to sing:

> When Kirov was killed they allowed free trade in bread;
> when Stalin is killed, all the kolkhozes will be divided up.

The emergence of a real enemy in Hitler seemed to justify Stalin's increasing insistence on vigilance. The rationalism of his critics had to be broken by fear and show trials that would demonstrate that all the mistakes and disasters had been the fault of criminal subordinates. Soviet citizens had to lose confidence in all subordinate leaders so that in desperation they would cling to the illusion that only Stalin could save them in an increasingly dangerous world.

A revolver shot in Leningrad on 1 December 1934 set off the machinery of terror. Nikolayev, a Young Communist, fired the shot; it killed Kirov, the secretary of the Leningrad Party organization. That same evening, Stalin issued the following (illegal) decree:

I. Investigative agencies are directed to speed up the cases of those accused of the preparation or execution of acts of terror;

II. Judicial organs are directed not to hold up the execution of death sentences pertaining to crimes of this category in order to consider the possibility of pardon because the Presidium of the Central Executive Committee of the U.S.S.R. does not consider as possible the reception of petitions of this sort;

III. The organs of the Commissariat of Internal Affairs are directed to execute the death sentences against criminals of the above-mentioned category immediately after the passage of sentences.

This directive 'became the basis for mass acts of abuse against socialist legality', Nikita Khrushchev later declared.

Nikolayev and a number of alleged sympathizers were tried and executed on the spot. No references to Nikolayev's testimony were ever made in the trials that followed. Zhdanov replaced the dead Kirov in Leningrad and went ahead with purging the party organization of supposed supporters of the former Leningrad Party boss, Zinoviev. But so far, Stalin limited himself to deporting the suspects, after a trial in which they admitted their moral complicity in the murder.

Some eighteen months later matters took a sensational turn when no lesser personalities than Zinoviev and Kamenev, together with some others, were charged with collaborating with others to overthrow the Soviet State. They worked, it was alleged, under the leadership of the exiled Trotsky. The accused men, well prepared by endless beatings and all-night interrogations and by threats against their dependants, confessed and were duly executed. On the face of it, this was in response to popular demand expressed in countless resolutions demanding their execution even before the trial. Even former Trotskyites, such as Christian Rakovsky, begged for a chance to execute their former comrades personally. Now the reign of terror began in real earnest, spurred on by Stalin who made it clear that a lack of zeal in this important matter could cost even the members of his Politburo dear. In a telegram to the Politburo Stalin and Zhdanov demanded that Yezhov replace Yagoda as head of the N.K.V.D. 'Yagoda has definitely proved himself incapable of unmasking the Trotskyite–Zinovievite block. The O.G.P.U. is four years behind in this matter. This is noted by all Party members . . .'

The N.K.V.D. accordingly began to catch up on those four lost years. At the beginning of 1937 a further group of Old Bolsheviks trod the same path to death. They also confessed to incredible crimes of treason. Early the next year the purge reached out to the Red Army and swept away Marshal Tukhachevsky, Chief of the Red Army, and Admiral Orlov, Commander-in-Chief of the Red Navy; and in March 1938, a final group of twenty-one of the highest Soviet personalities, including Rykov, Bukharin, and Yagoda, was charged with collaborating with foreign powers to dismember the Soviet Union, overthrow socialism, and restore capitalism. They too were found guilty and executed.

The men in the dock were of course only the most notable victims (and only those among the notables whose spirits could be broken or tamed were brought to trial; others perished secretly). Unnumbered thousands of less prominent people perished or were deported. Among the prominent victims were all the members of Lenin's Politburo (apart from Stalin himself and Trotsky), many ambassadors, most of the surviving Old Bolsheviks, the top leadership of the Red Army, the upper and middle levels of the Communist Party, and many members of the organization of Red partisans. Those deported fell into the hands of a special department of the N.K.V.D. set up in 1934. It bore the title GULAG: 'Chief Administration of Corrective Labour Camps and Labour Settlements'. Throughout the 1930s, the islands of the GULAG archipelago spread from the original outposts in the north of European Russia to every corner of Stalin's realm. Then, quite suddenly, the purges ceased in 1939. A collective amnesia seized the citizens who had quaked for years. 'Only a few weeks after the arrest of Yezhov it was quite exceptional to hear the arrests spoken about at all.' After a brief period of semi-frankness in 1956–64 about the awfulness of those times, the curtain has descended on them once more. All the military leaders were publicly rehabilitated under Khrushchev but not a single political leader has ever been publicly restored to a place of honour in the Soviet pantheon. To this day, the vast majority of Soviet people are 'vigilant' in their dealings with foreigners; the old openness of the 'broad Russian nature' is a thing of the past. Brutally reminded as they were of their own vulnerability, the vydvizhentsy, the formerly working-class engineers recruited in the late twenties, now moved into the command positions in Stalin's militarized society. Their relief at being spared must have been mixed with gratitude to the patron who had given them their chance. They are the Brezhnev–Kosygin generation, the inheritors of Stalinism.

CHAPTER 19

The Revolution and the World

The revolutionary state established by the Bolsheviks inherited many tsarist institutions, but few were more embarrassing than the Ministry of Foreign Affairs, now renamed the People's Commissariat of Foreign Affairs (Narkomindel). Its first Bolshevik incumbent was Trotsky. Apparently, this was Sverdlov's idea: 'Lev Davydovich should be set up against the rest of Europe', he suggested. Trotsky approached his new responsibilities in a spirit of celebrated flippancy. 'I will issue a few revolutionary proclamations to the peoples of the world, and then shut up shop.' He recalls that one of the high points of his work was to authorize a slanging match through the ether between the Bolsheviks' sole radio station at Tsarskoe Selo and the French government station broadcasting from the Eiffel Tower. In the end, he succeeded in getting the French to modify the tone of their propaganda. During his short tenure of the Foreign Commissariat, Trotsky took a number of other actions with far greater immediate importance. He authorized the publication of all the Allied Secret Treaties with the result that President Wilson had to incorporate a demand for open diplomacy in his Fourteen Points, and he authorized the diversion of 2,000,000 rubles for political work abroad.

Trotsky's flippancy did not go very deep. He knew, as did all the Bolsheviks, that they had come to power by claiming that they could bring peace to Russia. If they failed to do so, Soviet power might not last long. He also knew that peace with the Germans was only part of a very complicated equation, since a separate peace would be a breach of the 1914 Treaty of Paris and would bring down the wrath of the Entente. Trotsky employed the classic methods of diplomacy to suggest to the British diplomatic agent Lockhart that the Bolsheviks might continue the war with more Allied assistance, if they could not secure an acceptable peace from the Germans and Austrians. His appeals to the workers of the central powers did not go entirely unanswered. There was a wave of strikes in Austria and Germany. Julius Braunthal, a participant, described them as 'spontaneous movements of the workers, generated by a sudden reduction of the bread rations, and inflamed by the insolent attitude of the German militarists at Brest-Litovsk'. But as Otto Bauer, the Austrian socialist, put it, 'With strikes alone you can't compel an imperialist government to sign revolutionary peace proposals'. This failure cost Trotsky a great deal of the prestige he had won in the party since the summer of 1917.

The Foreign Commissariat, the Red Army, propaganda, all were traditional expressions of state power despite their new clothing. The Russian revolution also contributed something entirely new to statecraft, the Communist International or Comintern. There were some precedents for ideological solidarity across national frontiers in Russian history. Ivan III had used the devotion of the west Russian nobility to Orthodoxy to subvert Novgorod and Lithuania. The Georgians had appealed to Orthodox Russia to deliver them from Islam as early as the reign of Ivan the Terrible. Throughout the eighteenth and nineteenth centuries, the tsarist state had made intermittent use of appeals to Pan-Slav and Pan-Orthodox sentiment in the Balkans. There were also precedents for the Communist International in the first two socialist internationals, the first founded by Marx himself. Since capitalism was an international force, it was clear that only the combined force of the proletariat of all, or most, of the industrialized countries could overthrow it. Ever since the collapse of the Socialist International into competing patriotisms in 1914, Lenin had been thinking of ways of creating new forms of international proletarian solidarity. While he disliked the pacifism of many of the participants in the Zimmerwald and Kienthal conferences during the Great War, he had attended them in the hope of converting European socialism to his own policy of replacing international war by class war. In the 'April Theses', Lenin described the need for a Communist International as 'urgent'. Finally, the Bolsheviks were apprehensive about the possibility that the 'general association of nations' foreseen by Woodrow Wilson in January 1918 would become a 'bankers' international'.

Lenin had justified the timing of the Russian October revolution by referring to the imminence of revolution in Europe. The British shop stewards' movement, the mutinies in the French Army in the spring of 1917, the insurrections in Turin and Barcelona in summer 1917, the gradual re-emergence of an anti-war strike movement in Germany and Austria, all seemed to justify this confidence. Though Lenin had foreseen that socialist revolution might come first to Russia as the weakest link in capitalism, he had not imagined that the Russian revolution might be successful on its own. With the collapse of the central monarchies in November 1918, and the creation of workers' and soldiers' councils throughout Germany, relief seemed imminent. And so, in a sense, it was. No longer could the German Army guarantee the brutal provisions of the Treaty of Brest-Litovsk. Yet the German revolution did not take the course hoped for. At their national congress in December 1918, the German Soviets followed the lead of the nationalist Social Democrats and voted power back to the provisional government of Ebert and Scheidemann pending the convocation of a democratically elected National Assembly. Early in January 1919, left Socialists and Communists took over the printing presses in Berlin. It was a Social-Democrat, the self-styled 'bloodhound' Noske, who called in the army to put them down. The soldiery went on to murder Rosa Luxemburg and Karl Liebknecht, the head and heart of revolutionary socialism in Germany.

By January 1919, it appeared to the Russian Bolsheviks that it was the absence of a true Bolshevik party that was holding up the European revolution. Invitations therefore went out to some thirty-eight socialist organizations the Bolsheviks considered eligible for consideration as members of a Communist International. With the sole exception of the Japanese socialists, all these groups were from capitalist countries of European culture. The First Congress of the Communist International convened in Moscow in March 1919. The German Communist Eberlein considered the formation of a unified Communist International premature, but news of the creation of Soviet Republics in Bavaria and Hungary persuaded the majority of delegates that the time was ripe. Simultaneous attempts to re-create a Social Democrat International in Bern were also cited as a reason for immediate action. By the time the Second Congress of the Comintern met in July 1920, working-class militancy had declined almost everywhere in Europe save in northern Italy, whereas the Bolsheviks were much more secure in Russia. The Second Congress voted itself a statute based on the premise that 'the Communist International should represent a single, universal Communist Party, of which the parties operating in every country form individual sections'. A hierarchical relationship was established between the supreme organ of the International, the Executive Committee (E.C.C.I.), and the member parties; for socialists like Gramsci, this was 'the first germ of a world workers' government'. Bilateral relations were strictly discouraged. The Congress was faced with the need to spell out what this would mean in practice when Frossard and Cachin, from the French Socialist Party, indicated their desire to see their own party affiliated to the Comintern. But the leaders of the S.F.I.O. were in favour of Allied intervention in Russia, the leaders of their trade-union federation, the C.G.T., were discouraging strikes, and their parliamentarians were dead set against revolution. To avert the danger of 'dilution', the Comintern established the famous Twenty-One Conditions for admission. These included tight control over the party press, regular purges of reformists, the creation of parallel secret organizations, propaganda among troops, agitation among the peasants, hostility to pacifism, an end to relations with reformist organizations, support for colonial independence, party cells in the trade unions to reveal the treason of the 'social patriots', attempts to create Communist unions, and so on. They must be based on 'democratic centralism'.

At the present moment of relentless civil war, the Communist Party cannot fulfil its role unless it is organized in the most centralized fashion, unless an iron discipline, bordering on military discipline, is admitted into it, and unless its central organ is provided with extensive powers, exercises an unchallenged authority, benefits from the unanimous confidence of the militants.

This was all a bit steep for the French. As Frossard put it later, 'When we read them, we said to ourselves: "Bah! These are just statutes, they will apply them more or less, we shall sort it out as best we can. It'll all work out".' He could not have been more mistaken.

Although the Second Congress saw the beginnings of a debate about the significance of Asia to world communism, the major objective of the Comintern was to assume the political leadership of the working class in the advanced capitalist countries. But only in Germany and Austria did Social Democrats come to power after the First World War with the result, in Lenin's words, that 'the majority of the workers in Britain still support the British Scheidemanns and Kerenskys; since they have not yet experienced a government composed of such men . . .' The left wing of European socialism had grown up as a specifically pacifist movement during the First World War. Peace had returned to Western Europe in 1918, but not to Russia. The Spartakists had been put down in Berlin, the communists and socialists in Munich and Budapest. The workers' movement in Vienna was completely paralysed by the consideration that socialist revolution now meant not peace but war, and possibly martyrdom. Lenin himself had observed the 'corrupting' influence of imperialism on the working class of England. Patriotic English workers were not keen on losing the Empire and patriotic French workers were not prepared to forego reparations from Germany. Though some 360,000 Germans did join the Communist Party by late 1920, there were many others who felt that Germany might get better peace terms by remaining with a constitutional order resembling that of the former Entente powers.

In 1921, the Comintern expelled Paul Levi and Clara Zetkin from the Communist Party of Germany and ordered docile new leaders, Thalheimer and Brandler, to mount another insurrection. Again, it failed and the Communist Party lost half its members. Once more the German proletariat had failed the Russian revolution. This time appropriate lessons were drawn, though this had as much to do with the stabilization of Soviet power in Russia and the introduction of the N.E.P. as with the German experience. The Comintern had little more success in Italy, where Fascism was gathering its forces. The struggle against reformism in the Italian Socialist Party was conducted at a time when the working class was in retreat, when the Fascists themselves were appropriating Bolshevik slogans. The Italians found the Twenty-One Conditions so hard to swallow that the entire Socialist Party was expelled from the Comintern. Russian influence in the new C.P.I. was thrown behind Bordiga, who was more sectarian and less concerned with the broader dimensions of socialist revolution than Gramsci. In France, the Comintern's insistence on controlling the party press created immense tensions between the party's intellectuals and workers. A personal intervention by the Comintern envoy, Manuilsky, failed to overcome ferocious resistance to Muscovite domination by Frossard. When it emerged that he and many other leading French Communists had not even resigned their membership of Free Masonry, the traditional road to office in the French Republic, they were all expelled.

One of the first British socialists to show an interest in the Communist International was Sylvia Pankhurst; but she was soon expelled from the movement, condemned by her hostility to participation in parliamentary elections and by her reluctance to part with a journal she had nursed through thick and thin. With few exceptions, the tiny Communist Party of Great Britain was recruited from continental refugees and from Celts, especially the miners of Fifeshire and South Wales, who saw in the Russian revolution a consummation of the ideals that had inspired the 1916 Rising in Dublin. A section of Daniel De Leon's International Workers of the World ('Wobblies') joined the Comintern in the United States. They were subjected to a wave of hysterical persecution, beaten up by the American Legion, sacked from their jobs, and deported in the famous 'Soviet Ark'. The judicial murder of the Italian anarchists Sacco and Vanzetti followed a pattern already employed against the 'Wobbly' songwriter, Joe Hill, in 1915. Even non-Communists were victimized; the New York State Assembly expelled its five socialists as a reprisal for bomb outrages committed against well-known anti-Communists.

By 1921 it was clear that, for the time being, the future of world Communism was identical with the future of the Soviet State. The cautious collaboration with capitalism, towards which Lenin had looked forward in the spring of 1918, was now an urgent necessity. Lenin was fully aware of the dangers of this course. The aim must be to thwart the formation of any capitalist united front. 'Our foreign policy while we are alone,' said Lenin, 'and while the capitalist world is strong, consists . . . in our exploiting contradictions.'

But what contradictions? The post-1918 world offered, it would seem, quite a choice. There was the conflict between France and Britain, the conflict between the United States and Japan, the conflict between France and the United States. But in actual fact only one conflict offered itself for serious exploitation: the contradiction between victors and vanquished in the First World War, between Germany and the Allied powers.

But why should Lenin pick on Germany as Russia's foothold in the capitalist camp? He was in fact merely reading the signs of the times:

On the one hand, our existence depends on the presence of radical differences between the imperialist powers, and, on the other, on the Entente's victory and the Peace of Versailles having thrown the vast majority of the German nation into a situation it is impossible for them to live in. The Peace of Versailles has created a situation in which Germany cannot even dream of a breathing-space, or of not being plundered . . . naturally, her only means of salvation lies in an alliance with Soviet Russia, a country towards which her eyes are therefore turning. They are furiously opposing Soviet Russia; they detest the Bolsheviks, and shoot down their own Communists in the manner of real whiteguards. The German bourgeois government has an implacable hatred of the Bolsheviks, but such is its international position that, against its own desires, the government is driven towards peace with Soviet Russia.*

Lenin hoped, of course, that he would be able to combine support for the German bourgeoisie in its struggle against the imperialists with a proof 'to those people, conscious of the bourgeois yoke, that there is no salvation for them outside the Soviet Republic'. In other words, the objective was still world revolution, but in the meantime an alliance of German and Russian nations was possible.

Lenin's diagnosis of the situation in Germany derived from the pro-Russian orientation of German policy ever since the collapse of November 1918. The Germans had refused to join in the blockade of 1919 imposed on Russia by the Western powers; and in 1920, at the time of the Russian advance on Warsaw, they had refused to allow France and England to transport munitions across Germany in a hasty attempt to succour the Poles. It was then that Lenin noticed the emergence of a strange phenomenon in Germany

* V. I. Lenin, *Collected Works*, vol. 31 (Moscow, 1966), pp. 475–6.

– what he called 'a reactionary-revolutionary'. 'Everyone in Germany,' he noted, 'even the blackest reactionaries and monarchists, said that the Bolsheviks would save us, when they saw the Versailles peace splitting at all its seams, that it is the Red Army which has declared war on all capitalists.' His analysis dovetailed with that of Winston Churchill who wrote:

> The reactionary Germans would of course be delighted to see the downfall of Poland at the hands of the Bolsheviks, for they fully understand that a strong Poland standing between Germany and Russia is the one thing that will baulk their plans for [an imperialist] reconstruction and revenge.*

The new-found warmth shown by the German reactionaries for Russian Bolshevism contrasted favourably with the continuing hostility of the Social Democrats and their attempts to achieve a revision of Versailles by improving relations with Britain and France. It was in this context that, in 1925, the German Communists refused to endorse the Social Democratic candidate for the German presidency. This ensured the victory of Marshal von Hindenburg who ultimately nominated Hitler as Chancellor.

While civil war and intervention lasted, the main agencies of Bolshevik foreign policy were the Red Army and the Comintern. With the stabilization of the new regime in 1920–21, the time had come to bring other institutions into play; in many ways, of course, the Commissariats of Foreign Affairs and Foreign Trade were simply continuations of their tsarist equivalents. The Foreign Commissariat was even headed by a former career diplomat who had defected to the Bolsheviks during the 1905 revolution. George Chicherin and his assistant, Maxim Litvinov, were thoroughly reassuring figures in the eyes of Europe: Chicherin's aristocratic background and Litvinov's English wife seemed to guarantee their good behaviour. Their reign in the Foreign Ministry was to last right up to 1939.

For much of the inter-war period, the Commissariat of Foreign Trade was just as important as diplomacy. Most European countries refused to recognize the Soviet regime until 1924, and the U.S.A. maintained its non-recognition until a decade later. Yet

* *The World Crisis – The Aftermath* (London, 1929), p. 265.

American economic aid was vital to Russia in saving the Volga region from famine in 1922 and in providing the technology for the First Five-Year Plan after 1928. Before 1917, Leonid Krassin, the future Commissar of Foreign Trade, had combined underground Bolshevik activities with the St Petersburg representation of Siemens-Schückert. The excellent contacts he had built with European industrial circles were now of great use.

Lenin's policy of rapprochement with the capitalist world had its first notable success with the signature of the Anglo-Soviet commercial treaty in March 1921. This, wrote Maisky, the future Soviet Ambassador to London, 'served as a door opening on to the arena of world politics'. Two months later it was followed by a Soviet–German trade treaty. The main feature of this was a German undertaking to recognize the Soviet government as the sole government of Russia. Later that year, the Russo-German link was strengthened by the formation of a number of mixed companies, and the allocation of Soviet mineral and trading concessions to a number of influential German industrialists.

The climax came on the morning of Easter Sunday, 1922. This was the Soviet–German treaty signed at Rapallo immediately after the refusal of the British and French to re-admit Soviet Russia to the European concert of nations. It annulled all mutual claims between the two countries; it re-established full diplomatic and consular relations; and it pledged the two governments 'to co-operate in a spirit of mutual goodwill in meeting the economic needs of both countries'. The treaty shocked France and Britain. Lloyd George feared the development of what he termed 'a fierce friendship', between the two 'pariah-nations' of Europe. The French even tried to secure the annulment of the treaty.

What did the treaty of Rapallo mean to Russian diplomacy? Its published terms were innocuous enough. But there was certainly substance to justify the fears of the West. The Western powers thenceforward lost the capacity to dominate events in Central and Eastern Europe. There could be no more question of squeezing Germany to the uttermost. There could also be no question of ever forming a united capitalist front against Russia. To Germany, Rapallo constituted a weapon in the struggle against Versailles. The bargain sealed in Rapallo obliged the Soviet Union to support the German national struggle against Versailles. But it also obliged Germany to remain neutral in any concerted capitalist moves. Come what may, there would always stretch before the western borders of the Soviet Union this vast buffer zone of neutralized territory.

On this basis there grew up a very close rapprochement between the two countries; closer relations developed, in fact, between these two states, the one capitalist, the other communist, than would ever again develop between the Soviet Union and a state with a differing social structure.

These relations were not merely diplomatic and economic. A common Soviet–German diplomacy marched hand in hand with a secret military understanding on re-armament. The revolutionary demand for open diplomacy was soon abandoned. Negotiations in 1921–2 conducted under the authority of Trotsky, on the one hand, and the chief of the new German *Reichswehr*, General von Seeckt, on the other, led to the establishment in the Soviet Union of German factories for the production of poison gas, aeroplanes, and artillery shells. This arrangement enabled Germany to circumvent the disarmament clauses of the Treaty of Versailles. It also familiarized the Red Army with the most progressive Western military techniques. German credits for the later industrialization of the Soviet Union also helped to consolidate the relationship.

There was considerable improvement as well in Soviet relations with the other powers. In 1924 – paradoxically enough, hard on the heels of a last Comintern attempt to foster revolution in Europe – the Soviet regime was suddenly recognized *de jure* by a whole host of important powers. They included Great Britain, under its first Labour government, France, Italy, Norway, Sweden, Denmark, Austria, Hungary, and Greece. Only the United States, among the great powers, still withheld recognition. Relations were hardly normal; at the end of the twenties, Mayakovsky described how his Soviet passport was handled like a bomb by Western immigration officials. His own visits to the West were almost as provocative, if not quite as scandalous, as Yesenin's famous trip to America with Isadora Duncan.

In June 1921, the Third Congress of the Communist International met to hear Trotsky explain the new realities facing international Communism. 'Only now,' he admitted, 'do we see and feel that we are not immediately close to our final aim, to the conquest of power on the world scale, to the world revolution. We told ourselves back in 1919 that it was a question of months, but now we say that it is perhaps a question of several years.' Still, contradictions between capitalist powers were sure to bring about another world war quite soon; this would lead to another revolution, presumably in Germany, the country with the largest Communist Party after Russia. This would restore the hegemony of the European proletariat over the world Communist movement. The prestige of the Communist Party would rise since the reformist trade unions and parties were trying to force the workers to return to work on conditions worse than those that prevailed before the Great War. The European proletariat 'demands an improvement in its lot, which is at present *absolutely* incompatible with the *objective* possibilities of capitalism'. For the immediate future, the Communist Party must abandon insurrection for 'united front' tactics. These involved joint campaigning with reformist trade unionists for concrete improvements in working-class conditions, enabling the Communists to demonstrate that they were the vanguard of the working class. It was to make it clear that no dilution of Communist discipline was suggested, that Paul Levi was expelled from the German Communist Party for publicly criticizing the monolithic methods of the Comintern. We now know that most of this analysis was mistaken, to put it charitably. Even at the time, however, it was obvious that the tactics recommended by the Comintern were not entirely satisfactory. For a start, why should it be assumed that insurrection was out of the question in Bulgaria, for example, just because a 'united front' with reformists was an undoubted necessity for the English comrades? The Communist parties had spent two years purging themselves of reformists, sparing no epithets in the process. The thought of cooperation was now as obnoxious to many Communists, as it was to the reformists themselves.

There was naturally a widespread desire for an end to splits and name-calling among the European working class. One symptom of this was the emergence of a so-called Two-and-a-Half International, led by the Austrian Socialist Party, Marxist in ideology but reformist in tactics, which tried to re-unite Communists and Socialists. In an attempt to gain sympathy among the working-class militants, leaders of both Communist and Social Democratic Internationals agreed to meet in Berlin in April 1922. This was to be the last time that all the heirs to Marxism were to meet at one table. Victor Serge described the scene:

These men presented a striking physical contrast. The Socialists, Abramovich, Vandervelde, and Friedrich Adler had the fine profiles of Western intellectuals and the behaviour of competent lawyers; their whole comportment expressed moderation. Facing them was Clara Zetkin's solid, powerful old face, the mobile, sardonic features of Radek, and Bukharin's impervious geniality.

The Communists suggested a short-term alliance between Communists and socialists; after the victory over the bourgeoisie, the latter could then be removed from the scene. As Vandervelde put it, 'no secret is made of the intention to stifle us and poison us after embracing us . . .' In Radek's view, on the other hand, the socialists were only at the conference because the workers forced them to be; they would also force them to ally themselves with the Communists. This cut little ice with the socialists who rejected arguments that they had betrayed the European revolution and focused attention on Russian conduct towards socialists. At that very moment, Menshevik Georgia was under Red Army occupation and the Soviet government was conducting its show trial of S.R. leaders. In due course, the European proletariat gave its own answer to the debate. Between 1921 and 1928, the number of Communists in capitalist countries fell from 900,000 to 450,000 whereas the number of Social Democrats rose from three to six million.

In 1923, Germany defaulted on its reparations payments to France and the French Army marched into the Ruhr. Powerless to resist, the German government embarked on a policy of passive opposition, encouraging disobedience among its citizens in the occupied zone and inflating the currency. To the Comintern leadership, particularly Zinoviev, it seemed that the moment had come. The Comintern went so far as to push the 'Schlageter Line'. This policy, called after a German civilian killed by French soldiers who was canonized by the German right, endorsed almost any manifestation of German patriotism on the grounds that the Germans were being subjected to colonial treatment by the French. The Comintern instructed the Communists to enter coalition governments in Saxony and Thuringia; the revolution was timed for the anniversary of the October revolution. At the last minute, the insanity of the operation became so apparent that it was called off, but the message failed to reach the Hamburg comrades who came out for a brief moment of glory and a longer appointment with death. In the same month, Adolf Hitler and General Ludendorff mounted their Putsch in Munich. This was also put down, but they were more leniently treated than their Communist equivalents. The sad experience of the Comintern in Germany echoed that in Bulgaria where the Communists had stood by and watched the peasants and their leader Stambolisky murdered in the summer without lifting a finger to help, only to be ordered in the autumn to conduct a revolution on their own. Deprived of peasant allies in this totally peasant country, the Bulgarian Communists were easily put down. In both Germany and Bulgaria, young 'left-wing' leaders emerged, eager to help the Comintern shuffle off the responsibility for these defeats by heaping the blame on Thalheimer, Brandler, and Dimitrov. The last and most foolish example of Zinoviev's penchant for 'putschism' came in December 1924 when the Estonian Communists gave their lives, perhaps to efface the memory of Zinoviev's 'strike-breaking' in 1917, or to give him a weapon with which to beat off Stalin's attacks.

By 1922, the French Communists numbered some 60,000. Their leaders threw themselves fearlessly into the struggle against the occupation of the Ruhr, striving desperately to revive proletarian internationalism by organizing a propaganda campaign and strike action. *L'Humanité* looked hard for evidence of strikes but found only the female shop-assistants of Paris withholding their labour. A party agitator called Lozeray was sent to prison for ten years for sedition among the French soldiers in the Ruhr. Such was the patriotism of the French workers that the struggle to build the Communist Party had taken place in the total absence of mass actions by the working class.

In 1924, the attention of the Comintern turned to Britain, where the attempts of the Labour Party to replace the Liberals as the main vehicle of social progress were finally showing some success. The general election of December 1923 had given no party a majority in the House of Commons. When Baldwin was defeated by the House in January 1924, King George V called for Ramsay MacDonald, leader of the largest party, to form a new government. From the point of view of the Bolsheviks, this was ideal. A minority government of reformists was certain to disillusion the working class and hasten the growth of a true Communist Party. In the meantime, there were advantages to Russia herself from the new situation. MacDonald swiftly recognized the Soviet Union and signed a commercial treaty; a British loan was also negotiated, though the fall of the government meant that it was never made. The minority government finally decided to go to the country on an issue directly involving relations with Communists (its own inability to prosecute the Communist newspaper for sedition) and the election campaign was fought partly on a letter, allegedly written by Zinoviev, recommending the infiltration of the Labour Party and the armed forces. As we have already seen, it would not have been surprising had Zinoviev written such a letter and Aino Kuusinen insists that he did. But, as published, the letter bore all the marks of a forgery. To the British left, the Conservative victory in 1924 was secured by a fraud. Their alienation from the establishment had indeed been intensified.

One symptom of the increasing radicalization of the British trade unions was their agreement, in 1925, to the creation of an Anglo-Soviet Trade-Union Committee. It was the Conservative decision to return to the gold standard, however, and the recovery of the Ruhr coalfields in 1924 that brought real disaster to the British coal miners. Threatened with lower wages for longer hours in 1925, they eventually precipitated the General Strike in 1926. After nine days, it was called off. The militants felt betrayed; the Communist Party had neither warned them of what to expect nor did it now call upon them to continue the strike. The Soviet trade unions did not even resign from the Anglo-Soviet Committee. Only the miners, desperate for some hope of succour, turned to the Communist Party in any appreciable numbers; membership doubled in 1926 but declined thereafter.

An even clearer illustration of the priorities and methods of Stalin in foreign affairs was provided by the visit of an I.R.A. delegation to Russia in 1925. Following the Irish Treaty of 1921, the head of the then I.R.A., Michael Collins, had become Irish Prime Minister. Unable to accept anything less than a fully sovereign Irish Republic, a minority of I.R.A. men broke away and, after a short civil war, continued an underground existence. The political leadership was provided by Eamonn de Valera but the reformed I.R.A. contained a few revolutionary socialists who thought it might be possible to secure arms from Russia. Murray, Russell, and Boland took a look at Soviet arms in Leningrad and then met Stalin in Moscow. Stalin asked for guarantees that Soviet arms would not fall into the wrong hands and stunned them by producing a list of arms seized from the I.R.A., prepared by the Irish government. He let them know that his main fear was that captured Soviet arms would be made a pretext for an invasion of Russia by Britain. He also made it clear that he had had them under observation throughout their journey and that he had a low opinion of their security. The gulf between the two parties was emphasized when the I.R.A. men told a Soviet Communist they had hanged no bishops. 'Ah, you people are not serious at all', came the sardonic reply.

If the transference of the centre of gravity of Marxism came as a disconcerting experience to the Bolsheviks, the prospect of its further progress towards the east filled them with anxiety. This particular confrontation between theory and practice in the hands of Marxists who were also Europeans first occurred within the borders of the Soviet Union. The overwhelming majority of non-European citizens of the revolution were Moslems. Just as the Europeans came to revolutionary Marxism by way of some of the egalitarian and Messianic traditions of Christianity, so there were Moslems who hoped to marry equivalent strains in Islam with the liberating possibilities of Marxism. The egalitarian tradition of the *Khawarij* and the messianic possibilities of Mahdism had already been greeted by Al-Afghani as providing the starting points for a liberating theory, conducted in a spirit of *ijtihad*, or free inquiry. He was not a revolutionary himself, but he was capable of seeing the revolutionary implications of his ideas:

O you poor fellah [he wrote of the Egyptian peasantry]. You break the heart of the earth in order to draw sustenance from it and support your family. Why do you not break the heart of your oppressor? Why do you not break the heart of those who eat the fruit of your labour?

The man who tried to bring about a synthesis of revolutionary Islam and Marxism in Russia was the Tatar intellectual, Sultan Galiev. We must remember that the Tatars had once ruled most of the Eurasian plain. Like the Russians themselves, they were scattered over a wide area, with concentrations of Tatar population and culture around Kazan and in the Crimea. For them, the revolution offered something like a condominium with the Russians, since they alone of the Islamic peoples of the Russian Empire had developed an intelligentsia.

Sultan Galiev joined the Bolshevik Party, becoming President of the Central Muslim Commissariat and Stalin's assistant in the Commissariat of Nationalities. He, like many of his fellow Moslems, looked forward to the creation of a Turanian Republic uniting all the Soviet Moslems and a Turkish Communist Party separate from that of the European Russian Communists. As a Moslem Communist complained in 1919:

We were still obliged to endure a contemptuous attitude on the part of the former privileged classes towards the indigenous masses. This attitude is that of the communists, who retain a mentality of oppressors and regard the Moslems as their subjects.

Or as Safarov, Lenin's emissary in Central Asia, expressed it, 'Under tsarist colonialism, it was the privilege of the Russians to belong to the industrial proletariat. For this reason, the dictatorship of the proletariat took on a typically colonialist aspect'.* Statements like these posed a direct challenge to the concept of 'proletarian hegemony' to which both Lenin and Stalin adhered. Lenin had never had the time or interest to investigate Islamic culture with an open mind; as for Stalin, his growing power was based on precisely the elements criticized by Safarov.

The denouement was inevitable. Sultan Galiev was purged and vilified. He was the first Communist whom Stalin had removed

* H. Carrère d'Encausse and Stuart Schram, *Marxism and Asia* (London, 1969), p. 32.

from the party and imprisoned without being given an opportunity to defend himself; this in itself speaks volumes for party sentiment about 'nationalist deviations'. Inevitably, Sultan Galiev developed a more and more nationalist point of view that denied the importance of class struggles within Moslem nations. 'The Moslem peoples are proletarian nations,' he wrote: '. . . It may be stated that the national movement in the Moslem countries has the character of a socialist revolution.' But Sultan Galiev was not destined to see any authentic revolutions of this kind. The man who might have created a synthesis of Islam and socialism helped instead to build the White Sea Canal.

The Soviet government made two attempts to export revolution to areas on their Asian frontiers during the twenties. In 1920 they supported the creation of a 'Gilan Soviet Republic' in northern Iran, but retired when they feared Reza Shah might turn to the British for support in ejecting them from his country. More successful was their intervention in Outer Mongolia. In this case, there was no pretence of supporting a proletarian revolution, a nonsense in view of the economic structure of this vast but sparsely populated land of herdspeople. Outer Mongolia was technically Chinese territory; the Soviets were provided with a pretext for invasion by the activities of a White Russian adventurer, Baron Ungern-Sternberg, who announced that he was holding Mongolia for Tsar Michael. The techniques used successfully in Mongolia were those of camouflage and gradualism. First of all, a 'revolutionary' party was formed under the leadership of Sukhe Bator on Soviet soil; a provisional government of liberation was formed and then a native army. After a successful invasion by both Soviet and Mongolian armies, a broad coalition was formed which even accepted the theocratic monarchy. Buryat Mongols and other Russified Asians assumed responsible posts in the administration. With the death of the Bogdo Gegen in 1924, the First Great Khuraldan declared Mongolia to be a 'People's Republic'. This one and only successful attempt to export revolution in the inter-war period employed tactics imitated in every particular in the treatment of North Korea and Eastern Europe after the Second World War.

The decisive factor in the revolutions in Central Asia and Mongolia had been the Red Army. For the Comintern to have any greater degree of success in Asia, with all the benefits that might bring for the security of the Soviet Union, the emphasis would have to be on the recruitment of indigenous allies. Once more, however, there was a certain tension between the immediate needs of the Soviet State and the demands of the revolutionaries of the countries in question. This emerged at the Second Congress of the Comintern in July 1920, when the Indian M. N. Roy had to be persuaded that 'the co-operation of the bourgeois nationalist revolutionary forces is useful'. For Roy, 'the first and most necessary task is the formation of communist parties which will organize the peasants and workers and lead them to the revolution and to the establishment of Soviet Republics'.

The formation of Communist parties in Asia was not well regarded by non-Communist nationalists. The first to test the priorities of the Soviet government was Kemal Atatürk. In 1920 he had secured Soviet economic, military and diplomatic support, including some 10,000,000 gold rubles for his struggle against Greece and the Entente powers. A month and a half before the alliance with Russia was signed, he had the Communist leader Mustafa Subhi and fourteen other Communists arrested and strangled. To avoid a discussion of this unhappy precedent, which had gained enormously in relevance in view of the Russian efforts to normalize relations with capitalist powers everywhere, Zinoviev cut discussion of Asia to a minimum at the Third Comintern Congress in July 1921. Roy minced no words calling this 'worthy rather of a Congress of the Second International'.

Russia's most important neighbour in Asia is China and, ultimately, it was to be China where Soviet Communism would gain its greatest victory after Russia itself, only to suffer its greatest defeat. Until the late nineteenth century, most Chinese had continued to believe in the superiority of Chinese civilization. The adjustment to the challenge of Western society, which had taken place in Russia over ten, often troubled, generations, had to be accomplished by the Chinese in two. Scarcely had the Chinese Communist Party been founded in 1920, recruited from among those Chinese anxious to fight the class struggle, than the Comintern instructed them to join the nationalist Kuomintang Party as individuals, while retaining their own organization. This was in line with the 'united front' line which prevailed after 1921, but, as in Germany, it implied the exposure of the local Communists to the appeals of nationalism. Li Ta-chao went so far as to predict that 'racial struggles will inevitably break out, and these struggles will take the form of wars between white and coloured men and will merge with the "class struggle"'.

In 1925, Stalin announced that the Kuomintang had become a 'workers' and peasant's party', it was admitted to the Comintern as a 'sympathizing party', and its new leader Chiang Kai-shek was elected an honorary member of the Comintern Presidium. But Chiang belonged to a more muscular brand of nationalism than the revered Sun Yat-sen, and immediately began to clamp down on the activities of the Chinese Communists. When the Communist leader Chen Tu-hsiu proposed breaking with the Kuomintang, Stalin insisted they remain within it. Chiang then embarked, with Soviet military assistance, on his 'northern expedition' to re-unify China.

The Communist organizations in Shanghai rose to overthrow the existing authorities and greeted Chiang as a liberator. Stalin had been repeatedly warned that Chiang would turn against the Communists, but in a speech in the Bolshoi Theatre he rejected this advice. 'We are told that Chiang Kai-shek is making ready to turn against us again. I know that he is playing a cunning game with us, but it is he that will be crushed. We shall squeeze him like a lemon and then be rid of him.' On the following day came the news that Chiang had slaughtered the Shanghai Communists with swords and machine guns. Stalin persisted in hoping that his alliance with the 'left' Kuomintang in Wuhan would remain in force, thereby condemning another group of Chinese Communists to extinction. Finally, bitterly taunted by the Trotskyist opposition, Stalin insisted on a rising by the Canton Communists which was put down in its turn. Almost the entire proletarian strength of the Chinese Communist Party had been massacred. Since the Leader was now deemed infallible, the unfortunate Chen was made to shoulder the blame for the débâcle. Chen ended his days as a liberal democrat. The leadership of the Chinese Communists eventually passed to the peasant leader Mao Tse-tung. Mao paid

lip-service to the notion of 'proletarian hegemony' in whose name
Li Li-san and Wang Ming dashed thousands of Chinese Communists against the Kuomintang strongholds in the towns. Only
when this policy had brought about the virtual elimination of
proletarian Chinese Communism did Mao assume the leadership
of the party in 1935. When he heard the news of the dissolution of
the Comintern in 1943, Mao commented drily:

Since the Seventh World Congress of the Communist International in
1935, the Communist International has not intervened in the internal
affairs of the Chinese Communist Party. And yet, the Chinese Communist
Party has done its work very well . . .

The destruction of the Chinese Communists was one of a series
of setbacks suffered by Soviet diplomacy in 1927. Some of these
have been described earlier.* Coming as it did in the middle of
Stalin's fight with the 'left opposition', the Chinese débâcle was an
intolerable embarrassment. But Stalin had no intention of letting
his prestige be affected by a foreign disaster as Trotsky's and
Zinoviev's had been on previous occasions. When they circulated
a memorandum itemizing his mistakes in China, Stalin simply
read them out of the party.

During 1928, the struggle between Stalin and Bukharin began.
For Stalin, it was not accidental that the man who opposed his
assault on the peasantry should also stand in the way of his Russification of the Comintern. Bukharin sympathized with those
western Communists who foresaw that they would have to use
more flexible tactics if 'united fronts' with the left-wing socialists
of Europe were to have any success. After removing Bukharin
from the E.C.C.I., Stalin nominated Manuilsky and Kuusinen to
lay down the new line. It was to bear the title 'class against class'.
This new line declared that 'the aims of the Fascists and the social
Fascists [Social Democrats] are the same'. Following this analysis
the left wing of 'social Fascism' operated with pacifist, democratic,
and 'socialist' slogans, but these would disappear in time. 'Since
social Fascism openly shows itself up as Fascism, it will no longer
be difficult to win the majority of the working class in Germany
for the proletarian revolution.'

* See pp. 353–4 above.

In 1928, the German Communists were instructed to withdraw from Social Democrat trade unions to struggle for independent organizations. By January 1931, the Communists controlled a mere 4 per cent of the factory committees as opposed to the Social Democrats' 84 per cent. The world depression which followed 1929 had led to a considerable increase in the Communist vote (up to four and a half million in 1930) and this encouraged the party in its militancy. The significance of the six and a half million votes cast for Hitler escaped it. In August 1931, the Communists even supported the Nazis and Stalhelm nationalists in a referendum campaign against the Prussian Social Democratic government. Right up to the spring of 1933 they continued to campaign for a German Soviet Republic, without ever planning an insurrection. With Hitler in power, the E.C.C.I. declared:

The establishment of open fascist dictatorship, which destroys all the democratic illusions of the masses and frees them from the influence of Social Democracy, speeds up the process of Germany's evolution towards the proletarian revolution.

By the time this was printed, Thälmann and many other German Communists were under lock and key, many of them never to emerge. George Dimitrov's heroic defiance of Göring at the Reichstag Fire Trial provided an enormous boost for Communist prestige in Britain and France, but it had no impact on German society at all.

The German Communists were not the only casualties of the 'class against class' line. In Japan, all those opposed to militarism had been placed on the defensive by the authoritarian Peace Preservation Law of 1925. Despite this, the most democratic election ever fought in Japan before the war, the election of 1928, showed popular support for moderate foreign policies. In this delicate situation, the Communists proclaimed that 'Opposition to the war was not from pacifist scruples but as a part of a struggle to topple the present government and establish a new government of workers and peasants'. The slogans were 'Overthrow the Monarchy' and 'Protect the Soviet Union'. Anyone who opposed them was the enemy. In the United States, the sectarian demand was for the creation of a 'Negro Republic' in the southern states.

This was good for the recruitment of black Americans who became disillusioned later when the line changed and Soviet policy began to make overtures to white leaders like Roosevelt whose attitudes on race relations were rather moderate.

To the last minute, the hope persisted in the Kremlin that Rapallo might yet be saved. Until the beginning of 1934, Stalin and Litvinov were saying that 'we Marxists are the last people who can be reproached for allowing feelings to prevail over our policy . . . Fascism is not the issue . . . external policy counts, not internal'. Hitler no longer needed Stalin's unwitting assistance to take power in Germany; in the absence of Anglo-French resistance, he did not yet need it to carve up Eastern Europe. If the era of illusions was not entirely past, a more realistic phase in Soviet foreign policy was about to begin.

FROM THE POPULAR FRONT TO THE GRAND ALLIANCE

The Soviet leaders had responded to the supposed war scare in 1927 with hysteria. They replied to Hitler's unfriendliness with a humble plea for continued amity. The difference was that in the first instance the threat of war existed only in that realm of 'objective reality' supposedly derived from Marxist analysis, while in the second case the threat of war was unmistakably present no matter what your preferred philosophy. For Hitler's success in taking over and smashing the opposition in Germany had come hard on the heels of a major re-orientation in the East. In 1931, Japan had occupied the whole of Manchuria (North East China) and had begun the process of creating a puppet state under the last Chinese Emperor. Imperial princes had assumed the key positions in the army and navy so that criticism of Japanese aggression now became tantamount to treason. The Communist Party was outlawed and any suggestion of Communist ideas was used as a weapon against moderate opponents of militarism. Chiang Kai-shek regarded the Communists in China as his main enemy but he had to maintain face so he briefly retired rather than accept Japanese aggression. To force the Chinese to accept the new situation, the Japanese attacked Shanghai. For the first time, western residents of the foreign concessions witnessed the calculated use of atrocities against a civilian population as a matter of policy. On 15 May 1932, the militarists murdered Inukai, the last constitutional Prime Minister of Japan before the war.

As early as 1927, the Soviet government had responded to threats from abroad with pacifist propaganda. This was Litvinov's policy of complete and immediate disarmament. In 1932, the Soviet Union signed non-aggression treaties with the Baltic states, Poland, and France. But this was not enough. By the end of 1933, Litvinov went so far as to say that 'Any state, even the most imperialist, may at one time or another become profoundly pacifist'. In November 1933, the new administration of Franklin Roosevelt recognized the Soviet Union. In return, the Soviet government accepted that American intervention in Siberia had been aimed not against Bolshevism, but against the Japanese. The Russians also had to promise 'not to permit the formation or residence' on U.S. territory 'of any organization or group ... which has as its aim the overthrow or the preparation of the overthrow ... of the political or social order of the whole or any part of the United States'. A rapprochement with the French and Anglo-Saxon bourgeoisies was as far as things went at this stage.

France and Spain were to see the greatest successes of the Popular Front policy; had it not been for Hitler and Pilsudski the opportunity might never have arisen. In the wake of Fascist successes in Italy and Germany, and the patent inability of the Third Republic to solve any of France's major economic and social problems, the early 1930s saw the vigorous growth of a number of Fascist leagues; the largest and most important was Colonel De La Rocque's *Croix du Feu*. Early in 1934, the Third Republic was embarrassed by one of its periodic scandals of corruption associated with a Russian Jewish exile called Stavisky. Massive riots broke out in January and February 1934. The police and army chiefs were sympathetic to the Fascist rioters. Only their own lack of nerve prevented a *coup d'état*. During this period, the French Communists were on the streets fighting the police side by side with the French Fascists. All this was changed by the German–Polish Non-Aggression Pact of January 1934. In May 1934, Foreign Minister Barthou offered to sign a mutual assistance pact with Russia and to sponsor the entry of the Soviet Union into the League of Nations. The British were warned that if they blocked Soviet entry to the League, France might conclude a military alliance with Russia. Simultaneously, *Pravda* published an article which cut across the prevailing orthodoxies of official Comintern policy. Communists could now propose joint action not just to the rank-and-file militants of socialist parties, but to their leaders. The Communist leadership, which had just expelled Doriot (a future Fascist) for anti-Fascist activities, was now able to offer the bourgeois Radical Party partnership in a 'broad people's front'. Despite the assassination of Barthou, a Franco-Soviet Pact was signed in 1935 to complement the pact signed by the Soviet Union and Czechoslovakia the year before. In 1935, the French Communists justified their novel support for a 'bourgeois' army in a poster campaign with the slogan 'Stalin was right'.

In September 1934, the Soviet Union joined the League of Nations and was elected a permanent member of the Council. Henceforward, although there were tentative efforts to come to terms with Hitler, the Soviets were on the side of the angels. From this platform, day in day out, Litvinov preached the necessity of a strong League, the principles of collective security, and the indivisibility of peace. The 1936 'Stalin Constitution' played its part in fostering a respectable image of Soviet society. These were the years when a section of the intelligentsia of the capitalist West, disillusioned by the growth of mass unemployment and militarism, began to see in the Soviet Union the answer to all their hopes. To some extent this was a matter of wish-fulfilment. The Webbs, who claimed to have discovered no less than a New Civilization in Russia, asserted rather unconvincingly that 'old people are always absorbed in something, usually themselves; we prefer to be absorbed in the Soviet Union'. Stalin humoured these visitors by seeing some of them personally and exposing them to his very real charm and intelligence. He also saw that the most elaborate measures were taken to insulate them from any criticisms that might be made by Soviet citizens or bourgeois journalists resident in Russia.

Between 1934 and 1936 the nature of Fascism became more and more apparent. In Austria, the clerical Fascist Chancellor Dolfuss proscribed the socialists and, after a short civil war, created a Fascist corporate state. The Nazis hoped to capitalize on Austrian divisions and assassinated Dolfuss. Encouraged by Mussolini, Vice-Chancellor Schuschnigg resisted the Nazi coup, offered a free passage to Germany for the assassins, and then executed them. In 1933, the League had condemned Japanese aggression in Manchuria. The Japanese replied by leaving the League and invading the Chinese province of Jehol. In June 1935 the Chinese were induced to agree to a truce in North China, but in the autumn of the same year the Japanese began to suggest that it was desirable that the northern provinces of China become autonomous and friendly to Japan. Meanwhile, the Italians were flexing their muscles. After a series of attempts to extort territory from Ethiopia during 1934, the Italians invaded the country in 1935. Neither the bellicose rhetoric of Pierre Laval, nor the pacific rhetoric of Litvinov, Ramsay MacDonald, and Roosevelt, seemed able to stem the tide. Anglo-French relations were at a low ebb at this time. The French were mesmerized by the growing power of Germany and were therefore prepared to retain the friendship of Italy by making concessions in Africa. The British feared that the 'New Roman Empire' would disrupt Imperial communications with India, so they tried to gain German support against Italy by making a naval agreement with Germany in 1935.

At the beginning of 1936, Hitler prepared to take on France and Britain directly by re-militarizing the Rhineland, an area of Germany along the French border which the Germans had undertaken to leave demilitarized under the Treaty of Versailles. Foreign Minister Flandin asked Stanley Baldwin what the British would do if this happened. Baldwin replied by asking him what France would do. When Hitler re-militarized the Rhineland on 7 March no one did anything at all. Nor was appeasement a monopoly of conservative circles in the British government. The French socialist newspaper *Populaire* declared:

... Hitler has torn up a treaty, he has broken all his promises, but at the same time he speaks of Peace and of Geneva [seat of the League]. We must take him at his word.

To Stalin, it was becoming more and more obvious that an alliance with France was not worth much unless supported by the British. Yet the British were only very slowly waking up to the danger posed by Fascism; most British conservatives still considered Communism to be a greater danger.

Stalin had authorized the discontinuation of attacks on socialists and verbal campaigns in favour of Soviet republics to gain the support of bourgeois circles in France and Britain for the national interests of the Soviet Union. The restoration of relative unity to the leadership of the working class in Western Europe was perceived by the workers, and many of the peasants, of France and Spain in quite a different light. With their organizations preparing to attack the ultra right, they felt the time had come for an all-out assault on the bourgeois capitalist order of society. In February and May 1936, first the Spanish and then the French people voted in Popular Front governments. They had shown their strength through the ballot box; according to the new French Premier elect, Léon Blum, this did not give them a mandate for social revolution. To the consternation of Stalin and the jubilation of the exiled Trotsky, the workers and peasants showed that they thought otherwise. In Spain, they released political prisoners, forced employers to re-employ victimized workers, took over the land, and went on strike for better conditions and the suppression of Fascism. To the anarchist masses it seemed that the end of capitalism was near while the socialists acclaimed Largo Caballero as the 'Spanish Lenin'. In France, a wave of sit-in strikes commenced; by the time Blum took up office in June, a third of a million workers were on strike. On 7 June, Blum reached an agreement with the union leaders for wage increases and the right to collective bargaining. He promised that the government would legislate for a forty-hour week and two weeks' paid holiday for all. Four days later, the number of strikers had risen to nearly two million. While Trotsky was greeting the 'French Revolution', Stalin's mouthpiece, Maurice Thorez, was making his plea for a return to work: 'You have to know not only how to start a strike but how to end it'. The workers would not respond until they had got action as well as promises. In the words of one historian: 'Within ten days Parliament, which had resisted since the end of the Great War acting on such measures, had by an overwhelming vote given the country the only important social legislation of the Third Republic.' *

The right-wing parties were not inactive all this time. In France, they had greeted Blum's appointment with a colossal outburst of vituperative antisemitism. Later on they would drive Salengro, the Interior Minister, to suicide by vilifying his war record. A much more powerful weapon was the flight of gold. In Spain, right- and left-wing assassins gunned down leaders they loathed. On 17 July, General Franco proclaimed the beginning of the 'National Uprising'. On the following day, Salengro banned the Fascist leagues in France. When Giral, the Spanish Prime Minister, asked Blum for arms, Blum agreed that France would supply them; but when the French right got to hear of this agreement, they began a ferocious campaign against arms deliveries to Spain. Some days later, Blum saw Eden. 'Are you going to send arms to the Spanish Republicans?' Eden asked. Blum confirmed that he was. 'It's your affair, but I ask you one thing. I beg of you: be prudent.'

For Stalin, the events in France and Spain were a nightmare. Nothing was more certain to drive the British into the arms of Hitler than successful socialist revolutions in Western Europe. On the other hand, a total desertion of the left in Western Europe was an impossibility for a regime which claimed to lead the world socialist revolution. The most urgent requirement was for military assistance to Spain. This was only partly a matter of arms. Following Franco's rising, the strength of the working classes in Madrid, Valencia, Barcelona, and the north had been sufficient to check the generals' advance. Only in Old Castille and Navarre, relatively backward socially and economically, did the right have any mass support. On the other hand, a bare handful of officers remained loyal to the Republic. It fell to the Comintern to organize the dispatch of military experts under the overall command of General Berzin, and to form the famous International Brigades led entirely by Communists, but which recruited men (and a few women) of many different persuasions. At last the exiled German and Italian Communists had an opportunity to stand up and fight their enemies, for the aid of the Comintern to the Republic was more than matched by the aid sent by Mussolini and Hitler to

* W. L. Shirer, *The Collapse of the Third Republic* (London, 1970), pp. 276–7.

Franco. In an action that foreshadowed the civil war of 1943–5, the Italian Communists and Socialists under Nenni and Longó decisively defeated Roatta's Fascist Italian corps north of Guadalajara. The military activity of the Communists evoked unbounded admiration from all who observed them. Len Crome, an English medical officer, wrote later: 'I saw that the Communists did most of the fighting, were most steadfast and that without them it would have been impossible to continue resisting the Fascists'.* Spaniards went into battle for 'Estalin' just as Russians would a few years later. Yet in the end, all this heroism was in vain for the Spanish Republic collapsed just seven months before the beginning of the Second World War.

Already in August 1936, the British had forced France to agree to refrain from sending arms to Spain – unilaterally if need be. The massive Italian and German aid to Franco, which had come at the very beginning of the civil war, was followed by substantial aid for the Republic from Russia – in return for the gold in the Bank of Spain – and from Cardénas's radical regime in Mexico. The British response to all this was the creation of a 'Non-Intervention Committee' of the League of Nations to prevent any arms or military aid reaching either side in Spain. What had begun as sanctimonious priggishness degenerated into sheer hypocrisy when Britain and France failed to challenge the continued blatant support given to Franco by Italy and Germany. Even Soviet support for Spain was not entirely unlimited, however. President Azaña warned his Ambassador in Moscow in 1937 of his fears:

I think that, contrary to what is often supposed, there is a limit to Russia's co-operation, which is not set by the possible blockade but by Britain's official friendship. In my view, the U.S.S.R. will do nothing to help us that might do serious harm to their relations with Britain or compromise their position in the policy of seeking friends in the West.

In many ways, the political intervention of the Soviet Union in Spain was as significant as its military assistance. From the outset, Soviet influence in Spain was committed to opposing all manifestations of 'Communismo libertario'. Under Communist influence, the left-wing socialist administration of Largo Caballero

* Len Crome, in *History Workshop Journal*, 9 (Oxford, 1980), p. 126.

restored the State and a viable army, restored private ownership of the means of production, and a large degree of freedom for the bourgeois press. To some extent, many of these policies were essential if the Republic was to fight effectively. From May 1937, however, when Negrín replaced Largo Caballero, the Communists took the initiative in suppressing the anarchists and the alleged-Trotskyists of the P.O.U.M. party. The Soviet government had made occasional use of the security organs abroad ever since the revolution. The enticement of Savinkov back to recantation and a mysterious death in the Lubyanka, and the fool's tour given to discredit the monarchist Shulgin, had both taken place in the twenties. They were followed in the thirties by the kidnapping of the White General Miller and the hunting down of Trotsky's family. Still, these were Russians. The liquidation of an entire political leadership of a socialist party in an Allied state was something quite new, a portent of post-war developments in Eastern Europe. This was the period of the show trials in Moscow and the Spanish Communists hoped to emulate them in a trial of Andres Nín, the P.O.U.M. leader. But this conflicted with pledges of personal security given by Premier Negrín, and so Nín was murdered instead. It all added up to a situation in which victory began to appear as threatening to the libertarian left and anarchists in Spain as defeat. The increasing unpopularity of the Communists even permitted Azaña and Prieto to reduce Communist influence in the government and the army, facilitating the eventual collapse of the Republic with Colonel Casado's mutiny in 1939.

On 25 November, Stalin's fears of encirclement were given tangible form when Germany and Japan signed the Anti-Comintern Pact. Just twenty days later, pressure on the eastern front was relieved when Chiang Kai-shek was kidnapped by one of his subordinates and forced to agree on joint action with Chou En-lai against the Japanese and a cessation of the Chinese civil war. Surprisingly, Chiang remained fairly loyal to this agreement despite the terrible price exacted by the Japanese at the Rape of Nanking in 1937.

In Japan meanwhile, the army, imbued with a fanatical anti-Communism and bored by winning easy victories over the Chinese, was anxious for war with Russia. The imperial clique which dominated foreign policy formation was more interested, however, in the economic advantages of expansion southwards, towards the oil of the Dutch East Indies (Indonesia). Still, they felt obliged to let the army show what it could do against the Russians. In the summer of 1938, the Japanese army attacked Soviet forces near Vladivostok but were repulsed partly because the Japanese air force showed little interest in backing them up. A year later, at the height of the negotiations for a pact between Germany and the Soviet Union, the Japanese mounted an invasion of Outer Mongolia which was repulsed by Lieutenant General Zhukov at the bloody battle of Khalkin Gol (Nomonhan). The effect of these skirmishes was to drive Stalin in the direction of an accommodation with Hitler, a move to which the British had unwittingly contributed.

In retrospect it seems obvious that the British and Russians had an overriding common interest in the defeat of Fascism. At the time, however, all they seemed to share was an awareness of their own weakness which led each to try to deflect aggression on to the other. Stalin's weakness lay in the explosive hostilities which had followed collectivization; his awareness of them was signalled to all the world in the purge trials which, incidentally, exterminated many of the senior military men with experience as observers of the German and Japanese forces. Britain's weakness lay in the centrifugal forces which were already beginning to break up the Empire and which would be likely to develop in the event of a further war. In Europe, Britain's position depended on a French army whose leaders were profoundly anti-Communist and determined to avoid a situation in which the French would once again take a beating such as they had suffered in the First World War.

The overall result was to leave the Soviet Union isolated. In isolation the Russians saw the progress of the British policy of appeasement and its fruit in German and Italian expansion – the re-occupation of the Rhineland, the conquest of Abyssinia (Ethiopia), the *Anschluss* with Austria, the dismemberment of Czechoslovakia, a neighbour of the Soviet Union on whose fate the Russians were not even consulted. The policy of collective security had not one success to chalk up. All the moderation of the Communists of France and Spain, even the damping down of colonial nationalisms, had made no difference. On each occasion that the Soviet Union proposed international action to deter aggression, or an international conference, as after the *Anschluss* and again after the final annexation of Czechoslovakia, it was shrugged off by the British.

Small wonder that Stalin felt justified in abandoning the quest for collective security, or any rapprochement with the West. In March 1939 he diagnosed the attitude of the Western powers in terms of contempt! Their policy, he said, was tantamount to saying: 'Let every country defend itself against the aggressor as it will and can, our interest is not at stake, we shall bargain with the aggressors and with their victims'. But Stalin did not at once translate this discouraging diagnosis into practical politics. The switch, in the years immediately before and after Hitler's assumption of power, from Germany and Rapallo to the Western powers and the League, had been prepared most gradually, with every line of retreat covered and every line of advance carefully prospected. Similarly, it was only with the utmost caution that the decision was now taken to turn away from the West and seek an accommodation with Hitler.

The first very tentative move in this direction seems to go back to September 1938, at the climax of the Munich crisis. Stalin was scared by Munich and the whole policy of appeasement, seeing in it an encouragement to Hitler to turn his armies against Russia. It was then that *Pravda* suddenly tarred the democracies and the Fascist states with the same brush, declaring that the Soviet Union saw 'no difference between German and English robbers'. But it was not until August 1939, almost a year later, that the irrevocable decision was taken to yield to German remonstrances, to co-operate in the fourth partition of Poland, and thus to unleash the Second World War. In the meantime, the reluctance, not to say refusal, of the British government to enter into any alliance with Russia had become manifest. After the German occupation of Prague there had been the rejection of the Soviet proposal for a conference at Bucharest; then there had been the British guarantee to Poland without provision for further approach to the Soviet government; finally, there had been the inability of the Anglo-French military mission to Moscow to tackle the question of how

Russia might help Poland. But the Soviet government, Stalin later told Churchill, was 'sure' that a mere diplomatic line-up of Britain, France, and Russia would not restrain Hitler. Such an agreement would need teeth.

As late as the beginning of August 1939, Schulenburg, the German Ambassador to Moscow, was reporting to Berlin that it would take a 'considerable effort on our part to cause the Soviet government to swing about'. Helped in part by the Japanese army, Schulenburg's efforts were sufficient. Perhaps they did not, by this time, have to be so considerable. On the night of 23–4 August, Molotov and Ribbentrop finally concluded the agreement that protected Hitler's rear for the imminent war against Poland and 'bought in' the Soviet government as his collaborators by sharing with them in the partition of Eastern Europe.

It was now that the centralization of the world Communist movement became most obviously counter-productive. From Stalin's point of view it would have been ideal if he could have made his pact with Hitler while the Western Communists continued to build up resistance to Fascism in Europe. Unlike Roosevelt, however, Hitler was not to be fooled about the true relations between Moscow and the Communist parties and he demanded that they engage in defeatist propaganda in France and Britain. This enabled the French government to proscribe the Communist Party and imprison its leaders; there they waited for the Gestapo. In Britain, the government suppressed the *Daily Worker*. Several hundred European Communists exiled in Russia were handed over to the Gestapo as a goodwill gesture.

In return for Soviet quiescence in the East and the offer of naval facilities to the German fleet, Stalin acquired the right to treat a zone on the western borders of the Soviet Union as he saw fit. His first move was to assert a military protectorate over the Baltic republics. He then demanded that the Finns cede him a strip of land in Karelia and a number of islands in the Gulf of Finland. Despite the moderate advice of Mannerheim, the Finnish government refused to make any concessions. They had built strong defences in Karelia and had no confidence that, if they handed them over, they would not be occupied just as the Czechs had been. Kuusinen now felt his moment of glory had arrived and persuaded Stalin to recognize his 'government' in the occupied village of Terijoki, as the true government of Finland.

He immediately called on the Red Army to 'liberate' Finland from the bourgeoisie. At the same time, the Finnish Communists were urged to revolt. But the Red Finns of 1918 had been educated by collectivization and the purges in Russia and, with the exception of the party cadres, there was no disloyalty. Even more humiliating was the poor showing of the Red Army which took such a long job to break the Finns that there was a real risk of Anglo-French intervention on behalf of Finland. The League of Nations, from which Japan, Germany, and Italy had withdrawn, now found the courage to denounce Soviet aggression. By March 1940, the Finns were forced to sue for peace. They had lost a tenth of their territory and a tenth of their population was evacuated to avoid falling under Soviet rule. Kuusinen's 'government' was forgotten. With the alarming success of Hitler's armies in Scandinavia and the Netherlands in the spring of 1940, Stalin decided that he had better gobble up what remained to him quickly while Hitler was still busy in the West. The Baltic states begged to be admitted to the Soviet Union and Romania handed over Bessarabia, which was provided for in the German–Soviet pact, and Bukovina, which was not.

This latter strongly suggests that the Soviet Union did not have a great deal of confidence in the German ally – which was indeed the case. And this uneasiness was in fact considerably strengthened when the first of Stalin's major miscalculations became manifest with the precipitate fall of France. Comintern policy had not helped morale, of course, and the continuing hostility of the French Communists towards the 'imperialist war' allowed General de Gaulle to become the unchallenged leader of resistance after June 1940. Stalin had considerably overestimated French strength. It had been no part of his policy that Germany should so soon be freed from active campaigning in the West. On the contrary, he had hoped for, if not banked on, a much more protracted German involvement far from the Russian frontier. This would have given Russia a correspondingly protracted breathing-space to prepare for the probable struggle ahead.

The consequence, therefore, was an outbreak of Russo-German

friction immediately after the fall of France in the summer of 1940. But it did not reach its climax until November 1940. In a Berlin air-raid shelter, to which Churchill had helpfully driven the negotiators, the issues were defined and the incompatible long-term interests of the two allies made manifest. Their disputes turned largely on a classical source of Russo-Teutonic disharmony – the Balkans and south-east Europe. This was precisely the area where the basis had been laid for the outbreak of the First World War. Was Bulgaria, for example, in the Russian sphere of influence or not? This was one of the critical questions raised by Molotov, Stalin's stony-faced broker of realpolitik, to the sound of exploding British bombs. Hitler, on the other hand, preferred to talk of the 'warm seas' of the Indian Ocean and slices of 'Greater Asia' in a general endeavour to divert Russia away from Europe and eastwards into conflict with the British. But Molotov was more concerned with what would happen *before* the British Empire was partitioned. There was not only Bulgaria; there was Finland, from which Molotov proposed Germany must withdraw her troops; there were the Dardanelles, where Russia desired to establish land and naval bases; there was 'the area south of Batum and Baku in the general direction of the Persian Gulf [which must be] recognized as the centre of gravity of the aspirations of the Soviet Union'.

All this far outstripped German willingness. Hard on the heels of these abortive negotiations followed Hitler's instructions for Operation Barbarossa: 'the German Armed Forces must be prepared to crush Soviet Russia in a quick campaign even before the conclusion of the war against England'. Until the last minute, Stalin refused to give credence to the rumours and made every attempt to patch things up with the Germans. Had Hitler been a more rational individual, things might have turned out differently. When the attack finally came, Stalin was taken totally by surprise. Soviet dissidents have alleged with some plausibility that his surprise was partly due to his conviction that Soviet and German society were developing along broadly similar totalitarian lines and that this made them logical partners for future collaboration. They cite Stalin's assumption of the Premiership as evidence that he was about to embark on a series of personal meetings with his fellow leader of a kind that might ensure a lasting totalitarian peace, 'a century of great darkness', as the ex-Communist Chen Tu-hsiu put it.

Following the German invasion of Russia, the Comintern made its final turn. It was now the sacred duty of Communists everywhere to join in the struggle of the 'freedom-loving nations'. And join in they did. They joined the Allied Armies, they encouraged the colonial peoples and those in Latin America to support the Allies, they fought in the hills of France, Italy and Yugoslavia, and in the jungles of Viet Nam and Indonesia. Everywhere, the military emergency brought out those qualities of energy, loyalty, bravery, and discipline for which the Communists were justly famed, securing them a prestige and influence far greater than anything won by their propaganda. Two years later the Comintern was abolished. As Stalin put it:

> The dissolution of the Communist International is proper and timely because it facilitates the organization of the common onslaught of all freedom-loving nations against the common enemy – Hitlerism.

In a remarkable valedictory, the E.C.C.I. had admitted that the Comintern 'has even become a drag on the further strengthening of the national working-class parties'.

The dissolution of the Comintern came not before time. It is typical that it was dissolved by Stalin with the purely formal consultation of the E.C.C.I. itself (let alone foreign Communist Parties). Some indication of its degeneration is given by the dates of its Congresses: 1919, 1920, 1921, 1922, 1924, 1928, 1935. Between 1935 and its dissolution the 'parliament' of world Communism never met once. Stalin's own attitude towards it was revealed by his reference to it as a 'shaky enterprise', and a saying of the early thirties that 'one Soviet tractor is worth more than ten good foreign Communists' sums up the feelings of his followers. It had failed desperately in its principal task, the recruitment of the proletariat of the advanced capitalist countries. Between 1921 and 1931 the membership of the Comintern outside Russia had fallen from nearly 900,000 to around 330,000. Even the defeats of 1944–5 did not bring back the German Communists lost in the triumph of Nazism. Within the parties of the Comintern, each twist of policy provided an opportunity for a quasi-monastic discipline of informing on fellow members and emotional self-criticism. But if this helped to keep the cadres loyal to the myth of the Russian revolution, the rank-and-file were characterized by something of the 'fluidity' of which Stalin complained in quite a different context. The result was a party in which only the cadres had any memory, a party lacking in precisely that accumulation of theory and experience without which a Communist Party is a merely bureaucratic phenomenon. This was not just Stalin's fault. It was Leon Trotsky who advised that the cohesion of the Central Committee of the French Communist Party would be improved if one-third of its members were full-time Party functionaries. When, in 1927, the Communist parties prided themselves on denouncing Trotsky's views without having read them, they were committing themselves to blind obedience to Stalin's wishes. With the increasing authoritarianism of the movement after 1928, there was a tendency for defectors to move right across the political spectrum towards Fascism, e.g. Doriot in France and Sano and Nabeyama in Japan. The invariable use of scapegoats induced cynicism and even hatred among ex-members of the party who might have been quite happy to function as allies. All this induced paralysis in those who remained. As General Walter (Swierczewski) told a British volunteer in Spain:

Look at Heiner, look at Richard. They will never be good soldiers. Why? They are not afraid to die. Not afraid of fascists. They are undoubtedly able people. But they are afraid of one thing. They go about in deadly fear of losing their party card. That is all they can think of and it paralyses them.

The influence of the Comintern on Communists, ex-Communists, and even anti-Communists in socialist circles throughout the world is still incalculable. So far from ceasing with the demise of the Comintern, it has increased as older socialists, for whom ethics had a certain autonomy, have been replaced by younger socialists for whom ethics cannot be seen in isolation from the class struggle, and for whom Lenin's party is still the ideal model.

The history of the attempt of the Russian Communists to control the world socialist movement through the Comintern was therefore a terrible failure. It would be wrong to leave it at that. The power of the Comintern rested on the need of millions of people throughout the world to believe in a secular paradise which would justify their present sufferings. For western intellectuals and workers, peasants in China and Viet Nam, the newly literate of the colonial countries, and for all those threatened directly by Fascism, the Soviet Union spelled hope. This hope gave them tremendous élan and energy. As Jimmy Lane, a young militant of the twenties, said later:

It was a very exhilarating period particularly for us youngsters in that 20–22 age group. You've got to remember that the Russian revolution had only occurred nine years before, in 1917, and that is why we felt that the revolution was just round the corner. Our whole life was based on the fact that capitalism was on its way out and before long we would be in the forefront of a new world which we were going to usher in.

This worker lived in Battersea, London, where proletarian internationalism was sufficient of a reality for Saklatvala, an Indian Communist, to gain election to Parliament in those years. Richard Wright, the American writer, found himself treated like a human being for the first time by white people, when he went along to Communist meetings. When Paul Robeson, the great black American artist, arrived in Russia in 1935, he said: 'In Soviet Russia I breathe freely for the first time in my life'. In May 1941, E. M. Winterton could still write:

The Soviet Union stands aside from the imperialist struggles, towering amid the warring states like a different world. Tranquil strength, peaceful constructive work, cultural, intellectual and moral progress shine out from its frontiers like a beacon.

The moral fervour of Communism was maintained by a succession of martyrdoms and examples of resistance. Luxemburg, Liebknecht, Gramsci, and Thälmann inspired their comrades long after they were removed from active politics. As late as 1944, the Gestapo liquidated an underground German Communist organization, executing 400 of them. Even within the Auschwitz concentration camp, there was a Communist–Socialist resistance organization led by Józef Cyrankiewicz, future Prime Minister and President of Poland. In Sakai prison, Osaka, Matsumoto Sōichirō defied innumerable beatings and refused to bow towards the Imperial Palace as all the other prisoners did every morning. But would all this have been possible had they known what is now known about Soviet socialism?

CHAPTER 20

The War and the Cold War

The new society shaped by Stalin and his imitators was now subjected to the ultimate test of invasion by the most powerful, barbarous, and efficient military machine ever seen in European history. When the Red flag at last flew over the Reichstag building in Berlin in May 1945, the Russians experienced an unforgettable moment of euphoria, but this was short-lived. The regime now found itself in competition with America at the height of its power and self-confidence. However far-fetched it may seem to us, many Russians perceived these events as successive challenges from 'the West'. The nature of these two challenges dictated very different responses. To Hitler, the Slavs were 'sub-humans' and no match for his 'master race'. He succeeded in recruiting some support among the national minorities and even the Russian General Vlasov and his army. These were the exceptions. It was the brutality of the German armies that ensured the success of Stalin's patriotic appeals to the Russian people. The war brought the Russian government and the Russian people together and gave Soviet power a legitimacy it had never yet enjoyed. In relating how the security organs had come to him in the night during the war and 'I was not afraid', a contemporary Jewish 'dissident' explains 'it was not *their* war, but *our* war'. It is no accident that Leonid Brezhnev began his memoirs not with collectivization, nor with the five-year plans, but with his war service. Mohamed Heikal, one of the most privileged observers of Soviet government since the war, describes it as 'far and away the most memorable period in the lives of the present generation of Soviet leadership'.

Between June and December 1941, the Red Army suffered one military disaster after another. In the initial rout, immense armies were surrounded and smashed, together with the air force and Baltic fleet. Pasternak wrote that 'autumn was advancing in the steps of calamity' but the Soviet people, now deprived of private radio sets, had to make do with hints about the 'direction' of the

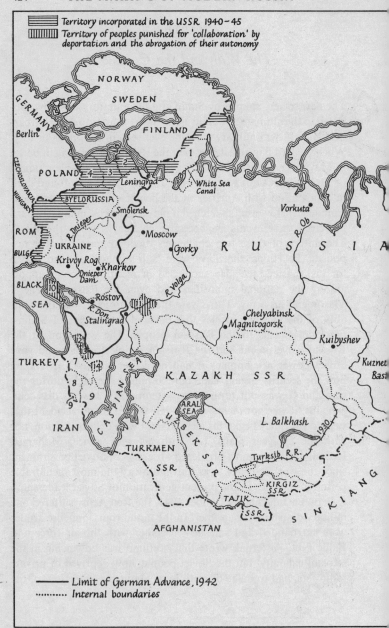

Territory incorporated in the USSR 1940–45

Territory of peoples punished for 'collaboration' by deportation and the abrogation of their autonomy

NORWAY

SWEDEN

GERMANY

Berlin

FINLAND

1

CZECHOSLOVAKIA

HUNGARY

POLAND   4   3   2

Leningrad

White Sea Canal

BYELORUSSIA

Smolensk

Vorkuta

R. Ob

ROM

BULG

UKRAINE

R. Dnieper

Moscow

R U S S I A

Krivoy Rog

Dnieper Dam

Kharkov

Gorky

BLACK SEA

Rostov

R. Don

Stalingrad

R. Volga

Chelyabinsk

Magnitogorsk

Kuibyshev

Kuznet Basi

TURKEY   7

8

9

9   9

CASPIAN SEA

K A Z A K H   S S R

ARAL SEA

L. Balkhash

1930

IRAN

TURKMEN SSR

U Z B E K   S S R

Turksib R.R.

KIRGIZ SSR

S I N K I A N G

TAJIK SSR

AFGHANISTAN

———— Limit of German Advance, 1942

··········· Internal boundaries

6. The Soviet Union 1930–50

1. Karelo-Finnish SSR
2. Estonian SSR
3. Latvian SSR
4. Lithuanian SSR
5. Kaliningrad Region
6. Moldavian SSR
7. Georgian SSR
8. Armenian SSR
9. Azerbaijan SSR
10. Crimean Tatar ASSR
11. Volga-German ASSR
12. Karachaev-Cherkessian Autonomous Region
13. Chechen-Ingush ASSR
14. Kabardino-Balkar ASSR
15. Jewish Autonomous Region

0   500   1000 Miles

German armies. 'A few days ago, our troops withdrew from Smolensk' was an ominous epitaph on an action in August that turned rout into orderly withdrawal. Despite this, by Christmas 1941 the German armies stood before the gates of Leningrad and Moscow; Rostov and Kharkov were already in their hands. Gone were the Baltic states, Belorussia, the Ukraine, and much of the Russian interior. Perhaps four million fighting men were lost while 65 million civilians faced the tragic choice of treason, passive collaboration, or death. Russia now had to face war and winter without the Dnieper industrial complex and the Ukrainian granary. For millions of Soviet citizens, this is a disaster that can never be forgotten. To this very day it may determine their status, or lack of it, in society; former prisoners or collaborators still find their careers and social standing affected. The questions it prompts still nag: why was the Red Army defeated? Could more lives have been saved if Leningrad and other cities had been properly evacuated? Whose fault was it? 'Damn you, year forty-one' wrote the poet Gudzenko, but for twenty years this line could not be published. Stalin knew what the trouble was. There must be 'wreckers'. General Pavlov of the Belorussian Military District and his staff were shot. With few exceptions, Soviet prisoners of war were regarded as traitors, then, and for many years after the war. It has to be said that Stalin was utterly consistent in this. When he discovered that his own son, Jacob, had been taken prisoner, he ordered the arrest of Jacob's wife 'to find out what was behind it'. Since Stalin's death it has become clear, not least from Soviet memoirs and military histories, that much of the blame for the early defeats lies with Stalin himself, and most of the rest with the system over which he presided.

Stalin personally made the crucial assumptions underlying Soviet military conduct in the summer of 1941. He had banked on a long war in the West and was unprepared for the rapid defeat of France. Misled perhaps by the prejudices against Jews and democrats that he shared with Hitler, Stalin hoped for a longer and more fruitful alliance with the Führer. His hostility to the Finnish Social Democrats pushed Finland to the Right and into the arms of the Germans during 1940–41, ensuring the total blockade of Leningrad during the 900 fearful days of siege. It was Stalin who wilfully disregarded the mass of precise information from anti-Nazi Germans, Soviet agents, and the Allied governments about the impending attack. He insisted that there should be no build-up of frontier forces, no German reconnaissance planes were to be shot down, even artillery fire must not be returned. Nothing was to be done to give Hitler a pretext for attack. The Generals were not allowed to prepare defensive tactics and the Soviet people were encouraged to believe that the German soldiers were just waiting for a chance to desert their Junker officers to join their class brothers in the Soviet Union. In 1937–8, it had been Stalin who ordered the execution and removal of tens of thousands of Red Army officers, including its ablest commanders. He knew the limitations of Voroshilov, Budyenny, and Timoshenko but he placed these ageing and discredited cavalrymen in command of the Army. The cynicism of his purge of the officers was revealed by the recall to the colours of former 'enemies of the people' such as Rokossovsky, Govorov, and Gorbatov who were now judged fit to command armies. Stalin's conduct did not cease to be dangerous once the war had begun. When he had recovered from his breakdowns of June and October 1941, he constantly harried his commanders, sending his trustees to spy on them, forcing them to fly through snow and fog to report to him in person, denying them authority and prestige. Like Hitler, he sacrificed men, at Stalingrad, Kharkov, and elsewhere, for reasons of prestige.

When Ehrenburg offered his propagandist services, Stalin's henchman, Shcherbakov, warned: 'Now don't you go being original . . .' The system with its tendency to promote blinkered loyalists and its discouragement of initiatives must be blamed for the failure of Soviet industry to make full use of the breathing space gained in 1939. At the outbreak of war, Russia's planes and tanks were too few and largely obsolete; she lacked vehicles and automatic rifles; her officers preferred the telephone to radio communication.

By 3 July 1941, Stalin had recovered sufficiently from the shock of invasion and retreat to be able to broadcast to his people. He spoke in a monotone, breathing heavily and stopping to sip water from time to time. Ironically, these very frailties lent him a humanity which impressed his listeners. There were traces of the Stalin they knew all too well, 'merciless struggle . . . against all deserters and panic mongers'. What remained in their memory, however, were his opening words: 'Comrades, citizens, brothers and sisters . . . I am speaking to you, my friends!' He had taken a first step towards policies of reconciliation and his listeners knew it. In Russia, as in England, the worst phase of the war made people desperately anxious for leadership and Stalin's words met this need. With the loss of the borderlands and the Ukraine, the war was becoming more and more Russian in character. To this day, it is the unarmed and ill-clad volunteers of 1941, the dying schoolchildren of Leningrad, the tank soldiers who saved Moscow, and the sappers in the ruins of Stalingrad that sum up the war for the Russians. Stalin had become thoroughly Russified himself and found the Russification of the war accorded with his own feelings. On the twenty-fourth anniversary of the revolution, to the sound of German guns, Stalin answered German insults to the Russian people with a Russian Pantheon of heroes that added Alexander Nevsky and Dmitri Donskoy to such progressive figures as Plekhanov and Lenin. The war also produced authentic new heroes. The war-leaders Zhukov, Rokossovsky, Konev, and Chuikov were no longer merely the creatures of the propaganda machine. During the summer of 1942, as the extent of Nazi atrocities became known, Simonov, Surkev, and Ehrenburg wrote hate propaganda about the Germans that was better literature, because more deeply felt, than people had known for some time. A kind of subterranean public opinion began to emerge. The politics of both national reconciliation and social stratification were reflected in the rehabilitation of the officer corps in 1942. Soviet officers now became independent of their political commissars; once more, even in disciplining other ranks, they were granted shoulder boards, special decorations and bound by a new code of etiquette that prohibited them from travelling on public transport. After just two weeks of war, atheist propaganda was suppressed and in 1942 the camps were scoured for Orthodox churchmen. In 1943, the Moscow Patriarchate was re-established, with its seminaries and journal. Bereaved mothers could now obtain the consolation of the liturgy. This was no one-way bargain. At the end of the war Metropolitan Nikolai Krutitsky thanked 'Our common father Joseph Vissarionovich'. and willingly joined in the suppression of the Uniate hierarchy in the re-united Ukraine. The Orthodox Church had resumed its traditional role as servant of the State; its bishops were now members of the Nomenklatura. For the Russians, however, the war inspired a rare unanimity. The immense courage, self-sacrifice, and capacity for responsibility shown by Russians in all walks of life induced a new mood of self-confidence and respect. As a Russian woman told Alexander Werth: 'For the first time in my life, I think we are a very great people, perhaps the greatest people in the world'.

The war is still the greatest folk memory of the Soviet people today. Every year on 9 May, Soviet citizens gather for the most unforced and spontaneous of all Soviet festivals, Victory Day. They gather in Brest, the scene of the early defeats, where an immense head, bowed but not broken, expresses the determination of the men who died in the fortress knowing that their deaths would make no practical difference. They gather before the painful monument to the starving civilians of Leningrad and remember those who suffered its 900 days of agony. They gather on the endless staircase that leads to the massive, triumphant figure of Winged Victory at Volgograd, once Stalingrad, to commemorate those who smashed the pride of the German Army. Wherever there is any place of special note, and in all major population centres, these monuments have grown up, the secular cathedrals of Soviet society. At the heart of each of them is an 'eternal flame',

... the fire of millions of hearts who have not faltered in battle, the fire of burning hatred towards the enemy and of boundless love towards the Motherland; the fire of faith in the great cause of Lenin which led our people to victory.

But the war did nothing to lighten the darker aspects of Soviet life. As before and since, these were assiduously protected from public scrutiny. At the very top, unscrupulous scheming still dominated politics. Malenkov and Beria seemed as concerned to discredit Zhdanov as to save Leningrad or the Second Strike Army that tried to rescue it. Zhdanov and his entourage continued to eat luxuriously in starving Leningrad and this was typical of the conduct of what Stalin himself called the 'damned caste' of the Nomenklatura. The N.K.V.D. continued its unsavoury operations in the rear. During 1940, they were busy dealing with the political and cultural elites of the Baltic countries and with the soldiers returning from their brief captivity in Finland. In 1941, they massacred all the 'enemies of the people' they could who might otherwise have been captured by the Germans. These included some 14,000 Polish officers and Maria Spiridonova, Lenin's left S.R. ally of 1917. At the beginning of the war they evacuated all the Soviet Germans they could lay their hands on, Communists and all, to desolate dugouts in the Kazakh steppe. As the German Army withdrew from the Caucasus and the Ukraine, whole peoples, the Crimean Tatars, Chechens, Meskhetians and others, were denounced as 'traitor peoples' and bundled off to starve in Central Asia with no regard to individual guilt, age, or sex. A special organization (S.M.E.R.S.H.) was established to shoot soldiers returning from German encirclement. Prisoners of war, on returning from Germany at the end of the war, were welcomed with flags, flowers, and bands. After the photographs had been taken, the politically doubtful were shot at once and the rest deported to camps.

In 1944 the N.K.V.D. troops at last saw real action against the Ukrainian partisans and the Polish Home Army. As the Red Army reached Eastern Europe, Stalin personally condoned rape and pillage inflicted by Soviet soldiers on enemy and Allied peoples alike. Once more, the uneasy memory of crimes committed left behind it a network of men with an interest in secrecy.

The conflict with America which began in 1946 was less difficult for the regime; it cast a shadow over the reconstruction of the country but did not seriously impede it. It had a military dimension in that, in 1945, American forces faced Soviet forces in Europe, the Middle East, and the Far East, and for several years thereafter the Americans had a monopoly of nuclear weapons. Unlike the traditional imperialisms of the Old World, the 'American Way of Life' competed with Soviet Communism in appealing to the common man and woman. It promised personal freedom and affluence to all and posed the greatest ideological challenge that Soviet power had ever faced. An impoverished and devastated Soviet state had little to answer with save austerity, hard labour, hysterical campaigns against 'cosmopolitanism' and a resumption of terror. Not until Stalin's death in 1953 did the Soviet leaders find a more sophisticated response to the challenge of the West.

In Russia, as in the West, post-war xenophobia was a natural reaction once exaggerated wartime enthusiasm for the allies was replaced by more sober assessments. The Russian people were immensely heartened by the promptness with which Churchill offered them an alliance in 1941, but Churchill was known to be both anti-Russian and anti-Communist and as the war went on this seemed a plausible explanation of his apparent dilly-dallying over the Second Front. The literary intelligentsia found the alliance with the Free French much more congenial, though this was unfortunately not of decisive military significance. It was the alliance with America, and Franklin Roosevelt personally, that evoked most enthusiasm. Very early in the war Young Communists, on seeing stills from American films for the first time, were moved to remark: 'Once Hitler's beaten, perhaps things will be different for us here too!' Apart from a dry statistical account of Land-Lease published after D-Day, the Soviet press played down American aid. This did not prevent Russian soldiers from noticing how much they relied on American vehicles nor from remarking, as they opened American foodstuffs, 'I'm opening the Second Front'. V.E. Day in Moscow witnessed spontaneous mass demonstrations of friendship outside the U.S. Embassy in Moscow. They would have been grateful to any allies, of course, but some of the enthusiasm undoubtedly sprang from the fact that they associated the Western Allies with democracy. The new-found courage of ordinary people had political significance. Even an enthusiastic Stalinist like A. N. Tolstoy could see it: 'People aren't the same', he muttered. They had learnt that they could think for themselves once more. So what did they think about the Hollywood films, the comfortable homes they saw as they liberated Eastern Europe, the news that trickled back to Leningrad in letters from New York? There is no reason to think that any of this weakened their patriotism; if anything German affluence filled them with cold hatred for those who, owning so much themselves had yet been greedy for the meagre personal wealth of the Russians. In the West Ukraine and the Baltic territories, the remnants of a capitalist class survived, but few Russians had any reason to want the heights of the economy returned to capitalism. Among the peasantry, the desire to see the collective farms abandoned was probably much greater.

Politically the most important common thread was an awareness that they had been deceived by their leaders: working people 'pauperized by capitalism' were richer than the working class of the 'workers' state'. They wanted, if not full democracy, at least greater openness and tolerance in government and less austerity. Most people exonerated Stalin from the crimes and stupidities of the pre-war years, blaming the 'sycophants' around him, but the more perceptive noted grimly that 'he hasn't changed either . . .' Much later, after the death of Marshal Zhukov, Brodsky would catch the tragic paradox of the soldiers who 'marching triumphant through foreign cities, shook with cold terror when they came home'.

The Nomenklatura itself was fully aware of these feelings and had expressed its concern about them in the party press during the war. They remembered how the Russian conquerors of Napoleon in 1814 had become the Decembrist conspirators of 1825; they knew that tolerance in the Western borderlands was incompatible with the transformation of society in those areas; they knew that openness in Russia itself was incompatible with their regime of power and privilege. As Churchill rightly observed, 'they fear our friendship more than our enmity'. They continued to hold a monopoly of power and they proceeded to show it. Popular generals and writers were removed from public view, marriages with foreigners (even citizens of 'socialist countries') were banned, rules for admission to the party were tightened up, and critics of Stalin (like Alexander Solzhenitsyn) were packed off to the camps. In a speech in 1946, in which he sounded confident about international relations, Stalin disabused those who thought he might have mellowed during the war. Everything done in the past had been correct, he insisted: collectivization, industrialization, the purges and the conduct of the war. 'Our social system has won . . . our *political* system has won.'

The most important task facing Russia in 1945 was that of reconstruction. Where were the resources to come from? The Americans cut off Land-Lease immediately the fighting stopped, causing financial crisis in Britain and shortage in Russia. Despite this chilling experience, both government and people in the Soviet Union continued to hope for American financial assistance. Such hopes were tempered by an awareness that even had Roosevelt lived on, American capitalists might have baulked at rebuilding Communism. A sympton of American attitudes was the apportionment of U.N.R.R.A. aid to Poland which received $400m whereas the Ukraine, with a larger population, only received $180m. Another source of aid that proved disappointing was reparations. The Allies soon cut off reparations from Western Germany to Russia. Extracting reparations from Eastern Germany and Manchuria, conquered from the Japanese in the summer war of 1945, proved a handicap in developing friendly relations with the local peoples. Until 1956, however, the Russians did exploit their power for economic advantage in these areas but this was not sufficient to restore the shattered economy without inflicting serious privations on the Soviet people. As before, priority for investment went into heavy industry, electrification, and communications. The Western territories liberated from the Germans were to be restored to their pre-war level of activity but the hinterland, the Volga, Urals, and Siberian regions must be transformed. Stalin looked forward to 'a situation where our industry can produce annually up to fifty million tons of pig iron, up to sixty million tons of steel, up to 500 million tons of coal, and up to sixty million tons of oil'. Only then did Stalin consider that Russia could be 'guaranteed against all possible accidents'. In fact these targets were all achieved by, or soon after Stalin's death, together with the production of the 'workers' bomb' in 1949. By 1950, Russia had become the world's second industrial power.

This economic 'Resurrection', as Brezhnev has justly called it, demanded the utmost in sweat and tears from managers, engineers, and workers. Considering what the Russian people had already endured, it was as remarkable an achievement as anything in Soviet history.

Stalin believed that the peasantry could still be exploited in the interests of industrialization, although many of the demobilized peasant soldiers never returned to the land after the war. In justifying the abolition of private agriculture in the Ukraine Belorussia, and the Baltic states, the Central Committee claimed that 'thanks to the kolkhoz system the Soviet Union has become the country of advanced agriculture'. Not until 1968 was Fyodor Abramov finally permitted to describe what life was really like in a kolkhoz just after the war. The almost entirely female work-force had been subjected to ruthless exploitation, forced to sub-scribe to the Victory loan and forced to pay taxes in kind on livestock and fruit trees.

The abolition of food rationing was promised for 1947. It was preceded by a currency 'reform' that virtually confiscated private savings, removed the profits of black-marketeers and private traders under the Germans, and ensured that the re-distribution of the social product was wholly restored to the planning system controlled by the Nomenklatura. Prices were stabilized for con-sumer goods but they remained in very short supply. The 1946 Plan set aside substantial resources for housing but most of this went on rehousing the twenty-five million people still living in dugouts at the end of the war. The low priority that local bosses, harried for maximum coal and steel outputs, gave to housing led to atrocious communal housing conditions. Extended families often occupied single rooms and fought for their turn in the kit-chens and bathrooms they shared with the whole block. The edu-cational effort of the regime never slackened, on the other hand, and with gratifying results for the health, welfare, and cultural life of the people. Between 1940 and 1958, the number of people with secondary specialist education rose from one and a half million to four and a half million, the number of graduates from one million to three million and the number of doctors from one hundred and fifty thousand to five hundred and fifty-four thousand.

The dramatic upheavals that shook the Nomenklatura between 1936 and 1945 had removed those Old Bolsheviks to whom Marx-ist ideals mattered more than power and privilege. The N.K.V.D. even took hostages from the families of Kalinin, Molotov, and Mikoyan to test the loyalty of the highest in the land. On the other hand, the disgrace of Yezhov, officially blamed for all the innocent blood spilt in the thirties, took place without any public fuss. He was not forced to confess to anything and it is not even certain he was executed. Nor did his family suffer as so many others did for the sins of their relatives. Some commentators have claimed that the purges proved that the Nomenklatura could not be a ruling class. This is not convincing; no one has yet suggested that Ivan the Terrible abolished feudalism just because he purged the boyars. Still, no ruling group can enjoy a situation in which it lacks personal security. Stalin had sought not a class structure, but a command structure: for him, the 3–4,000 leading officials were 'generals' and so on. He clearly despised behaviour reminiscent of that of a ruling class or caste. Yet, at the same time, he saw that they received the differential rewards that made his system run, the *payoks* and extra allowances in plain envelopes. (There are suggestions that the latter practice was a form of suspended blackmail, since anyone objecting to privilege could be shown to have taken unofficial payments.) The system of privilege existing in the Soviet Union was introduced in exactly the same form in Eastern Europe after the war, where it provoked some disgruntled comment among local socialists. Here is how it was described by Wolfgang Leonhard, one of its beneficiaries:

There was also an exact gradation of rank in the distribution of the famous *payoks*, those great parcels of food, cigarettes, tobacco, drinks and chocolate which we received regularly in addition to our ration cards and our meals at the Central Committee. These *payoks* were not only for middle-grade and senior Party officials, but also for officials in the Government and economic administration, as well as for scientists, specialists, poets and artists; but they were on a sharply graduated scale. Everything depended on the function of the recipient and whether he was a V.I.P.

Another kind of insight into the social structure of Stalin's Russia and the values it cultivated is provided by the official literature of the time. The use of literature as a substitute for honest communication between government and people had begun in the thirties. It gained immensely in significance during the war but it was in the post-war period that such literature gained a virtual monopoly of permitted discussion of sensitive matters affecting the everyday lives of the population. Much of this literature was escapist for the majority since it described as normal the lifestyles of members of the Nomenklatura or cultural elite. It did not discuss the lives of poor collective farmers nor the lives of

Politburo members. Yet the themes it dealt with had much wider resonance. There was a gentle mocking at the kind of proletarian pride that does not seek self-improvement, at the kind of Old Bolshevik egalitarianism that does not seek material reward, at the kind of feminism that eschews the 'double burden', the cultivation of femininity and the massaging of male morale. What survived has been called 'vestigial and systemic *meshchanstvo*', a petty-bourgeois acquisitiveness compounded of old matriarchal dreams of domestic decency and the materialism of Nomenklaturists whose appetites were sharpened by their insecurity. In the words of the sociologist critic, Vera Dunham:

> The former went on craving for sweets and pink lampshades. The latter craved affluence braced by power . . . Stalinist fiction abounds with emotional scenes in which peasant mothers, wearing humble black aprons, with their hair pulled tight into primordial knots, hands and faces weather-beaten, visit their V.I.P. sons. They either bask in their sons' glory or, on occasion, needle them. And the sons, having arrived, refurbish meshchanstvo from strength, as a gift to their worn-out mothers.

Thus, the post-war Nomenklaturists had a quite different view of the sources of political deviation from that of their predecessors. As Leonid Brezhnev puts it, with characteristic insensitivity:

> . . . any man with no love for the mother who gave him life, who fed and brought him up, strikes me personally as suspect. It is not for nothing that people speak of the Motherland. The person who can abandon and forget his mother will also be a bad son of the Motherland.

The political history of post-war Russia remains very obscure. Stalin's advancing age and indifferent health intensified the struggle amongst his potential successors. Malenkov and Beria were still doing their utmost to discredit Zhdanov. In the summer of 1946 they insinuated that Zhdanov had been guilty of a lack of ideological vigilance. Zhdanov responded by unleashing a pogrom against 'degenerate' trends in Russian culture, claiming to defend it against 'kow-towing' to the West. At a poetry recital in Moscow that summer, a predominantly young audience cheered Pasternak and Akhmatova but gave a cold reception to 'approved' poets. The party's cultural bosses and their informers traced the source of this ideological pollution to the editorial boards of two Len-

ingrad literary journals. Since the boards had been approved by
Zhdanov, it was clear he must do something drastic to save his
position. He accepted the criticism and tore into two Leningrad
writers, the novelist and journalist Zoshchenko and the poetess
Akhmatova. The phrase he used of Akhmatova, 'not exactly a
nun, not exactly a whore, but half nun and half whore . . .', has
stuck in the craw of the Russian literary intelligentsia ever since.
In Soviet politics, counter-attack is often the best form of defence.
Having disposed of the literature of individual emotions, Zhdanov
now attacked the history of philosophy written by Alexandrov, a
Malenkov protégé, who had fallen 'captive of bourgeois historians'. He also used this opportunity to attack Sartre and Einstein,
progressive western intellectuals opposed to the Cold War, who
enjoyed great popularity among the Russian intelligentsia. The
campaign against 'kow-towing' reached its zenith in 1948, the year
when East and West finally split irrevocably. Again, Zhdanov
orchestrated the efforts of the charlatans and the envious medio-
crities. Thus, Trofim Lysenko, the vitalist for whom genetics was
a 'bourgeois pseudo-science', and Tikhon Khrennikov, who criticized Shostakovich, Prokofiev, Miaskovsky, and Khachaturian
for their 'formalism', became tsars of biology and music. The
party continued to proscribe cybernetics, empirical sociology, and
non-Pavlovian psychology. The prominence given to claims that
nineteenth-century Russian scientists such as Tsiolkovsky and
Popov had discovered rocketry and radio were cited as proof that
the Soviet Union could do without Western bourgeois expertise, a
message calculated to flatter the masses and stifle the doubts of
the intelligentsia. Criminal sanctions were not forgotten either. It
became a crime to listen to foreign radio stations; they were also
jammed, just in case. As for Andrei Zhdanov, his work done, he
fell ill or was poisoned and died in August 1948. His rivals came to
Leningrad and removed his immediate supporters, more fodder
for the GULAG.

'Zhdanovism' has certain similarities with the 'McCarthyism'
that followed it in the U.S.A. Both discredited domestic opposi-
tions by associating them with foreign subversion. Both left a
swath of ruined lives and cultural impoverishment. But the developments that followed 'Zhdanovism' in the Soviet Union

claimed many more victims than those claimed by xenophobic hysteria in the U.S.A. The nature of Stalin's antisemitism is open to debate. Unlike Hitler, he always had Jews about him and he allowed his relatives to marry Jews. Jewish Stalinists served him loyally in the N.K.V.D. and elsewhere. On the other hand, he did not hide his own antisemitic prejudices. These became public in the routine caricatures of 'rootless cosmopolitans' with prominent noses and 'Jewish' surnames in brackets which appeared in the late forties and early fifties. Jews had been spared the attention of Zhdanov so far, partly because of the sensitivities of Western socialists and partly because Zionism had brought relatively progressive social forms to the Middle East, and individual Jews had largely created the Middle Eastern Communist parties. Moreover, in the United Nations debates of 1947–8, Gromyko, the Soviet representative, enthusiastically encouraged the emergence of Jewish statehood in Israel.

But when Golda Meir, the first Israeli Ambassador to the Soviet Union, visited the Moscow Synagogue in 1948, Russian Jews gave her an enthusiastic welcome. This was disturbing particularly as it soon became obvious that Zionism meant 'capitulation' to the Americans. It was now intolerable that the Jews should continue to transmit ideological contamination, just because they had relatives and sympathies abroad, at a time when such contacts were being denied to Russian intellectuals.

In December 1948 the Jewish Anti-Fascist Committee was dissolved. At the beginning of 1949 the Supreme Soviet restored the death penalty, in response to popular demand, so it was said. The first to be shot were Jewish 'wreckers' in the Stalin motor works. Later that year Stalin's senior economist, N. Voznesensky, and another senior politician were shot. Neither was Jewish but evidently the re-imposition of totalitarianism was to be no respecter of persons. For those with Jewish wives already inside, like Molotov, or at liberty, like Voroshilov, the end of the game did not look attractive. They knew Stalin better than anyone. A despot always envies those who promise to survive him. It seems possible that they refused to act out their allotted roles and denounce one another. Instead they tried to consolidate their position by foisting Party Congress on Stalin so that they might be re-elected to the

Politburo. Stalin played games with them all, upstaging the Congress with his publication of *Economic Problems of Socialism in the U.S.S.R.,* replacing the small Politburo with a large Presidium to dilute the oligarchs' power, intervening in arcane disputes about linguistics and posing as the protector of the Jews.

Stalin had once called on his supporters not to attack his rivals on the grounds that they were all Jews. According to senior party members his tactics on this occasion were equally cynical. 'Many cases of hooligan attacks on worthy Jews have been reported,' he told the Politburo in 1952. 'I think, comrades, that we must save our Jews, protect them. It would be better to re-settle all of them away from Moscow and Leningrad in a safe place.' Inevitably, the minister deputed to compile the list of worthy Jews was Kaganovich, himself a Jew. Camps were prepared in Birobidzhan, the Jewish Autonomous S.S.R. on the Chinese frontier. Some years later Khrushchev found these camps unfit for grain storage. The oligarchs still failed to denounce one another. At the end of January 1953, *Pravda* announced the discovery of a 'terrorist group of doctors', mostly Jews. They were accused of the murder of Shcherbakov and Zhdanov, and of trying to kill Stalin and a series of generals. Dr Lydia Timashuk, the Kremlin radiologist who had 'discovered' the plot, was awarded the Order of Lenin. There was some logic in the choice of doctors as victims of Stalin's last purge; they were indeed failing to win his last battle. Still, Beria must have trembled; Yagoda had been only four years behind while he was at least eight. He knew the price of failure and he had failed to discover the plot himself. The anxieties of the heirs were only removed when, on 2 March 1953, the old tyrant was found dead at his dacha.

Stalin's last years were probably something of an anti-climax. He even walked out of the celebrations for his own seventieth birthday. He had long since defeated all the enemies that really mattered, while Mao's victory in China indicated that his days of sole leadership of the Communist movement were numbered. The fear he emanated turned his companions to stone and there was an undertone of sadism to the drunken parties he forced them to endure. His daughter recalls that 'he saw enemies everywhere. It had reached the point of being pathological, of persecution mania, and it was all a result of being lonely and desolate'. The despot who peoples the world with real enemies is finally indistinguishable from the paranoid schizophrenic whose world is inhabited by imaginary ones. Deranged or not, Stalin remains a towering figure in world history. He had galvanized the forces that built a new form of society, presided over an ultimately triumphant war, and by careful diplomacy had made Russia the second greatest power on earth. He had destroyed the country ways, thrown down old gods, decimated muzhiks and mullahs, priests and intellectuals, engineers and writers. He died as he had lived, a remote, cruel deity, but for many, a deity all the same. Despite the intermittent efforts of his successors, it will be a long time before the world is free of the terrible spell cast by Joseph Stalin.

CHAPTER 21

Leaders and Dissidents

Stalin's immediate heirs soon showed that they were unable to rule by terror and unfit to represent any higher rationality. His own paranoia had seen to it that they were among the most ill-educated, xenophobic and mutually suspicious group ever to hold power in a major industrial state. It is only fair to add that several of them quickly showed that they were aware of their own deficiencies. The 'Doctors' Plot' had threatened them all but the sigh of relief they breathed at Stalin's death was brief. Now they saw threats in one another. Above all, they feared Lavrentii Beria, head of the M.V.D. (the former N.K.V.D.). For four months, in the spring and early summer of 1953, vital decisions on future policy were subordinated to the overriding need they all felt to save their skins. In denouncing the 'Doctors' Plot', Beria had intended to regain control of the security organs, not discredit them. Yet the public denunciation of this provocation fatally undermined the logic of twenty-five years of propaganda. If some 'enemies of the people' were victims of slander, why not others?

Apparently, it was Nikita Khrushchev who mustered the courage to call in Zhukov and the army to arrest Beria in June 1953. For once roles were reversed as Army generals arrested and executed the leaders of the security organs. But when political prisoners started to call the M.V.D. men 'Beria-ites' and loose tongues began to wag throughout the land, the Nomenklatura was perplexed. They had not intended to dispense with the security organs entirely. Now they would have to legitimize their position and policies by appealing to rationality. This meant paying more attention to the views of the technocrats, but what would they demand in return? And how far should the intelligentsia as a whole be permitted to enter public debate and influence the 'general line'?

Under Nikita Khrushchev, the Leader from 1957 to 1964, the Nomenklatura was itself deeply divided on the answers to these questions; Khrushchev was driven to demagogic posturing which raised more hopes than it could hope to satisfy. Not that this brash and garrulous man required much driving. Since 1970, Leonid Brezhnev has presided over a more cohesive and competent ruling group. He has integrated the technocrats, both civil and military, by the generous use of privileges and material rewards while inhibiting them from the exercise of corporate power. The rest of the intelligentsia has been brought to heel. They have been inhibited from entering an open debate on policy by an increasingly scientific array of incentives and disincentives. Nothing illustrates this better than the success of the government in transforming foreign contacts, so feared by Stalin, into carrots proffered to obedient members of the intelligentsia. Throughout the period since Stalin's death, the leadership has attempted to recruit a representative cadre of workers, including members of national minorities, into the party. An army of wives and children of the ruling group seek, on the contrary, to become a hereditary class, thereby denying the working-class party members promotion to the Nomenklatura and threatening the legitimacy of the regime.

In 1953 *Pravda* carried articles extolling 'collective leadership'; by the end of 1957, Khrushchev had expelled all his rivals from the Party Presidium. In 1964 *Pravda* carried articles extolling 'collective leadership'; by 1970, Leonid Brezhnev had achieved the leading position in the Politburo. This repetition is not likely to be accidental though the forthcoming dispute over the succession to Leonid Brezhnev may change our views.

To begin with, it shows that the Soviet regime, like its every subdivision, requires 'one-man management' (*yedinonachaliye*). It is interesting to note that, on both occasions, the successful contender defeated a figure closely associated with the central planning organs of the economy. The failures, Georgi Malenkov and Alexei Kosygin, might have been expected to articulate the views of the managerial technocrats. Their failure indicates that direct supervision of the process of re-distribution does not in itself confer predominance within the ruling group. Both Khrushchev and Brezhnev were associated with the central party apparatus. They were also the contenders with the widest experience, particularly of dealing with the non-Russian nationalities of the Soviet

Union. Their victories were certainly victories of the party over the State machine. At every level in society it is the party secretary who draws up agendas, drafts resolutions and reports, makes the keynote speech, selects or rejects candidates for party membership and posts in the Nomenklatura. From the late 1930s, Stalin had found it easier to rule through the security organs and government bureaucracies, but with the security organs downgraded and the specialized bureaucracies unable to resolve their differences, only the Party could impose consensus. As two Hungarian sociologists have recently put it: 'The Party stands guard over socialism's highest achievement, the political co-ordination of the economy and the consequent integration of individual bureaucracies'.*

A closer look at the careers of Khrushchev and Brezhnev illustrates the qualities required of the leader. The Soviet leader must have proved himself an unflinching practitioner of 'socialist humanism'; in other words, his hand must not shake when it comes to suppressing the enemies of 'socialism', particularly when his boss needs help. At the suggestion of Kaganovich, his first patron, Khrushchev demanded the repression of the Trotskyites, cleared the Bukharinites out of the Moscow Industrial Academy, bullied and cajoled the forced and free labour in the mud of the Moscow Metro and helped extinguish the last flickers of Ukrainian sentiment in the party. In 1947, Stalin broke up the relationship between Kaganovich and Khrushchev by sending Kaganovich to breathe down Khrushchev's neck in the Ukraine. Khrushchev successfully stood up to Kaganovich and was rewarded in 1949 with the job of keeping an eye on Malenkov in the party secretariat.

Brezhnev first showed his mettle in the villages and factories during collectivization and rapid industrialization. Khrushchev, his first patron, needed fellow Russians, untainted by Ukrainian feeling, well-versed in Stalinist dialectics, and possessed of the ruthless energy to direct industrial construction. During the war both Khrushchev and Brezhnev were army commissars. Khrushchev had to stay on to the end in the city of Kiev, despite his pleas to Stalin to evacuate its doomed defenders. Brezhnev was junior

*G. Konrád and I. Szelényi, *The Intellectuals on the Road to Class Power* (London, 1979), p. 161.

and therefore closer to the front-line where men had to be galvanized into laying down their lives 'for Stalin'. After the war, Brezhnev became Khrushchev's miracle worker. He restored the Dnieper Hydro-Electric Station and Steel Works to full production within two years. In 1951 he supervised the export of grain from starving Moldavia, and in 1956 he presented Khrushchev with the bumper harvest from the Virgin Lands that stopped the mouths of Kaganovich and Molotov.

It is striking that after the death of Stalin and after the fall of Khrushchev, the successful clique has discredited its opponents by denouncing the pacific policies and consumer goods orientation which, once victorious, it has itself adopted. What this appears to show is that, given a choice, the Nomenklatura feels happier about a leader who offers to extract the maximum surplus product by emphasizing heavy industry and arms production.

Once the patron of a clique, a leader (rukovoditel) becomes The Leader (vozhd), he becomes entitled to the ultimate prerequisite in the Soviet Union, as in ancient Rome, a 'personality cult'. The leader, like the Japanese Emperor, can do no wrong; scapegoats must be found for all failures that cannot be concealed. This is not just a product of 'Asiatic despotism' or the insistence of 'scientific socialism' that there can be only one correct line. Political integration requires such a cult irrespective of the personal modesty of a Lenin or the craving for self-glorification of a Stalin. If all the party secretaries and managers are to play the same tune at the same time they need a conductor. For this purpose the leader is presented as society's senior philosopher, Lenin's heir. His collected works will be found on the shelves of every ambitious bureaucrat. The leader may be invested with all manner of desirable attributes, like the 'common touch' (Khrushchev) or martial valour (Brezhnev). He will also be required to anathematize deviations or errors. At moments of crisis or transition, as in 1957 or 1970, it is possible to fall back on appropriate versions of the Lenin cult – suitable anniversaries fell with providential felicity.

The contents of the cults of Khrushchev and Brezhnev reveal a clear progression in the development of Soviet society, not least in presenting Khrushchev as a peasant agitator and Brezhnev as a working-class engineer. By the time of his death, Stalin's heirs had begun to find the stark insistence on ruthlessness and obedience in his cult unsuitable. It implied the waste of human resources; it eliminated intelligent specialists and tied up too much man-power in the security apparatus. The message conveyed by Khrushchev's cult was that bosses at all levels should be aware of shortcomings, see what could be learned from the capitalists and commit themselves to overtaking the Americans. Brezhnev's cult insists on the dignity of authority, not for him the banging of shoes on the U.N. rostrum. His elegant suits betray the concern for basic decencies (*kulturnost*) of the ruling group created by Stalin. His promotion as Marshal of the Soviet Union in 1976 suggests that leadership requires courage. The Brezhnev cult insists that authority be both rational and successful. Leaders must be able to delegate to Communist technocrats and must exercise repressive tolerance towards the faint-hearted. Enemies are to be punished, not 'liquidated'.

To some extent, both leaders have tried to match their own cults with their performance. Unlike Stalin, Khrushchev left the warts in his official photographs. More seriously, he was the author of the party's frankest ever statement on agriculture in September 1953, though this, like his increasingly spectacular attacks on Stalin, was more a tactical device to discredit his opponents than a case of frankness for its own sake. He visited Britain and the U.S.A. and met Nixon, then U.S. Vice-President, at the American Exhibition in Moscow. He personally promised to overtake America in the production of meat, milk, and butter by 1960 and to win the race to the moon. When Stalin died, millions had wept for an idol. No one mourned Khrushchev in 1964. He had asked to be judged by his performance and he had failed. While still very powerful in matters of policy and personnel, Brezhnev is neither a despot like Stalin, nor a self-willed dictator like Khrushchev. If anything, he is chairman of 'U.S.S.R. Ltd' with a firm belief that his product is better for the customer than all its rivals. As such he has consistently fostered expertise at the top (one of his recruits to the Politburo is a Ph.D.), taking care to see that the professional bureaucracies are fully integrated in policy-making. Thus, the Ministers of Defence, Foreign Affairs and the Committee of State Security (the K.G.B., successor to the M.V.D.) are members of the Politburo.

The expulsions from Brezhnev's Politburo have been equally significant. Where Khrushchev was forced to sack whole groups of Politburo or Presidium members over major policy issues, Brezhnev has expelled individuals.

Stalin's personality cult did not just fade away at his death. It had lasted too long, appealed to too many atavistic weaknesses, rationalized too many mass crimes, and facilitated too many dramatic promotions. There is still a 'Stalinist' party in the Soviet Union: retired M.V.D. men and their equivalents in the cultural elite, retired soldiers nostalgic for deferential youth and pavements promptly cleared of snow, Georgians who overlook Stalin's extermination of their own national intelligentsia (because of the way he terrified everyone else?). Finally, there were also a number of ambitious middle bureaucrats frustrated by gerontocracy with an obvious interest in a clear-out at the top.

There is also an anti-Stalin 'party'. Its rank-and-file comprises members of harassed religious and ethnic groups whose parents were massacred by Stalin. For the intelligentsia of Russia and the minorities, the Stalin cult is a barometer of the willingness of the Nomenklatura to permit them to participate in policy formation, the broken promise of socialism. The history of Soviet culture since 1953 is largely a story of de-Stalinization until 1964 and the resistance of intellectuals to partial re-Stalinization since.

'The Thaw' of 1953 (the phrase was coined by Ehrenburg's novel of that name) inaugurated a franker and more accessible style of leadership. This encouraged those 'at liberty' to overcome the 'atomist' isolation induced by terror. A public opinion unregimented by government became a possibility. The political prisoners, who had always enjoyed much greater mental freedom in the camps, exploded in revolts and strikes; this was premature. Still, as the influential pulled their own friends and relations out of the camps (more than 10,000 well-connected individuals by 1955), the scale and horror of the penal system became an intolerable embarrassment. This became acute when the German prisoners-of-war were sent home after Chancellor Adenauer's visit to Moscow in 1955. The Nomenklatura faced a terrible dilemma. They could not make any progress towards becoming a secure ruling class as long as they lacked personal security. But the reduction of the level of fear carried the risk that their privileged status would become public knowledge. They tried to have it both ways by re-asserting party control over the security organs (reduced in size and re-named the K.G.B.), but they did all they could to slow down the process of release and re-habilitation.

An opportunity for a decisive break with the past occurred at the Twentieth Party Congress in 1956. To the consternation of Molotov, Voroshilov and Kaganovich, Khrushchev used a proce-dural dodge to evade collective responsibility and delivered an unscheduled speech on the night of 24 February. This 'secret speech' has reverberated around the world for a quarter of a century without ever being de-classified in the Soviet Union. For the first time, the Great Terror was accurately described:

> Arbitrary behaviour by one person encouraged and permitted arbi-trariness in others. Mass arrests and deportations of many thousands of people, execution without trial and without normal investigation created conditions of insecurity, fear and even desperation.

The language was harsh but the criticism restricted in scope. Stalin was charged with doing away with 'many thousands of honest and innocent Communists', all of them loyal Stalinists. He was also accused of unjustified harshness towards the 'punished peoples' and the Russians captured by the Germans during the war. No tears were shed for those falsely labelled kulaks, for those who had refused to abandon their traditional cultures, nor for the 'bourgeois' specialists. There could be no full rehabilitation of Stalin's political opponents within the party, nor for those who had confessed in public trials. In differing from Stalin, Trotsky and Bukharin had challenged one of the central levers of control in Soviet society, a unitary ideology. Trotsky's policy positions were not mentioned but the Bukharinites were attacked for their reluctance to permit the subjugation of the entire economy by Stalin's Nomenklatura:

> Let us consider for a moment what would have happened if in 1928–9 the political line of right deviation had prevailed among us, or orientation towards 'cotton-dress industrialization', or towards the kulak etc. We

would not now have a powerful heavy industry, we would not have the kolkhozes, we would find ourselves disarmed and weak in a capitalist encirclement.

To demonstrate that his speech was squarely grounded in Leninist precedent, Khrushchev read out the texts of Lenin's testament and of sharp letters written by Krupskaya and Lenin to Stalin in 1922.

One of the motives for keeping the speech secret was that it was bound to undermine the reputations of those in the West who had defended the show trials as 'genuine' and 'fair' (D. N. Pritt). There is every reason to believe that Maurice Thorez, secretary of the French Communist Party, was particularly urgent with his pleas to Khrushchev to keep the lid on further disclosures. Despite these attempts, and the limitations of the speech itself, it came as a shattering revelation to hundreds of millions of people. Within months the world Communist movement was in disarray and Eastern Europe in turmoil. Economic and political changes in the area had already begun to cause unease but now the Poles threw out their Soviet 'advisers' while the Hungarians demolished Stalin's statue and, briefly, his system. Within the Soviet Union, M.V.D. troops fired on Georgians demonstrating *for* Stalin and Lithuanians demonstrating *against* Stalinism.

There followed nine years of hope and confusion. With the ousting of the 'anti-party group' (Molotov, Kaganovich, Malenkov, etc.) in 1957, hopes were high but no offer of participation was made to the intelligentsia. Vladimir Dudintsev's worthy novel, *Not by Bread Alone*, whose positive hero is a Communist engineer thwarted by the dead hand of the Nomenklaturist who blocks his project, was bitterly attacked. In the same year, Boris Pasternak's novel *Doctor Zhivago* was rejected for publication but, by this time, Pasternak had sent a copy to Italy where it appeared in print in 1958. He was promptly awarded the Nobel Prize for Literature. Pasternak was now subjected to a campaign of vilification and persecution and forced to renounce the Prize. He had sinned in many ways: his characters had good words for religious faith and harsh ones for collectivization. Implicitly, they exposed the cardboard 'positive heroes' of 'socialist realism'. Perhaps worst of all was the overwhelming power of Pasternak's mystical liturgy to the

Russian countryside and the sheer literary quality that contrasted so painfully with the dross of most official literature.

If such experiences were disappointing, the intelligentsia still had a great deal to be pleased with. Friends and relatives were returning home from the camps or being posthumously rehabilitated or even published. They could read Dostoyevsky and Bulgakov, listen to Stravinsky and Rakhmaninov. They could do professional work of a quality that would not disgrace them in the eyes of 'Europe'. Their lives improved in comfort and privacy. Many, worn out by their experiences, were content to leave it at that. For a small minority, this was not good enough. They believed that only justice would prevent a recurrence of Stalinism. While they were realistic enough to sense that there could be no Nuremburg trials, they wanted the facts of past crimes to be known.

A major step towards a re-evaluation of Stalin's role was the publication in 1960 of an official war history that discussed the tragedy of 1941. In the following year, Khrushchev, in difficulties with his social and economic policies, saw a further instalment of de-Stalinization as a useful way of undercutting his critics. At the Twenty-Second Party Congress in 1961, he publicly denounced Stalin and had Stalin's remains removed from the Lenin Mausoleum on Red Square. A year later, he went so far as to authorize the publication of Yevgeny Yevtushenko's poem, *The Heirs of Stalin*, which sharply attacked Stalinists in the party, and also Alexander Solzhenitsyn's *A Day in the Life of Ivan Denisovich*. Solzhenitsyn's novella was a literary masterpiece and an evocation of Stalinism as it was experienced by millions of ordinary Russians. It prompted scores of ex-prisoners to record their own experiences and show them to their friends or mail them to the literary journals. To the 'liberal' editor of *New World*, Alexander Tvardovsky, it even seemed possible to urge that censorship be left to Communist editors (i.e. intellectuals) rather than the unseen hacks of *Glavlit* (agents of the Nomenklatura). For a moment panic seized the former jailers as they thought that they might actually be identified. In the words of an M.V.D. colonel, it would be an 'outrage' to try security men for 'the murders of years gone by'. They were simply carrying out orders.

Schooled in decades of chicanery, the Stalinists set about the character-assassination of Solzhenitsyn, the man who had come to symbolize the strivings of the intellectuals for participation in public life. By lying about his war record and leaking his unpublished writings to the West, they presented him as 'anti-Soviet', denied him a Lenin Prize and had his novels *First Circle*, and *Cancer Ward* rejected. Self-publishing (*samizdat*) on the chain-letter principle had already reached substantial proportions when in 1961 Valery Tarsis began to give interviews to Western journalists. When these were re-broadcast to the Soviet Union by the B.B.C., the regime was threatened with a loss of its monopoly over information. In its search for 'scientific' sanctions, the K.G.B. received the assistance of the Serbsky Institute of Forensic Psychiatry. To Professor Snezhnevsky and his school, it is axiomatic that in a society without exploitation, only the mad protest. The compulsory in-patient 'treatment' of Tarsis in 1961, and General Grigorenko in 1964, were early examples of a practice that has since become routine.

Khrushchev's fall in October 1964 was enthusiastically greeted by the Stalinists and by the spring of 1965 it began to appear that their idol might be fully re-instated. Stalinist generals were promoted and their memoirs published; on V.E. Day, Brezhnev himself praised Stalin's war record. Later that year, the dogmatic Sergei Trapeznikov was placed in charge of the party's culture department and Sinyavsky and Daniel, two young Russian writers, the latter also Jewish, were charged with criminal libel. The 'liberal' intelligentsia, from Ehrenburg to Yevtushenko, came to their defence. The new leadership authorized a campaign to 'work over' public opinion by methods that recalled a grimmer past. A month *before* the trial, the newspapers assumed their guilt and began to publish indignant letters expostulating with the renegades. Sinyavsky and Daniel were sentenced to seven and five years' imprisonment but at the Twenty-third Party Congress in 1966, Mikhail Sholokhov still found it possible to lament the alleged scrupulosity of the trial and the leniency of the sentences.

Protests against the Sinyavsky–Daniel trial formed part of the charges against the writers Galanskov and Ginzburg who were tried early in 1968. This really was a watershed as literary opposition now moved into political activity and the human rights movement was born. Thus began an everlasting cycle of repression, protest, and repression that continues to this day. The human rights or democratic movement has given birth to characteristic institutions: the *samizdat* journal, *A Chronicle of Current Events*, which has recorded violations of freedom of speech in cool, legalistic prose ever since 1968 and the Initiative Group for the Defence of Human Rights in the Soviet Union, formed in 1969, the first in a series of overlapping groups, each with its own specific objectives and membership. The tactics of the movement have been determined by the scientific and literary intellectuals of the capitals but much heavier penalties have been inflicted on the rank-and-file, especially the members of national minorities: Ukrainians, Lithuanians, Armenians, Crimean Tatars, Germans, and Jews. This discrimination may not last. In 1980, Anatolii Shcharansky was tried on a charge that carries an option of the death penalty.

The anti-Zionist and antisemitic propaganda that accompanied the 1967 Six-Day War intensified a determined movement for 'Return to Israel' (*Aliyah*) among many Soviet Jews. Supported by Jews and others in the U.S.A., they are the only dissident group to have gained something of their objective, the right to emigrate, although it is at the price of harassment and persecution. Ironically, the regime has found emigration more convenient than it first thought and has since even expelled a number of non-Jewish 'dissidents' as Zionists. Khrushchev's virulent anti-religious campaign was at first moderated by his successors, but in 1975 they confirmed the 1929 Regulations designed to secure the elimination of organized religion in one or two generations. Many fundamentalist Christians and Roman Catholics could not accept this and have since suffered for their faith. This too has been reported by the *Chronicle*. Unlike the radical intellectuals of tsarist Russia, Soviet democrats have so far sought greater security and justice *within* the system by challenging the government to observe the freedoms promised in its own constitutions of 1936 and 1977.

The 1968 'Prague Spring' and August intervention in Czechoslovakia signified that the Nomenklatura would not countenance a society of open debate, a potential 'dictatorship of the intelligentsia' within the 'Socialist Commonwealth'. Re-Stalinization reached its peak in the late 1960s. Plans for a full rehabilitation to coincide with the ninetieth anniversary of Stalin's birth in 1969 were thwarted by foreign Communists and by Brezhnev's desire for detente, the urgency of which was illustrated by border clashes with China in that year. The ardent Stalinists had to be content with the rehabilitation of Stalin's war record and a modest statue within the Kremlin. Both liberalization in Czechoslovakia and re-Stalinization encouraged those on the 'extreme' wings of the party to identify themselves. Opportunist Stalinists like Shelepin were thereafter gradually demoted while the anti-Stalinists were expelled from the party. Solzhenitsyn stuck to the rules as long as there was any hope of publication but then resumed the work of 'naming names' abandoned by the government in 1964. The appearance of *The GULAG Archipelago* in Paris in 1973 led to Solzhenitsyn's expulsion from the Soviet Union a few months later. In this factually scrupulous but passionate history of repression in the Soviet Union, Solzhenitsyn successfully refutes Stalin's assertion that 'the death of a man is a tragedy; the death of a thousand is statistics'. Through this work, the imploring shades of millions of emaciated and tortured kulaks, workers and intellectuals will long haunt the intelligentsia of the whole world.

Under Brezhnev, the institutions of the intelligentsia have been systematically purged of all those who put professionalism before obedience to authority. Empirical sociology, revived under Khrushchev, had begun to gnaw away at the claims of the regime. It had discovered increased stratification, working-class alienation and surviving sexual inequality. In 1971–2 the Institute of Applied Social Research in Moscow was purged of a third of its staff, recalling the suppression of the Social Sciences Institute of the Academy of Sciences during the cultural revolution. As the new Director put it: 'Sociology is a party science'. Similar purges occurred in many other academic institutions and at the secondary schools attended by children of the Nomenklatura and cultural elite who were shocked to find that their own children were being taught by 'Zionists', were reading *samizdat*, and trying to discover what Bukharin and Trotsky had really said. On the whole, however, the professional autonomy won during the Khrushchev era was maintained; Soviet historians can defend almost any position concerning Russian history before 1917 as long as they indicate a general sympathy for Leninism.

By the mid 1970s, disillusioned with the new leadership, Soviet intellectuals such as the physicist, Academician Andrei Sakharov, were looking increasingly to the Western intelligentsia for support and inspiration. This mood was reinforced by Brezhnev's own diplomacy. To secure the ratification of the *status quo* in Europe, Brezhnev had the Soviet Union ratify the U.N. Human Rights' Covenants in 1973 and agree to freer movement of people and information in the 1975 Helsinki Agreements. Attempts by groups of intellectuals in Moscow, Kiev, Vilnius, and other cities to monitor Soviet non-implementation of these agreements were regarded as a treasonable impertinence by the government and punished accordingly. Towards the end of the 1970s, Soviet intellectuals became aware of the limited interest and power of the Western intelligentsia and began to look for allies with more muscle. The traditional claim that the Soviet state is a 'socialist state of workers and peasants', and the Soviet government's attempts to foster fraternal relations with Western trade unions, encouraged some worker-intellectuals in the Soviet Union to appeal to the Western labour movement. In 1978, they went a stage further by trying to establish a free trade union which would articulate worker grievances. The bitter road towards an alliance between the marginal intellectuals and the workers has been indicated by these brave people. It may never come to anything. If it does, its adherents must be prepared for trials even greater than those that faced the populists of the 1870s.

In 1978, Alexander Zinoviev's satire, *The Yawning Heights*, reached the West. Like Bulgakov, whose novel *The Master and Margarita* satirized Soviet society of the late 1930s, Zinoviev has had to devise a new form and a new language to convey his portrait of the Soviet intelligentsia today. It is a tale of tedium, cowardice, obscenity, bureaucratic absurdity, and mediocrity. Its title, a pun on the official goal of 'the radiant heights' of Communism, suggests that the socialist millennium may be neither the paradise promised by the prophets, nor the hell depicted by its enemies, but merely a state of absurd boredom. Paraphrasing Marx paraphrasing Hegel, Zinoviev asks how many times a farce has to be repeated before it becomes a tragedy. *The Yawning Heights* portrays the current alienation of the Soviet intelligentsia, with a mordant eye for idiosyncracy and a passionate despair that belies the discovery that convictions do not count. Like all great works of this genre, its relevance is not restricted to one place or time.

Since the late 1960s, when the 'Democratic Movement' began to move beyond description to prescription, it has become less united over objectives and more quarrelsome in temper. The Ukrainian Valentyn Moroz was ostracized by fellow Ukrainian dissidents for alleged antisemitism and the Russian Roy Medvedev for his allegiance to Marxism. Zinoviev's impartiality has made him generally disliked while no one wants to say a word for the film director Sergo Paradzhanov, victimized for his independence of spirit on homosexual charges. So far, neither Solzhenitsyn's reactionary Utopia, Sakharov's westernizing liberalism, nor the conceptually inert socialism of the Medvedev twins, have provided any convincing alternative to the *status quo*. Mikhail Voslensky's description of *The Nomenklatura*, published in 1980, marks some advance in analysis but is short on hopeful prescription. If the historic role of the marginal intelligentsia is to reassimilate Russian socialism to European humanism then it has made a small, though very courageous, beginning.

CHAPTER 22

Mature Socialism: Promise and Reality

In 1980, some British critics of Soviet foreign and domestic policies suggested that an excellent television series on the Russian language should not be screened. They feared lest the sight of ordinary Russians attending to their mundane affairs blunt the edge of the hostility felt by many ordinary Anglo-Saxons towards the policies of the Soviet government. Undoubtedly, when reporting on Russia the Western Press and television concentrate on the struggles and ordeals faced by 'dissidents'. One of the reasons for this is that these intellectuals share in Western values to a greater extent than most Soviet citizens. In a sense, the objections made by dissidents to Soviet society and government policy are those most Western intellectuals would make if forced to live in Russia. In their objections to the malpractices of the authorities, Soviet dissidents have been forced to refer to the ideal, and often unreal, promises made by Soviet aspirational documents. A case in point is Zhores Medvedev's examination of the censorship of correspondence in the light of the Constitutional statement that 'the secrecy of correspondence is guaranteed by law'. Yet, in the view of the Brezhnev leadership, the Soviet Union has become a society of 'mature socialism'. How has this come about and what does it mean for those who live in it?

In justifying the Virgin Lands campaign of the mid 1950s, Leonid Brezhnev said: 'It is not just an economic necessity, it is also a political matter. Let the whole world recognize yet again that we Communists are capable of solving major tasks in a very short period of time.' This concern with gigantic developments, and the legitimacy they confer on the party, has not slackened. Over the last two decades the Soviet Union has built the world's greatest hydro-electric stations at Bratsk and on the Angara as well as helping the Egyptians build the Aswan High Dam. They have built up the Tyumen oil and gas fields at a remarkable rate and are now completing the Baikal-Amur Main Line (B.A.M.), giving the Russian presence in Siberia greater depth. We cannot, of course, cost such 'externalities' as environmental degradation or industrial disease though there have been convincing reports of serious pollution in Lake Baikal and complaints that snow is rarely white near industrial installations. Nor can we establish the opportunity cost of tying up so much capital in prestige projects; we cannot know how many Russians will continue to bump along potholed roads in old cars just so that the B.A.M. can be built. Russians are not unaware of these possible criticisms and yet many of them still take pride in grandiose achievements. Much less is said about the achievements of the Soviet defence industry, though television viewers on Air Force Day must get some impression of the power and variety of Soviet armaments. Within the lifetime of a generation Admiral Gorshkov has presided over the achievement of the ambition of Peter the Great. Russia now boasts the world's second greatest navy. More recently, the Soviet Union has reached nuclear parity with the U.S.A.

The strengths and weaknesses of the Soviet approach to priority projects was well illustrated by the development of rocketry. Although nuclear weapons were available to Stalin, he had no reliable means of delivering them to targets in the United States. Soviet scientists discovered that rockets developed from the German V-2 could be simply tied together to produce the thrust required. This led to the initial Soviet successes in the space race; the first Sputnik (1957), Yuri Gagarin's space flight (1961), and the first rocket to the moon (1966). To Khrushchev, trying hard to overcome resistance to the idea that there was no more need to expect major war, these successes provided an enormous advantage. The Soviet programme then suffered some major disasters and it was the Americans who first landed on the moon; so far no Russians have followed them. Soviet failure in the moon race was due to the relative backwardness of the Soviet Union in cybernetics, miniaturized components, and plastics. Where Khrushchev was willing to take risks to beat the Americans, his more rational successors, like their counterparts in other countries, have cut down the astronomic expenditure required for interplanetary exploration and have settled for an effective defence system. It is worth remembering that Soviet military production is tested in the world market.

It finds plenty of buyers, but, even in an area of such vital import-ance to the Nomenklatura as military equipment, Soviet produc-tion remains technologically conservative. The Mig-25 aircraft turned over to the Japanese by a defecting Soviet pilot in 1978 was found to be much less formidable than U.S. analysts had expected and 'it was equipped with twenty-year-old, tube-type electronics'.

It is axiomatic that a socialist economy should be able to maintain a high level of investment, untroubled as it is by crises of over-production, underconsumption and 'stagflation'. One of the major roles of the party has been in rationalizing the deferment of consumption so that there could be a maximum of accumulation. Thus, capital investment by state and co-operative organizations (apart from collective farms) increased sixty times between 1928 and 1962 and six times between 1940 and 1962. Brezhnev claimed in 1979 that one-fifth of national income is still re-invested in the Soviet Union. How do we assess the overall results of this stupen-dous programme of investment? Official statistics are often not comparable with Western statistics for many reasons: past purges of the statisticians, the continuation of the tradition implied by the slogan 'statistics on the class front', the incentive at all levels to claim to have met norms, changing price indices and problems of definition. We can also not assume that an item, e.g. a car, is comparable with its Western equivalent in view of poorer quality control, the dearth of spare parts, and minimal provision for ser-vicing. However, the franker tone of Soviet speeches and articles on the economy since Stalin, plus the opportunities for direct observation that have grown with detente, permit a tentative assessment of Soviet economic performance. Stalin's assumption that impressive gross output of raw materials like coal, oil, steel, and electricity would guarantee the Soviet Union 'against all kinds of eventualities' reckoned without the dynamism of post-war capi-talism. His successors set about creating massive chemical, syn-thetic fibre, plastics, and electronics industries and rehabilitated the computer. Again, there were impressive quantitative results: the production of synthetic resins and fibres more than trebled between 1958 and 1965.

After Stalin's death, the dogma that the production of producer goods must take place at a faster rate than the production of consumer goods was abandoned. Despite this, the traditions of the Nomenklatura and the demands of security still tend to lead to a situation in which norms are more often met in the production of raw materials and machine tools than in consumer goods. Officially, it was claimed that the rate of growth (a somewhat dubious concept) had declined from around 20 per cent during Stalin's last years to around 10 per cent in the last years of Khrushchev. Western re-computations of Soviet statistics, making allowances for such things as changing prices, suggest that the average annual growth rate 1928–55 (excluding the war years) was 4·4 per cent. This is exactly the same as the rate of growth officially claimed for the late seventies. In fact, the true rate since 1953 is probably nearer 3·5 per cent. Increasingly, there is a tendency for gross output to fall below the targets set by the Plan even in such traditional success areas as electricity, coal, oil and steel production. The current malaise of the Soviet economy is all too reminiscent of difficulties experienced elsewhere. Summing up the contemporary views of Soviet economists, Alec Nove concludes:

It is not disputed that the rate of increase in the productivity of labour and the yield on capital investment have been falling, as has the level of profitability. Industrial and construction costs have edged upwards, and new machinery in particular is often much dearer, and not much more productive, than the models it replaces.

Can there be such a thing as falling rates of profit in 'socialist' society?

In the Soviet Union the demands of socialism and modernization have combined to foster a massive expansion of educational and health provision. The number of doctors rose from 347,000 in 1958 to 484,000 in 1965 and 733,000 in 1975; hospital beds from only 791,000 in 1958 to 2·2 million in 1965 and over 3 million in 1975. The number of teachers also rose, though less spectacularly, from 1·7 million in 1956 to 2·4 million in 1965 and 2·6 million in 1975. Apart from the services they provide for the general population, these jobs create improved opportunities for career satisfaction for women. The vast majority of Soviet doctors and teachers are women, though women are also well represented in such professions as engineering, technical occupations, and law. Western feminists may criticize the concentration of women in 'caring' occupations but for the women themselves it is surely a promotion and not a demotion to become a doctor rather than an unskilled factory worker.

After many years of neglect, Soviet housing was in an appalling state at Stalin's death. Khrushchev insisted on a massive housing programme. Unfortunately, some of the designs for mass housing were unnecessarily drab and have since been nicknamed *Khrushchoby* (Khrushchev slums). More recent designs have better amenities and are aesthetically more pleasing. The housing programme was significant as the first major industrial programme to bring direct material benefits to ordinary Soviet citizens on a large scale. Under the Brezhnev leadership, there has been a slackening of tempo in housing construction, though over two million dwellings, mostly flats, are built each year.

Since Stalin's death there have been two major drives to improve the standard of living of the people as a whole. Under Khrushchev, this was focused on an improvement in food production and housing. Events in Poland in 1970, when the working class demonstrated their discontent in a spectacular manner, led the Brezhnev–Kosygin leadership to promise to saturate the market with consumer goods. Again, quantitative results have been impressive. The number of new television sets went up from 1·7 million in 1960 to 6·7 million in 1970 and 7 million in 1976. This might be dismissed as part of a plan to bring official propaganda into every home. The same cannot be said of the production of refrigerators and cars which also rose impressively. The half a million fridges produced in 1960 catered for a tiny proportion of demand. In 1970 4·1 million were produced and in 1976 5·8 million. Car production rose from 139,000 in 1960 to 344,000 in 1970 and 1·2 million in 1976. In 1974, an American expert calculated that between 1950 and 1970, Soviet food consumption had doubled, disposable income quadrupled, time at work had been shortened, welfare benefits increased and consumption of goods had vastly increased. While Soviet workers are still probably only half as well off as those in Britain, they are incomparably better off than they have ever been.

Unfortunately, the quality of Soviet goods is still a constant headache. Shoes seem to be an extreme case. In 1973, every eighth pair of shoes produced had to be written off. We cannot assume that the quality of the remainder was acceptable by Western standards. The poor quality of Soviet goods and the refusal of the government to import consumer goods in any quantity has led to a frantic obsession among many Soviet consumers with the acquisition of imported goods. In 1958 a young Russian confided in an American friend that 'one of the worst tragedies of his life had been missing the [World Youth] festival. His friends had met many interesting people and had bought foreign clothes'. In 1958, this could still be dismissed as a consequence of the deprivations suffered in Stalin's time. In 1980, however, the Young Communist newspaper criticized a young Russian woman for living *entirely* from sales of Western consumer goods privately imported by influential relatives. Western visitors to the Soviet Union are still assailed by requests to sell things made abroad: rumours that Western or even East European goods are to be sold still create immediate impatient queuing. For some experts, the poor quality of Soviet products is the result of cultural factors, especially the recent arrival of unskilled ex-peasants into the industrial labour force. They point out that quality is higher in East Germany and Czechoslovakia which have a tradition of craftsmanship that goes back generations. On the other hand, the experience of East Asia suggests that not all peasant cultures produce the kind of sloppy workmanship that seems to lie behind the poor quality of Soviet goods.

Some of the blame for the deceleration of growth rates and poor quality must lie with the economic system. To some extent the slow-down in growth rates must reflect the increasing difficulty of the central planning of a sophisticated modern economy. There were hopes that the mismatch of supply and demand could be overcome by computerization. These have now been abandoned by the Soviet computer planners themselves. In a modern economy requiring millions of separate items whose design constantly changes, the computer programmes are out of date before they have been set up. In economies in which technology changes rapidly computers cannot entirely substitute for the market in indicating what quantities of particular items will be required in future. The problems posed by norms fixed by the central plan are indicated by many aprocryphal stories. There was the fictional firm that fulfilled its weight norm for nails in one month by making one huge (and unusable) nail. (A numerical norm might have resulted in millions of minute and equally unusable nails.)

The market also performs another function, rewarding those who produce what consumers want and punishing those who do not. This is particularly important in enforcing relatively high quality. In the Soviet system, the individual consumer has little *economic* influence over the central planning organizations which allocate investment, nor the intermediate levels of economic management which have to translate indicators from the centre into goods. The motivations of factory managers are bound up with achieving norms laid down by their superiors. This does not always help quality. Goods produced during the last hectic 'storming' days of a planning period are known to be particularly suspect.

Part of the reason for both declining growth rates and poor quality must be sought in the performance of the work force, the Soviet working class. Foreign socialists, such as René Dumont, have noted the 'modest pace of work' in Soviet factories. Stalin's successors have had to abandon his draconic labour legislation but they have found it politically impossible to re-introduce unemployment on a significant scale. Nor does the consumer goods market operate in such a way as to provide reliable incentives for hard work. Priority of access to lists and queues for the best consumer goods goes to those with influence, not money. It is well known that all the major cities in the Soviet Union have shops which only accept foreign currency; this is quite apart from the closed shops for the Nomenklatura. Under these circumstances, there is no guarantee that a worker's bonus will actually buy anything he or she really desires. This is one reason for the colossal savings of the Soviet people. Even more fundamental is the question of work norms. Workers who achieve significant increases in production may be rewarded with a bonus in one year but find that the norm for the next year is based on the new rate of production. Soviet planners function as eternally vigilant rate-fixers. Given the highly centralized nature of Soviet planning, there is thus a deep-seated antagonism between the interests of the workers and those of the planners installed by the Nomenklatura. This is, in many respects, analogous to the antagonism between labour and capital in capitalism.

An indication of the price paid by the Soviet economy for this antagonism was provided by the experiment conducted in 1967 at the Shchekino Chemical Combine in Tula. The intention was to keep the total wage fund static while reducing the number of workers, thereby increasing the earnings of the remainder and providing an incentive for improved labour productivity. Between 1967 and 1974, the volume of production rose two and a half times, 1,500 workers were dismissed, labour productivity more than trebled and average wages rose by nearly 50 per cent; the profitability of the enterprise also improved. The slogans about overtaking the Americans might take on entirely new meaning if this kind of experiment could be generalized to the whole of the economy. Unfortunately, it has not been widely followed. The initial results at Shchekino were not maintained indefinitely. Once a certain amount of labour had been shed there were no 'extra' wages to be divided up. The planners cheated by altering production norms and shaving the wages fund despite their previous promises. Shchekino workers found that the maximum 30 per cent addition to their wages did not radically alter their standard of living.

AGRICULTURE

The passing of Stalin was an unmitigated blessing for Soviet collective farmers and agriculture. After a quarter of a century of systematic exploitation, the Russian countryside was near to exhaustion by 1953. Nikita Khrushchev had the merit of seeing that this could not continue without an agrarian crisis that would bring famine, once more, to the towns. In 1953, he introduced changes in the pricing system for procurements which resulted in a massive infusion of cash into the countryside. Simultaneously, he announced a relaxation of restrictions on private plots: Stalin's taxes in kind had been so severe as to discourage the keeping of livestock and even the growing of fruit trees. Old debts were cancelled. There was massive investment in farm machinery and in the education of technical personnel. These changes seem to have improved the attitude of the collective farmers towards the Communist Party, which made it possible to set up primary party organizations on collective farms for the first time. Khrushchev extended the right to farm private allotments to town dwellers and he launched the campaign to open up the dry steppe-lands of North Kazakhstan. These 'Virgin Lands' offered a temporary solution to the immediate threat of grain shortages and, if carefully husbanded, they might have offered a more permanent insurance policy against bad weather and crop failure in the Ukraine. Initially, Khrushchev's reforms brought spectacular successes that helped him to oust Malenkov from the premiership in 1955 and defeat the 'anti-party group' in 1957. Between 1953 and 1958, the grain harvested increased from 80 million tonnes to 136 million tonnes and the yield per hectare from 7 to 11 centners. Over the same period, meat production increased from 6 to 8 million tonnes. Even more spectacular gains were registered in the farming of some industrial crops like sugar beet (50 per cent up), and by produce farmed largely on private plots such as milk (61 per cent up), eggs (44 per cent up) and wool (36 per cent up).

The achievements of Khrushchev's first years were subsequently squandered in an orgy of *shablon* or pseudo-planning. The errors he perpetrated were partly suggested by pseudo-scientists such as Lysenko and sycophantic local party bosses, but this does not exonerate him. In 1947, Khrushchev had nearly been ruined by Lysenko's attempt to foist spring wheat on the Ukraine where he was party secretary, and he had met many an opportunist in the party cadres. But Khrushchev was very much a man of the First Five-Year Plan in his belief in the ability of Communists to perform economic miracles. The catalogue of disasters makes sad reading. Khrushchev was obsessed with planting corn (maize) everywhere after a visit to the United States in which he learnt that all Americans eat bacon for breakfast while American pigs eat corn. But corn requires more fertilizer and more labour than other cereals and it will not ripen in the Soviet Union, which has a colder climate than the U.S.A. He encouraged Larionov, the party boss in Ryazan, to stampede the other regional bosses into doubling meat deliveries in 1959. While Ryazan party officials went on livestock-buying raids into other regions, in most areas the result was a mass slaughter of animals.

The increasing prosperity of some collective farms and the realization that the collective farmers were no longer a danger to the 'dictatorship of the proletariat' persuaded Khrushchev that the Machine Tractor Stations were no longer required. He seized on a successful experiment in Stavropol Territory in 1957 where M.T.S.s had been merged with the collective farms. Such integration might well have been a good thing with proper preparation and financing but Khruschchev ordered *all* M.T.S.s to sell off *all* their equipment, acquired over many years, to the collective farms, with no depreciation allowances, within the single year of 1958. Collective farm funds dried up, demand for new machinery collapsed and the trained mechanics of the M.T.S.s abandoned the land for the towns rather than accept the 'passportless' status of collective farmer.

The bill for Khrushchev's 'hair-brained schemes' was presented in the 1960s: the meat disaster (1960), the failure of the corn crop (1962), the failure of the wheat crop (including ecological disasters of salination and desertification in the no-longer Virgin Lands) in 1963 and 1965. 1963 also saw the mass slaughter of pigs deprived of adequate fodder. Stalin's successors have been neither willing nor able to let the workers starve so they have been forced to endure the humiliation of importing grain from the capitalists. This has become such a cornerstone of economic detente that neither the right-wing authoritarians in Argentina nor the farmers of the American mid west have ever accepted its interruption on political grounds. The instinct to seek out a scapegoat was not dead. In his fury at the collective farmers, Khrushchev closed many of their churches and cut their plots in half, driving still more off the land.

Brezhnev and Kosygin moved swiftly to repair the damage. In 1965 the size of the private plots was once more doubled and townspeople were again encouraged to cultivate their allotments. The proportion of total agricultural output from private farming (which occupies less than 1 per cent of arable land) is steadily decreasing, but in 1975 it still amounted to 27 per cent. It provides little grain or fodder but many vital foodstuffs and some welcome products like honey. In 1973 this sector supplied 62 per cent of the potatoes, 32 per cent of the fruit and vegetables, 47 per cent of the eggs and 34 per cent of the meat and milk. So far from exploiting agriculture in favour of industry, the leadership now in office has provided massive sustained investments for agriculture. In 1973 agricultural investment was almost a quarter of total investments. By Soviet standards there has been a lavish provision of farm-buildings, electrification and machinery. Although it pays low prices for grain and sugar beet, the State now pays a massive subsidy of nineteen thousand million rubles (1977) a year to obtain meat at a price that rewards the farmer without enraging the consumer. Overcoming shortages is quite another matter. Allowing for the vagaries of the weather, there has been a steady improvement in the grain harvest. The effects of this are partly concealed by the increase in population, the demand of the peasants themselves for city-baked bread, and the use of grain for fodder. Food supply still differs radically from place to place. In Moscow you can buy a wide variety of cheap processed foods in the State shops and high quality fresh food at great expense in the thirty private markets. In villages in the Urals, on the other hand, peasants may eat meat less than once a week. Altogether, modest improvements in agricultural output are occurring, but at an exceptionally high cost in industrialized inputs.

Marxists have always dreamed of overcoming the differences between town and country. In Khrushchev's time, this was symbolized by the rather absurd erection of small blocks of flats in the middle of villages with unpaved streets. The Brezhnev years have seen major steps taken towards the assimilation of the rural population into the working class. In 1966, collective farmers began to receive salaries, pensions, and family benefits that put them on a par with unskilled urban workers. The long-resented stigma of inferiority is gradually being overcome. Since 1976, members of collective farms have begun to receive internal passports after their sixteenth birthdays. The process should be complete by the late 1980s. Investment in agriculture has also taken forms designed to overcome the frightful cultural emptiness of rural life by providing improved medical, social, and cultural facilities. The

Ukrainian dissident, Leonid Plyushch, went to work as a village teacher during the Khrushchev years:

> I was immediately struck by the poverty of the villagers. A third of them had tuberculosis. Some peasants had their own cows but had to give all the milk to the collective farm. My landlady had a daughter of six who almost never drank milk. Living standards, I must say, improved greatly after 1964: the peasants acquired television sets and in some cases even cars.

Undoubtedly conditions in the countryside have improved. Yet pockets of rural poverty remain and collective farmers still suffer from poorer educational and medical facilities, fewer amenities and a severe shortage of consumer goods in village shops. Until these remaining differences have been overcome the flight from the land will continue.

THE PEOPLE AND THE NOMENKLATURA

Despite all the efforts of the security organs, we are gradually coming to realize that the Soviet regime suffered a real crisis in the 1960s and early 1970s. Emboldened by the relaxation of terror, their hopes first raised and then dashed by Khrushchev, workers in Temirtau, one of the rapidly growing towns of the Virgin Lands, erupted in strikes and riots in October 1959. This is the first case known so far of such a major disturbance by Soviet workers since the 1920s. The most massive and heroic outburst of worker discontent took place on 2 June 1962 in Novocherkassk, where sixty to eighty people were shot down after demonstrating against food price rises, wage cuts and contemptuous treatment by local bosses. It seems probable that this was followed by secret trials, executions, and the dispersal of other witnesses to penal establishments like the uranium mines in Uzbekistan where life expectancy is rather short. However, both workers and authorities drew the conclusion from these experiences that direct confrontation does not pay. Since then the government has adopted subtler, Western-style tactics for putting over price rises and wage reductions and has encouraged managers to study industrial psychology. There have been serious attempts to ensure that the party continues to recruit a cadre of loyal workers enjoying significant privileges and to oblige educational institutions to pursue policies of 'positive discrimination' towards working-class young people and adults. During the early years of the Brezhnev–Kosygin leadership the workers enjoyed significant improvements in standards of living, and while these have been more modest recently, the efforts continue. In 1977, a new constitution was adopted proclaiming the Soviet Union to be 'a socialist state of all the people' as opposed to the 'socialist state of workers and peasants' defined in the 1936 constitution. To some extent this reflected the reality that workers and peasants were no longer members of classes with potentially antagonistic relations. On the other hand, the Nomenklaturists breathed a sigh of relief: they would no longer have to justify their membership of the ruling group by referring to an increasingly tenuous connection with the industrial working class.

The potential antagonisms within Soviet society have certainly been blunted by improving working-class living standards. The antagonisms have not been entirely overcome, however. For one thing, working-class poverty is still far from absent. In a letter to the American Federation of Labour written in 1975, an Odessa worker Leonid Sery described his circumstances as follows:

... our family budget comprises 200–240 rubles a month for eight persons. Or thirty rubles a piece. We cannot feed ourselves properly for this sum, even if you work from state prices, without mentioning the [private] markets, where everything is dear. For a half-starved existence here it is necessary to have at least 60 rubles a month per person, that is apart from clothes, footwear, rent and other outgoings. We often cannot buy the children milk. We cook borshch once a month on pay day, we rarely see meat and our permanent diet is bread and tea, sometimes with butter. In a word, we just manage not to die of hunger. We have no fridge, nowhere even to keep our food ...

Those tempted to blame Sery and his wife for having so many children should remember that it is the policy of the Soviet government to increase the population. The working-class dissident Anatoly Marchenko described conditions in the Irkutsk region, to which he had been exiled. At a time when average wages stood at 160 rubles a month, women working in local sawmills were getting 120 for hard manual labour. He calculated that 160 rubles would buy one and a half decent suits, a third of a black and white television set, a flight to Moscow and back from Chuna, two wheels for an economical 'Moskvich' car, or three to five children's coats. Prices in the local shops included meat at 2 rubles a kilo, dried fruits at 1.60 rubles a kilo, milk at 28 kopecks a litre, eggs at 90 kopecks to 1.30 rubles for ten, butter at 3.60 rubles. 'But in the shops, more often than not, none of that is there. If you succeed in buying something from a private trader, then you have to pay almost double in addition: a kilo of pork at 4 rubles, milk at 40 kopecks a litre.' Resentment at poverty is probably even greater at a time when some of the better-qualified workers have begun to experience a degree of affluence. It is intensified by the sense of powerlessness that afflicts those workers who do complain in ways not provided for by the system. As Sery puts it:

> We are workers, and here a worker does not even have the right to demand a wage increase. We have the right only to work, to remain silent without complaining and to receive for our work pathetic kopecks without [sufficient] allowance for our families.

Soviet sociologists have supplied additional evidence of alienation among Soviet workers. In 1966, a study of 2,665 workers under thirty employed in twenty-five Leningrad factories showed that job satisfaction varied 'from a negative attitude among heavy, unskilled manual labour to a highly positive one among the highly skilled and the panel operator setters'. Surveys conducted in more remote locations among the full age range might have discovered an even higher incidence of alienation. Labour turnover remains high in unskilled jobs, as does absenteeism. This is often connected with alcoholism. One Soviet author claimed in 1977 that a 10 per cent improvement in labour productivity would result if on-the-job drunkenness were eliminated.

Strikes have never been forbidden by law in the Soviet Union, but since 1929 none have been officially admitted. Nevertheless, forms of non-co-operation do exist. Valery Chalidze has described the 'Russian strike' as follows:

> For example, a machine-tool has broken in a shop, they call a fitter to mend the machine-tool. An hour later a foreman comes and asks if the machine-tool is mended. The fitters are sitting down and smoking. He asks

why the machine-tool isn't mended. They answer: 'We went to the tool store, but they're closed and we need a tool to mend the machine-tool'. The foreman goes to the store, gets the tool and gives it to them. He returns an hour later and again they're sitting and smoking and to the question why the machine-tool isn't mended they say that a bolt is required and they went to the turner who could make the bolt but that he is ill . . .

There have been very few successful attempts to overcome low labour productivity by creating structures that would guarantee rewards for higher productivity. The Shchekino experiment worked well for a time but ground to a halt once a certain level of efficiency had been reached. Ultimately, it foundered against the refusal of the central planners to permit uncertainty in the wages fund. In agriculture, an attempt was made to harness the self-interest of farm-workers through the *zveno*, or link, experiments in the late 1960s. In its most radical form, this allocated sections of collective farms to teams of self-managing farm-workers. In some cases, it emerged that the members of the *zveno* were all related to one another and this smacked of de-collectivization. Not the least threatening aspect of the reform was the prospect of redundancy for tens of thousands of rural supervisors.

It would, of course, be quite wrong to give the impression that the majority of Soviet workers are consciously critical of the entire system or that they are merely awaiting an opportunity to engage in more organized forms of class struggle. Late industrial society offers them a variety of private satisfactions which go a long way towards making life tolerable. If the television programmes are rather dull, the young can play pop music and the older can stroll in the country picking mushrooms. Pets are popular and so is sport of every conceivable variety. Many sporting activities are organized by the trade-union committees of the larger factories and this brings us to another feature of Soviet society that Western critics often forget. Throughout Soviet society, participation in decision-making is compulsory for all. In practice the less skilled take little part and women tend to drop out after their second child. Still, the majority do participate and the more highly educated the higher the degree of participation. Factory or trade-union committees and their equivalents in institutions like hospitals and schools involve everyone from the lowest grade of manual labour to the director of the institution. Their central task is to negotiate the collective agreement that ratifies norms and takes crucial decisions on the division of the wages fund. Their meetings also provide opportunities for discussion of such matters as holidays, meals, and crèche facilities. Workers can and do complain to their trade-union representatives about breaches of safety regulations and unfair dismissals. There seems no reason to doubt that these channels can be utilized with success by individuals with fairly modest individual problems. Even Sery admits that he received a small grant from his trade-union branch. A worker with a less serious grievance might perhaps have been satisfied with this. The encouragement given by the regime to complaints in the form of letters to the leading newspapers and to State and party institutions must also not be forgotten. Literally millions of these are posted each year and they are thoroughly analysed by the bodies that receive them before they re-direct them to the appropriate authority. Side by side with the re-assertion of the right to complain (in the correct manner), there has been a return under Brezhnev to an intensification of labour discipline and a return to moral incentives. There has been a resurrection of the old tradition of 'voluntary' unpaid Saturday working. According to one author, in 1975 some 140 million people created production worth a billion rubles in this way. Far more striking has been the emergence under Brezhnev of a whole system of rituals sanctifying almost every aspect of life in the Soviet Union. We say 'almost' advisedly. There is little sign that admission into the intelligentsia, the party or the Nomenklatura is likely to be ritualized. Rituals are designed for those who do not see their relationship to society quite so clearly. Of course there have always been some rituals in Soviet society, such as the parades to mark the anniversary of the revolution and May Day, the funerals of political leaders, and the ceremonies of initiation into the junior branches of the Communist Party. The demand for a more comprehensive approach towards ritual seems to have come in the late fifties and early sixties from those involved in the anti-religious campaigns in the two formerly Lutheran republics of Latvia and Estonia. At first they sought rituals that would sanctify the rites of passage of individuals. Rites for births, weddings, and funerals were gradually evolved. One advantage of these is that they facilitate marriages between Russians and members of other nationalities. Such rites provide the State with an opportunity to assert its interest in the family, 'the primary cell in our society'. They are, however, voluntary and their appeal is based on the fundamental desire of the participants for dignity and meaning in life.

Less voluntary are some of the newer collective rituals, such as the rite of initiation into the working class. This started in the early 1960s in Leningrad and has since spread widely. Torchlight processions, speeches, oath-taking, the kissing of the factory banner, and films of the heroic past of the factory are some of the means used to inculcate a sense of pride in membership of the factory and the working class. There are other rituals – for instance the Handing Over of the First Wage, designed to inhibit the orgy of drunkenness which traditionally marked this moment in the lives of young male workers. Labour holidays have been held in centres such as Magnitogorsk, where, in 1974, the whole city was involved in celebrations to mark the pouring of the 200 millionth ton of steel. In some parts of the Soviet Union, families have been invited to register themselves as 'Workers' Dynasties'. During factory celebrations, several generations of the same family relate their exploits in a way that brings them home to those of the younger generation who cannot easily imagine what times were like in the past. Such has been the growth of ritual that some of its experts have tentatively suggested special education and regular remuneration for those involved.

If the new rituals have had modest successes among the Russians, Ukrainians and some of the Baltic peoples, they have been much less successful in undercutting traditional loyalties elsewhere. In Catholic Lithuania they have made very little headway; after football riots in Vilnius in the late 1970s elaborate police measures have been taken to avert anti-Russian riots there. The Moslem peoples of the Caucasus participate in some of the rituals that do not offend against their religious beliefs, but show little sign of abandoning their traditional ideas. Educated by the Russians to know their own traditions better, the peoples of Central Asia have created a new sense of *Umma* or Islamic community in which Communist officials license the building of mosques, underground secret societies proselytize, and women concentrate on the task of reproducing the race. The fertility of Central Asian Moslem women is such that by the end of the century 40 per cent of all Soviet teenagers will be Asian Moslems. In the face of such evidence of national identity, the Nomenklatura responds in the spirit of the old imperial adage, divide and rule. In April 1978, Georgian students demonstrated against a proposal that would have made Russian the principal language of the Georgian S.S.R. Fifteen months later, the Abkhazian minority in Georgia rioted and demanded to be taken into the Russian Republic. The relatively mild vocabulary of anti-Zionist propaganda in *Pravda* is translated by common militiamen into shouts of 'You lousy Yid!' In the Tatar Republic, Russian officials cuss Tatars for their rudeness in speaking Tatar in front of them; in Kazakhstan Ukrainians, forced to leave the heartland of Ukrainian culture by the State's failure to provide jobs there, find themselves obliged to teach Kazakhs in the Virgin Lands the benefits of Soviet (Russian-language) culture.

During the gathering of the last Soviet census, the students and other volunteers collecting the forms were embarrassed to find themselves involved in constant doorstep arguments about the question: 'Who is the head of the family?' In the end, this question had to be withdrawn. Soviet women had defeated the Central Statistical Administration. Undoubtedly, women have gained enormously from Soviet society. The most obvious gains have been greater individual freedom, equal rights to marriage and divorce, guarantees of support for their children, equality of education, and formal equality of opportunity and reward in employment. They have, however, paid a very high price for these advances. In particular, they have had to shoulder the 'double burden'. To this day, Soviet men are less than fully socialized to helping in the home. This situation cannot be helped, of course, by the tiny size of many Soviet kitchens and bathroom facilities. It is only in the last twenty years that the economy has begun to lighten this burden a little by providing convenience foods and household appliances to save domestic labour. For a long time, the only real provision made by the factories and enterprises was the crèche, without which the women could not have worked at all. Soviet women are increasingly objecting to the 'double burden'; this seems to be a factor in rising divorce rates. Another of the prices paid by Soviet women, though they themselves demanded this at least as much as men, was the restoration of traditional attitudes towards sexual morality. With the abolition of unemployment in the first Five-Year Plan, the humane methods employed by Kollontai for treating former prostitutes were abandoned for more down-to-earth methods against these 'deserters from the labour front'. For many years, permitted expressions of sexuality were few and far between and, with the inevitable exception of wartime lapses and official sanction for reproduction by 'women alone' after the war, restricted to marriage. Homosexuality was, and is, illegal. The appalling housing conditions of those years meant that no one had much privacy. Reliable contraceptives are still not available for most Soviet women so they have to put up with abortion on demand. Recently, a group of Christian women in Leningrad published an appeal for a restoration of the rights of motherhood. The government has gone some way to meeting this demand by promising a year's maternity leave. This concession is probably motivated as much by fear of the fertility of Central Asian women as by sympathy for the claims of motherhood.

During the 1960s, there was widespread speculation in the West that the Soviet Union was turning into a technocracy. It was suggested that the managers of Soviet enterprises formed a caste whose interests were sufficiently cohesive to enable them to influence policy collectively at the highest levels. To a large extent, attempts to overcome stagnation in the economy seemed to turn on the ability of the government to get the managers to behave in the way they wanted them to. Thus, Malenkov tried to co-ordinate economic planning by creating a number of super-ministries. Khrushchev went even further, abolishing the centralized industrial ministries in 1957 and replacing them with regional economic councils. Finally, in 1962, he went so far as to split the party itself into industrial and agricultural wings (shades of the S.R. Party!). These organizational revolutions, together with Khrushchev's attempts to increase the turnover of party membership, did more than agricultural disasters, de-Stalinization, or the row with China to secure his fall. The moment seemed right for a measure of economic decentralization. For some years there was a lively discussion of alternatives and some cautious, small-scale experimentation. The apogee of the movement came in 1966 with the publication of Lisichkin's *Plan and Market*, a well-argued case for market socialism. Other reformers were more modest, emphasizing the freeing of the managers to an extent that would permit the central planners to concentrate on major decisions of economic strategy. In 1965, Kosygin was able to reduce the number of compulsory planning indicators facing managers, thereby giving them more freedom and removing potential sources of conflict between technocratic managers and the central planning bodies. In practice, the centre, and even local party bosses, have tried to shackle the managers once more. In the late 1970s, Brezhnev has authorized some even more cautious experiments, this time in varying the organizational structure of enterprises so that they are on the right scale for the decisions they have to take. This piece of common sense is not likely to secure a greater identity of interests between the managers and the central planners.

The shooting of 'speculators' has been a feature of Soviet society since war communism but the early Brezhnev years also saw a wave of repression directed at managers, many of them Jews. Some were sacked for exchanging raw materials without authorization, while others were imprisoned for misappropriating State property. So far from constituting a technocracy, it is increasingly clear that the position of Soviet managers is far from enviable. Even the enormous power they have over the work-force is not all it seems. Studies of Leningrad trade-union committees suggest that a large proportion of dismissals ordered by managers are rescinded by the courts. The manager stands at the fulcrum of the downward pressure exerted by the Nomenklatura and the upward resistance offered by the Soviet working class. In theory he is solely responsible, that is what one-man-management means. In practice he is often forced to carry out plans he knows to be impossible and is hemmed in by a network of committees over which he has very little control. He has every incentive to understate plant capacity so as to avoid having to meet impossible norms. So far from having a common interest with his fellow managers, he is constantly in competition with them for the allocation of resources. It is hardly any wonder that the reforming managers from whom theorists like Liberman and Lisichkin sought economic advances were outnumbered by less imaginative and courageous colleagues to whom the only answer was, and still is, to seek political patronage among one of the cliques of the Nomenklatura.

The ruling Nomenklatura in the Soviet Union goes to elaborate lengths to conceal its existence from ordinary Soviet citizens. Despite this, its contours, lifestyle, privileges, and beliefs are very gradually becoming clearer; this is one of the unavoidable consequences of detente. M. Voslensky considers that there were, in 1970, approximately 100,000 first-rank and 150,000 second-rank members of the Nomenklaturas of party and State. In addition, a further half million Nomenklaturists were active in the economy and national culture. Together with their wives and children, this constitutes a class of some three million persons, or less than 1.5 per cent of the population. Such figures as may be gleaned from official publications suggest that the Nomenklatura is not growing with the economy but remaining static in number or even shrinking slightly, a sign of its consolidation as a class.

The perquisites of power in the Soviet Union are strictly graded according to status. Andrei Gromyko had to serve sixteen years as Foreign Minister before, in 1973, he was admitted to the Politburo and qualified for top-rank status. The most public sign of this was his $75,000 hand-tooled Zil limousine. For the second echelon, there are Chaikas which barge down the reserved central lane of the main Moscow avenues. Lesser fry have to be content with a chauffeur-driven car, probably a Volga, from the Central Committee or government car pool. For the most part, however, the benefits of Nomenklatura status are carefully concealed from public view. In theory, income differentials are quite modest. A bestselling author whose book is filmed can make up to 150,000 rubles for it. This dwarfs the sumptuous salary of a marshal (2,000 rubles a month) and makes the General Secretary's 900 rubles look paltry. This is not the whole story, however. An elaborate system of invisible extras ensure that no member of the Nomenklatura is ever short of anything. Thus, a Head of Section in the

Central Committee Secretariat receives only 450 rubles a month. The value of his holiday benefits brings this up to 530 rubles. The coupons (*Kremlyovka*) he receives for elite groceries and cooked take-away meals take it up to around 750 rubles. There is a premium of 10 per cent for a working knowledge of one foreign language or 20 per cent for two. For all this, he pays a maximum income tax of 13 per cent on his basic salary only. An article in a journal can bring in a further 300 rubles. His foreign travel enables him to import foreign goods untaxed which can be sold at a massive profit. This is without considering invisibles such as the Kremlin medical service, his flat – enormous by Soviet standards – and his dacha.

This makes no allowance for outright corruption and the corrupt extortion of sexual favours. Although these privileges do not remotely compare with the comforts available to Western capitalists, an ordinary Soviet worker, with an average wage of 167 rubles, has every reason to envy the Nomenklaturists.

Stalin denied the Nomenklatura personal security by having many of them executed. With the execution of Beria, this painful chapter in the history of the Nomenklatura was closed. In 1957, the 'anti-party group' was removed from the Politburo but they did not lose their status as members of the Nomenklatura. This was illustrated by the fact that Molotov even served as Soviet representative on the U.N. Atomic Energy Commission in Vienna for a time. Following *his* fall, Khrushchev became a pensioner of the party occupying Nomenklatura premises in the centre of Moscow. Anastas Mikoyan was allowed to live out his days on a real old aristocratic estate. According to those who have been through Soviet penal institutions, there is reason to believe that even those who go so far over the top that they fall foul of the law receive totally different treatment in prison than do normal prisoners. Not even such events as the attempt to assassinate Brezhnev in 1969 or the explosion in the Moscow Metro in 1978 have been able to shake the unruffled calm of the leadership and the determination of the Nomenklatura to avoid a return to the insecurity of Stalin's time.

To become a ruling class, the Nomenklatura needs to overcome the problem of auto-reproduction. There are many signs that the solution is well in hand. Lenin and Krupskaya had no children so their status was never a problem. Both Stalin's sons received military positions of Nomenklatura status, Vasily Stalin becoming an air force General at thirty; his daughter was content with membership of the cultural elite. Khrushchev's son-in-law, Alexei Adzhubei, became editor of the government newspaper, *Izvestiya*, but he fell with his patron. This does not mean that he was dropped from the Nomenklatura. Brezhnev has gone one better. His son, Yuri, is First Deputy Minister of Foreign Trade and a candidate member of the Central Committee; his son-in-law Lieutenant General Yuri Churbanov is First Deputy Minister of Internal Affairs and another candidate member of the Central Committee. Many similar cases could be cited. Even if these individuals lose their positions in the political leadership after Brezhnev's departure, it seems probable that they will still retain positions high up in the Nomenklatura just as Mikoyan's two sons do today. After the 1917 revolution, the future Nomenklatura was recruited from the workers, the peasants, and the intelligentsia. So it appears to some Western observers that it does not constitute a class. Thus, Brezhnev is a worker. The coming generation will show whether such recruitment from below is still possible on any scale.

There is, none the less, an understandable curiosity about the views of the Nomenklatura. Are they sclerotic Communists or sheer cynics? Like other Soviet children, young offspring of the Nomenklatura learn 'to have a warm love for V. I. Lenin' and 'to have a feeling of gratitude to the Communist Party and the Soviet government'. A detailed study of Lenin's work is not really necessary for those who do not wish to become ideologues; Marxism–Leninism is a compulsory part of education at all levels but it takes a strong-minded teacher to fail the children of the Nomenklatura. The Soviet equivalent of the Church of England's Thirty-Nine Articles is the 1961 Party Programme which new members are obliged to memorize. It includes the following statements:

During the coming decade [1961–70], in constructing the material basis of Communism, the Soviet Union will have surpassed, in terms of income per head, the U.S.A., the richest and most powerful capitalist state . . .

. . demeaning physical work will have disappeared . . .

... after the end of the first decade [i.e. 1970], there will no longer be any poorly paid workers or employees in the country ...

The memoirs of disillusioned idealists such as Lev Kopelev and Leonid Plyushch reveal that many young people do accept Communist ideals with enthusiasm. We also know that the party tends to get rid of 'starry-eyed idealists'. Those of the Brezhnev generation may well feel vindicated by the three great triumphs of the party in revolution, socialist construction, and war. For their progeny, 'Communism' is an obligatory ideology. Voslensky's account of 'A Day in the Life of Denis Ivanovich', a Head of Section in the Secretariat of the Central Committee, suggests that immediate considerations of power are far too pressing to leave much time for thoughts of an increasingly remote future.

Of one thing we may be sure. The Nomenklaturists are sincerely grateful to the party and the government. They are probably equally sincere in detesting the dissident intellectuals who implicitly challenge them for the leadership of society. They may even believe their own propaganda which suggests that the dissidents are either morally degenerate spokesmen for capitalism, out to inflict mass unemployment on the workers, or 'Zionists', out to dismember the Soviet State. On the other hand, some of them are probably sober and intelligent patriots who would like to carry out useful reforms – such at least is the opinion of the Medvedev twins. With a generational change imminent, we shall soon know which of these faces of the Nomenklatura is the true one.

CHAPTER 23

'The Stronghold Sure'

At the end of July 1941, Joseph Stalin told Harry Hopkins, President Roosevelt's closest adviser, that '. . . Hitler's greatest weakness was found in the vast numbers of oppressed people who hated Hitler and the immoral ways of his government'. Only the U.S.A. could provide the encouragement Hitler's enemies needed and 'the world influence of the President and the government of the United States was enormous'. As if this mixture of truth and flattery were not enough, Stalin even offered to let American troops fight the Germans on Russian soil. Only utter desperation could have prompted this last offer from Stalin; he was invoking the New World to redress the balance of the Old with an enthusiasm unsurpassed by Canning or Churchill. Since those grim days of 1941, relations with the U.S.A. have been the central concern of Soviet strategy, even as the Soviet Union has gradually risen from the status of humble petitioner to that of joint super-power. Of course the Allied politicians thrown together by Hitler's megalomania had reservations about each other's policies, but, as Eden and Harriman have insisted, there was also real warmth among the Allied statesmen; such feelings were not all on one side.

By March 1947, these feelings were a thing of the past. In justifying his determination to renew the American commitment to Europe, President Truman described Communism as 'based upon the will of a minority forcibly imposed upon the majority. It relies on terror and oppression, a controlled press and radio, fixed elections and the suppression of personal freedoms'. But to the Soviet leaders 'the frank expansionist programme of the United States' was 'highly reminiscent of the reckless programme . . . of the fascist aggressors'. In the ensuing 'Cold War', a rising tide of mutually reinforcing hysteria and militarism in both 'camps' tempted the Americans to abuse their nuclear monopoly. The Russians had little but pacifist agitation around the famous Stockholm Appeal to protect them. Presidents Truman and

Eisenhower were barely able to contain the pressures for action; they were very slow to respond to the more relaxed mood in Moscow after Stalin's death in 1953. It was not until two years later that Eisenhower could finally declare: 'I do know that the people of the world want peace.'

Real peace has been slow in coming. Crises over the Middle East in 1958, the Berlin Wall in 1961, and Cuba in 1962 brought thermonuclear disaster closer than ever. The surrogate war of the Space Race may have brought co-existence closer by suggesting that the opponent was more like a football team than a band of assassins. Since the mid fifties, a succession of Soviet and American leaders has made apparently sincere attempts to achieve a secure framework for 'peaceful co-existence'. There have been some real achievements in the realms of scientific co-operation, environmental protection, and arms limitation.

But after the collapse of the second U.S.–Soviet arms limitation treaty, the Soviet occupation of Afghanistan, martial law in Poland, Western disillusion with the Helsinki Agreements, and the resumption of the arms race, the fragility of this framework is apparent. To understand both the 'Cold War' of the late forties and early fifties and the difficulties upon which detente has foundered, the wartime years when the two future super-powers adopted strategic objectives that were mutually irreconcilable must be borne in mind.

In 1917, the United States took over the leadership of democratic republicanism from war-weary France; in 1947, she inherited the quasi-imperial position vacated by war-bled England. Both events brought America into conflict with the Soviet Union, the heir to Muscovy and Petrine Russia, the home of world revolution and an example of national emancipation for Latin America, Africa and Asia. Over many decades the competition has assumed a rationale of its own, with its own emotional dynamics. For Ostrovsky's hero, it was clear that the struggle would only end when 'we will take off for America to finish off the bourgeoisie there'. In 1966, Mikhail Sholokhov exulted in a Soviet space success, adding 'but the delight goes further than that: we've left the Americans behind again!'

What did the Soviet leaders hope for from the victory of 1945?

Quite naturally, they wanted an end to Russia's age-old nightmare of invasion. With the promised withdrawal of American forces from Europe and Asia, the Soviet army would be the only major land force in Eurasia. Russia would obtain secure frontiers realizing the ancient and modern aspirations of the Russian state. Her Communist friends would be freely elected to lead governments of the neighbouring countries by populations grateful for their liberation by the Red Army. Beyond this 'cordon sanitaire' in reverse, chaos in China and the gradual decline of the European colonial empires would inaugurate an era of alliances with progressive elements and collaboration with European bourgeois nationalists, such as General de Gaulle. The Russians expected the U.S.A. to continue to dominate the Americas and the islands off the east coast of Asia and to offer the Soviet Union massive reconstruction loans, not out of charity or altruism, of course, but in an effort to avert a post-war slump in the U.S.A. itself. These were the hopes of such cautious realists as Stalin and Molotov, hopes confided in the Allies and never discouraged by them during the war. They have constituted the strategic objectives of Soviet foreign policy ever since.

Between 1945 and 1952, nearly all these hopes were disappointed. The spectacular demonstration of American nuclear power in Japan cast a shadow over the hard-won victories of the Red Army. The Allies refused to recognize Russia's new Baltic coastline and thwarted Russian hopes in Iran, Turkey, and North Africa. The liberated peoples of Eastern Europe showed insufficent gratitude for their liberation and had to be dragooned into 'Friendship Treaties'. China regained her unity under self-willed Communist leaders who were only fully, if temporarily, brought to heel by the outbreak of the Korean War in 1950. After failing to use the international control of nuclear power as a stepping stone to an inevitably American dominated world government in 1946, the Americans re-introduced their armies into the Old World, bolstered the weakened Imperial powers of Western Europe, and rebuilt the conquered German and Japanese economies as bulwarks against Communism.

Not all of this was the consequence of Russian policy. The Soviet government certainly made a number of important concessions to avert the 'Cold War', particularly during the establishment of the United Nations' Organization. Stalin adhered loyally to the spheres of influence he had carved out with Churchill at Yalta and Potsdam. In the immediate aftermath of war, he instructed the Communists of France, Italy, Czechoslovakia, and Yugoslavia not to attempt to take power on their own; only the Yugoslavs turned a deaf ear. Stalin continued to respect the British position in Greece, despite the temptations offered by the civil war there. Russia finally withdrew from northern Iran and withdrew her claims on Turkey in the face of determined local opposition. Finland was treated with great leniency. There was, however, a grudging quality about many Soviet concessions that wore down the goodwill of even the best-disposed Western negotiators. Molotov and Vishinsky, the principal Soviet spokesmen in the post-war period, showed little awareness of the need to woo men like Harriman so that they could counter the propaganda of Polish officers, anti-Communist businessmen, and the Vatican, who hoped to exploit American power to extort further concessions from the Russians. During the negotiations of the 1970s, Soviet diplomats showed that they had learned valuable lessons from these failures. Even so, Kissinger's memoirs suggest that Soviet boorishness in negotiations is not entirely dead.

Soviet offences were numerous. They protested when S.S. generals tried (without success) to make a separate peace with the West, though they had no compunction about failing to pass on Japanese overtures to America until Russia was ready to march into Manchuria. Stalin was not to know that the Americans had broken the Japanese cipher, thereby divesting him of joint responsibility for Hiroshima and Nagasaki. The Russians treated Allied prisoners of war in Eastern Europe shabbily. By the spring of 1945, they had already imposed Communist-dominated governments on Poland, Bulgaria, and Romania. They insisted on arbitrary interpretations of Allied agreements on Poland and refused to allow the West to monitor them. Russian rapacity in Germany and Manchuria threatened to land the Americans with an enormous relief bill. Russia's refusal even to discuss the internationalization of nuclear power helped to create the atmosphere in which the betrayals of scientists such as Klaus Fuchs helped to pave the way for McCarthyism. American brinkmanship was sometimes met by Soviet rashness as the 'Cold War' got under way. The Russian blockade of Berlin in 1948 was a breach of Allied agreements. Soviet support for Kim Il-sung's invasion of *South* Korea in 1950 (whoever fired the first shot) were as dangerous as General MacArthur's subsequent threats to use nuclear weapons on China. The essential point on which they could not agree, as Maxim Litvinov, the former Soviet Foreign Minister, confided to more than one friendly American just after the war, was that Russia was determined to develop its sphere of influence whatever the Allies decided.

In 1918 France had emerged from a war fought largely on her own soil with her own blood only to find her Anglo-Saxon Allies insensitive to her demands for security. This was exactly Russia's position in 1945, with the difference that, unlike Clémenceau, Stalin had the power to enforce Russian demands. Any Russian government which failed to use victory to achieve security would have forfeited the support of the Russian people. Stalin hoped that this could be achieved with the assent of the Anglo-Saxons but he would not be bound by them. As the Red Army swept the Germans westwards in 1944–5, the 'in-gathering of the Russian lands' was finally completed as western Belorussia and Ukraine, Bessarabia, and Bukovina were re-incorporated. Despite real friendship with Czechoslovakia, the incorporation of Trans-Carpathian Ukraine was never a matter for negotiation. The Czechs were eventually asked to accede to a *fait accompli*. No latter-day Hrushevsky would ever again preach Ukrainian nationalism across the Carpathian mountains. The Baltic littoral acquired by the eighteenth-century tsarinas was reannexed and consolidated by the absorption in the Russian Republic of northern East Prussia, cleansed of its Prussians. Leningrad and Murmansk were protected by a neutral Finland, cut off from its outlet to the Arctic, its capital overawed by a naval base manned by weekly trainloads of Soviet sailors through Helsinki Station. The Finns were forced to pay reparations and try their ex-President but they were not occupied.

In Asia, the Soviet Union exploited China's weakness to annex Tuva in 1944 and further consolidated her far-eastern borders as a result of the August 1945 war against Japan. Though he had suggested to the Japanese in 1941 that 'we are both Asiatics', V.J. Day brought out the Eurocentrism of Stalin and the Soviet military establishment. The 'defeat of the Russian troops in 1904 left a bitter memory in the minds of our people. Our people waited and believed that this blot would one day be erased' In annexing the southernmost of the Kurile Islands, Stalin was turning the tables with a vengeance since these islands had never been Russian. This transformed the Sea of Okhotsk into a Soviet lake, but in recent years it has provided Japanese military circles with a welcome argument to overcome pacifist sentiment at home in order to comply with the suggestions made by America and China that they should re-arm against Russia. This is perhaps the clearest case of how Russia's desire for security can seem menacing to others, leading to an actual deterioration in that very security. Only to the south did Stalin fail to achieve the historic ambitions of some Imperial Russian statesmen, ambitions in which he had been irresponsibly encouraged by Churchill in Teheran. Iran offered no warm-water port. Turkey, benefiting from cast-iron diplomatic agreements and stiffening Allied attitudes, refused to modify the Straits Convention, refused to grant a naval base, and refused to return the territories taken from Russia in 1920. Thus ended Stalin's largely successful attempt to revise the frontiers of the Soviet Union. They endure to this day, a monument to Russia's understandable but obsessive concern for security at home and abroad: tens of thousands of miles of barbed wire, K.G.B. frontier guards, planes and patrolboats, the best that modern repressive technology can devise.

The conversion of Poland into a loyal ally of Russia taxed Soviet resourcefulness to the limit; it has demanded qualities of ruthlessness and patience and a determination to invest whatever may be necessary to achieve the result desired. The enthusiasm shown for the Polish-born Pope John Paul II in 1979, and the temporary achievement by the Polish working class of the right to strike in 1980, show how very far from ideal the Polish situation remains in Soviet eyes. Only a combination of fear and opportunism can have induced the Brezhnev leadership to take on another such challenge in Afghanistan in 1979, though the

Afghans may lack the cohesion of the Poles. This sense of Polish solidarity, which still causes such disquiet in Moscow, stems from the determination of the Polish priesthood and gentry, throughout the nineteenth century, to recover their lost nationhood. Marxism had little impact on this sentiment: Rosa Luxemburg's largely Jewish Social Democrats made few if any concessions to Polish nationalism; and she found Germany a more fruitful field for her endeavours. When Communism first appeared in Poland, it was in the guise of Comandarm Tukhachevsky's armies in 1920, when they offered to impose a Dzerzhinsky government at the point of the bayonet. The 'Fourth Partition' of 1939 and the widespread beliefs that the Soviet Union had massacred the Polish officers at Katyn, and had betrayed the Warsaw Rising against the Germans, all conspired to inflame anti-Russian sentiment. Massacres and deportations by Hitler and Stalin had combined to remove most of the Jewish, Orthodox, and Lutheran citizens of pre-war Poland, so that the Poles of 1945 were the most homogeneously Catholic nation in the world, loyal children of Pius XII. The mere tens of thousands of Polish Communists in 1945 included an embarrassing proportion of Jews. Many obligingly changed their names, only to have this thrown in their faces after 1967. The free elections promised to the Allies simply could not, for the foreseeable future, produce the friendly neighbour promised to the Russians and it was the Russians who were present in force to arbitrate between these incompatible promises.

Stalin invested all his diplomatic skill into weaning Churchill and the Polish Peasant Party leader, Mikołajczik, away from the more conservative officers in London. He isolated the Polish Right from Western opinion by demanding that they accept as Poland's eastern frontier the ethnic line charted by Lord Curzon, the British Foreign Secretary, in 1920. He suggested to the Americans that Churchill's obduracy over Poland was the result of his class sympathies. 'Poland,' he remarked to Harriman in 1946, 'needs democrats who will look after the interests of the people, not Tory landlords'. A major land reform in Poland after 1946 gave most peasants a material interest in the new regime and eliminated the troublesome gentry 'as a class'. A wedge was driven between the Poles and the West, including the Pope, by Russian insistence that

Poland annex the whole of German Silesia. For many years this went unrecognized by the West and the Church. The Russians counted correctly on the Polish peasantry knowing the value of the bird in the hand. The new Polish government appropriated the symbols of Polish nationalism and attended Mass; they inaugurated a grandiose plan to restore the baroque splendours of Warsaw, and they attacked the conservative Quebec government, which refused to return the Polish crown jewels. Mikołajczik lasted just long enough to persuade the bulk of the underground 'Home Army' to abandon their guerilla war against the Russian and Polish Communists. By January 1947, the new realities were put to the test. A 500,000-strong Workers' Party was able to fix the promised 'free elections' by arrests, intimidation, and some straightforward ballot-rigging. Mikołajczik avoided the fate of some other non-Communist leaders in Eastern Europe by going into exile.

Russia's two other East European Allies presented fewer initial difficulties. While Stalin was plainly worried because the Yugoslavs were pushing their social revolution too fast, he did not altogether object to Tito's elimination of British influence from the Eastern Adriatic. In Czechoslovakia, Soviet aims were achieved promptly, and in an atmosphere of real amity. Many Slovaks had participated willingly in the anti-Bolshevist crusade in 1941, but the honour of Slovakia was saved by a spirited anti-German revolt in 1944. The Czechs had learnt in 1938 that the Western powers could not guarantee their security and Beneš was now determined to rule with Stalin's blessing. The Communist Gottwald ordered his militants to postpone the revolution that was theirs for the taking in 1945. The Soviet Army was present but popular, the Czech Army under the control of friendly officers, and in the free elections of 1945 the Communists gained 43·5 per cent of the vote. Stalin was anxious to reciprocate, and at a time of real famine in Russia he sent 200,000 tons of grain to Czechoslovakia, a gesture that evoked genuine gratitude.

With the sole exception of Bulgaria, the former enemy areas of Eastern Europe contained few friends of the Soviet Union. Limited Allied sympathy for the local populations gave Stalin a much freer hand in dealing with them. He brought to bear traditional Russian dreams of Orthodox unity and Slav solidarity but his fundamental motive was the creation of a buffer zone sufficiently deep to absorb any repetition of July 1941. Throughout Eastern Europe, the Soviet Army provided protection and logistics for Soviet-trained and native Communists, who rebuilt their shattered parties, weaned left-wing or opportunist socialists from independent or anti-Soviet leaders, and suborned conservative bureaucrats and soldiers. Soviet Ambassadors and Commanders secured the suppression of real and alleged Fascists and collaborators. Russian Orthodox bishops advised their brethren to accept the new conditions with humility. The M.V.D. purged the internal security forces, repatriated exiled White Russians and hunted down interesting papers. These included the German records of German–Soviet dealings since the twenties; they might have had an unfortunate effect on the attitude of Western socialists had they been published. There were also the Gestapo files which would show which Communists had been broken. These unfortunate people were not exposed so long as they remained unconditionally loyal to the Soviet Union and its agents.

Pre-existing patterns of authoritarianism prepared the populations of Eastern Europe for the new masters. Most leading anti-Communist politicians had left already, so that the remaining obstacles to Soviet and Communist influence were few: the tactical acumen of some moderate conservatives such as King Michael of Romania; popular reaction to Red Army misbehaviour; occasional Soviet tactical errors such as the free elections in Austria and Hungary, showing negligible support for the Communists; and, above all, Stalin's own desire to avoid the final show-down with the West. From the end of the war until late 1947, Soviet policy aimed to seize the levers of power in Eastern Europe, to create subservient, but still pluralistic regimes. Reforms were limited to those all socialists and democrats could agree on; some nationalizations, land reform, free education and health services. Local Communists such as Laszlo Rajk in Hungary who wanted to go faster were sharply slapped down.

Stalin gave little overt sign of fearing America's nuclear monopoly until 1950, but he and his spokesmen demonstrated an obsessive fear of America's economic might. This fear was not entirely misplaced. During 1947, the Americans helped to eliminate Communists from the governments of Italy, France, and Belgium, and to persuade even the Czech and Polish Communists to consider participation in Secretary of State Marshall's plan for economic reconstruction *without the Soviet Union*. The Soviet Union itself could not participate without revealing the weakness of its economy, thereby inviting the Americans to 'up the ante'. Suddenly, the Soviet leaders faced the prospect of a Europe dominated by the U.S. dollar; even their most dependable friends in the buffer zone seemed captivated by the prospect. The Soviet Union insisted that no East European state, not even Finland, should participate in the Marshall plan, and in September, Zhdanov announced the formation of the Cominform, a new organization to unite the European Communist Parties. From that moment on, the formation of a block of monolithic Sovietized States began.

The first act in the tragedy took place in Prague, where the non-Communist ministers overplayed their hand by resigning in protest at the Communization of the police. Nationwide meetings of the Communist-led National Front and some quiet pressure by army and police chiefs persuaded President Beneš to replace the ministers by nominees of the Communist Party. The apparent suicide of Jan Masaryk, the Czech Foreign Minister, was the only blemish on what appeared to be a perfectly constitutional assumption of sole power by the Communists. Throughout Eastern Europe, it was now 'discovered' that the independent leaders of socialist and peasant parties had been Western spies. Western socialists were dismayed when Dimitrov, hero of the Reichstag Fire trial, had the socialist Petkov executed in Bulgaria. Many of the non-Communist leaders simply fled to the West. The rump socialist parties that remained expressed a unanimous desire to merge with the Communists. One major obstacle prevented the total subordination of Eastern Europe to Stalin's will, the single truly independent Communist regime in Yugoslavia. Yugoslavia's disobedience threatened Stalin with a world war when all he wanted was the consolidation of his buffer zone. The Yugoslavs had aided the Greek Communists in the British sphere of influence and challenged the Allies over Trieste. They had been disobedient in other ways, eliminating the forms of 'bourgeois democracy' before this was convenient for Stalin and refusing to submit to Soviet economic exploitation by so-called 'joint companies'. Most serious of all, as the Cominform itself made clear, was the refusal of the Yugoslavs to tolerate the creation within Yugoslavia of a party within the Party, responsible only to the Soviet M.V.D. Twenty years later, Raúl Castro would denounce similar activities in Cuba and emerge unscathed. What made the Yugoslavs even more of a menace was the prestige they enjoyed among the other East European Communists, some of whom, such as Dimitrov in Bulgaria, were willing to join Tito in creating a socialist Balkan Federation which might be less amenable to Soviet control.

Apparently, Stalin expected the Yugoslav Communists, led by two Soviet agents in the Politburo, to throw out Tito's closest supporters and accept Soviet rule. When Tito met the challenge head-on and submitted to the Yugoslav people a detailed account of all the matters at issue, Yugoslavia was expelled from the world Communist movement as 'Fascist'. The Yugoslavs had previously criticized the West European Communist Parties for their inclination towards parliamentarianism, and this was now used to isolate Yugoslavia from their moral support. All forms of economic aid were cut off and threatening manoeuvres conducted by Soviet troops in neighbouring countries. The maltreatment of *three* Soviet citizens by the Yugoslav secret police was cited in a violent propaganda offensive: 'Would it not be more correct to say,' fulminated the Soviet media, 'that a regime under which people are ill-treated in this way is a Fascist, Gestapo regime?' Inexorably, the Yugoslavs were pushed towards an accommodation with the Americans as the only way of maintaining their independence, an experience to be shared by Mao and Sadat many years later. Despite Khrushchev's rapprochement with Tito in 1956 and Brezhnev's pilgrimage to his graveside, the Soviet government has never brought itself to recognize Yugoslavia's unconditional right to independence. Once again, however, Stalin's caution was manifest. He did not invade Yugoslavia, afraid perhaps of the resistance the Yugoslavs might put up and the opportunity this might offer the Americans to intervene in his Balkan sphere of influence.

The failure of Soviet policy in Yugoslavia shook Stalin; no

Communist Party had ever before defied him with impunity. It intensified his determination to subject the rest of Eastern Europe to totalitarian control and increased his chronic fear of 'treason'. In the three years after the breach with Yugoslavia, the region was transformed in two simultaneous processes. The societies were re-structured so that they could be totally controlled by the local Communist Parties. This involved the total and final suppression of all non-Communist political activity, the favouring of heavy industry, the collectivization of agriculture, and the emasculation of the Churches, especially the hated Catholic Church which was busy inspiring anti-Communism from San Francisco to Saigon.

The second process saw the conversion of the East European Communist parties into Soviet-style armies of obedient robots – obedient, that is, to Moscow. For this to succeed, questioning intellectuals had to be eliminated and the rank-and-file inoculated against the virus of independent thinking. As in the Soviet Union before the war, show trials served this dual purpose admirably. Throughout Eastern Europe, the security forces were ordered to find agents of Titoism and Imperialism among the highest ranking members of the Communist parties. It is to the credit of the local secret police that they sometimes made the mistake of looking for real evidence; they were quickly instructed by personnel seconded by the M.V.D. Often the most vigorous of the initial purgers, such as Rudolf Slansky in Czechoslovakia, ended as victims. Confes-sions were sometimes extracted by blackmail, more often by force, but drugs were used more frequently than they had been in the Soviet show trials. The resulting theatre was staged with panache.

In Czechoslovakia and Hungary, as in the Soviet Union itself, some of the leading victims were Jewish Communists. However, in Poland and Hungary other Jewish Communists were among those promoted because of the purges. Stalin was prepared to exploit other people's antisemitism but it did not determine his own actions. It was precisely in Czechoslovakia, the country with the warmest feelings for the Soviet Union and the highest proportion of socialist intellectuals, that casualties were highest. This is a chilling thought for those who believe that Soviet socialism would be more tolerant if introduced into a West European society. The Communists who have come to power in Czechoslovakia since

1969 have also been far more vindictive than Kadar in Hungary.

After 1949, Soviet personnel were installed openly or secretly in all important offices and ministries of state throughout Eastern Europe, a system which excited much resentment. Only in Finland was a possible Communist coup discouraged, though the Finns had to agree to military consultations in a new treaty. Perhaps the fear that Sweden might conclude an alliance with the Americans dissuaded the Russians from Sovietizing Finland. To a large extent, the situation established in Eastern Europe by the early 1950s is the situation that still obtains.

Soviet armed forces suppressed revolts in East Berlin in 1953, and in Hungary in 1956: they intervened to re-impose a harshly intolerant authoritarian regime in Czechoslovakia in 1968. The threat of Soviet intervention has been a constant factor in Polish politics since 1956, leading to the military coup of 1981. A similar threat was made against Romania in 1968–9. Only the barrier presented by Yugoslavia prevented intervention in Albania after 1960. Bulgaria alone, surrounded by her national enemies and still grateful for her liberation, has never had to be encouraged in her loyalty by threats of naked force. A review of these interventions and threats of intervention shows clearly enough which aspects of the *status quo* Soviet leaders regard as essential and which as marginal or unimportant.

Since Stalin's death, the Soviet government has accepted the need to avoid gratuitous offence to national sensibilities. This was signalled by the removal in 1956 of Marshal Rokossovsky, a Soviet citizen, as Poland's Defence Minister, and by the abolition of the Cominform. The Soviet government has accepted locally negotiated compromises with the farmers, leading to de-collectivization in Poland and Hungary. Since the deaths of Stalin and Pius XII, State and major Churches in Eastern Europe have achieved a *modus vivendi*, the extent of the concessions to the Churches depending on pragmatic assessments of the extent of local support for them. In cultural affairs and the supply of consumer goods, concessions have been made to intellectuals and workers. Some scope has been permitted to reformist technocrats, especially in Hungary, to experiment with greater managerial freedom.

On the other hand, Romania's striving for economic independence and an independent foreign policy have been enormously resented by the Soviet government and are tolerated rather than accepted. Equally unpalatable have been the repeated attempts made by Polish workers since 1970 to achieve the right to strike under representative trade unions, a concession that would hamstring centralized planning methods. Where then does the Soviet Union draw the line? The creation of the buffer zone in Eastern Europe arose from a desire for military and political security and it will be defended against any threat, whether it be the desire of the East Germans for re-unification with West Germany (as in 1953), or the desire of the Hungarians for neutrality (in 1956). In 1980, Polish Communists reminded the leaders of Solidarity that Poland lies in 'the immediate security zone of the socialist super-power'. This is not just a question of armies; the Yugoslav and Romanian welcomes for Chairman Hua in 1979 were also perceived as a threat. Above all, the machinery of control, the monopolistic position of the local Communist parties, must not be attenuated. It does not matter if the opponents of Communist hegemony are bourgeois nationalists, spontaneous movements of workers, or reformist Communist functionaries. The Soviet leadership is especially wary of attempts by the intellectuals as a quasi-class to usurp what they believe to be the role of the party. This means that reliable comrades must exercise a vigilant censorship over all forms of public debate – above all, when it comes to discussions of the origins, and therefore the legitimacy, of the current order in Eastern Europe. Only as a last resort has the Soviet Union used military power, as this has a destabilizing effect throughout the world. Less disturbing internationally is the technique of a military coup by the local armed forces, first attempted in Poland in 1981. The similarity of this to military coups in right-wing dictatorships was strikingly illustrated when General Jaruzelski introduced it with a speech which echoed that of his right-wing Turkish counterpart, General Evren, in almost every particular.

Soviet policy in Eastern Europe has had some important successes in modernizing social and economic structures of the more backward countries in the region. But the awareness that they lack real independence continues to irk many people in Eastern Europe, particularly in the more advanced areas such as Czechoslovakia and East Germany, and in those with a homogeneous nationalist tradition, such as Poland. Since the West finally accepted Soviet hegemony in the region in the treaties of the mid 1970s and in the Helsinki Agreements of 1975, the major threats to Soviet power have come from indigenous forces. Even in Poland, where they have massive popular support, they show little sign of being able to reverse the results of the war.

The gains made by the Soviet Union in Eastern Europe after the war, and more recently in the Third World, have been totally overshadowed in Soviet eyes by the threats that have emerged in East Asia, where, in 1980, a 'Greater East Asia Co-Prosperity Sphere' looked far more feasible than when it was openly proclaimed by the Japanese militarists in the 1930s. Who in 1945 could have foreseen that the co-leader of a Communist China would in 1978 rehabilitate Emperor Hirohito and urge the Japanese to rearm against Communist Russia? In their dealings with China, the Russians initially showed complacency and greed. After Stalin's death, they revealed a total inability to share the leadership of the 'socialist camp'. Towards both China and Japan, the Soviet Union has acted with a total lack of the tact and courtesy that they themselves demand from the West. There is nothing new about this. In 1945, Stalin told U.S. Secretary of State Byrnes that 'all Chinese are boasters who exaggerate the forces of their opponents as well as their own'. Stalin felt that the Chinese Communists, despite their rhetoric, had done little more to hurt the Japanese than the Kuomintang, and he associated peasant guerillas with the disorderly bands of peasant anarchists that had plagued Soviet power in the 1920s. He counted on continuing Chinese disunity and weakness, taking advantage of it to annex Tuva in 1944, and to extort from Chiang Kai-shek the 'independence' of Outer Mongolia in 1946. After removing the Japanese, he reclaimed Imperial Russia's extra-territorial position in the Chinese north-east. The Chinese Communists were allowed to seize Japanese arms there but that was all. Stalin's pre-war attempts to oust Mao from the leadership of the Chinese Party were well known to Mao himself, while the Soviet correspondent in Yenan relayed Mao's Chinese nationalism and contempt for Stalin to Moscow.

The Soviet press greeted Mao's victory in the Chinese revolution very coolly; his wife was subjected to various petty humiliations while undergoing medical treatment in Moscow at this time. At the end of 1949, Mao visited Moscow to conclude a treaty of alliance. Again, there was little public or private rejoicing. Mao came as a potential equal, but returned, six fraught weeks later, as a reluctant satellite, conceding the Soviet Union's quasi-colonial position in Singkiang and the north-east, a one-sided military alliance, and a Soviet veto over Chinese foreign relations. Khrushchev later conceded that this had been an 'insult to the Chinese people'. For a time the Korean war brought real cordiality to Sino-Soviet relations: far from negotiating with the Americans, the Chinese had given them a bloody nose at a time when the Americans were at the apogee of their military and economic power. Soviet respect for the Chinese was immensely enhanced by this and this was reflected in greater economic assistance. In 1954, the new and unstable Soviet leadership renounced Russia's quasi-colonial privileges in China, though they absolutely refused to alter the status of Outer Mongolia. The Chinese paid a very high price for all this. They lost 300,000 men in Korea including one of Mao's sons; they lost the opportunity for the speedy re-incorporation of Taiwan, and the benefits that might have flowed from economic and political relations with the West. They even had to pay the Russians hard cash for the arms they used in Korea.

No reliable independent witnesses were present when the first shots were fired in the Korean war, and Western revisionist historians have convincingly shown the strong interest General MacArthur, President Rhee of South Korea, and Chiang Kai-shek all had in the war. But Stalin and President Kim of North Korea had an equal interest in the war, and the striking initial successes of the North Koreans suggest that they were not exactly unprepared for the conflict. In retrospect, it seems foolish of both Stalin and Truman to have left two inflexible Korean regimes face to face with no restraining leash, unless they wanted them to settle the affairs of Korea on their own. In any event, the results of the war were gratifying to both incipient super-powers: both 'camps' were whipped into line behind their leadership. The subsequent and consequent international isolation of China became a powerful diplomatic weapon in the hands of Khrushchev for a number of years. He became fond of suggesting that the West would have to deal with Russia for fear of the terrible Chinese. One can hardly blame him for using a myth concocted in the U.S.A. It was nearly twenty years before Nixon and Kissinger were able to call this absurd bluff and establish cordial relations with Mao Tse-tung in person.

There seems little doubt that the whole Chinese leadership hoped that, after Stalin's death, the entire Communist movement would develop a pattern of collective leadership in which the Chinese revolution would occupy some sort of vice-chairmanship. A divided Soviet leadership was in no position to undertake such a radical move and Khrushchev's rapprochement with Tito and denunciation of Stalin were made, in true Stalin style, with no warning to anyone outside the Soviet Union, least of all the Chinese. When the Soviet leadership found itself in difficulties in Eastern Europe, it was prepared to lean on Chinese support; Chinese agreement was also essential for concluding the wars in Korea and Viet Nam in 1953–4. But if the Chinese thought they had gained a position of equality with the Russians, they were soon disabused. Khrushchev was not prepared to sacrifice his improving relations with President Eisenhower for the sake of Taiwan, nor would he disavow the 'goulash Communism' that appalled Chinese puritanism.

Mao's assumption of the mantle of Communism's senior philosopher–statesman irked Khrushchev intensely, particularly when the Chinese embarked on the 'Great Leap Forward', an ambitious series of economic experiments, and suggested that they might achieve Communism before the Russians. By 1959–60, the Chinese had achieved some industrial advances but at an appalling cost in terms of universal hunger. Now a confident Soviet leadership confronted a divided Chinese leadership and cancelled an agreement to supply the Chinese with nuclear weapons, signalled to the West and India her refusal to support China's aims in Taiwan and the Himalayas, encouraged the defection of tens of thousands of

Chinese citizens from Singkiang, and cut off all economic and technical aid. The Chinese replied with the criticism that the Russians were soft on 'revisionism' and that their views on nuclear weapons and the ex-colonial countries were blunting the class struggle everywhere. The July 1963 Test Ban Treaty between the Soviet Union and the West was denounced in Peking as 'a U.S.–Soviet alliance against China pure and simple'. The Chinese proceeded to explode their own bomb on the day Nikita Khrushchev fell from office.

The Brezhnev leadership has made several attempts to stabilize relations with China; but the 1969 border clashes, Soviet hints at a unilateral elimination of Chinese nuclear forces, and recent Soviet support for Viet Nam against China show just how fraught relations really are. One small bonus has been an intensification of Soviet patriotism: the slogan 'Siberia is Ours!' is one nearly all Soviet citizens can echo.

One casualty of Sino-Soviet tension was the international Communist movement. The insecurity of Khrushchev's position as leader of world Communism led him to convene a world Communist Congress in Moscow in 1957, the first since the Seventh Congress of the Comintern in 1935. In the wake of Khrushchev's revelations a year earlier, it began to look as though the world Communist movement might begin to play the role of super-ego to the Soviet State suggested by the Comintern statutes many years earlier. This was not to be. Differences over Yugoslav 'revisionism', the extent of the independence of the West European Parties, and Soviet relations with China soon split the movement wide open. The last Congress to bring all Parties together took place in Moscow in 1960. On relations between socialist states, it said:

Fraternal friendship and mutual assistance of peoples, born of the socialist system, have superseded the political isolation and national egoism typical of capitalism.

Since then, revisionism has gained ground in the European Communist Parties, some of whom have even claimed the label 'Eurocommunist' since the mid 1970s, while the ideas of Trotsky have had a significant effect on younger socialists. If the Soviet Union can still command the loyalty of most of the world's Communist parties, this is increasingly a question of tactical necessity. The old emotional loyalty to the Soviet Union is the property of a declining number of older militants.

The Soviet debacle in China has been fully as great as the American 'loss' of China in 1949. It has been compounded by the failure of the Soviet leadership to create a positive relationship with Japan, a nation which in 1980 achieved the same Gross National Product as the Soviet Union itself. With the exception of a brief period during the mid 1970s when the Soviet Union sought Japanese assistance in the development of Siberia, the Russians have been victims of their inability to decide between an alliance with Japanese capitalism and their support for the Japanese pacifist opposition. During the immediate post-war period, when it was firmly excluded from the occupation of Japan, the Soviet Union aligned itself with the pacifists and socialists in Japan in their efforts decisively to weaken Japan's traditional ruling class. By refusing to deal with the Japanese at the American-sponsored San Francisco Peace Conference in 1952, the Russians lost the chance to exploit remaining Japanese weakness. Subsequently, their refusal to return the two southernmost Kurile islands and the tactless conduct of the Soviet navy have been exploited by the revived forces of Japanese conservatism to nudge the Japanese people into an acceptance of the idea that Japan should replace the U.S.A. as the leading military power in East Asia. The Russians have still to find a formula for dealing with both East Asian giants; they are paying a very high price for these failures.

Soviet foreign policy has had a number of impressive successes in the Third World, and Admiral Gorshkov's navy finds a welcome haven in every continent and ocean. Two facts must be grasped, however, for these successes to be seen in perspective: first is the enormous help given to this policy by the errors of the West; second is that, despite this help, Soviet policy has suffered setback after setback in the Third World and this same fate may yet befall some of her more recent successes. The countries of Asia became independent around 1950, those of Africa some ten years later. For many of the leaders of the new nations, the Soviet Union had been a source of inspiration. As Jawaharlal Nehru put it:

Russia, following the great Lenin, looked into the future and thought only of what was to be, while other countries lay numbed under the dead hand of the past and spent their energy in preserving the useless relics of a bygone age. In particular, I was impressed by the reports of the great progress made by the backward regions of Central Asia under the Soviet regime ... the presence and example of the Soviets was a bright and heartening phenomenon in a dark and dismal world.

In view of this fund of goodwill, it is all the more surprising that the Soviet Union has found it so difficult to forge firm alliances with Third-World countries. Purges of Soviet experts on Asia as 'Trotskyites' in the thirties, a tendency to prejudge 'bourgeois nationalists', and an excessively monolithic foreign policy all played their part.

During the 1930s and 1940s, the willingness of Communist trade unionists in Latin America to do deals with dictators such as Peron in Argentina, Vargas in Brazil, and Batista in Cuba alienated the libertarian intelligentsia and helped divide the potential revolutionary movement. It took the Cuban Communist Party years to overcome this division in its own ranks. During the war, the Communists in India and Indonesia were instructed to support the colonial power, a wartime ally of the Soviet Union, against the nationalists. By 1948, they were being instructed to sabotage the creation of peaceful relations between the newly independent countries and the former colonial powers. Again, this isolated the Communists and inoculated the middle classes against Communism, especially in Indonesia where an abortive coup in 1948 anticipated the debacle of 1964.

The *volte face* of the Soviet government over Israel has already been mentioned. It left a bitter taste – all the more so when the Soviet Union began to disseminate antisemitic propaganda; and Arab nationalists have never forgotten that, without Czech arms, Israel might have been strangled at birth. Ironically, it was the Chinese success at the 1955 Bandung Conference of Non-Aligned Countries that finally persuaded the new Soviet leaders that they would have to re-examine their prejudices concerning 'bourgeois nationalists'. The first overtures came via the Chinese from the new Egyptian leader, Colonel Nasser, even though he had recently been denounced by the Egyptian Communists, and the Soviet press, as a 'Fascist'. Within a year, he had become a Soviet hero, refusing to join an anti-Soviet alliance, demanding real independence for Egypt, with Czech arms and Soviet economic assistance if need be. During the ensuing Anglo-French *folie de grandeur* at Suez in 1956, some rather unspecific Soviet threats to use rockets against the aggressors convinced many members of the intelligentsia in the Third World that the Soviet Union was indeed their best friend. From preaching total mistrust of bourgeois nationalists during the early 1950s, the Soviet Party had moved so far as to sanction the absorption of the Egyptian Communist Party into Nasser's Arab Socialist Union in 1965. The only precedent for this was the discouraging experience of the Chinese Communists who joined the Kuomintang, on Stalin's orders, in 1925.

Already, however, the tactics of infiltration were beginning to fall before a series of brutal counter-strokes by right-wing officers and politicians. These people represented middle-class aspirations towards American life-styles or merely fatigue at the inefficiency of the socialism of rhetoric. During the mid 1960s came the fall of Goulart in Brazil, Nkrumah in Ghana, Ben Bella in Algeria, and the massacre of nearly one million Communists and socialists in Indonesia, following the bungled coup by pro-Communist officers in 1964. These all suggested that the new flexible tactics had failed and provided much grist for the Chinese propaganda mill.

These disasters were compounded by the humiliating defeat of the Egyptians, with their massive stocks of Soviet equipment, during the October War of 1967. Nasser never really recovered from this shock and died within three years. By 1972, his successor Anwar Sadat had thrown Soviet advisers out of Egypt and levered them out of the rest of the Arab world. The Soviet failure to understand the Arabs is part of their general failure to understand the force of modern nationalism, but it is partly explained by the fact that they have no real interest in the emergence of an enormous Arab Federation on their southern flanks. Their influence in the Arab world has been entirely negative, depending on Israel to force the Arabs to look for support to another great power rather than Israel's patron. For this reason, they have been neither willing nor able to move the Arabs towards peace. Their sympathy for the

Palestinians is not convincing in view of their refusal to allow the Tatars back to Crimea or the Meskhetians to Georgia. They might have used Jewish emigration as a means of pressure on Israel; instead they have traded it off for economic and military concessions by the West. In short, Henry Kissinger was at least half right when he said to Sadat: 'The Soviet Union can only offer you war, we can give you peace'. In the early 1980s, it is still the case that the only real allies of the Soviet Union in the Middle East are a shaky Syria and the Palestine Liberation Organization.

If Cuba has been the Soviet Union's greatest success story in the Third World so far, it has been strictly by courtesy of the United States. Fidel Castro's 26th July Movement was on very bad terms with the Cuban Communists when it seized power at the beginning of 1960. It was the Americans whose insensitivity and economic bullying converted Castro into a Communist. Cuban–Soviet friendship has flowered since, though not without repeated tensions. Castro's delight at receiving a nuclear umbrella in October 1962 turned to chagrin when it was withdrawn without consultation; no Latin American nationalist could be happy with a mere verbal pledge of non-intervention from an American president. The Soviet government publicly criticized Che Guevara's attempts to ignite guerrilla war in the Bolivian countryside in the late 1960s, while Castro had his brother publicly denounce Soviet attempts to subvert the Cuban Communist Party in 1968. In the 1970s, Castro did his best to swallow his disapproval of Allende's parliamentary road to socialism in Chile, the model approved in the Soviet Union. Since 1973, when Allende and his supporters were massacred in Chile, Cuban and Soviet policy-makers have drawn closer together in a new-found humility forged by the common experience of failure. In the late 1970s, they began to give their cautious support to a heterodox coalition of Central American revolutionaries struggling to break free from local oligarchies and U.S. monopolies.

Soviet policy in Africa has benefited immensely from Cuban collaboration. Soviet logistics and cash and Cuban personnel have helped consolidate quasi-Soviet regimes in the ex-Portuguese colonies of Guinea-Bissau, Angola, and Mozambique, and more recently in Ethiopia, a former ally of the United States. Like the

P.L.O., the African National Congress of South Africa (Azania) is deeply indebted to the Soviet Union for its moral and material support for their efforts to overthrow the apartheid regime in that country.

China's rapprochement with the U.S.A. in 1969 facilitated the American withdrawal from Viet Nam by demonstrating that 'monolithic Asian Communism' was a figment of President Johnson's imagination. Subsequent Vietnamese disillusion with China has made Viet Nam one of the Soviet Union's closest allies. Soviet military aid to Viet Nam, which was very modest by Egyptian standards during the period when the American forces were seriously trying to win the war, became much more lavish as the Americans began to pull out. The Soviet Union supported the effective re-unification of Viet Nam in 1975 and the re-assertion of traditional Vietnamese predominance in Indo-China. In clashes with China in 1980, the Vietnamese showed how valuable military experience and sophisticated equipment can be. It was a savage irony that found the Soviet Union supporting the elimination by Viet Nam of one of the most pathological distortions of socialism yet seen – the Pol Pot regime in Kampuchea – just as the Western powers launched a campaign in favour of human rights. This is not an isolated occurrence. It was the Soviet Union's support that enabled India to liberate Bangladesh from Yahya Khan's Pakistani dictatorship in 1971 and the Russians gave the subsequent democratic Bhutto regime in Pakistan a massive loan. In Afghanistan, the replacement of Hafizullah Amin's indigenous Communist regime by the Soviet puppet, Babrak Karmal, in 1979, was irregular in international law, but it was an undoubted improvement in terms of 'human rights'. (The principal motive of the Russians was probably fear lest a resurgence of Islamic nationalism might spread from Iran into Soviet Central Asia.)

The Soviet Union has also, of course, supported some obnoxious regimes in Eastern Europe and it has done some shady deals with terrorist regimes like that of Idi Amin in Uganda. More recently, it has apparently worked closely with Argentina to sabotage the U.N. Human Rights Commission. However, the Soviet Union has been largely successful in suggesting that Russia and not China is the 'stronghold sure of the friendship of the peoples', in the words of the Hymn of the Soviet Union. In so doing, it has reinforced its own legitimacy. Young Soviet engineers in Cuba and Ethiopia can feel involved in a continuing anti-imperialist struggle in a way that is scarcely possible in today's hedonistic Soviet society. Despite this marginal asset and the increasing technical competence of Soviet diplomats, bankers and K.G.B. men, Soviet successes have been as much the result of the 'contradictions of capitalism' as of their own plans or plots.

From a conventional point of view, Soviet foreign policy since the last war has been a failure. The modest distance that has begun to appear between the policies of Bonn and Washington since 1982 is of minor significance compared with the fact that all the major concentrations of power in the world (U.S.A., Europe, China, and Japan) are opponents of the Soviet Union. The alliances with Cuba, Viet Nam, and some African and Arab countries cannot compare in importance with the forces aligned against Russia. There is also no sign that India will take any risks to help Viet Nam or Afghanistan on Russia's behalf. A close examination of Soviet foreign policy suggests that it is as often conventionally opportunist as it is principled; Stalin's use of 'joint companies' in Communist-ruled countries after the war and his plea for an African territory are cases in point. The Soviet government is often torn between short-term accommodations with capitalists and a strategic interest in revolutionary movements. The essential continuities of Russian policy are striking, however, and nowhere more so than in France where the Communists have on three occasions (1936, 1944, 1968) opposed revolution with Russian blessing.

The Eternal Flame

The Great Russian people created an identity for themselves in the forests of north-east Europe after their retreat from the heartland of old Rus. As James Billington reminds us, fire was an awesome phenomenon for these dwellers of the forest. For the pre-Christian Russians, Perun, the Russian Thor, occupied a central place in the pantheon. His Christianized version, Ilya of Murom, Elijah in another guise, sent down fire on the heads of his enemies and ascended to Heaven in a chariot of fire. The icons of Rublev depict the furnace of Hell that awaits those who fail the test of life. This fascination with fire has not gone from Russian culture. The most remarkable example of Russian music and dance this century is 'The Firebird' by Stravinsky and Diaghilev.

For dwellers in the forest, fire was a helpmate and an enemy. It was by a process of cut and burn that new settlements arose in the forest, but the friend could so easily turn into a raging enemy, destroying everything in its path. The first step towards a future greatness was taken when the Russians began to assimilate the Finns in their midst. A crucial element in this conversion was the use of religious emotionalism, a form of ideology. Traditionally, flaming candles were immersed in the waters blessed on Epiphany to remind men and women that Christ came to 'baptize with the Holy Ghost and with fire'. Fire was also the agency by which those possessed of the arcane secrets of the smithy converted rock into iron, the basic material for sword and axe alike. Ivan Peresvetov, the sixteenth-century apologist for autocracy, wanted to set up a factory for making shields, but the Time of Troubles soon brought devastating new combinations of steel and fire to Russia. The Russians found themselves forced to modernize or perish. Their response was to hire Andreas Vinnius from Holland, a supersmith of his time; in the twentieth century Stalin was to bring Max MacMurray from Cleveland to do the same at Magnitogorsk. The Pouring of the 200 Millionth Ton of Steel at Magnitogorsk in 1974 celebrated a contemporary instalment of a perennial Russian theme.

Fire was also a weapon in its own right: when masters were harsh, peasants might 'let loose the red rooster'. Soviet historians believe that the fires of 1547, that for a time brought Ivan IV to his senses, were a form of deliberate social protest. In his study of crowds, Elias Canetti writes:

Fire is the same wherever it breaks out: it spreads rapidly; it is contagious and insatiable; it can break out anywhere, and with great suddenness; it is multiple; it is destructive; it has an enemy; it dies; it acts as though it were alive, and is so treated.

This aptly describes the periodic rebellions in Russian history and, with one arguable exception, the great revolution accomplished for Russia and for the world by the arsonist whose journal bore the name *Iskra* (The Spark). Fire was also a weapon of last resort for those who had lost the desire to live in a polluted world. The Old Believers doomed on earth converted themselves into flames, the quicker to reach heaven; rather the holocaust than a loss of faith. In 1812, the Russians reduced Napoleon's victories to ashes, rendering the sublime ridiculous, by permitting the fiery destruction of their capital. At the heart of all the great Soviet war memorials, an 'eternal flame' commemorates those who fell in the last great conflagration and expresses the hope that there will never be another. Fire, then, is inseparable from the four main themes of Russian history: expansion, modernization, liberation, and survival.

In his work on Mao Tsetung, Stuart Schram has defined the phases by which China modernized as 'tradition-orientated nationalism', 'radical Westernization', and 'revolutionary nationalism'. This schema has an obvious relevance to the Russian experience. In the seventeenth century, Patriarch Philaret and Tsar Alexis combined xenophobia with a free use of Western military technology; Peter embarked on a ruthless policy of military westernization; and Catherine attempted to import Western ideas wholesale. The transition to revolutionary nationalism was delayed for another century, however. A feature of this 'hiatus' was the emergence of a superfluous caste of 'over-educated' persons; Gogol's comical experiences in attempting to gain a well-paid professorship with minimal qualifications were an incident in the disillusion of the intelligentsia with the market, an essential stage in the introduction of socialist ideas into Russia. Nevertheless, the attitudes of both intelligentsia and peasantry during the 1917 revolution suggest that capitalist individualism had made greater headway among the Russians than anyone had suspected. The triumph of revolutionary nationalism was accomplished in two stages, the revolutionary predominating under Lenin and the nationalistic emerging more strongly under Stalin, though neither element was entirely lacking from either phase. In 1931, Stalin turned to Russian national sentiment to legitimize the ruthless drive for industrialization to which he had just committed the country. He suggested that Russian history was a story of defeats rather than expansion:

. . . the history of old Russia is the history of defeats due to backwardness. She was beaten by the Mongol khans. She was beaten by the Turkish beys. She was beaten by the Swedish feudal barons. She was beaten by the Polish-Lithuanian 'squires'. She was beaten by the Anglo-French capitalists. She was beaten by the Japanese barons. All beat her for her backwardness . . .

Stalin's revolutionary nationalism was responsible for the massive purges of the late 1930s. To some extent, they marked the cultural reunification of the Russian people; the old intelligentsia, whose values derived from aristocratic predecessors such as the Decembrists, were merged with the new Soviet 'intelligentsia', recruited from the workers and peasantry. On the other hand, the hope of socialists everywhere that Stalin might pioneer the final resolution of national problems was disappointed. Within the Soviet Union, militiamen still arrest orthodox Jews for trying to say a kaddish at the Babi Yar memorial, while over the Amur River frontier soldiers of two 'socialist' states confront one another with modern weapons at the ready. Beyond the borders of the Soviet Union, the government has alternated between gravely underestimating the power of modern nationalism and concluding tactical, and sometimes over-cynical, alliances with nationalist movements.

Whether or not the theme of modernization in Russian history is now exhausted, we cannot but pause to consider the pathos that fascinates us in the Russian nineteenth century. With the creation by Pushkin and his predecessors of a language with the polish and sophistication of any in Europe, with an endless potential for revitalization through contact with the verse and prose of the people, a great literature was born. Gogol, Tolstoy, Dostoyevsky, Turgenev, Chekhov, and even Gorky belong to the common wealth of all who read. The other arts, although less universal, made their own contribution. Foreign architects seem to have built the majority of Russia's most famous buildings but Zakharov's Admiralty is among the most striking and original creations of the neo-classical movement. Tchaikovsky's symphonies have universal appeal, and Mussorgsky's 'popular music dramas' are among the most overwhelming of all operas. In dancing and painting, Russian men and women made a quite disproportionate contribution to the development of post-impressionist techniques throughout the world. Nor should we forget the influence of Russians on the 'minor' and domestic arts.

Modernization was, of course, the sequel to backwardness. Russia is poor in soil and climate compared with the United States. For many centuries she was uniquely vulnerable to invasion; she suffered several centuries of isolation from advances in European culture and emerged with a peculiarly despotic form of government, which was both a defence and also an obstacle to further development. Enduring backwardness in tsarist Russia was the consequence of a pattern of social and economic relations defined by a militarized state with a limited understanding of economics, a fragile capitalist class, a fear of innovators as possible subversives, and a servile labour force. In principle, these relationships should have been abolished by the revolution. The massive importation of Western technology during the 1970s suggests that these relations have in fact been substantially reproduced; the enterprise director has replaced the pre-revolutionary capitalist. Zhores Medvedev's study of the obstacles to the circulation of scientific information demonstrates graphically just how the State impedes progress precisely in those areas in which it desires it. While the average Nomenklaturist is certainly more interested in economics than the average tsarist pomeshchik, he is unwilling to permit the agricultural workers an economic freedom that would undermine his political control and afraid, so far, to subject the workers to unemployment on the scale required to induce higher productivity.

The original ideology of liberation for the Russian people was the idea of a 'true tsar' who would grant the land to the peasants. The nineteenth century saw the creation of a new ideology, that of the anarchists, led by Michael Bakunin among others, who sought to realize the ancient dream of the peasantry in a Russia that would avoid the trials of industrialization and the alienation induced by the division of labour. It was, however, Marxism that ultimately took root and inspired the successful revolution that replaced the tsars. There were many reasons for this. For the people, a traditional view that 'he who trades, steals', the insistence of the quasi-feudal governing class on attaching 'estate' labels to individuals right up to 1917, and the experience of proletarianization in the massive, often foreign-owned, factories – all this appeared to square with Marxist doctrine. For the most revolutionary of the intelligentsia, Marxism offered something else: a signpost towards the overthrow of autocracy and the introduction of a truly rational regime. For Lenin, above all, the possibility of creating a Marxist sociology or a Marxist psychology meant next to nothing. For all his years in Western Europe, he showed almost no comprehension of the mentality of West Europeans.

From the rich and complex thought of Marx, Lenin extracted above all certain recipes for the conquest of power. This was his strength, and also his weakness, as history has shown.*

The performance of Marxism in its Russian laboratory has been impressive in many respects. The Bolsheviks expropriated the exploiters and won the admiration of revolutionary socialists throughout the world for so doing. They achieved better health and education for all and social mobility for hundreds of thousands of working people. Soviet women have achieved civil independence, the right to abortion (though this has at times been

*Hélène Carrère d'Encausse and Stuart Schram, *Marxism and Asia* (London, 1969), p. 31.

withdrawn), and easier access than in tsarist times to education and careers. Members of national minorities have become as literate as the Russians, and non-Europeans in the Soviet Union came to occupy key positions in the economy at a time when most Europeans were still insisting that they were simply incapable of them.

As a doctrine claiming to be 'scientific', Marxism presupposes a wide area of intellectual freedom, but the Russian Marxists inherited and reinforced a tradition in which dissent was coterminous with crime. In 1922, Alexandra Kollontai told Ignazio Silone: 'If you happen to read in the papers that Lenin has had me arrested for stealing the silver spoons in the Kremlin, that simply means that I'm not entirely in agreement with him about some little problem of agricultural or industrial policy'. The enormously enhanced power of the State, especially after 1928, combined with the destruction of private property rights, has enabled the Soviet rulers to repress criticism and impose uniformity of expression without parallel, even in tsarist times. Only outside Russia has it been possible to publish unhindered the works of such authors as Pasternak, Solzhenitsyn, and Nadezhda Mandelshtam. 'Partyness' is no longer invoked against cybernetics or genetics but plate tectonics is still criticized on ideological grounds and topology can anticipate determined resistance in the Soviet Union.

After three generations it is time to ask whether the ruling group that emerged from the revolution has not, in fact, become a parasitical ruling class? Much of the evidence presented here suggests that it has. Its capacity to achieve further advances towards modernizing or socialist objectives does appear to have declined. It seems to have become a clearly defined group appropriating the surplus product, to be able to secure substantial, though not unlimited, material advantages, to have secured a large degree of personal inviolability, and to be close to the solution of the problem of auto-reproduction. Western scholars, both hostile and sympathetic towards the Soviet regime, object to considering the Nomenklatura a class on the grounds that there is no private ownership of the means of production and that status is not heritable. Of course these criteria would lead one to the nonsensical conclusion that medieval bishops were not members of a ruling class. There is also a tendency for Western theorists to argue from the alleged social background of current senior members of the Nomenklatura. No one doubts that Khrushchev and Brezhnev once came from working-class families. This says nothing about those recruited more recently, still less about those to be recruited in the coming generation. Since the death of Stalin, no one has met any ordinary Soviet worker who claims descent from a Nomenklatura family. A more serious objection to the idea that the Nomenklatura is a class stems from their inability, so far, to subject the Soviet working class to a really efficient form of exploitation. For the Soviet working class, the introduction of the market, mass unemployment and all, would represent the erosion of the last major 'conquest' of Stalin's second revolution. Equally intriguing is the apparent disappearance of autocracy. Has the Nomenklatura succeeded where aristocracy and gentry failed in making the government of Russia a purely class dictatorship?

The erosion of socialist idealism in Russia was not unrelated to the failure of socialist revolution in the West. In both, the changing structure of employment generated hopes for social promotion and self-betterment rather than egalitarian comradeship. The erosion of the very idea of the socialist Utopia has followed the success of capitalism in devising and providing consumer goods which represent an alternative path to liberation and fulfilment, particularly for women. Long before the Soviet State was willing or able to satisfy these urges on any scale, photographs cut from wartime American magazines adorned the rooms of countless hundreds of thousands of Russians; the same process can be observed in China today. Despite the hopes of its prophet and chronicler, permanent revolution is a contradiction in terms. The revolutionary flame dies, and while it may arise in a different place or at a different time, it cannot remain at white heat in one place once it has absorbed all the available combustible material. The time comes when the booming intonation of a Mayakovsky or the geometric predictability of a Lissitsky lose their power to move. It is then that the shades of the Gulag emerge to force the survivors to count the full cost of their experiments.

During the Russian civil war, Gorky spoke to some peasants about the exposure of monkish trickery in staging supposed miracles. The peasants agreed with him and said that it was now time to expose the doctors as well. When queried, the peasants looked embarrassed. Haltingly, they explained what they meant:

> Of course, you don't believe this . . . but they say that now it's possible to poison the wind, and that would be the end of every living thing, man and beast. Now everyone is vicious, no one has any pity.

For Gorky, this was evidence of the congenital stupidity of the Russian peasant. Reminiscing about the decade that followed, Brezhnev wrote: '. . . everywhere in the Urals I noticed the familiar smell of industry mingling with the scents of the fields and meadows . . .' The consequences of all this are no different in the Soviet Union than they are elsewhere. '. . . As the nation's economy continues to develop through 1980,' states an official report, 'atmospheric pollution may maintain, and in some cases exceed, levels extremely hazardous for health in some industrial centers of the Soviet Union'. There is strong evidence that the world's worst nuclear disaster so far occurred in the Urals in 1957. There cannot, in fact, be fires without smoke. Paragraph 18 of the 1977 constitution guarantees the protection of the environment and this is one area in which limited public policing of economic institutions has been a reality. Experience suggests, however, that where the key facts are State secrets and the offenders powerful organizations within the State, environmental factors will often be sacrificed to the imperatives of economic development.

The engine of economic growth in Russia and elsewhere has been the harnessing of the energies of more and more people to productive tasks. The rising aspirations of these people now threaten the world with serious problems of pollution and resource depletion. Yet the Soviet Union is alone among the major powers in having a policy of encouraging increased fertility. To some extent this is because Soviet economic planners have not yet discovered how to maintain high rates of growth without a constantly increasing supply of labour. This also reflects demographic anxieties about China and the composition of the Soviet population itself. The Soviet Union contains its own North–South problem, a division between a mostly European post-Christian North and a largely Asiatic Islamic South. While the average Russian woman bears two children, the average Uzbek woman bears four. In 1981, new plans were announced for discriminatory child and maternity benefits to encourage fertility in the Northern zone. This may sound like encouraging reproduction in Tunbridge Wells or Westchester County while discouraging it in Brixton or the Bronx, but it must be set against social and economic progress in Soviet Central Asia unequalled throughout Asia, with the sole exception of Japan and, more recently, a few small East Asian societies and the oil-soaked states of the Gulf.

The Soviet Union boycotted the Cancún conference in 1982, called to discuss the North–South divide, and its own record on aid to poorer countries has been mixed. It largely ignores the needs of the poorest and is generally 'fiscally conservative'. On the other hand, it has concentrated its aid on creating new industries in the countries aided, its loans have been at low rates of interest, it has accepted goods in lieu of hard currency in repayment, and it has acquired no permanent stake in the countries concerned.

If the North–South divide presents the most alarming prospect of the polarization of humanity in the long term, the immediate risks are those arising from the present polarization of the world behind two armed superpowers. During the early 1970s, there were hopes that the 'Cold War' had been abandoned for an era of 'detente'. J. K. Galbraith even looked forward to a process of 'convergence' whereby co-operation between East and West would lead to an exchange of attractive features. It was hoped that the East would become more democratic and open in its politics, and leave more room for consumer choice in economics. In the West, there would be a greater willingness to accept some need for centralized planning and greater progress towards better health and welfare programmes for the masses. Unhappily, other possibilities soon emerged, symbolized by the deportation from the Soviet Union of Bukovsky in handcuffs marked 'Made in the U.S.A.'.

The Soviet invasion of Afghanistan in 1979 was preceded by the American refusal to ratify the Soviet–American Trade Treaty and by clear indications that the Republicans would block the second Treaty on Arms Limitation. The beginning of the 1980s saw preparations for an imminent resumption of the arms race on a scale that threatened to de-stabilize the concept of deterrence, already weakened by the proliferation of nuclear arms and the growth of the idea that a limited war might be fought in Europe. In view of everything that has been said about the greater dynamism of capitalism in exploiting new technology, from pocket calculators to pornography, it seems reasonable to assume that a new generation of weapons is more necessary to the 'military–industrial complex' in the West than to the Soviet Nomenklatura. On the other hand, the creation of military bureaucracies in the Soviet Union becomes an obstacle to actual disarmament. Thus, whereas major technological 'improvements' in weapons of mass destruction have tended to come from the United States, obstacles to the verification of arms control agreements have come mainly from the Soviet Union. They turned down the Baruch Plan for monitoring nuclear power just after the last war, President Eisenhower's 'Open Skies' proposal in the 1950s, and the proposals of the neutral countries for the impartial monitoring of the treaty banning biological weapons in 1972. Recent Soviet support for anti-nuclear, and even pacifist movements in Western Europe has not been echoed within Russia itself, because the Russians always emphasize the defensive nature of their own armaments.

Even so, starting from a lower economic level as they do, Soviet citizens will pay dearly if current threats to intensify the arms race are realized. Defensive arms are no less costly than offensive. Defence spending concentrates investment in limited areas of high technology, provides very limited employment opportunities and then only for a highly qualified minority, starves the civilian sector of investment and depresses popular levels of consumption. An intensification of the arms race at a moment when the Soviet leadership is due to change might well consolidate popular support for the Nomenklatura and lead to an extension of quasi-totalitarian controls over the Soviet people. It could easily lead also to the re-institution of mass unemployment there, either openly or in covert ways. On the other hand, a more pacific development of the Soviet economy might permit both workers and intellectuals to extend their autonomy in different ways so that Chekhov's ordinary Russians could begin to build lives less oppressed by the prophetic burdens of the past.

Further Reading

This list of books is limited to works written in English or available in English translation. Many of the titles listed themselves contain bibliographies which will serve as a guide for further study.

1. DOCUMENTS

T. Riha, ed., *Readings in Russian Civilization* (Chicago, 1964).

G. Vernadsky, ed., *A Source Book for Russian History from Early Times to 1917* (New Haven, Conn., and London, 1972).

W. F. Reddaway, ed., *Documents of Catherine the Great* (London, 1931).

D. von Mohrenschildt, ed., *The Russian Revolution of 1917* (London and Toronto, 1971).

M. McCauley, ed., *The Russian Revolution and the Soviet State 1917–1921: Documents* (London, 1975).

1903: The First Ordinary Congress of the RSDLP, trans. B. Pearce (London, 1980).

R. V. Daniels, ed., *A Documentary History of Communism* (New York, 1960).

The Bolsheviks and the October Revolution (London, 1974).

J. L. H. Keep, ed., *The Debate on Soviet Power* (Oxford, 1979).

L. D. Trotsky, *The Age of Permanent Revolution*, ed. I. Deutscher (New York, 1964).

T. P. Whitney, ed. *Khrushchev Speaks* (Ann Arbor, Mich., 1963).

L. I. Brezhnev, *Socialism, Democracy and Human Rights* (Oxford, 1980).

Jane Degras, ed., *The Communist International 1919–1943: Documents* (London, 1956–65).

Baku Congress of Peoples of the East (London, 1977).

A. Z. Rubinstein, ed., *The Foreign Policy of the Soviet Union* (New York, 1960).

H. L. Roberts, ed., *The Anti-Stalin Campaign and International Communism* (New York, 1956).

2. GENERAL HISTORIES

J. Blum, *Lord and Peasant in Russia from the Ninth to the Nineteenth Century* (Princeton, N.J., 1961).

M. T. Florinsky, *Russia, A History and an Interpretation* (New York, 1953).

G. Vernadsky, *A History of Russia* (New Haven, Conn.. 1969).

J. Billington, *The Icon and the Axe* (London, 1966).

M. Cherniavsky, *Tsar and People: Studies in Russian Myths* (London, 1961).

History of the U.S.S.R. (Moscow, 1977).

N. Riasanovsky, *A History of Russia* (Oxford and New York, 1977).

R. Pipes, *Russia under the Old Regime* (London, 1974).

3. SPECIAL ASPECTS

(a) *Historiography*

C. E. Black, ed., *Rewriting Russian History* (New York, 1956).

A. G. Mazour, *Modern Russian Historiography* (New York, 1958).

J. L. H. Keep, ed., *Contemporary History in the Soviet Mirror* (London, 1964).

(b) *Economic History*

P. I. Lyashchenko, *History of the National Economy of Russia to the 1917 Revolution* (New York, 1949).

M. Dobb, *Soviet Economic Development Since 1917* (London, 1966).

A. Nove, *An Economic History of the U.S.S.R.* (London, 1976).

(c) *Sociology*

G. Konrád and I. Szélenyi, *The Intellectuals on the Road to Class Power* (London, 1979).

D. L. Ransel, ed., *The Family in Imperial Russia* (Urbana, Chicago and London, 1978).

Dorothy Atkinson *et al.*, eds., *Women in Russia* (Stanford, Cal., 1977).

(d) *Psychology and Anthropology*

E. H. Erikson, 'The Legend of Maxim Gorky's Youth' in *Childhood and Society* (London, 1965).

S. P. Dunn and Ethel Dunn, *The Peasants of Central Russia* (New York, 1967).

(e) *Literature*

D. S. Mirsky, *A History of Russian Literature* (London, 1964).

P. N. Milyukov, *Outlines of Russian Culture* (Philadelphia, Pa., 1943).

M. Slonim, *An Outline of Russian Literature* (Oxford, 1958).

J. Lavrin, *A Panorama of Russian Literature* (London, 1973).
R. Hingley, *Russian Writers and Soviet Society 1917–1978* (London, 1979).

(f) *The Fine Arts*
Tamara Talbot Rice, *Russian Art* (London and New York, 1963).
J. Milner, *Russian Revolutionary Art* (London, 1979).

(g) *Armed Forces and Secret Police*
R. Hingley, *The Russian Secret Police* (London, 1970).
J. Erickson, *The Soviet High Command 1918–1945* (London, 1962).

4. BEFORE PETER THE GREAT

N. K. Chadwick, *The Beginning of Russian History* (Cambridge, 1946).
I. Boba, *Nomads, Northmen and Slavs* (The Hague, Wiesbaden, 1967).
D. Obolensky, *The Byzantine Commonwealth* (London, 1971).
B. D. Grekov, *The Culture of Kievan Rus* (Moscow, 1947).
B. Spuler, *The Mongols in History* (London, 1971).
G. Vernadsky, *Mongols and Russians* (New Haven, Conn., 1953).
J. L. I. Fennell, *Ivan the Great of Moscow* (London, 1961); *The Emergence of Moscow 1304–1359* (London, 1968); trans. and ed., *The Correspondence between Prince A. M. Kurbsky and Tsar Ivan IV of Russia 1564–1579* (Cambridge, 1955); trans. and ed., *Prince A. M. Kurbsky's History of Ivan IV* (Cambridge, 1965).
R. J. Kerner, *The Urge to the Sea* (Berkeley, Cal., 1942).
F. Carr, *Ivan the Terrible* (Newton Abbot, 1981).
Valerie A. Tumins, ed., *Tsar Ivan IV's Reply to Jan Rokyta* (The Hague and Paris, 1971).
B. Nørretranders, *The Shaping of Czardom under Ivan Groznyj* (London, 1971).
L. E. Berry and R. O. Crummey, eds., *Rude and Barbarous Kingdom* (Madison, Milwaukee and London, 1968).
I. Grey, *Boris Godunov: The Tragic Tsar* (London, 1973).
C. J. Halperin, *The Russian Land and the Russian Tsar* (London, 1976).
R. E. F. Smith, *The Enserfment of the Russian Peasantry* (Cambridge, 1968); *Peasant Farming in Muscovy* (Cambridge, 1977).
S. H. Baron, ed., *The Travels of Olearius in Seventeenth Century Russia* (Stanford, Cal., 1967).
P. Bushkovitch, *The Merchants of Moscow 1580–1650* (Cambridge, 1980).
P. Longworth, *Tsar Alexis* (in preparation), *The Cossacks* (London, 1969).
Zinaida Shakhovskoy, *Precursors of Peter the Great* (London, 1964).

G. A. Maloney, *Russian Hesychasm* (The Hague, 1973).

J. M. Hittle, *The Service City: State and Townsmen in Russia, 1600–1800* (Cambridge, Mass., 1979).

J. T. Alexander, *Bubonic Plague in Early Modern Russia* (Baltimore, Md., and London, 1980).

P. Dukes, *The Making of Russian Absolutism 1613–1801* (London, 1982).

5. THE EIGHTEENTH CENTURY

M. S. Anderson, *Peter the Great* (London, 1978).

J. Cracraft, *The Church Reform of Peter the Great* (London, 1971).

M. Raeff, ed., *Peter the Great Changes Russia* (Lexington, Mass., 1972).

V. O. Klyuchevsky, *Peter the Great* (London, 1958).

M. Raeff, *Plans for Political Reform in Imperial Russia 1730–1905* (Englewood Cliffs, N.J., 1966).

C. Marsden, *Palmyra of the North: The First Days of St. Petersburg* (London, 1942).

J. L. H. Keep, *The Secret Chancellery, the Guards and the Dynastic Crisis of 1704–1741* (London, 1976).

P. Longworth, *The Three Empresses: Catherine I, Anne and Elizabeth of Russia* (London, 1972).

D. Ransel, *The Politics of Catherinian Russia* (New Haven, Conn., and London, 1975).

R. E. Jones, *The Emancipation of the Russian Nobility 1762–1785* (Princeton, N. J., 1973).

G. L. Freeze, *The Russian Levites: Parish Clergy in the Eighteenth Century* (Cambridge, Mass., 1977).

Prince M. M. Shcherbatov, *On the Corruption of Morals in Russia* (Cambridge, 1969).

D. Maroger, ed., *The Memoirs of Catherine the Great* (London, 1955).

P. Dukes, *Catherine the Great and the Russian Nobility* (Cambridge, 1967).

Isabel de Madariaga, *Russian in the Age of Catherine the Great* (London, 1981).

Miriam Kochan, *Life in Russia under Catherine the Great* (New York and London, 1969).

J. T. Alexander, *Emperor of the Cossacks* (Lawrence, Ks., 1973).

K. A. Papmehl, *Freedom of Expression in Eighteenth Century Russia* (The Hague, 1971).

D. M. Lang, *The First Russian Radical: Alexander Radishchev* (London, 1960).

P. Longworth, *The Art of Victory. The Life and Achievements of Generalissimo Suvorov* (London, 1965).

6. THE NINETEENTH CENTURY

H. Seton-Watson, *The Russian Empire 1801–1917* (Oxford, 1967).

E. V. Tarle, *Napoleon's Invasion of Russia, 1812* (London, 1942).

A. W. Palmer, *Alexander I* (London, 1974).

M. Raeff, *Michael Speransky: Statesman of Imperial Russia 1772–1839* (The Hague, 1969).

M. R. H. Jenkins, *Arakcheev* (London, 1969).

W. L. Blackwell, *The Beginnings of Russian Industrialization 1800–1860* (Princeton, N.J., 1968).

A. Nikitenko, *The Diary of a Russian Censor* (Amherst, Mass., 1975).

A. Mazour, *The First Russian Revolution* (Berkeley, Cal., 1937).

N. V. Riasanovsky, *A Parting of the Ways: Government and the Educated Public in Russia 1801–1855* (Oxford, 1976).

A. Seaton, *The Crimean War: A Russian Chronicle* (London, 1972).

W. B. Lincoln, *Nicholas I* (London, 1978).

Baron von Haxthausen, *The Russian Empire* (London, 1968).

A. I. Herzen, *My Past and Thoughts*, London, 1974.

M. Malia, *Alexander Herzen and the Birth of Russian Socialism 1812–1855* (London, 1961).

I. Berlin, *Russian Thinkers* (London, 1978).

A. Yarmolinsky, *The Road to Revolution* (London, 1957).

S. Monas, *The Third Section* (Cambridge, Mass., 1961).

E. Lampert, *Studies in Rebellion* (London, 1957).

R. Hare, *Portraits of Russian Personalities* (Oxford, 1959).

C. E. Black, ed., *The Transformation of Russian Society* (Cambridge, Mass., 1961).

D. Footman, *Red Prelude, A Life of A. I. Zhelyabov* (London, 1944).

J. H. Billington, *Mikhailovsky and Russian Populism* (Oxford, 1958).

G. T. Robinson, *Rural Russia under the Old Regime* (New York, 1943).

S. Levin, *Youth in Revolt* (New York, 1930).

James Joll, *The Anarchists* (London, 1964).

W. E. Mosse, *Alexander II and the Modernization of Russia* (London, 1958).

A. J. Richter, ed. and intr., *The Politics of Autocracy: Letters of Alexander II to Prince A. I. Bariatinskii 1857–1864* (Paris and The Hague, 1966).

W. B. Lincoln, *Nikolai Miliutin, An Enlightened Russian Bureaucrat* (Newtonville, Mass., 1977).

T. Emmons, *The Russian Landed Gentry and the Peasant Emancipation of 1861* (Cambridge, 1968).

P. A. Zayonchkovsky, *The Abolition of Serfdom in Russia* (Gulf Breeze, Fla., 1978); *The Russian Autocracy in Crisis 1878–1882* (Gulf Breeze,

Fla., 1979); *The Russian Autocracy under Alexander III* (Gulf Breeze Fla., 1978).

C. E. Timberlake, ed., *Essays on Russian Liberalism* (Columbia, Mo., 1972).

W. Vucinich, *The Peasants in Nineteenth-Century Russia* (Stanford, Cal., 1970).

Vera Broido, *Apostles into Terrorists* (London, 1978).

Cathy Porter, *Fathers and Daughters* (London, 1976).

P. Kropotkin, *Memoirs of a Revolutionist* (New York, 1962).

H. Troyat, *Tolstoy* (New York and London, 1967).

J. Frankel, *Prophecy and Politics: Socialism. Nationalism and the Russian Jews 1862–1917* (Cambridge, 1981).

F. Venturi, *Roots of Revolution* (London, 1960).

S. H. Baron, *Plekhanov, the Father of Russian Marxism* (London, 1963).

R. E. MacMaster, *Danilevsky: A Russian Totalitarian Philosopher* (Cambridge, Mass., 1967).

T. H. von Laue, *Sergei Witte and the Industrialization of Russia* (New York and London, 1963).

S. Yu. Witte, *The Memoirs of Count Witte* (London, 1921).

E. J. Simmons, ed., *Continuity and Change in Russian and Soviet Thought* (Cambridge, Mass., 1955).

L. Schapiro, *Rationalism and Nationalism in Russian Nineteenth-Century Political Thought* (New Haven, Conn., 1967).

K. P. Pobednonostsev, *Reflections of a Russian Statesman* (Ann Arbor, Mich., 1965).

R. F. Byrnes, *Pobednonostsev: His Life and Thought* (Bloomington, Ind., and London, 1968).

E. C. Thaden, *Conservative Nationalism in Nineteenth Century Russia* (Seattle, Wash., 1964).

T. C. Owen, *Capitalism and Politics in Russia: A Social History of the Moscow Merchants 1855–1905* (Cambridge, 1981).

R. W. Tolf, *The Russian Rockefellers* (Stanford, Cal., 1976).

Olga Crisp, *Studies in the Russian Economy before 1914* (London, 1976).

P. L. Alston, *Education and the State in Tsarist Russia* (Stanford, Cal., 1969).

K. Paustovsky, *Story of a Life* (London, 1964).

R. A. Pierce, *Russian Central Asia 1867–1917* (Berkeley and Los Angeles, Cal., 1960).

7. FROM 1905 TO THE WAR

S. M. Schwarz, *The Russian Revolution of 1905* (Chicago, Ill., and London, 1967).

S. Harcave, *First Blood: The Russian Revolution of 1905* (London, 1964).

P. N. Milyukov, *Russia and its Crisis* (London, 1962).

G. Katkov *et al.*, eds., *Russia Enters the Twentieth Century 1874–1917* (London, 1971).

T. Riha, *A Russian European: Paul Miliukov in Russian Politics*, (Notre Dame, Ind., and London, 1969).

H. D. Mehlinger and J. M. Thompson, *Count Witte and the Tsarist Government in the 1905 Revolution* (Bloomington, Ind., and London, 1974).

J. L. H. Keep, *The Rise of Social Democracy in Russia* (Oxford, 1963).

L. Haimson, *The Russian Marxists and the Origins of Bolshevism* (Cambridge, Mass., 1955).

A. K. Wildman, *The Making of a Workers' Revolution* (Chicago, Ill., and London, 1967).

D. Lane, *The Roots of Russian Communism* (London, 1968).

J. Schneidermann, *Sergei Zubatov and Revolutionary Marxism* (Ithaca, N.Y., and London, 1976).

B. D. Wolfe, *Three who Made a Revolution* (London, 1967).

I. Getzler, *Martov* (Cambridge, 1967).

T. Dan, *The Origins of Bolshevism* (London, 1964).

L. Schapiro, *The Origins of the Communist Autocracy* (London, 1966).

L. D. Trotsky, *1905* (London, 1971).

O. Anweiler, *The Soviets* (New York, 1974).

Mary S. Conroy, *Peter Arkad'evich Stolypin* (Boulder, Colo., 1976).

R. B. McKean, *The Russian Constitutional Monarchy 1907–1917* (London, 1977).

G. A. Hosking, *The Russian Constitutional Experiment: Government and Duma 1907–1914* (Cambridge, 1973).

D. Treadgold, *The Great Siberian Migration* (Princeton, N.J., 1957).

Sir D. Mackenzie Wallace, *Russia* (New York and London, 1970).

K. K. Pahlen, *Mission to Turkestan* (London, 1964).

M. Samuel, *Blood Accusation* (New York, 1966).

R. K. Massie, *Nicholas and Alexandra* (London, 1968).

L. Kochan, *Russia in Revolution 1890–1918* (London, 1966).

8. THE REVOLUTION

M. T. Florinsky, *The End of the Russian Empire* (New York, 1931).

W. D. Rosenberg, *Liberals in the Russian Revolution* (Princeton, N.J., 1974).

P. N. Milyukov, *Political Memoirs 1905–1917* (Ann Arbor, Mich., 1967).

Florence Farmborough, *Nurse at the Russian Front* (London, 1974).

R. H. Bruce Lockhart, *Memoirs of a British Agent* (London, 1932).

A. F. Kerensky, *The Kerensky Memoirs* (London, 1965).

V. M. Chernov, *The Great Russian Revolution* (New Haven, Conn., 1936).

W. H. Roobol, *Tsereteli – A Democrat in the Russian Revolution* (The Hague, 1976).

O. H. Radkey, *The Agrarian Foes of Bolshevism* (New York, 1958); *The Unknown Civil War in Soviet Russia* (Stanford, Cal., 1976).

G. Katkov, *Russia 1917. The February Revolution* (London, 1967); *The Kornilov Affair* (London, 1980).

M. Ferro, *The Russian Revolution of February 1917* (London, 1972); *October 1917. A Social History of the Russian Revolution* (London, 1980).

J. L. H. Keep, *The Russian Revolution: A Study in Mass Mobilization* (London, 1976).

R. Pethybridge, *The Spread of the Russian Revolution* (London, 1972).

A. Rabinowitch, *Prelude to Bolshevism* (London, 1978); *The Bolsheviks come to Power* (New York and London, 1976).

R. V. Daniels, *Red October* (London, 1967).

P. N. Sobelev *et al.*, eds., *The Great October Socialist Revolution* (Moscow, 1977).

W. H. Chamberlin, *The Russian Revolution: 1917–1921* (New York and London, 1935).

Diane Koenker, *Moscow Workers and the 1917 Revolution* (Princeton, N.J., 1981).

R. G. Suny, *The Baku Commune* (Princeton, N.J., 1972).

A. Ulam, *Lenin and the Bolsheviks* (London, 1969).

L. Fisher, *Life of Lenin* (London, 1964).

I. Deutscher, *Lenin's Childhood* (London, 1970); *Trotsky* (London, 1954–70).

L. D. Trotsky, *The History of the Russian Revolution* (London, 1932–3); *Lenin* (London, 1925); *My Life* (London, 1975); *How the Revolution Armed Itself* (London, 1981).

S. F. Cohen, *Bukharin and the Bolshevik Revolution* (Oxford, 1971).

R. C. Elwood, ed., *Reconsiderations on the Russian Revolution* (Cambridge, Mass., 1976).

Cathy Porter, *Alexandra Kollontai* (London, 1980).

Alix Holt, ed., *Selected Writings of Alexandra Kollontai* (London, 1977).

I. Steinberg, *Spiridonova* (London, 1935).

N. N. Sukhanov, *The Russian Revolution 1917* (Oxford, 1955).

John Reed, *Ten Days that Shook the World* (New York, 1960; Harmondsworth, 1982).

M. Brinton, *The Bolsheviks and Workers' Control* (London, 1970).

L. Schapiro, *The Communist Party of the Soviet Union* (London, 1970).

M. P. Price, *Reminiscences of the Russian Revolution* (London, 1921).

T. Shanin, *The Awkward Class* (Oxford, 1972).

R. E. F. Smith, *The Russian Peasant 1920 and 1984* (London, 1977).

P. Kenez, *Civil War in South Russia* (Berkeley and Los Angeles, Cal., 1971–7).

J. Bradley, *Civil War in Russia 1917–1920* (London, 1974).

R. Luckett, *The White Generals* (London, 1971).

R. E. Pipes, *The Formation of the Soviet Union* (London, 1964).

P. Avrich, *The Anarchists in the Russian Revolution* (London, 1973).

P. Arshinov, *History of the Makhnovist Movement 1918–1921* (Detroit and Chicago, Ill., 1974).

V. Serge, *Memoirs of a Revolutionary* (London, 1963).

M. Lewin, *Lenin's Last Struggle* (New York, 1968).

E. H. Carr, *A History of Soviet Russia* (London, 1950–78).

Hélène Carrère d'Encausse, *A History of the Soviet Union* (London, 1981).

9. STALIN'S RUSSIA

C. Bettelheim, *Class Struggles in the U.S.S.R.* (London, 1976–8).

E. Preobrazhensky, *The Crisis of Soviet Industrialization* (New York, 1979).

A. Erlich, *The Soviet Industrialization Debate* (Cambridge, Mass., 1960).

Aino Kuusinen, *Before and After Stalin* (London, 1974).

R. Fülöp-Miller, *The Mind and Face of Bolshevism* (London and New York, 1927).

T. Beeson, *Discretion and Valour* (London, 1974).

G. Vins, *Three Generations of Suffering* (London, 1976).

A. S. Makarenko, *The Road to Life* (Moscow, 1951).

G. J. Massell, *The Surrogate Proletariat* (Princeton, N.J., 1974).

R. Pethybridge, *The Social Prelude to Stalinism* (London, 1979).

T H. Von Laue, *Why Lenin? Why Stalin?* (New York, 1964).

A Nove, *Was Stalin Really Necessary?* (London, 1964).

R. V. Daniels, *The Conscience of the Revolution* (Cambridge, Mass., 1960).

Sheila Fitzpatrick, *The Commissariat of Enlightenment* (Cambridge, 1970); *Education and Social Mobility in the Soviet Union 1921–1934* (Cambridge, 1979); ed., *Cultural Revolution in Russia 1928–1931* (Bloomington, Ind., and London, 1978).

E H. Carr, *The Russian Revolution from Lenin to Stalin 1917–1929* (London, 1979).

Sir J. Maynard, *The Russian Peasant and Other Studies* (London, 1942; New York, 1962).

M. Lewin, *Russian Peasants and Soviet Power* (London, 1968).

N. Jasny, *The Socialized Agriculture of the U.S.S.R.* (Stanford, Cal., 1949).

M. Fainsod, *Smolensk under Soviet Rule* (London, 1958).

H. R. Knickerbocker, *The Soviet Five-Year Plan and its Effects on World Trade* (London, 1931).

D. Granick, *Soviet Metal-Fabricating and Economic Development: Practice versus Policy* (Madison, Milwaukee and London, 1967).

T. Seibert, *Red Russia* (London, 1932).

W. H. Chamberlin, *Russia's Iron Age* (Boston, Mass., 1934).

L. D. Trotsky, *The Revolution Betrayed* (London, 1967); *Stalin* (London, 1968).

I. Deutscher, *Stalin* (Oxford, 1949).

A. Ulam, *Stalin* (London, 1974).

Svetlana Alliluyeva, *Twenty Letters to a Friend* (London, 1967).

R. A. Medvedev, *Let History Judge* (London, 1972); *Problems in the Literary Biography of Mikhail Sholokhov* (Cambridge, 1977).

R. Conquest, *The Great Terror* (London, 1968); *Kolyma* (London, 1978).

A. Solzhenitsyn, *The Gulag Archipelago* (London, 1974–8).

Yevgenia Ginzburg, *Into the Whirlwind* (London, 1967).

Nadezhda Mandelshtam, *Hope Against Hope* (London, 1971); *Hope Abandoned* (London, 1974).

Violet Connolly, *Soviet Tempo* (London, 1938).

A. Werth, *Russia at War 1941–1945* (London, 1964); *Russia in the Post-War Years* (London, 1971).

I. Ehrenburg, *Men, Years, Life* (London, 1962–6).

A. Dallin, *German Rule in Russia 1941–45* (London, 1981).

J. A. Armstrong, *Ukrainian Nationalism 1939–45* (New York, 1955).

Harrison E. Salisbury, *The Siege of Leningrad* (London, 1969).

V. I. Chuikov, *The Beginning of the Road* (London, 1963); *The End of the Third Reich* (London, 1967).

G. K. Zhukov, *Memoirs* (London, 1971).

M. Djilas, *Conversations with Stalin* (London, 1962); *The New Class* (New York, 1957).

V. Kravchenko, *I Chose Freedom* (London, 1947).

N. S. Khrushchev, *Khrushchev Remembers* (London, 1971).

L. I. Brezhnev, *How it Was* (Oxford, 1979); *Reminiscences* (Moscow, 1981).

Vera Dunham, *In Stalin's Time* (Cambridge, 1976).

W. Leonhard, *Child of the Revolution* (London, 1979).

D. Javorsky, *The Lysenko Affair* (Cambridge, Mass., 1970).

E. Ashby, *Scientists in Russia* (London, 1947).

J. F. Hough and M. Fainsod, *How the Soviet Union is Governed* (London, 1979).

M. McCauley, *The Soviet Union Since 1917* (London, 1981).

A. Bennigsen and C. Lemercier-Quelquejay, *Islam in the Soviet Union* (London, 1967).

10. THE SOVIET UNION SINCE 1953

S. Bialer, *Stalin's Successors* (Cambridge, 1980).

E. Crankshaw, *Khrushchev: A Biography* (London, 1968).

M. Frankland, *Khrushchev* (London, 1966).

A. Werth, *Russia under Khrushchev* (Westport, Conn., 1975).

R. A. Medvedev, *On Socialist Democracy* (London, 1975); and Zh. A. Medvedev, *Khrushchev: The Years in Power* (Oxford, 1977).

Zh. A. Medvedev, *Nuclear Disaster in the Urals* (London, 1979); *The Medvedev Papers* (London, 1971).

L. I. Brezhnev, *The Virgin Lands* (Moscow, 1978).

M. Tatu, *Power in the Kremlin* (London, 1968).

J. Dornberg, *Brezhnev, the Masks of Power* (London, 1974).

A. Brown and M. Kaser, eds., *The Soviet Union Since the Fall of Khrushchev* (London, 1978).

J. F. Hough, *The Soviet Prefects* (Cambridge, Mass., 1969); *Soviet Leadership in Transition* (Washington, D.C., 1980).

D. Lane, *The Socialist Industrial State* (London, 1976); *Politics and Society in the U.S.S.R.* (London, 1978).

M. Matthews, *Class and Society in Soviet Russia* (London, 1977).

A. Szymanski, *Is the Red Flag Still Flying?* (London, 1979).

J. R. Millar, ed., *The Soviet Rural Community* (Urbana, Ill., 1971).

A. Nove, *The Soviet Economic System* (London, 1977).

Sally Belfrage, *A Room in Moscow* (London, 1958).

L. van der Post, *Journey into Russia* (London, 1964).

J. Miller, *Life in Russia Today* (London and New York, 1969).

H. Smith, *The Russians* (London, 1976).

P. B. Reddaway, ed., *Uncensored Russia* (London, 1972).

I. Dzyuba, *Internationalism or Russification* (New York, 1973).

V. Moroz, *Boomerang* (Baltimore, Md., Paris and Toronto, 1974).

A. Amalrik, *Will the Soviet Union Survive until 1984?* (London, 1970).

Gyuzel Amalrik, *Memories of a Tatar Childhood* (London, 1979).

V. Bukovsky, *To Build a Castle* (London, 1978).

L. Plyushch, *History's Carnival* (London, 1979).

V. Haynes and Olga Semyonova, eds., *Workers against the Gulag* (London, 1979).

A. D. Sakharov, *Progress, Coexistence and Intellectual Freedom* (London,

1968); *My Country and the World* (London, 1975); *Alarm and Hope* (London, 1979).

'B. Komarov'. *The Destruction of Nature in the Soviet Union* (London, 1978).

Christel Lane, *The Rituals of Rulers* (Cambridge, 1981).

Hélène Carrère d'Encausse, *Decline of an Empire* (New York, 1979).

11. RUSSIA AND THE WORLD

O. Halecki, *Borderlands of Western Civilization* (New York, 1952).

T. Hunczak, ed., *Russian Imperialism from Ivan the Great to the Revolution* (Brunswick, N.J., 1974).

A. G. Cross, ed., *Great Britain and Russia in the Eighteenth Century* (Norwich, 1977).

A. Lobanov-Rostovsky, *Russia and Europe 1789–1825* (Charoltte, N.C., 1947).

N. E. Saul, *Russia and the Mediterranean 1797–1807* (Chicago and London, 1970).

John H. Gleeson, *The Genesis of Russophobia in Great Britain* (Harvard, 1950).

I. J. Lederer, ed., *Russian Foreign Policy* (New Haven, Conn., and London, 1962).

B. H. Sumner, *Russia and the Balkans 1870–1880* (Oxford, 1937).

Barbara Jelavich, *A Century of Russian Foreign Policy 1814–1914* (Philadelphia, Pa., 1964).

R. Wade, *The Russian Search for Peace February–October 1917* (Stanford, Cal., 1969).

J. Silverlight, *The Victors' Dilemma* (London, 1970).

A. J. Toynbee, ed., *The Impact of the Russian Revolution 1917–1967* (Oxford, 1967).

P. Dukes, *October and the World* (London, 1979).

G. Kennan, *Soviet Foreign Policy 1917–1941* (New York, 1960); *Russia and the West under Lenin and Stalin* (New York, 1961).

A. Ulam, *The Rivals: America and Russia since World War 1* (New York, 1971).

T. T. Hammond, ed., *The Anatomy of Communist Takeovers* (New Haven, Conn., and London, 1975).

S. R. Schram and H. Carrère d'Encausse, *Marxism and Asia* (London, 1969).

Nina Berberova, *The Italics are Mine* (London and Harlow, 1969).

F. Claudín, *The Communist Movement* (London, 1975).

R. H. Crossman, ed., *The God that Failed* (New York, 1950).

W. Averell Harriman and E. Abel: *Special Envoy to Churchill and Stalin 1941–1946* (London, 1976).

N. Tolstoy, *Victims of Yalta* (London, 1977).

B. Ponomaryov *et al.*; *History of Soviet Foreign Policy 1945–1970* (Moscow, 1974).

I. Deutscher, *Marxism in Our Time* (Berkeley, Cal., 1971).

M. H. Heikal, *Sphinx and Commissar* (London, 1978).

S. E. Gorshkov, *The Sea Power of the State* (Oxford, 1979).

A. Ulam, *Expansion and Coexistence* (New York, 1974).

Alva R. Myrdal, *The Game of Disarmament* (New York, 1978).

C. Levinson, *Vodka-Cola* (London, 1980).

S. S. Kaplan, *Diplomacy of Power* (Washington, D.C., 1981).

12. COMPARATIVE WORKS

P. Anderson, *Lineages of the Absolutist State* (London, 1974).

R. Barrington Moore, *The Social Origins of Democracy and Dictatorship* (London, 1967).

E. Canetti, *Crowds and Power* (London, 1962).

A. Gerschenkron, *Economic Backwardness in Historical Perspective* (London, 1965).

A. Giddens, *The Social Structure of Advanced Societies* (London, 1973).

Index